BUILDING THE INFORMATION SOCIETY

IFIP – The International Federation for Information Processing

IFIP was founded in 1960 under the auspices of UNESCO, following the First World Computer Congress held in Paris the previous year. An umbrella organization for societies working in information processing, IFIP's aim is two-fold: to support information processing within its member countries and to encourage technology transfer to developing nations. As its mission statement clearly states,

> *IFIP's mission is to be the leading, truly international, apolitical organization which encourages and assists in the development, exploitation and application of information technology for the benefit of all people.*

IFIP is a non-profit making organization, run almost solely by 2500 volunteers. It operates through a number of technical committees, which organize events and publications. IFIP's events range from an international congress to local seminars, but the most important are:

- The IFIP World Computer Congress, held every second year;
- Open conferences;
- Working conferences.

The flagship event is the IFIP World Computer Congress, at which both invited and contributed papers are presented. Contributed papers are rigorously refereed and the rejection rate is high.

As with the Congress, participation in the open conferences is open to all and papers may be invited or submitted. Again, submitted papers are stringently refereed.

The working conferences are structured differently. They are usually run by a working group and attendance is small and by invitation only. Their purpose is to create an atmosphere conducive to innovation and development. Refereeing is less rigorous and papers are subjected to extensive group discussion.

Publications arising from IFIP events vary. The papers presented at the IFIP World Computer Congress and at open conferences are published as conference proceedings, while the results of the working conferences are often published as collections of selected and edited papers.

Any national society whose primary activity is in information may apply to become a full member of IFIP, although full membership is restricted to one society per country. Full members are entitled to vote at the annual General Assembly, National societies preferring a less committed involvement may apply for associate or corresponding membership. Associate members enjoy the same benefits as full members, but without voting rights. Corresponding members are not represented in IFIP bodies. Affiliated membership is open to non-national societies, and individual and honorary membership schemes are also offered.

BUILDING THE INFORMATION SOCIETY

IFIP 18th World Computer Congress
Topical Sessions
22–27 August 2004
Toulouse, France

Edited by

René Jacquart
ONERA
France

SPRINGER SCIENCE+BUSINESS MEDIA, LLC

Library of Congress Cataloging-in-Publication Data

A C.I.P. Catalogue record for this book is available from the Library of Congress.

Building the Information Society
Edited by René Jacquart

DOI 10.1007/978-1-4020-8157-6

Originally published by Kluwer Academic Publishers in 2004
MyCopy version of the original edition 2004

Printed on acid-free paper.
www.springer.com/mycopy

Contents

Preface

This book consists of the collection of articles or extended abstracts which have been written for the support of the so-called "Topical day/session" track during the 18th IFIP World Computer Congress, held in Toulouse from August 22-27, 2004.

I thank all the organizers, co-ordinators and contributors of these Topical Days for their involvement in the success of this track and for the success of the WCC itself.

The identification of topics and potential contributors was done with the strong support of Jean-Claude Laprie and Reino Kurki-Suonio. The evaluation of contribution and the selection was done by a specific committee. I would like to thank here: Algirdas Avižienis, Marie-Claude Gaudel, Takashi Nanya, Gus Olling and Jean-Jacques Quisquater.

The final edition of this book was made possible thanks to the effective work and support of Noëlle Desblancs, under the guidance and advices of Leon Strous and Yana Lambert. Many thanks for them.

René Jacquart (Topical Day Program Chair)

Contributors

Topic Number / Name(s)/Affiliation

1 **Patrick Ziegler, Klaus R. Dittrich;** U. Zurich, Switzerland
Guy Pierra, Yamine Ait Ameur ; LISI/ENSMA. Poitiers. France
Domenico Beneventano, Sonia Bergamaschi; U. di Modena e Reggio Emilia. Italy
Chantal Reynaud ; LRI, Orsay, France

2. **Mark Cavazza, Fred Charles, Steven J. Mead;** U. Teesside, UK
Adrian David Cheok, Goh Kok Hwee, Liu Wei, Jason Teo, Teo Sze Lee, Farzam Farbiz, Lee Chang Ping; National U. Singapore, Singapore
Matthias Rauterberg; Technical U. Eindhoven, Netherlands
Ryohei Nakatsu, Takenori Wama, Masayuki Higuchi; Kwansei Gakuin U., Japan
Hajime Sakamoto, Hajime Laboratory, Kobe, Japan
Naoko Tosa; Entertainment Computing Laboratory, Japan
Henry Thomas; France Telecom R&D, France

3 **Algirdas Avižienis;** UCLA, USA and Vytautas Magnus U., Kaunas, Lithuania
Jean-Claude Laprie, Yves Deswarte, David Powell; LAAS-CNRS, France
Miloš D. Ercegovac, David A. Rennels; UCLA, USA
Yoshihiro Tohma; Tokyo Denki U., Japan,
Masao Mukaidono; Meiji U., Kawasaki, Japan
Ravishankar K. Iyer, William H. Sanders, Janak H. Patel, Z. Kalbarczyk; UIUC, USA
Tom Anderson, Brian Randell, Alexander Romanovsky; U. Newcastle, UK

Pascal Traverse, Isabelle Lacaze, Jean Souyris; Airbus, France
Ying C. Yeh; Boeing Corporation, Seattle, WA, USA
Hermann Kopetz; U. Technology, Vienna, Austria
Michele Morganti; Siemens Mobile Communications, Milan, Italy
Shobha Vasudevan, Jacob A. Abraham; U. Texas at Austin, USA
Luca Simoncini; U. Pisa and PDCC, Italy
Andrea Bondavalli; U. Florence and PDCC, Italy
Felicita Di Giandomenico, Silvano Chiaradonna; ISTI-CNR, Pisa and PDCC, Italy
Daniel P. Siewiorek, Roy A. Maxion, Priya Narasimhan; Carnegie Mellon U., Pittsburgh, USA
Hirokazu Ihara; Hiro Systems Laboratory Tokyo, Japan
Motohisa Funabashi; Hitachi Ltd, Kawasaki, Japan

4 **Patrick Cousot, Laurent Mauborgne;** École Normale Supérieure, Paris, France
Radhia Cousot; CNRS, Ecole Polytechnique Palaiseau, France
Tal Lev-Ami, Roman Manevich, Mooly Sagiv; Tel-Aviv University, Israel
Christian Ferdinand, Rheinhold Heckmann; AbsInt GmbH, Saarbruecken, Germany
Jean Souyris; Airbus France, Toulouse

5 **Laurence Nigay;** CLIPS-IMAG, France
Marie-Luce Bourguet; Queen Mary University London, UK
Yamine Ait Ameur; U. de Poitiers, France
Nadjet Kamel; LRIA-USTHB, Alger, Algérie
Fabio Paternò; ISTI-CNRS, Italy
Quentin Limbourg; Jean Vanderdonckt; UCL, Belgium
Dave Raggett; W3C/Canon
Philipp Hoschka; W3C
Max Froumentin; W3C/INRIA, France

6 **Denis Cavallucci;** INSA Strasbourg, France
Noel Leon, Jorge Guttierez, Carlos Castillo; Center for Product Innovation and Development, Campus Monterrey, Mexico
Oscar Martinez; Dept. of Mech. Eng. ITESM, Monterrey, Mexico
Rosario Vidal, Elena Mulet, M. Jose Bellés; U. Jaume I, Spain
Belinda López-Mesa; Luleå University Technology, Sweden
Graham Thompson; UMIST, Manchester, UK
Gaetano Cascini; University of Firenza, Italy
Valeri Souchkov; Insytec B.V, The Netherlands
Michael S. Slocum; Breakthrough Management Systems, USA

Sergei Ikovenko; International TRIZ Association, USA/Russia

7 **Odile Laurent, Christian Bougnol, Denis Favre-Felix, Jean-Pierre Heckmann, Sylvain Metge, Jean Souyris;** Airbus, France
Christel Seguin, Guy Durrieu, Virginie Wiels, Charles Castel, Pierre Bieber, Christophe Kehren; ONERA, France
Neil Audsley, Iain Bate, Steve Crook-Dawkins, John McDermid; U. York, UK
Steven P. Miller; Rockwell Collins, USA

8 *Details not available at press time*

9 **Xavier Delgado;** Polytechnic U. Catalonia, Barcelona, Spain
Marie-Christine Jené; ITACA, Spain
Erik Duval, Stefaan Ternier; KUL, Belgium
Philippe Vidal, Julien Broisin, Daniel Marquie; U. Paul Sabatier, IRIT, France
Gérard-Michel Cochard; U. Picardy, France

10 **Vijay Masurkar;** Sun Microsystems, Inc., Burlington, MA, USA
Emilio Mordini; Centre for Science, Society and Citizenship, Rome, Italy
Diane Whitehouse; European Commission, Belgium
Penny Duquenoy; School of Computing Science, Middlesex University, London, UK

11 **Dines Bjørner;** National U. Singapore, Singapore
Peter Chiang, Morten S.T. Jacobsen, Jens Kielsgaard Hansen, Michael P. Madsen; DTU Lyngby, Denmark
Denis Sabatier; Clearsy, France
Alistair A. McEwan, Jim Woodcock; U. Kent, UK
Martin Penicka; Czech Technical U., Czech Republic
Wolfgang Reif, Frank Ortmeier, Andreas Thums, Gerhard Schellhorn; Augsburg University, Germany
Takahiko Ogino; RTRI, Tokyo, Japan
Theo C. Giras, Zongli Lin; U. Virgina, USA

12 **Philippe David;** ESA, The Netherlands
Hélène Waeselynck, Yves Crouzet; LAAS-CNRS, France
Carl E. Landwehr; NSF, USA
Cristina Gacek; University of Newcastle upon Tyne, UK
Shigeru Chiba; Tokyo Institute of Technology, Japan
Cyrille Comar, Franco Gasperoni; Ada Core, ACT Europe, France
Jiri Gaisler; Gaisler Research, Gôteborg, Sweden

Serge Goiffon, Pierre Gaufillet; Airbus, France
Jean-Michel Tanneau; THALES Research & Technology, Orsay, France

13 **Nouredine Hadjsaid;** INP Grenoble, France
Christophe Andrieu; Schneider Electric, France
Rune Gustavsson; Blekinge Institute of Technology, Sweden

14 **Hirochika Inoue;** Digital Human Research Center, AIST, Japan
Raja Chatila, Georges Giralt; LAAS-CNRS, France
Kerstin Dautenhahn; U. Hertfordshire, UK
Oussama Khatib; Stanford U., USA
Gerhard Sagerer; Bielefeld University, Germany
Ben Krose; U. Amsterdam, Netherlands
Ruediger Dillmann; Karlsruhe U., Germany
Roland Siegwart; EPFL, Switzerland
Kurt Konolige; SRI International, USA

Topic 1

Semantic Integration of Heterogeneous Data

Organisers:

Yamine Ait Ameur
LISI/ENSMA. Poitiers. France
yamine@ensma.fr

Guy Pierra
LISI/ENSMA. Poitiers. France
pierra@ensma.fr

Engineering, trade and management oriented activities rely on a wide variety of data sources all over the world and are performed by means of various computer-supported systems. Such activities require not only that local data may be processed, but also that global data might be searched, compared and understood by computers systems, and that their meaning descriptions be available in computer - interpretable representations. Therefore, formal representation, sharing and exchange of data meaning representations appear as a prerequisite to allow semantic integration of data.

Over the last decade a number of new approaches were proposed for data meaning representation and for semantic integration of data. These approaches have all in common to use computer-interpretable representations of data meaning. Representations may be ontology's, thesauri or domain model, and various description languages and logic have been used for description and for reasoning, but these approaches opened new perspectives on integration of heterogeneous data.

The purpose of this topical day is to bring together researchers, engineers, standard developers and practitioners interested in the advance and application of semantic integration of heterogeneous data to review and discuss some typical example of data integration projects.

THREE DECADES OF DATA INTEGRATION — ALL PROBLEMS SOLVED?

Patrick Ziegler and Klaus R. Dittrich
Database Technology Research Group, Department of Informatics, University of Zurich Winterthurerstrasse 190, CH-8057 Zürich, Switzerland
{pziegler|dittrich}@ifi.unizh.ch

Abstract Data integration is one of the older research fields in the database area and has emerged shortly after database systems were first introduced into the business world. In this paper, we briefly introduce the problem of integration and, based on an architectural perspective, give an overview of approaches to address the integration issue. We discuss the evolution from structural to semantic integration and provide a short outlook on our own research in the SIRUP (Semantic Integration Reflecting User-specific semantic Perspectives) approach.

Keywords: Data integration, integration approaches, semantic integration

1. Introduction

In today's business world, it is typical that enterprises run different but co-existing information systems. Employing these systems, enterprises struggle to realize business opportunities in highly competitive markets. In this setting, the integration of existing information systems is becoming more and more indispensable in order to dynamically meet business and customer needs while leveraging long-term investments in existing IT infrastructure.

In general, integration of multiple information systems aims at combining selected systems so that they form a unified new whole and give users the illusion of interacting with one single information system. The reason for integration is twofold: First, given a set of existing information systems, an integrated view can be created to facilitate information access and reuse through a single information access point. Second, given a certain information need, data from different complementing information systems is to be combined to gain a more comprehensive basis to satisfy the need.

There is a manifold of applications that benefit from integrated information. For instance, in the area of business intelligence (BI), integrated information can be used for querying and reporting on business activities, for statistical analysis, online analytical processing (OLAP), and data mining in order to enable forecasting, decision making, enterprise-wide planning, and, in the end, to gain sustainable competitive advantages. For customer relationship management (CRM), integrated information on individual customers, business environment trends, and current sales can be used to improve customer services. Enterprise information portals (EIP) present integrated company information as personalized web sites and represent single information access points primarily for employees, but also for customers, business partners, and the public. Last, but not least, in the area of e-commerce and e-business, integrated information enables and facilitates business transactions and services over computer networks.

Similar to information, IT services and applications can be integrated, either to provide a single service access point or to provide more comprehensive services to meet business requirements. For instance, integrated workflow and document management systems can be used within enterprises to leverage intraorganizational collaboration. Based on the ideas of business process reengineering (BPR), integrated IT services and applications that support business processes can help to reduce time-to-market and to provide added-value products and services. That way, interconnecting building blocks from selected IT services and applications enables supply chain management within individual enterprises as well as cooperation beyond the boundaries of traditional enterprises, as in interorganizational cooperation, business process networks (BPN), and virtual organizations. Thus, it is possible to bypass intermediaries and to enable direct interaction between supply and demand, as in business-to-business (B2B), business-to-consumer (B2C), and business-to-employee (B2E) transactions.[1] These trends are fueled by XML that is becoming *the* industry standard for data exchange as well as by web services that provide interoperability between various software applications running on different platforms.

In the enterprise context, the integration problem is commonly referred to as enterprise integration (EI). Enterprise integration denotes the capability to integrate information and functionalities from a variety of information systems in an enterprise. This encompasses enterprise information integration (EII) that concerns integration on the data and information level and enterprise application integration (EAI) that considers integration on the level of application logic. In this paper, we focus on the integration of information and, in particular, highlight integration solutions that are provided by the database community. Our goal is to give, based on an architectural perspective, a database-centric overview of principal approaches to the integration problem and to il-

[1] Similarly, processes like government-to-government (G2G), government-to-citizen (G2C), and government-to-business (G2B) are used in e-government.

lustrate some frequently used approaches. Additionally, we provide an outlook to semantic integration that is needed in all integration examples given above and that will form a key factor for future integration solutions.

This paper is structured as follows: In the following Sect. 2, we sketch the problem of integration. Sect. 3 presents principal approaches to address the integration issue. In Sect. 4, the evolution from structural to current semantic integration approaches is discussed. Sect. 5 concludes the paper.

2. The Problem of Integration

Integration of multiple information systems generally aims at combining selected systems so that they form a unified new whole and give users the illusion of interacting with one single information system. Users are provided with a homogeneous logical view of data that is physically distributed over heterogeneous data sources. For this, all data has to be represented using the same abstraction principles (unified global data model and unified semantics). This task includes detection and resolution of schema and data conflicts regarding structure and semantics.

In general, information systems are not designed for integration. Thus, whenever integrated access to different source systems is desired, the sources and their data that do not fit together have to be coalesced by additional adaptation and reconciliation functionality. Note that there is not *the* one single integration problem. While the goal is always to provide a homogeneous, unified view on data from different sources, the particular integration task may depend on (1) the architectural view of an information system (see Fig. 1), (2) the content and functionality of the component systems, (3) the kind of information that is managed by component systems (alphanumeric data, multimedia data; structured, semi-structured, unstructured data), (4) requirements concerning autonomy of component systems, (5) intended use of the integrated information system (read-only or write access), (6) performance requirements, and (7) the available resources (time, money, human resources, know-how, etc.) [Dittrich and Jonscher, 1999].

Additionally, several kinds of heterogeneity typically have to be considered. These include differences in (1) hardware and operating systems, (2) data management software, (3) data models, schemas, and data semantics, (4) middleware, (5) user interfaces, and (6) business rules and integrity constraints.

3. Approaches to Integration

In this section, we apply an architectural perspective to give an overview of the different ways to address the integration problem. The presented classification is based on [Dittrich and Jonscher, 1999] and distinguishes integration approaches according to the level of abstraction where integration is performed.

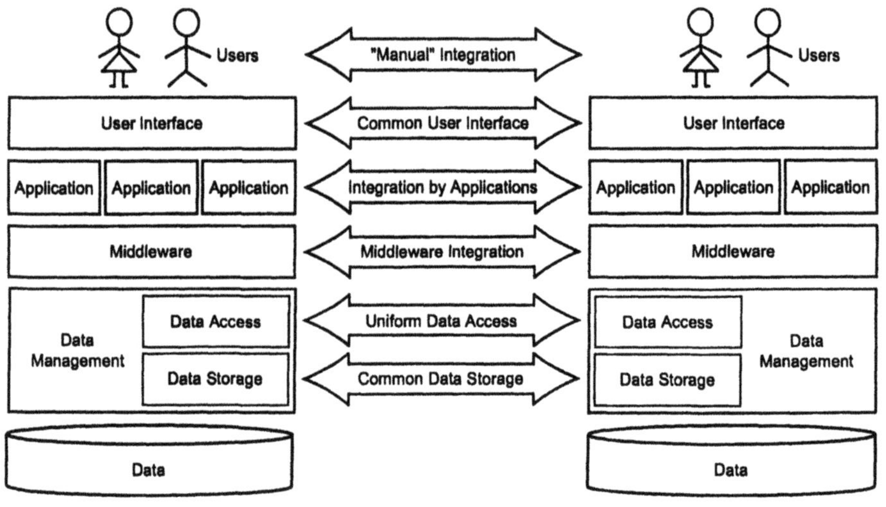

Figure 1. General Integration Approaches on Different Architectural Levels

Information systems can be described using a layered architecture, as shown in Fig. 1: On the topmost layer, users access data and services through various interfaces that run on top of different applications. Applications may use middleware — transaction processing (TP) monitors, message-oriented middleware (MOM), SQL-middleware, etc. — to access data via a data access layer. The data itself is managed by a data storage system. Usually, database management systems (DBMS) are used to combine the data access and storage layer.

Customarily, the integration problem can be addressed on each of the presented system layers. For this, the following general approaches — as illustrated in Fig. 1 — are available:

Manual Integration. Here, users directly interact with all relevant information systems and manually integrate selected data. That is, users have to deal with different user interfaces and query languages. Additionally, users need to have detailed knowledge on location, logical data representation, and data semantics.

Common User Interface. In this case, the user is supplied with a common user interface (e.g., a web browser) that provides a uniform look and feel. Data from relevant information systems is still separately presented so that homogenization and integration of data yet has to be done by the users (for instance, as in search engines).

Integration by Applications. This approach uses integration applications that access various data sources and return integrated results to the user. This solution is practical for a small number of component systems. However, applications become increasingly fat as the number of system interfaces and data formats to homogenize and integrate grows.

Integration by Middleware. Middleware provides reusable functionality that is generally used to solve dedicated aspects of the integration problem, e.g., as done by SQL-middleware. While applications are relieved from implementing common integration functionality, integration efforts are still needed in applications.[2] Additionally, different middleware tools usually have to be combined to build integrated systems.

Uniform Data Access. In this case, a logical integration of data is accomplished at the data access level. Global applications are provided with a unified global view of physically distributed data, though only virtual data is available on this level. However, global provision of physically integrated data can be time-consuming since data access, homogenization, and integration have to be done at runtime.

Common Data Storage. Here, physical data integration is performed by transferring data to a new data storage; local sources can either be retired or remain operational. In general, physical data integration provides fast data access. However, if local data sources are retired, applications that access them have to be migrated to the new data storage as well. In case local data sources remain operational, periodical refreshing of the common data storage needs to be considered.

In practice, concrete integration solutions are realized based on the presented six general integration approaches. Important examples include:

- *Mediated query systems* represent a uniform data access solution by providing a single point for read-only querying access to various data sources. A mediator [Wiederhold, 1992] that contains a global query processor is employed to send subqueries to local data sources; returned local query results are then combined.

- *Portals* as another form of uniform data access are personalized doorways to the internet or intranet where each user is provided with information tailored to his information needs. Usually, web mining is applied

[2]For instance, SQL-middleware provides a single access point to send SQL queries to all connected component systems. However, query results are not integrated into one single, homogeneous result set.

to determine user-profiles by click-stream analysis; that way, information the user might be interested in can be retrieved and presented.

- *Data warehouses* realize a common data storage approach to integration. Data from several operational sources (on-line transaction processing systems, OLTP) are extracted, transformed, and loaded (ETL) into a data warehouse. Then, analysis, such as online analytical processing (OLAP), can be performed on cubes of integrated and aggregated data.

- *Operational data stores* are a second example of a common data storage. Here, a "warehouse with fresh data" is built by immediately[3] propagating updates in local data sources to the data store. Thus, up-to-date integrated data is available for decision support. Unlike in data warehouses, data is neither cleansed nor aggregated nor are data histories supported.

- *Federated database systems (FDBMS)* achieve a uniform data access solution by logically integrating data from underlying local DBMS. Federated database systems are fully-fledged DBMS; that is, they implement their own data model, support global queries, global transactions, and global access control. Usually, the five-level reference architecture by [Sheth and Larson, 1990] is employed for building FDBMS.

- *Workflow management systems (WFMS)* allow to implement business processes where each single step is executed by a different application or user. Generally, WFMS support modeling, execution, and maintenance of processes that are comprised of interactions between applications and human users. WFMS represent an integration-by-application approach.

- *Integration by web services* performs integration through software components (i.e., web services) that support machine-to-machine interaction over a network by XML-based messages that are conveyed by internet protocols. Depending on their offered integration functionality, web services either represent a uniform data access approach or a common data access interface for later manual or application-based integration.

- *Peer-to-peer (P2P) integration* is a decentralized approach to integration between distributed, autonomous peers where data can be mutually shared and integrated. P2P integration constitutes, depending on the provided integration functionality, either a uniform data access approach or a data access interface for subsequent manual or application-based integration.

[3]That is, not within the same transaction but within a period of time that is reasonable according to the particular application requirements.

4. From Structural to Semantic Integration

Database technology was introduced in enterprises since the late 1960s to support (initially rather simple) business applications. As the number of applications and data repositories rapidly grew, the need for integrated data became apparent. As a consequence, first integration approaches in the form of multidatabase systems [Hurson and Bright, 1991] were developed around 1980 — e.g., MULTIBASE [Landers and Rosenberg, 1982]. This was a first cornerstone in a remarkable history of research in the area of data integration. The evolution continued over mediators (e.g., Garlic [Carey et al., 1995]) and agent systems (e.g., InfoSleuth [Bayardo et al., 1997]) to recent ontology-based (e.g., OBSERVER [Mena et al., 1996]), peer-to-peer (P2P) (e.g., Hyperion [Arenas et al., 2003]), and web service-based integration approaches (e.g., Active XML [Abiteboul et al., 2002]).

In general, early integration approaches were based on a relational or functional data model and realized rather tightly-coupled solutions by providing one single global schema. To overcome their limitations concerning the aspects of abstraction, classification, and taxonomies, object-oriented integration approaches [Bukhres and Elmagarmid, 1996] were adopted to perform structural homogenization and integration of data. With the advent of the internet and web technologies, the focus shifted from integrating purely well-structured data to also incorporating semi- and unstructured data while architecturally, loosely-coupled mediator and agent systems became popular.

However, integration is more than just a structural or technical problem. Technically, it is rather easy to connect different relational DBMS (e.g., via ODBC or JDBC). More demanding is to integrate data described by different data models; even worse are the problems caused by data with heterogeneous semantics. For instance, having only the name "loss" to denote a relation in an enterprise information system does not provide sufficient information to doubtlessly decide whether the represented loss is a book loss, a realized loss, or a future expected loss and whether the values of the tuples reflect only a roughly estimated loss or a precisely quantified loss. Integrating two "loss" relations with (implicit) heterogeneous semantics leads to erroneous results and completely senseless conclusions. Therefore, explicit and precise semantics of integratable data are essential for semantically correct and meaningful integration results. Note that none of the integration approaches in Sect. 3 helps to resolve semantic heterogeneity; neither is XML that only provides structural information a solution.

In the database area, semantics can be regarded as people's interpretation of data and schema items according to their understanding of the world in a certain context. In data integration, the type of semantics considered is generally real-world semantics that are concerned with the "mapping of objects in the model or computational world onto the real world [...] [and] the issues that involve human interpretation, or meaning and use of data and information" [Ouksel and Sheth, 1999]. In this setting, semantic integration is the task of grouping, combining or completing data from different sources by taking into account explicit and precise data semantics in order to avoid that semantically incompatible data is structurally merged. That is, semantic integration has to ensure that only data related to the same or sufficiently[4] similar real-world entity or concept is merged. A prerequisite for this is to resolve semantic ambiguity concerning integratable data by explicit metadata to elicit all relevant implicit assumptions and underlying context information.

One idea to overcome semantic heterogeneity in the database area is to exhaustively specify the intended real-world semantics of all data and schema elements. Unfortunately, it is impossible to completely define what a data or schema element denotes or means in the database world [Sheth et al., 1993]. Therefore, database schemas do typically not provide enough explicit semantics to interpret data always consistently and unambiguously [Sheth and Larson, 1990]. These problems are further worsened by the fact that semantics may be embodied in data models, conceptual schemas, application programs, the data itself, and the minds of users. Moreover, there are no absolute semantics that are valid for all potential users; semantics are relative [García-Solaco et al., 1996]. These difficulties concerning semantics are the reason for many still open research challenges in the area of integration.

Ontologies — which can be defined as explicit, formal descriptions of concepts and their relationships that exist in a certain universe of discourse, together with a shared vocabulary to refer to these concepts — can contribute to solve the problem of semantic heterogeneity. Compared with other classification schemes, such as taxonomies, thesauri, or keywords, ontologies allow more complete and more precise domain models [Huhns and Singh, 1997]. With respect to an ontology a particular user group commits to, the semantics of data provided by data sources for integration can be made explicit. Based on this shared understanding, the danger of semantic heterogeneity can be reduced. For instance, ontologies can be applied in the area of the Semantic Web to explicitly connect information from web documents to its definition and context in machine-processable form; that way, semantic services, such as semantic document retrieval, can be provided.

In database research, *single* domain models and ontologies were first applied to overcome semantic heterogeneity. As in SIMS [Arens et al., 1993], a domain model is used as a single ontology to which the contents of data sources are mapped. That way, queries expressed in terms of the global ontology can be asked. In general, single-ontology approaches are useful for

[4]How much similarity is considered as sufficient depends on the particular information need and application area.

integration problems where all information sources to be integrated provide nearly the same view on a domain [Wache et al., 2001]. In case the domain views of the sources differ, finding a common view becomes difficult. To overcome this problem, multi-ontology approaches like OBSERVER [Mena et al., 1996] describe each data source with its own ontology; then, these local ontologies have to be mapped, either to a global ontology or between each other, to establish a common understanding.

Mapping all data to one single domain model forces users to adapt to one single conceptualization of the world. This contrasts to the fact that receivers of integrated data widely differ in their conceptual interpretation of and preference for data — they are generally situated in different real-world contexts and have different conceptual models of the world in mind [Goh et al., 1994]. COIN [Goh et al., 1994] was one of the first research projects to consider the different contexts data providers and data receivers are situated in.

In our own research, we continue the trend of taking into account user-specific aspects in the process of semantic integration. We address the problem how user-specific mental domain models and user-specific semantics of concepts (e.g., "loss") can be reflected in the data integration process. In the SIRUP (Semantic Integration Reflecting User-specific semantic Perspectives) approach, we investigate how data — equipped with explicit, queryable semantics — can be effectively pre-integrated on a conceptual level. That way, we aim at enabling users to perform declarative data integration by conceptual modeling of their individual ways to perceive a domain of interest.

5. Conclusions

In this paper, we gave an overview of issues and principal approaches in the area of integration seen from a database perspective. Even though data integration is one of the older research topics in the database area, there is yet no silver bullet solution and there is none to be expected in the near future. The most difficult integration problems are caused by semantic heterogeneity; they are being addressed in current research focusing on applying explicit, formalized data semantics to provide semantics-aware integration solutions. Despite this, considerable work remains to be done for the vision of truly user-specific semantic integration in form of efficient and scalable solutions to become true.

References

Abiteboul, Serge, Benjelloun, Omar, and Milo, Tova (2002). Web Services and Data Integration. In Ling, Tok Wang, Dayal, Umeshwar, Bertino, Elisa, Ng, Wee Keong, and Goh, Angela, editors, *Third International Conference on Web Information Systems Engineering (WISE 2002)*, pages 3–7, Singapore, December 12–14. IEEE Computer Society.

Arenas, Marcelo, et al. (2003). The Hyperion Project: From Data Integration to Data Coordination. *SIGMOD Record*, 32(3):53–58.

Arens, Yigal, et al. (1993). Retrieving and Integrating Data from Multiple Information Sources. *International Journal of Cooperative Information Systems (IJCIS)*, 2(2):127–158.

Bayardo, Roberto J., et al. (1997). InfoSleuth: Agent-Based Semantic Integration of Information in Open and Dynamic Environments. In *1997 ACM SIGMOD International Conference on Management of Data (SIGMOD 1997)*, pages 195–206, Tucson, Arizona, USA. ACM.

Bukhres, Omran A. and Elmagarmid, Ahmed K., editors (1996). *Object-Oriented Multidatabase Systems: A Solution for Advanced Applications*. Prentice-Hall.

Carey, M.J., et al. (1995). Towards Heterogeneous Multimedia Information Systems: The Garlic Approach. In *5th International Workshop on Research Issues in Data Engineering-Distributed Object Management (RIDE-DOM 1995)*, pages 124–131, Taipei, Taiwan, March 6–7.

Dittrich, Klaus R. and Jonscher, Dirk (1999). All Together Now — Towards Integrating the World's Information Systems. In Masunaga, Yoshifumi and Spaccapietra, Stefano, editors, *Advances in Multimedia and Databases for the New Century*, pages 109–123, Kyoto, Japan, November 30 – December 2. World Scientific Press.

García-Solaco, Manuel, Saltor, Fèlix, and Castellanos, Malú (1996). Semantic Heterogeneity in Multidatabase Systems. In Bukhres, Omran A. and Elmagarmid, Ahmed K., editors, *Object-Oriented Multidatabase Systems. A Solution for Advanced Applications*, pages 129–202. Prentice-Hall.

Goh, Cheng Hian, Madnick, Stuart E., and Siegel, Michael (1994). Context Interchange: Overcoming the Challenges of Large-Scale Interoperable Database Systems in a Dynamic Environment. In *Third International Conference on Information and Knowledge Management (CIKM 1994)*, pages 337–346, Gaithersburg, USA, November 29 – December 2. ACM.

Huhns, Michael N. and Singh, Munindar P. (1997). Agents on the Web: Ontologies for Agents. *IEEE Internet Computing*, 1(6):81–83.

Hurson, Ali R. and Bright, M. W. (1991). Multidatabase Systems: An Advanced Concept in Handling Distributed Data. *Advances in Computers*, 32:149–200.

Landers, Terry and Rosenberg, Ronni L. (1982). An Overview of MULTIBASE. In Schneider, Hans-Jochen, editor, *Second International Symposium on Distributed Data Bases (DDB 1982)*, pages 153–184, Berlin, Germany, September 1–3. North-Holland.

Mena, Eduardo, et al. (1996). OBSERVER: An Approach for Query Processing in Global Information Systems based on Interoperation across Pre-existing Ontologies. In *First IFCIS International Conference on Cooperative Information Systems (CoopIS 1996)*, pages 14–25, Brussels, Belgium, June 19–21. IEEE Computer Society.

Ouksel, Aris M. and Sheth, Amit P. (1999). Semantic Interoperability in Global Information Systems: A Brief Introduction to the Research Area and the Special Section. *SIGMOD Record*, 28(1):5–12.

Sheth, Amit P., Gala, Sunit K., and Navathe, Shamkant B. (1993). On Automatic Reasoning for Schema Integration. *International Journal of Intelligent and Cooperative Information Systems*, 2(1):23–50.

Sheth, Amit P. and Larson, James A. (1990). Federated Database Systems for Managing Distributed, Heterogeneous, and Autonomous Databases. *ACM Computing Surveys*, 22(3):183–236.

Wache, H., et al. (2001). Ontology-Based Integration of Information — A Survey of Existing Approaches. In Stuckenschmidt, H., editor, *IJCAI-2001 Workshop on Ontologies and Information Sharing*, pages 108–117, Seattle, USA, April 4–5.

Wiederhold, Gio (1992). Mediators in the Architecture of Future Information Systems. *IEEE Computer*, 25(3):38–49.

THE PLIB ONTOLOGY-BASED APPROACH TO DATA INTEGRATION

Guy Pierra
Laboratory of Applied Computer Science (LISI)
National Engineering School for Mechanics and Aerotechnics (ENSMA), Poitiers
86960 Futuroscope Cedex - France
pierra@ensma.fr

Abstract This paper presents an overview of the integration approach developed in the PLIB project (officially ISO 132584 "parts Library"). This approach is based on (1) an ontology model, (2) an ontology mapping model, and (3) an ontology-based database model (OBDB).

1. Introduction

The semantic heterogeneity has been identified as the most challenging issue of data integration since it requires to understand the relationship between data and real world objects to be able to map various conceptualization often based on various point of views. In the traditional data integration approach, domain semantics is encoded in a procedural form. More recent approaches (Wache, 2001) explicitly represent domain semantics through ontologies. The commonality of most of these approaches is that data integration is considered *a posteriori*, once the data sources have been set up.

The goal of this paper is to give an overview of the *a priori* approach developed over the last 10 years in the PLIB project to provide for automatic integration of engineering component databases and catalogues (ISO, 2004). The PLIB approach is based on three ideas, leading to the development of three resources. (1) In a number of structured activity domains, a precise shared vocabulary is already existing to allow person-to-person communication. It should be possible to make this vocabulary computers sensible in the form a shared ontology. A *context-explicit ontology model*, known is the PLIB ontology model, has been developed. (2) The main characteristic of human activity is to innovate, this means to create specific extensions of existing concepts and practices. An *on-*

tology mapping model allowing a user to define its own ontology as a specialization of a shared ontology has been developed. (3) Integrating data require human and/or computer understanding of data meaning. We have developed a new database model, called *Ontology-Based Database (OBDB)* where each database contains its own ontology.

We presents an overview of these three models in the three following sections.

2. Overview of PLIB ontology

The role of a PLIB ontology is twofold. First it is intended to support user interfaces at the knowledge level, both for graphical access and for queries. Second, it provides for automatic integration. PLIB ontologies are: (1) object-flavored (the word is captured by classes and properties), (2) property-oriented (class are only defined when required to define the domain of some properties), (3) conceptual (each entry is a concept defined by a number of facets, both formal and informal, and not a term), (4) multilingual (each entry is associated with a globally unique identifier (GUI), words used in some facets may appear in any number of languages) (5) formal (the PLIB ontology model is specified in EXPRESS); (6) modular (an ontology may reference another ontology); (7) consensual (both the model (Kashyap et al., 1996), and domain ontologies result from standardization consensus).

2.1 Minimizing context-sensitivity

Importance of a context representation for the semantic integration of heterogeneous database was already underlined by a number of researchers in multidatabase systems, both at the schema definition level (Kashyap et al., 1996), and at the property value level (Goh et al., 1999). To ensure the feasibility to reach a consensus on an ontology definition (Pierra, 2003), a PLIB ontology minimizes context sensitivity: (1) definition context explication is done by associating with each properties, the higher class where it is meaningful and with each class the properties applicable to each class; (2) value context explication is done by associating with each *context-dependent property* value its evaluation context represented as a set of *context parameter*-value pairs (properties whose values are not context-sensitive are called *characteristic properties*), (3) value scaling explication is done at the schema level by associating each quantitative property type both with a dimensional equation and with a unit, and (4) to avoid context bias when choosing the properties associated with a class, each class is associated, at the ontology level, with all the properties that are essential for its instances, at least in a very broad context.

2.2 Formal definition of PLIB ontologies

Formally, a single PLIB ontology may be defined as a 6-tuple : $O = < C, P, IsA, PropCont, ClassCont, ValCont >$, where: (1) C is the set of classes used to describe the concepts of a given domain; (2) P is the set of properties used to describe the instances of C. P is partitioned into P_{val} (characteristics properties), P_{fonc} (context dependent properties) and P_{cont} (context parameters); (3) $IsA : C \rightarrow C$ is a partial function, the semantic of which is subsumption; (4) $PropCont : P \rightarrow C$ associates to each property the higher class where it is *meaningful* (the property is said to be *visible* for this class); (5) $ClassCont : C \rightarrow 2^P$ associates which each class all the properties that are applicable to every instances of this class (rigid properties); (6) $ValCont : P_{fonc} \rightarrow 2^{P_{cont}}$ associates to each context dependent properties the context parameters of which its value depends.

Axioms specify that: (1) IsA defines a single hierarchy, (2) visible and applicable properties are both inherited, and (3) only visible property may become applicable.

EXAMPLE 1 *Figure 1 (a) presents a single ontology. Class hierarchy is represented by indentation. $P = \{mass\}$. The mass properties applies to hardware and components, but not to software and simulation models. mass is visible at the level of resources : $PropCont(mass) = resources$, with a definition s. t. "the mass of a resource that is a material object". It becomes applicable in hardware and components: ClassCont (hardware) = $\{mass\}$; ClassCont (component) = $\{mass\}$.*

3. Inter-ontology mappings

PLIB does not assume that all data sources use the same ontology. Each data source may build its local ontology without any external reference. It may also build it based upon one or several reference ontologies (i. e., standard ones). A class of a local ontology may be described as *subsumed* by one or several other class(es) defined in other ontologies. This means that each instance of the former is also instance of the latter. This relationship is named *case-of.* Though case-of relationship the subsumed class may either import properties (their GUI and definitions are preserved) or map properties (the properties are different but they are semantically equivalent) that are defined in the referenced class(es). It may also define additional properties.

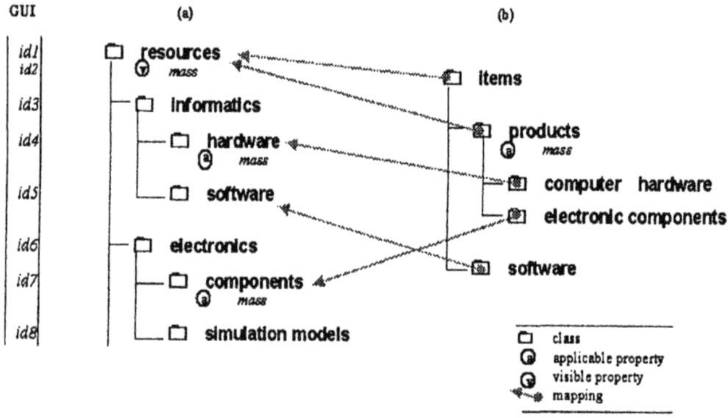

Figure 1. An example of a reference ontology (a) and of an user defined ontology (b)

A PLIB ontology O_m that includes mapping onto one (or several) other ontologies (called a *PLIB ontology*) may be formally defined as a couple: $O_m =< O, M >$, where : O is a single PLIB ontology, and $M = \{m_i\}$, is a mapping defined as a set of mapping objects.

Each mapping object has four attributes :
$m =< domain, range, import, map >$, where: (1) $domain \in C$ defines the class that is mapped onto an external class by a *case-of* relationship; (2) $range \in GUI \subset \{string\}$ is the globally unique identifier of the external class onto which the $m.domain$ class is mapped; (3) $import \in 2^P$ is a set of properties visible or applicable in the $m.range$ class that are imported in $ClassCont(m.domain)$; (4) $map \subset \{(p, id) \mid p \in P \wedge id \in GUI \subset \{string\}\}$ defines the mapping of properties defined in the $m.domain$ class with equivalent properties visible or applicable in the $m.range$ class. The latter are identified by their GUIs.

EXAMPLE 2 *Figure 1 (b) present a (user-defined) ontology mapped on a reference ontology (a). C = {items, products, computer hardware, electronic components, software} and P = {mass}. $M = m1, m2, m3, m4$ with $m_1 = (item, id1, (), ())$; $m_2 = (products, id1, (id2), ())$; $m_3 =$ (computer hardware, id4, (), ()) ; $m_4 =$ (electronic components, id7, (), ()). We note that no properties are mapped, they are all imported.*

Axioms (1) and (2) for single ontologies hold. Axiom (3) states that only imported or visible properties may become applicable. As shown by example 2, the structure of a (user) ontology may be quite different from the one of a standard ontology she references. Nevertheless, a

system storing the user ontology $< O, M >$ may automatically answer queries against the standard ontology(ies) on which O is mapped.

4. Ontology-based database

We call *ontology-based data base* (OBDB) a database (1) that explicitly represent an ontology, possibly including a mapping onto other ontologies, (2) whose schema refers to the ontology for each of its represented entities and properties and (3) whose each data may be interpreted in a consistent way using the meaning defined for the corresponding ontology entry. An OBDB is not required to populate either all the classes of its ontology or all the properties defined for a given class.

Formally, an OBDB is a quadruplet $OBDB =< O_m, I, Sch, Pop >$, where: (1) O is a PLIB ontology ($O_m =< O, M >$); (2) I is the set of instances of the database; (3) $Sch : C \to 2^P$ associates to each ontology class c_i of C the properties which are effectively used to describe the instances of the class c_i; (4) $Pop : C \to 2^I$ that associates to each class (leaf class or not) those own instances. The following axiom, that states that only applicable properties for a class may be used for describing instances of this class, holds :

$$\forall c_i \in C, Sch(c_i) \subset Applic(c_i) \tag{1}$$

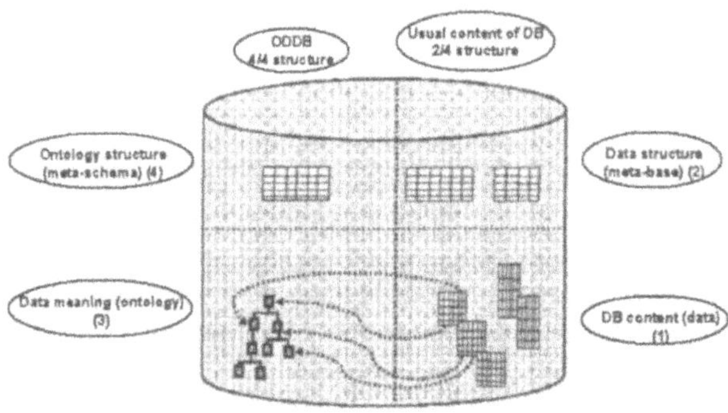

Figure 2. The OntoDB model for OBDB

The OntoDB architecture model we have proposed for OBDB, and prototyped in various environments, defines four different parts (see figure 2). The *ontology part* contains ontology definition as instances of the ontology model (that may be PLIB or any other model represented as a set of objets). In order to make the system generic with respect to

ontology model evolution, the *meta-schema part* records, in a reflexive meta-model, both the ontology model (or models) and its own structure. The *data part*, contains description of object instances (belonging to the ontology domain) described in terms of ontology class belonging and ontology property values. But, unlike individuals of description logic that may be described by any number of class belonging and by any existing properties (if they are not associated with specific constraints) thus making difficult storage indexing, in the OntoDB model instance data must obey to two assumptions. (A1) Each instance must belong to one only class, called its *base class* (and to all of its superclasses). (A2) Each instance may be only described by properties that are applicable property for its base class. With these two assumptions, each class may be associated with a view of which each row describes an instance that defines this class as its base class, and of which columns are the subset of applicable properties that were selected to constitute the schema of this class. Finally, the *meta-base part* (that allows in any DBMS to record data schema) is used for recording how the above view is defined on terms of table structure.

5. Conclusion

The PLIB integration approach allows both: (1) an autonomy of the various data sources, each one having its own ontology, and (2)an automatic integration. To the best of my knowledge, It is the first approach that fulfil these two conditions. An increasing number of B2B e-commerce actors are moving in the direction of PLIB.

References

L. Bellatreche, G. Pierra, D. Nguyen Xuan and H. Dehainsala, An Automated Information Integration Technique using an Ontology-based Database Approach. in *Proc. of 10th ISPE Int. Conf. on Concurrent Engineering*(2003)

C.H. Goh, S. Bressan, S. Madnick, M. Siegel, Context Interchange: New Features and Formalisms for the Intelligent Integration of Information, *ACM Transactions on Information Systems* 17(3) (1999) pp. 270-293.

ISO 13584-25. 2004. *Industrial Automation Systems and Intregration - Parts Library - Part 25: Logical model of supplier library with aggregate values and explicit content*, (ISO, Geneva, 2004)

V. Kashyap and A. Sheth, Semantic and schematic similarities between database objects: a context-based approach, *The VLDB Journal*, 5 (1996) pp. 276-304.

G. Pierra, Context-Explication in Conceptual Ontologies: The PLIB Approach. in *Proc. of 10th ISPE Int. Conf. on Concurrent Engineering* (2003)

H. Wache, T. Vgele, U. Visser, H. Stuckenschmidt, Ontology-Based Integration of Information: A Survey of Existing Approaches, in *Proc. of the IJCAI-01 Workshop: Ontologies and Information Sharing*, Seattle, WA, (2001) pp. 108-117

THE MOMIS METHODOLOGY FOR INTEGRATING HETEROGENEOUS DATA SOURCES*

Domenico Beneventano and Sonia Bergamaschi
Dipartimento di Ingegneria dell'Informazione
Università degli Studi di Modena e Reggio Emilia
Via Vignolese 905 – 41100 - Modena

Abstract: The Mediator EnvirOnment for Multiple Information Sources (MOMIS) aims at constructing synthesized, integrated descriptions of the information coming from multiple heterogeneous sources, in order to provide the user with a global virtual view of the sources independent from their location and the level of heterogeneity of their data. Such a global virtual view is a conceptualization of the underlying domain and then may be thought of as an ontology describing the involved sources. In this article we explore the framework's main elements and discuss how the output of the integration process can be exploited to create a conceptualization of the underlying domain.

Keyword: Ontologies, Heterogeneous Sources, Mediator, Global As View, WordNet

1. INTRODUCTION

Nowadays the Web is a huge collection of data and its expansion rate is very high. Web users need new ways to exploit all this available information and possibilities. A *new vision of the Web*, the Semantic Web, where resources are annotated with machine-processable metadata providing them with background knowledge and meaning, arises. A fundamental component of the Semantic Web is the ontology; this "*explicit specification of a conceptualization*"[1] allows information providers to give a understandable meaning to their documents.

MOMIS[2] is a framework for information extraction and integration of heterogeneous information sources, developed by the DBGroup (www.dbgroup.unimo.it) at the University of Modena and Reggio Emilia

---

* This research has been partially supported by EU IST-SEWASIE

(UNIMORE). The system implements a semi-automatic methodology for data integration that follows the *Global as View* (GAV) approach[3]. The result of the integration process is a global schema, which provides a reconciled, integrated and virtual view of the underlying sources, GVV (Global Virtual View). The GVV is composed of a set of (global) classes that represent the information contained in the sources, and it is the result of the integration process, i.e. a conceptualization of the underlying domain (domain ontology) for the integrated sources. The GVV is then semi-automatically annotated according to a lexical ontology. With reference to the Semantic Web area, where generally the annotation process consists of providing a web page with semantic markups according to an ontology, we firstly markup the local metadata descriptions and then the MOMIS system generates an annotated conceptualization of the sources. Moreover, our approach "builds" the domain ontology as the synthesis of the integration process, while the usual approach in the Semantic Web is based on "a priori" existence of ontology.

A comparison of MOMIS with others mediator systems is proposed in Table 1 (TSIMMIS[4], GARLIC[5], SIMS[6], Infomaster[7], Information Manifold[8], Observer[9]).

	MOMIS	**TSIMMIS**	**GARLIC**	**SIMS**	**Infomaster**	**IM**	**Observer**
Developer	UNIMORE University	Stanford University	IBM Almaden	ISI-USC	Stanford University	AT&T Research	Saragozza University
Sources	Structured and semistruct.	Semistruct.	Heterog.	Semistruct.	Semistruct.	Web pages	Heterog.
Data Model	ODL$_{I^3}$	OEM/MSL	GDL	Loom	KIF/KQML	Extended Relational	-
Description Logic	OLCD[10]	-	-	Loom	-	CARIN	CLASSIC
Approach	GAV	GAV	GAV	GAV/ LAV	GAV	LAV	GAV
Global View Creation	semi-automatic	manual	manual	based on wrapper description	manual	manual	automatic (DL based)
Query	Only for relational sources	Yes	Yes	Yes	Yes	Yes	Yes
Status of the project	Evolving in the Sewasie project	Completed	Evolving in other projects	Evolving in other projects	Completed	Completed	Completed

Table 1. Mediator system comparison.

2. THE MOMIS INTEGRATION METHODOLOGY

In this section, we describe the information integration process for building the GVV. The process is shown in Figure 1.

The ODL$_{I3}$ Language

As a common data model for integrating a given set of local information sources, MOMIS uses an object-oriented language called ODL$_{I3}$, which is an evolution of the OODBMS standard language ODL. ODL$_{I3}$ extends ODL with the following relationships expressing intra- and inter-schema knowledge for the source schemas: SYN (synonym of), BT (broader terms), NT (narrower terms) and RT (related terms). By means of ODL$_{I3}$, only one language is exploited to describe both the sources (the input of the synthesis process) and the GVV (the result of the process). The translation of ODL$_{I3}$ descriptions into one of the Semantic Web standards such as RDF, DAML+OIL, OWL is a straightforward process. In fact, from a general perspective an ODL$_{I3}$ concept corresponds to a *Class* of a the Semantic Web standard, and ODL$_{I3}$ relationships are translated into *properties*.

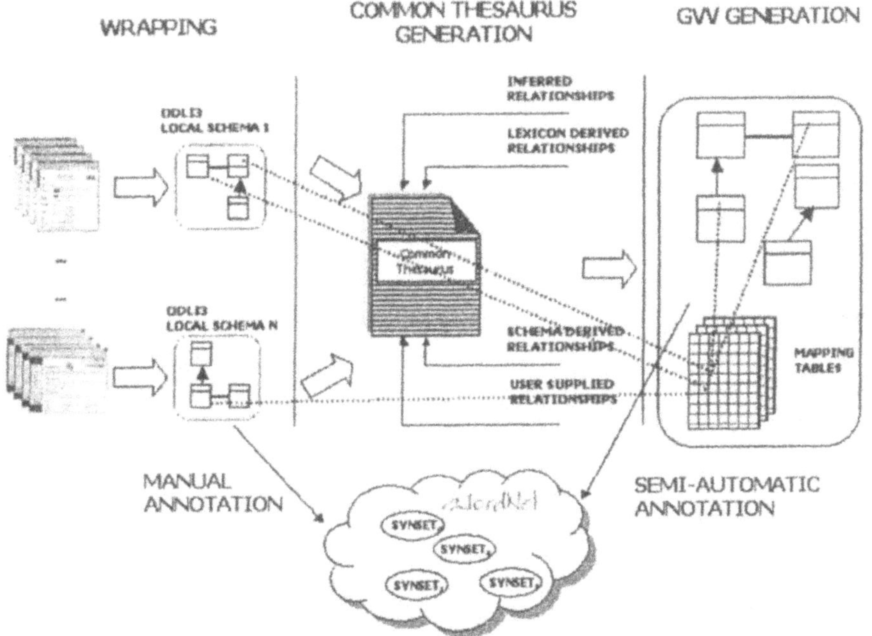

Figure 1. Overview of the ontology-generation process. The figure shows the local schemas' generation, where local schemas are annotated according to the lexical ontology WordNet, the Common Thesaurus generation, and finally the GVV global classes. In particular, these ones are connected by means of mapping tables to the local schemas and are (semi-automatically) annotated according to WordNet.

Wrapping: extracting data structure for sources

A wrapper logically converts the source data structure into the ODL_{I3} model. The wrapper architecture and interfaces are crucial, because wrappers are the focal point for managing the diversity of data sources. For conventional structured information sources (e.g. relational databases), schema description is always available and can be directly translated. For semistructured information sources, a schema description is in general not directly available at the sources. A basic characteristic of semistructured data is that they are "self-describing" hence information associated with the schema is specified within data. Thus, a wrapper has to implement a methodology to extract and explicitly represent the conceptual schema of a semi-structured source. We developed a wrapper for XML/DTDs files. By using that wrapper, DTD elements are translated into semi-structured objects, according to different proposed methods[11].

Manual annotation of a local source with WordNet

For each element of the local schema, the integration designer has to manually choose the appropriate meaning in the WordNet[12] lexical system. The annotation phase is composed of two different steps: in the *Word Form choice* step, the WordNet morphologic processor aids the designer by suggesting a word form corresponding to the given term; in the *Meaning choice* step the designer can choose to map an element on zero, one or more senses. The annotation assigns a name (this name can be the original one or a word form chosen from the designer), and a set of meanings, to each local class and attribute of the local schema.

Common Thesaurus Generation

MOMIS constructs a Common Thesaurus describing intra and inter-schema knowledge in the form of SYN, BT, NT, and RT relationships. The Common Thesaurus is constructed through an incremental process in which the following relationships are added:

schema-derived relationships: relationships holding at intra-schema level are automatically extracted by analyzing each schema separately. For example, analyzing XML data files, BT/NT relationships are generated from couples IDs/IDREFs and RT relationships from nested elements.

lexicon-derived relationship: we exploit the annotation phase in order to translate relationships holding at the lexical level into relationships to be added to the Common Thesaurus. For example, the hypernymy lexical relation is translated into a BT relationship.

designer-supplied relationships: new relationships can be supplied directly by the designer, to capture specific domain knowledge. If a nonsense or wrong relationship is inserted, the subsequent integration process can produce a wrong global schema;

inferred relationships: Description Logics (DL) techniques of ODB-Tools[13] are exploited to infer new relationships, by means of subsumption computation applied to a "virtual schema" obtained by interpreting BT/NT as subclass relationships and RT as domain attributes.

Global Virtual View (GVV) Generation

The MOMIS methodology allows us to identify similar ODL_{I^3} classes, that is, classes that describe the same or semantically related concept in different sources. To this end, *affinity coefficients* are evaluated for all possible pairs of ODL_{I^3} classes, based on the relationships in the Common Thesaurus properly strengthened. Affinity coefficients determine the degree of matching of two classes based on their names (*Name Affinity* coefficient) and their attributes (*Structural Affinity* coefficient) and are fused into the *Global Affinity* coefficient, calculated by means of the linear combination of the two coefficients[14]. Global affinity coefficients are then used by a hierarchical clustering algorithm, to classify ODL_{I^3} classes according to their degree of affinity.

For each cluster Cl, a Global Class GC, with a set of Global Attributes $GA_1, \ldots, GA_N$, and a Mapping Table MT, expressing mappings between local and global attributes, are defined. The Mapping Table is a table whose columns represent the local classes, which belong to the Global Class and whose rows represent the global attributes. An element `MT[GA][LC]` is a function which represents how local attributes of LC are mapped into the global attribute GA : `MT[GA][LC]= f(LAS)` where LAS is a subset of the local attributes of LC.

Global Virtual View (GVV) Annotation

To annotate a GVV means to assign a name and a set (eventually empty) of meanings to each global element (class or attribute).

In order to semi-automatically associate an annotation to each global class, we consider the set of all its "broadest" local classes, w.r.t. the relationships included in the Common Thesaurus. On the basis of this set, the designer will annotate the global class as follows:

name choice: the designer is responsible for the choice of the name: the system only suggests a list of possible names. The designer may select a name within the proposed list or introduce a new one.

meaning choice: the union of the meanings of the "broadest" local classes are proposed to the designer as meanings of the Global Class; the designer may change this set.

A similar approach is used for Global Attributes Annotation.

3. CONCLUSION AND FUTURE WORK

MOMIS supports the semiautomatic building and annotation of domain ontologies by integrating the schemas of information sources. The MOMIS framework is currently adopted in the Semantic Web Agents in

Integrated Economies (SEWASIE) European research project (www.sewasie.org), coordinated by UNIMORE. SEWASIE aims at implementing an advanced search engine that enables intelligent access to heterogeneous data sources on the Web via semantic enrichment, providing the basis for structured secure Web-based communication. To achieve this goal, SEWASIE creates a virtual network based on Sewasie information nodes (SINodes), which consist of managed information sources, wrappers, and a metadata repository. SINodes metadata represent GVVs of the overall information sources that each manage. To maintain the GVV of a SINode, we are investigating two distinct aspects: the system overload in maintaining the built ontologies and the effects of inserting new sources that could modify existing ontologies. Future work will addresses the improving of the annotation phase by allowing the designer to face multilingual environments, that is adopting a multiligual lexical database.

REFERENCES

1. T. R. Gruber. A translation approach to portable ontologies. *Knowledge Acquisition*, 5(2):199-220, 1993.
2. S. Bergamaschi, S. Castano, D. Beneventano, M. Vincini: "Semantic Integration of Heterogeneous Information Sources", *DKE*, Vol. 36, Num. 1, Pages 215-249, 2001.
3. M. Lenzerini Data Integration: A Theoretical Perspective. *PODS '02*: 233-246, 2002.
4. S. Chawathe, Garcia Molina, H., J. Hammer, K. Ireland, Y. Papakostantinou, J.Ullman and J. Widom. The TSIMMIS project: Integration of heterogeneous information sources. *IPSJ Conference*, Tokyo, Japan, 1994.
5. M.J. Carey, L.M. Haas, P.M. Schwarz, M. Arya, W.F. Cody, R. Fagin, M. Flickner, A. Luniewski, W. Niblack, D. Petkovic, J. Thomas II, J.H. Williams, and E.L. Wimmers, Towards heterogeneous multimedia information systems: The Garlic approach. *IBM Almaden Research Center,* San Jose, CA 95120, 1996.
6. Y. Arens, C. A. Knoblock, and C. Hsu. Query processing in the sims information mediator. *Advanced Planning Technology*, 1996.
7. M. R. Genesereth, A. M. Keller, and O. M. Duschka. Infomaster: An information integration system. *SIGMOD'97*, pages 539--542, Tucson, Arizona, USA, 1997. ACM Press.
8. T. Kirk, A. Y. Levy, Y. Sagiv, and D. Srivastava. The information manifold. *AAAI Spring Symposium on Information Gathering from Heterogeneous*, 1995.
9. E. Mena, A. Illarramendi, V. Kashyap, and A. P. Sheth. Observer: An approach for query processing in global information systems based on interoperation across preexisting ontologies. *Distributed and Parallel Databases*, 8(2):223--271, 2000.
10 D. Beneventano, S. Bergamaschi, S. Lodi and C. Sartori, Consistency Checking in Complex Object Database Schemata *IEEE TKDE.*, vol. 10, no. 4, 1998, pp. 576–598.
11 S. Abiteboul, P. Buneman, and D. Suciu. Data on the Web - From Relations to Semistructured Data and XML. Morgan Kaufmann, 2000.
12. A.G. Miller. A lexical database for English. *Communications of the ACM,* 38(11):39:41,1995.
13. D. Beneventano, S. Bergamaschi, C. Sartori, M. Vincini ODB-QOptimizer: a tool for semantic query optimization in OODB. *ICDE'97*, UK, April 1997.
14. S. Castano, V. De Antonellis, S. De Capitani di Vimercati. Global viewing of heterogeneous data sources. *IEEE TKDE*, 13(2), 2001.

BUILDING SCALABLE MEDIATOR SYSTEMS

Chantal Reynaud
University of Paris-Sud, CNRS (L.R.I.) & INRIA (Fiuturs), orsay, France; University of Paris X-Nanterre, France.

Abstract: This paper deals with PICSEL mediator systems which integrate services. We propose a scalable approach which exploits standardized specifications provided by normalization organisms. The paper focuses on the use of such specifications to automate the construction of the mediator. An illustration in the tourism domain with OTA specifications is given.

Key words: Service integration, mediation, scalability.

1. INTRODUCTION

In the recent years, considerable research work has been done on data mediation systems between users and multiple data sources leading to integration systems related to a same domain. A mediator system provides a uniform interface for querying collections of pre-existing data sources that were created independently. Several data mediation systems have been implemented. They have proved to be suitable for building specialized data servers over a reasonable number of data sources (Chawathe et al., 1994; Genesereth et al., 1997; Kirk et al. 1995).

A mediator system is composed of two parts, a part which contains knowledge corresponding to the application domain of the system and a query engine which is generic. The knowledge part is composed first of a single mediated schema, also called ontology, which is a description of the application domain. Second, it is composed of a set of source descriptions expressed as views over the ontology. They model the correspondence between the ontology and the schemas of the data sources.

Research works have developed languages for describing the mediated schema, the content of data sources and the users' queries (Etzioni et al.,

1994; Papakonstantinou et al., 1995). Other research works addressed the issue of providing sound and complete algorithms for rewriting queries using views over data sources. The information integration context is typical of the need of rewriting queries using views for answering queries because users of data integration systems do not pose queries directly to the sources in which data are stored but to a set of virtual relations that have been designed to provide a uniform and homogeneous access to a domain of interest. The rewriting problem that has been extensively studied concerns the pure relational setting (Halevy, 2001).

Improving scalability is a problem which is now studied in the setting of peer-to-peer computing (Milojicic et al., 2002) but it had not received a lot of attention in the setting of centralized mediator systems. This paper deals with this problem in the setting of the PICSEL project (Goasdoue et al., 2000), a collaboration with France Telecom R&D. A first project, PICSEL1, was dedicated to the construction of a declarative development platform of a mediator system. A very rich knowledge representation language, CARIN, has been proposed to model application domains and the content of the sources. Algorithms have been designed for rewriting queries over data sources in an efficient way. We also proposed a representation of an ontology of a real application domain, the tourism domain, in CARIN. We defined methodological guidelines to represent the ontology given this particular language. However, in spite of these results, building the ontology remains a difficult and very time consuming task preventing the deployment and the scalability of mediator systems.

Consequently we aimed, in a new project, PICSEL2, at automating the construction of the ontology in the PICSEL setting. We considered that resources were XML documents and we used PICSEL to build a mediator in the tourism domain by automating the construction of the ontology from XML documents corresponding to standardized messages specifications provided by Open Travel Alliance, OTA (www.opentravel.com), in the travel industry. This application was very interesting because it has allowed to go beyond the initial objective of the project. Domain standards reuse not only allows the automation of the construction of the ontology but of all the knowledge part. Moreover, suitable user interfaces have been automatically generated from the ontology and XML messages have been automatically written from query plans. As a result, the approach improves scalability avoiding strong dependency between the system and the available resources.

The paper is organized as follows. Section 2 provides the general description of the PICSEL2 approach. In section 3, we present the automation of the construction of the mediator. Section 4 focuses on the interface part.

2. GENERAL DESCRIPTION OF THE PICSEL2 APPROACH

PICSEL2 approach aims at building a scalable mediator-based integration system PICSEL with available resources restricted to XML documents. Improving scalability needs automation. As the query engine is generic, the part of the system concerned by automation is the knowledge-based part of the system, that is the construction of the ontology and the description of the contents of the available resources.

The specificity of the approach is that automation is based on XML standardized specifications provided by organizations for the exchange of structured e-business messages. Thus, the approach allows services integration instead of data sources integration. Consequently, the ontology whose construction is automated (cf. 3.1) describes the services of a domain. The second part of the knowledge part of the mediator describes the functionalities of available services, this part being also automatically generated (cf. 3.2).

Moreover, the goal of the approach is to increase independency between available service providers and the system. Thus, available services are decoupled into two parts. Decoupling of services includes information hiding based on the difference on internal business and public message exchange protocol interface descriptions. Coupling of the mediator systems with services is achieved via interfaces. The names of the performed messages are mentioned in the public part of these interfaces using a language of description of services (for example WSDL).

In this setting, a user query, formulated on the ontology thanks to an interface dynamically generated from the ontology (cf. 4.1), is relative to a service. It is translated into a set of queries using their descriptions. Then the queries are performed by available service providers. Wrappers are usually needed at this step in data sources integration systems. In our approach, they are replaced by a generic module which automatically translates the set of queries into XML documents corresponding to standardized messages (cf. 4.2).

In respect to this approach, we built a mediator system integrating services (air booking, hotel reservation, ...) from standardized specifications defined by the Open Travel Alliance. OTA is a non-profit organization working to define industry-wide, e-business specifications. Our application exploited 115 OTA XML-Schemas defining the elements to be used in messages when searching for availability and booking in the travel industry.

3. AUTOMATISATION OF THE CONSTRUCTION OF THE MEDIATOR

In a first sub-section we describe the building of the ontology, then the generation of the service descriptions.

3.1 Semi-automated construction of the ontology

The building of the ontology is a two-step process. First, a very simple version, guided by standardized specifications, is manually built. We consider all the messages (e.g. AirAvailabilityRequirement) for which a content is defined by the normalization organism that is considered. Then, we group the messages into categories (e.g. AirBookingService). As a consequence, we obtain the two first levels of a class hierarchy. Names of the classes in level 2 are names of standardized messages. Names of the classes in level 1 are names of categories. The name of the root class denotes the domain of interest (e.g. tourism service).

In a second step, the initial hierarchy is enriched from standardized specifications in a semi-automatic way. Indeed we ask the ontology designer to valid and modify, if needed, the enrichment. A set of classes, a set of properties which characterize classes and a set of relations among classes are extracted from XML-schemas associated to XML documents provided by the standardization organism. More details about heuristics used in this process are given in (Giraldo and Reynaud, 2002). Then, the extracted elements are structured. That means connecting the two-level initial class hierarchy with the output of the extraction phase. Thanks to common classes (terms of level 2 in the initial hierarchy correspond to names of the messages and are root elements in the XML-schemas), the connection can be automated. Finally, the model is automatically represented in CARIN.

3.2 Automated generation of service descriptions

In PICSEL the description of the content of each data source is given in terms of a set of logical implications $v_i(X) \Rightarrow p(X)$ establishing a link between a view v_i and the domain relation p whose instances can be found in the source. The use of PICSEL to integrate services leads to define for each service as many views as messages the service is able to perform. The logical implications are generated in an automatic way from the names of the messages extracted from the public part of the services. For example, S_1-v_1 $\Rightarrow$ AirAvailabilityRequirement could be one implication defining a view with v_1 the name of the view that is associated with

AirAvailabilityRequirement in the ontology, a class corresponding to a name of a message the service S_1 is able to perform. This implication says that the service S_1 fulfills searching for availability of flights.

These view definitions are not sufficient. A user must be able to precisely define the service he is looking for. For example, he must be able to express that he wishes to have a flight from the airport CDG. Thus, a view associated with the relation corresponding to the departure airport in the ontology must be defined. More generally, we have to define views for all the elements composing the messages services providers can perform. As all data composing the messages are already represented in the ontology, such views are automatically generated.

4. INTERFACING PICSEL2 MEDIATOR SYSTEM

This section deals both with end-users and service providers interface.

4.1 End-users interfaces for querying

End-users interfaces are automatically generated from the ontology. Their design is based on the fact that there are optional terms in the ontology, indicated by the cardinalities in the XML-Schemas, not all of the same technical level. Three ordered levels of difficulties are distinguished: low, medium and high. When a user wants to query the mediator system, he has to precise his level to access the system through a suitable interface which only presents terms in the ontology he is able to understand, i.e. terms with a level lower than his level. By reducing the number of terms that a low-level user can used in his query, the system becomes quite usable by non-expert users. The terms of the ontology are visualized in a graphical form and each user navigates the ontology as he likes. Moreover, the graphically specified query is automatically translated in CARIN.

4.2 Providers interfaces for translating query plans

We designed an interface to generate XML documents corresponding to the messages that must be performed by the service providers mentioned in the query plans of the PICSEL mediator. The interface is the equivalent of a wrapper. In our setting, it is a generic interface usable for all the service providers. The components and the structure of the messages come from the XML-Schemas. The rewritings given by the PICSEL query engine provide the values of the elements to insert into the various XML documents understood by the service providers mentioned in the query plans.

5. CONCLUSION

We presented a scalable approach based on standards reuse to integrate multiple services using the PICSEL mediator system. The main point is to increase automation. We shown that PICSEL2 approach allows to automate the knowledge part of PICSEL. Moreover, the building of interfaces with end-users and service providers can also be automated, which is, in addition to the fact that the approach allows an easy and fast construction of such systems, an important point to increase their deployment.

REFERENCES

Chawathe S., Garcia-Molina H., Hammer J., Ireland K, Papakonstantinou Y., Ullman J. D., Widom J., 1994, The TSIMMIS project: Integration of heterogeneous information sources, In 16th Meeting of the Information Processing Society of Japan, Tokyo , p 7-18.

Etzioni O., Weld D., 1994, "A Softbot-Based Interface to the Internet", Communications of the ACM, v 37, n 7, p 72-76.

Genesereth M. R., Keller A. M., Duschka O. M., 1997, Infomaster: an information integration system, In Joan M. Peckman (ed), proceedings, ACM SIGMOD International Conference on Management of Data: SIGMOD 1997: May 13-15, 1997, Tucson, Arizona, USA, v 26, n 2, SIGMOD Record (ACM Special Interest Group on Management of Data), p 539-542, New-York, NY 10036, USA. ACM Press.

Giraldo G., Reynaud C., 2002, Construction semi-automatique d'ontologies à partir de DTDs relatives à un même domaine, Journées Francophones d'Ingénierie des Connaissances.

Goasdoue F., Lattes V., Rousset M.-C., 2000, The use of CARIN language and algorithms for Integration Information: the PICSEL system, International Journal of Cooperative Information Systems, v 9, n 4, p 383-401.

Halevy A., 2001, Answering queries using views: A Survey, VLDB Journal.

Kirk T., Levy A. Y., Sagiv Y., Srivastava D., 1995, "The Information Manifold", In C. Knoblock & A. Levy (eds*)*, Information Gathering from Heterogeneous, Distributed Environments, AAAI Spring Symposium Series, Stanford University, California.

Milojicic D. J., Kalogeraki V., Lukose R., Nagaraja K., Pruyne J., Richard B., Rollins S., Xu Z., 2002, Peer-to-Peer Computing, Technical report HPL, 57, HP Labs.

Papakonstantinou Y., Garcia-Molina H., Widom J., 1995, Object exchange across heterogeneous information sources, In P. S. Yu and A. L. Chen (eds.), 11th Conference on Data Engineering, Taipei, Taiwan, IEEE Computer Society, p 251-260.

REPRESENTATION OF PROCEDURAL KNOWLEDGE AND ITS USE TO COMPUTE A FORM OF SUBSUMPTION

Yamine AIT AMEUR
LISI/ENSMA-Université de Poitiers
BP 109. Site du Futuroscope. 86960 Futuroscope Cedex. France.
yamine@ensma.fr

Abstract This paper shows the possibility to describe language based representations by model based representations. This uniform representation is useful for model integrations and helps to compute a form of subsumption.

Keywords: Data modelling languages, Procedural knowledge, Derivation, Constraints.

1. Introduction

Nowadays, computer aided engineering activities like specification, design, maintenance, simulation, etc. involve the use of electronic data which require the use of complex data models. These developments led to a wide class of heterogeneous data models. As a consequence, the processes of sharing, exchanging and integrating data and data models become complex as well. The origin of the work outlined in this paper is CAD which involves several industrial parts descriptions defined by several part suppliers and supported by several CAD systems and LMS (Library Management Systems). Usually these parts need to be assembled (or composed) in order to incrementally build more complex parts which are themselves stored in such LMS in order to be shared and/or exchanged. Thus, part descriptions are heterogeneous.

Meta-modelling and model transformation techniques have been put into practice in order to promote model integration and reduce heterogeneity. We propose a meta model approach allowing to handle procedural knowledge in order to increase integration of data models which use procedural knowledge for derivation and constraint expressions and we give the benefits of this approach for computing a particular form of subsumption.

Before giving the overview of our approach, let us review the following toy example. Let us consider two descriptions of a screw. $Screw\_R$ defined by the $Head\_Ray$ and $Length$ properties and $Screw\_Diameter$ defined by the $Head\_Diameter$ and $Length$ properties. These two descriptions of a common screw are different. However, the expression $Head\_Diameter = 2 * Head\_Ray$ (Resp. $Head\_Ray = Head\_Diameter/2$) may be used in order to relate the two descriptions and integrate them. Indeed, using the expression $Head\_Diameter = 2*Head\_Ray$ (Resp. $Head\_Ray = Head\_Diameter/2$) instances of $Screw\_R$ (Resp. $Screw\_D$) may become instances of $Screw\_D$ (Resp. $Screw\_R$) encoding here a form of subsumption. Therefore, there is a need of representing in the data models to be integrated the expression $Head\_Diameter = 2*Head\_Ray$ (Resp. $Head\_Ray = Head\_Diameter/2$). More generally, there is a need of representing the procedural knowledge either for encoding not only expressions like in this simple example, but also possible constraints (logical expressions) on data (e.g. $Head\_ Diameter < 2 * Length$).

Continuing this example, two questions arise: (1) where are these expressions represented in the data model ? (2) How are they represented ?

At the ontological (dictionary) level is the answer to the first question. Indeed, the properties of $Head\_Diameter$ and $Head\_ray$ associated to the concept of a $Screw\_D$ or a $Screw\_R$ (classes of instances) shall be uniquely and universally defined in a shared ontology (or dictionary). For example, they can be represented as derived attributes. In this paper, we do not focus on the ontology representation aspect, we suppose that such an ontology exists. The reader may refer to (Pierra, 2004) available in these proceedings for ontology modelling.

Several different answers for the second question are possible (abstract syntax, languages, data-models, etc.). We have chosen to represent the procedural knowledge using data models. The main reason is uniformity of the representation. Indeed, both structural, descriptive and procedural knowledge are represented using the same technology, the same modelling language and the same data model independently of any programming language and platform. We do not separate the data models from the models for expressions. Indeed, expressions become properties (encoded in derived attributes or in constraints) of the elements they contribute to describe.

Finally, one can continue this toy example by introducing another level of heterogeneity that can be solved in the same manner by associating heterogeneous units to the properties (centimeters for the $Head\_Ray$ and inches for the $Head\_Diameter$.

The rest of this paper gives an overview of our approach for representing procedural knowledge using data models and meta-modelling techniques issued from the work developed by (Bernstein, 2003,Ait-Ameur et al., 2000, Ait-Ameur et al., 1995b, Ait-Ameur et al., 1995a and Ait-Ameur and Wiedmer, 1998).

2. Modelling and language representation

In classical data engineering, data models are built in order to capture and to formalize the structure, the semantics, the representation, etc. of a set of data they intend to characterize. Different categories of knowledge are represented in these models (structural, descriptive and procedural). The problem of handling heterogeneous models and integrating them has been addressed by several researchers issued from different research areas (database systems, knowledge engineering, CAD systems etc.). In this context approaches promoting integration have been proposed (standards, exchange formats, meta-models, etc.).

Formal modelling languages are used to represent and to encode these data models. They offer the possibility to assert that given data, commonly named instances, fit with a given data model. These languages offer a set of basic modelling concepts (objects, attributes, derived attributes, constraints, etc.) allowing to describe data models which represent structural, descriptive and procedural knowledge. Again the use of these languages leads to a wide variety of heterogeneous data models that need to be integrated.

The integration data models requires to be able to formally talk about all the concepts described by these models. In practice, one can consider that models are represented as instances of meta models (themselves expressed in a modelling language) shared by all the parties involved during integration. The possibility to express complex data models depends on the richness of the meta-model which depends itself on the modelling power offered by the modelling language. According to (Bernstein, 2003), we define a model to be the set of objects, each of which has properties, and relationships between objects. Objects, properties and relationships have types. Three layers are required to describe the whole model technology.

1- *models* are defined by instances of objects, properties and relationships. Models definition is based on an explicit set extension description;

2- *meta-models* are the type definitions for the objects of the models. They describe the types the different objects belong to;

3- *meta-meta-models* is the language where models and meta-models are expressed.

The complexity of meta-model descriptions depends on the meta-meta-model language. The more this language is powerful, the more models are expressive. The richness of the models depends on the kind of knowledge that can be written within this language (availability of procedural, structural and descriptive knowledge). Model management systems are systems that implement models, meta-models and operators between models (Bernstein, 2003).

The models, we are dealing with in this paper, are sets of objects, with a root object, each of which has an identity and attributes (properties). Objects can be related by the is_a relationship (generalization-specialization), has_a relationship (part-of). Objects, attributes and relationships can be typed by built-in types or can be constrained. The typing expressions depend on the typing power supplied by the meta-model and by the meta-meta-model.

Notice that the concepts introduced in the meta-model are present in almost all the available modelling languages, and depending on the meta-meta-model, it is possible to define complex types, constraints, derivation functions and so on, that will be used at the meta-model level.

Language representation. Procedural knowledge is described by a language of expressions involving operands and operators, allowing to express either derivations or constraints. Encoding this kind of knowledge requires representing the grammar to derive all the suited expressions. Let us consider a production rule which describes simple numeric expressions defined by $E ::= E + E|E * E|Cst|Var$. If we consider a modelling language with the is_a relationship then, figure 1 represents the previous production rule. A root concept (inside a box) represents an expression E. Add_E and Mul_E are concepts (represented inside boxes) for addition and multiplication with two attributes that are expressions, introducing recursive descriptions. Consider now,

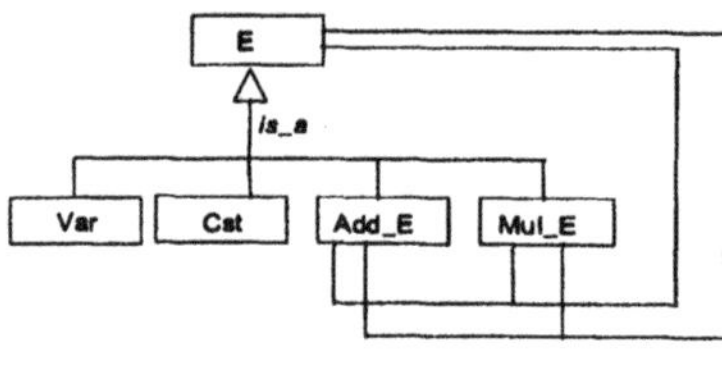

Figure 1. A simple example of a model for simple expressions with one non terminal and recursion.

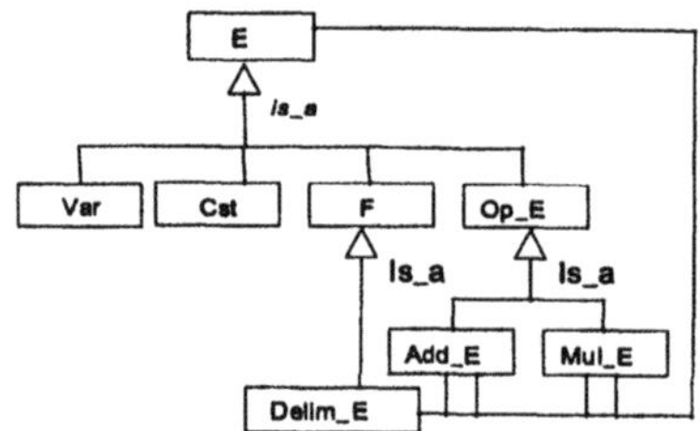

Figure 2. A simple example of a model for simple expressions with two non terminals and recursion.

the production rules $E ::= E \ op \ E|Cst|Var|F$, $op ::= +|*$ and $F ::= (E)$ with a case of indirect recursion. Using the same modelling language, figure 2 shows the translation of this set of production rules.

In both cases, a finite graph represents these production rules. The is_a relationship allows to encode the left and right hand sides of a production rule. Recursion is represented either by direct referencing or by indirect referencing through intermediate non terminals. These two simple examples show that it is possible to encode classical BNF grammars in modelling languages with a small set of basic concepts.

Formal grammars. The previous approach can be generalized to handle any kind of BNF grammar. A BNF grammar G is classically defined by a 4-tuple $G = (T, N, A, P)$. A production rule $F ::= E_1 | \cdots | E_n$, where $F \in N$ and $E_i \in (T \cup N)^*$, allows to rewrite the non terminal symbol F into one of the E_i. Using the same mechanism as described previously, it is possible to represent any production rule issued from such grammars and encode it by a data model with F as root.

Static semantics. In classical language processing, we denote by static semantics all the information that can be expressed (i.e. computed) on models in their static context. Usually, analyzers, type checkers, model checkers, theorem provers, abstract interpretation, are used to perform such a static analyses. In models static analysis is expressed by analyzing the relevant information embedded in the concepts. The set of instances of the model is not built nor provided.

Several features related to static semantics can be encoded for such grammars. Among them: enrichment of models by adding attributes using the is_a relationship for example, enrichment of models by adding types for constraining attributes domains, enrichment of models by adding constraints which express relevant static properties of the model (for example asserting that the underlying graph of an expression is a DAG). All these enrichments can be written although the set of all the instances is not known (static aspect).

Dynamic semantics and evaluation. In programming languages dynamic semantics is related to execution, interpretation and evaluation. In relational database systems, dynamic semantics is related to query executions. In model based representations, the expression of dynamic semantics is possible when instances of models are available and are evolving dynamically. In this case, adding, removing, modifying, querying of instances become possible. It is required that the meta-meta-modelling language is equipped with instance management operators. Depending on the power of the procedural knowledge encoded in the meta-meta-model language, it is possible to reach the level of a programming language or of a verification procedure, etc. If we come back to our example of figures 1 and 2, dynamic semantics can be expressed by writing an evaluator of an expression described in the concept E. To write this evaluator, it is necessary to have an instance of the model described by these figures and values associated to the variables.

Required characteristics for the meta modelling language. Naturally, the meta-meta-model language shall be powerful enough to support a logic allowing to encode derived attributes and to write and check constraints. The expression power and the resolution procedure of this logic express the kind of constraints that can be described. We have experimented the EXPRESS language (Schenck and Wilson, 1994) which offers, in a common language, all these features and an operational available tool.

3. Conclusion

This paper showed the importance of modelling the procedural knowledge for data integration processes. It suggested a data model oriented approach allowing to encode expressions and more generally grammars by data models. The advantage of such a representation is the possibility to have all the data model characteristics encoded in a single and common framework based on data models and data modelling languages. When used in an ontology, it allows to describe expressions transformations for subsumption purposes. We have experimented this approach in several projects by encoding complex data models for representing procedural knowledge. Moreover, we have used this approach for encoding the procedural knowledge of the PLIB ontology (Ait-Ameur et al., 2000, Ait-Ameur et al., 1995b, Ait-Ameur et al., 1995a and Ait-Ameur and Wiedmer, 1998). In this work, generic expressions, numeric, boolean, string expressions, expressions for aggregates and relational database expressions were encoded using this approach.

References

Ait-Ameur, Y., Besnard, F., Girard, P., Pierra, G., and Potier, J. C. (1995a). Formal Specification and Metaprogramming in the EXPRESS Language. In *International Conference on Software Engineering and Knowledge Engineering*, pages 181–189. KSI Institute in Corporation with ACM Sigsoft and IEEE.

Ait-Ameur, Y., Pierra, G., and Sardet, E. (1995b). Using The EXPRESS Language For Metaptogramming. In *Express User Group Conference*. Grenoble, France.

Ait-Ameur, Y., Pierra, G., and Sardet, E. (2000). An Object Oriented Approach to Represent Procedural Knowledge in Heterogeneous Information Systems. In *International Conference on Object Oriented Information Systems, OOIS'2000*, pages 303–315. Choudhury-Patel-De Cesare, Editors, Springer Verlag.

Ait-Ameur, Y. and Wiedmer, H. (1998). *General resources*. ISO-IS 13584-20. ISO Geneve, 88 pages.

Bernstein, P. (2003). Applying Model Management to Classical Meta Data Problems. In *Proceedings of the CIDR conference*.

Pierra, G. (2004). The PLIB ontology-based approach to data integration. In *Topical day on Semantic Integration of Heterogeneous Data*. IFIP World Computer Congress, Toulouse - France.

Schenck, D. and Wilson, P. (1994). *Information Modelling The EXPRESS Way*. Oxford University Press.

Topic 2

Virtual Realities and New Entertainment

Organiser:

Ryohei Nakatsu
Kwansei Gakuin University, Japan
nakatsu@ksc.kwansei.ac.jp

Although various kinds of virtual reality (VR) technologies have been studied and developed, VR has been adopted to only a few applications. We believe that entertainment is the most appropriate application area of VR. Recently by the advancement of computers and networks, new types of entertainment have been emerging such as video games, entertainment robots, and network games. By applying VR technologies we can expect that more and more new entertainment will emerge. Also it is expected that various kinds of business and education applications would emerge starting from these new entertainment.

The goal of this topical day is to give the audience the information on the most advanced VR technologies and the possibilities of new entertainment utilizing these technologies. Since our lectures have very different backgrounds and expertise, it is expected that the audience would grasp the whole trends in the area of VR and entertainment through the talk of the lecturers.

DEVELOPING RE-USABLE INTERACTIVE STORYTELLING TECHNOLOGIES

Marc Cavazza, Fred Charles and Steven J. Mead
School of Computing, University of Teesside, TS1 3BA, Middlesbrough, UK
(http://www-scm.tees.ac.uk/virtualstorytelling)
{m.o.cavazza, f,charles, steven.j.mead}@tees.ac.uk

Abstract: Despite the growing interest in Interactive Storytelling (IS), there have been only a small number of implemented demonstrators and few have attempted at developing a re-usable IS technology. In this paper we describe such an IS engine, which is the result of several years of experimentation in the field. The system is based on a game engine for its visualisation component, while the narrative generation component implements a variant of HTN Planning. After an introduction to the principles underlying the system, we introduce the associated production process and discuss authoring problems as well as tools we have developed to facilitate the use of the technology.

Key words: Interactive Narratives, Virtual Storytelling, Artificial Actors.

1. INTRODUCTION AND STATE OF THE ART

One of the most ambitious aspects of developing Interactive Storytelling (IS) as a new medium consists in establishing technologies supporting interactive narratives. With the recent development of IS, there is now an emerging consensus among those teams who have developed substantial IS prototypes [Cavazza et al., 2002] [Mateas and Stern, 2002] [Swartout et al., 2001] [Young, 2001] on which computing technologies are central to that endeavour. IS technologies should support the real-time presentation of a story whose plot is generated dynamically, so as to accommodate the result of user intervention. At the same time, the existence of narrative formalisms (plot-based or character-based) guarantees plot coherence and provide practical solutions to the narrative control problem. Both aspects, dynamic generation of situations and the representation of a story baseline, can be addressed using Artificial Intelligence techniques. From a formal perspective the backbone of the narrative is constituted by a sequence of actions: it hence comes as no surprise that AI planning is considered by many as a central technology for IS [Cavazza et al., 2002] [Young, 2001]. However, attention should also be paid to the representation component of IS technologies, as it conditions the authoring of the story baseline which should play an essential role in plot coherence and narrative control.

As a result of several years of experimenting with these issues, we have produced various research prototypes, which recently have demonstrated some potential for scalability. In this paper we are presenting the IS engine we have developed as a technology which, even if far from being mature, can be shared among the research community.

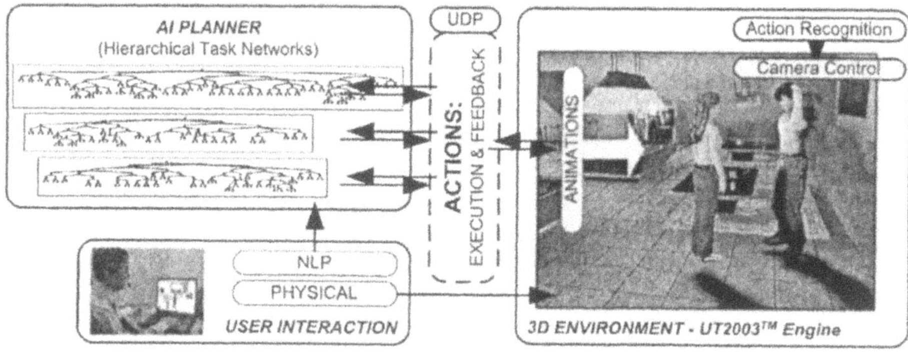

Figure 1. System overview.

2. SYSTEM ARCHITECTURE

Our technology (Figure 1) is developed on top of a computer game engine (UT 2003™, Epic Games), which is an approach inspired from foundational work in IS [Young, 1999] [Young, 2000]. The game engine ensures real-time visualisation (including camera control) as well as basic interaction mechanisms (between agents, between agents and objects, etc.). We have developed several additional layers (amounting to a total of 10 000 lines of C++ code and 8000 lines of UnrealScript code) corresponding to the narrative engine, which is essentially a HTN planner determining for each virtual actor what action it should take next. The actions selected are passed to the engine, in which they are associated to corresponding scripts describing the physical realisation of the action (including specific animations). The planner communicates with the visualisation engine using UDP socket connections. The two mechanisms for story generation are interaction between agents and user intervention. The latter is essentially mediated by speech input, which is why the system accepts data from an off-the-shelf speech recognition system. The recognised utterance is further processed into templates that can be interpreted in terms of narrative content.

3. STORY GENERATION AND PERFORMANCE

To a large extent, the system's approach has been generalised from the study of specific story genres, such as the sitcom genre. More recent experiments with another narrative genre would suggest that the system is not strongly biased towards its early supporting examples; however, it is likely that some assumptions such as task decomposability would fail to properly represent certain kind of narratives. Even within the subset of genres for which the approach is appropriate, system performance should be judged by the system's ability to generate relevant (ideally, interesting) stories and by its potential for scalability. The whole field still lacks metrics for the evaluation of a story's narrative qualities. This is why a basic measure of story generation consists in recording beats [Mateas and Stern, 2002], as a minimal (semantic) unit of narrative action, probably assimilable to a narrative function. Mateas and Stern have proposed an evaluation metric for the maturity of IS techniques, which consisted in being able to generate a 10-minute story comprising at least one beat per minute.

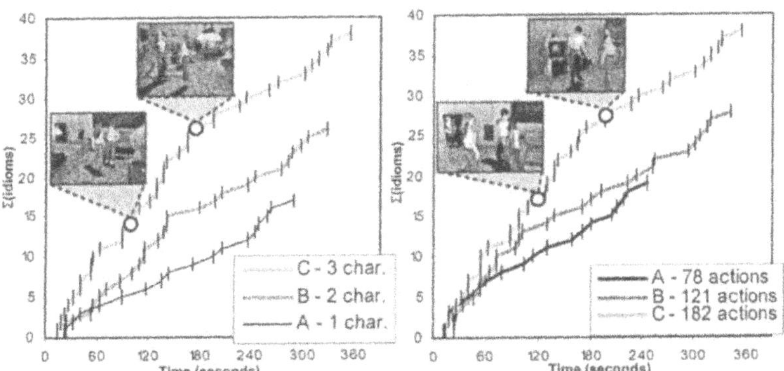

Figure 2. Scalability of character-based storytelling.

We have conducted several scalability experiments demonstrating the increase in story sophistication as the individual characters roles are made more complex [Charles and Cavazza, 2003]. Figure 2 shows the increase in story duration and number of situations generated (measured through film idioms, a formalisation of situations used in Film Studies) for various versions of a same story, each version differing by the complexity of individual characters' roles.

4. THE DEVELOPMENT PROCESS

The creation of an interactive narrative with our system proceeds through several steps which are summarised on Figure 3. Once again it is helpful to keep in mind the distinction between story generation and presentation; in other words, generating the sequence of actions and for each of these actions, staging them in real-time in the most appropriate fashion.

The first aspect consists in creating all the visual elements for the interactive story: the virtual stage can be developed as a UT 2003™ level for which the editor provides sophisticated features. The 3D contents can be imported from popular modelling packages and the textures can be generated from various image formats, apart from an extensive range existing in the system's own library (we do not discuss character's animations as these are related to the definition of primitive actions in the next section).

Figure 3. Integration of creative contents in the virtual environment.

Probably the most central part of authoring an IS system is to instantiate the knowledge representation underlying the story generation system. In our approach, this consists in formalising the role of each character into an HTN. This is done by identifying various phases of the character's role, then expressing them as a decomposition of tasks into sub-tasks. Because we have developed a specific graphic interface for that purpose, we will describe this process in the next section.

The generation of actions for each character is based on a role formalised as an HTN, which decomposes the role into independent tasks, ordered chronologically, until these tasks can be solved through elementary actions. The system relies on the native mechanisms of UT 2003™ for many of these actions (such as path planning, walking, grabbing objects, etc.). However, once terminal actions have been identified a script should be generated for its enactment encapsulating all relevant system primitives. As for the visual presentation, many actions require specific animations to be imported into the system (actions such as sitting, or kissing, are obviously not part of the native library of a first-person shooting game).

In our character-based approach, it is not possible (and not even desirable) to incorporate within each single character's role an anticipation of all possible situations that can arise dynamically from the interaction between characters. Hence it can be necessary to complement the top-down approach with the bottom-up description of situated reasoning that would react to such situation.

Finally, as spoken utterances are the most appropriate interface for user interventions in the story [Cavazza et al., 2002] [Mateas and Stern, 2002], there is a need to author these aspects as well. However this kind of authoring depends on the specific speech recognition component adopted, which is why we shall not discuss it here.

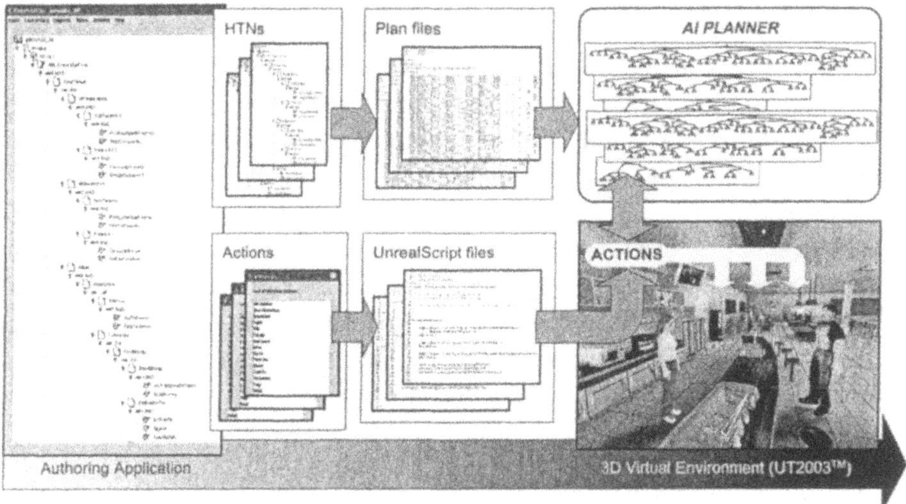

Figure 4. From story authoring to dynamic story generation.

5. THE AUTHORING INTERFACE

One of the limiting factors of the development of IS is likely to be the difficulty to author interactive narratives. Despite the dynamic nature of such stories, whose generative aspects depend not only from user intervention but also from internal interactions between the story characters, the value of the baseline narrative still plays an essential role in underlying the overall consistency of the narrative. At this early stage it remains unclear whether interactive stories will be created by traditional scriptwriters or by a new breed of story designers, closer to those creating computer games. In order to remain as neutral as possible on this issue, we have devised a user interface supporting the authoring of characters' roles in our IS engine. This interface does not address the whole content production chain as discussed above, but is centred on its most technical aspect, which is the definition of role-plans for the IS characters (Figure 4). We have previously discussed the authoring problems associated with planning formalisms in IS [Cavazza et al., 2002], and have concluded that one of the benefits of HTN formalisms are their visual and integrated nature. We hypothesised that this visual nature should facilitate authoring by content creators, who would proceed by incremental task decomposition when describing a character's role, relying on the intuitive semantics of the formalism.

6. CONCLUSIONS

We have described a fully implemented IS prototype, for which we claim a possible re-use of its underlying technology. We have identified several key steps in the production process and have developed user-friendly interfaces to facilitate some aspects of authoring identified as critical for the use of the technology.

We have only recently started to distribute alpha versions of the system, which have been used for teaching AI-based animation and multi-agent systems at our institution, as well as others. Despite only implementing one possible paradigm of IS, we hope it could be useful, not only to researchers in IS but also in related areas such as training and edutainment, which can develop applications on top of these technologies.

Acknowledgements

We would like to give credits to the designers of the character models, Demiurge Studios.

References

Cavazza M, Charles F, Mead SJ. Character-based Interactive Storytelling", IEEE Intelligent Systems, 17(4), 2002.

Charles F and Cavazza M. Exploring the Scalability of Character-based Storytelling. ACM Joint Conference on Autonomous Agents and Multi-Agent Systems, New York, USA, 2004 (to appear).

Mateas M, Stern A. A Behavior Language for Story-based Believable Agents", IEEE Intelligent Systems, 17(4), 2002.

Swartout W, Hill R, Gratch J, Johnson WL, Kyriakakis C, LaBore C, Lindheim R, Marsella S, Miraglia D, Moore B, Morie J, Rickel J, Thiebaux M, Tuch L, Whitney R, Douglas J. Toward the Holodeck: Integrating Graphics, Sound, Character and Story. Proceedings of the Autonomous Agents 2001 Conference; Montreal, Canada, 2001.

Young RM. Notes on the Use of Plan Structures in the Creation of Interactive Plot. AAAI Fall Symposium on Narrative Intelligence. AAAI Press, 1999.

Young RM. Creating Interactive Narrative Structures: The Potential for AI Approaches. AAAI Spring Symposium in Artificial Intelligence and Entertainment. AAAI Press, 2000.

Young RM, An Overview of the Mimesis Architecture: Integrating Intelligent Narrative Control into an Existing Gaming Environment, Working Notes of the AAAI Spring Symposium on Artificial Intelligence and Interactive Entertainment, AAAI Press, 2001.

CONNECTING THE REAL WORLD AND VIRTUAL WORLD THROUGH GAMING

Adrian David Cheok, Goh Kok Hwee, Liu Wei, Jason Teo, Teo Sze Lee, Farzam Farbiz, Lee Shang Ping
Mixed Reality Lab, National University of Singapore

Abstract This paper presents two novel interactive game entertainment systems named by Human Pacman and Touch spaced that ventures to embed the natural physical world seamlessly with a fantasy virtual playground by capitalizing on mobile computing, wireless LAN, ubiquitous computing, and motion-tracking technologies. We can connect seamlessly the computer virtual world to our real world through these game systems. Human Pacman and Touch space are physical role-playing augmented-reality computer fantasy together with real human-social and mobile gaming. They recapture human touch and physical interaction real-world environment as essential elements of the game play, whilst also maintaining the exciting fantasy features of traditional computer entertainment. It emphasizes collaboration and competition between players in a wide indoor and outdoor physical area which allows natural wide-area human-physical movements.

Keywords: Collaboration, Physical interaction, Social computing, Wearable computing, Tangible interaction, Ubiquitous computing

1. Introduction

In the pre-computer age, games were designed and played out in the physical world with the use of real-world properties, such as physical objects, our sense of space, and spatial relations. Nowadays, computer games focus the user's attention mainly on the computer screen or a 2-D/3-D virtual environment, thereby, constraining physical interactions. However, there seems to be a growing interest in physical gaming and entertainment, even in industry. Commercial arcade games have recently seen a growing trend of games that require human-physical movement as part of interaction. For example, dancing games such as Dance Dance Revolution and ParaParaParadise are based on players dancing in time with a musical dance tune and moving graphical objects. However, these systems still force the person to stand in more or less the same spot, and focus on a computer screen in front of them. Nevertheless, the underpinning philosophy is similar.

In this paper we propose two novel game systems that we developed in our laboratory which bring both features of physical gaming and computer gaming together. In a better word, our systems connect the real world and physical interaction between players to the computer world (virtual world) through the game space. The players can have social interaction with each others and physical movements like traditional games and at the same time they will enjoy interacting with virtual objects (e.g. monsters, witches, ...) in both real and virtual environment. All the players' movements in real world are tracked by the game system to update their virtual world in real time.

The organization of the paper is as follows. We illustrate our game system, Human Pacman, in Section 2 and then in Section 3 we give the explanation of the second system, Touch Space. In Section 4 we provide the conclusion.

2. Human Pacman

In recent years, the world has seen the proliferation of highly portable devices, such as personal digital assistants (PDAs), laptops, and cellular telephones. Trends in computing environment development also suggest that users are gradually being freed from the constraints of stationary desktop computing with the explosive expansion in mobile computing and networking infrastructure. With this technological progress in mind, we have developed human Pacman , a genre of computer entertainment that is based on real-world-physical, social, and wide-area mobile-interactive entertainment. The novelty of this computer game has the following aspects: first, the players physically and immersively role-play the characters of the Pacman and the Ghosts, as if a fantasy computer digital world has merged with the real physical world. Second, users can move about freely in the real world over wide area indoor and outdoor spaces whilst maintaining seamless networked social contact with human players in both the real and virtual world. Third, human Pacman also explores novel tangible aspects of human physical movement and perception, both in the player's environment and in the interaction with the digital world. In other words, objects in the real world are embedded and take on a real-time link and meaning with objects in the virtual world. For example, to devour the virtual "enemy", the player has to tap on the real physical enemy's shoulder; to obtain a virtual "magic" cookie, the player has to physically pick up a real physical treasure box with an embedded Bluetooth device attached. Human Pacman ventures to elevate the sense of thrill and suspended disbelief of the players in this untypical computer game. . Each of the novel interactions mentioned is summarized in Table 1.

Human Pacman features a centralized client-server architecture that is made up of four main entities, namely, a central server, client wearable computers, helper laptops, and Bluetooth-embedded objects. Wireless LAN serves as a communication highway between the wearable computers, the helper computers (laptops), and the server desktop computer.

In this game the players are assigned to two opposing teams, namely the Pacman team and the Ghost team. The former consists of two Pacmen and two Helpers; correspondingly, the latter consists of two Ghosts and two Helpers. Each Pacman or Ghost is in coalition with one Helper, promoting collaboration and interaction between the users. Since a Helper player is essentially participating in the game play remotely by using a computer terminal over a wireless LAN, human Pacman can effectively be expanded to include online players anywhere on Earth who can view and collaborate, via the Internet, with real human Pacmen and Ghosts who are immersed in the physical playground.

Ever since its introduction by Namco to Japanese arcade fans in 1979, Pacman has gone through numerous stages of development. Yet, the ultimate goal of the game remains fundamentally unchanged. We have designed human Pacman to be in close resemblance to the original Pacman in terms of game objectives so that the players' learning curves are very much leveled to the point where they can pick up the game in very little time and enjoy the associated familiarity. Basically, the goal of the Pacman team is to collect all virtual plain cookies and hidden special cookies in Pac-World whilst avoiding the Ghosts. On the other hand, the aim of the Ghost team is to devour all Pacmen in Pac-World. To add to the excitement of the game play, after "eating" a special cookie, a Pacman gains Ghost-devouring capability and, henceforth, can attack her enemy for a limited period of time.

Pac-World is a fantasy world existing simultaneously in physical reality, in AR and VR modes. Pacmen and Ghosts, who are walking around in the real world with their networked wearable computers and HMD, view the world in AR mode. Helpers, on the other hand, can view it in VR mode since they are stationed in front of networked computers. Most importantly, there is a direct and real-time link between the wide-area physical world and the virtual Pac-World at all times, thus, providing the users with a ubiquitous and seamless merging of the fantasy digital world and the realistic physical world. Here we have converted the real world to a fantasy virtual playground by ingraining the latter with direct physical correspondences.

The real-time position of each mobile user is sent periodically to the server through the wireless LAN. Upon receiving the position data, the server sends an update to each wearable computer detailing the position of the other mobile players, as well as the positions of all "non-eaten" plain cookies.

Pacman has to physically move within the game area to collect all virtual plain cookies overlaid in the real world, by walking through them as seen through her HMD. Such a physical action is reflected visually in Pac-World through the disappearance of the cookie in both the AR and VR mode. When she walks through the cookie, the cookie disappears. This collection is also reflected in real time in the virtual Pac-World (seen by the Helpers) and the Pac-World map (seen by both Pacmen and Ghosts) through the disappearance of the cookie in the corresponding location.

In addition, she has to find and collect special cookies in the virtual Pac-World. These are directly linked and represented by Bluetooth-embedded objects. This creates a sense of presence and immersion within the virtual Pac-World, as well as a feeling of active participation in the real world. Pacman collects a special cookie by touching real Bluetooth-embedded objects placed in different parts of the game area. When the Pacman is within range of the Bluetooth object (a distance of about 10 m), communication takes place between the wearable computer and the Bluetooth device.

The collection of the special cookie exemplifies a natural tangible interaction involving physically interacting with this object through human touch. Pacman is able to hold a real object naturally in her hands as should be in real-life treasure finding. Such a tangible action provides the player with a sense of touch in the fantasy domain of the game play. The Ghost can devour a Pacman by tapping on a capacitive sensor attached to a Pacman's shoulder. Likewise, a Ghost can be devoured by Pacmen endowed with Ghost-devouring powers. Such tangible physical interaction between humans, commonly found in traditional games such as hide-and-seek and the classic "catching" game, is now revived in this computer gaming arena.

Each Pacman and Ghost will be assigned a partner Helper who acts as an intelligence, advisor, and coordinator in her quest to achieve her goal. To enhance the gaming experience for both Pacmen and Ghosts, these players in the physical world with wearable computers are not able to see enemy mobile units (the positions of the enemies are not shown on the virtual map, and there is no AR labeling on them) and hidden special cookies. The Helper, who is in VR mode and sees all, guides her partner by messaging her with important information. This promotes collaboration and interaction between players through the internet.

3. Touch Space

In Touch-Space, the games are situated and carried out in the physical world, and they recognize the physical co-location of players and objects in the world as essential elements of the game mechanics. Players must walk around within a large room-size area and pick up real objects to physically interact with the game space, in the similar way as they are playing a traditional non-computer game. What enhances the physical space is that the real object and real envi-

Table 1. Detailed descriptions of the features of human Pacman

Feature	*Details*
Physical gaming	Players are physically role-playing the characters of Pacman and Ghosts; with wearable computers donned, they use free bodily movements as part of interaction between each person, between the real and virtual world, and among objects in the real wide-area landscapes and virtual environments
Social gaming	Players interact both directly with other players when they are in physical proximity, or indirectly via the wireless LAN network by real-time messaging. There is a coherent networked social contact among
Mobile gaming	players in both the real and virtual worlds, as well as throughout their boundaries. People from all around the world can also participate in the human Pacman experience by viewing and collaborating in real time over the internet with the physical human Pacmen and Ghosts who are immersed in the physical-real-world game Players are free to move about in the indoor/outdoor space without being constrained to the 2D/3D screen of desktop computers
Ubiquitous computing	Everyday objects throughout the environment seamlessly have a real-time fantasy digital world link and meaning. There is automatic communication between wearable computers and Bluetooth devices embedded in physical objects used in game play
Tangible interaction	Throughout the game, people interact in a graspable and tangible manner. For example, players need to physically pick up objects to collect them digitally, or to tap on the shoulder of other players to devour them
Outdoor wide-area gaming arena	Large outdoor areas can be set up for the game whereby players carry out their respective missions for the role they play. This could even be linked throughout cities

ronment may be augmented with virtual objects or virtual figures. Thus, the benefits and excitement of computer entertainment is also incorporated into the physical space. The system supports multiple simultaneous participants playing together, while maintaining the social, non-mediated interaction between players. Through a seamless traversable interface, the players can transit to and from fully immersive virtual environment. Thus, players will experience a novel full spectrum game experience ranging from physical reality, augmented reality, to virtual reality, in a seamless way featured with tangible interfaces and social interaction.

The story of the game is as follows: a princess is captured by a witch and is trapped in the witch's castle that is located in a mysterious land. To play the game, firstly the two players need to find two map pieces of the mysterious land and other necessary treasures. Secondly, they should fly above the land

and look for the castle, after then, they need to fight and defeat the witch. Finally, they enter the castle to find the princess, and thus they complete the game mission. Thus, the game consists of three main game stages stages.

Touch-Space is an exploration of the embodied interaction within a mixed reality collaborative setting. The result of the project is a unique game space which combines the interactions of natural human to human, human to physical world and human to virtual world, and provides a novel game experience ranging from physical reality, augmented reality, to virtual reality.

4. Conclusion

The continual propagation of digital communication and entertainment in recent years has forced many changes in societal psyche and lifestyle, that is, how we think, work, and play. With physical and mobile gaming gaining popularity, traditional paradigms of entertainment will irrevocably shake one from the stale television set inertia. We believe that human Pacman and Touch Space herald the conjuration and growth of a new genre of computer game that are built on mobility, physical actions, and the real world as a playground. Reality, in this case, is becoming more exotic than fantasy because of the mixed reality element in the game play. On the other hand, emphasis on physical actions might even bring forth the evolvement of professional physical gaming as a competitive sport of the future, for example "Pacman International League". Furthermore, by providing seamless transition between physical world and virtual world, the players can enjoy both tangible physical game experience and fantasy virtual game experience and, therefore, a higher than ever level of sensory gratification is obtained. These games connect the computer generated virtual world to our real world to each other.

We envision a new type of game experience that has two main features: integrated ubiquitous context-awareness and sociality into the computer interaction context, which entails ubiquitous, tangible, and social computing (and thus directly applies the theory of embodied interaction); and a seamless merging of physical world, augmented world and virtual world exploration experience.

POSITIVE EFFECTS OF ENTERTAINMENT TECHNOLOGY ON HUMAN BEHAVIOUR

Matthias Rauterberg
Technical University Eindhoven (The Netherlands)

Abstract: Worldwide the pros and cons of games and social behaviour are discussed. In Western countries the discussion is focussing on violent game and media content; in Japan on intensive game usage and the impact on the intellectual development of children. A lot is already discussed on the harmful and negative effects of entertainment technology on human behaviour, therefore we decided to focus primarily on the positive effects. Based on an online document search we could find and select 393 online available publications according the following categories: meta review (N=34), meta analysis (N=13), literature review (N=38), literature survey (N=36), empirical study (N=91), survey study (N=44), design study (N=91), any other document (N=46). In this paper a first preliminary overview over positive effects of entertainment technology on human behaviour is presented and discussed. The drawn recommendations can support developers and designers in entertainment industry.

Key words: Meta review, entertainment, positive effect, behaviour, recommendations.

1. INTRODUCTION

This paper focuses on users' growing use of entertainment technology at work, in school and at home, and the impact of this technology on their behaviour. Nearly every working and living place has computers, and over two-thirds of children in high industrialized countries have computers in their homes as well [7] [12]. All of us would probably agree that adults and children (normal, impaired and disabled) need to become competent users to be prepared for life and work in the future. Especially children's growing use of entertainment technologies brings with it both the risk of possible harm and the promise of enriched learning, well-being and positive development. Entertainment technology covers a broad range of products and services:

movie, music, TV (including upcoming interactive TV), VCR, VOD (including music on demand), computer game, game console, video arcade, gambling machine, internet (e.g. chat room, board and card games, MUD), intelligent toy, edutainment, simulation, VR, and upcoming service robots [2] [21] [24] [30].

2. META REVIEW APPROACH

This paper presents the preliminary results of a literature search and review. We searched for the following keywords (context specific in different combinations): 'academic achievement, altruism, ANOVA, attainment, children, computer, education, edutainment, entertainment, gamble, game, meta analysis, PDF, performance, pet, positive effect, religion, robot, school record, review, survey, technology, therapy, user study, video', using the following search engines/databases: 'ACM Digital Library, IEEE Computer Society Digital Library, Internet via Google, ISI web of science, Kluwer online, LookSmart, Prenctice Hall, Science Direct, Scirus for scientific information, SpringerLink, Wiley interScience'. We could find, select and process 393 online available publications (e.g. DOC, RTF, PDF or HTML format) according the following categories: meta review (N=34), meta analysis (N=13), literature review (N=38), literature survey (N=36), empirical study (N=91), survey study (N=44), design study (N=91), any other document (N=46) (for a complete reference list see [27]). The preliminary and selective results presented in this paper summarize research so far available on how the use of entertainment technology affects human's daily life in a *positive* and promising manner.

3. GENERAL REMARKS

It has to be pointed out that addiction, racism, sexism, violence, etc are not new inventions of the entertainment and game industry and would not disappear from the world, where games abolished. They should better be seen as a reflection of underlying dimensions of a society or culture into economical and social accepted artifacts [6]. In this respect a criticism of games can not be separated from a fundamental critique of the society which produce, accept and promote these games. It could be shown [35] that misunderstanding is endemic in the Western culture because most of the Western societies tend to believe that the best way to a common goal is by rigorous and often aggressive dispute. There for a lot confrontational public forums are established, from congressional politics to media hearings. The author argues that thoughtful debate and real understanding gets lost in all these disputes. She suggests to consider other methods of communication and offers a survey of mostly non-Western ways of dealing with conflict, including the use of intermediaries and rituals.

It is our responsibility as researchers, engineers, politicians, parents and educators to pay attention to all relevant issues, and to discuss them in the proper context of references and values, so that entertainment industry can be enabled to make correct choices for their future developments (see e.g. [2] [11] [23]). How can we get an appropriate orientation, given the fact that controversial discussions take place (see [1] [7] [13] [14] [32])?

4. RESULTS AND RECOMMENDATIONS

4.1 EFFECTS IN EDUCATIONAL CONTEXT

Academic performance: In a research program the use of electronic communication and games with children was investigated in both classroom and after-school settings for nearly 15 years [9]. The after-school programs was called "The Fifth Dimension", and include the typical uses of home computers, such as educational software, computer games, searching the Internet, and multi-user dungeons (MUD) activities. Subject matter includes social development, geography, communications, reading, writing, math, social studies, health, technology, language, and problem solving. The computer games and Internet activities are based in a social and cognitive context that includes a ladder of challenges [25]. This research program effects include advances in reading [31] and mathematics [8] [10], computer knowledge, following directions, grammar and school achievement tests [9].

A considerable body of research has examined the effects of computer use on *academic performance*. Reviews of this literature typically conclude that the results are preliminary (e.g., [29], [33]). Although benefits of computer use have been observed, they typically depend on a variety of factors (mainly on *context of use* and *content*). The only positive cognitive effect have been consistently observed is *visual-spatial skills*. Gaming in 2D or 3D applications contributes to visual-spatial skills, at least when these skills are assessed immediately after the computer activity [34].

General development: Games require the use of logic, memory, problem solving and critical thinking skills, visualization and discovery [34]. Their use requires that players manipulate objects using electronic tools and develop an understanding of the game as a complex system. Play is an effective teaching strategy both inside and outside school. According to "Goldstein more than 40 studies concludes that play enhances early development by at least 33%" [36]. Play with games and toys are an important part of child development to acquire a variety of skills for life, such as motor-coordination, social and cognitive skills [15]. As societies become increasingly concerned about the physical and psychological well-being of children, the value of playing and learning is getting crucial [22]. Players can progress from newcomer to expert, in particular in belonging to a *social* system [11].

Play: People who have been allowed and encouraged to play stand the best chance of becoming healthy, happy and productive members of society [33]. Some positive aspects of playing can promote literacy, thinking, reflecting and creativity [16] [31].

Teaching: If computer games are to become part of educational settings, it is crucial to question existing stereotypes and to ensure that the culture of games players in education conforms to neither [13]. It is teachers' stereotypes that resist change and not people; therefore, by interrogating conceptions of these stereotypes it is possible to avoid falling into the error of believing them to be exclusive descriptors of games players [11].

4.2 EFFECTS ON SOCIAL BEHAVIOUR

Collaboration: Collaborative game playing necessitates the development of social skills, for example in order to decide on, define and agree goals. All of these features should be usefully incorporated into next generation of computer games that will support positive effects on the social and intellectual development of the users. In a meta-analysis study [17] 122 empirical studies on the effect of competition on result of players' improvement are reviewed. This meta-analysis included every study that could be found on achievement in (a) co-operative, (b) competitive and/or (c) individualistic tasks (not only games and play). 65 studies found that (a) co-operation tasks promotes higher achievement than (b) competitive tasks, 8 found the reverse, and 36 found no statistically significant difference. Co-operation tasks promoted higher achievement than (c) individualistic tasks in 108 studies, while 6 found the reverse, and 42 found no difference. The superiority of co-operation could be justified for higher achievement for all subject areas and all age groups [17] (see also [18]).

Prosocial behaviour: The results of a meta analysis about positive effects of television on social behaviour indicate clearly that *prosocial content* of entertainment technology does have positive effects as follows [20]: "(1) Children exposed to prosocial content have more positive social interactions, show more altruistic behavior and self-control, and have less stereotyped views of others. (2) The strongest effects of prosocial content were found for measures of altruism. (3) Relying on children's ability to pick out the moral messages from programs which feature violence or conflict and some prosocial resolution may backfire, leading to more aggression than merely showing the conflict. (4) Effects of prosocial content are often strongest when viewing is combined with discussion. (5) The effect sizes overall ranged from small to medium. (6) Effects of prosocial content were strongest for pre-school and grade-school children, diminishing in adolescence. (7) Effects are somewhat stronger for girls than for boys" (p. 19). In a more recent literature review the following results are presented [34]: (1) "game playing did not impact the social network and characteristics of interactions among children" (p. 17); (2) "socially anxious and lonely people find more honest and intimate human relationships with others on the Internet than in the real world, and they tend to successfully integrate these online relationships into their offline lives" (p. 20).

Recommendations: Cole's results [9] indicate that well designed computer games and Internet activities for home use can have a lasting positive impact on children's academic performance. The design of entertainment product should focus on prosocial and altruistic content (e.g. Tamagotchi [4], Robota [3], Kismet [5], Affect-Support Agent [19]). Based on the results of Johnson's meta-analysis co-operative entertainment systems are strongly recommended [17]. The results of an experimental study show that separated audio communication line per team should be provided to increase co-operation among team members [26].

4.3 THERAPEUTIC EFFECTS

Health Care: The introduction of the 'mental commit' robot pet Paro in a hospital environment showed promising results: the mood of children and elderly patients could be positively changed [23]. Turnin et al [38] could find a positive influence of a computer game on 2000 children for nutritional teaching. "In conclusion, it is possible for children to learn good eating habits by playing computer games" (p. 239).

Hyperactivity: Early research suggests that active play may reduce impulsivity thereby helping children with attention deficit and hyperactivity disorder (ADHD, see [37]). Goldstein concludes [14] that play is of fundamental importance to children, but it is not always recognized and fully appreciated by adults and society. Playing is fun and contributes to children's happiness, but it is also vital to their health and well-being.

Phobia: Using a low-cost commercial computer game VR application with head mounted display applied to phobic and non-phobic persons resulted in a sufficient amount of immersion and presence for the phobic patients to be useful for therapeutic settings [28].

Recommendations: "The phobogenic effectiveness of the inexpensive hardware and software used in this study shows that VR technology is sufficiently advanced for VR exposure therapy to move into the clinical mainstream" ([28] p. 475). The authors conclude that low cost, therapeutic VR applications based on desktop VR games are superior to their expensive commercial counterparts. Mental commit robots and computer games with proper content have positive health effects as well.

5. CONCLUSIONS

So far, two main conclusions can be drawn: (1) not the technology in its self, but the *content* of the product or service really matters, (2) the *context of use* is almost as important as the content. If the content and the context of use is properly designed, *positive* effects on the users can be achieved. The following contents and contexts of use can maximize positive effects on human behaviour of different age (children, adults, elderly): prosocial content, game like computer aided instructions/learning application, robot pets, in a multi-user, collaborative or therapeutic setting.

6. REFERENCES

[1] Anderson, C. & Bushman, B. (2002). Effects of media violence on society. *Science*, Vol. 295, No. 3, pp. 2377-2379.

[2] Berman, S. (2004). Media and entertainment 2010. *Report*, IBM Business Consulting Sevices.

[3] Billard, A. (2003). Robota: clever toy and educational tool. *Robotics and Autonomous Systems*, Vol. 42, pp. 259-269.

[4] Bloch, L.-R. & Lemish, D. (1999). Disposable love. *new media & society*, Vol. 3, pp. 283-303.

[5] Breazeal, C. (2003). Toward sociable robots. *Robotics and Autonomous Systems*, Vol. 42, pp. 167-175.

[6] Breuer, H. (2001). Kultivation und Imagination in den neuen Medien [Cultivation and imagination in new media]. *PhD Thesis*, O.-v.-G.-Universität Magdeburg, Germany.

[7] Calvert, S., Jordan, A.B. & Cocking, R.R. (2002). *Children in the digital age: the role of entertainment technologies in children's development.* Praeger Publishers.

[8] Clements, D. H. (2000). From exercises and tasks to problems and projects – unique contributions of computers to innovative mathematics education. *Journal of Mathematical Behavior*, Vol. 19, No. 1, pp. 9–47.

[9] Cole, M. (1996). *Cultural psychology: a once and future discipline.* Harvard Press.

[10] Cox, M. & Abbott, M. (2004, eds.). A review of the research literature relating to ICT and attainment. *Report*, retrieved April 27, 2004 from www.becta.org.uk

[11] Cox, M. & Webb, M. (2004, eds.). An investigation of the research evidence relating to ICT pedagogy. *Report*, retrieved April 27, 2004 from www.becta.org.uk

[12] Durkin, K. & Aisbett, K. (1999). Computer Games and Australians today. *Report*, Office of Film and Literature Classification, Sydney, Australia.

[13] Garthwait, A. (2001). Factors influencing technology's effect on student achievement and a caution about reading the research. *Occasional Paper No. 40,* a publication of the College of Education & Human Development, University of Maine, USA.

[14] Goldstein, J. (2000). Effects of electronic games on children. *Testimonial Statement* to US senate committee on Commerce, Science and Transportation, March 2000, USA.

[15] Goldstein, J. & Raessens, J. (2004, in press). *Handbook of computer game studies.* Cambridge, MA: MIT Press.

[16] Hartung, P. J. (2002). Development through work and play. *Journal of Vocational Behavior*, Vol. 61, pp. 424-438.

[17] Johnson, D. W., Maruyama, G., Johnson, R.T., Nelson, D., & Skon, L. (1981). Effects of co-operative, competitive and individualistic goal structures on achievement: A meta-analysis. *Psychological Bulletin*, Vol. 89, pp. 47-62.

[18] Kerlin, B A. (1992). Cognitive engagement style-self regulated learning and cooperative learning. Retrieved April 27, 2004 from http://kerlins.net/bobbi/research/myresearch/srl/

[19] Klein, J., Moon, Y. & Picard, R. (2002). This computer responds to frustration: theory, design, results and implications. *Interacting with Computers*, Vol. 14, pp. 119-140.

[20] Mares, M.-L. (1996). Positive effects of television on social behavior: a meat analysis. *Report Series No. 3*, The Annenberg Public Policy Center, Pennsylvania, USA.

[21] Nakatsu, R. & Hoshino, J. (2003; eds.). *Entertainment computing-technologies and applications.* Kluwer Academic Press.

[22] National Science Foundation (2001). The application and implications of information technologies in the home: where are the data and what do they say? *Report No. NSF 01-313*, Division of Science Resources Studies, USA.

[23] No author (2003). Therapeutic robot. *AIST Today International Edition*, No. 9, pp. 2-3.

[24] Pek, Z. (2003). What is entertainment technology? A short overview. *Online document* retrieved May 7, 2004 from www.nb2bc.co.uk/pdfs/entertaintech.pdf

[25] Priest, J., Coe, R., Evershead, B. & Bush, N. (2004). An exploration of the use of ICT at the millennium primary school, Greenwich. *Report* available at www.becta.org.uk

[26] Rauterberg, M. (2003). Determinantes for collaboration in networked multi-user games. In: R. Nakatsu & J. Hoshino (eds.), *Entertainment computing-technologies and applications* (pp. 313-321). Kluwer Academic Press

[27] Rauterberg, M. (2004). Entertainment technology and human behaviour: complete reference list. *Report*, Industrial Design, Technical University Eindhoven, Netherlands.

[28] Robillard, G., Bouchard, S., Fournier, T. & Renaud, P. (2003). Anxiety and presence during VR immersion: a comparative study of the reactions of phobic and non-phobic participants in therapeutic virtual environments derived from computer games. *CyberPsychology & Behavior*, Vol. 6, No. 5, pp. 467-477.

[29] Roschelle, J. M., Pea, R. D., Hoadley, C. M., Gordon, D. N., & Means, B. M. (2000). Changing how and what children learn in school with computer-based technologies. *Children and Computer Technology*, Vol. 10, No. 2, pp. 76-101.

[30] Rose, B. & Lenski, J. (2003). Internet and multimedia 10: the emerging difital consumer. *Report*, Arbitron Internet broadcast Services & Edison Media Research.

[31] Saracho, O. N. & Spodek, B. (1998). A play foundation for family literacy. *International Journal of Educational Research*, Vol. 29, pp. 41-50.

[32] Shields, M. & Behrmann, R. (2000). Children and computer technology: analysis and recommendations. *Children and Computer Technology*, Vol. 10, No. 2, pp. 4-30.

[33] Subrahmanyam, K., Kraut, R. E., Greenfield, P. M. & Gross, E. F. (2000). The impact of home computer use on children's activities and development. *Children and Computer Technology*, Vol. 10, No. 2, pp. 123-144.

[34] Subrahmanyam, K., Greenfield, P. M., Kraut, R. E. & Gross, E. F. (2001). The impact of computer use on children's and adolescents' development. *Applied Developmental Psychology*, Vol. 22, pp. 7-30.

[35] Tannen, D. (1999). *The Argument Culture: Stopping America's war of words.* Ballantine

[36] Toy Industries of Europe (2004). Play as key to child development as formal education. *Press Release*, Retrieved May 7, 2004 from www.tietoy.org/press/Nuremberg_VoP_Seminar_English.pdf

[37] Tuchman, R. (2000). The treatment of learning disabilities. *International Pediatrics*, Vol. 15, No. 2, pp. 91-96.

[38] Turnin, M.C., Couvaras, O., Jouret, B., Tauber, M. T., Bolzonella, C., Fabre, D., Tauber, J. P. & Hanaire-Broutin, H. (2000). Learning good eating habits playing computer games at school: a 2000 children evaluation. *Diabetes Research and Clinical Practice*, Vol. 50, No. 1001, p. 239.

REALIZATION OF TAI-CHI MOTION USING A HUMANOID ROBOT

Physical interactions with humanoid robot

Takenori Wama[1], Masayuki Higuchi[1], Hajime Sakamoto[2], Ryohei Nakatsu[1]

[1] Kwansei Gakuin University, School of Science and Technology
2-1 Gakuen, Sanda, 669-1337 Japan
{scbc0057, x78072, nakatsu}@ksc.kwansei.ac.jp,
http://www.ksc.kwansei.ac.jp
http://ist.ksc.kwansei.ac.jp/index.html

[2] Hajime Laboratory
Kobe, Japan
h_sakamoto@cam.hi-ho.ne.jp
http://www.hajimerobot.co.jp/

Abstract: Even though in recent years research and development of humanoid robots has increased, the major topics of research generally focus on how to make a robot perform specific motions such as walking. However, walking is only one of the complicated motions humans can perform. For robots to play an active role in society as our partner, they must be able to simulate precisely various kinds of human actions . We chose tai-chi as an example of complicated human actions and succeeded in programming a robot to perform the 24 fundamental tai-chi actions.

Key words: robot, physical interaction, communication

1. INTRODUCTION

Many companies and universities are currently doing research and development into humanoid robots. These robots are equipped with a certain amount of flexibility at their robotic "joints," making it possible for them to perform various motions. However, most of these studies investigate little outside of rising or walking actions, ignoring the rest of the actions that humans can perform. As a result, little research has fully investigated and utilized robotic flexibility. Indeed, since walking and rising are good examples of complicated and dynamic actions, it is valuable to study them. At the same time, however, it is expected that in the near future humanoid robots will be introduced into society to become our partner at home and in the workplace. Therefore, robots must not only walk or rise but also do various kinds of human-like operations naturally. Robots must also use these motions to communicate with humans. Based on this basic concept, we tried to reproduce smooth full body actions in a commercially available humanoid robot. We selected the motions of *tai-chi*, a Chinese martial art form, because smooth movements condensed from all human actions for exercising the entire body are essential to it. Therefore, our goal is to design tai-chi actions, install them, and develop a humanoid robot that can perform them.

2. HUMANOID ROBOT

We decided to use a robot developed at the Hajime Laboratory to reproduce the smooth exercises of tai-chi. This humanoid robot was equipped with 22 servomotors, enabling it to simulate the smooth, human-like motions by simultaneously controlling all of these motors. The hardware specifications of the robot are shown in Table 1, and its appearance is shown in Fig. 1.

Table 1. Specification of the humanoid robot used for experiment

Size / Weight	34cm / 1.7kg
Flexibility	22 (leg 12, arm 8, waist 1, head 1)
CPU	SH2/7047F
Motor	KO PDS-2144, FUTABA S3003, FUTABA S3102, FUTABA S3103
Battery	DC6V

3. TAI-CHI

There are five major schools of tai-chi: Chin, Kure, Son, Bu and Yo, which is the most commonly practiced style. Yo's extended version has been officially established by the Chinese government. As an established tai-chi, there are 24 formula, 48 formula, 88 formula, and etc. In creating tai-chi motions, we chose the 24 formula tai-chi because even though it is the simplest form of tai-chi, it still contains the strong points of the other schools.

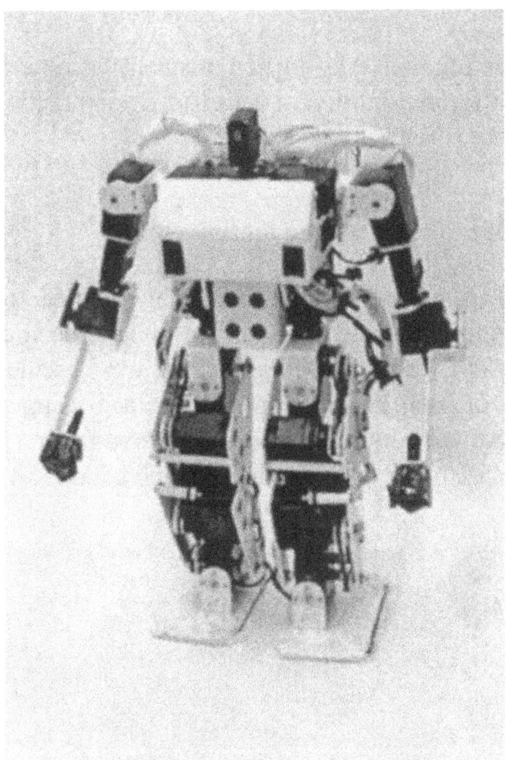

Fig. 1. Appearance of the humanoid robot

4. MOTION EDITOR

A motion editor was used to design the robot's motion as shown in Fig. 2. Fig. 2 also shows the *Front*, *Right*, and *Top* views for the robot's front, right, and above positions, respectively. In the *Perspective* view, we can rotate the robot image 360 degrees in any direction to gain a panoramic view. The angle of each motor is controlled by the parameter in the upper right part of the figure. The number in the left-hand side shows the data assigned to each motor, and the right-hand side number shows the angle of each motor. The transition time for each motion is decided by the parameter in the lower right part of the figure. Moreover, since we can create and store 32 motions in one file, 24 files were created to store all of the 24 formula tai-chi motions.

5. MOTION DESIGN

Basically, each motion was created manually using a motion editor. By connecting each created motion, a series of smooth actions was generated. The detailed process is described below.

5.1 Creation of motion with the motion editor

As described in section 4, we exhaustively studied each tai-chi motion through magazines and videos. Then we divided each continuous motion into a series of short, key motions; key frames were decided for each motion. Next, a portion of each key motion was decided using the motion editor, which then output the control data for each servomotor. In the process, we had to create each motion, maintaining as much balance as possible.

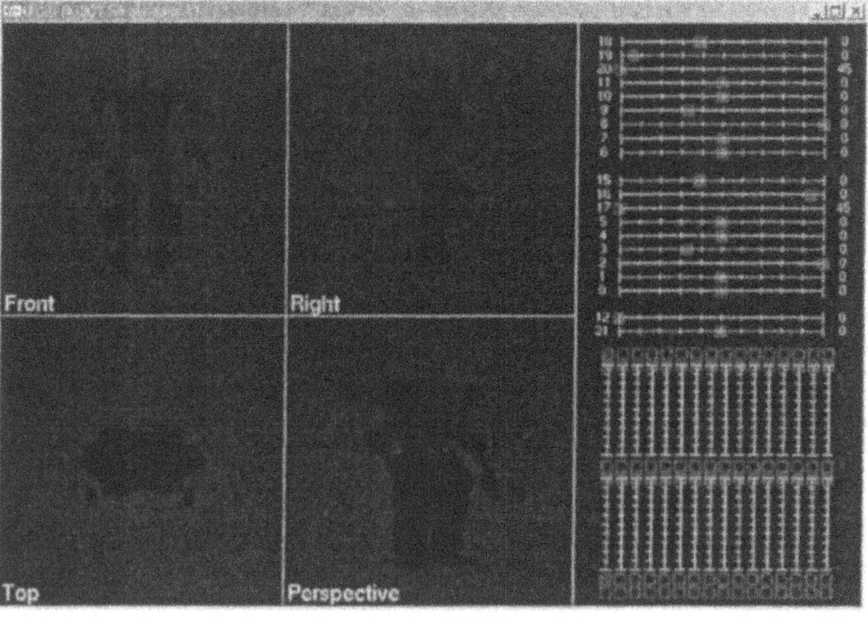

Fig. 2. User interface screen of the motion editor

5.2 Check of continuous action

Before connecting the motion created in section 5.1 to a series of motions, it was necessary to investigate any incongruities by comparing the motion with that of human tai-chi motion from magazines and videos. Tai-chi, essentially, is comprised of a series of continuous actions that do not stop from beginning to end. When the robot does tai-chi, however, there is a short pause when the motion is connected because of the specifications of the motion editor that we used. However, if we concentrate on watching the tai-chi motion of the robot, however, there is no little sense of incongruity.

5.3 Motion adjustment on an actual robot

Each tai-chi motion created in section 5.2 was then installed into the robot and checked. Since the robot's center-of-gravity could only be checked during simulations with the actual physical robot, this whole process was the most important and time consuming. Sometimes small differences in the center-of-gravity between the computer graphics robot and the physical robot couldn't be recognized on the motion editor. If the robot fell down during a tai-chi motion, the motor angle had to be adjusted. A key frame between two key frames had to be carried out. In this way, we investigated for incongruity in the series of robot motions, eventually obtaining complete motion data.

6. DEMONSTRATION OF TAI-CHI MOTION BASED ON HUMAN ROBOT INTERACTION

We extended our study and added a speech recognition tool called *Julian* to the robot, enabling it to perform a tai-chi demonstration based on communication with humans. When a user utters a command sentence, the key words are extracted by the speech recognition tool, converted into the control command for the robot, and sent to it (Fig. 3). The control data for each motion itself is loaded in the robot's microcomputer. Corresponding to the control command sent from the Server PC, the microcomputer reads out suitable control data to control the robot movement.

At various exhibitions we demonstrated our robot having easy conversations with the audience and showing them various tai-chi motions. In the future, various applications are possible based on such interaction between humans and this type of humanoid robot. For example, a robot can talk or chat with humans and act as their partner. It can also entertain humans by showing them tai-chi or dancing with them. Moreover, such forms of entertainment that currently use computer characters as fighting games and role-playing games could be performed with humanoid robots. In the near future there could be a growing market for such interactive games.

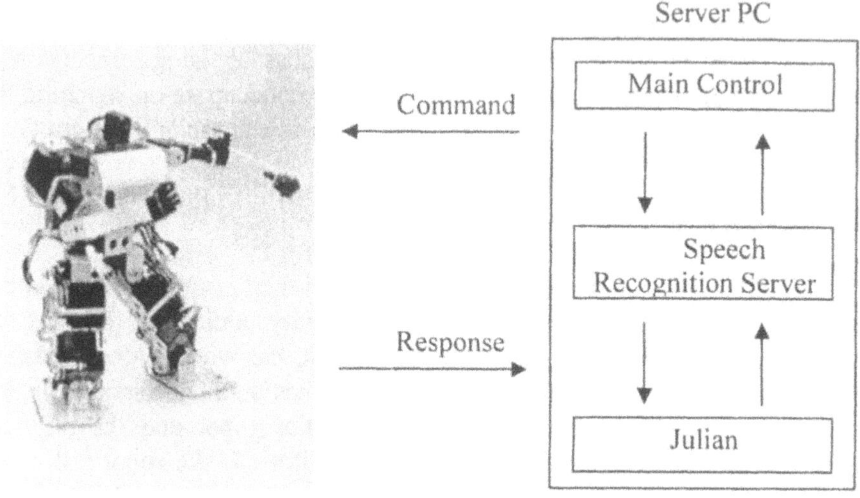

Fig. 3. Composition of the conversation system using the robot

7. CONCLUSION

In this paper we investigated the realization of tai-chi motions for a humanoid robot and created a control data base of human-like tai-chi motions. However, tai-chi is only one of the complicated motions and actions of humans. A humanoid robot must be able to perform various human-like motions, so a robot needs to be capable of autonomous motion, action, and behavior.

For the autonomy of a robot, there are many research issues. We want to prepare a database containing various kinds of fundamental motions and achieve any desired motions and actions by combining these basic motion units. For the preparation of such a database, it is necessary for the motion editor to grasp the center-of-gravity balance and make it easy for the user to design robot motions. In addition, it is necessary to introduce new technologies for the humanoid robot. For example, if a robot encounters stairs, it must use image processing to recognize their height and inclination. Thus, research of image processing is also required. Research on accurate speech recognition is also needed.

At present the functions of humanoid robots are very limited. However, we believe that someday such autonomous robots as science fiction *Androids* from movies will emerge and be introduced into society.

STORYTELLING FOR RECREATING OUR SELVES: ZENETIC COMPUTER

Naoko Tosa
Massachusetts Institute of Technology /JST,
N52-390, 265 Massachusetts Ave. Cambridge, MA USA, : Japan Science Technology Coporation "Interaction & Intelligence" 2-2-2, Hikaridai, Seika-cho, Soraku-gun, Kyoto 619-0288, Japan,
mail:naoko@mit.edu

Abstract: We present an interactive storytelling system that aims to help us "recreate" our conscious selves by calling on traditional Japanese concepts and media. "Recreating our selves" means the process of reconciling our conscious 'daily self' and our 'hidden self'. This requires deep stimulations which are difficult to achieve through conventional logic based interactions. Users create, enter and dynamically interact with a virtual world expressed as 3D "Sansui" ink painting, encountering fragments of stories and ambiguous provocations. The user physically interacts with the system through various media including a Sumie (ink painting), a rake in a Zen rock garden, touching screen images, drawing or clapping hands. The interaction system includes a dynamical chaos engine which is used to couple activity of the user to the generation of high dimensional context and evolution of the storytelling.

Key words:

1. INTRODUCTION

We have developed an interactive storytelling system that aims to help us "recreate" our conscious selves by calling on Buddhist principles, Asian philosophy, and traditional Japanese culture through the inspirational media of traditional ink paintings, kimono and haiku. "Recreating ourselves" means the process of making the consciousness of our 'daily self' meet that of our 'hidden self'. through stimulation of activity deep within us. It is difficult to achieve this through traditional logic-based interactions. Our system is a new approach which incorporates traditional media and methods in an interactive computer system. The interactive storytelling stimulates deep imagination and allows users to develop connections between their hidden selves, full of imagination and creative energy, and their daily conscious selves, which directly interpret the ambient reality [1].

2. PHILOSOPHY OF ZENETIC COMPUTER

The user creates a virtual world by manipulating 3D images of Asian sansui ink painting on a computer display with an intuitive and enjoyable interface tool. These images, which typically symbolize nature and philosophical precepts, provide a dramatic departure from our view of daily experience. This awakens us from our daily consciousness and gives free reign to subconscious imagination[2]. Based on the user's sansui design, the system infers his or her internal consciousness and generates a story that the user can 'enter' via the computer display. This story further shakes the user's consciousness. This is not a complete story, such as those in the movies or novels, but fragments of short stories. Experiencing these episodic stories makes users feel uneasy and arouses their subconscious desire to construct a whole story by linking the fragments. In each of these inchoate stories, the system stimulates interaction through Zen dialogue or haiku as a form of allegorical communication. The user is asked questions that do not have "correct" answers. He or she is forced to deal with these ambiguous provocations while subconsciously struggling to answer the questions.

This subconscious effort inspires the user to find ways of linking the stories into an original whole. The user responds to objects presented by the interactive system, whether a graphic image or a provocative statement, by manipulating input media, such as a virtual calligraphy brush or rake of a Zen rock garden, on-screen images, or simply clapping hands. Coupled with the subconscious effort exerted to link the fragmentary stories, these user interactions decrease the gap between daily self and hidden self. This process of bringing our selves together is called MA-Interaction; ma is a Japanese concept that stresses the ephemeral quality of experience. In the final phase, the user has a dialogue with a "bull," which is used as a metaphor of our hidden self in Zen Buddhism. Through this dialogue, users experience a virtual unification of their daily self and their unconscious self into a recreated conscious self.

3. TECHNICAL REALIZATION

Key technologies used to realize the system include a digital 3D *sansui* ink-painting engine which allows the users themselves to compose an ink painting to enter, a neural network engine which classifies the user's 'hidden personality' revealed in the ink painting into Buddhist Goun categories, and a dynamical chaos engine which is injected with signals from Goun categories and other user actions to generate high dimensional data for the context and evolution of the storytelling. The following are the main components of the system structure.

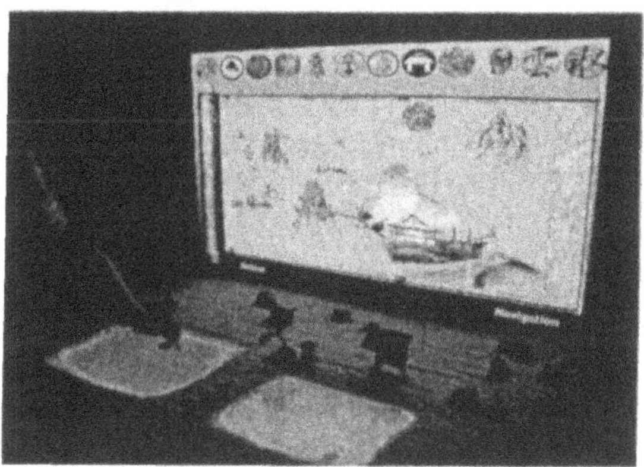

Figure 1. User make ink painting by ZENetic Computer

3.1 Software Integration [3]

The flow of the system is as follows:

1) User makes 3D Sansui ink-painting picture by manipulating symbolic icons
2) User's hidden self is classified into Goun categories.
3) User enters the Sansui picture and a journey begins. Haiku is used to generate story fragments that are presented in Sansui.
4) User experiences various stages of MA-Interaction (User may experience Steps 3 and 4 several times).
5) Finally, the Ten Bulls Story Interaction takes place.

3.2 Hardware Structure

Figure 1 shows the overall hardware structure of the Zenetic Computer System.

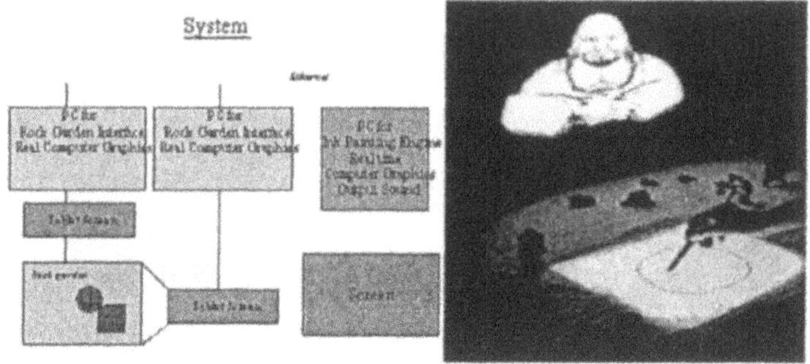

Figure 2. ZENeticComputer System *Figure 3.* ZEN dialogue Interaction

3.3 3D Sansui Ink-painting engine

A key part of the system is the user interaction with a digital 3D ink-painting engine. Depending on how users compose their initial ink-painting, the system classifies their intrinsic personality using a neural network. The personality corresponds to a point in a Goun space. Goun is a categorization from Buddhism based on the view that five basic spirits and materials make up the world. The five categories of personality based on goun can be summarized as follows.

a) 色 *Shiki* is how nature and materials actually exist.
b) 受 *Jyu* is the intuitive impression.
c) 想 *So* is the perceived image.
d) 行 *Gyo* is the process of mind that activates your behavior.
e) 識 *Shiki* is the deep mental process that lies behind all of the above processes

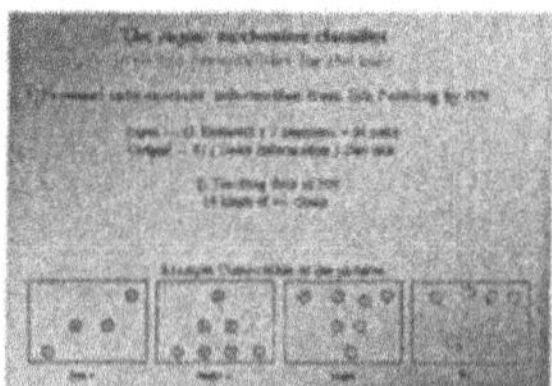

Figure 4. Examples of neural-net classification of the composition of pictures created by a user into Buddhist Goun categories corresponding to "hidden self".

User data is also obtained at later times from various interactions between the user and the system, and used to determine a pseudo Goun personality. Depending on how the user is affected by the evolving story, the pseudo Goun personality may differ from the intrinsic (=hidden) personality. Conversely, the difference between the pseudo personality and the intrinsic personality will affect the evolving story via an engine, called a chaos engine.

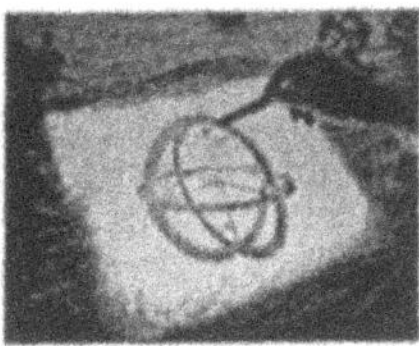

Figure 5. Compass for navigation in your ink painting world.

3.4 Storytelling generated by chaos engine

A dynamical chaos engine is used to couple activity of the user, via the difference between the pseudo personality and the intrinsic personality, to the generation of high dimensional context and evolution of the storytelling. The chaos engine consists of three dynamic components, which we call agents. We name the three agents, User, Target and Master. The agents each have internal chaotic dynamics, and also move around in Goun space. The three agents are coupled so that there is an interplay between their motions in the Goun space and the synchronization [4] of their internal dynamics. The transient dynamics of the chaos engine are sampled and used to create the sounds and images experienced by the user, and also to control the evolution of the story.

In the current implementation of the chaos engine for the ZENetic computer, the position of the User agent corresponds to the user's pseudo personality, and the position of the Target agent corresponds to the momentary view of the user's pseudo personality obtained from the latest user interaction. The User agent starts at the position of the intrinsic personality and tends to move toward the position of the Target agent. The User agent is coupled to the Target via the Master in such away that if there is no interference from the Master, the User tends to synchronize to the Target and move toward the Target position, so that the User and Target become identical. On the other hand, if there is interference from the Master, it is more difficult for the User to synchronize with the Target, and so less likely that the User will reach the Target. The strength of the Master's interference depends inversely on the distance between the pseudo personality and the hidden personality - the smaller the distance, the stronger the influence of the Master, and hence the more difficult it is for the User to synchronize and merge with the Target.

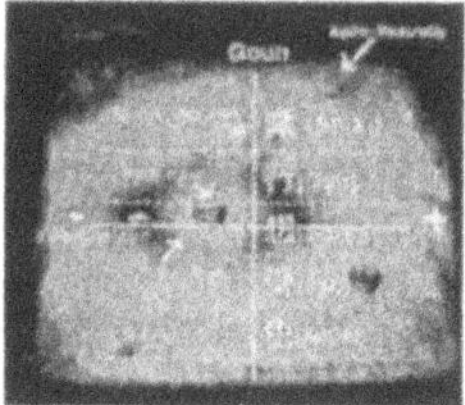

Figure 6. Visualization of your own Chaos engine in ZENetic Computer ZENetic Computer.

4. CONCLUSIONS AND FUTURE WORK

Real-time interaction with individual consciousness and subconscious is a long-term challenge for computer systems. Interactive storytelling is a frontier which allows us to explore this challenge. Science says that human consciousness may have a chaotic nature. By incorporating chaotic mechanisms, our system aims to provide a rich and dynamic interaction which entangles the conscious and subconscious. Responses to questionnaires from users who have experienced the ZENetic Computer show that they tend to feel relaxed and stimulated in a way that they had never felt before. Both English and Japanese versions have been developed. This system will be exhibited at the MIT Museum, KODAIJI - ZEN Temple (Kyoto, Japan) and around the world. [5]

5. ACKNOWLEDGMENTS

This research was supported in part by the Telecommunications Advancement Organization of Japan. Thanks to Dr. Peter Davis for helping to design and tune the chaos engine.

6. REFERENCES

1. S. Matsuoka,"The Science of the beauties of nature," Shunjusha (1994) (In Japanese)
2. S. Matsuoka, "Sansui Thought" Gogatsu shobo (2003) (In Japanese)
3. N. Tosa, Chapter19: Expression of emotion unconsciousness with art and technology, "AFFECTIVE MINDS," ELSEVIER, pp. 183-201 (2000)
4. Y. Liu, P. Davis, "Dual synchronization of chaos", Physical Review E, 61 pp. R2176-R2179 (2000)
5. http://web.mit.edu/~naoko/

INTERACTION IN A SENSITIVE HOUSE

Future room that senses human mood and respond to it

Henry Thomas

France Telecom R&D, 4 rue du Clos Courtel, BP 91226, 35512 Cesson Sévigné cedex, France- mail:henry.thomas@francetelecom.com

Abstract: We describe a sensitive and multimedia house conceived at France telecom R&D Studio creative, and the way we experiment interface for that house. Interaction can be explicit, such as bike, carpet-pad that control directly multimedia content. Interaction can also be indirect, making use of emotion analysis. We are working with multimedia artist Naoko Tosa to investigate the latter category of interactions.

Key words: interaction, emotions, pervasive computing

1. INTRODUCTION

The *Creative studio* is a part of France Telecom's R&D centre. It was launched in 1997 to promote innovation in communication services. Its main thrust is to build up usages, services and customer awareness in an innovative process traditionally governed by a technical and scientific structure. The *Creative studio* complement the R&D approach with new methods borrowed from human sciences, creativity and artistic creation. Coming up with ideas gathered from different input, we design concept-services, simple illustrations together with scenarios of use. From the scenarios and illustration, we obtain reactions, comments from marketing teams, projects teams or future customers, or from potential users. This helps us to refine the concept, to end up with a precise definition of the product.

2. THE SENSITIVE HOUSE

We are testing our services in a simulation of a house, which is around 100 square meters. It is designed to be modular and to allow a rapid reconfiguration, either from the technical side (electronic, routing of video, sound and computer signals) or from the furniture point of view. Thus, we are able to adapt to different ways of life. The aim is to have a familiar environment, in which user can describe their existing practice, and also develop new ones. We use the house in several different ways, which can be contradictory sometimes:

- A *domestic house* to test automated element of comfort.
- A *secure house* in which we can test the security of persons and goods.
- An *adaptative house* in which we develop new ideas and concept about the living space and its components (ambient intelligence, pervasive computing).
- A *sensitive and multimedia house* which is more oriented on leisure, permanently connected to the world. It relies on the perspective of broadband access, and on the ability for the user to interact naturally and easily with services. It is this latter house that is the subject of this article.

Figure 1. The sensitive house. Left side, the view shows from left to right 1) the back a plasma display (see right picture), two projection screen to create data projection, or panorama live videos, 3) the kitchen space, which integrate a display screen. The right picture displays the large plasma screen, also use for video conferencing, with to PhD students mimicking end-users.

To interact with the user, we devised information appliances [3] in the shape of objects. An information appliance is an intelligent object that performs one function (for instance give the weather forecast with a single push on an unique button). The different appliances in the house cooperate in order to provide the desired result. In the sensitive house, you will find a variety of sensors and object that allows direct control over "things" (comfort, medias) and other sensors that work in a more elaborate and indirect way, such as emotions.

3. HETEROGENEITY OF SENSOR

Our goal is to provide different interactors in the house, suited for each member of the family, depending on his needs and moods. We developed, alone or in cooperation with artists and designers, several concept services.

- A bicycle, that enable users to navigate trough 3D content[2] and inside a travelogue[1].
- A sensitive carpet, similar in principle to a Playstation-2 dance pad, though this carpet is much wider : 2 meters by 3 meter, with an accuracy of 15 cm. With the carpet, one can navigate in a 3D world.
- A video tracking system: a camera mounted on the ceiling is able to identify a point of light. The pictures and sounds of the room will be modified according to the movements.

All these navigation system were developed separately and do not interoperate. What if Jane user is tired does not want to bike, but want to sit on the floor and still interact? What if Jon wants to move freely inside the house? Jane could use the sensitive carpet, and Jon exploits the video tracking feature. We are reengineering our demos, so that input devices are all permutable, just like a PC gamer could use a Joystick, a game pad or a keyboard. To achieve this result, we choose to use the VRPN abstraction layer. VRPN met all of our requirements. *"The Virtual-Reality Peripheral Network (VRPN) is a set of classes within a library and a set of servers that are designed to implement a network-transparent interface between application programs and the set of physical devices (tracker, etc.) used in a virtual-reality (VR) system. The idea is to have a PC or other host at each VR station that controls the peripherals (tracker, button device, haptic device, analog inputs, sound, etc)"*[4]. VRPN application domain was only the world of 3D modeling and cinema studio. We propose to use it in the house. Using this layer will open combinations that were not suspected before: navigation in a CDROM with a bike or a carpet, 3D world navigation via a carpet. Apart from the multi sensors aspect, this opens up possibilities for disabled people. This allows to simply switching to a "preferred input device".

4. INTUITIVE CONTROL

However, all these systems are used for explicit control / movement into 2D or 3D world, or to control a video playback. We want to develop systems that allow intuitive control. The aim of such systems is to be able to address issues such as:

- How Jane can set the ambient of the house without having to use a control interface that explicitly addresses all lights and blinds?
- How John can browse a huge CD collection (either local or network based), looking for a music that suits its mood?

One answer is to detect the user *mood* and to (re)act accordingly. The reaction could be to propose an ambient for the house (combination of light sound, pictures). The same way, we could find a record in a huge library of CD that is adequate for John's mood.

We established a partnership with the Japanese multimedia artist Naoko Tosa to integrate her interactive piece of work "The Zenetic computer" [5] inside the sensible house. ZENetic Computer is an interactive experience that evokes "self-awakening, a particular cognitive response to processing reality via subliminal consciousness. It uses stories portrayed in sumi-e (ink painting), haiku and kimono which display features of eastern philosophy, and Zen in particular. Visitors create their own sumi-e and stories on a large rice paper screen, while learning about Zen, Japanese art, and themselves.

The ZENetic computer uses the ink painting and interactions to induce an emotional state for the visitor, and then tries to bring the visitor, through a sequence of interactions to a higher awakening. We believe that such devices can be used in the future to interact with services. Imagine a scenario in which you come back home. You do not want to interact with a PC computer to specify an ambient (music, videos etc.). You could just sit and place different special objects on a surface, or do a drawing, just like the one we often do during a boring phone call. The house can then analyze the pattern of object, or the drawing to induce your mental state, and go through patterns learnt to find the ambient that fits your mood, without having to go through introspection.

Figure 2. The Zenetic computer in the sensitive house. The plasma screen is used for main display, while a large rock garden (in front of the author) integrates a sensitive screen for interaction. Smells are emitted by the yellow box in the back, and videos are projected on the wall behind. A very dark ambient is used.

5. CONCLUSION

The field of domestic interfaces and interaction is quite wide and we focus mainly on the two directions described:

- Low level interactors such a bike, carpet that we use to directly control media (video, pictures, 3D)
- High level interactors that deal with emotion, and allow the user to explore a non explicit dialog with the house, based on the building of a language, specific the house and its inhabitants.

6. REFERENCES

[1] "IBIS interactive travelogue", Rob White, 2000, http://www.veloquence.com
[2] "Using a Bicycle Interface for Interaction and Games", Henry Thomas, Rob White,. 10th International Conference on Human - Computer Interaction, June 22-26, 2003
[4] VRPN, University of northern California http://www.cs.unc.edu/Research/vrpn/
[3] "The Invisible computer", Donald A. Norman, MIT Press, 1999
[5] Naoko Tosa, Chapter 19: Expression of emotion unconsciousness with art and technology, "Affective minds", Elsevier, pp. 183201 (200)

Algirdas Avižienis

Topic 3

Fault Tolerance for Trustworthy and Dependable Information Infrastructures

Organiser:

Jean Arlat
LAAS-CNRS, France
jean.arlat@laas.fr

The wide variety of vulnerabilities, outages and failures that may affect information processing systems and infrastructures constitute increasing worries in most today's technology deployments. These concerns extend beyond the classical application domains (such as space, power production, telecommunications, transportation, etc.) and reach all information infrastructures (such as the Internet) and impact more societal domains that increasingly rely on the proper behavior of these infrastructures. Even embedded systems, that could be classically considered as closed systems, are now impacted by the cross-coupling that is establishing between the dedicated computerized control systems supporting the critical applications, and the overall information infrastructures.

The goal of these Topical Days is to provide a state-of-the-art review of the emerging problems and challenges, and anticipate potential solutions and research avenues to cope with these issues.

This event is organized by IFIP WG 10.4 on Dependable Computing and Fault Tolerance, in the honor of Prof. Algirdas Avižienis, whose pioneering and leading work has shaped the discipline of fault-tolerant and dependable computing.

DEPENDABLE SYSTEMS OF THE FUTURE: WHAT IS STILL NEEDED?

Algirdas Avižienis
Vytautas Magnus University, Kaunas, Lithuania and University of California, Los Angeles, USA — aviz@adm.vdu.lt

Abstract: It is concluded that hardware is not being adequately employed to provide system fault tolerance. A design principle called the "immune system paradigm" is presented and a hardware-implemented fault tolerance infrastructure is proposed as the means to use hardware more effectively in building dependable systems of the future.

Key words: dependable systems; immune system paradigm; fault tolerance infrastructure

1. WHAT IS THIS ALL ABOUT?

Predicting the future is not a dependable activity when breakthroughs and inventions are forecast; however, when a missing link in the chain of evolution is identified, the dependability of the prediction is likely to be more trustworthy. At least, that is my hope in presenting my thoughts on one link that I consider to be essential in building truly dependable systems in the future.

We find an interesting paradox in contemporary computing systems: they are used to provide protection for various critical infrastructures of our society, such as electrical power, transportation, communication, etc., but they do not possess an identifiable protective infrastructure of their own. Such an infrastructure should be (1) generic, that is, suitable for a variety of "client" computing systems, (2) transparent to the client's software, but able to communicate with it, (3) compatible with and able to support other defenses that the client system employs, and (4) fully self-protected by fault tolerance, immune to the client's faults, including design faults, and to attacks by malicious software.

It is my goal to suggest what a protective infrastructure with the above properties should be like and to illustrate the concept with an architecture first presented at DSN 2000 [1] and its generalization to a hierarchy of protective infrastructures implemented entirely in hardware. I am convinced that in the first fifty years of our computer age hardware has not been adequately exploited (not even close to its full potential!) to assure system dependability, and that this omission needs to be corrected if we are going to cope with the proliferating threats to dependable and secure computing.

In the following sections, I present (1) a look at contemporary methods of protecting high-availability systems and their shortcomings, (2) the principle of design I call "the immune system paradigm", and (3) the architecture of a hierarchical fault tolerance infrastructure evolved from the infrastructure of [1].

2. FAULT TOLERANCE IN CONTEMPORARY SYSTEMS

Fault tolerance defenses in current high performance and availability platforms (servers, communication processors, etc.) are found at four different hardware levels: component (chip, cartridge, etc.), board, platform (chassis), and cluster of platforms.

2.1 Component Level Fault Tolerance

At the component level, the error detection and recovery mechanisms are part of the component's hardware and firmware. In general, we find very limited error detection and poor error containment in COTS processors. For example, in Pentium and P6 processors error detection by parity only covers the caches and busses, except for the data bus which has an error correcting code, as does the main memory. All the complex logic of arithmetic and instruction processing remains unchecked. Recovery choices are "reset" actions of varying severity. The cancellation in April 1998 of the duplex "FRC" mode of operation eliminated most of the error containment boundary. All internal error detection and recovery logic remains entirely unchecked as well [2,3].

Similar error coverage and containment deficiencies are found in the high-end processors of most other manufacturers. The exceptions are IBM S/390 G5 and G6 processors that internally duplicate the arithmetic and instruction handling units and provide extensive error detection or correction and transient recovery for the entire processor [4]. Near 100% error detection and containment are attained in the G5 and G6 processors, which carry on the legacy of fault tolerance from the IBM 9020 – the last TCM mainframe.

Intel also has a record of building fault-tolerant systems [5]. The original design of the Pentium and P6 family of processors (except P4) includes the FRC (functional redundancy checking) mode of operation. In FRC two processors operate as a master/checker pair that receives the same inputs. The checker internally compares its outputs to those of the master and issues the FRCERR signal when a disagreement is found. The master enters the Machine Check state upon receiving FRCERR [6]. Operation in the FRC mode provides near 100% error detection at the master's output and also makes the output an error containment boundary. In April 1998 a set of specification changes was issued by Intel: "The XXX processor will not use the FRCERR pin. All references to these pins will be removed from the specification." (The XXX stands for all processors from Pentium to Pentium III). Deletion of the FRC mode left the Pentium and P6 processors with very limited error detection and containment. No further explanation was provided by Intel for the change. Our conjecture is that asynchronous inputs could not be properly handled in the FRC mode. Intel did not reply to our inquiry about the cause of FRC deletion.

Processors that do not have adequate error detection and containment can be made fault-tolerant by forming a self-checking pair with comparison (e.g., the FRC mode) or a triplet with majority voting on the outputs. Since the FRC mode deletion, there is a second deficiency of contemporary processors: they do not (or cannot) provide hardware support for comparison or voting operations.

2.2 Fault Tolerance at Higher Levels

At the board level, complete redundant hardware as well as software components are used to assure very high availability. The "hot standby" approach is especially widely used in the fields of embedded systems and telecommunications. Hot standby duplexing selectively duplicates the most critical subsystems, such as the CPU, power supplies, cooling fans, etc. Less costly fault tolerance techniques such as ECC, RAID, N+1 sparing, etc. are used for the remaining subsystems. The CPU boards present the greatest challenge: to detect faults in both CPUs and to execute a rapid switchover to the hot standby CPU when the active CPU is faulty. A good example of the state-of-the-art is the Ziatech high availability architecture [7]. The critical elements that execute CPU switchover are three hardware modules and four software modules for each CPU. These modules must be operational to make a switchover possible, but they are not protected by fault tolerance themselves.

At the platform level a widely used technique is Intelligent Platform Management (IPM) that requires the introduction of the IPM hardware subsystem into the platform [8]. It consists of additional COTS hardware (buses and controllers) and firmware that provides autonomous monitoring and recovery functions. Also provided are logging and inventory functions [8]. The effectiveness of the IPM monitoring and recovery functions is limited by the error information outputs and recovery commands of the COTS processors of the platform. For example, the P6 processors [6] have only a set of "reset" commands and five error signals (after deletion of FRCERR) whose coverage was estimated to be very limited [3].

The IPM subsystem of [8] itself is not protected by fault tolerance. The cost of adding fault tolerance may be high because of the multiple functions of the IPM. The Version 1.5 of the IPM Interface Specification (implementation independent) has 395 pages, which represent a lot of functionality to be protected. Furthermore, the IPM does not support comparison or voting for redundant multi-channel (duplex or triplex) computing.

A cluster is a group of two or more complete platforms (nodes) in a network configuration. Upon failure of one node, its workload is distributed among the remaining nodes. There are many different implementations of the generic concept of "clustering." Their common characteristic is that they are managed by cluster software such as Microsoft Cluster Service, Extreme Linux, etc. The main disadvantages for telecommunication or embedded systems are: (1) the relatively long recovery time (seconds); (2) the cost of complete replication, including power consumption, replication of peripherals, etc.

The four approaches discussed above are at different levels and can be implemented in different combinations. The integration of the different error detection, recovery and logging techniques is a major challenge when two or more approaches are combined in the same platform.

2.3 The Design Fault Problem

None of the approaches described above address the problem of tolerating design faults in hardware ("errata") and in software ("bugs") of the COTS processors. Yet a study of eight models of the Pentium and P6 processors [2] shows that by April 1999 from 45 to 101 errata had been discovered, and from 30 to 60 had remained unfixed in the latest versions ("steppings") of the processors. The discovery of errata is a continuing process. For example, consider the Pentium III [9]. The first specification update (March 1999) listed 44 errata of which 36 remained unfixed in five steppings (until May 2001). From March 1999 to May 2001 35 new errata were discovered of which 22 remained unfixed. Other manufacturers also publish errata lists, but those of Intel are most comprehensive and well organized.

Most of the errata are triggered by rare events and are unlikely to cause system failures; yet the designers of high-dependability systems cannot ignore their existence and the fact that more errata will be discovered after a system design is complete. Continuing growth of processor complexity and the advent of new technologies indicate that the errata problem will remain and may get worse in the future.

The most effective method of design fault tolerance is design diversity, i.e., multichannel computing in which each channel employs independently designed hardware and software [10], as in the Boeing 777 Primary Flight Control Computer [11]. The Boeing and other diverse designs employ diverse COTS processors and custom hardware and software because the COTS processors do not support multichannel computing. Design fault tolerance by means of design diversity will become much less costly if it can be supported by COTS hardware elements. It is also important to note that design diversity provides support for the detection and neutralization of malicious logic [12].

2.4 Limitations of the Four Approaches

The implementation of defenses at all or some of the above described four levels has led to the market appearance of many high-availability platforms (advertised as 99.999% or better) for server, telecommunications, embedded and other applications. However, all four approaches show deficiencies that impose limits on their effectiveness.

At the component level the Intel P6 and Itanium processors, as well as those of most other manufacturers (except IBM's G5 and G6) have a low error detection and containment coverage, leaving instruction handling and arithmetic entirely unchecked. After executing the Reset command most of the existing checks (bus ECC, parity, etc) are disabled and must be enabled by software that sets bits in the (unprotected) Power-On Configuration register. In general, critical recovery decisions are handed off to software.

At the board level, such as in "hot standby" [7], unprotected "hard core" hardware and software elements handle the critical switchover procedure.

At the platform level the Intelligent Platform Management (IPM) hardware subsystem handles both critical recovery decisions and voluminous logging, configuration record keeping and communication management operations. The critical IPM element is the Baseboard Management Controller (BMC) [8] that is itself unprotected and depends on interaction with software to carry out its functions.

At the cluster level that is software-controlled the disadvantages are long recovery times and the high cost of complete system (chassis) replication.

In summary, the weaknesses are:

1. The presence of unprotected "hard core" elements, especially in the error detection and recovery management hardware and software;
2. The commingling of hardware and software defenses: both must succeed in order to attain recovery;
3. The absence of built-in support for multiple-channel computing that provides high coverage and containment, especially when design diversity is employed to attain design fault tolerance.

It is my conclusion that during the explosive evolution of hardware over the past 25 years, computer hardware has not been adequately utilized for the assurance of system dependability or survivability.

3. A DESIGN PRINCIPLE: THE IMMUNE SYSTEM PARADIGM

At the beginning, I identified four attributes that were needed by a fault tolerance infrastructure (FTI), which I see as the "missing link" in the defenses of contemporary systems, as reviewed in the preceding section. The FTI should be generic, transparent to the client's software, compatible with defenses used by the client, and fully self-protected. It is evident that an all-hardware FTI would be most likely to meet those goals, since stored programs do not need to be protected. The FTI needs non-volatile storage for record-keeping and ROM microcode for sequencing operations

While looking for a convenient way to explain the approach to system designers as well as to their customers and interested members of the public, I noted [13] that the immune system of the human body serves in a similar manner as my proposed hardware FTI in a computing system.

To develop the argument, I use the following three analogies:

1. the body is analogous to hardware,
2. consciousness is analogous to software,
3. the immune system is analogous to the fault tolerance infrastructure.

Four fundamental attributes of the immune system are particularly relevant [14]:

1. It functions (i.e., detects and reacts to threats) continuously and autonomously, independently of consciousness.
2. Its elements (lymph nodes, other lymphoid organs, lymphocytes) are distributed throughout the body, serving all its organs.
3. It has its own communication links – the network of lymphatic vessels.
4. Its elements (cells, organs, and vessels) themselves are self-defended, redundant and in several cases diverse.

Now we can identify the properties that the FTI must have in order to justify the immune system analogy. They are as follows:

1a. The FTI consists of hardware and firmware elements only.

1b The FTI is independent of (requires no support from) any software of the client platform, but can communicate with it.

1c. The FTI supports (provides protected decision algorithms for) multichannel computing of the client platform, including diverse hardware and software channels to provide design fault tolerance for the client platform.

2 The FTI is compatible with (i.e. protects) a wide range of client platform components, including processors, memories, supporting chipsets, discs, power supplies, fans and various peripherals.

3. Elements of the FTI are distributed throughout the client platform and are interconnected by their own autonomous communication links.

4 The FTI is fully fault-tolerant itself, requiring no external support. It is not susceptible to attacks by intrusion or malicious software and is not affected by natural or design faults of the client platform.

A different and independently devised analogy of the immune system is the "Artificial Immune System" (AIS) of S. Forrest and S. A. Hofmeyr [15]. Its origins are in computer security research, where the motivating objective was protection against illegal intrusions. The analogy of the body is a local-area broadcast network, and the AIS protects it by detecting connections that are not normally observed on the LAN. Immune responses are not included in the model of the AIS, while they are the essence of the FTI.

4. ARCHITECTURE OF THE FAULT TOLERANCE INFRASTRUCTURE

The FTI is a system composed of four types of special-purpose controllers called "nodes". The nodes are ASICs (Application-Specific Integrated Circuits) that are controlled by hard-wired sequencers or by read-only microcode. The basic structure of the FTI is shown in Figure 1.

The figure does not show the redundant nodes needed for fault tolerance of the FTI itself. The C (Computing) node is a COTS processor or other hardware component of the client system being protected by the FTI. One A (Adapter) node is provided for each C node. All error signal outputs and recovery command inputs of the C node are connected to its A node. Within the FTI, all A nodes are connected to one M (Monitor) node via the M (Monitor) bus. Each A node also has a direct input (the A line) to the M node. The A nodes convey the C node error messages to the M node. They also receive recovery commands from the M node and issue them to C node

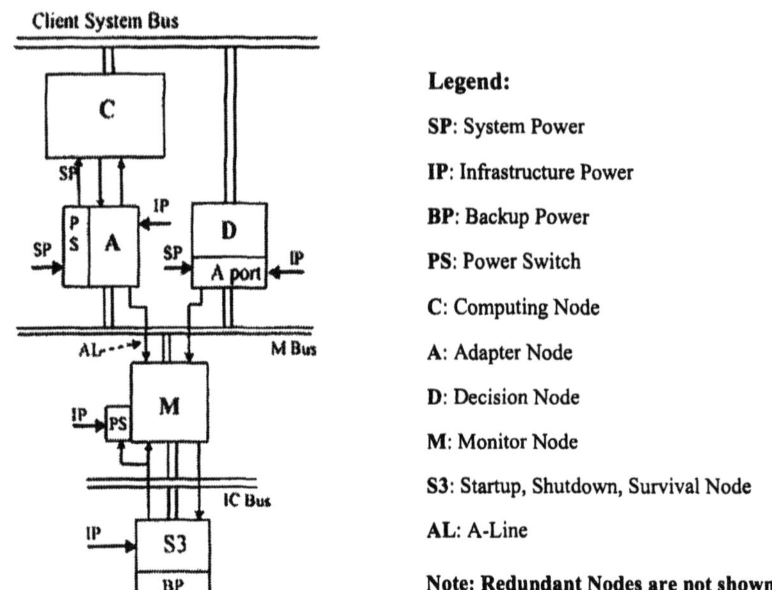

Figure 1 – The Fault Tolerance Infrastructure

inputs. The A line serves to request M node attention for an incoming error message.

The M node stores in ROM the responses to error signals from every type of C node and the sequences for its own recovery. It also stores system configuration and system time data and its own activity records. The M node is connected to the S3 (Startup, Shutdown, Survival) node.

The functions of the S3 node are to control power-on and power-off sequences for the entire system, to generate fault-tolerant clock signals and to provide non-volatile, radiation-hardened storage for system time and configuration. The S3 node has a backup power supply (a battery) and remains on at all times during the life of the FTI.

The D (Decision) node provides fault-tolerant comparison and voting services for the C nodes, including decision algorithms for N-version software executing on diverse processors (C nodes). Fast response of the D node is assured by hardware implementation of the decision algorithms. The D node also keeps a log of disagreements in the decisions. The second function of the D node is to serve as a communication link between the software of the C nodes and the M node. C nodes may request configuration and M node activity data or send power control commands. The D node has a built-in A node (the A port) that links it to the M node.

Another function of the FTI is to provide fault tolerant power management for the entire host system, including individual power switches for every C node, as shown in Figure 1. Every node except the S3 has a power switch. The FTI has its own fault-tolerant power supply (IP).

5. FAULT TOLERANCE OF THE FTI

The partitioning of the FTI is motivated by the need to make it fault-tolerant. The A and D nodes are self-checking pairs, since high error detection coverage is essential, while spare C and D nodes can be provided for recovery under M node control. The M node must be continuously available, therefore triplication and voting (TMR) is used, with spare M nodes added for longer life.

The S3 nodes manage M node replacement and also shut the system down in the case of catastrophic events (temporary power loss, heavy radiation, etc.). They are protected by the use of two or more self-checking pairs with backup power. S3 nodes were separated from M nodes to make the node that must survive catastrophic events as small as possible.

The all-hardware implementation of the FTI makes it safe from software bugs and external attacks. The one exception is the power management command from C to M nodes (via the D node) which could be used to shut the system down. Special protection is needed here. Hardware design faults in the FTI nodes could be handled by design diversity of self-checking pairs and of M nodes, although the logic of the nodes is very simple and their complete verification should be possible.

When interconnected, the FTI and the COTS "client" platform form a computing system that is protected against most causes of system failure. This system is called DiSTARS: Diversifiable Self Testing And Repairing System and is discussed in detail in [1]. DiSTARS is the first example of an implementation of the immune system paradigm. Much detail of implementation of the FTI is presented in the U.S. patent application disclosure "Self-Testing and -Repairing Fault Tolerance Infrastructure for Computer Systems" by A. Avižienis, filed June 19, 2001.

The use of the FTI is likely to be affordable for most computer systems, since the A, M, D, and S3 nodes have a simple internal structure, as shown in the above mentioned disclosure. It is more interesting to consider that there are some truly challenging missions that can only be justified if their computers with the FTI have very high coverage with respect to design faults and to catastrophic transients due to radiation. Furthermore, extensive sparing and efficient power management can also be provided by the FTI. Given that the MTBF of contemporary processor and memory chips is approaching 1000 years, missions that can be contemplated include the 1000-day manned mission to Mars [16] with the dependability of a 10-hour flight of a commercial airliner. Another fascinating possibility is unmanned very long life interstellar missions using a fault-tolerant relay chain of modest-cost DiSTARS type spacecraft [17]. Both missions are discussed in [1].

6. IN CONCLUSION: THE FTI WILL EVOLVE

The goal of the FTI is to use hardware more extensively and more effectively than it is being done currently in providing fault tolerance for very dependable high-performance platforms.

The DiSTARS illustration considered Intel's P6 family of processors and their supporting chipsets as the COTS elements of the host platform. These elements were not designed to utilize the FTI, which is introduced by a "retrofit."

When the FTI is provided, the processors (C nodes) can be designed to contain Adapter (A) ports, similar to those of the D node of DiSTARS. The FTI becomes simpler (the A nodes are not needed) and the FTI is used to the fullest extent when COTS processors are designed with the FTI in mind. It is also quite conceivable that the D node can be built into the processor as a "D port" as well. That leaves only the Monitor and S3 nodes as separate and independent components that are needed to implement the FTI.

A further benefit of the FTI's existence is the ability to simplify higher-level defenses that require software participation. The presence of an effective FTI simplifies the error detection and recovery requirements for system software. Currently the functions of the FTI are carried out by software, such as the Machine Check Handler in P6 family processors [6].

It is very reasonable to predict that adoption of the FTI in platform designs will lead to a better structured and more cost-effective overall dependability assurance architecture, since the other levels of protection will be supported by hardware that is missing in today's designs.

A much more drastic evolutionary step of the FTI concept is the introduction of a hierarchy of FTIs. The FTI described in [1] served a collection of COTS components located in reasonable proximity and communicating via system busses. Most likely it would be the FTIb for one board or blade. However, an FTI structure can also be incorporated in the processor chip itself. The on-chip FTIp locally manages recovery, sparing, and power management. Its Mp nodes and S3p nodes serve as the A port of the chip and communicate with the Mb nodes of the board-level FTIb. The on-chip S3p node would be simplified, since backup power is not needed at the chip level.

The next extension of the hierarchy is to install a chassis-level FTIc, where the chassis contains several boards, each with its own FTIb that contains Db, Mb and S3b nodes. The Mb and S3b nodes now serve as the A port of the board and communicate with the Mc node of the FTIc. Considering Figure 1, C is now a board and A is its Mb, D is Dc, M is Mc and S3 is S3c of the chassis, located on their own board or on one of the other boards. The S3c node has the highest shutdown and startup authority, and the S3b nodes may be simplified. The C node can also be a monitor, printer or any other peripheral; they either have an A port built in, or an A node has to be custom designed for communication with the Mc.

It is important to note that the individual A lines, M buses and IC buses for FTI communications must be provided at each level of the hierarchy. For this reason a direct extension of the hierarchy from chassis to clusters and local networks is more problematic, but feasible. The question that remains to be resolved here is whether a single chassis can be given the authority to command shutdowns of other members of the cluster or LAN, or whether only status information will be exchanged between the Mc nodes, which then act independently. A detailed study of the hierarchical structuring is currently in progress.

ACKNOWLEDGMENTS

Ever since I wrote my first program for the ILLIAC I in 1954 and worked on the first dependability problem at JPL in 1955-56, I have been most lucky to work with and to learn from true friends: mentors, colleagues, and young researchers chasing the Ph. D. prize.

University of Illinois professors James E. Robertson and David E. Muller were mentors and role models for my academic career, and working with Ed McCluskey in the old Computer Group, later Society, taught me how to get good people to work for free and be happy about it.

The University of Illinois, Caltech's Jet Propulsion Laboratory, and the UCLA Computer Science Department will remain in my memories as places of hard work, accomplishment, and the great pleasure of shared achievement. To each one of my 31 Ph.D. winners – thanks for the challenge of keeping up with your efforts, and the same thanks go to my "UCLA club" of visiting scholars from Europe, Japan, and China who truly enriched our environment.

A most rewarding experience has been the hard work and play with my friends in the IEEE Computer Society's TC on Fault-Tolerant Computing and in the IFIP Working Group 10.4 on Dependable Computing and Fault Tolerance. Many thanks for your dedication and friendship in working toward our common goals.

The fall of the Iron Curtain allowed me the unexpected privilege to return to my native Lithuania in 1990 and to lead as Rector the revival of Vytautas Magnus University (closed by the Soviet regime) in the city of my birth – Kaunas. Starting with 180 students in 1989, VMU now has an enrolment of over 8000, including over 1000 graduate students. Many thanks to my friends and colleagues in several EU countries for inviting me – and VMU – to take part in efforts to find a place for dependable oomputing in the developing European Research Area.

Finally, and most importantly – thanks to my wife Jurate and my sons Rimas and Audrius for patiently and lovingly sharing the sometimes frantic life of a restless academic competitor.

REFERENCES

[1] A. Avižienis, A fault tolerance infrastructure for dependable computing with high performance COTS components, *Proc. of the Int. Conference on Dependable Systems and Networks (DSN 2000)*, New York, June 2000, pages 492-500.

[2] A. Avižienis and Y. He, Microprocessor entomology: A taxonomy of design faults in COTS microprocessors. In J. Rushby and C.B. Weinstock, editors, Dependable Computing for Critical Applications 7, IEEE Computer Society Press, 1999, pp. 3-23.

[3] Y. He and A. Avižienis. Assessment of the applicability of COTS microprocessors in high confidence computing systems: A case study. *Proceedings of ICDSN 2000*, June 2000.

[4] T.J. Slegel et al. IBM's S/390 G5 microprocessor design. *IEEE Micro*, 19(2):12-23, March/April 1999.

[5] D. Johnson. The Intel 432: a VLSI architecture for fault-tolerant computer systems. Computer 17(8):40-49, August 1984.

[6] Intel Corp. P6 Family of Processors Hardware Developer's Manual, September 1998. Order No. 244001-001.

[7] Ziatech Corp. Redundant CPU Architecture for High Availability Systems. "White paper," October 1999, available at www.ziatech.com.

[8] Intel Corp. The Pentium II Xeon Processor Server Platform System Management Guide, June 1998. Order No. 243835-001.

[9] Intel Corp. Intel Pentium III Processor Specification Update, May 2001. Order No. 244453-029.

[10] A. Avižienis and J.P.J. Kelly. Fault tolerance by design diversity: concepts and experiments. *Computer*, 17(8):67-80, August 1984.

[11] Y.C. Yeh. Dependability of the 777 primary flight control system, in R.K. Iyer et al., editors, *Dependable Computing for Critical Applications 5*, IEEE Computer Society Press, 1997, pp. 3-17.

[12] M.K. Joseph and A. Avižienis. A fault tolerance approach to computer viruses. *Proc. Of the 1988 IEEE Symposium on Security and Privacy*, April 1988, pp.52-58.

[13] A. Avižienis. Toward systematic design of fault-tolerant systems. *Computer*, 30(4):51-58, April 1997.

[14] G.J.V. Nossal. Life, death and the immune system. *Scientific American*, 269(33)52-62, September 1993.

[15] S.A. Hofmeyr and S. Forrest. Immunity by design: An artificial immune system. *Proc. 1999 Genetic and Evolutionary Computation Conference*, pages 1289-1296. Morgan-Kaufmann, 1999.

[16] Special report: sending astronauts to Mars. *Scientific American*, 282(3):40-63, March 2000.

[17] A. Avižienis. The hundred year spacecraft. *Proceedings of the 1st NASA/DoD Workshop on Evolvable Hardware*, Pasadena, CA, July 1999, pp.233-239.

DEPENDABILITY AND ITS THREATS: A TAXONOMY

Algirdas Avižienis*, Jean-Claude Laprie**, Brian Randell***
** Vytautas Magnus University, Kaunas, Lithuania and University of California, Los Angeles, USA — aviz@adm.vdu.lt*
*** LAAS-CNRS, 7 avenue du Colonel Roche, 31077 Toulouse Cedex 04, France, jean-claude laprie@laas.fr*
**** School of Computing Science, University of Newcastle upon Tyne, UK brian.randell@newcastle.ac.uk*

Abstract: This paper gives the main definitions relating to dependability, a generic concept including as special case such attributes as reliability, availability, safety, confidentiality, integrity, maintainability, etc. Basic definitions are given first. They are then commented upon, and supplemented by additional definitions, which address the threats to dependability (faults, errors, failures), and the attributes of dependability. The discussion on the attributes encompasses the relationship of dependability with security, survivability and trustworthiness.

Key words: Dependability, availability, reliability, safety, confidentiality, integrity, maintainability, security, survivability, trustworthiness, faults, errors, failures.

1. ORIGINS AND INTEGRATION OF THE CONCEPTS

The delivery of correct computing and communication services has been a concern of their providers and users since the earliest days. In the July 1834 issue of the *Edinburgh Review,* Dr. Dionysius Lardner published the article "Babbage's calculating engine", in which he wrote:

> *"The most certain and effectual check upon errors which arise in the process of computation, is to cause the same computations to be made by separate and independent computers; and this check is rendered still more decisive if they make their computations by different methods".*

It must be noted that the term "computer" in the previous quotation refers to a person who performs computations, and not the "calculating engine".

The first generation of electronic computers (late 1940's to mid-50's) used rather unreliable components, therefore practical techniques were employed to improve their reliability, such as error control codes, duplexing with comparison, triplication with voting, diagnostics to locate failed components, etc. At the same time J. von Neumann [von Neumann 1956], E. F. Moore and C. E. Shannon [Moore & Shannon 1956], and their successors developed theories of using redundancy to build reliable logic structures from less reliable components, whose faults were masked by the presence of multiple redundant components. The theories of masking redundancy were unified by W. H. Pierce as the concept of *failure tolerance* in 1965 [Pierce 1965].

In 1967, A. Avižienis integrated masking with the practical techniques of error detection, fault diagnosis, and recovery into the concept of fault-tolerant systems [Avižienis 1967]. In the reliability modeling field, the major event was the introduction of the coverage concept by Bouricius, Carter and Schneider [Bouricius *et al.* 1969]. Work on software fault tolerance was initiated by Elmendorf [Elmendorf 1972], later it was complemented by recovery blocks [Randell 1975], and by N-version programming [Avižienis & Chen, 1977].

The formation of the *IEEE-CS TC on Fault-Tolerant Computing* in 1970 and of *IFIP WG 10.4 Dependable Computing and Fault Tolerance* in 1980 accelerated the emergence of a consistent set of concepts and terminology. Seven position papers were presented in 1982 at FTCS-12 in a special session on fundamental concepts of fault tolerance [FTCS 1982], and J.-C. Laprie formulated a synthesis in 1985 [Laprie 1985]. Further work by members of IFIP WG 10.4, led by J.-C. Laprie, resulted in the 1992 book *Dependability: Basic Concepts and Terminology* [Laprie 1992], in which the English text was also translated into French, German, Italian, and Japanese.

In this book, intentional faults (malicious logic, intrusions) were listed along with accidental faults (physical, design, or interaction faults). Exploratory research on the integration of fault tolerance and the defenses against deliberately malicious faults, i.e., security threats, was started in the mid-80's [Dobson & Randell 1986], [Joseph & Avižienis 1988], [Fray *et al.* 1986].

The first IFIP Working Conference on Dependable Computing for Critical Applications (DCCA) was held in 1989. This and the six Working Conferences that followed fostered the interaction of the dependability and security communities, and advanced the integration of security (confidentiality, integrity and availability) into the framework of dependable computing. Since 2000, the DCCA Working Conference together with the FTCS became parts of the International Conference on Dependable Systems and Networks (DSN).

2. THE BASIC CONCEPTS

In this section we present a basic set of definitions (in **bold** typeface) that will be used throughout the entire discussion of the taxonomy of dependable computing. The definitions are general enough to cover the entire range of computing and communication systems, from individual logic gates to networks of computers with human operators and users.

2.1 System Function, Behavior, Structure, and Service

A **system** in our taxonomy is an entity that interacts with other entities, i.e., other systems, including hardware, software, humans, and the physical world with its natural phenomena. These other systems are the **environment** of the given system. The **system boundary** is the common frontier between the system and its environment.

Computing and communication systems are characterized by four fundamental properties: functionality, performance, dependability, and cost. Those four properties are collectively influenced by two other properties: usability and adaptability. The **function** of such a system is what the system is intended to do and is described by the **functional specification** in terms of functionality and performance. Dependability and cost have separate specifications. The **behavior** of a system is what the system does to implement its function and is described by a sequence of states. The **total state** of a given system is the set of the following states: computation, communication, stored information, interconnection, and physical condition.

The **structure** of a system is what enables it to generate the behavior. From a structural viewpoint, a system is a set of components bound together in order to interact, where each **component** is another system, etc. The recursion stops when a component is considered to be **atomic**: any further internal structure cannot be discerned, or is not of interest and can be ignored.

The **service** delivered by a system (the *provider*) is its behavior as it is perceived by its user(s); a **user** is another system that receives service from the provider. The part of the provider's system boundary where service delivery takes place is the **service interface**. The part of the provider's total state that is perceivable at the service interface is its **external state**; the remaining part is its **internal state**. The delivered service is a sequence of the provider's external states. We note that a system may sequentially or simultaneously be a provider and a user with respect to another system, i.e., deliver service to and receive service from that other system.

It is usual to have a hierarchical view of a system structure. The relation *is composed of*, or *is decomposed into*, induces a hierarchy; however it relates only to the list of the system components. A hierarchy that takes into account the system behavior is the relation *uses* [Parnas 1974, Ghezzi *et al.*

1991] or *depends upon* [Parnas 1972, Cristian 1991]: a component *a* uses, or depends upon, a component *b* if the correctness of *b*'s service delivery is necessary for the correctness of *a*'s service delivery.

We have up to now used the singular for function and service. A system generally implements more than one function, and delivers more than one service. Function and service can be thus seen as composed of function items and of service items. For the sake of simplicity, we shall simply use the plural — functions, services — when it is necessary to distinguish several function or service items.

2.2 The Threats: Failures, Errors, Faults

Correct service is delivered when the service implements the system function. A **service failure** is an event that occurs when the delivered service deviates from correct service. A service fails either because it does not comply with the functional specification, or because this specification did not adequately describe the system function. A service failure is a **transition** from correct service to incorrect service, i.e., to not implementing the system function. The period of delivery of incorrect service is a **service outage**. The transition from incorrect service to correct service is a **service restoration.** The deviation from correct service may assume different forms that are called **service failure modes** and are ranked according to **failure severities.** A detailed taxonomy of failure modes is presented in Section 4.

Since a service is a sequence of the system's external states, a service failure means that at least one (or more) external state of the system deviates from the correct service state. The deviation is called an **error**. The adjudged or hypothesized cause of an error is called a **fault**. In most cases a fault first causes an error in the service state of a component that is a part of the internal state of the system and the external state is not immediately affected.

For this reason the definition of an **error** is: the part of the total state of the system that may lead to its subsequent service failure. It is important to note that many errors do not reach the system's external state and cause a failure. A fault is **active** when it causes an error, otherwise it is **dormant.**

When the functional specification of a system includes a set of several functions, the failure of one or more of the services implementing the functions may leave the system in a **degraded mode** that still offers a subset of needed services to the user. The specification may identify several such modes, e.g., slow service, limited service, emergency service, etc. Here we say that the system has suffered a **partial failure** of its functionality or performance. **Development failures** and **dependability failures** that are discussed in Section 4 also can be partial failures.

2.3 Dependability and its Attributes

The general, qualitative, definition of **dependability** is: the ability to deliver service that can justifiably be trusted. This definition stresses the need for justification of trust. The alternate, quantitative, definition that provides the criterion for deciding if the service is dependable is: **dependability** of a system is the ability to avoid service failures that are more frequent and more severe than is acceptable to the user(s).

As developed over the past three decades, dependability is an integrating concept that encompasses the following attributes:

- **availability**: readiness for correct service;
- **reliability:** continuity of correct service;
- **safety:** absence of catastrophic consequences on the user(s) and the environment;
- **confidentiality:** absence of unauthorized disclosure of information;
- **integrity:** absence of improper system alterations;
- **maintainability**: ability to undergo, modifications, and repairs.

Security is the concurrent existence of a) availability for authorized users only, b) confidentiality, and c) integrity with 'improper' meaning 'unauthorized'.

The **dependability specification** of a system must include the requirements for the dependability attributes in terms of the acceptable frequency and severity of failures for the specified classes of faults and a given use environment. One or more attributes may not be required at all for a given system.

The taxonomy of the attributes of dependability is presented in Section 5.

2.4 The Means to Attain Dependability

Over the course of the past fifty years many means to attain the attributes of dependability have been developed. Those means can be grouped into four major categories:

- **fault prevention**: means to prevent the occurrence or introduction of faults;
- **fault tolerance**: means to avoid service failures in the presence of faults;
- **fault removal**: means to reduce the number and severity of faults;
- **fault forecasting**: means to estimate the present number, the future incidence, and the likely consequences of faults.

Fault prevention and fault tolerance aim to provide the ability to deliver a service that can be trusted, while fault removal and fault forecasting aim to reach confidence in that ability by justifying that the functional and dependability specifications are adequate and that the system is likely to meet them.

The schema of the complete taxonomy of dependable computing as outlined in this section is shown in Figure 2.1.

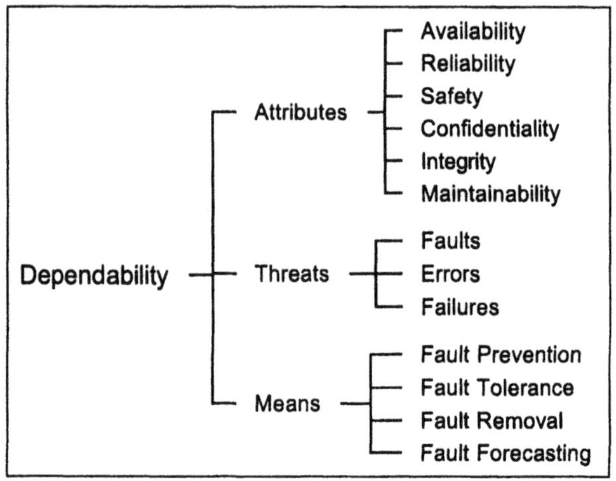

Figure 2.1: The dependability tree

3. THE TAXONOMY OF FAULTS

3.1 System Life Cycle: Phases and Environments

In this and the next section we present the taxonomy of threats that may affect a system during its entire life. The **life cycle** of a system consists of two phases: *development* and *use.*

The development phase includes all activities from presentation of the user's initial concept to the decision that the system has passed all acceptance tests and is ready to be deployed for use in its user's environment. During the development phase the system is interacting with the development environment and *development faults* may be introduced into the system by the environment. ***The development environment*** of a system consists of the following elements:

1. the *physical world* with its natural phenomena;
2. *human developers*, some possibly lacking competence or having malicious objectives;
3. *development tools*: software and hardware used by the developers to assist them in the development process;
4. *production and test facilities.*

The use phase of a system's life begins when the system is accepted for use and starts the delivery of its services to the users. Use consists of alternating periods of correct service delivery (to be called ***service delivery***), service outage, and service shutdown. A ***service outage*** is caused by a service failure. It is the period when incorrect service (including no service at all) is delivered at the service interface. A ***service shutdown*** is an intentional halt of service by an authorized entity. ***Maintenance*** actions may take place during all three periods of the use phase.

During the use phase the system interacts with its *use environment* and may be adversely affected by faults originating in it. The ***use environment*** consists of the following elements:

1. *the physical world* with its natural phenomena;
2. *the administrators* (including maintainers): entities (humans, other systems) that have the authority to manage, modify, repair and use the system; some authorized humans may lack competence or have malicious objectives;
3. *the users:* entities that receive service at the service interfaces;
4. *the providers:* entities that deliver services to the system at its service interfaces;
5. *the fixed resources:* entities that are not users, but provide specialized services to the system, such as information sources (e.g., GPS, time, etc.), communication links, power sources, cooling airflow, etc.
6. *the intruders*: malicious entities that have no authority but attempt to intrude into the system and to alter service or halt it, alter the system's functionality or performance, or to access confidential information. They are hackers, malicious insiders, agents of hostile governments or organizations, and info-terrorists.

As used here, the term ***maintenance***, following common usage, includes not only repairs, but also all modifications of the system that take place during the use phase of system life. Therefore maintenance is a development process, and the preceding discussion of development applies to maintenance as well. The various forms of maintenance are summarized in Figure 3.1.

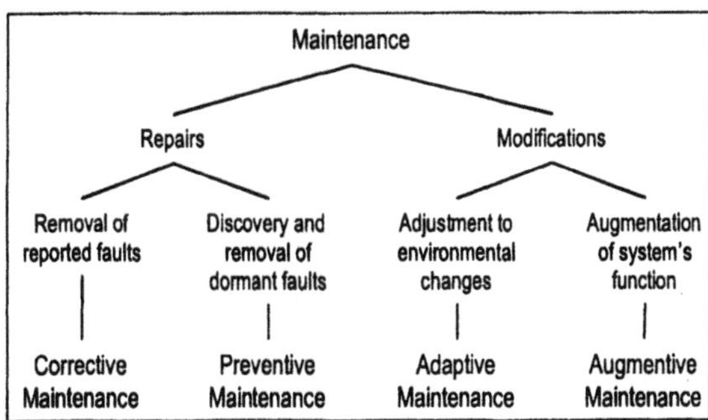

Figure 3.1: The various forms of maintenance

It is noteworthy that repair and fault tolerance are related concepts; the distinction between fault tolerance and maintenance in this paper is that maintenance involves the participation of an external agent, e.g., a repairman, test equipment, remote reloading of software. Furthermore, repair is part of fault removal (during the use phase), and fault forecasting usually considers repair situations.

3.2 A Taxonomy of Faults

All faults that may affect a system during its life are classified according to eight basic viewpoints that are shown in Figure 3.2. These fault classes are called *elementary faults.*

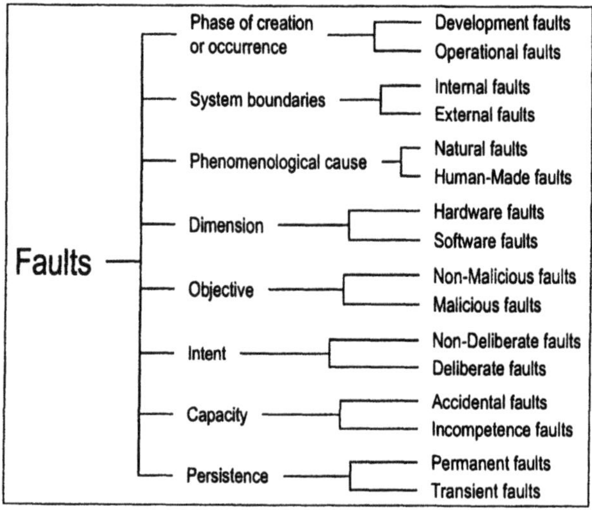

Figure 3.2: The elementary fault classes

The classification criteria are as follows:

1. The *phase* of system life during which the faults originate:

- **development faults** that occur during (a) system development, (b) maintenance during the use phase, and (c) generation of procedures to operate or to maintain the system;
- **operational faults** that occur during service delivery of the use phase.

2. The *location* of the faults with respect to the system boundary:

- **internal faults** that originate inside the system boundary;
- **external faults** that originate outside the system boundary and propagate errors into the system by interaction or interference.

3. The *phenomenological cause* of the faults:

- **natural faults** that are caused by natural phenomena without human participation;
- **human-made faults** that result from human actions.

4. The *dimension* in which the faults originate:
- **hardware (physical) faults** that originate in, or affect, hardware;
- **software (information) faults** that affect software, i.e., programs or data.

5. The *objective* of introducing the faults:
- **malicious faults** that are introduced by a human with the malicious objective of causing harm to the system;
- **non-malicious faults** that are introduced without a malicious objective.

6. The *intent* of the human(s) who caused the faults:
- **deliberate faults** that are the result of a harmful decision;
- **non-deliberate faults** that are introduced without awareness.

7. The *capacity* of the human(s) who introduced the faults:
- **accidental faults** that are introduced inadvertently;
- **incompetence faults** that result from lack of professional competence by the authorized human(s), or from inadequacy of the development organization.

8. The *temporal persistence* of the faults:
- **permanent faults** whose presence is assumed to be continuous in time;
- **transient faults** whose presence is bounded in time.

If all combinations of the eight elementary fault classes were possible, there would be 256 different *combined fault classes*. In fact, the number of likely combinations is 31; they are shown in Figures 3.3 and 3.4.

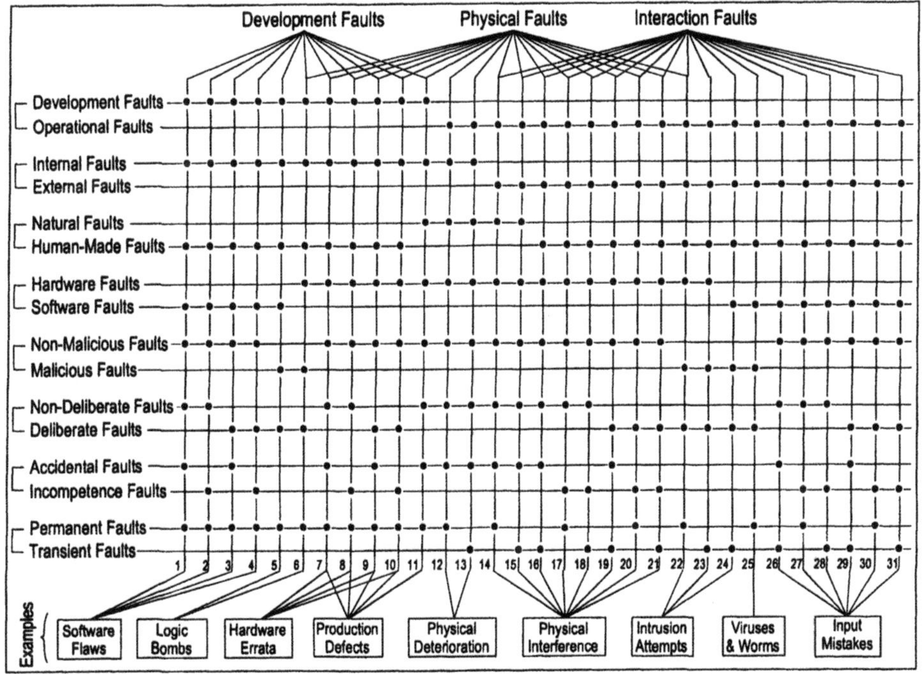

Figure 3.3: The classes of combined faults

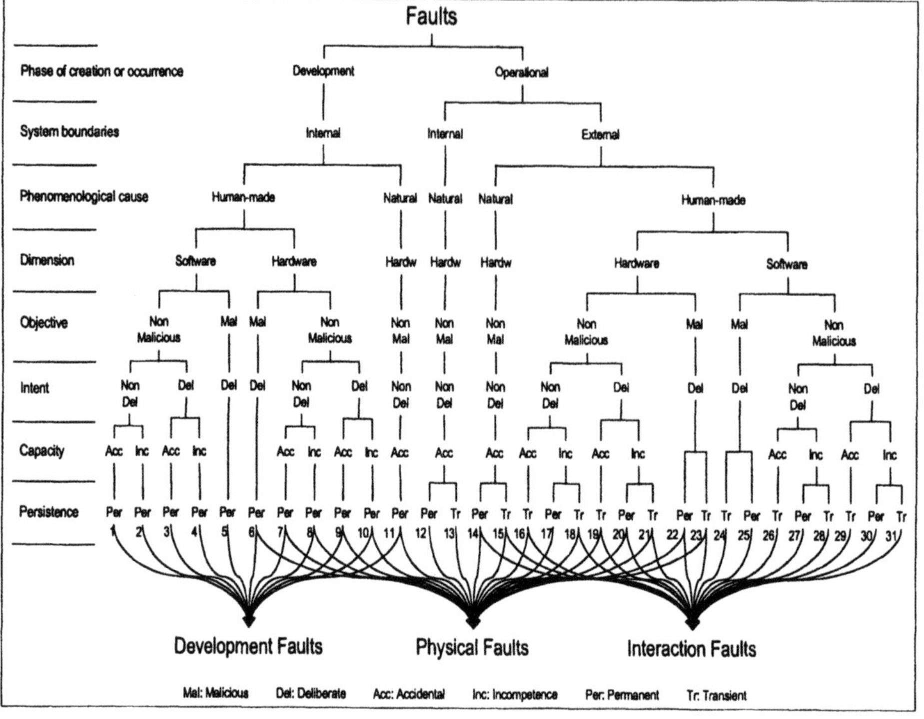

Figure 3.4: Tree representation of combined faults

The combined faults of Figures 3.3 and 3.4 are shown to belong to three major partially overlapping groupings:

- **development faults** that include all fault classes occurring during development;
- **physical faults** that include all fault classes that affect hardware;
- **interaction faults** that include all external faults.

The boxes at the bottom of Figure 3.3 identify the names of some illustrative fault classes.

3.3 On Human-Made Faults

The definition of human-made faults (that result from harmful human actions) includes absence of actions when actions should be performed, i.e., **omission faults**, or simply **omissions**. Performing wrong actions leads to **commission faults**.

The two basic classes of human-made faults are distinguished by the *objective* of the developer or of the humans interacting with the system during its use:

- ***malicious faults***, introduced during either system development with the intent to cause harm to the system during its use (#5-#6), or directly during use (#22-#25)

- ***non-malicious faults*** (#1-#4, #7-#21, #26-#31), introduced without malicious objectives.

Malicious human-made faults are introduced by a developer with the malicious objective to alter the functioning of the system during use. The goals of such faults are: (1) to disrupt or halt service, (2) to access confidential information, or (3) to improperly modify the system. They are grouped into two classes:

- *potentially harmful components* (#5, #6): Trojan horses, trapdoors, logic or timing bombs;
- deliberately introduced software or hardware *vulnerabilities or human-made faults*..

The goals of malicious faults are: (1) to disrupt or halt service (thus provoking *denials-of-service*), (2) to access confidential information, or (3) to improperly modify the system. They fall into two classes:

1. **Malicious logic faults**, that encompass development faults such as *Trojan horses*, logic or timing *bombs*, and *trapdoors*, as well as operational faults such as *viruses*, *worms,* or *zombies*. Definitions for these faults are as follows [Landwehr *et al.* 1994, Powell & Stroud 2003]:
   - **logic bomb**: *malicious logic* that remains dormant in the host system till a certain time or an event occurs, or certain conditions are met, and then deletes files, slows down or crashes the host system, etc.
   - **Trojan horse**: *malicious logic* performing, or able to perform, an illegitimate action while giving the impression of being legitimate; the illegitimate action can be the disclosure or modification of information (attack against confidentiality or integrity) or a *logic bomb*;
   - **trapdoor**: *malicious logic* that provides a means of circumventing access control mechanisms;
   - **virus**: *malicious logic* that replicates itself and joins another program when it is executed, thereby turning into a *Trojan horse*; a virus can carry a *logic bomb*;
   - **worm**: *malicious logic* that replicates itself and propagates without the users being aware of it; a worm can also carry a *logic bomb*;
   - **zombie**: *malicious logic* that can be triggered by an attacker in order to mount a coordinated attack.
2. **Intrusion attempts**, that are operational external faults. The external character of intrusion attempts does not exclude the possibility that they may be performed by system operators or administrators who are exceeding their rights, and intrusion attempts may use physical means to cause faults: power fluctuation, radiation, wire-tapping, etc.

Non-malicious human-made faults can be partitioned according to the developer's intent:

- *non-deliberate* faults that are due to *mistakes,* that is, *unintended actions* of which the developer, operator, maintainer, etc. is not aware,
- *deliberate* faults that are due to *bad decisions,* that is, *intended actions* that are wrong and causes faults.

Deliberate, non-malicious, development faults result generally from tradeoffs, either a) aimed at preserving acceptable performance, at facilitating system utilization, or b) induced by economic considerations. Deliberate, non-malicious interaction faults may result from the action of an operator either aimed at overcoming an unforeseen situation, or deliberately violating an operating procedure without having realized the possibly damaging consequences of this action. Deliberate non-malicious faults share the property that often it is recognized that they were faults only *after* an unacceptable system behavior, thus a failure, has ensued; the developer(s) or operator(s) did not realize that the consequence of their decision was a fault.

It is often considered that both mistakes and bad decisions are *accidental*, as long as they are not made with malicious objectives. However, *not all* mistakes and bad decisions by non-malicious persons are accidents. Some very harmful mistakes and very bad decisions are made by persons who lack professional competence to do the job they have undertaken. A complete fault taxonomy should not conceal this cause of faults, therefore we introduce a further partitioning of both classes of non-malicious human-made faults into (1*) accidental faults*, and (2) *incompetence faults.* The structure of this human-made fault taxonomy is shown in Figure 3.5.

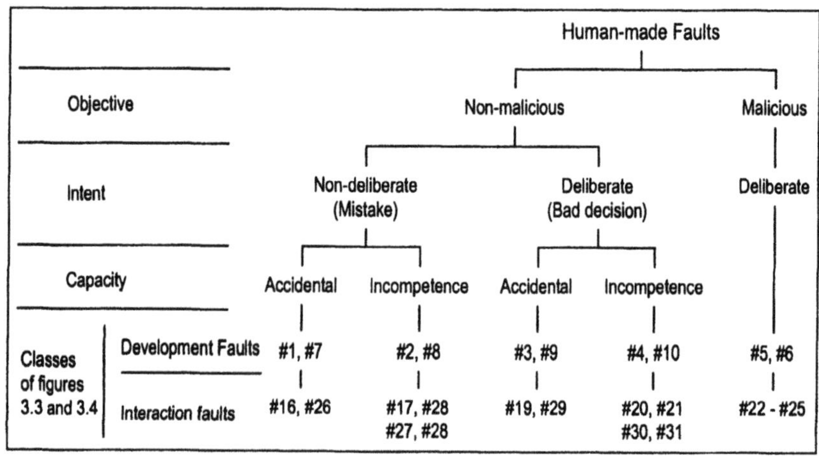

Figure 3.5: Classification of human-made faults

The question of how to recognize incompetence faults becomes important when a mistake or a bad decision has consequences that lead to economic losses, injuries, or loss of human lives. In such cases independent professional judgment by a board of inquiry or legal proceedings in a court of law will decide if professional malpractice was involved.

Thus far the discussion of incompetence faults has dealt with individuals. However, human-made efforts have failed because a team or an entire organization did not have the organizational competence to do the job. A good example of organizational incompetence is the human-made failure of the AAS air traffic control system described in Section 4.2.

The purpose of this fault taxonomy is to present a complete and structured view of the universe of faults. The explicit introduction of incompetence faults in the taxonomy serves as a reminder that incompetence at individual and organizational level is a serious threat in the human-made development and use of dependable systems..

The non-malicious development faults exist in hardware and in software. In hardware, especially in microprocessors, some development faults are discovered after production has started [Avižienis & He 1999]. Such faults are called "errata" and are listed in specification updates [Intel 2001]. The finding of errata continues throughout the life of the processors, therefore new specification updates are issued periodically. Some development faults are introduced because human-made tools are faulty. The best known of such "secondary" human-made faults is the Pentium division erratum [Meyer 1994].

Designing a system always recurs to some extent to incorporating off-the-shelf (OTS) components. The use of OTS components introduces additional dependability problems. They may come with known development faults, and may contain unknown faults as well (bugs, vulnerabilities, undiscovered errata, etc.). Their specifications may be incomplete or even incorrect. This problem is especially serious when *legacy* OTS components are used that come from previously designed and used systems, and must be retained in the new system because of the user's needs.

Some development faults affecting software can cause **software aging** [Huang *et al.* 1995], i.e., progressively accrued error conditions resulting in performance degradation or complete failure. Examples are [Castelli *et al.* 2001] memory bloating and leaking, unterminated threads, unreleased file-locks, data corruption, storage space fragmentation, accumulation of round-off errors.

3.4 On Interaction Faults

Interaction faults occur during the use phase, therefore they are all *operational* faults. They are caused by elements of the use environment (see Section 3.1) interacting with the system, therefore they are all *external.* Most classes originate due to some human action in the use environment, therefore they are *human-made*. They are fault classes #16-#31 in Figures 3.3 and 3.4. An exception are external natural faults (#14-#15) caused by cosmic rays, solar flares, etc. Here nature interacts with the system without human participation.

A broad class of human-made operational faults are **configuration faults**, i.e., wrong setting of parameters that can affect security, networking, storage, middleware, etc. [Gray 2001]. Such faults can occur during configuration changes performed during adaptive or augmentative maintenance performed concurrently with system operation (e.g., introduction of a new software version on a network server); they are then called **reconfiguration faults** [Wood 1994].

A common feature of interaction faults is that, in order to be 'successful', they usually necessitate the prior presence of a **vulnerability**, i.e. an internal fault that enables an external fault to harm the system. Vulnerabilities can be development or operational faults; they can be malicious or non-malicious, as can be the external fault that exploit them. There are interesting and obvious similarities between an intrusion attempt and a physical external fault that 'exploits' a lack of shielding. A vulnerability can result from a deliberate development fault, for economic or for usability reasons, thus resulting in limited protections, or even in their absence.

3.5 On Physical Faults

Physical faults shown on Figure 3.3 fall into three categories: purely natural faults (#12-#15), physical development faults (#6-#11), and physical interaction faults (#16-#23). Development and interaction faults have been discussed in the preceding sections. The purely natural faults are either internal (#12-#13), due to natural processes that cause physical deterioration, or external (#14-#15), due to natural processes that originate outside the system boundaries and cause physical interference by penetrating the hardware boundary of the system (radiation, etc.) or by entering via service interfaces (power transients, noisy input lines, etc.).

4. THE TAXONOMY OF FAILURES AND ERRORS

4.1 Service Failures

In Section 2.2 a ***service failure*** (called simply "failure" in this section) is defined as an event that occurs when the delivered service deviates from correct service. The different ways in which the deviation is manifested are a system's *service failure modes*. Each mode can have more than one *service failure severity*.

The occurrence of a failure was defined in Section 2 with respect to the function of a system, not with respect to the description of the function stated in the functional specification: a service delivery complying with the specification may be unacceptable for the system user(s), thus uncovering a specification fault, i.e., revealing the fact that the specification did not adequately describe the system function(s). Such specification faults can be either omissions or commission faults (misinterpretations, unwarranted assumptions, inconsistencies, typographical mistakes). In such circumstances, the fact that the event is undesired (and is in fact a failure) may happen to be recognized only after its occurrence, for instance via its consequences. So failures can be subjective, disputable, i.e., require judgment to identify and characterize.

The failure modes characterize incorrect service according to four viewpoints: a) the failure domain, b) the detectability of failures, c) the consistency of failures, and d) the consequences of failures on the environment.

The *failure domain* viewpoint leads us to distinguish:

- **content failures**: the content of the information delivered at the service interface (i.e., the service content) deviates from implementing the system function;
- **timing failures**: the time of arrival or the duration of the information delivered at the service interface (i.e., the timing of service delivery) deviates from implementing the system function.

These definitions can be specialized: a) the content can be in numerical or non-numerical sets (e.g., alphabets, graphics, colors, sounds), and b) a timing failure may be **early** or **late**, depending on whether the service is delivered too early or too late. Late failures with correct information are **performance failures** [Cristian 1991]; these can relate to the two aspects of the notion of performance: responsiveness or throughput [Muntz 2000]. Failures when both information and timing are incorrect fall into two classes:

- **halt failure**, or simply **halt**, when the service is *halted* (external state becomes constant, i.e., system activity, if there is any, is no longer perceptible to the users); a special case of halt is **silent failure**, or simply **silence**, when no service at all is delivered at the service interface (e.g., no messages are sent in a distributed system);
- **erratic failures** otherwise, i.e., when a service is delivered (not halted), but is *erratic* (e.g., babbling).

Figure 4.1 summarizes the failure modes with respect to the failure domain viewpoint.

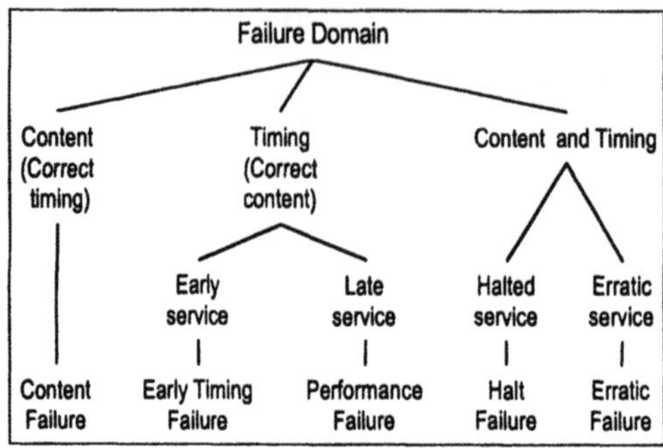

Figure 4.1: Failure modes with respect to the failure domain viewpoint

The detectability viewpoint addresses the signaling of losses of functions to the user(s). The losses result in reduced modes of service. Signaling at the service interface originates from detecting mechanisms in the system that check the correctness of the delivered service. When the losses are detected and signaled by a warning signal, then **signaled failures** occur. Otherwise, they are **unsignaled failures**. The detecting mechanisms themselves have two failure modes: a) signaling a loss of function when they no failure has actually occurred, that is a **false alarm**, b) not signaling a function loss, that is an *unsignaled failure*. Upon detecting the loss of one or more functions, the system retains a specified reduced set of functions and signals a degraded mode of service to the user(s). Degraded modes may range from minor reductions to emergency service and safe shutdown.

The **consistency** of failures leads us to distinguish, when a system has two or more users:

- **consistent failures**: the incorrect service is perceived identically by all system users;
- **inconsistent failures**: some or all system users perceive differently incorrect service[1]; inconsistent failures are usually called, after [Lamppost *et al.* 1982], *Byzantine failures*.

Grading the ***consequences of the failures*** upon the system environment enables failure **severities** to be defined. The failure modes are ordered into severity levels, to which are generally associated maximum acceptable probabilities of occurrence. The number, the labeling and the definition of the severity levels, as well as the acceptable probabilities of occurrence, are application-related, and involve the dependability attributes for the considered application(s). Examples of criteria for determining the classes of failure severities are:

- for availability, the outage duration,
- for safety, the possibility of human lives to be endangered,
- for confidentiality, the type of information that may be unduly disclosed,

[1] Some users may actually perceive correct service.

- for integrity, the extent of the corruption of data and the ability to recover from these corruptions.

Generally speaking, two limiting levels can be defined according to the relation between the benefit (in the broad sense of the term, not limited to economic considerations) provided by the service delivered in the absence of failure and the consequences of failures:

- **minor failures**, where the harmful consequences are of similar cost as the benefit provided by correct service delivery;
- **catastrophic failures**, where the cost of harmful consequences is orders of magnitude, or even incommensurably, higher than the benefit provided by correct service delivery.

Figure 4.2 summarizes the failure modes.

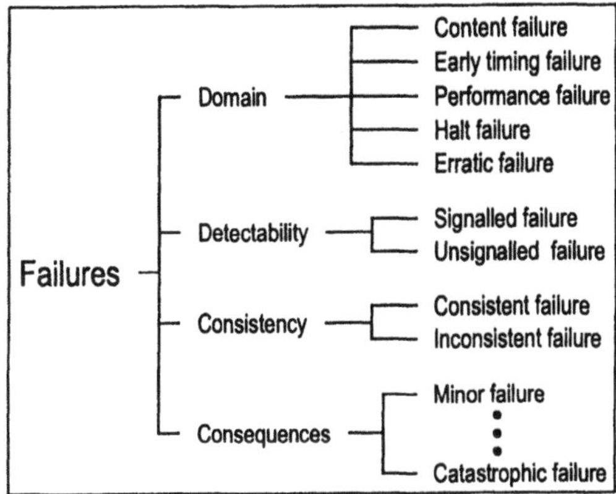

Figure 4.2: Failure modes

Systems that are designed and implemented so that they fail only in specific modes of failure described in the dependability specification and only to an acceptable extent, are **fail-controlled systems**, e.g., with stuck output as opposed to delivering erratic values, silence as opposed to babbling, consistent as opposed to inconsistent failures. A system whose failures are to an acceptable extent halting failures only, is a **fail-halt system**; the situations of stuck service and of silence lead respectively to **fail-passive systems** and to **fail-silent systems** [Powell *et al.* 1988]. A system whose failures are, to an acceptable extent, all minor ones is a **fail-safe system**.

As defined in Section 2, delivery of incorrect service is an *outage*, which lasts until *service restoration. The* outage duration may vary significantly, depending on the actions involved for service restoration after a failure occurred: a) automatic or operator-assisted recovery, restart or reboot, b) corrective maintenance. Correction of development faults is usually performed off-line, after service restoration, and the upgraded components resulting from fault correction are then introduced at some appropriate time, with or without interruption of system operation. Preemptive interruption of system operation for an upgrade or for preventive maintenance is a **service shutdown**[2].

4.2 Development Failures

A **development failure** causes the development process to be terminated before the system is accepted for use. There are two aspects of development failures:

1. *Budget failure*: the allocated funds are exhausted before the system passes acceptance testing.
2. *Schedule failure*: the projected delivery schedule slips to a point in the future where the system would be technologically obsolete or functionally inadequate for the user's needs.

The principal causes of development failures are:

1. Too *numerous specification changes initiated by the user*. They have the same impact on the development process as the detection of specification faults, requiring re-design with possibility of new development faults being introduced.
2. *Inadequate design*. The functionality and/or performance goals cannot be met.
3. *Too many faults*. Introduction of an excessive number of development faults and/or inadequate capability of fault removal during development.
4. *Insufficient dependability*. The dependability forecasting by analytical and experimental means shows that the specified dependability goals cannot be met.
5. *Faulty (too low) estimates of development costs*, either in funds, or in time needed, or both. They are usually due to an underestimate of the complexity of the system to be developed.

Budget and/or schedule *overruns* occur when the development is completed, but the funds or time needed to complete the effort exceed the original estimates. The overruns are *partial development failures*, i.e., failures of lesser severity than project termination. Another form of partial development failure is *downgrading*: the developed system is delivered with less functionality, lower performance, or is predicted to have lower dependability than required in the original system specification.

Development failures, overruns, and downgrades have a very negative impact on the user community, as exemplified by Figure 4.3.

[2] Service shutdowns are also called *planned outage*, as opposed to outages consecutive to failures, that are then called *unplanned outages*.

	1994	2002
Number of surveyed projects	8,380	13,522
Successful projects (completed on-time and on-budget, with all features and functions as initially specified)	16%	34%
Challenged projects (completed and operational but over-budget, over the time estimate, and offers fewer features and functions than originally specified)	53%	51%
Canceled projects	31%	15%
Overruns for challenged projects	89%	82%
Left functions for challenged projects	61%	52%
Total estimated budget for software projects in the USA, in $ billion	250	225
Estimated lost value for software projects in the USA, in $ billion	81	38

(a) Large software projects [www.standishgroup.com]

The Advanced Automation System (AAS) was intended to replace the aging air traffic control systems in the USA [Hunt & Kloster 1987]. In 1984 the FAA awarded competitive design phase contracts to IBM and Hughes Aircraft Co. In July 1988 an acquisition phase contract of $3.5 billion was awarded to IBM, and the program cost, including supporting efforts, was estimated by the FAA to be $4.8 billion. In 1994 FAA estimated that the program would cost $7 billion, with key segments as much as eight years behind schedule. The AAS as originally conceived, was terminated in June 1994, and an investigation showed that $2.6 billion were spent, of which $1.5 billion was completely wasted. Of the five program segments, only the simplest one was completed, one was restructured under a new contract, and three were terminated. The main causes of development failure were reported to be (1) overambitious plans, (2) poor oversight of software development, (3) FAA's inability to stabilize requirements, and (4) a poor statement of work in the original contract [US DOT, 1998].

(b) The AAS system

Figure 4.3: Development failures

4.3 Dependability Failures

It is expected that faults of various kinds will affect the system during its use phase. The faults may cause unacceptably degraded performance or total failure to deliver the specified service. For this reason a *dependability specification* is agreed upon that states the goals for each dependability attribute: availability, reliability, safety, confidentiality, integrity, and manageability.

The specification explicitly identifies the *classes of faults* that are expected and the *use environment* in which the system will operate. The dependability specification may also require safeguards against certain undesirable or dangerous conditions. Furthermore, the inclusion of specific fault prevention or fault tolerance techniques may be required by the user.

A **dependability failure** occurs when the given system fails more frequently or more severely than acceptable to the user(s).

Dependability and cost are not part of the functional specification. For this reason we call them the *meta-functional specification.* We object to the often used term "non-functional", since that also means "failed". A complete system specification consists of both, as shown in Figure 4.4.

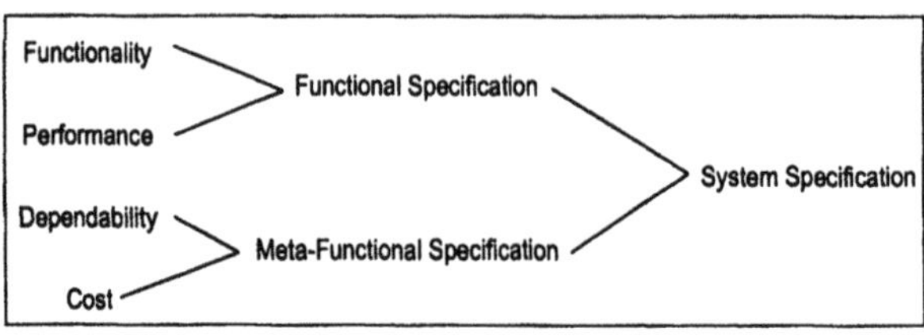

Figure 4.4: Elements of the system specification

The dependability specification can contain also faults. Omission faults can occur in description of the use environment or in choice of the classes of faults to be prevented or tolerated. Another class of faults is the unjustified choice of very high requirements for one or more attributes that raises the cost of development and may lead to a cost overrun or even a development failure. For example, the AAS complete outage limit of 3 seconds per year was changed to 5 minutes per year for the new contract in 1994 [US DOT 1998].

4.4 Errors

An **error** has been defined in Section 2.2 as the part of a system's total state that may lead to a failure — a failure occurs when the error causes the delivered service to deviate from correct service. The cause of the error has been called a fault.

An error is **detected** if its presence is indicated by an *error message* or *error signal*. Errors that are present but not detected are **latent** errors.

Since a system consists of a set of interacting components, the total state is the set of its component states. The definition implies that a fault originally causes an error within the state of one (or more) components, but service failure will not occur as long as the external state of that component is not part of the external state of the system. Whenever the error becomes a part of the external state of the component, a service failure of that component occurs, but the error remains internal to the entire system

Whether or not an error will actually lead to a failure depends on two factors:

1. The structure of the system, and especially the nature of any redundancy that exists in it:
   - *intentional* redundancy, introduced to provide fault tolerance, that is explicitly intended to prevent an error from leading to service failure,

- *unintentional* redundancy (it is in practice difficult if not impossible to build a system without any form of redundancy) that may have the same — presumably unexpected — result as intentional redundancy.

2. The behavior of the system: the part of the state that contains an error may never be needed for service, or an error may be eliminated (e.g., when overwritten) before it leads to a failure.

A convenient classification of errors is to describe them in terms of the elementary service failures that they cause, using the terminology of Section 4.1: content *vs.* timing errors, detected *vs.* latent errors, consistent *vs.* inconsistent errors when the service goes to two or more users, minor *vs.* catastrophic errors.

Some faults (e.g., a burst of electromagnetic radiation) can simultaneously cause errors in more than one component. Such errors are called **multiple related errors**. **Single errors** are errors that affect one component only.

4.5 The Pathology of Failure: Relationship between Faults, Errors and Failures

The creation and manifestation mechanisms of faults, errors, and failures are illustrated by Figure 4.5, and summarized as follows:

1. A fault is **active** when it produces an error, otherwise it is **dormant**. An active fault is either a) an internal fault that was previously dormant and that has been activated by the computation process or environmental conditions, or b) an external fault. **Fault activation** is the application of an input (the activation pattern) to a component that causes a dormant fault to become active. Most internal faults cycle between their dormant and active states.
2. Error propagation within a given component (i.e., *internal* propagation) is caused by the computation process: an error is successively transformed into other errors. Error propagation from one component (C1) to another component (C2) that receives service from C1 (i.e., *external* propagation) occurs when, through internal propagation, an error reaches the service interface of component C1. At this time, service delivered by C2 to C1 becomes incorrect, and the ensuing failure of C1 appears as an external fault to C2 and propagates the error into C2.
3. A service failure occurs when an error is propagated to the service interface and causes the service delivered by the system to deviate from correct service. A failure of a component causes a permanent or transient fault in the system that contains the component. Failure of a system causes a permanent or transient external fault for the other system(s) that interact with the given system.

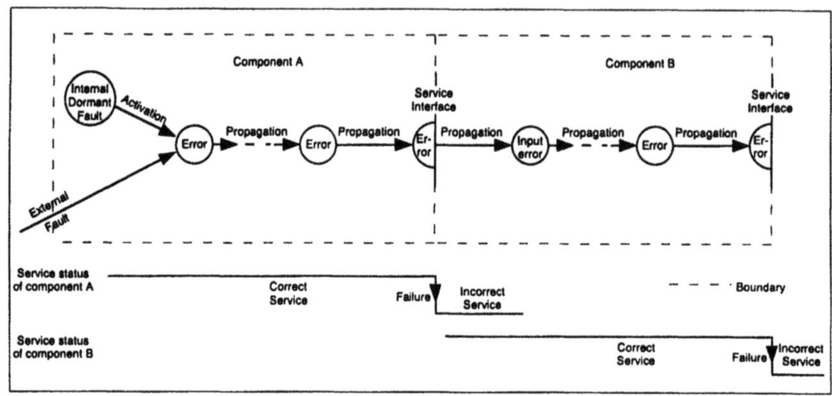

Figure 4.5: Error propagation

These mechanisms enable the 'fundamental chain' to be completed, as indicated by Figure 4.6.

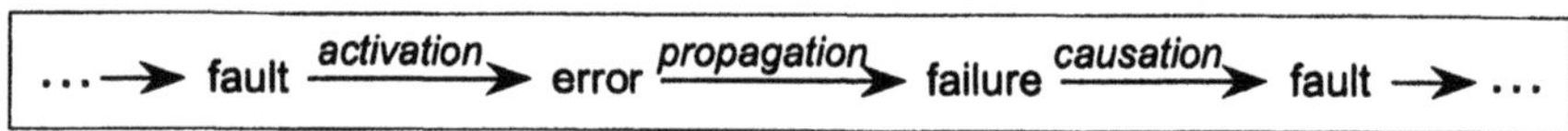

Figure 4.6: The fundamental chain of dependability threats

The arrows in this chain express a causality relationship between faults, errors and failures. They should be interpreted generically: by propagation, several errors can be generated before a failure occurs. Propagation, and thus instantiation(s) of the chain, can occur via the two fundamentals dimensions associated to the definitions of systems given in Section 2.1: interaction and composition.

Some illustrative examples of fault pathology are given in Figure 4.7. From those examples, it is easily understood that fault dormancy may vary considerably, depending upon the fault, the given system's utilization, etc.

The ability to identify the activation pattern of a fault that caused one or more errors is the **fault activation reproducibility**. Faults can be categorized according to their activation reproducibility: faults whose activation is reproducible are called **solid**, or **hard**, faults, whereas faults whose activation is not systematically reproducible are **elusive**, or **soft**, faults. Most residual development faults in large and complex software are elusive faults: they are intricate enough that their activation conditions depend on complex combinations of internal state and external requests, that occur rarely and can be very difficult to reproduce [Gray 86]. Other examples of elusive faults are:

- 'pattern sensitive' faults in semiconductor memories, changes in the parameters of a hardware component (effects of temperature variation, delay in timing due to parasitic capacitance, etc.);

- conditions — affecting either hardware or software — that occur when the system load exceeds a certain level, causing e.g. marginal timing and synchronization.

- A short circuit occurring in an integrated circuit is a *failure* (with respect to the function of the circuit); the consequence (connection stuck at a Boolean value, modification of the circuit function, etc.) is a *fault* that will remain dormant as long as it is not activated. Upon activation (invoking the faulty component and uncovering the fault by an appropriate input pattern), the fault becomes active and produces an error, which is likely to propagate and create other errors. If and when the propagated error(s) affect(s) the delivered service (in information content and/or in the timing of delivery), a failure occurs.
- The result of an error by a programmer leads to a failure to write the correct instruction or data, that in turn results in a *(dormant) fault* in the written software (faulty instruction(s) or data); upon activation (invoking the component where the fault resides and triggering the faulty instruction, instruction sequence or data by an appropriate input pattern) the fault becomes *active* and produces an error; if and when the error affects the delivered service (in information content and/or in the timing of delivery), a *failure* occurs. This example is not restricted to accidental faults: a logic bomb is created by a malicious programmer; it will remain dormant until activated (e.g. at some predetermined date); it then produces an error that may lead to a storage overflow or to slowing down the program execution; as a consequence, service delivery will suffer from a so-called denial-of-service.
- The result of an error by a specifier' leads to a failure to describe a function, that in turn results in a *fault* in the written specification, e.g. incomplete description of the function. The implemented system therefore does not incorporate the missing (sub-)function. When the input data are such that the service corresponding to the missing function should be delivered, the actual service delivered will be different from expected service, i.e., an *error* will be perceived by the user, and a *failure* will thus occur.
- An inappropriate human-system interaction performed by an operator during the operation of the system is an external *fault* (from the system viewpoint); the resulting altered processed data is an *error;* etc.
- An error in reasoning leads to a maintenance or operating manual writer's failure to write correct directives, that in turn results in a *fault* in the corresponding manual (faulty directives) that will remain dormant as long as the directives are not acted upon in order to address a given situation, etc.

Figure 4-7: Examples illustrating fault pathology

The similarity of the manifestation of elusive development faults and of transient physical faults leads to both classes being grouped together as **intermittent faults**. Errors produced by intermittent faults are usually termed **soft errors.**

Situations involving multiple faults and/or failures are frequently encountered. Given a system with defined boundaries, a **single fault** is a fault caused by *one* adverse physical event or *one* harmful human action. **Multiple faults** are *two or more* concurrent, overlapping, or sequential single faults whose consequences, i.e., errors, overlap in time, that is, the errors due to these faults are concurrently present in the system. Consideration of multiple faults leads one to distinguish a) **independent faults**, that are attributed to different causes, and b) **related faults**, that are attributed to a common cause. Related faults generally cause *similar errors*, i.e., errors that cannot be distinguished by whatever detection mechanisms are being employed, whereas independent faults usually cause *distinct errors*. However, it may happen that independent faults lead to similar errors [Avižienis & Kelly 1984], or that related faults lead to distinct errors. The failures caused by similar errors are **common-mode failures**.

5- DEPENDABILITY AND ITS ATTRIBUTES

In Section 2, we have presented two alternate definitions of dependability:

1. A qualitative definition: the ability to deliver service that can justifiably be trusted.
2. A quantitative definition: the ability of a system to avoid failures that are more frequent or more severe than is acceptable to the user(s).

The definitions of dependability that exist in current standards differ from our definitions. Two such differing definitions are:

- "The collective term used to describe the availability performance and its influencing factors: reliability performance, maintainability performance and maintenance support performance" [ISO 1992].
- "The extent to which the system can be relied upon to perform exclusively and correctly the system task(s) under defined operational and environmental conditions over a defined period of time, or at a given instant of time" [IEC 1992].

The ISO definition is clearly centered upon availability. This is no surprise as this definition can be traced back to the definition given by the international organization for telephony, the CCITT [CCITT 1984], at a time when availability was the main concern to telephone operating companies. However, the willingness to grant dependability with a generic character is noteworthy, since it goes beyond availability as it was usually defined, and relates it to reliability and maintainability. In this respect, the ISO/CCITT definition is consistent with the definition given in [Hosford 1960] for dependability: "the probability that a system will operate when needed". The second definition, from [IEC 1992], introduces the notion of reliance, and as such is much closer to our definitions.

Other concepts similar to dependability exist, as survivability and trustworthiness. They are presented and compared to dependability in Figure 5.1.

A side-by-side comparison leads to the conclusion that all three concepts are essentially equivalent in their goals and address similar threats. Trustworthiness omits the explicit listing of internal faults, although its goal implies that they also must be considered. Such faults are implicitly considered in survivability via the (component) failures. Survivability was present in the late sixties in the military standards, where it was defined as a system capacity to resist hostile environments so that the system can fulfill its mission (see, e.g., MIL-STD-721 or DOD-D-5000.3); it was redefined recently, as described in Figure 5.1. Trustworthiness was used in a study sponsored by the National Research Council, referenced in Figure 5.1. One difference must be noted. Survivability and trustworthiness have the threats explicitly listed in the definitions, while both definitions of dependability leave the choice open: the threats can be either all the faults of Figure 3.3 and Figure 3.4, or a selected subset of them, e.g., 'dependability with respect to development faults', etc.

Concept	Dependability	Survivability	Trustworthiness
Goal	1) ability to deliver service that can justifiably be trusted 2) ability of a system to avoid failures that are more frequent or more severe than is acceptable to the user(s)	capability of a system to fulfill its mission in a timely manner	assurance that a system will perform as expected
Threats present	1) development faults (e.g., software flaws, hardware errata, malicious logic) 2) physical faults (e.g., production defects, physical deterioration) 3) interaction faults (e.g., physical interference, input mistakes, attacks, including viruses, worms, intrusions)	1) attacks (e.g., intrusions, probes, denials of service) 2) failures (internally generated events due to, e.g., software design errors, hardware degradation, human errors, corrupted data) 3) accidents (externally generated events such as natural disasters)	1) hostile attacks (from hackers or insiders) 2) environmental disruptions (accidental disruptions, either man-made or natural) 3) human and operator errors (e.g., software flaws, mistakes by human operators)
Reference	This paper	"Survivable network systems" [Ellison *et al.* 1999]	"Trust in cyberspace" [Schneider 1999]

Figure 5.1: Dependability, survivability and trustworthiness

The attributes of dependability that have been defined in Section 2 may be of varying importance depending on the application intended for the given computing system: availability, integrity and maintainability are generally required, although to a varying degree depending on the application, whereas reliability, safety, confidentiality may or may not be required according to the application. The extent to which a system possesses the attributes of dependability should be considered in a relative, probabilistic, sense, and not in an absolute, deterministic sense: due to the unavoidable presence or occurrence of faults, systems are never totally available, reliable, safe, or secure.

The definition given for integrity — absence of improper system state alterations — goes beyond the usual definitions, that a) relate to the notion of authorized actions only, and, b) focus on information (e.g., prevention of the unauthorized amendment or deletion of information [CEC 1991], assurance of approved data alterations [Jacob 1991]): a) naturally, when a system implements an authorization policy, 'improper' encompasses 'unauthorized', b) 'improper alterations' encompass actions that prevent (correct) upgrades of information, and c) 'system state' includes system modifications or damages.

The definition given for maintainability intentionally goes beyond corrective and preventive maintenance, and encompasses the other forms of maintenance defined in section 3, i.e., adaptive and augmentative maintenance.

Security has not been introduced as a single attribute of dependability. This is in agreement with the usual definitions of security, that view it as a *composite* notion, namely "the combination of confidentiality, the prevention of the unauthorized disclosure of information, integrity, the prevention of the unauthorized amendment or deletion of information, and availability, the prevention of the unauthorized withholding of information" [CEC 1991, Pfleeger 2000]. A unified definition for **security** is: the absence of unauthorized access to, or handling of, system state. The relationship between dependability and security is illustrated by Figure 5.2.

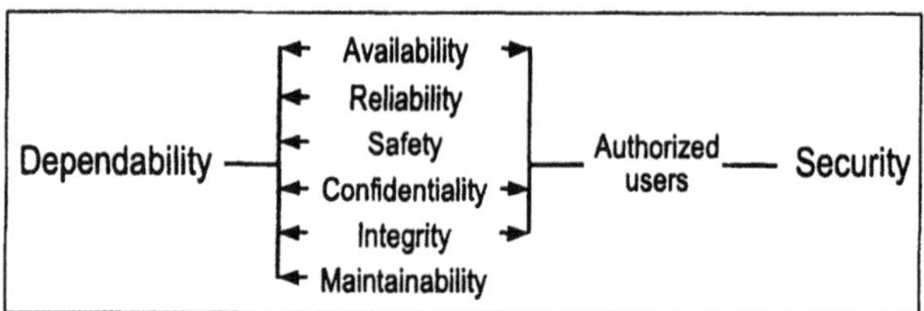

Figure 5.2: Dependability and security

In their definitions, availability and reliability emphasize the avoidance of failures, while safety and security emphasize the avoidance of a specific class of failures (catastrophic failures, unauthorized access or handling of information, respectively). Reliability and availability are thus closer to each other than they are to safety on one hand, and to security on the other; reliability and availability can thus be grouped together, and be collectively defined as the avoidance or minimization of service outages.

Besides the attributes defined in Section 2, and discussed above, other, *secondary*, attributes can be defined, which refine or specialize the *primary* attributes as defined in Section 2. An example of specializing secondary attribute is **robustness**, i.e., dependability with respect to external faults, that characterizes a system reaction to a specific class of faults.

The notion of secondary attributes is especially relevant for security, when we distinguish among various types of information [Cachin *et al.* 2000]. Examples of such secondary attributes are:

- **accountability**: availability and integrity of the identity of the person who performed an operation,
- **authenticity**: integrity of a message content and origin, and possibly of some other information, such as the time of emission,
- **non-repudiability**: availability and integrity of the identity of the sender of a message (non-repudiation of the origin), or of the receiver (non-repudiation of reception).

Dependability classes are generally defined via the analysis of failure frequencies and severities, and of outage durations, for the dependabilty attributes that are of concern for a given application. This analysis may be conducted directly, or indirectly, via risk assessment (see, e.g., [Grigonis 2001] for availability, [RTCA/EUROCAE 1992] for safety, and [ISO/IEC 1999] for security).

The variations in the emphasis placed on the different attributes of dependability directly influence the balance of the techniques (fault prevention, tolerance, removal and forecasting) to be employed in order to make the resulting system dependable. This problem is all the more difficult as some of the attributes are conflicting (e.g., availability and safety, availability and security), necessitating that trade-offs be made. Regarding the three main development dimensions of a computing system besides functionality, i.e., cost, performance and dependability, the problem is further exacerbated by the fact that the dependability dimension is less understood than the cost-performance development space [Siewiorek & Johnson 1992].

6. CONCLUSION

Increasingly, individuals and organizations are developing or procuring sophisticated computing systems on whose services they need to place great reliance — whether to service a set of cash dispensers, control a satellite constellation, an airplane, a nuclear plant, or a radiation therapy device, or to maintain the confidentiality of a sensitive data base. In differing circumstances, the focus will be on differing properties of such services — e.g., on the average real-time response achieved, the likelihood of producing the required results, the ability to avoid failures that could be catastrophic to the system's environment, or the degree to which deliberate intrusions can be prevented. The notion of dependability provides a very convenient means of subsuming these various concerns within a single conceptual framework. Dependability includes as special cases such properties as availability, reliability, safety, confidentiality, integrity, maintainability. It also provides the means of addressing the problem that what a user usually needs from a system is an *appropriate balance* of these properties.

A major strength of the dependability concept, as it is formulated in this paper, is its integrative nature, that enables to put into perspective the more classical notions of reliability, availability, safety, security, maintainability, that are then seen as attributes of dependability. The fault-error-failure model is central to the understanding and mastering of the various threats that may affect a system, and it enables a unified presentation of these threats, while preserving their specificities via the various fault classes that can be defined. The model provided for the means for dependability is extremely useful, as those means are much more orthogonal to each other than the more classical classification according to the attributes of dependability, with respect to which the design of any real system has to perform trade-offs due to the fact that these attributes tend to conflict with each other.

What has been presented is an attempt to document a minimum consensus within the community in order to facilitate fruitful technical interactions. The associated terminology effort is not an end in itself: words are only of interest because they unequivocally label concepts, and enable ideas and viewpoints to be shared.

REFERENCES

[Avižienis 1967] A. Avižienis, "Design of fault-tolerant computers", in *Proc. 1967 Fall Joint Computer Conf., AFIPS Conf. Proc. Vol. 31,* pp. 733-743, 1967.

[Avižienis & Chen, 1977] A. Avižienis and L. Chen, "On the implementation of N-version programming for software fault tolerance during execution", in *Proc. IEEE COMPSAC 77*, pp. 149-155, Nov. 1977.

[Avižienis & He 1999] A. Avižienis, Y. He, "Microprocessor entomology: a taxonomy of design faults in COTS microprocessors", in Dependable Computing for Critical Applications 7, C.B. Weinstock and J. Rushby, eds, IEEE CS Press, 1999, pp. 3-23.

[Avižienis & Kelly 1984] A. Avižienis, J.P.J. Kelly, "Fault tolerance by design diversity: concepts and experiments", *Computer,* vol. 17, no. 8, Aug. 1984, pp. 67-80.

[Bouricius *et al.* 1969] W.G. Bouricius, W.C. Carter, and P.R. Schneider, "Reliability modeling techniques for self-repairing computer systems", in *Proceedings of 24th National Conference of ACM,* pp. 295-309, 1969.

[Cachin *et al.* 2000] C. Cachin, J. Camenisch, M. Dacier, Y. Deswarte, J. Dobson, D. Horne, K. Kursawe, J.-C. Laprie, J.C. Lebraud, D. Long, T. McCutcheon, J. Muller, F. Petzold, B. Pfitzmann, D. Powell, B. Randell, M. Schunter, V. Shoup, P. Veríssimo, G. Trouessin, R.J. Stroud, M. Waidner, I. Welch, "Malicious- and Accidental-Fault Tolerance in Internet Applications: reference model and use cases", LAAS report no. 00280, MAFTIA, Project IST-1999-11583, Aug. 2000, 113p.

[Castelli *et al.* 2001] V. Castelli, R.E. Harper, P. Heidelberger, S.W. Hunter, K.S. Trivedi, K. Vaidyanathan, W.P. Zeggert, "Proactive management of software aging", *IBM J. Res.& Dev.*, vol. 45, no. 2, March 201, pp. 311-332.

[CCITT 1984] Termes et définitions concernant la qualité de service, la disponibilité et la fiabilité, Recommandation G 106, CCITT, 1984; in French.

[CEC 1991] *Information Technology Security Evaluation Criteria,* Harmonized criteria of France, Germany, the Netherlands, the United Kingdom, Commission of the European Communities, 1991.

[Cristian 1991] F. Cristian, "Understanding Fault-Tolerant Distributed Systems", *Com. of the ACM*, vol. 34, no. 2, pp. 56-78, 1991.

[Dobson & Randell 1986] J.E. Dobson and B. Randell. Building reliable secure computing systems out of unreliable insecure compnents. In *Proc. of the 1986 IEEE Symp. Security and Privacy*, pp. 187-193, April 1986.

[Ellison *et al.* 1999] R.J. Ellison, D.A. Fischer, R.C. Linger, H.F. Lipson, T. Longstaff, N.R. Mead, "Survivable network systems: an emerging discipline", Technical Report CMU/SEI-97-TR-013, November 1997, revised May 1999.

[Elmendorf 1972] W.R. Elmendorf, "Fault-tolerant programming", in *Proc. 2nd IEEE Int. Symp. on Fault-Tolerant Computing (FTCS-2),* Newton, Massachusetts, June 1972, pp. 79-83.

[Fray *et al.* 1986] J.-M. Fray, Y. Deswarte, D. Powell, "Intrusion tolerance using fine-grain fragmentation-scattering", in *Proc. 1986 IEEE Symp. on Security and Privacy,* Oakland, April 1986, pp. 194-201.

[FTCS 1982] Special session. Fundamental concepts of fault tolerance. In *Digest of FTCS-12*, pages 3-38, June 1982.

[Ghezzi *et al.* 1991] C. Ghezzi, M. Jazayeri, D. Mandrioli, *Fundamentals of Software Engineering*, Prentice-Hall, 1991.

[Gray 2001] J. Gray, "Functionality, Availability, Agility, Manageability, Scalability -- the New Priorities of Application Design", *in Proc. HPTS 2001*, Asilomar, April 2001.

[Grigonis 2001] R. Grigonis, "Fault-resilience for communications convergence", *Special Supplement to CMP Media's Converging Communications Group*, Spring 2001.

[Hosford 1960] J.E. Hosford, "Measures of dependability", *Operations Research,* vol. 8, no. 1, 1960, pp. 204-206.

[Huang *et al.* 1995] Y. Huang, C. Kintala, N. Kolettis, N.D. Fulton, "Software rejuvenation: analysis, module and applications", in *Proc. 25th IEEE Int. Symp. on Fault-Tolerant Computing (FTCS-25),* Pasadena, California, June 1995, pp. .

[Hunt & Kloster 1987] V.R. Hunt & G.V. Kloster, editors, "The FAA's Advanced Automation Program", special issue, *Computer*, February 1987.

[IEC 1992] Industrial-process measurement and control — Evaluation of system properties for the purpose of system assessment. Part 5: Assessment of system dependability, Draft, Publication 1069-5, International Electrotechnical Commission (IEC) Secretariat, Feb. 1992.

[Intel 2001] Intel Corp. Intel Pentium III Processor Specification Update, May 2001. Order No.244453-029.

[ISO 1992] Quality Concepts and Terminology, Part one: Geberic Terms and Definitions, Document ISO/TC 176/SC 1 N 93, Feb. 1992.

[ISO/IEC 1999] *Common Criteria for Information Technology Security Evaluation*, ISO/IEC Standard 15408, August 1999.

[Jacob 1991] J. Jacob. "The Basic Integrity Theorem", in *Proc. Int. Symp. on Security and Privacy,* pp. 89-97, Oakland, CA, USA, 1991.

[Joseph & Avižienis 1988] M.K. Joseph and A. Avižienis, "A fault tolerance approach to computer viruses", in *Proc. of the 1988 IEEE Symposium on Security and Privacy,* pages 52-58, April 1988.

[Lamport *et al.* 1982] L. Lamport, R. Shostak, M. Pease, "The Byzantine generals problem", *ACM Trans.on Programming Languages and Systems,* vol. 4, no. 3, July 1982, pp. 382-401.

[Landwehr *et al.* 1994] C.E. Landwher, A.R. Bull, J.P. McDermott, W.S. Choi, "A Taxonomy of Computer Program Security Flaws", *ACM Computing Surv.*, vol. 26, no. 3, pp. 211-254, 1994.

[Laprie 1985] J.-C. Laprie. Dependable computing and fault tolerance: concepts and terminology. In *Proc. 15th IEEE Int. Symp. on Fault-Tolerant Computing (FTCS-15)*, Ann Arbor, June 1985, pp. 2-11, .

[Laprie 1992] J.-C. Laprie, editor, *Dependability: Basic Concepts and Terminology*, Springer-Verlag, 1992.

[Meyer 1994] Meyer, Michael, "A 'Lesson' for Intel: How It Mishandled the Pentium Flap", *Newsweek*, December 12, 1994, p.58.

[Moore & Shannon 1956] E.F. Moore and C.E. Shannon, "Reliable circuits using less reliable relays", *J. Franklin Institute*, 262:191-208 and 281-297, Sept/Oc. 1956.

[Muntz 2000] R.R. Muntz, "Performance measurement and evaluation", in *Encyclopedia of Computer Science*, A.Ralston, E.D. Reilly, D. Hemmendinger, eds, Nature Publishing Group, 2000.

[Parnas 1972] D. Parnas, "On thecriteria to be used in decomposing systems into modules", Comunications of the ACM, vol. 15, no. 12, Dec. 1972, pp. 1053-1058.

[Parnas 1974] D. Parnas, "On a 'buzzword': hierarchical structure", in *Proc. Information Processing 74"*.

[Pfleeger 2000] C.P. Pfleeger, "Data security", in *Encyclopedia of Computer Science*, A.Ralston, E.D. Reilly, D. Hemmendinger, eds, Nature Publishing Group, 2000, pp. 504-507.

[Pierce 1965] W.H. Pierce, *Failure-Tolerant Computer Design*, Academic Press, 1965.

[Powell *et al.* 1988] D. Powell, G. Bonn, D. Seaton, P. Veríssimo, F. Waeselynck, "The Delta-4 approach to dependability in open distributed computing systems", in *Proc. 18th IEEE Int. Symp. on Fault-Tolerant Computing (FTCS-18)*, Tokyo, Japan, June 1988, pp. 246-251.

[Powell & Stroud 2003] D. Powell, R. Stroud, editors, "Conceptual Model and Architecture of MAFTIA", MAFTIA, Project IST-1999-11583, Jan. 2003, 123p.

[Randell 1975] B. Randell, "System structure for software fault tolerance", *IEEE Transactions on Software Engineering*, SE-1:1220-232, 1975.

[RTCA/EUROCAE 1992] *Software considerations in airborne systems and equipment certification*, DO-178-B/ED-12-B, Requirements and Technical Concepts for Aviation/European Organisation for Civil Aviation Equipment, 1992.

[Schneider 1999] F. Schneider, ed., *Trust in Cyberspace*, National Academy Press, 1999.

[Siewiorek & Johnson 1992] D.P. Siewiorek, D. Johnson, "A design methodology for high reliability systems: the Intel 432", in D.P. Siewiorek, R.S. Swarz, *Reliable Computer Systems, Design and Evaluation*, Digital Press, 1992, pp. 737-767.

[US DOT 1998] USA Department of Transportation, Office of Inspector General, Audit Report: Advance Automation System, Report No. AV-1998-113, April 15, 1998.

[von Neumann 1956] J. von Neumann, "Probabilistic logics and the synthesis of reliable organisms from unreliable components", in C. E. Shannon and J. McCarthy, editors, *Annals of Math Studies*, numbers 34, pages 43-98. Princeton Univ. Press, 1956.

[Wood 1994] A. Wood, "NonStop availability in a client/server environment", Tandem Technical Report 94.1, March 1994.

CURRENT RESEARCH ACTIVITIES ON DEPENDABLE COMPUTING AND OTHER DEPENDABILITY ISSUES IN JAPAN

Yoshihiro Tohma[1] and Masao Mukaidono[2]

[1]Tokyo Denki University, tohma@sie.dendai.ac.jp; [2]Meiji University, masao@cs.meiji.ac.jp

Abstract: Current research activities on dependable computing and other related dependability issues in Japan are reviewed. When considering the dependable computing, an emphasis is put on architectural aspects of computing systems, though the dependable computing is not limited to them, but ranges very broadly. Not only technical issues but also some organizational activities are also touched.

Key words: fault tolerance; mobile computing; COTS; Internet; grid computing; feature interaction; fail-safe; organizational activities.

1. INTRODUCTION

Taking this opportunity of Topical Day for commemorating Prof. Al Avižienis's outstanding contributions to the advancement of fault tolerance and dependable computing, it is our pleasure and honor to present a paper, reviewing research activities on dependable computing and other dependability issues currently conducted in Japan. However, this paper is not intended to make a comprehensive survey, but to introduce some research outcomes simply based on the authors' view.

When looking at research activities, we first focused our attention to architectural aspects of dependable computing systems with new features, and further argued some extension of the application of dependability concept to other technical worlds.

2. NEW PARADIGMS OF DEPENDABLE COMPUTING

These days, every thing such as the configuration of computing systems, the requirement to them, and the computing paradigm are changing rapidly. Stand-alone computing systems make no longer any sense, but are almost networked. The scale of a computing system and its clients is ever exploding concurrently with its non-stop provision of services. It is required to provide different services of not only scientific computation but also support or assistance to the daily life of individuals. Mobile and/or ubiquitous computing are new demands. The way of computation is changing. Computing will be shared with servers distributed over a network(s) in a form of, say, grids.

Facing these trends, dependable computing is becoming more significant in different ways.

2.1 Fault tolerance in mobile computing

In mobile computing environment, computing unit in such equipments as cellular phone, PDA, etc. must be light and small for portable purposes. Therefore, LSI's in such equipments are produced by sub-micron fabrication technologies. This means that those computing units are becoming very vulnerable to cosmic ray and/or artificially made radiation such as alpha particle and prone to suffer transient errors. Since continuous and real-time services are mandatory in mobile computing, it is required and becomes more important to implement countermeasures against transient errors, which can recover the computing units quickly.

T. Sato proposed to implement the fault detection and recovery mechanism in superscalar processors (Sato 2003) with the at most 8-way dynamic scheduling, focusing on transient errors in the logic and arithmetic units in the processor. Other parts can be protected effectively by means of ECC and/or parity check. The essence of error detection is simply the duplicated execution of an instruction and the comparison between the both results.

As shown in Fig. 1, instructions are first stored in the register update unit (RUU), of which primary role is to carry out the dynamic scheduling, and then dispatched to functional units. When an instruction in RUU is committed (with the necessary control and data ready), it is again dispatched. Its execution result is compared to that of the first execution of the instruction.

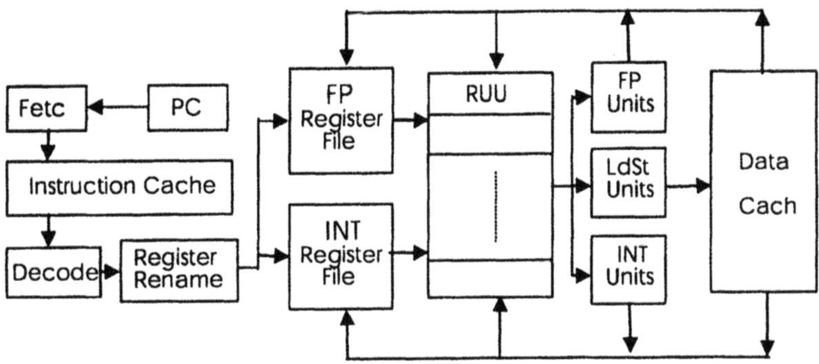

Figure 1. Error detection.

When the mismatch happens, the recovery by hardware (instead of relying on OS) is activated transparently. Regarding the occurrence of an error to be a misspeculation of data, the transparent hardware recovery here uses the existing mechanism to reissue an instruction upon the misspeculation of data.

What we are mostly concerned with is the performance degradation caused by the introduction of fault tolerance. The percentage increase of execution cycles in the error-free operation was measured for various benchmarks of SPEC2000 and MediaBench suites. Thanks to the superscalaring (Mendelson 2000), the overheads in SPEC200 and MediaBench are 44.2% and 44.7%, respectively, in average, even though every instruction is executed twice. The more detailed investigation to reduce the overhead revealed that earlier speculative update of branch prediction table at the stage of instruction decode together with the elimination of redundant memory access is effective. Finally, the overhead was reduced to about 30% in average by incorporating the above two techniques. He notes that the limitation of hardware resources greatly influences the performance degradation and therefore, it could be lessened further, if microprocessors would have sufficient hardware resources.

2.2 Use of COTS for dependable Internet services

As Internet extends not only to computer professionals but also to common people, various services which range from purely engineering computations to daily supports for individuals such as multimedia delivery, online entertainments, VoIP, e-commerce, e-government, and etc. are carried outd on it. Thus, Internet has become an important social infrastructure, and the importance of dependable computing on Internet is recognized even by common people.

On the other hand, the cost to implement dependability measure for Internet should not be much, because they should be incorporated widely and commonly. Traditional dependable computing systems in critical applications use proprietary hardware such as voting and fault isolation circuitries with proprietary OS. They are main sources of the cost. Instead of using such proprietary components, Mishima and Akaike proposed ways to implement fault tolerance measure (Mishima and Akaike 2003), using COTS components of commodity hardware (computers and networks) and software (OS and applications), which are not modified, nor re-compiled, and nor vendor-specific.

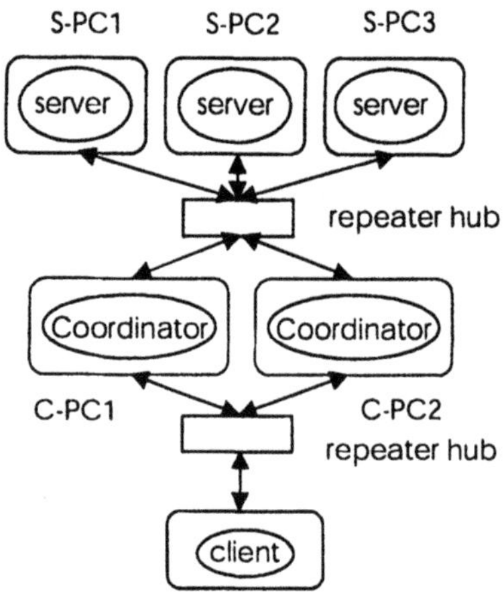

Figure 2. Fault tolerance measure for servers.

Although Internet services are carried out in the coordinated relationship of servers and clients, the malfunction of servers is much more serious than that of clients. Therefore, they simply considered ways to realize dependable servers. Since many services on Internet are real-time operations, the fault tolerance of servers based on the primary-backup is not applicable. Therefore, the fundamental idea is to use the active replication of servers as shown in Fig. 2, which needs less time to make the recovery than that of the primary-backup. Three servers on different PC's (denoted S-PC's) are employed to simply perform the TMR operation. However, the key issue here is to make the fault tolerance measure as much transparent as possible, because in the use of COTS components, the modifications of both hardware and software components in servers and clients should be kept unnecessary. To realize the transparency, a control function called *Coordinator* is inserted between a client and triplicate servers. In addition to IP address of Coordinator itself "CDR", it has another IP address "IPVD" (IP address as Virtual Server) by which the client views the Coordinator as a single virtual server. The communication between the Coordinator and the clients are carried out by referring to the client's IP address "C" and "IPVD". Similarly, the Coordinator communicates to each of the replicate servers, using "CDR" and the server's IP address "S" in addition to "C", as shown in Fig. 3.

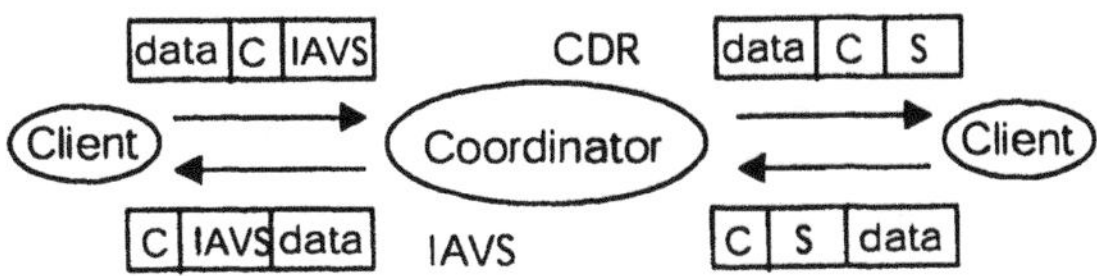

Figure 3. Packet flow control.

When a client communicates to the servers, the Coordinator must manage the loose synchronization among the replicated servers and make the adjudication. To reduce the response time to the client, it responds quickly to the client as soon as the first and the second responses from the replicated servers agree.

In order to tolerate the malfunction of Coordinator itself, the primary-backup and the active replication of Coordinators were considered. The experiments of the performance evaluation show that the former is better than the latter in terms of the round trip time. It is speculated that the active replication of Coordinators causes more congestion of packets, resulting in the performance degradation.

2.3 Fault tolerance in new computation paradigm

Today, computers exist ubiquitously, and are connected to each other through a network(s). However, they do not necessarily run always. Therefore, such an idea is a natural consequence that computing power distributed over a network should be shared by different users. They should not necessarily reside in a corporation but across enterprises. In a way, computers make a form of virtual grid over a network and they perform services in the coordination. This computation paradigm is called *grid computing*.

A computer over a network may participate in different grids. Further, it decides for itself whether it participates in a coordinated service or not. In this sense, the grid computing is a paradigm of *distributive* and *autonomous* computing.

Another incentive to such distributive and autonomous computing is the continuous expansion of a computing system over network(s). The number of computing facilities on a network ever increases. Further, the territory of a computing system over a network is becoming more and more boundary-less.

The configuration and scale of a computing system over network(s) changes dynamically. In such circumstances, it is hard to manage whole computing system by a single centralized mechanism. We should rely on the autonomous computing distributed over the network.

A typical example of computational model of grid computing is as shown in Fig. 4 (Foster 2002), where computers of two categories are included, the *registry* and the (computing) *servers*. First, a user sends his/her inquiry to the registry about what service(s) he/her requests. The registry responds to the user's request, retuning ID's of server(s) which can perform the requested service(s). Then, the user sends message(s) to such server(s), requesting the service(s). The requested server(s) execute the necessary operation(s) and return the result(s) to the user. If necessary, the requested server may sends its own request to other servers.

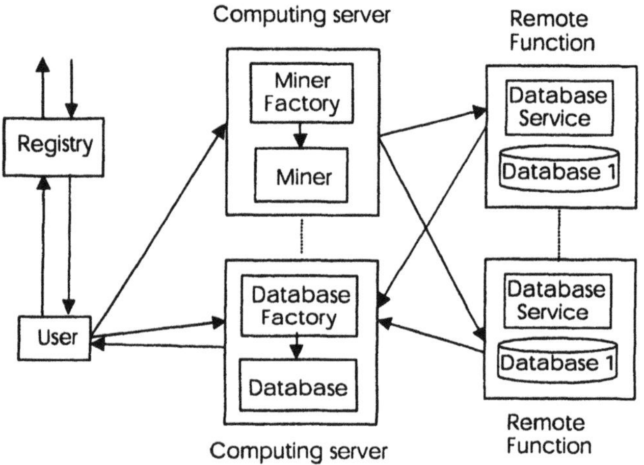

Figure 4. Operational model of the grid computing.

Issues concerned with the incorporation of fault tolerance into such environments are argued (Tohma 2003). First, the registry plays a key role to the fault tolerance in such a computational environment. It must tell the user the fault-free servers which can satisfy the user's request, excluding faulty ones. Therefore, it must also maintain the information of which servers are fault-free and which are faulty. The fault tolerance of the registry itself is crucial.

There may be many servers of similar functionalities in such an environment. Therefore, in contrast to the case of the registry, a faulty server can easily be replaced by another fault-free one.

Servers execute their computation in the message-driven way. Therefore, the most difficult problem is by what way the user or a requesting server can recognize the occurrence of faults in the requested servers. Or reversely by what way can the requested servers notify it to the user or a requesting server? The concept of neighborhood and its consensus is advantageous in alleviating this difficulty. However, since the neighborhood consists of three servers of similar functionalities and the user or a requesting server must send a message to each of three servers in a neighborhood, the nine-fold of a message are transmitted through the network in the worst case. Further, each server in a neighborhood exchanges its computational result to each other. Thus, the communication overhead is considerable.

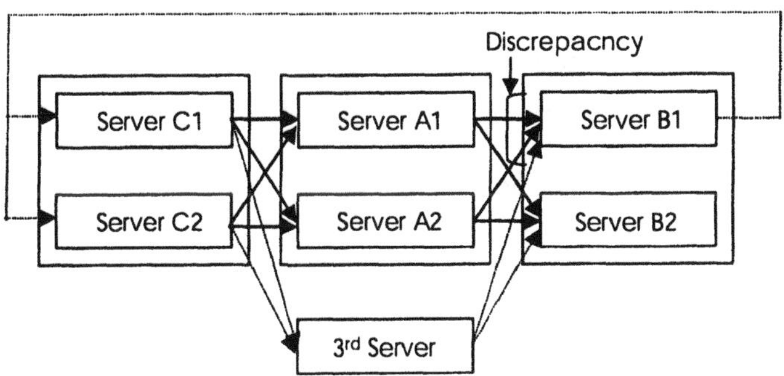

Figure 5. Duplicated operation in a pair.

Instead, it is proposed that the computation is normally duplicated in a pair of servers as shown in Fig.5. When the operation of a server in a pair is abnormal, a discrepancy between the paired computational results is found at the input of servers in the succeeding pair. Then, the server in the succeeding pair requests the re-computation by the third server which receives the necessary inputs from the preceding pair and provides its result to the succeeding pair. Since each server in the succeeding pair receives three-fold inputs, it can restore the correct input.

Servers in a pair are not necessarily the same one, and may reside remotely to each other on a network. The use of differently designed servers in pairs may benefit by the design diversity against the intrusion.

However, the grid computing needs more detailed investigation about how granularity or atomicity the functionality of grid computing needs, what language should be developed to describe services requested by users, etc.

2.4 New frontier of dependable computing

One of the clearest characteristic to contemporary computing systems is the continuous augmentation of their functionality. New functions and/or capabilities are added rather independently even under the continuation of services so far provided to users. Then, a new type of harassments arises, that is, functions and/or capabilities added newly may conflict to other functions which already reside in the system and make some of them not to work properly. This is called the *feature interaction.*

Typical examples of feature interaction can be found in telephony systems. Consider, for example, that function OCS (Originating Call Screening) to make connection from subscribers A to C prohibited has been installed. However, if new function CF (Call Forwarding) to have telephone call from A to subscriber B automatically forwarded to C is added, and if A calls B, A is connected to C by way of B. The intention of OCS not to connect A to C is thus violated. In recent intelligent communication systems, the feature interaction has become one of real problems against providing dependable communication services.

The difficulty is how to find (detect) possible feature interaction, when functions and/or capabilities are added to a communication system without considering mutual interactions to each other.

Generally, a service is specified by the sets of subscribers, rules, predicates, and events. Further, to describe rules in a general form, variables are introduced and are instantiated, when rules are applied to actual situations. Rules of such forms as $r : pre-condition\,[event]\,post-condition$ define post-conditions to which pre-conditions are reduced, when rules are applied to preconditions and the events are activated. Pre-conditions are represented by predicates and/or the negations of predicates, while post-conditions by predicates only.

A state is defined to be a set of predicates with their variables instantiated. For example, assume that subscribers are A and B, variables x and y, respectively. Further, the predicates are $\{idle(x),\ dialtone(x),\ busytone(x),\ calling(x,y),\ talk(x,y)\}$. Then, $\{dialtone(A), dialtone(B)\}$ is a state. When A dials B, pre-condition $\{dialtone(A), \neg idle(B)\}$ invokes such a rule $dialtone(x), \neg idle(y)[dial(x,y)]busytone(x)$ and post-condition $busytone(A)$ results by the execution of event $dial(A,B)$. Thus, state $\{dialtone(A), dialtone(B)\}$ transfers to a new state $\{busytone(A), dialtone(B)\}$ as shown in Fig.6.

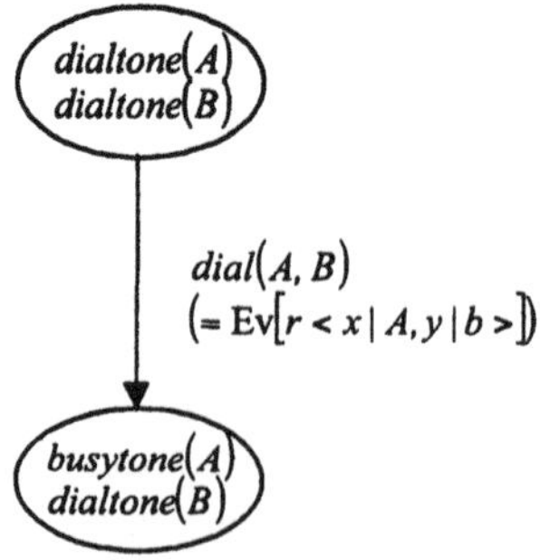

Figure 6. State transition.

In this way, all state transitions are defined for the set of rules of a service. The feature interaction can be detected by checking the existence of paths from the initial state to states (reachability check) where the feature interaction holds.

When analyzing real situations, the number of states becomes prohibitively large in general. To cope with this state explosion, the state space and the state transition relation as well as the condition of feature interaction are represented symbolically by Boolean functions, which are calculated by symbolic model checking tools. However, such Boolean formula is lengthy so that its simplification is still one of challenging issues.

Yokogawa, et al proposed a new way of representation (encoding) (Yokogawa 2003), noting that only a small fraction of state variables are usually involved in each state transition. Since the size of formula can be reduced, this new way benefits often in the possibility to explore larger state space. The considered services are as follows:

- Call Waiting (CW) allows subscribers to receive the second incoming call while they are already talking.
- Call Forwarding (CF) allows subscribers to have their incoming call forwarded to another address.
- Originating Call Screening (OCS) allows subscribers to specify in the screening list their outgoing calls to be either restricted or allowed.
- Terminating Call Screening (TCS) allows subscribers to specify in the screening list their incoming calls to be either restricted or allowed.
- Denied Origination (DO) allows subscribers to disable any call originating from the terminal. Only terminating calls are permitted.
- Denied Transmission (DT) allows subscribers to disable any call terminating at the terminal. Only originating calls are permitted.
- Direct Connect (DC) is the so-called hot-line service. When x subscribes to DC and it specifies y as the destination address, x is directly calling y simply by offhooking.

As the feature interactions, the *nondeterminism* and the *invariant violation* are considered. The nondeterminism is the situation such that two or more functionalities of different services can be activated simultaneously and therefore, which functionality should be actually performed is not determined. The invariant is a property to be held at any time.

The experiment was conducted to detect the nondeterminism for 11 combinations of services with four subscribers. The performance improvement is shown in Table 1. Times in column 'Trad.scheme' are measured by using an implementation of Chaff (Moskewicz 2001) and represented relative to those in column 'time', respectively: The latter are obtained by using the new method. The invariant violation was also checked very efficiently.

Table 1. Comparison of performance of detecting the nondeterminism.

Combination	time	Trad.scheme
CW+CF	1	1634
CW+DT	1	44.1
CW+OCS	1	113.8
CW+TCS	1	386.9
CF+DT	1	2676
CF+OCS	1	1966
CF+TCS	1	3255
DC+DO	1	43.5
DT+OCS	1	38.2
DT+TCS	1	93
OCS+TCS	1	101

3. EXTENDED APPLICATION OF DEPENDABILITY CONCEPT TO OTHER WORLDS

Modern dependable computing has many application fields from business information systems including financial, data communications, and etc. to online real time control systems including chemical process, manufacture, aerospace, etc. The concept of dependability has many aspects such as reliability, maintainability, safety, evaluation, etc. and fundamentally it covers many systems not only computing and structural systems but also social and human systems such as organizations and inspections. That is, we can extend the concept of dependability into many other worlds, and it has potentially huge application fields in the real world.

In these applications the most critical one will be a system, which affects a person's life, that is, a safety system. Safety has a strong relation with reliability but is fundamentally different concept from reliability. "Reliability" targets to maintain the given functions, but "safety" targets to avoid dangerous situations in which a sense of values of related person or current society is concerned. For example, if a bullet train is stopped from a fault of safety devise, the safety is maintained (high) but the reliability is lost (low).

In this section two activities on safety issues, which are currently conducted in Japan, are explained. One is an activity on the attempt to construct Map on Safety, which systematizes the safety concepts and safety technologies applied commonly to many safety fields. The other is harmonized activity on safety standard of machinery in Japan with international safety standards.

3.1 Map on Safety or Safety Mandala

This is an attempt toward establishing a new overall discipline on safety (which we would like to call newly "safenology") by unifying safety engineering and safety science with social and humanity sciences. For the first step of the purpose we list up many key words concerning or related to safety and cluster them into categories, which consist of three hierarchal levels and one appendix as shown in Fig. 7. We would like to call it the Map on Safety (first we called it safety map, but we prefer now to call it safety Mandala, which means, in Buddhism, a map illustrating the structure of conceptual essences) (Mukaidono 2002).

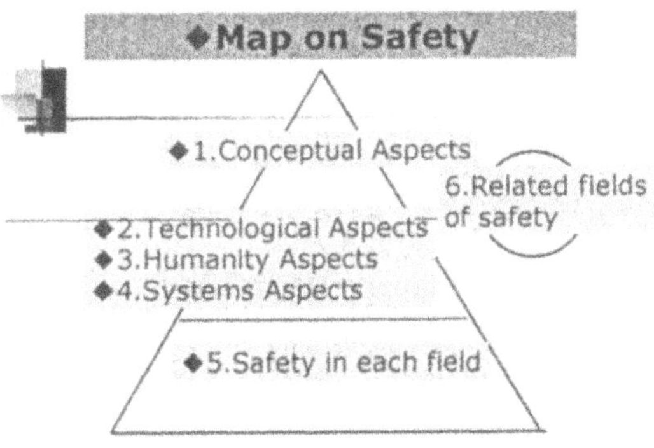

Figure 7. Map on safety.

The first level of the map on safety is (1) Conceptual Aspects, which includes fundamental concepts on safety. The second level is made of three categories (2) Technological Aspects, (3) Humanity Aspects, and (4) Systems Aspects, which are commonly used in many fields of safety. The third level of safety on map is (5) Safety in each field, which consists of each domain specific safety such as machine safety, chemical safety, nuclear power safety, etc. The appendix is (6) Related fields of safety.

The following are examples of key words clustered into each category.

(1) Conceptual Aspects

(1-1) What is safety

Definitions of safety, risk, tolerable risk, hazards, danger, safety target

(1-2) A sense of values in safety

Responsibility, safety versus cost/efficiency/ethics/convenience, safety culture

(1-3) Humanity in safety

Mistakes, habit, human's reliability

(1-4) Structure of safety

Defend what, from what, how, under what name ?

(2) Technological Aspects
Technologies on evaluation, prevention, maintenance, damage reduction, prevention, inherent safety design, fault tolerance, fail safe, fail soft, and fool proof

(3) Humanity Aspects
Human machine interface, miss uses, ergonomics, education, peace in mind

(4) Systems Aspects
Management, assessment, standardization, regulation and norm, certification

(5) Safety in each field
Machine safety, nuclear power safety, traffic safety, chemical safety, product safety, material safety, food safety

(6) Related fields of safety
Crisis management, security, insurance, court systems, law

3.2 Recent activities in standardisation on safety of machinery in Japan

Standards for safety of machinery started from Europe. EN292 (Safety of Machinery--Basic concepts, general principle for design) was originated from British and German safety standards came into effect on 1991, and used as harmonized standards of EC Machine Directives, which are mandatory. ISO/TC199 (Safety of Machinery) was established to discuss ISO12100 (Safety of Machinery—Basic concepts, general principle for design) based on EN292 and related many international standards of safety of machinery. Japan has JIS (Japan Industrial Standard) systems but not enough for machine safety. According to TBT (Technical Barriers to Trade) agreement, Japan started in 1995 to harmonize JIS with international standards, and the safety of machinery standards are introduced actively into JIS based on ISO/TC199. We started the research for developing international safety standards, for example, vision-based protective devices and electronic safety control circuit module based on fail safe technology. Furthermore, in the cooperation with **Asia-Pacific** countries, we are pushing researches and making efforts to propose the international safety standards to ISO and IEC.

The following is a short history of the safety machinery standards in Japan and Europe.

- 1989 (Europe) EC Machine directives
- 1990 (International) ISO/IEC guide 51: Safety Aspects - Guidelines for their inclusion in standards
- 1991 (Europe) EN292: Safety of Machinery - Basic concepts, general principle for design

- 1991 (International) ISO/TC199: Safety of Machinery
- 1992 (International) ISO/TR12100: Safety of Machinery - Basic concepts, general principle for design
- 1995 (International) TBT (Technical Barriers to Trade) agreement
- 1995 (Japan) Declaration to harmonize JIS (Japan Industrial Standard) with ISO, IEC within 5 years
- 1998 (Japan) TR B 0008, 0009 (corresponding to ISO/TR12100)
- 2001 (Japan) Guideline for comprehensive safety norm on Machinery (corresponding to ISO/TR12100) into effect by Ministry of Labor, Health and Welfare
- 2001 (Japan) Asia-Pacific Machinery Safety Seminar started every year (China, Korea, Thailand, Singapore, India, Philippines)
- 2001 (Japan) Research for developing International Safety Standards
  (1) Development of vision-based protective device
  (2) Electronic control circuit module
- 2003 (International) ISO12100: Safety of Machinery - Basic concepts, general principle for design
- 2004 (Japan) JS B 970 (corresponding to ISO12100)

4. CONCLUSION

As technological innovation emerges, we face always new challenges to dependable computing. This paper has reviewed researches as well as organizational activities currently conducted in Japan, noting their new characteristic and nature.

REFERENCES

Foster, I., Kessselman, S., Nick, J. M. and Tuecke, S., 2002, Grid Services for Distributed System Integration, Computers, *IEEE Computer*, Vol. 35, No. 6, pp. 37-46, June 2002.

Mishia, T and Akaike, T., 2003, PREGMA: A New Fault Tolerant Cluster Using COTS Components for Internet Services, *Transactions on Information and Systems, The Institute of Electronics, Information and Communication Engineers (IEICE)*, Vol. E86-D, No. 12, pp. 2517-2526, December 2003.

Mendelson, A. and Suri, A., 2000, Designing high-performance & reliable superscalar architecture - the out of order reliable superscalar (O3RS) approach; *Proc. IEEE/IFIP International Conference on Dependable Systems and Networks*, pp. 447-481, 2000.

Moskewicz, M. W., Madigan, C. F., Zhao, Y., Zhang, L, and Malik, S, 2001, Chaff: Engineering an efficient sat solver, *Proc. 39th Design Automation Conference*, 2001.

Mukaidono, M., 2002, The Map on Safety - Toward to establish a new overall discipline on safety, *Proc. 3rd International Forum on Safety Engineering and Science (IFSESIII)*, 2002. (See http://www.sys.cs.meiji.ac.jp/~masao/kouen/safetymandala.file/frame.htm.)

Sato, T., 2003, A Transparent and Transient Faults Tolerance Mechanism for Superscalar Processors, *Transactions on Information and Systems, IEICE*, Vol. E86-D, No. 12, pp. 2508-2516, December 2003.

Tohma, Y., 2003, Consideration of Fault Tolerance in Autonomic Computing Environment, *ibid*, 2503-2507.

Yokogawa, T., Tsuchiya, T., Nakamura, M., and Kikuno, T., 2003, Feature Interaction Detection by Bounded Model Checking, *ibid*, 2579-2587.

THE EVOLUTION OF DEPENDABLE COMPUTING AT THE UNIVERSITY OF ILLINOIS

R. K. Iyer, W. H. Sanders, J. H. Patel, Z. Kalbarczyk
Coordinated Science Laboratory and Electrical and Computer Engineering Dept.
University of Illinois at Urbana-Champaign, USA
{iyer, whs, patel, kalbar}@crhc.uiuc.edu

Abstract: The University of Illinois has been active in research in the dependable computing field for over 50 years. Fundamental ideas have been proposed and major contributions made by researchers at the University of Illinois in the areas of error detection and recovery, fault tolerance middleware, testing and diagnosis, experimental evaluation and benchmarking of system dependability, dependability modeling, and secure system design and validation. This paper traces the origins of these ideas and their development within the University of Illinois, as well as their influence upon research at other institutions, and outlines current research directions.

Key words: error detection and recovery, experimental evaluation of dependability, fault injection, dependability modeling, secure and survivable system design and validation.

1. INTRODUCTION

The University of Illinois, though nestled in cornfields far from any center of industry, has been surprisingly productive in the field of computers. The first electronic digital computer at the University was ORDVAC [92], built for the Ordnance Department and patterned after the machine developed at the Institute for Advanced Study, Princeton. One of the pioneers in the field of fault-tolerant computing was Professor S. Seshu, whose fundamental contributions to fault diagnosis and fault simulation laid the groundwork for continued research in the field. From those beginnings in the late 1950s and early 1960s, the research has continued at a strong pace at the University, where, at present, around 50 faculty and graduate students are active in the area.

Researchers at the University of Illinois have consistently contributed to the dependable computing community. Over the years they actively participated in primary symposiums on dependable systems, including the FTCS International Symposium on Fault-Tolerant Computing (now DSN, the International Conference on Dependable Systems and Networks), both by presentation of papers and by serving as program and general chairs. Program and general chairs who were at the University, or who have come from the University, include Professor Algirdas Avižienis (FTCS-1, 1971), Professor Gernot Metze (FTCS-2, 1972 and FTCS-4, 1974), Professor John Hayes (FTCS-7, 1977), Professor Jacob Abraham (FTCS-11, 1981 and FTCS-19, 1989), Professor Ravi Iyer (FTCS-19, 1989 and FTCS-25, 1995), Professor William H. Sanders (FTCS-29, 1999), and Dr. Zbigniew Kalbarczyk (DSN 2002).

We are delighted with this opportunity to participate in an event honoring Professor Algirdas Avižienis, a distinguished alumnus of the ECE Department of the University of Illinois and a founder of IFIP WG 10.4 and the Fault-Tolerant Computing Symposium.

2. EARLY COMPUTERS

When ILLIAC 1 (essentially a duplicate of ORDVAC) and ILLIAC II were built at the University of Illinois in the 1950s, fault diagnosis consisted of running a battery of programs that exercised different sections of the machine. These test programs typically compared answers computed two different ways (essentially emulating hardware multiplication in software) or tended to stress what was suspected to be a vulnerable part (e.g., punch and subsequently read a continuous stream of characters on paper tape). In ILLIAC I, a vacuum tube computer (about 2,500 tubes, consuming 35 KW), the maintenance engineers found it useful to vary supply and heater voltages by some margins, to tap tubes and chassis with a small plastic mallet while the test programs were running, and to use only replacement tubes that had been aged at least 100 hours. Special tests were used for the electrostatic *Williams-tube* memory to determine the *Read-Around Ratio* (RAR) for the day, i.e., the number of times a cell's neighbors could be bombarded between refreshes without altering the cell's contents. An RAR of 300 was considered pretty good [156]. By present-day standards, this approach was very primitive; no attempt was made to model faults systematically or to evaluate precisely which segments of the machine were covered by the tests. Yet the routine, preventive, marginal testing maintenance approach and the clinical experience of the maintenance engineers, coupled with the healthy skepticism of the users who didn't completely trust either their numerical methods or the computer, resulted in a highly reliable operation. Of course, the equivalent of the entire ILLIAC I, including its 1024-word memory, could now be put on one IC chip.

The approach to testing in ILLIAC II, a discrete-component transistor machine put in service in 1961, was quite similar. However, to simplify fault diagnosis, the arithmetic unit's control (involving the equivalent of about 100 flipflops) had been designed to operate asynchronously, using essentially a double handshake for each control signal and its acknowledgement. The basic idea came from the theory of speed-independent circuits developed at the University of Illinois [93]. A large percentage of failures would, therefore, simply cause the control to wait for the next step of the handshake sequence; the missing step could easily be identified from the indicator lights on the flipflops. By contrast, the logic for the lookahead control did not use handshaking and exhibited some failures that were extremely difficult to trace. (Incidentally, a subtle design bug in the arithmetic unit, (-2) * (-2) giving (-4), escaped detection by the tests using pseudo-random operands but was caught after about nine months by a numerical double-check built into a user's program.) Note again that no attempt was made to model faults systematically, although the handshake mechanism used in the ALU control exhibited the basic idea of what is now called *self-checking operation*.

3. TESTING AND DIAGNOSIS

3.1 Fault simulation and automatic test generation

In the early 1960s, S. Seshu [134], [135], [136] developed the *Sequential Analyzer*, which included a set of programs that can generate fault simulation data (for single, logical, stuck-line faults) for a given logic circuit and a given test sequence and also has the ability to generate test sequences for combinational as well as sequential circuits. Although these test sequences usually were not minimal, they were generated automatically. The Sequential Analyzer was applied directly, but on a limited scale, at Bell Telephone Laboratories to check for design errors in IC designs prior to production, to generate test sequences that could be incorporated into factory test equipment, and to improve diagnosis procedures for the No. 1 Electronic Switching System (ESS-1). It was also used extensively at the University of Illinois to study computer self-diagnosis when an unduplicated processor was performing checkout and diagnosis of itself [88], [90]. Again, this self-diagnosis procedure relied on the idea that a processor fault could cause the processor to stop prematurely. Fault simulators were soon available commercially. Chang, Manning, and Metze produced, as a tribute to Seshu, what is probably the first book devoted entirely to digital fault diagnosis

[20]. Marlett went on to write the first successful commercial software for automatic test generation in sequential circuits [89].

In the 1980s research continued on fault simulation and automatic test pattern generation (ATPG). Cheng completed his Ph.D. at Illinois under Patel and went on to produce the sequential circuit ATPG at AT&T Bell Labs [25]. Cheng later launched a start-up company (Check Logic Inc.) to produce commercial ATPG and fault simulation tools. Check Logic was later acquired by Mentor Graphics. Cheng's ATPG tools are still being offered by Mentor Graphics. Niermann, also a student of Patel, advanced the APTG and fault simulation algorithms even further [98]. Niermann and Patel launched Sunrise Test Systems in 1989 to productize the research tools from Illinois. Through subsequent acquisitions, Sunrise became a part of Synopsys Inc., which continues to offer these test tools and their derivatives. One of the most notable breakthroughs that came out of this research was a very fast, memory-efficient fault simulation algorithm, PROOFS [99]. The then-entrenched algorithm, Concurrent Fault Simulation [151], was replaced by PROOFS throughout academia and industry and is still the algorithm of choice for fault simulation of synchronous sequential circuits for simulating stuck-at faults and many other fault types. A number of researchers have used the PROOFS fault simulator for research in fault diagnosis, transient error propagation, and logic verification.

As the IC chip size grew, interconnect faults, such as opens and shorts, became far more dominant than transistor faults in the semiconductor manufacturing process. PROOFS was readily adapted to simulate resistive shorts in ICs [52], [114]. With the availability of accurate resistive bridge fault simulators, an ATPG for such faults was not far behind [37].

The late 1990s and beyond brought to the forefront the problem of test application time and test data volume in large scan-based circuits with close to a million flip-flops in scan. Research at Illinois on generating the smallest set of test vectors produced theoretical lower bounds as well as the vector set meeting these bounds in a majority of benchmark circuits [57]. However, reduction of vectors alone was not enough to bring down the test application time and data by large factors. Large reduction was achieved with a novel scan organization called the Illinois Scan Architecture [58], [61]. Illinois Scan is now in use in many large chips.

3.2 Fault models

Another area in which the research done at the University of Illinois proved to be seminal is fault representation [130], [131], [132]. Indistinguishable or dominated faults can easily be identified, a priori, from the network structure and be eliminated from further consideration. Other research in fault representation was carried out, primarily at Stanford University [91] and at Western Electric Company [148]. Further work by Hayes, Smith, and Metze at the University of Illinois concentrated on the analysis of multiple faults, including masking relationships [16], [60], and some surprising results concerning the undetectability of certain multiple faults, i.e., multiple redundancies that have no sub-redundancies [140] and extensions [138].

Detailed studies (by Banerjee and Abraham) at the transistor level indicated that the conventional stuck-at fault model is inadequate for modeling the effects of physical failures on MOS circuits [9]. Those studies were used to develop accurate, higher-level fault models for modules such as decoders and multiplexers, which include the effects of realistic physical failures. A new logical model, in the form of a multivalued algebra, has also been developed [11]. It can be used to model the effects of physical failures at the transistor level, since the model allows for strong interactions among all three terminals of a transistor. As interconnect became dominant in today's large multilayer chips, the focus shifted from transistor defects to interconnect defects, specifically bridges between signal lines in metal. As mentioned in the previous section, a number of fault simulation and ATPG tools were developed to target bridge faults [37], [52], [114].

3.3 Functional-level test generation

As complex chips such as memories and microprocessors began to be used widely in systems because of their increasing density and decreasing cost, the problem of testing these chips without the availability of information about their internal structure became acute. An interesting solution to this problem was initially obtained in the case of memories, for which a higher, functional-level fault model was developed; it was used as the basis for deriving tests. Thus, the initial fault model for memories included stuck bits in the memory as well as coupling between cells in a memory. An $O(n\log_2 n)$ algorithm, which will detect all the faults in the fault model, was developed by Thatte and Abraham [146]. This test generation algorithm was improved by Nair, Thatte, and Abraham [94] to one of complexity $O(n)$. The work was extended by others, including Suk and Reddy [145] at Iowa.

An extrapolation of the approach to testing memories, using only functional-level information, was used by Thatte and Abraham [147] to develop test generation procedures for microprocessors in a user environment. A general graph-theoretic model was developed at the register-transfer level to model any microprocessor using only information about its instruction set and the functions performed. A fault model was developed on a functional level, quite independent of the implementation details. These were used to generate test patterns for microprocessors. A fault simulation study on a real microprocessor showed extremely good fault coverage for tests developed using these procedures.

3.4 Testable design of regular structures

Techniques for deriving testable structures from high-level descriptions were studied in [1]. The generated structures in that case were cellular and interconnected in a tree structure, and a general algorithm to test those tree structures that grows only linearly with the size of the tree was developed.

In 1985, Cheng and Patel [27], [28], [29] developed a comprehensive theory of testing for multiple failures in iterative logic arrays. The theory provided the necessary and sufficient conditions for deriving small test sets and showed that testing for multiple faults required only slightly more effort than testing for single faults. Techniques for testing VLSI bit-serial processors and designing them for testability were also studied in [39].

3.5 Diagnosis and repair

The basic idea of computer self-diagnosis, posed (by Metze) in simplified form as a problem on the Electrical Engineering Ph.D. qualifying examination given in December 1965, led to abstract questions of mutual diagnosis of several computers; those questions were collectively known as the Connection Assignment Problem [109]. That study created an enormous amount of interest, and systems that use different fault models, more general test outcomes, other measures of diagnosability, probabilistic fault diagnosis, and diagnosis of intermittent faults are still being investigated at several different institutions. A survey paper [50] lists 26 derived papers. The idea of not having a global supervisor that detects failures and removes failed units was investigated in [3], in which a new technique for distributed systems, called *roving diagnosis*, was presented.

Diagnosis and repair became important in improving the yield of rectangular arrays of logic with spare rows and columns. Such arrays are common in processor arrays, PLAs, and static and dynamic random access memory chips (RAMs). Fuchs developed a graph theoretic model of such arrays to represent the relationship between faults and spares [78]. The model was used to improve the yield of RAMs [21]. Following that work, many others have published work on RAM yield improvement. In addition to RAMs, these methods are also in use for large cache memories in present-day microprocessors.

Logic diagnosis of defective chips became important in the 1990s as the chips began to have multi-millions of logic gates. Traditional methods of using full fault dictionaries were running into trouble from the explosive growth in the size of the dictionaries. The problem of size was first addressed at Illinois by Fuchs in collaboration with Intel Corp. [119]. Fuchs continued his work on diagnosis with many of his Ph.D. students [14], [59]. Much of that work is used today by semiconductor manufacturers for failure analysis of defective chips.

4. ERROR DETECTION AND RECOVERY

4.1 Self-checking circuits

Self-diagnosis concepts, coupled with the earlier, fundamental results on "dynamically checked computers" by Carter and Schneider [15], led to the formulation of Totally Self-Checking (TSC) circuits by Anderson and Metze [5], [6]. A TSC circuit uses inputs and outputs that are encoded in a suitable code, together with a TSC checker that indicates whether the output is a code word or a non-code word. TSC circuits satisfy the following properties: (1) only code word inputs are needed to diagram the circuit completely (self-checking property), and (2) no fault causes the circuit to output an incorrect code word, i.e., the output is either the correct code word or is an incorrect, non-code word (fault-secure property). Actually, these requirements can be relaxed somewhat for strongly fault-secure networks, which are a larger class of networks that achieve the totally self-checking goal [139], [141]. The main advantages of TSC circuits are that transient errors are either caught or have no effect, that the outputs can be trusted as long as the checkers indicate no error (i.e., that erroneous information is not propagated), and that the circuit diagnoses itself with normally occurring inputs. However, since the normally occurring inputs do not necessarily cycle through the inputs required for a complete test, the circuit nevertheless has to be taken out of service periodically for testing. It should also be mentioned that the problem of finding a code whose error protection capabilities match the error-generation capabilities of the logic is non-trivial (e.g., [48]). TSC research has also led to numerous extensions at other institutions, including Bell Telephone Laboratories, Stanford University, USC, and the University of Iowa, among others. The strongly fault-secure concept has also been adapted and extended, for example, by Jansch and Courtois [68].

4.2 Time redundancy

The use of time redundancy for checking errors in hardware gained renewed attention in a series of papers from Illinois starting in the late 1970s. The papers dealt with a variety of techniques and circuits. The first in a series of these results was a report on the fault detection capabilities of alternating logic in circuits by Reynolds and Metze [118]. The alternating logic used circuits, which were arranged to be functionally self-dual. Conditions were presented that, if satisfied by a circuit, guaranteed the detection of errors due to single stuck-at faults. The paper also discussed the application of alternating logic and sequential logic.

A method of error detection called *Recomputing with Shifted Operands (RESO)* was proposed and analyzed for arithmetic and logic units (ALU) by Patel and Fung [105]. That was the first time that a unified method was used for both arithmetic and logic operations. That paper also differed from the earlier papers on self-checking logic in that it assumed a far more general fault model, which was suitable for the emerging VLSI circuits. Depending on the number of shifts used for the recomputed step, a variable amount of fault coverage was provided. For example, if k shifts were used in an adder, then any $(k - 1)$ consecutive failed cells would be covered, although the cells may fail in any arbitrary way. The method of RESO was then applied to more complex circuits of multiply and divide arrays [106]. The method was extended to arbitrary one-dimensional iterative logic arrays [26]. Variants of RESO were also used for error correction in arithmetic operations [79] and data transmission [108].

4.3 Memory error detection and recovery

Abraham, Davidson, and Patel developed a new memory system design for tolerating errors due to single-event radiation upsets [2]. The design used coding, control duplication, and scrubbing to tolerate soft errors from single-event upsets, and had much lower cost than a straightforward application of redundancy. An analytical model for reliability of memory with scrubbing was also developed, and is now widely used in industry [121].

4.4 Application-aware techniques

The field of ***control-flow checking*** has been the focus of intense research over the last two decades and resulted in a number of hardware- and/or software-based schemes. Most of the existing solutions, however, are not preemptive in nature, i.e., often the system crashes before any error detection is triggered. PECOS (Preemptive Control Signatures) techniques developed by Bagchi and Iyer enable preemptive detection of errors in the execution flow of an application [7], [8]. The strengths of the technique are that (1) it is preemptive, i.e., the detection happens before a branch/jump is taken, and (2) it significantly reduces events of silent data corruption. PECOS was applied and evaluated on a call-processing application. Fault/error injection results show that use of PECOS eliminates silent data corruptions and application hangs, and the crash incidences of the entire call-processing application are reduced by almost three times. A generalization of preemptive checking is instruction checking, which is a focus of current work [95].

Data audits are traditionally used in the telecommunications industry and implement a broad range of custom and ad hoc application-level techniques for detecting and recovering from errors in a switching environment. In [8] Liu, Kalbarczyk, and Iyer presented design, implementation, and assessment of a dependability framework for a call-processing environment in a digital mobile telephone network controller. The framework contains a data audit subsystem to maintain the structural and semantic integrity of the database. The fault-injection-based evaluation of the proposed solution indicates that the data audit detects 85% of the errors and significantly reduces the incidence of escaped errors.

The semantic of application programs usually exhibits instruction-level parallelism, which can be exploited in a super-scalar architecture for increasing performance. However, there is a limit to this parallelism due to dependency between instructions, which forces the processor to execute the dependent instructions in separate cycles. For example, one instruction may use the result produced by a previous instruction as its operand. Failure of the processor to execute the instructions in the correct sequence may adversely affect the output of the program and therefore should be considered an error. ***Instruction sequence checking*** verifies (through monitoring the issue and execution of the instructions in the pipeline at runtime) whether a sequence of dependent instructions is executed in the correct order.

4.5 Checkpointing and recovery

Deployment of distributed applications supporting critical services, e.g., banking, aircraft control, or e-commerce, created a need for efficient error recovery mechanisms and algorithms. In this context an important research area, led by Fuchs and his students Wang, Alewine, and Neves, was the development of novel checkpointing and rollback recovery strategies.

Independent checkpointing for parallel and distributed systems allows maximum process autonomy, but suffers from possible domino effects (processes have to roll back an unbounded number of times as they attempt to find a consistent global state for recovery) and storage space overhead for maintaining multiple checkpoints and message logs. In [155] it was shown that transformation and decomposition can be successfully applied to the problem of efficiently identifying all discardable message logs to achieve optimal garbage collection, and hence optimize the space overhead and improve performance of checkpointing schemes.

Another research avenue pursued by Fuchs focused on investigation of the applicability of a compiler-assisted multiple instructions rollback scheme (a technique developed for recovery from transient processor failures) to aid in speculative execution repair. The work took advantage of the fact that many problems encountered during recovery from branch misprediction or from instruction re-execution due to exceptions in speculative execution architecture are similar to those encountered during multiple instructions rollback. Consequently, extensions to the compiler-assisted scheme were added to support branch and exception repair [4].

In subsequent work Neves and Fuchs [96] developed a new low-overhead coordinated checkpoint protocol for long-running parallel applications and high-availability applications. The protocol uses time to avoid all types of direct coordination (e.g., message exchanges and message tagging), reducing the overheads to almost a minimum. To ensure that rapid recoveries can be attained, the protocol guarantees small checkpoint latencies. The protocol was implemented and tested on a cluster of workstations, and the results show very small overhead. In [97] the RENEW toolset for rapid development and testing of checkpoint protocols with standard benchmarks was proposed.

4.6 Algorithm-based fault tolerance

An exciting new direction in the design of fault-tolerant systems was started when Huang and Abraham [63] developed matrix encoding schemes for detecting and correcting errors when matrix operations are performed using processor arrays. The schemes were generalized to the new system-level method of achieving high reliability called *algorithm-based fault tolerance (ABFT)*. The technique encodes data at a high level, and algorithms are designed to operate on the encoded data and produce encoded output data. The computation tasks within the algorithm are appropriately distributed among multiple computation units so that failure of one of the units affects only a portion of the output data, enabling the correct data to be recovered from the encoding [64]. This result was applied to matrix operations using multiple processor arrays. The work was generalized to linear arrays by Jou and Abraham [71] and also extended to Laplace equation solvers [65], as well as FFT networks [72]. [10] developed fault tolerance techniques for three powerful paradigms: the multiplex, the recursive combination, and the multiplex/demultiplex paradigms. In the proposed approach, processors that are idle during normal computation are used to check the results of other processors. In later work, a general theory of algorithm-based fault tolerance was developed that gives bounds on the processor and time overhead in the ABFT scheme [12]. This approach seems to be ideal for low-cost fault tolerance for special-purpose computations, including a wide class of signal-processing applications. The work has been extended in [85]. ABFT has been widely explored by a large number of researchers, more recently as part of the Remote Exploration and Experimentation (REE) program at the Jet Propulsion Laboratory [55].

5. MIDDLEWARE AND HARDWARE SUPPORT FOR FAULT TOLERANCE AND SECURITY

In the 1990s, the high cost of custom hardware solutions, plus the availability of inexpensive COTS hardware, led to development of methods for providing dependability via software middleware. In this spirit, several

University of Illinois projects were initiated that jointly provide reliability and security services. The solution space ranges from purely software approaches (ARMORs [71], AQuA [116], and ITUA [35]) to more recent work on hardware-based (or processor-level) support for error detection, masking of security vulnerabilities, and recovery under one umbrella, in a uniform, low-overhead manner (RSE [95]).

5.1 ARMOR high availability and security infrastructure

The ARMOR approach, proposed by Whisnant, Kalbarczyk, and Iyer, relies on a network of self-checking reconfigurable software modules, which collectively provide high availability and security to applications [71], [158]. The ARMOR infrastructure (consisting of multiple ARMOR processes) is designed to manage redundant resources across interconnected nodes, to foil security threats, to detect errors in both the user applications and the infrastructure components, and to recover quickly from failures when they occur. Because of the flexible ARMOR infrastructure, security protection and detection and recovery services can be added or removed depending on application requirements. The modular design ensures that there is a clear upgrade path through which additional protection capabilities can be added to the ARMOR infrastructure in the future. The architecture has been demonstrated and evaluated (using fault injection) on several real-world applications in the areas of telecommunication (e.g., call processing) [154] and scientific distributed computing (JPL-NAS Mars Rover application) [157].

5.2 A processor-level framework for high dependability and security

A middleware is effective in handling errors as long as they propagate and manifest at that level. Often, however, propagating lower-level errors crash the system (i.e., never reach the middleware level) or cause silent data corruption (i.e., generate latent errors) before being detected. Understanding of that fact, together with an increasing rate of soft errors due to CMOS scaling, led to renewed interest in supporting hardware/processor-based techniques. Recently, Nakka, Kalbarczyk, and Iyer proposed the Reliability and Security Engine (RSE), a hardware-level framework implemented as an integral part of a modern microprocessor and providing application-aware reliability and security support in the form of customizable hardware modules [95]. The detection mechanisms investigated include (1) the Memory Layout Randomization (MLR) Module, which randomizes the memory layout of a process in order to foil attackers who assume a fixed system layout, (2) the Data Dependency Tracking (DDT) Module, which tracks the dependencies among threads of a process and maintains checkpoints of shared memory pages in order to roll back the threads when an offending (potentially malicious) thread is terminated, and (3) the Instruction Checker Module (ICM), which checks an instruction for its validity or the control flow of the program just as the instruction enters the pipeline for execution. Performance simulations for the studied modules indicate low overhead of the proposed solutions.

5.3 AQuA and ITUA

At the network level, three factors have significantly lowered the ability to withstand hostile attacks on critical networked systems: (1) an economic mandate to construct systems with more cost-effective commercial off-the-shelf (COTS) solutions, thereby accepting known and unknown limitations; (2) the increasingly sophisticated nature of commonly available technologies, capable of mounting more complex and sustained attack patterns against these systems; and (3) the fact that systems are increasingly inter-networked and need to remain open to meet interoperability goals. The first of these factors makes it more likely that some systems will be compromised and corrupted by adversaries. The second makes it likely that preplanned, coordinated, and sustained attacks will be mounted against high-value systems. The third implies that effects of successful intrusion will be compounded as multiple systems are impacted. All of these factors have led to recent work in intrusion-tolerant networked systems.

Significant work on designing, implementing, and validating fault- and intrusion-tolerant systems has gone on at the University of Illinois, together with its industrial partners (most notably BBN Technologies) since the late 1990s. In the AQuA project [116], Sanders and his group (including Research Programmer M. Seri) developed the concept of a *property gateway*, which provides adaptation between different types of replication, each providing a different performance/fault-tolerance trade-off, depending on a high-level dependability specification [120],[133]. J. Ren's Ph.D. thesis work [117],[115], completed in 2001, documented much of the AQuA work. In addition to providing differing levels of dependability, AQuA provided tunable consistency and soft real-time performance using algorithms developed by S. Krishnamurthy as part of her Ph.D. thesis [77],[76].

In the ITUA project [35],[104], the AQuA approach was extended to include malicious attacks by combining redundancy management techniques (specifically countering faults resulting from a partially successful attack) and diversity with techniques that produce unpredictable (to the attacker) and variable responses to complicate the ability to preplan a coordinated attack. In the process, new Byzantine algorithms were developed [113],[112] that tolerate the characteristic Byzantine faults resulting from a class of staged, coordinated intrusions.

6. DEPENDABILITY MODELING

6.1 UltraSAN

When Sanders joined the University of Illinois in 1994 from the University of Arizona, he brought with him a team of people working on dependability modeling. Sanders's and his team's work in the early and mid-1990s was implemented in a software tool called *UltraSAN* [129].

UltraSAN was a software package for model-based evaluation of systems represented as stochastic activity networks (SANs) [127]. The model specification process in *UltraSAN* was carried out in a hierarchical fashion. Subsystems, specified as SANs, could be replicated and joined together in a composed model [126] using the "SAN-based reward models" that Sanders had introduced in his Ph.D. thesis in 1988 [122]. On top of the composed model, reward structures could be used to define performance, dependability, and performability measures [128]. To solve a specified model, *UltraSAN* provided analytic solvers [150] (developed by J. Tvedt) as well as discrete-event simulators (developed by R. Friere) [125]. When analytic solvers were used, the state space of the underlying stochastic process was first generated through reduced base model construction [126]. Using that approach, state-space lumping was automatically performed when SANs were replicated in the composed model, thus reducing the state-space size for the models. The models that could be solved analytically by *UltraSAN* included Markov models as well as certain models with deterministic delays [87],[86], which were developed by L. Malhis as part of his Ph.D work. Moreover, an importance sampling component, developed by D. Obal as part of his Master's thesis, was provided to speed up the simulation [101]. *UltraSAN* also contained novel methods for computing the distribution of reward accumulated in a finite interval developed by A. Qureshi as part of his Ph.D thesis [111],[110]. A. van Moorsel developed the theory for, and implemented, adaptive uniformization in *UltraSAN*, which significantly reduces the time to obtain a transient solution of many stiff Markov chains, particularly those that arise in dependability evaluation [152],[153]. Finally, although never implemented in *UltraSAN*, D. Obal significantly extended these methods in his Ph.D. thesis to the more general "graph"-based composed models [100] and path-based reward structures [102],[103].

UltraSAN was licensed a large number of sites for commercial use, and many universities for teaching and research. For example, it was used for many telecommunications applications at Motorola and was the primary dependability evaluation tool in the Iridium project. It has also been used to design disk drive controllers and system-managed storage software at IBM, and ATM and frame-relay networks at US West and Bellcore, among other applications.

6.2 Möbius

By the mid 1990s, it became clear that while the *UltraSAN* approach was successful at evaluating the dependability and performance of many systems, further work was needed to develop performance/dependability modeling frameworks and software environments that could predict the performance of complete networked computing systems, accounting for all system components, including the application itself, the operating system, and the underlying computing and communication hardware.

Ultimately, the experiences with *UltraSAN* showed that a framework should provide a method by which multiple, heterogeneous models can be composed together, each representing a different software or hardware module, component, or aspect of the system. The composition techniques developed should permit models to interact with one another by sharing state, events, or results, and should be scalable. A framework should also support multiple modeling languages (i.e., formalisms), as well as methods to combine models at different levels of resolution. Furthermore, a framework should support multiple model solution methods, including both simulation and analysis, that are efficient. Finally, a framework should be extensible, in the sense that it should be possible to add, with reasonably little effort, new modeling formalisms, composition and connection methods, and model solution techniques.

Those goals were realized in the performance/dependability/security evaluation framework developed at the University of Illinois known as *Möbius* [123],[41]. The first version of Möbius was released in 2001; T. Courtney coordinated the development of this and future versions. The fundamental ideas concerning the Möbius framework were developed by D. Deavours as part of his Ph.D. thesis [43],[42],[40]. Although Möbius was originally developed for studying the reliability, availability, and performance of computer and network systems, its use has expanded rapidly. It is now used for a broad range of discrete-event systems, from biochemical reactions within genes to the effects of malicious attackers on secure computer systems, in addition to the original applications.

That broad range of use is possible because of the flexibility found in Möbius, which comes from its support of multiple high-level modeling formalisms (e.g., Modest [13] and PEPA [34]) and multiple solution techniques. This flexibility allows users to represent their systems in modeling languages appropriate to their problem domains, and then accurately and efficiently solve the systems using the solution techniques best suited to the systems' size and complexity. Time- and space-efficient distributed discrete-event simulation and numerical solution are both supported.

The various components of the Möbius tool are divided into two categories: model specification components and model solution components. The Möbius tool is designed so that new formalisms can be implemented and employed if they adhere to the model-level AFI, as specified in a paper by Deavours and Sanders [43]. The model AFI views models as consisting of two sets of components: state variables, which store model state, and actions, which change model state. This design allows new model formalisms and editors to be incorporated without modification of the existing code, supporting the extensibility of the Möbius tool. Similarly, Derisavi, Kemper, Sanders, and Courtney [46] developed a state-level AFI to cleanly separate numerical solution algorithms from a state-level model representation. A. Christensen developed a connection method by which models could exchange results, in an ordered or fixed-point fashion, to build large system models [32].

Models can be solved, through interface to the state-level AFI, either analytically/numerically or by simulation. Innovative data structures, developed by S. Derisavi as part of his Ph.D work and based on multi-valued decision diagrams, are used to represent system models with tens of millions of states compactly [44],[45]. From each model, C++ source code is generated and compiled, and the object files are linked together to form a library archive [33]. The libraries are linked together along with the Möbius base libraries to form the executable for the solver. Most recently, D. Daly has developed methods for constructing approximate models that have smaller state spaces but bound the error induced by the state space reduction using stochastic ordering arguments [38], and V. Lam has developed path-based methods to solve for instant-of-time variables that do not require explicit representation of either a state-transition-rate matrix or solution vector [80].

Möbius has been distributed widely to other academic and industrial sites. There are now approximately 130 academic and industrial licensees of Möbius, and Illinois is now collaborating with the University of Twente in The Netherlands, Dortmund University, TU Dresden, and the Universität der Bundeswehr München in Germany, and the University of Florence in Italy to further enhance Möbius.

6.3 Depend

In the early 1990s Goswami and Iyer initiated the DEPEND project to develop a framework for designing dependable systems [51]. DEPEND is a simulation-based environment that supports the design of systems for fault tolerance and high availability. It takes as inputs both VHDL and C++ system description and produces as output dependability characteristics including fault coverage, availability, and performance. At the core of DEPEND are simulation engines supported by a fault injector, a set of fault dictionaries, and component libraries. The fault injector provides mechanisms to inject faults. The component libraries contain model-building blocks with detailed functional descriptions and characteristics. The fault dictionaries embody possible fault effects of the given fault types, devices, and circuits. DEPEND was developed with DARPA support and it was licensed to several companies and employed to simulate a number of industrial systems, including Integrity S2 from Tandem (now a division of HP).

7. EXPERIMENTAL EVALUATION / BENCHMARKING OF SYSTEM DEPENDABILITY

7.1 Fault injection

Fault injection has been used since the early days of experimental assessment of dependable systems as a mechanism to evaluate computing systems. At Illinois, research on fault/error injection was driven by failure data analysis of real systems. Tsai and Iyer employed stress-based fault injection to evaluate one of the first UNIX-based fault-tolerant systems developed by Tandem (now a division of HP). The stress-based approach ensures fault/error injection to system components when they are heavily used (i.e., highly stressed) [149]. This allowed meaningful comparison of systems and was an important step towards benchmarking. In order to facilitate automated fault/error injection experiments, NFTAPE, a sophisticated environment for software-implemented automated fault/error injection experiments, was developed [144], [143].

In more recent studies Gu, Kalbarczyk, and Iyer [53], [54] applied error injection to characterize Linux kernel behavior under errors that impact kernel code, kernel data, kernel stack, and processor system registers, and to provide an insight on how processor hardware architecture (instruction set architecture and register set) impacts kernel behavior in the presence of errors. Two target Linux-2.4.22 systems were used: the Intel Pentium 4 (P4) running RedHat Linux 9.0 and the Motorola PowerPC (G4) running YellowDog Linux 3.0. The study found, for example, that (1) the activation of errors is generally similar for both processors, but that the manifestation percentages are about twice as high for the Pentium 4, (2) less-compact fixed 32-bit data and stack access makes the G4 platform less sensitive to errors, and (3) the most severe crashes (those that require a complete reformatting of the file system on the disk) are caused by reversing the condition of a branch instruction. Since the recovery from such failures may take tens of minutes, those failures have a profound impact on availability.

An important research avenue pursued by Xu, Kalbarczyk, and Iyer is the exploration of the possibility of security violations due to errors. In [159] it was shown that naturally occurring hardware errors can cause security vulnerabilities in network applications such as an *FTP* (file transfer protocol) and *SSH* (secure shell). As a result, relatively passive but malicious users can exploit the vulnerabilities. While the likelihood of such events is small, considering the large number of systems operating in the field, the probability of such vulnerabilities cannot be neglected. In the following study, Chen, another student of Iyer, employed fault/error injection to experimentally evaluate and model the error-caused security vulnerabilities and the resulting security violations on two Linux kernel-based firewall facilities (*IPChains* and *Netfilter*) [22]. Using data on field failures, data from the error injection experiments, and system performance parameters such as processor cache miss and replacement rates, a SAN (Stochastic Activity Network) model was developed and simulated to predict the mean time to security vulnerability and the duration of the window of vulnerability under realistic conditions. The results indicate that the error-caused vulnerabilities can be a non-negligible source of security violations.

In parallel with that work, members of Sanders's group, which included R. Chandra, M. Cukier, D. Henke, K. Joshi, R. Lefever, and J. Pistole, worked to develop a new form of fault and attack injection for distributed systems in which the introduction of faults is triggered based on the global state of the system. In addition to developing the basic concepts, and supporting theorems related to global-state-based fault injection (GSBFI), they deployed Loki, a global-state-based fault injector [18],[36],[19],[17], and used it to experimentally evaluate two large-scale distributed systems. In particular, in [70] K. Joshi used Loki to assess the unavailability induced by a group membership protocol in Ensemble, a widely used group communication system. R. Lefever employed Loki to evaluate the effects of correlated network partitions on Coda, a popular distributed file system [82].

There are two benefits of using GSBFI. The first is the ability to validate a system when its fault models rely on states that are hard to target either because they are short-lived or because they occur infrequently. Examples include correlated faults, stress-based faults, and malicious faults. The second benefit is the ability to perform evaluations beyond the scope of fault forecasting. GSBFI can be used to estimate a broad range of conditional measures for use in system models to compute a variety of unconditional performance and dependability measures. Efforts are currently underway to apply GSBFI to the experimental evaluation of the survivability of systems by systematically injecting the effects of cyber attacks in a correlated manner.

7.2 Operational life monitoring and failure data analysis

The use of measured data to study failures in a real use environment has been the focus of active research for quite some time. Rossetti and Iyer [66] used measured data to study the effect of increasing workload on hardware and software fault tolerance. Analysis showed that the probability of a CPU-related error increases nonlinearly with increasing workload. The resulting increase in the error probability can be 50 to 100 times more than that at a low workload. Those results show that reliability models cannot be considered representative unless the system workload environment is taken into account, since the gain in performance is more than offset by degradation in reliability. Similar results relating to operating system reliability appeared in [67]. A novel experiment to obtain, for the first time, distributions of error latency was performed by Chillarege and Iyer [31]. The extension of that work to the study of various fault models appears in [30].

More recent studies by Kalyanakrishnam, Xu, Kalbarczyk, and Iyer focused on error and failure analysis of a LAN of Windows NT-based servers [75], [161] and reliability of Internet hosts [74] with particular focus on the importance of the user's perspective in assessing the systems. For example, while the measured availability of the LAN of Windows-based mail servers is 99%, the user-perceived availability is only 92% [75]. The study on Internet hosts' reliability showed that on average, a host remained unavailable to the user for 6.5 hours (during the 40-day experiment, i.e., approx. 2.5 days per year), which is an availability of about 99%. However, closer analysis of data revealed that an average (or mean value) is not always an adequate measure, because it may hide the reality experienced by the user. For example, a more detailed data breakdown revealed that (1) 45% of hosts had a total downtime ranging from 1,000 seconds to 7,000 seconds, and a median downtime of nearly an hour (i.e, approximately 9.5 hours per year), (2) 49% of hosts had a total downtime ranging from 7,000 seconds to 70,000 seconds and a median downtime of about 4.5 hours (i.e., approximately 40 hours per year), and (3) 6% of hosts had a total downtime ranging from 90,000 seconds to 120,000 seconds, and a median downtime of about 2.2 days (i.e., approx. 20 days per year).

8. SECURE SYSTEM DESIGN AND VALIDATION: FROM DATA ANALYSIS TO PROTECTION AND TOLERANCE MECHANISMS

Challenged by the increasing number and severity of malicious attacks, security has become an issue of primary importance in designing dependable systems. There is no better way to understand the security characteristics of computer systems than by direct measurement and analysis.

8.1 Measurement-driven security vulnerability analysis

In a seminal work, Chen, Kalbarczyk, and Iyer employed a combination of an in-depth analysis of real data on security vulnerabilities and a focused source-code examination to develop a finite state machine (FSM) model to depict and reason about the process of exploiting vulnerabilities and to extract logic predicates that need to be met to ensure vulnerability-free system implementation [24]. In the FSM approach, each predicate is represented as a primitive FSM (*pFSM*), and multiple pFSMs are combined to develop FSM models of vulnerable operations and possible exploitations. The proposed FSM methodology is demonstrated by analysis of several types of vulnerabilities reported in the *Bugtraq* [62] database: stack buffer overflow, integer overflow, heap overflow, file race condition, and format string vulnerabilities, which constitute 22% of all vulnerabilities in the database. For the studied vulnerabilities, three types of pFSMs were identified that can be used to analyze operations involved in exploitation of vulnerabilities and to identify the security checks to be performed at the elementary activity level.

A practical demonstration of the usefulness of the approach was the discovery of a new heap overflow vulnerability now published in *Bugtraq* (ID 6255). The discovery was made during construction of the FSM model for another known vulnerability of the *null HTTPD* application (a multithreaded web server for Linux and Windows platforms).

8.2 Vulnerability avoidance

The low-level analysis of severe security vulnerabilities indicates that a significant number of vulnerabilities are caused by programmers' improper use of library functions. For example, omitting buffer size checking before calling string manipulation functions, such as *strcpy* and *strcat*, causes many buffer overflow vulnerabilities. A common characteristic of many of these vulnerabilities is pointer taintedness. A pointer is tainted if a user input can directly or indirectly be used as a pointer value. Pointer taintedness that leads to vulnerabilities usually occurs as a consequence of low-level memory writes, typically hidden from the high-level code. Hence, a memory model is necessary for reasoning about pointer taintedness. In [23] the memory model is formally defined and applied to reasoning about pointer taintedness in commonly used library functions.

Reasoning about pointer taintedness makes it possible to extract security preconditions, which either correspond to already known vulnerability scenarios (e.g., format string vulnerability and heap corruption) or indicate the possibility of function invocation scenarios that may expose new vulnerabilities. This work will progress through (1) an investigation of approaches that reduce the amount of human intervention in the theorem-proving tasks using pointer-analysis techniques and heuristics, and (2) the exploration of the possibility of incorporating this technique into compiler-based static checking tools.

8.3 Protection mechanisms against security attacks

FSM-based analysis of vulnerabilities also indicates that security problems, such as buffer overflow, format string, integer overflow, and double-freeing of a heap buffer lead to Unauthorized Control Information Tampering (UCIT) in a target program. An additional survey (other than *Bugtraq*) of the 109 CERT security advisories issued over the past four years shows that UCIT vulnerabilities account for nearly 60% of all the CERT advisories. Transparent Runtime Randomization (TRR), proposed by Xu, Kalbarczyk, and Iyer, is a generalized approach to protect systems against a wide range of security attacks that exploit UCIT vulnerabilities [160]. The TRR technique dynamically and randomly relocates a program's stack, heap, shared libraries, and parts of its runtime control data structures inside the application memory address space. If a program's memory layout is different each time it runs, it foils the attacker's assumptions about the memory layout of the vulnerable program and makes the determination of critical address values difficult if not impossible. An incorrect address value for a critical memory element causes the target application to crash. Although a crash may not be desirable from reliability and availability perspectives, in the security domain, a crash is an acceptable option for the program being hijacked. TRR is implemented by changing the Linux dynamic program loader; hence, it is transparent to applications. TRR incurs less than 9% program startup overhead and no runtime overhead.

8.4 DPASA: Designing protection and adaptation into a survivability architecture

The AQuA and ITUA work, together with other work in intrusion-tolerant systems (e.g., [47],[49]) has suggested that it may be possible to build large-scale, networked intrusion-tolerant systems that can continue to provide specified services even when under sustained partially successful cyber attack. To test this hypothesis, the University of Illinois, together with partners at BBN, SRI, Draper Labs, Adventium Labs, and the University of Maryland, embarked upon a 2-year project called DPASA (Designing Protection and Adaptation into a Survivability Architecture) to design, implement, and validate a large-scale, intrusion-tolerant publish and subscribe system [142]. Team members from Illinois included A. Agbaria, T. Courtney, M. Ihde, J. Meyer (a consultant), W. Sanders, M. Seri, S.

Singh, and F. Stevens. The designed system was considered to be prototypical of many critical communication systems, and a good test of recently developed intrusion-tolerance techniques.

8.5 DPASA architecture

The publish and subscribe system developed consisted of multiple clients communicating with each other through a central core. Redundancy and diversity were used in the core, and the core consisted of four quadrants. Each quadrant was divided into three zones: the crumple zone, the operations zone, and the executive zone. The client-hosted components of the publish-subscribe middleware included a survivability delegate that intercepted the mission application's requests and managed communication with the core, including cryptographic manipulations, through DJM stubs. The crumple zone accommodated client-core communication via multiple access proxies which served as the first barrier between the core and clients after the isolation switch. The operational zone provided the PS&Q functionality and intrusion/fault detection mechanisms, such as the guardians. It contained several components, each with specific tasks. The PSQ component was responsible for performing publish, subscribe, and query operations requested by clients. The guardian and the correlator were responsible for performing intrusion detection in the core and IOs inside it. The downstream controller (DC) and the policy server (PS) components were responsible for specifying policies and forwarding control information to the autonomic distributed firewalls (ADF NICs) [107] installed on the hosts. Finally, the system manager (SM) of the Executive zone managed the core's actions.

The system also included intrusion detection system (IDS) [69] components for improving its survivability. The main components participating in the alert/response data flow were the IDS components: sensors, actuators, and local controllers (LC). IDS components were associated with many of the processing and communication components of the system. Sensors are dedicated to intrusion detection, actuators are mechanisms that carry out actions when commanded, and an LC is a control agent responsible for local survivability management functions.

8.6 DPASA architecture validation

A methodology for validating, in a quantitative manner, the survivability of the DPASA design was also developed. Efforts for quantitative validation of security have usually been based on formal methods [81], or have been informal, using "red teams" to try to compromise a system [84].

Probabilistic modeling has been receiving increasing attention as a mechanism to validate security [83], [124]. For example, work at Illinois by

Singh et al. [137] used probabilistic modeling to validate the ITUA intrusion-tolerant architecture, emphasizing the effects of intrusions on the system behavior and the ability of the intrusion-tolerant mechanisms to handle those effects, while using very simple assumptions about the discovery and exploitation of vulnerabilities by the attackers to achieve those intrusions. Shortly thereafter, Gupta et al. [56], in a paper resulting from two class projects in Sanders's graduate class, used a similar approach to evaluate the security and performance of several intrusion-tolerant server architectures. Probabilistic modeling is especially suited to intrusion-tolerant systems, since by definition, intrusion tolerance is a quantitative and probabilistic property of a system.

In the DPASA project, a probabilistic model was used to validate the system design, as documented in F. Stevens's Master's thesis [142]. The probabilistic model made use of an innovative attacker model. The attacker model had a sophisticated and detailed representation of various kinds of effects of intrusions on the behavior of system components (such as a variety of failure modes). It included a representation of the process of discovery of vulnerabilities (both in the operating system(s) and in the specific applications being used by the system) and their subsequent exploitation, and considered an aggressive spread of attacks through the system by taking into account the connectivity of the components of the system at both the infrastructure and the logical levels. Probabilistic modeling was used to compare different design configurations, allowing the designers of the system to make choices that maximized the intrusion tolerance provided by the system before they actually implemented the system. Lastly, the model was used to show that the system would meet a set of quantitative survivability requirements.

9. CONCLUDING REMARKS

The last 50 years have witnessed the introduction of multiple new ideas in dependable and secure computing and their development at the University of Illinois. With a strong commitment to this area of research by a large staff of researchers, we expect to see many more exciting results in the future. New research in application-aware error detection and recovery, fault tolerance middleware, benchmarking of system dependability, dependability modeling, and secure system design and validation continue to maintain Illinois's status as a leading center in fault-tolerant and secure computing research.

ACKNOWLEDGEMENTS

We would like to thank our past and current research sponsors for supporting this work, and our colleagues, both past and present, that also contributed to the research described herein. Our sponsors include the Gigascale Systems Research Center (GSRC/MARCO), the NSF (NSF CCR 99-02026, NSF CCR 00-86096 ITR, NSF ACI 0121658 ITR/AP, NSF EIA 99-75019, NSF INT 0233490, NSF CCR 0311616), MURI Grant N00014-01-1-0576, the Defense Advanced Research Projects Agency, the Jet Propulsion Laboratory, the Semiconductor Research Corporation, Motorola, and Pioneer Hybrid. We would also like to thank Ms. Jenny Applequist for her editorial assistance.

REFERENCES

[1] J. Abraham, D. Gajski, "Design of Testable Structures Defined by Simple Loops," *IEEE Trans. on Comp.*, C-30, 1981, pp. 875-884

[2] J. Abraham, E. Davidson, J. Patel, "Memory System Design for Tolerating Single-Event Upsets," *IEEE Trans. on Nuclear Science*, NS-30, No. 6, 1983, pp. 4339-4344.

[3] J. Abraham, G. Metze, "Roving Diagnosis for High-Performance Digital Systems," *Proc. Conf. on Information Sciences and Systems*, 1978, pp. 221-226.

[4] N. Alewine, K. Fuchs, W-M. Hwu, "Application of Compiler-Assisted Multiple Instruction Rollback Recovery to Speculative Execution," Technical Report CRHC-93-16, University of Illinois, 1993.

[5] D. Anderson, "Design of Self-Checking Digital Networks," Coordinated Science Laboratory Technical Report R527, University of Illinois, Urbana, Illinois, 1971.

[6] D. Anderson, G. Metze, "Design of Totally Self-Checking Circuits for m-out-of-n Codes," *IEEE Trans. on Comp.*, C-22, No. 3, 1973, pp. 263-269.

[7] S. Bagchi, "Hierarchical Error Detection in a SIFT Environment," Ph.D. Thesis, University of Illinois, 2000.

[8] S. Bagchi, Y. Liu, Z. Kalbarczyk, R. K. Iyer, Y. Levendel, L. Votta, "A Framework for Database Audit and Control Flow Checking for a Wireless Telephone Network Controller," *Proc. of Conf. on Dependable Systems and Networks, DSN'01*, July 2001, pp. 225-234.

[9] P. Banerjee, J. Abraham, "Characterization and Testing of Physical Failures in MOS Logic Circuits," *IEEE Design and Test*, 1, 1984, pp. 76-86

[10] P. Banerjee, J. Abraham, "Fault-Secure Algorithms for Multiple Processor Systems," *Proc. 11th Int. Symp. on Computer Architecture*, 1984, pp. 279-287.

[11] P. Banerjee, J. Abraham, "A Multivalued Algebra for Modeling Physical Failures in MOS VLSI Circuits," *IEEE Trans. on Computer-Aided Design*, CAD-4, No. 3, 1985, pp. 312-321.

[12] P. Banerjee, J. Abraham, "Bounds on Algorithm-Based Fault Tolerance in Multiple Processor Systems," *IEEE Trans. on Comp.*, C-35, No. 4, 1986, pp. 296-306.

[13] H. Bohnenkamp, T. Courtney, D. Daly, S. Derisavi, H. Hermanns, J.-P. Katoen, R. Klaren, V. V. Lam, W. H. Sanders, "On Integrating the Möbius and Modest Modeling Tools," *Proc. Int. Conf. on Dependable Systems and Networks*, San Francisco, CA, June 22-25, 2003, p. 671.

[14] V. Boppana, W. K. Fuchs, "Fault Dictionary Compaction by Output Sequence Removal," *Proc. IEEE/ACM Conf. Computer-Aided Design*, Nov. 1994, pp. 576-579.

[15] W. Carter, P. Schneider, "Design of Dynamically Checked Computers," *Proc. IFIP Congress 2*, 1968, pp. 878-883.
[16] C. Cha, "Multiple Fault Diagnosis in Combinational Networks," Coordinated Science Laboratory Technical Report R-650, University of Illinois, Urbana, Illinois, 1974.
[17] R. Chandra, M. Cukier, R. M. Lefever, W. H. Sanders, "Dynamic Node Management and Measure Estimation in a State-Driven Fault Injector," *Proc. 19th IEEE Symp. on Reliable Distributed Systems*, Nürnberg, Germany, October 16-18, 2000, pp. 248-257.
[18] R. Chandra, R. M. Lefever, M. Cukier, W. H. Sanders, "Loki: A State-Driven Fault Injector for Distributed Systems," *Proc. Int. Conf. on Dependable Systems and Networks (DSN-2000)*, New York, NY, June 25-28, 2000, pp. 237-242.
[19] R. Chandra, R. M. Lefever, K. Joshi, M. Cukier, W. H. Sanders, "A Global-State-Triggered Fault Injector for Distributed System Evaluation," *IEEE Trans. on Par. and Dist. Systems*, to appear.
[20] H. Chang, E. Manning, C. Metze, *Fault Diagnosis of Digital Systems*, Huntington, NY: Robert E. Krieger Publishing Company, 1970.
[21] M. Chang, W. Fuchs, J. Patel, "Diagnosis and Repair of Memory with Coupling Faults," *IEEE Trans. Comp.*, April 1989, pp. 493-500.
[22] S. Chen, J. Xu, Z. Kalbarczyk, R. K. Iyer, K. Whisnant, "Modeling and Evaluating the Security Threats of Transient Errors in Firewall Software," *Int. Journal on Performance Evaluation*, 56, March 2004, pp. 53-72.
[23] S. Chen, K. Pattabiraman, Z. Kalbarczyk, R. K. Iyer, "Formal Reasoning of Various Categories of Widely Exploited Security Vulnerabilities Using Pointer Taintedness Semantics," *Proc. 19th IFIP Int'l Information Security Conf. (SEC-2004)*, held as part of 18th IFIP World Computer Congress, August 2004.
[24] S. Chen, Z. Kalbarczyk, J. Xu, R. K. Iyer, "A Data-Driven Finite State Machine Model for Analyzing Security Vulnerabilities," *Proc. Int. Conf. on Dependable Systems and Networks, DSN'03*, June 2003, pp. 605-614.
[25] W. Cheng, "The BACK Algorithm for Sequential Test Generation," *Proc. IEEE Int. Conf. on Computer Design*, Oct 1988, pp. 66-69.
[26] W. Cheng, J. Patel, "Concurrent Error Detection in Iterative Logic Arrays," *Proc. 14th Int. Symp. on Fault-Tolerant Computing*, 1984, pp. 10-15.
[27] W. Cheng, J. Patel, "A Minimum Test Set for Multiple-Fault Detection in Ripple-Carry Adders," *Proc. Int. Conf. on Computer Design*, 1985, pp. 435-438.
[28] W. Cheng, J. Patel, "Multiple-Fault Detection in Iterative Logic Arrays," *Proc. Int. Test Conf.*, 1985, pp. 493-499.
[29] W. Cheng, J. Patel, "A Shortest Length Test Sequence for Sequential-Fault Detection in Ripple Carry Adders," *Proc. Int. Conf. on Computer-Aided Design*, 1985, pp. 71-73.
[30] R. Chillarege, R. K. Iyer, "Fault Latency in the Memory: An Experimental Study on VAX 11/780," *Proc. 16th Int. Symp. on Fault-Tolerant Computing*, 1986.
[31] R. Chillarege, R. K. Iyer, "The Effect of System Workload on Error Latency: An Experimental Study," *Proc. ACM SIGMETRICS Conf. on Measurement and Modeling of Computer Systems*, 1985, pp. 69-77.
[32] A. L. Christensen, "Result Specification and Model Connection in the Möbius Modeling Framework," Master's Thesis, University of Illinois, 2000.
[33] G. Clark, T. Courtney, D. Daly, D. Deavours, S. Derisavi, J. M. Doyle, W. H. Sanders, P. Webster, "The Möbius Modeling Tool," *Proc. 9th Int. Workshop on Petri Nets and Performance Models*, Aachen, Germany, September 11-14, 2001, pp. 241-250.
[34] G. Clark, W. H. Sanders, "Implementing a Stochastic Process Algebra within the Möbius Modeling Framework," in Luca de Alfaro and Stephen Gilmore (Eds.), *Process Algebra and Probabilistic Methods: Performance Modelling and Verification: Proc. Joint Int. Workshop, PAPM-PROBMIV 2001*, RWTH Aachen, Germany, September 12-14, 2001, *LNCS* no. 2165, Berlin: Springer, 2001, pp. 200-215.

[35] T. Courtney, J. Lyons, H. V. Ramasamy, W. H. Sanders, M. Seri, M. Atighetchi, P. Rubel, C. Jones, F. Webber, P. Pal, R. Watro, M. Cukier, J. Gossett, "Providing Intrusion Tolerance with ITUA," *Supplemental Volume Int. Conf. on Dependable Systems & Networks (DSN-2002)*, Washington, DC, June 23-26, 2002, pp. C-5-1 to C-5-3.

[36] M. Cukier, R. Chandra, D. Henke, J. Pistole, W. H. Sanders, "Fault Injection Based on a Partial View of the Global State of a Distributed System," *Proc. 18th IEEE Symp. on Reliable Distributed Systems*, Lausanne, Switzerland, October 19-22, 1999, pp. 168-177.

[37] J. Cusey, J. Patel, "BART: A Bridging Fault Test Generator for Sequential Circuits," *Proc. Int. Test Conf.*, Nov. 1997, pp. 838-847.

[38] D. Daly, P. Buchholz, W. H. Sanders, "An Approach for Bounding Reward Measures in Markov Models Using Aggregation," submitted for publication.

[39] T. Davis, R. Kunda, K. Fuchs, "Testing of Bit-Serial Multipliers," *Proc. Int. Conf. on Computer Design*, 1985, pp. 430-434.

[40] D. D. Deavours, "Formal Specification of the Möbius Modeling Framework," Doctoral Dissertation, University of Illinois, 2001.

[41] D. D. Deavours, G. Clark, T. Courtney, D. Daly, S. Derisavi, J. M. Doyle, W. H. Sanders, P. G. Webster, "The Möbius Framework and Its Implementation," *IEEE Trans. on Software Eng.*, 28, No. 10, October 2002, pp. 956-969.

[42] D. D. Deavours, W. H. Sanders, "The Möbius Execution Policy," *Proc. 9th Int. Workshop on Petri Nets and Performance Models*, Aachen, Germany, September 11-14, 2001, pp. 135-144.

[43] D. D. Deavours, W. H. Sanders, "Möbius: Framework and Atomic Models," *ibid.*, pp. 251-260.

[44] S. Derisavi, P. Kemper, W. H. Sanders, "Symbolic State-space Exploration and Numerical Analysis of State-sharing Composed Models," *Proc. 4th Int. Conf. on the Numerical Solution of Markov Chains*, Urbana, IL, USA, Sept. 3-5, 2003, pp. 167-189.

[45] S. Derisavi, P. Kemper, W. H. Sanders, "Symbolic State-space Exploration and Numerical Analysis of State-sharing Composed Models," *Linear Algebra and Its Applications (LAA)*, to appear.

[46] S. Derisavi, P. Kemper, W. H. Sanders, T. Courtney, "The Möbius State-level Abstract Functional Interface," *Performance Evaluation*, 54, No. 2, October 2003, pp. 105-128.

[47] Y. Deswarte, L. Blain, J. C. Fabre, "Intrusion Tolerance in Distributed Computing Systems," *Proc. IEEE Symp. on Research in Security & Privacy*, May 1991, pp. 110-121.

[48] J. Dussault, "On the Design of Self-Checking Systems under Various Fault Models," Coordinated Science Lab. Technical Report R-781, Univ. of Illinois, Urbana, IL, 1977.

[49] B. Dutertre, V. Crettaz, V. Stavridou, "Intrusion-tolerant Enclaves," *Proc. IEEE Int. Symp. on Security & Privacy*, Oakland, CA, May 2002, pp. 216–224.

[50] A. Friedman, L. Simoncini, "System-Level Fault Diagnosis," *Computer* (Spec. Issue on Fault-Tolerant Computing), 13, No. 3, 1980, pp. 47-53.

[51] K. Goswami, R. K. Iyer, L. Young, "DEPEND: A Simulation-Based Environment for System Level Dependability Analysis," *IEEE Trans. on Comp.*, vol. 46, no. 1, 1997, pp.60-74.

[52] G. Greenstein, J. Patel, "E-PROOFS: A CMOS Bridging Fault Simulator," *Proc. IEEE/ACM Conf. on Computer-Aided Design*, Nov. 1992, pp. 268 – 271.

[53] W. Gu, Z. Kalbarczyk, R. K. Iyer, "Error Sensitivity of the Linux Kernel Executing on PowerPC G4 and Pentium 4 Processors," *Proc. Conf. on Dependable Systems & Networks, DSN'04*, June 2004.

[54] W. Gu, Z. Kalbarczyk, R.K. Iyer, Z. Yang, "Characterization of Linux Kernel Behavior under Errors," *Proc. Conf. on Dependable Systems & Networks, DSN'03*, June 2003, pp. 459-468.

[55] J. Gunnels, D. Katz, E. Quintana-Orti, R. van de Geijn, "Fault-Tolerant High-Performance Matrix Multiplication: Theory and Practice," *Proc. Conf. on Dependable Systems and Networks, DSN'01*, July 2001, pp. 47-56.

[56] V. Gupta, V. Lam, H. V. Ramasamy, W. H. Sanders, S. Singh, "Dependability and Performance Evaluation of Intrusion-Tolerant Server Architectures," *Dependable Computing: Proc. First Latin-American Symposium (LADC 2003)*, São Paulo, Brazil, October 21-24, 2003, *LNCS* vol. 2847 (Rogério de Lemos, Taisy Silva Weber, and João Batista Camargo Jr., eds), Berlin: Springer, 2003, pp. 81-101.

[57] I. Hamzaoglu, J. Patel, "Test Set Compaction Algorithms for Combinational Circuits," *Proc. IEEE/ACM Int. Conf. Computer-Aided Design*, Nov. 1998, pp. 283-289.

[58] I. Hamzaoglu, J. Patel, "Reducing Test Application Time for Full Scan Embedded Cores," Proc. *29th Int. Symp. on Fault-Tolerant Computing*, June 1999, pp. 260-267.

[59] I. Hartanto, V. Boppana, W. Fuchs, J. Patel, "Diagnostic Test Generation for Sequential Circuits," *Proc. IEEE VLSI Test Symp.*, April 1997, pp. 196-202.

[60] J. Hayes, "A NAND Model for Fault Diagnosis in Combinational Logic Networks," *IEEE Trans. on Comp.*, C-20, 1971, pp. 1496-1506.

[61] F. Hsu, K. Butler, J. Patel, "A Case Study on the Implementation of the Illinois Scan Architecture," *Proc. Int. Test Conf.*, Oct-Nov 2001, pp. 538-547.

[62] http://www.securityfocus.com.

[63] K. Huang, J. Abraham, "Low-Cost Schemes for Fault Tolerance in Matrix Operations with Array Processors," *Proc. 12th Int. Symp. on Fault-Tolerant Computing*, 1982, pp. 330-337.

[64] K. Huang, J. Abraham, "Algorithm-Based Fault Tolerance for Matrix Operations," *IEEE Trans. on Comp.* (Spec. Issue Reliable & Fault-Tolerant Comp.), C-33, 1984, pp. 518-528.

[65] K. Huang, J. Abraham, "Fault-Tolerant Algorithms and their Applications to Solving Laplace Equations," *Proc. Int. Conf. on Parallel Processing*, 1984, pp. 117-122.

[66] R. K. Iyer, D. Rossetti, "A Measurement-Based Model for Workload Dependency of CPU Errors," *IEEE Trans. on Comp.*, C-35, No. 6, 1986.

[67] R. K. Iyer, D. Rossetti, "Effect of System Workload on Operating System Reliability: A Study on the IBM 3081," *IEEE Trans. on Software Eng.* (Spec. Issue Software Reliability, Part 1), 1985, pp. 1438-1448.

[68] I. Jansch, B. Courtois, "Strongly Language Disjoint Checkers," *Proc. 15th Int. Symp. on Fault-Tolerant Computing*, 1985, pp. 390-395.

[69] H. S. Javitz, A. Valdes, "The SRI IDES Statistical Anomaly Detector," *Proc. IEEE Symp. on Research in Security and Privacy*, Oakland, CA, May 1991, pp. 316-376.

[70] K. R. Joshi, M. Cukier, W. H. Sanders, "Experimental Evaluation of the Unavailability Induced by a Group Membership Protocol," *Dependable Computing EDCC-4: Proc. 4th European Dependable Computing Conf.*, Toulouse, France, Oct 23-25, 2002, pp. 140-158.

[71] J. Jou, J. Abraham, "Fault-Tolerant Matrix Operations on Multiple Processor Systems Using Weighted Checksums," *Proc. SPIE Conf.*, 1984, pp. 94-101.

[72] J. Jou, J. Abraham, "Fault-Tolerant FFT Networks," *Proc. Int. Symp. on Fault-Tolerant Computing*, 1985, pp. 338-343.

[73] Z. Kalbarczyk, R. K. Iyer, S. Bagchi, K. Whisnant, "Chameleon: A Software Infrastructure for Adaptive Fault Tolerance," *IEEE Trans. on Par. and Dist. Systems*, 10, No. 6, June 1999, pp. 560-579.

[74] M. Kalyanakrishnam, R. K. Iyer, J. Patel, "Reliability of Internet Hosts: A Case Study from End User's Perspective," *Proc. 6th Int. Conf. on Computer Communications and Networks*, Las Vegas, 1996, pp. 418-423.

[75] M. Kalyanakrishnam, Z. Kalbarczyk, R. Iyer, "Failure Data Analysis of LAN of Windows NT Based Computers," *Proc. of 18th Symp. on Reliable and Distributed Systems, SRDS '99*, Lausanne, Switzerland, 1999, pp. 178-187.

[76] S. Krishnamurthy, "An Adaptive Quality of Service Aware Middleware for Replicated Services," Ph.D. Thesis, University of Illinois, 2002.

[77] S. Krishnamurthy, W. H. Sanders, M. Cukier, "An Adaptive Quality of Service Aware Middleware for Replicated Services," *IEEE Trans. on Par. and Dist. Systems*, 14, No. 11, November 2003, pp. 1112-1125.

[78] S. Kuo, K. Fuchs, "Efficient Spare Allocation in Reconfigurable Arrays," *IEEE Design and Test*, Feb. 1987, pp. 24-31.

[79] S. Laha, J. Patel, "Error Correction in Arithmetic Operations using Time Redundancy," *Proc. 13th Int. Symp. on Fault-Tolerant Computing*, 1983, pp. 298-305.

[80] V. V. Lam, P. Buchholz, W. H. Sanders, "A Structured Path-Based Approach for Computing Transient Rewards of Large CTMCs," *Proc. 2004 Int. Conf. on Quantitative Evaluation of Systems (QEST)*, Twente, The Netherlands, September 27-30, 2004.

[81] C. Landwehr, "Formal Models for Computer Security," *Computer Surveys*, 13, No. 3, Sept. 1981.

[82] R. M. Lefever, M. Cukier, W. H. Sanders, "An Experimental Evaluation of Correlated Network Partitions in the Coda Distributed File System," *Proc. 22nd Int. Symp. on Reliable Distributed Systems (SRDS'03)*, Florence, Italy, October 6-8, 2003, pp. 273-282.

[83] B. Littlewood, S. Brocklehurst, N. Fenton, P. Mellor, S. Page, D. Wright, J. Dobson, J. McDermid, D. Gollmann, "Towards Operational Measures of Computer Security," *Journal of Computer Security*, vol. 2, no. 2-3, pp. 211-229, 1993.

[84] J. Lowry, "An Initial Foray into Understanding Adversary Planning and Courses of Action," *Proc. DARPA Information Survivability Conf. and Exposition II (DISCEX'01)*, pp. 123-133, 2001.

[85] F. Luk, "Algorithm-Based Fault Tolerance for Parallel Matrix Equation Solvers," *Proc. SPIE Conf. (Real-Time Signal Processing VIII)*, 564, 1985.

[86] L. Malhis, "Development and Application of an Efficient Method for the Solution of Stochastic Activity Networks with Deterministic Activities," Doctoral Dissertation, University of Arizona, 1996.

[87] L. Malhis and W. H. Sanders, "An Efficient Two-Stage Iterative Method for the Steady-State Analysis of Markov Regenerative Stochastic Petri Net Models," *Performance Evaluation*, 27&28, October 1996, pp. 583-601.

[88] E. Manning, "On Computer Self-Diagnosis: Part I and II," *IEEE Trans. Electronic Comp.*, EC-15, 1966, pp. 873-890.

[89] R. Marlett, "An Effective Test Generation System for Sequential Circuits," *Proc. Design Automation Conf.*, June 1986, pp. 250-256.

[90] R. Marlett, "On the Design and Testing of Self-Diagnosable Computers," Coordinated Science Laboratory Technical Report R-293, University of Illinois, Urbana, IL, 1966.

[91] E. McCluskey, F. Clegg, "Fault Equivalence in Combinational Logic Networks," *IEEE Trans. on Comp.*, C- 20, 1971, pp. 1286-1293.

[92] R. Meagher, J. Nash, "The ORDVAC," *Review of Electronic Digital Computers*, 1952, pp. 37-43.

[93] D. Muller, J. Bartky, "A Theory of Asynchronous Circuits," *Proc. Int. Symp. on Theory of Switching*, 1959, pp. 204-243.

[94] R. Nair, S. Thatte, J. Abraham, "Efficient Algorithms for Testing Semiconductor Random-Access Memories," *IEEE Trans. on Comp.*, C-27, No. 6, 1978, pp. 572-576.

[95] N. Nakka, J. Xu, Z. Kalbarczyk, R. K. Iyer, "An Architectural Framework for Providing Reliability and Security Support," *Proc. Conf. on Dependable Systems and Networks, DSN'04*, June 2004.

[96] N. Neves, K. Fuchs, "Coordinated Checkpointing Without Direct Coordination," *Proc. Int. Computer Performance and Dependability Symp. (IPDS)*, 1998.

[97] N. Neves, K. Fuchs, "RENEW: A Tool for Fast and Efficient Implementation of Checkpoint Protocols," *Proc. 28th Int. Symp. on Fault-Tolerant Computing*, 1998, pp.58-67.

[98] T. Niermann, J. Patel, "HITEC: A Test Generation Package for Sequential Circuits," *Proc. European Design Automation Conf.*, Feb. 2001, pp. 214-218.

[99] T. Niermann, W. Cheng and J. Patel, "PROOFS: A Fast Memory Efficient Sequential Circuit Fault Simulator," *IEEE Trans. On Computer-Aided Design*, Feb. 1992, pp. 198-207.

[100] W. D. Obal II, "Measure-Adaptive State-Space Construction Methods," Doctoral Dissertation, University of Arizona, 1998.

[101] W. D. Obal II, W. H. Sanders, "An Environment for Importance Sampling Based on Stochastic Activity Networks," *Proc. 13th Symp. on Reliable Distributed Systems*, Dana Point, CA, October, 1994, pp. 64-73.
[102] W. D. Obal II, W. H. Sanders, "State-Space Support for Path-based Reward Variables," *Proc. Int. Computer Performance and Dependability Symp. (IPDS)*, September 7-9, 1998, Durham, North Carolina, USA, pp. 228-237.
[103] W. D. Obal II, W. H. Sanders, "State-Space Support for Path-based Reward Variables," *Performance Evaluation*, 35, 1999, pp. 233-251.
[104] P. Pal, F. Webber, R. Schantz, J. Loyall, R. Watro, W. Sanders, M. Cukier, J. Gossett, "Survival by Defense-Enabling," *Proc. New Security Paradigms Workshop 2001*, Cloudcroft, New Mexico, September 11-13, 2001, pp. 71-78.
[105] J. Patel, L. Fung, "Concurrent Error Detection in ALUs by Recomputing with Shifted Operands," *IEEE Trans. on Comp.*, C-31, 1982, pp. 589-595.
[106] J. Patel, L. Fung, "Concurrent Error Detection in Multiply and Divide Arrays," *IEEE Trans. on Comp.*, C-32, 1983, pp. 417-422.
[107] C. Payne, T. Markham, "Architecture and Applications for a Distributed Embedded Firewall," *Proc. 17th Annual Computer Security Applications Conf. (ACSAC'01)*, New Orleans, Louisiana, October 2001.
[108] L. Pollard and J. Patel, "Correction of Errors in Data Transmission using Time Redundancy," *Proc. 13th Int. Symp. on Fault-Tolerant Computing*, 1983, pp. 314-317.
[109] F. Preparata, G. Metze, R. Chien, "On the Connection Assignment Problem of Diagnosable Systems," *IEEE Trans. on Electronic Comp.*, EC-16, No. 6, 1967, pp. 848-854.
[110] M. A. Qureshi, "Construction and Solution of Markov Reward Models," Doctoral Dissertation, University of Arizona, 1996.
[111] M. A. Qureshi, W. H. Sanders, "A New Methodology for Calculating Distributions of Reward Accumulated During a Finite Interval," *Proc. 26th Int. Symp. on Fault-Tolerant Computing*, Sendai, Japan, June 1996, pp. 116-125.
[112] H. V. Ramasamy, M. Cukier, W. H. Sanders, "Formal Verification of an Intrusion-Tolerant Group Membership Protocol," *IEICE Trans. on Information and Systems* Spec. issue on Dependable Computing, E86-D, No. 12, December 2003, pp. 2612-2622.
[113] H.V. Ramasamy, P. Pandey, J. Lyons, M. Cukier, W.H. Sanders, "Quantifying the Cost of Providing Intrusion Tolerance in Group Communication Systems," *Proc. Int. Conf. on Dependable Systems & Networks (DSN'02)*, Washington, DC, June 23-26, 2002, pp. 229-238.
[114] J. Rearick, J. Patel, "Fast and Accurate CMOS Bridging Fault Simulation," *Proc. Int. Test Conf.*, Oct. 1993, pp. 54-62.
[115] Y. Ren, "AQuA: A Framework for Providing Adaptive Fault Tolerance to Distributed Applications," Ph.D. thesis, University of Illinois at Urbana-Champaign, 2001.
[116] Y.(J.) Ren, D.E. Bakken, T. Courtney, M. Cukier, D.A. Karr, P. Rubel, C. Sabnis, W.H. Sanders, R.E. Schantz, M. Seri, "AQuA: An Adaptive Architecture that Provides Dependable Distributed Objects," *IEEE Trans. on Comp.*, 52, No. 1, January 2003, pp. 31-50.
[117] Y. Ren, M. Cukier, W.H. Sanders, "An Adaptive Algorithm for Tolerating Value Faults and Crash Failures," *IEEE Trans. on Par. & Dist. Systems*, 12, No. 2, Feb. 2001, pp. 173-192.
[118] D. Reynolds, C. Metze, "Fault Detection Capabilities of Alternating Logic," *IEEE Trans. on Comp.*, C-27, 1978, pp. 1093-1098.
[119] P. Ryan, S. Rawat, W. Fuchs, "Two-stage Fault Location," *Proc. Int. Test Conf.*, Oct. 1991, pp. 963-968.
[120] C. Sabnis, M. Cukier, J. Ren, P. Rubel, W. H. Sanders, D. E. Bakken, D. A. Karr, "Proteus: A Flexible Infrastructure to Implement Adaptive Fault Tolerance in AQuA," in C. B. Weinstock and J. Rushby (Eds.), *Dependable Computing for Critical Applications 7*, vol. 12 in *Dependable Computing and Fault-Tolerant Systems* (A. Avizienis, H. Kopetz, and J. C. Laprie, Eds.), pp. 149-168. Los Alamitos, CA: IEEE CS, 1999.
[121] A. Saleh, J. Serrano, J. Patel, "Reliability of Scrubbing Recovery Techniques for Memory Systems," *IEEE Trans. on Reliability*, April 1990, pp. 114-122.

[122] W. H. Sanders, "Construction and Solution of Performability Models Based on Stochastic Activity Networks," Doctoral Dissertation, University of Michigan, 1988.

[123] W. H. Sanders, "Integrated Frameworks for Multi-Level and Multi-Formalism Modeling," *Proc. of PNPM'99: 8th Int. Workshop on Petri Nets and Performance Models*, Zaragoza, Spain, September 8-10, 1999, pp. 2-9.

[124] W. H. Sanders, M. Cukier, F. Webber, P. Pal, R. Watro, "Probabilistic Validation of Intrusion Tolerance," *Supplemental Volume Int. Conf. on Dependable Systems & Networks (DSN-2002)*, Washington, DC, June 23-26, 2002, pp. B-78 to B-79.

[125] W. H. Sanders, R. S. Freire, "Efficient Simulation of Hierarchical Stochastic Activity Network Models," *Discrete Event Dynamic Systems: Theory and Applications*, 3, No. 2/3, July 1993, pp. 271-300.

[126] W. H. Sanders, J. F. Meyer, "Reduced Base Model Construction Methods for Stochastic Activity Networks," *IEEE Journal on Selected Areas in Communications*, special issue on *Computer-Aided Modeling, Analysis, and Design of Communication Networks*, vol. 9, no. 1, Jan. 1991, pp. 25-36.

[127] W. H. Sanders, J. F. Meyer, "Stochastic Activity Networks: Formal Definitions and Concepts," in E. Brinksma, H. Hermanns, and J. P. Katoen (Eds.), *Lectures on Formal Methods and Performance Analysis, First EEF/Euro Summer School on Trends in Computer Science, Berg en Dal, The Netherlands, July 3-7, 2000, Revised Lectures, LNCS* no. 2090, pp. 315-343. Berlin: Springer, 2001.

[128] W. H. Sanders, J. F. Meyer, "A Unified Approach for Specifying Measures of Performance, Dependability, and Performability," *Dependable Computing for Critical Applications*, Vol. 4 of *Dependable Computing and Fault-Tolerant Systems* (ed. A. Avizienis, H. Kopetz, and J. Laprie), Springer-Verlag, 1991, pp. 215-237.

[129] W.H. Sanders, W.D. Obal II, M.A. Qureshi, F.K. Widjanarko, "The *UltraSAN* Modeling Environment," *Performance Evaluation*, 24, No. 1, Oct.-Nov. 1995, pp. 89-115.

[130] D. Schertz, G. Metze, "A New Representation for Faults in Combinational Digital Circuits," *IEEE Trans. on Comp.*, C-21, No. 8, 1972, pp. 858-866.

[131] D. Schertz, "On the Representation of Digital Faults," Coordinated Science Laboratory Technical Report R418, University of Illinois, Urbana, Illinois, 1969.

[132] D. Schertz, G. Metze, "On the Indistinguishability of Faults in Digital Systems," *Proc. 6th Ann. Allerton Conf. on Circuit and System Theory*, 1968, pp. 752-760.

[133] M. Seri, T. Courtney, M. Cukier, V. Gupta, S. Krishnamurthy, J. Lyons, H. Ramasamy, J. Ren, W. H. Sanders, "A Configurable CORBA Gateway for Providing Adaptable System Properties," *Supplemental Volume Int. Conf. on Dependable Systems & Networks (DSN-2002)*, Washington, DC, June 23-26, 2002, pp. G-26 to G-30.

[134] S. Seshu, D. Freeman, "The Diagnosis of Asynchronous Sequential Switching Systems", *IRE Trans. on Electronic Comp.*, EC-11, No.4, 1962, pp. 459-465.

[135] S. Seshu, "The Logic Organizer and Diagnosis Programs", Coordinated Science Laboratory Technical Report R226, University of Illinois, Urbana, IL, 1964.

[136] S. Seshu, "On an Improved Diagnosis Program", *IEEE Trans. on Electronic Comp. EC-14*, No. 1, 1965, pp. 76-79.

[137] S. Singh, M. Cukier, W. H. Sanders, "Probabilistic Validation of an Intrusion-Tolerant Replication System," *Proc. Int. Conf. on Dependable Systems and Networks (DSN-2003)*, San Francisco, CA, June 22-25, 2003, pp. 615-624.

[138] J. Smith, "On Necessary and Sufficient Conditions for Multiple Fault Undetectability," *IEEE Trans. on Comp.*, C-28, 1979, pp. 801-802

[139] J. Smith, "The Design of Totally Self-Checking Combinational Circuits," Coordinated Science Laboratory Technical Report R-737, University of Illinois, Urbana, IL, 1976.

[140] J. Smith, G. Metze, "On the Existence of Combinational Networks with Arbitrary Multiple Redundancies," Coordinated Science Laboratory Technical Report R-692, University of Illinois, Urbana, IL, 1975.

[141] J. Smith, G. Metze, "Strongly Fault-Secure Logic Networks," *IEEE Trans. on Comp.*, C-27, No. 6, 1978, pp. 491-499.

[142] F. Stevens, "Validation of an Intrusion-Tolerant Information System Using Probabilistic Modeling," Master's Thesis, University of Illinois, 2004.

[143] D. Stott, B. Floering, D. Burke, Z. Kalbarczyk, R. K. Iyer, "NFTAPE: A Framework for Assessing Dependability in Distributed Systems with Lightweight Fault Injectors," *Proc. Int. Computer Performance & Dependability Symp. (IPDS)*, March 2000, pp. 91-100.

[144] D. Stott, P. Jones, M. Hamman, Z. Kalbarczyk, R. Iyer, "NFTAPE: Network Fault Tolerance and Performance Evaluator," *Proc. Int. Conf. on Dependable Systems and Networks, DSN'02*, June 2002, pp. 542.

[145] D. Suk, S. Reddy, "A March Test for Functional Faults in Semiconductor Random Access Memories," *IEEE Trans. on Comp.*, C-30, 1981, pp. 982-984.

[146] S. Thatte, J. Abraham, "Testing of Semiconductor Random Access Memories," *Proc. 7th Int. Symp. on Fault-Tolerant Computing*, 1977, pp. 81-87.

[147] S. Thatte, J. Abraham, "Test Generation for Microprocessors," *IEEE Trans. on Comp.*, C-29, No. 6, 1980, pp. 429-441.

[148] K. To, "Fault Folding for Irredundant and Redundant Combinational Circuits", *IEEE Trans. on Comp. C-22*, No. 11, 1973, pp. 1008-1015.

[149] T. Tsai, M-Ch. Hsueh, H. Zhao, Z. Kalbarczyk, R. K. Iyer, "Stress-based and Path-based Fault Injection," *IEEE Trans. on Comp.*, 48, No. 11, Nov. 1999, pp. 1183-1201.

[150] J. Tvedt, "Solution of Large-Sparse Stochastic Process Representations of Stochastic Activity Networks," Master's Thesis, University of Arizona, 1990.

[151] E. Ulrich and T. Baker, "The Concurrent Simulation of Nearly Identical Digital Systems," *Proc. 10th Design Automation Workshop*, June 1973, pp. 145-150.

[152] A. P. A. van Moorsel, W. H. Sanders, "Adaptive Uniformization," *ORSA Communications in Statistics: Stochastic Models*, 10, No. 3, August 1994, pp. 619-648.

[153] A. P. A. van Moorsel, W. H. Sanders, "Transient Solution of Markov Models by Combining Adaptive & Standard Uniformization," *IEEE Trans. on Reliability*, 46, No. 3, September 1997, pp. 430-440.

[154] L. Wang, Z. Kalbarczyk, R. K. Iyer, H. Vora, T. Chahande, "Checkpointing of Control Structures in Main Memory Database Systems," *Proc. Conf. on Dependable Systems and Networks, DSN'04*, June 2004.

[155] Y. Wang, K. Fuchs, "Optimal Message Log Reclamation for Independent Checkpointing," Technical Report CRHC-93-07, University of Illinois, 1993.

[156] D. Wheeler and J. Robertson, "Diagnostic Programs for the ILLIAC," *Proc. IRE 41*, 1953, pp. 1320-1325.

[157] K. Whisnant, R.K. Iyer, Z. Kalbarczyk, P.H. Jones III, D.A. Rennels, R. Some, "The Effects of an ARMOR-Based SIFT Environment on the Performance and Dependability of User Applications," *IEEE Trans. on Software Eng.*, 30, No. 4, April 2004, pp. 257-277.

[158] K. Whisnant, Z. Kalbarczyk, R. Iyer, "A System Model for Reconfigurable Software," *IBM Systems Journal*, 42, No. 1, 2003, pp. 45-59.

[159] J. Xu, S. Chen, Z. Kalbarczyk, R. K. Iyer, "An Experimental Study of Security Vulnerabilities Caused by Errors," *Proc. Conf. on Dependable Systems and Networks, DSN'01*, July 2001, pp. 421-430.

[160] J. Xu, Z. Kalbarczyk, R.K. Iyer, "Transparent Runtime Randomization for Security," *Proc. Symp. on Reliable and Distributed Systems, SRDS'03*, October 2003.

[161] J. Xu, Z. Kalbarczyk, R. Iyer, "Networked Windows NT System Filed Failure Data Analysis," *Proc. Pacific Rim Int. Symp. on Dependable Computing*, Hong Kong, 1999.

WRAPPING THE FUTURE

Tom Anderson, Brian Randell and Alexander Romanovsky
School of Computing Science, University of Newcastle upon Tyne, UK
{tom.anderson, brian.randell, alexander.romanovsky}@newcastle.ac.uk

Abstract: Enclosing a component within a software "wrapper" is a well-established way of adapting components for use in new environments. This paper presents an overview of an experimental evaluation of the use of a wrapper to protect against faults arising during the (simulated) operation of a practical and critical system; the specific context is a protective wrapper for an off-the-shelf software component at the heart of the control system of a steam raising boiler. Encouraged by the positive outcomes of this experimentation we seek to position protective wrappers as a basis for structuring the provision of fault tolerance in component-based open systems and networks. The paper addresses some key issues and developments relating wrappers to the provision of dependability in future computing systems.

Key words: dependability; off-the-shelf components; fault tolerance; protective wrapping.

Many siren voices, and some harsh economic facts, argue in favour of *off the shelf* (OTS) components as a way to reduce the costs of software system development. Compared with bespoke design and development, the OTS option offers a number of potential benefits, including: immediate availability, proven in use, low price due to amortisation. The increasing scale and complexity of modern software systems is a powerful driver for modularity in design, which clearly chimes with a structured and therefore such a component (or sub-system) based approach.

The need for economy is often most keenly felt in expensive systems, and this can certainly be the case for systems that have critical requirements (such as safety-critical systems). But it is in the nature of these systems that they really **must** deliver on their requirements; their operational behaviour must exhibit dependability; they must do what they are supposed to do, and must not do what is prohibited (well, almost always). With a completely bespoke development, designers can strive very hard to achieve a dependable system, and regulators can obtain access to extensive information on the development process (as well as the delivered product) in order to evaluate a documented justification that the system will meet its critical requirements (for example, a safety case). Utilisation of an OTS software component is likely to inhibit this evaluation, since – in the extreme case – the component may have to be viewed as a black box, with no information on its inner workings or its development; the proven-in-use evidence for the component's suitability may, or may not, be valid, but such evidence cannot be relied upon if it is merely anecdotal or does not relate to an identical use environment.

So, consider the situation where use of an OTS software component is feasible and there is a strong financial reason for doing so, but the component's behaviour needs to be trusted, and we have insufficient evidence to justify that trust. How can we proceed? The approach to be considered in this paper is a simple application of diversity to provide an architectural solution. The OTS component will be enclosed in a bespoke *protective wrapper* [Voa98, Arl02], a purpose designed additional component that intercepts all inputs to, and outputs from, the OTS component in order to monitor its behaviour. The aim is for the wrapper to deal with any problems arising from inadequate behaviour of the OTS component, ideally masking any such deleterious effects from the rest of the system. This is thus a special case of the more general use of software wrapping, a technology that has a long history of use as a means of adapting existing components for use in new environments.

1. THE DOTS PROJECT

DOTS – "Diversity with OTS components" – is a joint project at CSR (Centre for Software Reliability) in Newcastle and City Universities, funded by the UK EPSRC. Work at Newcastle is exploring architectural approaches to diversity in the presence of OTS items, while colleagues at City concentrate on assessment of the benefits that can be expected.

Our architectural exploration has concentrated on *protective wrapper technology*, a phrase that gives an appealing technical ring to this simplistic approach of enveloping a possibly suspect component. However, despite its apparent simplicity, there are a range of issues to consider and questions to be asked. We believe that our work gives some encouragement that positive answers may be given to the following questions:

- is protective wrapper technology feasible in practical systems?
- can protective wrappers detect and respond successfully to erroneous situations in practical systems?

In order to draw conclusions for practical systems we sought realism in our investigation. Experimentation with a real-world critical system would be fraught with peril, so we made use of a software model of a real-time software system. To maximise realism we adapted a model taken directly from industry: a Honeywell-supplied industrial grade simulation of a steam boiler and its associated control system. Written in Simulink [Mat], the model represents a real steam raising system in which a coal-fired boiler responds to demands for steam under the operational authority of an automated control system; the control system consists of a PID (i.e. Proportional, Integral and Derivative) controller together with a range of smart sensors, actuators, and configuration controls (collectively referred to as the ROS (rest of system)), as illustrated in Figure 1.

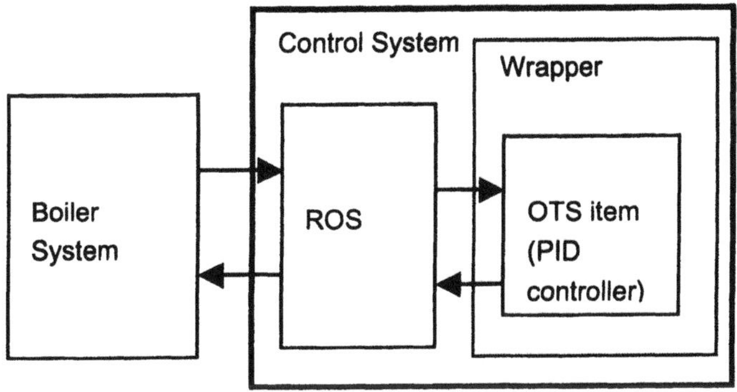

Figure 1. Boiler System and Control System

We chose to treat the PID controller as an OTS item, and then developed a (simulated) protective wrapper that can monitor and, when appropriate, modify all input/output signals between the PID controller and the rest of the control system. As a purely protective wrapper there was no intention to adjust or upgrade the PID controller's behaviour at the interface; the aim was simply to provide fault-tolerant elements that can detect and recover from errors. In designing the wrapper we only had access to limited information about the operation of the boiler and the control system; furthermore we deliberately ignored any details of the inner working of the PID controller, treating it as a black box. Ideally we would have wished for access to a full external specification of the PID controller, but the lack of this made our position even more realistic.

In creating our own, approximate, specification for the PID controller we built up a set of *Acceptable Behaviour Constraints* (ABCs) [Pop01] which stipulate what may be considered as acceptable behaviour at the interface between the PID controller and the rest of the control system.

2. ERROR DETECTION

Given the limitations of the scenario we were exploring our strategy for error detection was necessarily based on a systematic application of generic criteria. Erroneous situations can arise anywhere in the system, but the wrapper can only check for symptomatic "cues" at the interface to the PID controller. The wrapper was programmed to check inputs to the PID controller cyclically against constraints established as ABCs (missing, invalid, unacceptable, marginal or suspect values from the sensors or configuration variables). Similarly, outputs from the PID controller were also checked against ABCs (missing, invalid or unacceptable values intended for the actuators). Thus we were attempting to deal with both the PID's monitoring and its control activities.

To help inform the next stage of wrapper design we categorised these error cues as follows:

- unavailability of signal (inputs or outputs),
- signal violating specified constraints (usually out of range errors),
- excessive signal oscillations (in amplitude or frequency).

Additionally, we recognised that with respect to the safety of the system, some erroneous situations are much more acute than others. In a steam boiler, a key parameter is the "drum level"; this parameter measures the mass of water contained in the boiler drum more accurately than the "water level" (which is also monitored, of course). Too little water and the boiler tubes are exposed to heat stress, too much and water could go over the header causing corrosion. The danger of excessive steam pressure is obvious and explosive. Thus detected errors that concerned either steam pressure or the quantity of water in the drum were designated as needing an immediate and effectual response. (A boiler operated via a PID controller is one of the most widely deployed systems, installed in many industrial facilities and residential houses, for the safe and reliable generation of steam and/or hot water. Nevertheless, critical incidents in these systems lead to deaths and injuries every year [Nat03].)

3. ERROR RECOVERY

The purpose of error recovery is to transform a system state that contains errors to one that does not. *Backward* recovery returns the system to a previous state, prior to the incidence of error, and is unlikely to be available for OTS components. So our protective wrapper attempts to implement application-specific *forward* recovery, which does not discard the current state. Exception handling provides a general framework for such forward recovery.

We implemented three elementary recovery actions:

- H1: reset signal to normal value and alert operator
- H2: wait Δt, if error goes away no action taken; otherwise send alarm to operator and wait ΔT, no further action if error goes away; otherwise invoke H3 {delay times Δt and ΔT chosen by the wrapper designer}
- H3: shut system down and send alarm to operator.

We then devised a rationale for a recovery strategy in which:

- all errors for PID controller outputs invoke H1
- all errors from configuration controls invoke H1
- all PID input errors (except drum level and steam pressure) invoke H2
- excessive signal oscillation errors concerning drum level and steam pressure invoke H2
- all other errors concerning drum level and steam pressure invoke H3.

[Adopting this (or any other) recovery strategy for an actual boiler plant would, of course, require safety analysis and justification.]

In our experimental situation, having implemented a protective wrapper with a detection and recovery capability we need to observe how well the system responds. Initial test exercises gave very positive indications, and we have just completed a first phase of setting up a range of fault injection scenarios, running these, and recording the outcomes. Our fault injection scenarios involve signal communication faults (bias, random noise, stuck-at previous, stuck-at random) and faults that impinge directly on the algorithms of the PID controller (transient zeros, control parameter overwrites). A preliminary examination of the experimental data generated indicates that the wrapper has been very effective in reducing serious failures of the boiler system.

4. PROTECTIVE WRAPPING – WHAT NEXT?

Thus far we merely claim to have built a reasonably realistic, albeit rather simplistic, demonstrator of a protective wrapper in action to enhance the dependability of an industrial OTS component, with encouraging early results. The exercise of working with the demonstrator has helped us to address a number of specific concerns, which we consider in more detail elsewhere [And03a, And03b, And03c]. However, and much more significantly, we now discern a salient role for wrapper technology as a means for structuring, designing and building future ICT systems. We believe that protective wrapping has considerable promise as a uniform approach for incorporating fault tolerance into new and existing complex systems, particularly when these are organised and created as integrative networks of interacting components.

Openness is often considered to be one of the defining characteristics of the ICT systems that are expected to be widely deployed in future – systems that will support mobile access and that are pervasive of society; systems that deliver ambient "intelligence" in terms of services, information, processing and communication; networks of heterogeneous systems/components which interact with (and depend upon) other networks; sub-networks that combine and decompose dynamically. Openness allows on-line composition, reconfiguration, evolution and upgrading, performed on the basis of a dynamic analysis of the available information representing possible changes. This flexibility is made possible by features that can be used dynamically to select or devise optimal configurations, and then to realise these configurations by locating, deploying and integrating the appropriate components. Openness is usually understood in the widest possible sense, in that it should allow systems to deal with changes in: requirements, location (mobility), quality of service (QoS) characteristics, the environment, component behaviour, users' expectations, users' behaviour, etc. Clearly this must include dealing with changes due to accidental or malicious faults.

There is a significant challenge in identifying and developing fault tolerance solutions that fit the specific characteristics of open systems; protective wrapping has considerable potential to be one of the fundamental fault tolerance techniques needed, primarily because it sits well with the open network based approach but also because it provides such a simple but general starting point. Of course, there are numerous issues that will need to be examined further before that potential can be converted into a fully effective approach. Among these issues we can draw attention to:

- wrapper deficiencies – the role of a protective wrapper is to improve system dependability by providing an error detection and recovery capability, but there is always a risk in including defensive mechanisms for fault tolerance that by adding an additional software component new opportunities for erroneous computation may arise; the best general guidance is to keep wrappers as simple as possible
- formal development of wrappers – the need to minimise the risk of a protective wrapper introducing additional fault modes is not only a driver for simplicity in wrapper design, but also for adherence to stringent and rigorous development practice; we see a basis for progress here based on contracts derived from constraint-based specification of component interfaces (e.g. ABCs), and by exploiting compositional semantics
- timing issues – there is considerable scope for considering how best a protective wrapper should stipulate and monitor deadlines, and react to

delays; strategies and protocols from distributed systems work will need to be adapted for open networks

- scoping issues – the most simplistic image of a protective wrapper gives it full access to all communications across the wrapped component's interface and no access to any variables elsewhere in the system (either internal to the wrapped component or in its environment), but any realistic implementation is likely to deviate from this artifice; it will rarely be feasible or necessary to control each and every component interaction, access to internal values (though often undesirable and/or inhibited by lack of knowledge) may be possible and of benefit in special circumstances, and supplementary information about external conditions could be an invaluable guide to the operation of the wrapper (both for error detection and response)
- wrapper interactions – a set of protective wrappers in a network of wrapped components may need to be able to communicate and interact in order to best achieve their several and collective dependability objectives; imposing constraint and mediation on inter-wrapper communication is likely to involve approaches based on interactive consistency solutions

The above list of bulleted topics could be extended almost indefinitely, for instance with issues from specific dependability domains (safety and security, for example) and more general systems engineering concerns (modelling and requirements, for example) but instead we move on, to relate the technology of protective wrapping to anticipated developments in the dependability of systems more generally.

A recently-commissioned Foresight document [Jon04] identified a number of core directions for future research in dependability, including: dependability-explicit systems, cost-effective formal methods, architecture theory, and adaptivity. In the remainder of this paper we outline how advances in these four areas could impact on protective wrapper technology, and vice-versa.

Dependability-explicit system development [Kaâ00] is an emerging area of research which supports the explicit incorporation of dependability-related information into system development artefacts right through the development life-cycle, starting from the earliest phases of development, and continuing through to on-line support for maintaining, updating and exporting this dependability information within the operational system (with reference to the current state of the system and its environment). Examples of dependability information are fault descriptions, expected normal/abnormal behaviour, redundancy resources, mappings between errors and handlers, abnormal situations that components are capable of handling, failure frequency data, etc. Protective wrapping fits this approach extremely well, since such data will be relevant for informing decisions by the wrappers relating to error detection and recovery, potentially allowing the evolution of wrappers in response to changes in system and environment behaviour, and after network reconfiguration. Furthermore, wrappers are an obvious candidate mechanism for processing the dependability information, and publishing it across the network.

Research on *cost-effective formal methods* will contribute to overall system dependability by accumulating a set of advanced tools (operating within an open platform) for cutting-edge formal development methods focussed on fault tolerance, mobility and adaptivity. Formal models of future open systems will enable wrappers to be rigorously described, and the systems containing them to be formally analysed. A key research objective is the development of tools that can analyse the models of a system and a specific component, from that analysis determine requirements for a protective wrapper for the component, and then generate the wrapper model – with the long term objective that this analysis and generation can be performed fully automatically as an adaptive open system evolves.

Architecture theory research aims to provide methods for reasoning about dependability concerns at an architectural level much earlier in system development. Protective wrappers provide a major structuring approach that embodies fault tolerance capabilities (including confinement of error propagation, and exception handling), but they will need to have adequate architectural support. In particular, there is a need to introduce recursive architectural solutions that can integrate wrappers within the architectural styles that will be typical for future open systems. Wrappers will then serve as a cardinal structure for introducing and managing redundancy at the architectural level. The focus should be on preserving architectural representations throughout all development phases until runtime execution to enable dynamic changes of architecture to be made online to improve overall system dependability.

It seems clear that future systems will need to have *adaptivity*, so that they can respond to changing environments, altered patterns of use, modified requirements and more. They will need to be dynamically upgradeable and reconfigurable; they will need to have a capacity for adjustment and evolution. Despite this mutability, users will demand that the dependable delivery of service be sustained. Wrappers could provide the fundamental structure supporting component-level adaptation and evolution; protective wrappers could embody fault tolerant defences in support of dependable operation.

5. CONCLUSION – ONLY A BEGINNING!

Protective wrappers offer a simplicity of concept and a generality of applicability that is attractive and encouraging. But it must be acknowledged that this welcome simplicity defers many of the difficult issues to the next stage of research and development.

We close this paper with the observation that all computing systems are (eventually) embedded in groups of humans – that is, in society. Members of society will need future computing systems to be wrapped as a protective mechanism and, in turn, it may be appropriate (in effect) to wrap the users to protect the systems. Very basic protective wrappers are already essential to shield us from the excesses created by something as trivial as spam e-mails!

ACKNOWLEDGEMENT

This work was partially supported by the UK EPSRC DOTS project.

REFERENCES

[And03a] T. Anderson, M. Feng, S. Riddle, A. Romanovsky. Error Recovery for a Boiler System with OTS PID Controller, *CS Technical Report 798*, May 2003, School of Computing Science, Univ. of Newcastle (presented at ECOOP 2003, Darmstadt).

[And03b] T. Anderson, M. Feng, S. Riddle, A. Romanovsky. Protective Wrapper Development. *Proc. 2nd Int. Conf. on COTS-Based Software Systems*, Ottawa, Canada, February 2003, pp. 1-14.

[And03c] T. Anderson, M. Feng, S. Riddle, A. Romanovsky. Investigative Case Study: Protective Wrapping of OTS items in Simulated Environments. *CS Technical Report 821*, December 2003, School of Computing Science, Univ. of Newcastle (submitted to COMPSAC 2004).

[Arl02] J. Arlat, J.-C. Fabre, M. Rodríguez, F. Salles. Dependability of COTS Microkernel-Based Systems. *IEEE Trans. on Computers*. **51**, 2, 2002, pp. 138-163.

[Jon04]C. B. Jones, B. Randell. *Dependable Pervasive Systems*. Foresight report, DTI, UK. 2004.

[Kaâ00] M. Kaâniche, J.-C. Laprie, J.-P. Blanquart. A Dependability-Explicit Model for the Development of Computing Systems. *Proc. SAFECOMP 2000*. Rotterdam, The Netherlands, 2000, pp. 107-116.

[Mat] Mathworks, Using Simulink: reference guide, http://www.mathworks.com

[Nat03] The National Board of Boiler and Pressure Vessel Inspectors. *2002 National Board Incident Report*, http://www.nationalboard.org/incidents/02-IR.html, 2003.

[Pop01] P. Popov, S. Riddle, A. Romanovsky, L. Strigini. On Systematic Design of Protectors for Employing OTS Items. *Proc. 27th Euromicro Conf.*, Warsaw, Poland, September 2001, pp. 22-29.

[Voa98] J. Voas. Certifying OTS Software Components, *IEEE Computer* **31**, 1998, pp. 53-59.

FROM THE UNIVERSITY OF ILLINOIS VIA JPL AND UCLA TO VYTAUTAS MAGNUS UNIVERSITY: 50 YEARS OF COMPUTER ENGINEERING BY ALGIRDAS AVIŽIENIS

David A. Rennels[1] and Miloš D. Ercegovac
Computer Science Department
University of California, Los Angeles
rennels@cs.ucla.edu,milos@cs.ucla.edu

[1] *Also with the Jet Propulsion Laboratory*
Pasadena, California

Abstract This article surveys pioneering contributions of Algirdas Avižienis to the fields of fault-tolerance and dependable computing, digital arithmetic, and computer design, made during his 50-year long career in computer engineering.

Keywords: Dependable computing, fault-tolerance, arithmetic error codes, signed-digit arithmetic

1. Introduction

Algirdas Avižienis was born in Kaunas Lithuania in 1932, the son of a Lithuanian army officer. His family escaped the invasion of the Soviets during World War 2, and as a teenager, he and his family wound up in a displaced persons camp where he learned some of English reading Western novels. The family emigrated to Chicago, that then had a large Lithuanian community, and he worked his way through the University of Illinois. He has had a very successful career, becoming a senior professor, a leader of his research field, and a fellow of the IEEE; receiving numerous awards and an honorary doctorate, serving on many important advisory boards, and finally becoming the founding Rector of the re-established National Lithuanian University. A successful career is characterized by chance events, and a person who has to optimism to recognize opportunities in these events, and the creative abilities to take advantage of them and create something that has not existed before.

Al has done this and through a long career of teaching has made many friends and colleagues whose careers have been enhanced by his work.

2. Algirdas Avižienis and the Development of Fault-Tolerant Computing

Professor Algirdas Avižienis has been a leading figure in fault-tolerant computing for nearly a half-century, and his technical contributions have been seminal in its development. In addition, his leadership in founding the scholarly community of interest through IEEE and IFIP has shaped the growth of the field and greatly facilitated its development. This paper is a reflection on some of his major contributions, but it is not comprehensive – that would require a whole book.

The Beginning (1955-1962)

Upon finishing his MS at the University of Illinois (UIUC) in 1955, he took a job in sunny California with what was then a US Army Laboratory, Caltech's Jet Propulsion Laboratory (JPL), in Pasadena. There, he worked on developing the Corporal and Sergeant missiles - capable of carrying a nuclear warhead up to 100 miles. This was very early technology where target information was entered by turning dials (potentiometers) on the missile, and operator error under battlefield conditions would be catastrophic. This was Avižienis' first exposure to a problem of dependability for critical systems, and he came up with a design to enter the data using punched cards, automatically set the dials, and independently read out their settings. Although he claims that this, his first design was rather kludgy, he was told that parts of it were used in the subsequent Sergeant production models. The early JPL environment was very exciting, but he quickly realized that to take a leadership role, he would need a PhD. So after a year, he took leave of absence and went back to UIUC to finish a Ph.D. under the great computer arithmetic scholar, Jim Robertson. There he increased in wisdom and stature, and he also gained experience in logic design by designing parts of the ILLIAC II arithmetic unit.

While at UIUC new unexpected events and opportunities occurred that would propel him into the leadership of fault-tolerant computing. The USSR, launched Sputnik, the Army with JPL launched the first US satellite (Explorer 1) and an alarmed Congress passed the National Aeronautics and Space Act creating NASA. By the time that Avižienis returned to JPL in 1960, still in his twenties, JPL had been designated a NASA laboratory. Their mission of exploring space required computers that could last for up to 10 years in space without hope of external repair.

Furthermore the amount of electrical power from early solar arrays could only be a few tens of watts, and the state of integrated circuit technology that could be used in the space radiation environment (i.e., bipolar) was only a few gates or flip flops per chip.

Within a year or so (1961), Avižienis came up with the idea of creating a low-power, long life computer using self-repairing techniques by:

- partitioning a computer into modules of smaller size to obtain adequately low module failure rates;
- using codes to provide low cost concurrent error detection - allowing only one module of each type to be operating and thus saving power;
- providing a simple small hybrid redundant core (voting with unpowered spares) that would rollback and/or replace modules that detect errors.

Here, his graduate work in computer arithmetic fit perfectly, because the key to implementing modules that checked themselves lay in the use of low-cost coding techniques (product codes, residue codes) that are invariant under arithmetic. He spent the next few years refining the architectural approach and the coding techniques that could be used in implementing the needed computer modules. This involved partitioning logic onto chips such that single chip failures would remain detectable, and analyzing the coverage of various codes. Here he developed the clever idea of organizing a system in an k-bit serial fashion, so that code checking of either product or residue codes based on a modulus of $2^k - 1$ could be done by simply performing a simple modulo $2^k - 1$ addition of digits as they passed by [4].

While remaining a member of the JPL technical staff, Avižienis joined the faculty of UCLA in 1962 teaching undergraduate and graduate courses on computer design and computer arithmetic.

1962-1972 The STAR Computer Decade

Technical Contributions By 1965-66 his conceptual design had matured to the point where an initial product-coded arithmetic processor was built and tested, and plans were made to implement the complete computer (with the other modules using inverse residue codes). The machine was designated the JPL Self-Testing and Repairing (STAR) computer. In developing the computer, many new research issues were raised, and Avižienis took on a team of graduate student advisees (also working as JPL engineers) who have remained his friends and colleagues for nearly forty years. Among the research issues addressed were:

- how to program such a machine - resulting in the design of an operating system, assembler, and some of the earliest work on program rollback (John Rohr);
- how to do hardware design and evaluation of such a machine - resulting in a design methodology and some of the earliest work on experimental fault-injection tests (David Rennels);
- how to provide reliability prediction of the STAR Computer - resulting in the development of new hybrid redundancy models based on recursive integral equations (Frank Mathur);
- how to use such a machine as an automated repairman for its host spacecraft - resulting in the first comprehensive study of using fault-tolerant design on a spacecraft (George Gilley).

There was an air of excitement as the machine progressed, since nothing like this had been attempted before, and by the date of the First International Symposium on Fault-Tolerant Computing (FTCS 1) the machine was working and ready to be displayed. (As an aside, it almost wasn't ready. A laboratory power supply unexpectedly jumped from 5 to 50 volts, and this author spent the weekend before FTCS 1 soldering new IC flat-packs onto the circuit boards of one of the modules.)

The primary papers on the JPL-STAR Computer were published in 1971 [10, 11], and having coined the term *Fault-Tolerant Computing* Avižienis wrote an article in Computer Magazine giving an overview of what it meant [12]. Related papers were published over the next several years [40, 14, 15, 32, 46, 51].

Perhaps Avižienis' shortest publication of this period, was a letter to the editor of a national news weekly. Being a champion table tennis player at UIUC, he wrote to complain that "if they wanted to refer to table tennis as *ping pong* then they should also refer to basketball as *dribble drabble* or golf as *put put*".

Creating the IEEE Technical Committee on Fault-Tolerant Computing In initiating his STAR computer research, Avižienis visited and corresponded with others he could find who were doing advanced work in dependable systems, including the Saturn V at NASA Marshall, and the IBM Federal Systems Division. JPL subcontracts were awarded to the Stanford Research Institute (Now SRI) to design a voting power switch for the STAR computer, and the MIT Instrumentation Laboratory (now CS Draper Lab) for a read-only memory. Thus due to the STAR project, he had established contacts with many of the people who were to become the leading players in dependable computing.

Yet at that time there were few relevant conferences, and there were no regularly organized meetings or professional community dedicated to fault-tolerant computing. So Avižienis organized a Workshop on the Organization of Reliable Automata, sponsored by UCLA and the IEEE Technical Committee on Switching Circuit Theory and Logic Design in February 1966. The turnout and quality of work at this workshop demonstrated that a critical mass had been reached in this field, with representatives from MIT, MIT Instrumentation Laboratory, Stanford, SRI, UC Berkeley, Princeton, UIUC, IBM Research, University of Michigan, Bell Telephone Laboratories, Honeywell, Westinghouse, Universities of Kyoto and Osaka, Aerospace Corporation, et al.

In early 1969, Avižienis proposed to the IEEE that a new Technical Committee on Fault-Tolerant Computing be established, and it was approved in November 1969 with Avižienis as its first chair. The first order of business was to establish an annual conference, and the first International Symposium on Fault-Tolerant Computing took place in Pasadena, CA with Avižienis as general chair and Bill Carter as Program Chair. FTCS was international from the start, with papers from Japan, France and England as well as the US, and over the years, it has been hosted by research groups in Japan and in six European countries. Thirty four FTCS/DSN conferences later, one can say that the establishment of this community has had an enormous impact on dependable computing technology. It has influenced the careers and friendships of innumerable people involved in it.

1972-1980 The shift to UCLA

At the conclusion of the JPL STAR effort, Avižienis turned his primary attention to research at UCLA. He obtained a five-year National Science Foundation Grant titled Fault-Tolerant Computing that enabled the establishment of the Dependable Computing and Fault-Tolerant Systems (DC-FTS) Laboratory at UCLA. The scope of its research has been very broad, encompassing many aspects of fault-tolerant system architecture, dependability modeling, and even formal specifications and program correctness. It is estimated that about 200 publications, 31 PhD dissertations and 20 M.S. theses have resulted from research started by Avižienis at JPl and in the DC-FTS laboratory. Of the original thirty, five of the PhD's have gone on to university faculty positions and the rest to responsible positions in government and industry.

It was Avižienis' style to initiate many graduate student projects of his own, but also to draw upon the strengths at UCLA by involving other faculty as collaborators in applying fault-tolerance to new application areas. These areas and faculty collaborators are briefly described below:

- High Performance Numerical Processing (with Miloš Ercegovac and Tomás Lang) – Array processors and reconfigurable arrays for high speed numeric computation [16, 18, 20, 22, 29, 45, 54, 56] (3 PhDs)
- Memory systems (with Wesley Chu) – fault-tolerance of multiport memories [38]. (1 PhD)
- Database machines (with Alfonso Cardenas) – fault-tolerance issues in implementing associative processors [30]. (1 PhD)
- On-Line arithmetic and VLSI testing (with Miloš Ercegovac) – error coding algorithms for on-line arithmetic and design of testable CMOS chips [33, 42]. (2 PhDs)
- Computer networks (with Mario Gerla) – fault-tolerant ring networks and the use of Stochastic Petri nets to prove correctness and performance [34, 35].
- Modular systems composed of self-checking VLSI-based building blocks (with David Rennels and Miloš Ercegovac) [47].
- Formal specifications and program correctness (with David Martin) – compiler correctness and the syntheses of correct microprograms (2 PhDs)

Avižienis extended his work on error detecting codes used in the STAR computer with algorithms for two-dimensional residue codes which allowed error correction as well as detection [26]. Other studies were conducted to explore external monitoring and diagnosis.

He was especially interested in issues of fault-tolerant VLSI design and directed studies on self-checking VLSI design, yield enhancement, and techniques to enhance their testability. This resulted in techniques to use redundancy to improve chip yields [39] and to implement self-checking programmable logic arrays [57, 52].

He maintained his interest in reliability modeling and he directed the development of several new prediction models. A major advance in Markov modeling was contributed through the Ph.D. dissertation of Y. W. Ng, who devised an unified model that introduced transient faults degradability and repair [41]. The ARIES 76 reliability modeling system (written in APL) contained all these features and found wide acceptance for education, research, and in industry.

In about 1975 Avižienis turned his attention to the hard question of how to provide tolerance against software faults through Multi-Version Programming (MVP) alternatively called N-Version Programming. Here he proposed an approach akin to replication and voting in hardware, i.e., Multi-Version Software (MVS), that could be voted to override an error in any single version. All versions are partitioned into smaller modules whose results are individually voted. Thus all versions may have an error, but the system will continue correctly as long as there are not enough errors in the versions of any individual module to overwhelm the voting. An experiment was conducted using students in a software engineering class, and the results were satisfactory: faulty versions were outvoted and the redundant software continued to perform satisfactorily [19].

It was recognized however, that the dependability of MVS depended upon the availability of high quality specifications. It also depended on the various software versions not having related faults (i.e., maximizing diversity of the design). Furthermore it had yet to be applied to a critical real-world application. Thus the stage was set for continued investigation.

Design Diversity 1980-1990

During this period Avižienis organized and directed large scale experiments to explore the issues of multiversion software in depth.

Specification Languages To examine the effect of specification techniques on multi-version software, an experiment was designed in which three different specifications were used. The first was written in the formal specification language OBJ. The second specification language chosen was the non-formal PDL that was characteristic of current industry practice. English was employed as the third, or "control" specification language, since English had been used in the previous studies. Teams of programmers wrote MVP programs which were then run to determine the accuracy of the resulting code. Although there were errors in modules of some of the software versions, the MVP programs executed correctly when all versions were run and voted. It was determined that there were more code errors in software generated from the formal specification language than when using non-formal PDL [36, 23].

The DEDIX Testbed In order to provide a long-term research facility for design diversity experiments his research group implemented the DEDIX (DEsign DIversity eXperiment) system, a distributed supervisor and testbed for multiple-version software. It provided tools to supervise and monitor the execution of N diverse versions of an application program functioning as a fault-tolerant N-version software unit. DEDIX also provided Input/Output services and a transparent interface to the users writing individual versions, so that they need not be aware of the existence of multiple versions and the implementation of recovery algorithms. It began operation in 1965 [25]. The design team that implemented this system, in addition to Avižienis and John Kelly, included a remarkable international group. They included Per Gunningberg (Uppsala), Lorenzo Strigini (Pisa), Pascal Traverse (Toulouse) and Udo Voges (Karlsruhe).

To apply this methodology to a real-application, Avižienis collaborated with Honeywell/Sperry, who provided a problem of pitch control for automated landing systems [27]. A MVS experiment was conducted with the programming teams using different languages to further increase the diversity of their versions (C, Pascal, Modula2, Prolog, and T). Very few errors were found after acceptance testing, and the redundancy of the voted programs provided correct operation. Their paper concluded that the technology was ready for use in commercial applications. It was also concluded, however, that the specification and programming methodology developed over extensive experiments must be followed very carefully to preserve diversity [37].

As a result of Avižienis original MVS research, NASA initiated a Multi-University N-Version Programming Experiment in which UCLA and three universities were involved in writing N-version programs for control of a Redundant Strapped Down Inertial Measurement Unit. The results provided a large amount of data on preserving diversity in MVP programming, effectiveness of MVP, and methodologies for code testing.

Multi-version programming was somewhat controversial when it was started because it is a hard and open-ended problem without simple answers. It required building tools, conducting patient experiments involving teams of students, and its practical applications were seen to be limited and not provable. Only when one looks deeper into this does one recognize its major contributions to the *science* of dependable computing.

- First it asks one of the hardest of questions. How can we get correct operation when people make design mistakes? Then it explores the best ways we know how to do this – providing qualitative and quantitative results and insights.

- Second, the experiments provided extensive data on how programming errors are made and what procedures can be used to minimize these errors – thus providing invaluable data in software engineering. In the course of doing these experiments, diverse design has proven itself as an effective technique for program debugging and even finding errors in specifications.

- Third, there are highly critical applications where diverse design has been selected as the only way to meet stringent reliability requirements.

Following the MVP research, Avižienis turned his attention back to hardware architecture. He and a student have done an extensive study of design errors in modern microprocessors and, since retiring from UCLA he has developed a new distributed architecture for COTS components [28].

Creation of the IFIP Working Group 10.4 on Dependable Computing and Fault Tolerance

As the research community in fault-tolerant and dependable computing (that Al Avižienis had such a large part in building) became large, highly international and well established, it became clear that it should be represented in the International Federation of Information Processing. Al Avižienis was the primary person in establishing this IFIP working group in October 1980 and served as its first chairman. It has become a mechanism where leading international researchers regularly gather and address new issues that arise in this important technical area.

3. Contributions to Digital Arithmetic

In his landmark 1960 doctoral dissertation [2, 3] on signed-digit number systems and arithmetic algorithms, Aviženis provided the foundation and formalisms enabling their systematic use in the design of arithmetic units. Signed-digit number systems had been previously recognized as useful. They were used in the Booth multiplier recoding in radix 2 of the set {0,1} to {-1,0,1}, and similarly in higher radices $r > 2$. Likewise, the use of redundancy in quotient digit sets allowed faster division algorithms such as the SRT division [50] and led to generalized high-radix non-restoring division investigated in detail by Robertson [48] and others at the University of Illinois in the 60s and 70s [50, 49]. Interestingly, the potential advantages of signed-digit numbers were noticed by many early mathematicians including Augustine Cauchy who discussed signed-digit numbers as early as 1840.

Avižienis was first to propose and develop general algorithms for arithmetic operations on signed-digit representations to achieve a "closed" arithmetic system. His "totally parallel" addition algorithm elegantly eliminates the notorious carry problem by allowing redundancy in each digit position. This led to a two-step addition algorithm that can be executed in constant time, that is, independently of the number of digits. In other words, redundant arithmetic algorithms retain weighted representations while "decoupling" digit positions. As a consequence, one can also perform addition and other operations in the most-significant-digit-first manner. Thus Aviženis' work ultimately led to online arithmetic where all operations can be performed most-significant-digit-first (MSDF), generating the result digits while consuming the input digits [31]. As discussed by Avižienis in [5, 7], the MSDF class of arithmetic algorithms has inherent capabilities to perform variable-precision operations and to keep track of significance of generated digits .

The use of redundant number systems has become pervasive and represents one of the most important developments in the field of digital arithmetic. Avižienis' work on redundant representation systems provided much of the underlying framework, and it also provided a framework for studying other important techniques such as digit-set recoding, carry-save addition, and, as mentioned, online arithmetic. In [6] he developed arithmetic microsystems suitable for IC implementations based on signed-digit arithmetic. Further work on a universal arithmetic building element (ABE) and design methods for arithmetic processors was described in [8]. These ideas were applied in the design of combinational arithmetic systems for approximation of functions [55]. Complexity issues of redundant arithmetic were investigated in [17].

The first extensive use of signed-digit number system and algorithms was in the Illiac III computer as described in [1]. A quick look at the literature indicates that signed-digit number system have been frequently used in both general-purpose processors and in application-specific processors, in particular, in digital signal processors.

Aviženis is also widely known for his novel work on low-cost arithmetic error codes. In particular, he made original contributions to low-cost arithmetic error-detection and correction codes [13] and developed efficient algorithms for error-coded operands [15]. These algorithms were implemented in the radix-16 processor constructed for the Jet Propulsion Laboratory STAR computer mentioned above. The 1971 paper is a classic which was selected as the representative paper on the topic in the 1982 text on "Reliable System Design" by D. Siewiorek and R.S. Swarz. His ideas on error codes led to research in their applications in mass memories [43, 44]. In [22] the low-cost error codes have been investigated in the context of large high-performance computers, and they were extended to signed-digit operands in [21]. His two-dimensional low-cost residue and inverse residue codes are novel and appear to be very useful for checking of memories as well as of byte-oriented processors [24].

Besides mentoring a large number of PhD and MS students, Avižienis established at UCLA one of the first graduate courses in the USA dedicated to computer arithmetic algorithms and processors. He developed extensive notes and contributed a widely-known unified algorithmic specification [9].

Avižienis has been an active participant in the IEEE Symposia on Computer Arithmetic (ARITH) since the first workshop in 1969. For his seminal contributions to digital arithmetic he has been honored twice: he was invited as the keynote speaker to the 8th IEEE Symposium on Computer Arithmetic in 1978, Lake Como, Italy, and the proceedings of the 12th IEEE Symposium on Computer Arithmetic in 1995, Bath, England, were dedicated to him.

4. On to Even Bigger Things

Over the decades, Al Avižienis maintained close ties to both the Los Angeles and the international Lithuanian community – inviting visiting Lithuanian scholars to his home and frequently visiting Lithuania. One of his proudest accomplishments was working to build a local Lithuanian Boy Scout Camp in the mountains of Southern California. Due to this, fate intervened again when Lithuania achieved independence. His home town of Kaunas Lithuania was historically the Lithuanian academic center, and Avižienis and others saw the opportunity to re-open the National University of Lithuania, Vytautas Magnus University, previously closed by the Soviets, and establish western-style research and PhD programs. From 1990-1993 he served as the founding rector in re-starting this university.

This is probably his crowning accomplishment that will have a major impact on the development of Lithuania, and on the careers of many students. Starting with 180 first-year students, VMU currently has an enrolment of 7000, including about 800 Master's and 200 Doctorate students. After retiring as rector, Prof. Avižienis has served at VMU as a Research Professor and Professor Honoris Causa since 1994, working on fundamental concepts of dependable computing and on an Immune System Paradigm for design of fault-tolerant systems. He has served as a member of the Kaunas city council and will doubtlessly remain involved in community service in other ways in the future.

In his long career, Professor Avižienis has repeatedly demonstrated the ability to seize opportunities, offer innovative solutions to the new situations that present themselves, and in the process enrich the technology and the lives of those with whom he works. We will be expecting more new and interesting results from his efforts.

References

[1] Atkins, D. E., Design of the Arithmetic Units of ILLIAC III: Use of Redundancy and Higher Radix Methods", *IEEE Transactions on Computers*, C-19(8):720–733, August 1970.

[2] Avižienis, A., *A Study of Redundant Number Representations for Parallel Digital Computers*, Ph.D. Thesis, University of Illinois, Urbana, 1960.

[3] Avižienis, A., Signed Digit Number Representations for Fast Parallel Arithmetic, *IRE Transactions on Electronic Computers*, EC-10(9): 389-400, September 1961.

[4] Avižienis, A., A Study of the Effectiveness of Fault-Detecting Codes for Binary Arithmetic, Jet Propulsion Laboratory, Pasadena, California, Technical Report 32-711, September 1, 1965.

[5] Avižienis, A., On flexible implementation of digital computer arithmetic, *Proc. IFIP Congress*, pp. 664–670, 1962.

[6] Avižienis, A., Arithmetic microsystems for the synthesis of function generators, *Proc. of the IEEE*, 54(12):1910-1919, December 1966.

[7] Avižienis, A., Binary-compatible signed-digit arithmetic, *Proc. Fall Joint Computer Conference*, pp. 663–672, 1964.

[8] Avižienis, A. and C. Tung, A Universal Arithmetic Building Element (ABE) and Design Methods for Arithmetic Processors, *IEEE Transactions on Computers*, C-19(8):733–745, August 1970.

[9] Avižienis, A., Digital Computer Arithmetic: A Unified Algorithmic Specification, *Proceedings Symposium on Computers and Automata*, pp. 509-525, April 1971.

[10] Avižienis, A., Gilley, G. C., Mathur, F. P., Rennels, D. A., Rohr, J. A, Rubin, D. K., The STAR (Self-Testing-and-Repairing)Computer: An Investigation of the Theory and Practice of Fault-Tolerant Computer Design, *IEEE Trans. on Computers*, Vol. C-20, No. II, November 1971, pp. 1312-1321: also in *Digest of the 1971 International Symposium on Fault-Tolerant Computing*, Pasadena, CA, March 1971, pp. 92-96.

[11] Avižienis, A., Arithmetic Error Codes: Cost and Effectiveness Studies for Application in Digital System Design, *IEEE Trans. on Computers*, Vol. C-20, No. II, November 1971, pp. 1322-1330: also in *Digest of the 1971 International Symposium on Fault-Tolerant Computing*, Pasadena, CA, March 1971, pp. 118-121.

[12] Avižienis, A., Fault-Tolerant Computing An Overview, *IEEE Computer*, Vol. 4, No. I, February 1971, pp. 5-8.

[13] Avižienis, A., Arithmetic Error Codes: 'Cost and Effectiveness Studies for Application in Digital System Design, *IEEE Transactions on Computers*, C-20(11):1322-1331, November 1971.

[14] Avižienis, A., Rennels, D. A., Fault-Tolerance Experiments With The JPL STAR Computer, in *Digest of COMPCON '72* (Sixth Annual IEEE Computer Society Int. Conf.), San Francisco, California, 1972, pp. 321-324.

[15] Avižienis, A., Arithmetic Algorithms for Error-Coded Operands, *IEEE Trans. on Computers*, C-22(6):567-572, June 1973; also in *Digest of FTCS-2, the 2nd*

International Symposium on Fault-Tolerant Computing, Newton, MA, June 1972, pp. 25-29.

[16] Avižienis, A., Parhami, B., A Fault-Tolerant Parallel Computer System for Signal Processing, *Digest of FTCS-4, the 4th International Symposium on Fault-Tolerant Computing*, Champaign, IL., June 1974, pp. 2-8 - 2-13.

[17] A. Avižienis, Redundancy in number representations as an aspect of computational complexity of arithmetic functions, *Proc. 3rd IEEE Symposium on Computer Arithmetic*, pp. 87–89, 1975.

[18] Avižienis, A., Ercegovac, M., Lang, T., Sylvain, P., Thomasian, A., An Investigation of Fault-Tolerant Architectures for Large-Scale Numerical Computing, *Proceedings of the Symposium on High-Speed Computer & Algorithm Organization*, University of Illinois at Urbana-Champaign, April 1977, Academic Press, pp. 173-178.

[19] Avižienis, A., Chen, L., On the Implementation of N-version Programming for Software Fault Tolerance During Execution, *Proceedings COMPSAC 77*, (First IEEE-CS International Computer Software and Applications Conference), Chicago, November 1977, pp. 149-155.

[20] Avižienis, A., Bond, J. W. III, Fault Tolerance in Large Computing Systems, *Proceedings of the 3rd Jerusalem Conference on Information Technology*, Jerusalem, August 1978, pp. 9-16.

[21] A. Avižienis, Low-cost residue and inverse residue error-detecting codes for signed-digit arithmetic, *Proc. 5th IEEE Symposium on Computer Arithmetic*, pp. 165-168, 1981.

[22] A. Avižienis and C. S. Raghavendra, Applications for arithmetic error codes in large, high-performance computers, *Proc. 6th IEEE Symposium on Computer Arithmetic*, pp. 169-173, 1983.

[23] Avižienis, A., Kelly, J. P. J., Fault Tolerance by Design Diversity: Concepts and Experiments, *Computer*, Vol. 17, No. 8, August 1984, pp. 67-80.

[24] Avižienis, A., Arithmetic algorithms for operands encoded in two-dimensional low-cost arithmetic codes, *Proc. 7th IEEE Symposium on Computer Arithmetic*, pp. 285-292, 1985.

[25] Avižienis, A., Gunningberg, P., Kelly, J. P. J., Strigini, L., Traverse, P. J., Tso, K. S., Voges, U., The UCLA DEDIX system: a Distributed Testbed for Multiple-Version Software, *Digest of FTCS-15, the 15th International Symposium on Fault-Tolerant Computing*, Ann Arbor, Michigan, June 1985, pp. 126-134.

[26] Avižienis, A., Two-Dimensional Low-Cost Arithmetic Residue Codes: Effectiveness and Arithmetic Algorithms, *Digest of FTCS-16, the 16th International Symposium on Fault-Tolerant Computing*, Vienna, Austria, July 1986, pp. 330-336.

[27] Avižienis, A., Ball, D. E., On the Achievement of a Highly Dependable and Fault-Tolerant Air Traffic Control System, *Computer*, Vol. 20, No. 2, February 1987, pp. 84-90.

[28] Avižienis, A., A FaultTolerance Infrastructure for Dependable Computing with High-Performance Components, *Digest International Conference on Dependable Systems and Networks*, DSN 2000, New York, June 25-28, 2000, pp. 81-86.

[29] Baqai, I., Lang, T., Reliability Aspects of the ILLIAC IV Computer, *Proceedings of the 1976 International Conference on Parallel Processing*, August 1976, pp. 123-131.

[30] Cardenas, A. F., Alavian, F., Avižienis, A., Performance of Recovery Architectures in Parallel Associative Database Processors, *ACM Transactions on Database Systems*, Vol. 8, No. 3, September 1983, pp. 291-323.

[31] Ercegovac, M.D. and T. Lang, *Digital Arithmetic*, Morgan Kaufmann Publishers, San Francisco, 2004.

[32] Gilley, G. C., A Fault-Tolerant Spacecraft, *Digest of FTCS-2, the 2nd International Symposium on Fault-Tolerant Computing*, Newton, MA, June 1972, pp. 105-109.

[33] Gorji-Sinaki, A., *Error-Coded Algorithms for On-Line Arithmetic*, PhD Thesis, University of California, Los Angeles.

[34] Grnarov, A., Kleinrock, L., Gerla, M., A Highly Reliable Distributed Loop Architecture, *Digest of FTCS-IO, the 10th International Symposium on Fault-Tolerant Computing*, Kyoto, Japan, October 1980, pp. 319-324.

[35] Grnarov, A., Arlat, J., Avižienis, A., Modeling of Software Fault-Tolerance Strategies, *Proceedings of the 11th Annual Pittsburgh Modeling & Simulation Conference*, University of Pittsburgh, Pennsylvania, Vol. II, Part 2, May 1980, pp. 571- 578.

[36] Kelly, J. P. J., Avižienis. A., A Specification-oriented Multi-version Software Experiment, *Digest of FTCS-13, the 13th International Symposium on Fault-Tolerant Computing*, Milano, Italy, June 1983, pp. 120-126.

[37] Kelly, J. P.J. et al., A Large Scale Second Generation Experiment in Multi-Version Software: Description and Early Results, *Digest of FTCS 28, International Symposium on Fault-Tolerant Computing*, Tokyo, Japan, June 27-30, pp. 9-14.

[38] Korff, P., *A Multiaccess Memory*, Ph.D. thesis, UCLA Computer Science Department, University of California, Los Angeles, June 1976; also Technical Report UCLA-ENG-7607, July 1976.

[39] Mangir, T. E., Avižienis, A., Fault-Tolerant Design for VLSI: Effect of Interconnect Requirements on Yield Improvement of VLSI Designs, *IEEE Transactions on Computers*, Vol. C-31, No. 7, July 1982, pp. 609-616.

[40] Mathur, F. P., On Reliability Modeling and Analysis of Ultra-Reliable Fault-Tolerant Digital Systems, *IEEE Transactions on Computers*, Vol. C-20, No. II, November 1971, pp. 1376-1382.

[41] Ng, Y. W., Avižienis, A., A Unified Reliability Model for Fault-Tolerant Computers, *IEEE Transactions on Computers*, Vol. C-29, No. II, pp. 1002-1011, November 1980.

[42] Oklobdzija, V. G., Ercegovac, M. D., Testability Enhancement of VLSI Using Circuit Structures, *Proceedings of IEEE 1982 International Conference on Circuits and Computers*, New York, 1982.

[43] Parhami, B. and A. Avižienis, Application of arithmetic error codes for checking mass memories, *Digest of FTCS-3, the 3rd Int. Symposium on Fault-Tolerant Computing*, pp. 47-51, June 1973.

[44] Parhami, B. and A. Avižienis, Detection of storage errors in mass memories using low-cost arithmetic codes, *IEEE Transactions on Computers*, C-27(4):302-308, April 1978.

[45] Raghavendra, C. S., Avižienis, A., Ercegovac, M. D., Fault Tolerance in Binary Tree Architectures, *IEEE Transactions on Computers*, Vol. C-33, No. 6, June 1984, pp. 568-572.

[46] Rennels, D. A., Avižienis, A., RMS: A Reliability Modeling System for Self-Repairing Computers, *Digest of FTCS-3, the 3rd International Symposium on Fault-Tolerant Computing*, June 1973, pp. 131-135.

[47] Rennels, D. A., Avižienis, A., Ercegovac, M., A Study of Standard Building Blocks for the Design of Fault-Tolerant Distributed Computer Systems, *Digest of FTCS-8, the 8th International Symposium on Fault-Tolerant Computing*, Toulouse, France, June 1978, pp. 144-149.

[48] J. E. Robertson, A New Class of Digital Division Methods, *IRE Transactions Electronic Computers*, EC-7(3):88-92, September 1958.

[49] Robertson, J. E., *Introduction to Digital Computer Arithmetic*, Department of Computer Science, University of Illinois at Urbana-Champaign, File No. 599, 1964.

[50] Robertson, J. E., Arithmetic unit (Chapter 8) in On the design of very high-speed computer, Computer Science Department, University of Illinois at Urbana-Champaign, Technical Report No. 80, 1957

[51] Rohr, J. A., STAREX Self-Repair Routines: Software Recovery in The JPL-STAR Computer, *Digest of FTCS-3, the 3rd International Symposium on Fault-Tolerant Computing*, Palo Alto, California, June 1973, pp. 11-16.

[52] Sievers, M., Avižienis, A., Analysis of a Class of Totally Self-Checking Functions Implemented in a MOS LSI General Logic Structure, *Digest of FTCS-11, the 11th International Symposium on Fault-Tolerant Computing*, Portland, Maine, June 1981, pp. 256-261.

[53] Slekys, A. G. and A. Avižienis, A modified bi-imaginary number system, *Proc. 4th IEEE Symposium on Computer Arithmetic*, pp. 48–55, 1978.

[54] Sylvain, P., Vineberg, M., The Design and Evaluation of the Array Machine: A High-Level Language Processor, *Proceedings of Second Annual Symposium on Computer Architecture*, Houston, TX, January 1975, pp. 119-125.

[55] Tung, C. and Avižienis, A., Combinational arithmetic systems for the approximation of functions, *AFIPS Conference Proceedings 1970 Spring Joint Computer Conference*, pp. 95-107, 1970.

[56] Vineberg, M., Avižienis, A., Implementation of a Higher- Level Language on an Array Machine, *Proceedings of the International Workshop on Computer Architecture*, Grenoble, France, June 1973.

[57] Wang, S. L., Avižienis, A., The Design of Totally Self-Checking Circuits Using Programmable Logic Arrays, *Digest of FTCS-9, the 9th International Symposium on Fault-Tolerant Computing*, Madison, Wl, June 1979, pp. 173-180.

AIRBUS FLY-BY-WIRE: A TOTAL APPROACH TO DEPENDABILITY

Pascal Traverse, Isabelle Lacaze and Jean Souyris
Airbus, 316, route de Bayonne, 31060 Toulouse, France
{pascal.traverse, isabelle.lacaze, jean.souyris}@airbus.com

Abstract: This paper deals with the digital electrical flight control system of the Airbus airplanes. This system is built to very stringent dependability requirements both in terms of safety (the systems must not output erroneous signals) and availability. System safety and availability principles are presented with an emphasis on their evolution and on future challenges

Key words: dependability, fault-tolerance, safety, proof, human factors, system design, airplane, fly-by-wire, flight controls

1. INTRODUCTION

1.1 Background

The first electrical flight control system (a.k.a. Fly-by-Wire) for a civil aircraft was designed by Aerospatiale and installed on Concorde. This is an analogue, full-authority system for all control surfaces and copies the stick commands onto the control surfaces while adding stabilizing terms. A mechanical back-up system is provided on the three axes.

The first generation of electrical flight control systems with digital technology appeared on several civil aircraft at the start of the 1980's including the Airbus A310. These systems control the slats, flaps and spoilers. These systems have very stringent safety requirements (in the sense that the runaway of these control surfaces is generally classified as Catastrophic and must then be extremely improbable). However, loss of a function is permitted, as the only consequences are a supportable increase in the crew's workload.

The Airbus A320 was certified and entered into service in the first quarter of 1988. It is the first example of a second generation of civil electrical flight control aircraft, which is now a full family (A318, A319, A320, A321, A330, A340). The distinctive feature of these aircraft is that high-level control laws in normal operation control all control surfaces electrically and that the system is designed to be available under all circumstances.

This family of airplane has accrued a large and satisfactory service experience with more than 10000 pilots operating a Fly-by-Wire Airbus, and more than 40 million flight hours. Nevertheless, system architecture is permanently challenged to take benefit of technical progress and of this large in-service experience. Indeed, on top of the architecture level reached by A340[1, 2], A340-600, A380, and A400M are going steps further.

The A340-600 is the first significant change compared to the A320/A330/A340 baseline. It entered into service mid of 2002, introducing structural modes control, a full rudder electrical control and integration of autopilot inner loop with manual control laws. The full rudder electrical control is now part of all A330 and A340 definition.

A380 and A400M will be the first in-service aircraft with electrical actuation of control surfaces (a.k.a. Power-by-Wire). Additionally, new avionics principle are applied and a full autopilot and manual control integration is performed.

Other architectures are possible[3]. The family of architectures we have designed has the merit of having been built step-by-step, together with our products development and experience.

1.2 Fly-by-wire principle

On a conventional airplane, the pilot orders are transmitted to the actuators by an arrangement of mechanical components. In addition, computers are modifying pilot feels on the controls, and autopilot computers are able to control servo actuators that move the whole mechanical control chain.

The A320/A330/A340 Airbus flight control surfaces are all electrically controlled, and hydraulically activated.

The side-sticks are used to fly the aircraft in pitch and roll (and indirectly through turn co-ordination in yaw). The pilot inputs are interpreted by the flight controls computers that move the surfaces as necessary to achieve the desired flight path modification. In autopilot mode, the flight controls computers take their orders from the autopilot computers. With this respect, the flight controls are composed of five to seven computers, and the autopilot of two.

The aircraft response to surfaces movement is fed back to both autopilot and flight controls computers through specific sensors (Air Data and Inertial Reference Units - ADIRU, accelerometers, rate-gyro).

1.3 On failure and dependability

Flight control systems are built to very stringent dependability requirements both in terms of safety (the system must not output erroneous signals) and availability. Most, but not all, of these requirements are directly coming from Aviation Authorities (FAA, EASA, etc. refer to FAR/JAR 25[4]).

Remaining of the paper is structured around threat to safety and availability of the system[5], namely:

- Failures caused by physical faults such as electrical short-circuit, or mechanical rupture
- Design and manufacturing error
- Particular risks such as engine rotor burst
- Mishap at Man-Machine Interface

Interestingly, means against these threats to dependability are valuable protection against malicious faults and attacks, on top of classical security measures.

For each of these threats, the applicable airworthiness requirements are summarized; the solutions used on Airbus Fly-by-Wire are described, along with challenges to these solutions and future trends.

2. SYSTEMS FAILURES DUE TO PHYSICAL FAULTS

FAR/JAR 25.1309 that requires demonstrating that any combination of failures with catastrophic consequence is Extremely Improbable typically addresses failures. "Extremely Improbable" is translated in qualitative requirements (see § 3 to 5) and to a 10^{-9} probability per flight hours. Specifically for flight controls, FAR/JAR 25.671 requires that a catastrophic consequence must not be due to a single failure or a control surface jam or a pilot control jam. This qualitative requirement is on top of the probabilistic assessment.

To deal with the safety issue (the system must not output erroneous signals), the basic building blocks are the fail-safe command and monitoring computers. These computers have stringent safety requirements and are functionally composed of a command channel and a monitoring channel.

To ensure a sufficient availability level, a high level of redundancy is built into the system.

2.1 Command and monitoring computers

2.1.1 Computer architecture

Functionally, the computers have a command channel and a monitoring channel (see figure 1.a). The command channel ensures the function allocated to the computer (for example, control of a moving surface). The monitoring channel ensures that the command channel operates correctly. This type of computer has already been used for the autopilot computers of Concorde, and the Airbus aircraft.

These computers can be considered as being two different and independent computers placed side by side. These two (sub) computers have different functions and software and are placed adjacent to each other only to make aircraft maintenance easier. Both command and monitoring channels of one computer are active simultaneously, or waiting, again simultaneously, to go from stand-by to active state. When in stand-by mode, computers are powered in order to activate potential dormant faults and isolate them. The monitoring channel acts also on associated actuator: when deselecting the COM order, it switches off the actuator solenoid valve to set it in stand-by mode (figure 1.b).

Two types of computers are used in the A320 flight control system: the ELAC's (ELevator and Aileron Computers) and the SEC's (Spoiler and Elevator Computers). Each computer has a command channel and a monitoring one. Thus, four different entities coexist: command channel of ELAC computer, monitoring channel of ELAC computer, command channel of SEC computer, and monitoring channel of SEC computer. This leads to four different software packages.

Two types of computers are also used on the A340 and A380: the PRIM's (primary computers) and the SEC's (secondary computers). Although these computers are different, the basic safety principles are similar and described in this part of the paper.

In addition to the ELAC's and SEC's of the A320, two computers are used for rudder control (FAC). They are not redundant to the ELAC's and SEC's. On other Airbus, these rudder control functions are integrated in the PRIM's and SEC's.

2.1.2 Computer channel architecture

Each channel (figure 1.a) includes one or more processors, associated memories, input/output circuits, a power supply unit and specific software. When the results of one of these two channels diverges significantly, the channel or channels which detected this failure cut the links between the computer and the exterior.

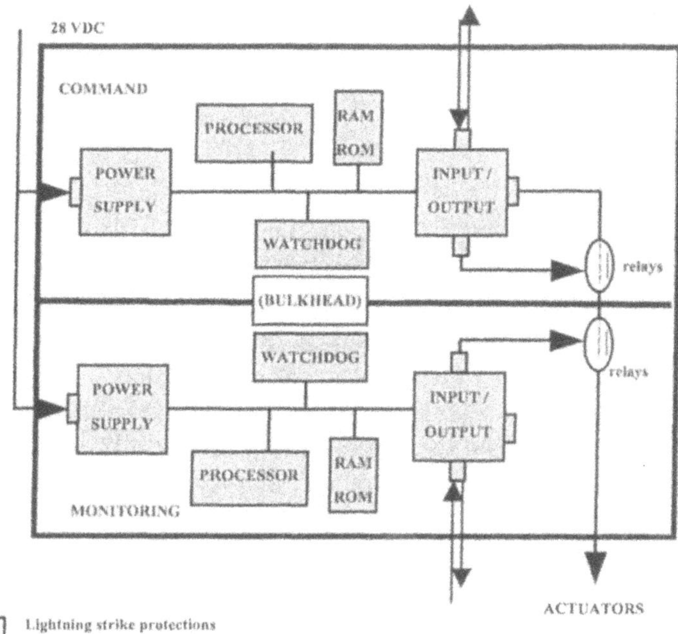

Figure 1.a: computer global architecture

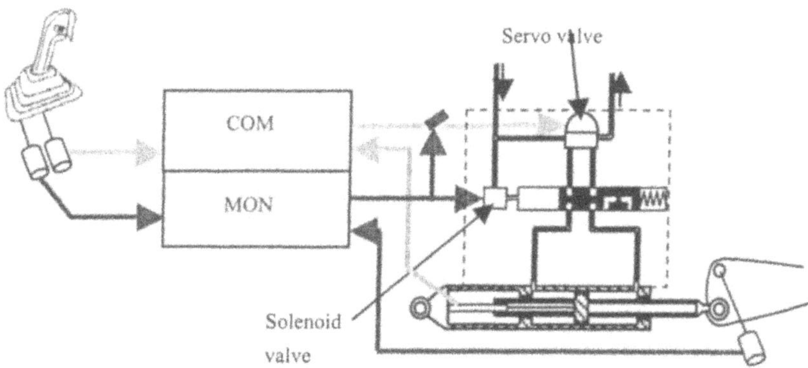

Figure 1.b: computer monitoring architecture

The system is designed so that the computer outputs are then in a dependable state (signal interrupt via relays). Failure detection is mainly achieved by comparing the difference between the command and monitoring commands with a predetermined threshold. This schema therefore allows the consequences of a failure of one of the computer's components to be detected and prevents the resulting error from propagating outside of the computer. This detection method is completed by monitoring for good execution of the program via its sequencing and memory encoding.

Flight control computers must be especially robust. They are protected against over voltages and under voltages, electromagnetic aggressions and indirect effects of lightning. They are cooled by a ventilation system but will operate correctly even if ventilation is lost.

2.1.3 Redundancy

The redundancy aspect is handled at system level. This paragraph only deals with the computer constraints making system reconfiguration possible. The functions of the system are divided out between all the computers so that each one is permanently active at least on one subassembly of its functions. For any given function, one computer is active the others are in standby ("hot spares"). As soon as the active computer interrupts its operation, one of the standby computers almost instantly changes to active mode without a jerk or with a limited jerk on the control surfaces. Typically, duplex computers are designed so that they permanently transmit healthy signals and so that the signals are interrupted at the same time as the "functional" outputs (to an actuator for example) following the detection of a failure.

2.1.4 Failure detection

Certain failures may remain masked a long time after their creation. A typical case is that of a monitoring channel made passive and detected only when the monitored channel itself fails. Tests are conducted periodically so that the probability of the occurrence of an undesirable event remains sufficiently low (i.e., to fulfill FAR/JAR 25.1309 quantitative requirement). Typically, a computer runs its self-tests and tests its peripherals during the power-up of the aircraft and therefore at least once a day.

2.2 Components redundancy

2.2.1 Power supplies

Primary power is coming from the engines to pressurize hydraulic systems and to generate electricity. Also, an auxiliary generator, batteries and a Ram Air Turbine (RAT) are available. If all engines shut down, the RAT is automatically extended. It then pressurizes a hydraulic system that drives a third electrical generator. The computers are connected to at least two electrical power supplies. The aircraft has three hydraulic systems (identified by a color, Green, Blue, and Yellow on figure 2 for A340-600) one of which is sufficient to control the aircraft.

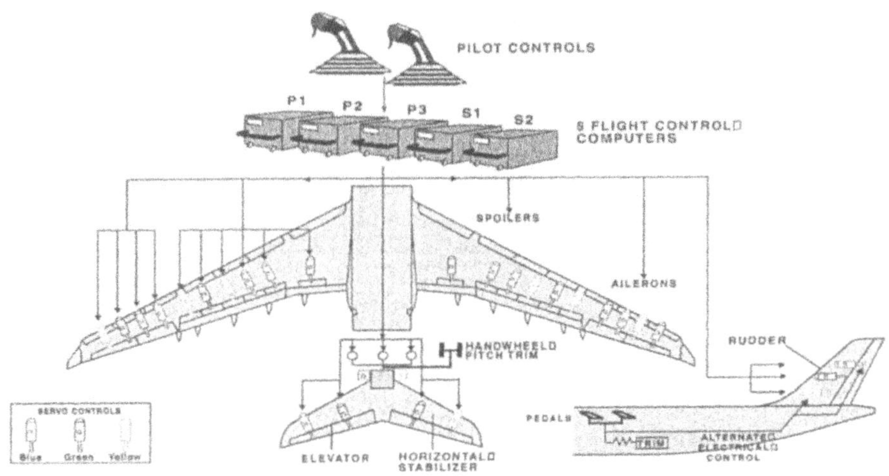

Figure 2: A340-600 system architecture

As a new technology of actuators is now available[6] (Electro Hydrostatic Actuator – EHA – see figure 3.a, compared to conventional servocontrol, figure 3.b) it is possible to take benefit of them. This is done on A380 and A400M. The 3 hydraulic power supplies are replaced by 4, 2 hydraulic ones and 2 electrical ones. RAT is providing directly electrical power. This provides a weight and cost saving along with an increased redundancy and survivability, which was the primary reason for the introduction of this technology.

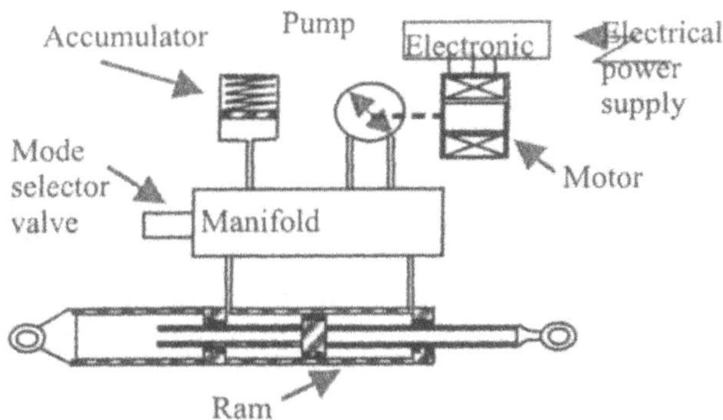

Figure 3.a: Electro-hydrostatic Actuator

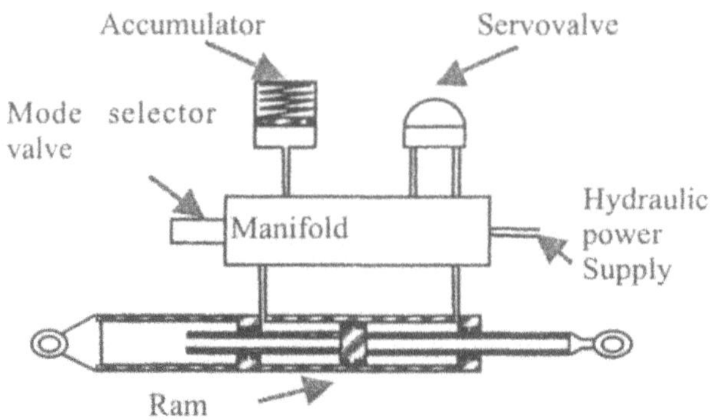

Figure 3.b: Hydraulic Servocontrol

2.2.2 Computers

The computers and actuators are also redundant. This is illustrated by the A340-600 pitch control (left and right elevator, plus Trimable Horizontal Stabilizer - THS). Four command and monitoring computers are used, one is sufficient to control the aircraft. In normal operation, one of the computers (PRIM1) controls the pitch, with one servocontrol pressurized by the Green hydraulic for the left elevator, one pressurized by the Green hydraulic on the right elevator, and by electric motor N°1 for the THS. The other computers control the other control surfaces. If PRIM1 or one of the actuators that it controls fails, PRIM2 takes over (with the servocontrols pressurized by the Blue hydraulic on left elevator, yellow on right side, and with THS motor N°2). Following same failure method, PRIM2 can hand over control to SEC1. Likewise, pitch control can be passed from one SEC to the other depending on the number of control surfaces that one of these computers can handle. Note that 3 computers would be sufficient to meet the safety objectives. The additional computer is fully justified by operational constraints: it is desirable to be able to tolerate a take-off with one computer failed. This defines the Minimum Equipment List (MEL).

2.2.3 Reconfiguration of flight control laws and flight envelope protections

Note that the laws are robust as designed with a sufficient stability margin[7-10]. Also, if the input vector of the system is far outside the maximum certified envelope, only a simple law, using the position of the sticks and the position of the control surfaces at input, is activated (this law is similar to the type of control available on a conventional aircraft).

The laws must be reconfigured if certain sensors are lost (in particular, the ADIRU's). The crew is clearly warned about the status of the control law. If the three ADIRU's are available (normal case), the pilot has full authority within a safe flight envelope. This safe flight envelope is provided by protections included in the control laws, by addition of protection orders to the pilot orders. Flight control is in G-load factor mode.

If only one ADIRU is available, it is partially monitored by comparison with other independent information sources (in particular, an accelerometer). In this case, the safe flight envelope is provided by warnings, as on a conventional aircraft. Flight control is still in G-load factor mode. If all ADIRU's are lost, the flight envelope protections are also lost and the flight control law is in a degraded mode: direct mode. This law has gains, which are a function of the aircraft configuration (the position of the slats and the flaps), and allows here again flight control similar to that of a conventional aircraft.

2.3 Challenges and trends

On computer side, there is no major change in sight, apart from physically cutting a COM/MON computer into two units. This coupled with an increase self-test capability could provide a reduction of spare needs. This will be applied on A380 PRIM. Another trend is to design fully portable software. This could be used to get exactly the same software on simulators as on airplane.

In term of communications between computers, a step has been done on A380 and A400M by using a deterministic Ethernet network, for non-critical data and functions. Next step could be to use more smart actuators, and thus a digital network between them and computers.

3. DESIGN AND MANUFACTURING ERRORS

These errors are addressed by FAR/JAR 25.1309 that mandates to follow a stringent development process, based on following guidelines:

- ARP4754/ED79[11] for aircraft system development
- DO178/ED12[12] for software development
- DO254/ED80[13] for hardware development

There is no clear requirement that a design must be design-fault-tolerant, except if the applicant wishes to reduce its development assurance effort.

On Airbus EFCS, both ways are used:

- Error-avoidance with a stringent development process
- Error-tolerance as well.

3.1 Error avoidance

Aviation guidelines are applied, with the highest level of Development Assurance Level (level A). A340-600 EFCS is even likely to be the first system to be certified according to ARP 4754 level A.

3.1.1 On computer functional specification

The specification of a computer includes, on the one hand, an "equipment and software development" technical specification used to design the hardware and, in part, the software, and, on the other hand, an "equipment functional specification" which accurately specifies the functions implemented by the software.

This functional specification is a key element in the Fly-by-Wire development process. It is designed by engineers skilled in automatic control and aircraft system sciences and used by software engineers. Although system and software engineers are knowledgeable in each other field, and are working in the same company with the same objective, it is mandatory that the functional specification be non-ambiguous for each discipline. It is written using a graphic computer-assisted method. Specification language is named SCADE, a derivative of a previous one: SAO. All of the computer functions are specified with this method: flight control laws, monitoring of data, actuators, slaving of control surfaces, reconfigurations, etc. Timing of these functions is very simple. Scheduling of operations is fixed and run continuously at a fixed period. One of the benefits of this method is that each symbol used has a formal definition with strict rules governing its interconnections. The specification is under the control of a configuration management tool and its syntax is partially checked automatically.

Hence, validation and verification activities are addressed in this paper in three steps: system architecture and integration, computer functional specification, computer software.

For the translation of functional specification into software, the use of automatic programming tools is becoming widespread. This tendency appeared on the A320 and since A340-600 both PRIM and SEC are programmed automatically for a significant part. Such a tool has as input the functional specification sheets, and a library of software packages, one package for each symbol utilized. The automatic programming tool links together the symbol packages.

The use of such tools has a positive impact on safety. An automatic tool ensures that a modification to the specification will be coded without stress even if this modification is to be embodied rapidly (situation encountered during the flight test phase for example). Also, automatic programming, through the use of a formal specification language, allows onboard code from one aircraft program to be used on another. Note that the functional specification validation tools (simulators) use an automatic programming tool. This tool has parts in common with the automatic programming tool used to generate codes for the flight control computers. This increases the validation power of the simulations.

3.1.2 System architecture and integration V&V

The system validation and verification proceeds through several steps:

- Peer review of the specifications, and their justification. This is done with the light of the lessons learned by scrutinizing incidents that occur in airline service
- Analysis, most notably the System Safety Assessment which, for a given failure condition, checks that the monitoring and reconfiguration logics allow to fulfill the quantitative and qualitative objectives, but also analysis of system performances, and integration with the structure
- Tests with a simulated system, taking credit to the automatic coding of the functional specification, with a coupling with a rigid aircraft model
- Test of equipment on a partial test-bench, with input simulation and observation of internal variables (for computers)
- Tests on iron bird and flight simulator. The iron bird is a test bench with all the system equipment, installed and powered as on aircraft. The flight simulator is another test bench with an aircraft cockpit, flight controls computers, and coupled with a rigid aircraft model. The iron bird and the flight simulator are coupled for some tests.
- Flight-tests, on up to four aircraft, fitted with a "heavy" flight test instrumentation. More than 10000 flight controls parameters are permanently monitored and recorded.

The working method for these tests is twofold. A deterministic way is used, based on a test program, with a test report answering. In addition, credit is taken of the daily use of these test facilities for work on other systems, for demonstration, or test engineer and pilot activity. If the behavior of the system is not found satisfactory, a Problem Report is raised, registered and investigated.

3.1.3 Verification and validation of functional specifications

Certain functional specification verification activities are performed on data processing tools (e.g., the syntax of the specification can be checked automatically). A configuration management tool is also available and used.

The specification is validated mainly by means of proofreading (in particular, during the safety analysis), analysis, and ground or flight tests (see § 3.1.2). Analyses are more or less aided by tools, and address topics such as uncertainties propagation and timing for robustness. Our target is validation at earliest possible stage. To achieve this, various simulation tools exist and this because the specifications were written in a formal language making the specification executable.

This makes it possible to simulate the complete flight control system: computers, actuators, sensors, and aircraft returns (OCASIME tool). It is also possible to inject with this tool some stimuli on data that would not be reachable on the real computer. The signals to be observed can be selected arbitrarily and are not limited to the inputs/outputs of a specification sheet. The test scenarios thus generated can be recorded and rerun later on the next version of the specification, for example. A global non-regression test is in place, allowing for each new standard of computer specification, to compare the test results of the previous version, and of the new version. This comparison allows detecting modification errors.

Also, the part of the specification that describes the flight control laws can be simulated in real time (same Ocasime tool) by accepting inputs from a real sidestick controller (in fact, simpler than an aircraft stick), and from the other aircraft controls. The results are provided on a simulated Aircraft Primary Flight Display for global acceptance, and in more detailed forms, for deep analysis. The Ocasime tool is coupled to an aerodynamic model of the aircraft.

Test scenarios are defined based on the functional objectives of the specification, including robustness and limit tests. Some formal proofs are performed too, but still on a very limited basis.

3.1.4 Software

The software is produced with the essential constraint that it must be verified and validated. Also, it must meet the world's most severe civil aviation standards (currently level A software to DO178B). The functional specification acts as interface between the aircraft manufacturer's world and the software designers' world. The major part of the flight control software specification is a copy of the functional specification. This avoids creating errors when translating the functional specification into the software specification. For this "functional" part of the software, validation is not required as covered by the work carried out on the functional specification.

Actually, the whole software is divided in five programs plus one library. The programs are: the applicative program, automatically produced from the functional specification, as mentioned above; the self-tests; the initialization and applicative tasks sequencing; the download function; the input/output software. The library is the set of basic code components that implement the graphical SCADE – or SAO – basic components (OR, AND, FILT, etc) of the functional specification.

With respect to the applicative (functional) program, checking that the applicative tasks are schedulable must be performed "at software level". Indeed, to make software verification easier, the various tasks are sequenced in a predetermined order with periodic scanning of the inputs. Only the clock can generate interrupts used to control task sequencing. This sequencing is deterministic. A part of the task sequencer validation consists in methodically evaluating the margin between the maximum execution time for each task (worst case) and the time allocated to this task.

Lets now focus on the non-applicative software parts. Their development (called *life-cycle* by DO 178B) requires to successively specify, design and write the code. The verification techniques used for getting confident in the results of each activity and on the whole program are traditionally based on tests, readings and intellectual analyses.

In A380 software development, tool-aided software proof techniques were introduced into the verification workbench.

Lets take a example of one of the most important software verification: Unit verification, which is used for demonstrating that the software components (like C routines), once coded, conforms their definition, made at design time.

An important criterion of the quality of a verification process is its *functional coverage*, regardless of the verification technique used. In Unit Verification, satisfying this criterion consists in making sure that for each design component, there exists a code component which is verified by a "verification entity" allowing for the checking of all the Low Level Requirements (DO 178B terminology) expressed for this component at design time.

When the verification technique is the *test*, these Low Level Requirements are verified by applying the so-called "equivalent class" method. Adequate *functional coverage* of the Low Level Requirements must be obtained for the range of values of the inputs of a code component. The term "adequate" does not mean that the tests are assumed to be exhaustive, which is practically impossible to achieve, but means that "equivalent classes" are defined for covering all expected behaviors. The test cases actually performed are the most representative of each "equivalent class".

When a tool-aided *proof* method is used for Unit Verification[14], the *functional coverage* of the Low Level Requirements is a lot more directly obtained. Indeed, the Low Level Requirements are expressed formally by first order predicates at design time, and the verification consists of applying the tool-aided proof method for demonstrating that these predicates hold on the code component, i.e., for all possible behaviors.

When the verification technique is the *test*, an additional criterion has to be fulfilled: the *structural coverage*. It consists, for each software component, of checking that 100% of the instructions, 100% of the decisions and 100% of the Modified Conditions/Modified Decisions are exercised during tests. These *structural coverage* criteria are completely specified by DO 178B.

Beyond Unit Verification, the following other verification activities benefit from tool-aided proof techniques: the safe stack maximum usage computation and the safe Worst Case Execution Time computation[15] for all functional tasks. This kind of automatic demonstration that a whole program actually possesses some characteristics is of great interest with respect to dependability properties.

The verification techniques, like those described above, and a possible additional verification effort have the approval of the various parties involved (aircraft manufacturer, equipment manufacturer, airworthiness authorities, designer, quality control).

The basic rule to be retained is that the software is made in the best possible way. This has been recognized by several experts in the software field both from industry and from the airworthiness authorities. Dissimilarity is an additional precaution that is not used to reduce the required software quality effort.

3.1.5 Challenges and trends

With respect to error-avoidance we are faced with the challenge to get the system right the first time. This leads more and more to move V&V upstream and to partially automate it. We have also an opportunity that is the level of formalism of functional specification language. This should make more way to prove formally properties of the system and to measure the structural coverage of the tests performed.

Applied to software verification, this leads to use formal verification (tool-aided proof methods, static analysis) widely. As stated in section 3.1.4, a first set of proof techniques has been introduced in the verification workbench, i.e., for Unit Verification, safe maximum stack usage and Worst Case Execution Time computations.

These first applications cover a small subset of all software verification objectives whereas the underlying theoretical framework, i.e., the Abstract Interpretation theory[16], makes it possible, in the future, to get other applications (as automatic tools) like: the proof of absence of Run Time Error[17]; the analysis of the quality of floating point calculus[18]; the proof of properties (predicates) on whole programs (not limited to Unit Verification).

Moreover, more assurance about the system will be obtained earlier in the development process by using Abstract Interpretation based verification tools for proving dependability properties by analysis of the formal functional specification.

The objective is the effective application of the Product Based Assurance concept in which the confidence in the program is not only based on the quality of its development (Process Based Assurance) but also on its properties, as a product.

3.2 Error tolerance

3.2.1 Dissimilarity

The flight control system was subjected to a very stringent design and manufacturing process and we can reasonably estimate that its safety level is compatible with its safety objectives. An additional protection has nevertheless been provided which consists in using two different types of computers: for example, A320's ELAC is based on 68010 microprocessors and the SEC on the 80186; A340's PRIM on 80386, and the SEC on 80286; A380's PRIM on Power PC and the SEC on Sharc processor. Automatic coding tools are different too.

Functional specification and hence the software are different too; ELAC and PRIM run the elaborate functions while SEC is simpler (less functions, less stringent passenger comfort requirements) and thus more robust.

Within a computer, COM and MON hardware are basically of a same design, but with different software.

We therefore have two different design and manufacturing teams with different microprocessors (and associated circuits), different computer architectures and different functional specifications (ELAC vs. PRIM on A320; PRIM vs. SEC on A330/A340/A380). At software level, the architecture of the system leads to use 4 software packages (ELAC/COM, ELAC/MON, SEC/COM, SEC/MON) when, functionally, one would suffice. This is still applicable to PRIM and SEC of A330/A340 and A380.

3.2.2 Data diversity

As part of a struggle against single point of failures, the system is loosely synchronized. Computers are synchronizing their data both internally (command/monitoring) and between them (PRIM1, 2 ...) but not their clocks. Hence, for a given piece of information computers are using different data, sampled at different time. This is felt as an additional robustness margin.

3.2.3 Challenges and trends

A challenge to error tolerance is the reduction of electronic component suppliers: it becomes more and more likely that if two design teams (one for PRIM, one for SEC) choose independently their components, they will end up with some in common. Hence, we have moved from this kind of "random" dissimilarity to a managed one, such that both computer design teams decide in common to take different components.

In-service experience has shown that PRIM/SEC dissimilarity is fully justified. Indeed, two cases showed that this dissimilarity was beneficial for system availability. During one A320 flight, both ELAC were lost following an air conditioning failure and the subsequent abnormal temperature rise. It appears that a batch of these computers was fitted with a component whose temperature operating range did not match exactly the specified range. During one A340 flight, a very peculiar hardware failure of a single component trapped all three PRIM logic temporarily (reset was effective).

EHA are also an opportunity to get dissimilar actuation power supplies: indeed, A380 and A400M will be able to tolerate a complete loss of hydraulic power.

4. PARTICULAR RISKS

Particular risks are spread within FAR/JAR. ARP 4761[19] tends to regroup most of them.

Basically, the concern with this type of event is that it can affect several redundancies in a single occurrence.

Airbus addresses this concern by building a robust system and qualifying its components accordingly (against vibration, temperature...). Additionally, emphasis is put on separating physically the system resources, segregating them, and by providing an ultimate back-up redundant to the EFCS.

4.1 Segregation

The electrical installation, in particular the many electrical connections, comprises a common-point risk. This is avoided by extensive segregation: in normal operation, two electrical generation systems exist without a single common point. Computers are divided in two sets associated to these two electrical generation systems. The links between computers are limited, the links used for monitoring are not routed with those used for command. We end up with at least four different electrical routes: COM of electrical system 1, MON of electrical system 1, COM of electrical system 2, MON of electrical system 2. This proved useful when a case of electrical arc tracking occurred: all the wires in a single bundle have been destroyed, but other

located elsewhere were sufficient to ensure continued safe flight and landing, with margin.
The destruction of a part of the aircraft is also taken into account: the computers are placed at three different locations, certain links to the actuators run under the floor, others overhead and others in the cargo compartment. Power supplies are also segregated. It is worth noting here again the benefit of EHA, as electrical power cables are easier to install and thus it is possible to get more space between all the power transmission lines (electrical cables and hydraulic pipes).

4.2 Ultimate back-up

In spite of all these precautions, a mechanical standby system has been conserved on A320 to A340. This mechanical system is connected to the trimmable horizontal stabilizer allowing the pitch axis and the rudder to be controlled providing direct control of the yaw axis and indirect control of the roll axis. The safety objectives for the fly-by-wire part of the system (PRIM's plus SEC's) have been defined without taking credit of this mechanical back-up.

A340-600 needs a precise rudder control to damp structural vibration. This is difficult to get with an ageing mechanical control, prone to threshold and freeplay. Hence, A340-600 rudder control is fully electrical (like an elevator or an aileron on A320 or basic A340). A new ultimate back-up has thus been designed, which is electrical with an autonomous power converter (from hydraulic to electricity), completely independent from the basic system of PRIM's and SEC's, integrating a yaw rate-gyro, pedals sensors, rudder servocontrol servoloop.

On A380 and A400M the last step is done: the mechanical linkage from cockpit control wheel to the actuator of the horizontal stabilizer is cancelled. Ultimate back-up is thus similar to A340-600 rudder one, but controlling rudder, one pair of elevators, and one pair of ailerons, based on pedals and sidesticks order. Technology is currently analog.

4.3 Challenges and trends

Fiber optics is used on A340-600 and A380 for the "Taxi Aid Camera System". This non-critical system is partially installed in the fin and in non-pressurized area. It should demonstrate that fiber optics can be used in this kind of difficult area and are compatible with standard airline maintenance practices. This will open the door to introduce this technology on civil fly-by-light systems. Current systems are sufficiently immune to electromagnetic interferences, and flight control system communication network needs a rather low bandwidth. Hence, optical fiber are not needed, nevertheless this could give some more installation margin.

5. HUMAN FACTOR IN FLIGHT CONTROL DEVELOPMENT

Since Human Factor is identified as important as a contributive factor in accidents and incidents[20], Airbus flight control system takes it into account in its process development.

This issue is extensively addressed by the aviation regulation with respect to aircraft stability and control and related issues (warning, piloting aid). Maintainability is also addressed in broad terms.

Airbus flight control system offers piloting aids such as flight envelope protections, some of them are available on non fly-by-wire airplane while others are specific, along with maintainability helping devices. Note that errors introduced by the designers are addressed in §3.

5.1 Human Factor in design development

The automation in Airbus fly-by-wire contributes to safety enhancement by reducing the crew workload, the fatigue, and providing situation awareness and a better survivability to extreme situations, not to mention better robustness to crew error.

5.1.1 Comfort

One of the constraints to optimize the control laws is the crew and passengers comfort, in order not to have too much oscillations or excessive G-load factor variation[8-10].

This optimization contributes to mitigate crew fatigue[21].

5.1.2 Situation awareness

The Airbus flight control system provides also information to the crew, in order to increase his situation awareness to an adequate level. On top of this information, the aircraft systems can provide warnings, with aural and visual cues.

The information displayed on PFD / FMA / ECAM (such as which AP mode is engaged or the stall speed indication on speed scale or the status of flight control on ECAM page) provide tools to the crew to interpret the situation and to maintain him in the automation loop (crew is not excluded of the aircraft control).

Another level of information is the warnings (visual or audio). Flight control system provides the necessary information to the Flight Warning Computer.

For instance, the T.O. CONFIG memos allow checking the good configuration of the aircraft before take-off (spoiler retracted, flap / slat in take-off configuration, etc.).

5.1.3 Reconfiguration

The auto-diagnostic of a failure and the automatic reconfiguration after this failure (see paragraph 2.2.3) contributes to reduce the crew workload.

For instance, in case of a servo-control control loss, the failure is automatically detected by monitoring of discrepancy between feedback loop and command loop. Then, the redundant servo-control of the impacted surface takes over from the failed one, with a totally transparency for crew.

5.1.4 Specific flight envelope protection

Several avionic equipments are already dedicated to flight envelope protection, providing information to the crew as:

- Audio alert on Traffic Collision Avoidance System (TCAS) in case of collision risk with another A/C, on Terrain Avoidance Warning System (TAWS) in case of terrain collision risk but also in case of too excessive sink rate.
- Situation awareness on meteorological radar with the display of storming area on Navigation Display.

The electrical flight control system contributes also to the safety enhancement of the aircraft through the set of protections[8, 22], which is an integral part of the flight control laws.

Structure protections are provided during normal flying (extreme G-load factor, excessive speed).

Another protection, called high angle-of-attack, prevents the aircraft from stalling. Airbrakes are also set to 0° in case the pilot commands full thrust on the engines or flight a high angle of attack regime.

These protections lighten the pilot's workload, in particular, during avoidance manoeuvres whether for an obstacle (near miss) or windshear. A pilot who must avoid another aircraft can concentrate on the path to be followed without worrying about the structural limits of the aircraft or a possible stall.

5.2 Human factor in maintainability

Electrical flight control system uses sensors all over the aircraft and inside the actuators. As a side effect, most system failures are readily detectable and a rather precise diagnostic can be done. Thus, hundreds of precise maintenance messages are targeting the exact Line Replaceable Unit.

This contributes to decision-making in case of a failure; by crew if a dispatch is proposed in MEL document, by maintenance team otherwise.

The flight control system is designed to propose the maximum of availability.

5.3 Human Factor in certification

The aviation rules (in particular FAR/JAR 25.1302) have been reviewed for A380 to put emphasis on the human error impact in system failure.

Through this new rule, the flight control design will be demonstrated to be adequate to the effects of crew errors, to the workload, and to provide an adequate feedback to the crew on aircraft situation.

That means that the flight control design, the interface with crew, the procedures in case of failure (Flight Crew Operating Manual - FCOM) and the training are adapted:

- Not to increase the crew workload
- To provide safety barriers which prevent a single human error to transform a minor or major failure into catastrophic failure.

5.4 Challenges and trends

A difficulty has been to fine-tune all the failure detection mechanism. A basic Airbus fly-by-wire choice is to prefer immediate failure detection by on-line monitorings to off-line tests during scheduled maintenance. This reduces the level of hidden failure when the aircraft is dispatched. Unfortunately, this can be a burden to the operator when such a monitoring is too "talkative". Challenge is thus to get that all these monitorings be perfectly matured when the airplane enters into service.

The trend is also to more integrate the system, to have more interaction with avionics systems and all surveillance systems. For instance, flight control system could automatically react to a collision risk, better control could be provided on ground[23].

On certification point of view, the Human Factor Working Groups have also proposed some recommendations on Airworthiness rules FAR/JAR 25.1301 and 25.1302, specifically on:

- *Error-tolerance*: The objective is to explicitly address design-related pilot error, to make errors detectable and reversible. The error effects must be apparent for flight crew.
- *Error-avoidance*: This rule would formally address design characteristics that lead to or contribute to error. For instance, the controls and system logic required for flight crew tasks must be provided in accessible usable and unambiguous form and must not induced pilot error. The integration within systems must also be addressed.

Airbus cockpits are already designed this way; the new rule adds formalism in the exercise.

6. CONCLUSION

Experience has shown that Airbus fly-by-wire is safe, and even features safety margins. Research has also shown that new technologies can be both cost effective and provide additional safety margins. Such technical improvements, when mature, are incorporated in aircraft design, such as Electrical Actuation on A380 and A400M.

Acknowledgements

The authors are indebted to Dominique Brière for continuous guidance and inspiration.

REFERENCES

1. D. Brière, and P. Traverse, *Airbus A320/A330/A340 electrical flight controls – a family of fault-tolerant systems*, Proc. 23rd IEEE Int. Symp. On Fault-Tolerant Computing (FTCS-23), Toulouse, France, pp. 616-623 (1993).
2. D. Brière, and P. Traverse, *Airbus electrical flight controls – a family of fault-tolerant systems*, Proc. RTO/SCI Symp. on Challenges in Dynamics, System Identification, Control and Handling Qualities for Land, Air, Sea and Space Vehicles, Berlin, Germany, RTO-MP-095, paper 29 (2002).
3. Topical Days on *Fault Tolerance for Trustworthy and Dependable Information Infrastructure,* IFIP World Computer Congress, Toulouse, France, Kluwer, (2004).
4. FAR/JAR 25, *Airworthiness Standards: Transport Category Airplane*, published by FAA, title 14, part 25, and *Certification Specifications for Large Aeroplanes*, published by EASA (former JAA), CS-25.
5. A. Avizienis, J.C. Laprie, and B. Randell, *Fundamental Concepts of Dependability*, LAAS report no. 01-145 (2001).
6. D. van den Bossche, *EHA application to commercial transports – the Aerospatiale approach*, Proceedings on conference on Recent Advances in Aerospace Hydraulics, Toulouse, France (1998) and *More electric control surface actuation*, Proceedings of Royal Aeronautical Society conference on More-Electric Aircraft, London, UK, 2004.
7. J. Farineau, *Lateral electric flight control laws of a civil aircraft based upon eigen structure assignment technique*, Proc. AIAA Guidance, Navigation and Control Conference, Boston, MA, USA (1989).
8. C. Favre, *Fly-by-wire for commercial aircraft: the Airbus experience*, International Journal of Control, vol. 59, No. 1, pp.139-157 (1994).
9. F. Kubica, T. Livet, X. LeTron, and A. Bucharles, *Parameter-robust flight control system for a flexible aircraft*, Control Engineering Practice, Vol. 3, No. 9, pp.1209-1215 (1995).
10. T. Livet, D. Fath, and F. Kubica, *Robust autopilot design for a highly flexible aircraft*, Proc. 13th IFAC World Congress, Vol. P, San Francisco, CA, USA, pp.279-284 (1995).

11. ARP 4754/ED79, *Certification Considerations for Highly-Integrated or Complex Systems*, published by SAE, no. ARP4754, and EUROCAE, no. ED79 (1996).
12. DO178B/ED12, *Software Considerations in Airborne Systems and Equipment Certification*, published by ARINC, no. DO178B, and EUROCAE, no. ED12, 1992.
13. DO254/ED80, *Design Assurance Guidance for Airborne Electronic Hardware*, published by ARINC, no. DO254, and EUROCAE, no. ED80 (2000).
14. F. Randimbivololona, J. Souyris, P. Baudin, A. Pacalet, J. Raguideau et D. Schoen. *Applying Formal Proof Techniques toAvionics Software: A pragmatic Approach.* FM99. LNCS 1709, Vol II.
15. S. Thesing, J. Souyris, R. Heckmann, F. Randimbivololona, M. Langenbach, R. Wilhelm, and C. Ferdinand*An Abstract Interpretation-Based Timing Validation of Hard Real-Time Avionics*, Proc. Int Conf. on Dependable Systems and Networks (DSN) (June 2003).
16. P. Cousot. *Interprétation abstraite*, Technique et Science Informatique, *Vol. 19, Nb 1-2-3.*, Hermès, Paris, France, pp. 155-164 (2000).
17. B. Blanchet, P. Cousot, R. Cousot, J. Feret, L. Mauborgne, A. Miné, D. Monniaux, and X. Rival.*A Static Analyzer for Large Safety-Critical Software,* Proc. PLDI 2003 - ACM SIGPLAN SIGSOFT Conf. on Programming Language Design and Implementation, Federated Computing Research Conference, San Diego, CA USA, pp. 196-207 (2003).
18. E. Goubault, M. Martel, and S. Putot. *Asserting the Precision of Floating-Point Computations: a Simple Abstract Interpreter* (Demo Paper), ESOP'2002, LNCS.
19. ARP 4761, *Guidelines and Methods for Conducting the Safety Assessment Process on Civil Airborne Systems*, published by SAE, no. ARP4761 (1996).
20. *Human Factors for Civil Flight Deck Design*, published by Ashgate (2004).
21. I. Lacaze, *Prise en compte du confort vibratoire dans la conception*, Paris V University Report (2002).
22. D. Chatrenet, *Les qualités de vol des avions de transport civil à commandes de vol électriques*, Proc. AGARD Conf. on Active Control Technology, Turin, Italy, AGARD-CP-560, paper 28 (1994).
23. J. Duprez, F. Mora-Camino and F. Villaume, *Robust control of the aircraft on ground lateral motion*, Proc. 24th ICAS Conf., Yokohama, Japan (2004).

UNIQUE DEPENDABILITY ISSUES FOR COMMERCIAL AIRPLANE FLY BY WIRE SYSTEMS

Ying C. (Bob) Yeh
Boeing Commercial Airplanes, Seattle, WA, USA – ying.c.yeh@boeing.com

Abstract: The fundamental concept of dependability is applied to the design of commercial airplane FBW systems beyond the lessons learned from the NASA FBW and industry/military FBW research and development projects. The considerations of generic errors and common mode failures play important role for configuring commercial airplane FBW system architectures and the FBW computer architectures.

Key words: Dependability, Fly-By-Wire (FBW)

1. INTRODUCTION

The NASA FBW projects provide the fundamental framework for functional integrity and functional availability requirements [1], [2] for the FBW computers. The Byzantine General Problems [3] and its solutions are illustrated in [1], [3], [4]. Further the lessons learned from the military FBW project [5] and other industry/academic experiences in dealing with generic faults [6], near-coincidence fault [7], and design paradigm [8] provide ground rules or derived design requirements for Boeing commercial airplane FBW programs [9], [10], [11].

A tutorial of fundamental concepts of dependability [12] can be used for referenced discussions. Two unique design requirements or design considerations for Commercial Airplane FBW are that of generic error/fault and common mode failure. The purpose of this article is to describe how these two requirements/considerations play an important role for the Commercial Airplane FBW computers [13], [14], [15].

2. GENERIC ERROR AND DISSIMILARITY CONSIDERATIONS

The concept of design diversity [16] [17] has played a central role in academic research and its follow on experiments [18] [19] while the commercial airplane industry is using dissimilarity for flight critical systems, such as Autopilot computers and the FBW research. The experiments [18] [19] has influenced the final decision for the 777 FBW system design [13]. The Airbus [15] and Boeing FBW computers design considerations for generic errors and dissimilarity considerations are studied [20] and can be summarized as follows.

Two types of computers are used in the A320 FBW system: the ELAC (Elevator and Aileron computers) and the SEC (Spoiler and Elevator computers). The ELAC is produced by Thomson-CSF using Motorola 68010 processor, and the SEC is produced by SFENA/Aerospatiale using Intel 80186 processor. Each computer consists of two channels: control channel and monitor channel. The software and its programming language of the control channel are different from that of the monitor channel. Likewise the software of ELAC is different from that of SEC. Thus at software level, the architecture leads to the use of 4 software packages.

Two types of computers are also used on A340: the PRIM (primary computers) and SEC (secondary computers). The basic design philosophy is similar to A320. The PRIM uses Intel 80386 processors with a difference in software. Further the control channel is programmed in Assembler, while the monitor channel is programmed in PL/M. The SEC uses Intel 80186 processors. Assembly language is used for control channel, and Pascal is used for the monitor channel. Also for dissimilarity reasons, only the PRIM computer is coded automatically (the SEC being coded manually) and that the PRIM automatic coding tool has two different coded translators, one for control channel and another for monitor channel.

In addition to the ELAC and SEC of the A320, two computers are used for rudder control (FAC). On A330 and A340 FBW, these rudder control functions are integrated in the PRIM and SEC.

The overview of Boeing 777 Primary Flight Control System (or FBW) is depicted in Figure 1. The Boeing FBW system design considerations [13] extend the concept of triple hardware resources (hydraulics, airplane electrical power, FBW ARINC 629 bus) to triple dissimilar processors and their Ada compilers to construct triple-triple redundant PFC (primary flight computer) [14]. Further, dissimilarity is invoked in the design and implementation of the PFC system where it is judged to be a necessary feature to satisfy critical minds of Boeing engineers. The design diversity issue [11] is integrated to the system design issue of dealing with all possible errors for a complex flight controls systems, experienced in Boeing and in industry/academia.

3. COMMON MODE FAILURE AND SINGLE POINT FAILURE

Common mode or common area faults [21] are considered for multiple redundant systems such as the FBW. Airplane susceptibility to common mode and common area damage is addressed by designing the systems to both component and functional separation requirement. This includes criteria for providing installations resistant to maintenance crew error or mishandling, such as the followings:

- impact of objects
- electrical faults
- electrical power failure
- electromagnetic environment
- lightning strike
- hydraulic failure
- structure damage
- radiation environment in the atmosphere
- ash cloud environment in the atmosphere
- fire
- rough or unsafe installation and maintenance

The single point failure consideration is integrated to the safety requirements. For instance, the derived 777 PFC safety requirements include numerical and non-numerical requirements as follows.

Safety requirements apply to PFC failures which could preclude continued safe flight and landing, and include both passive failures (loss of function without significant immediate airplane transient) and active failures (malfunction) with significant immediate airplane transient).

The numerical probability requirements are both 1.0E-10 per flight hour for functional integrity requirement (relative to active failures affecting 777 Airplane Structure) and functional availability requirement (relative to passive failures).

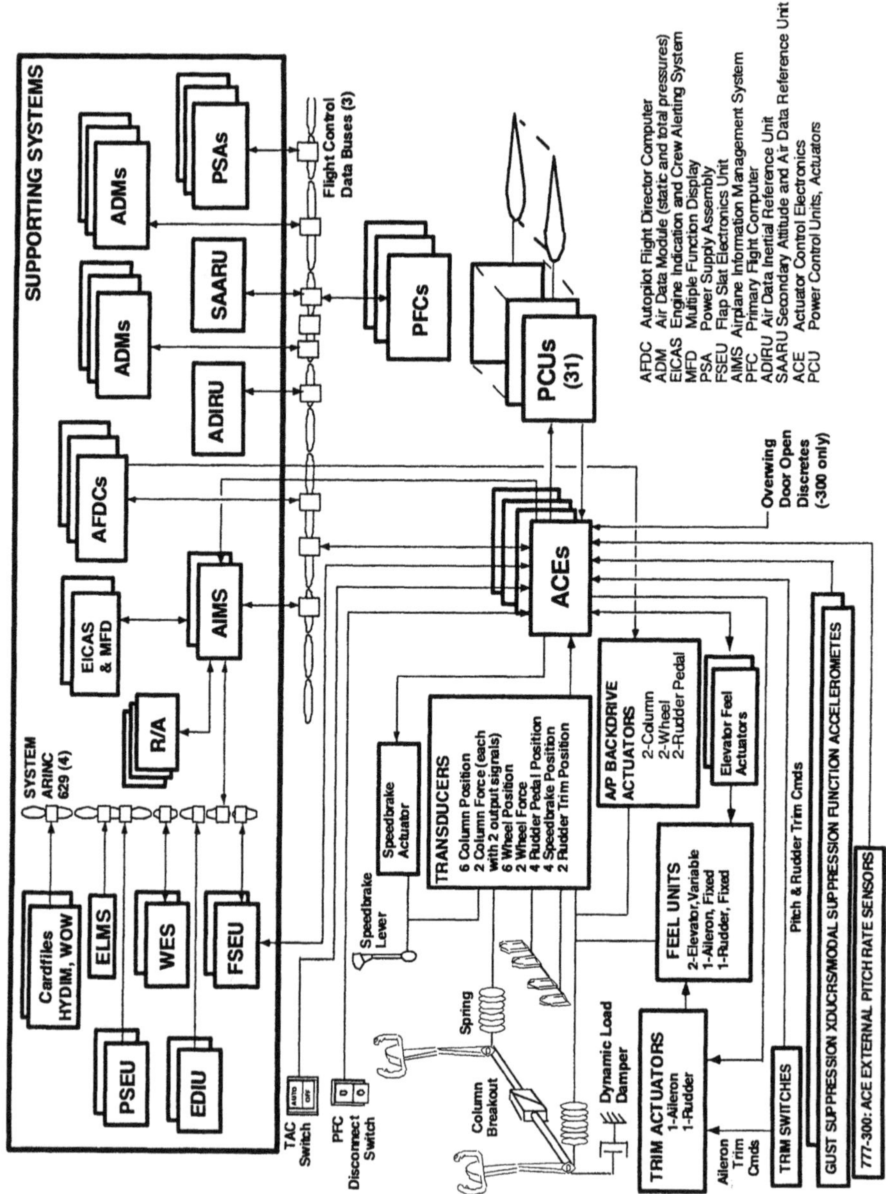

Figure 1. 777 Primary Flight Control System

The PFC is designed to comply with the following non-numerical safety requirements described as follows:

a) No single fault, including common mode hardware fault, regardless of probability of occurrence, shall result in an erroneous (assumed active failures for the worst case) transmission of output signals without a failure indication.
b) No single fault, including common mode hardware fault, regardless of probability of occurrence shall result in loss of function in more than one PFC channel.

Extensive validation process [22] is undertaken to comply with the 777 Flight Controls certification plan approved by the certification agencies, and to satisfy critical minds of Boeing engineers.

4. SUMMARY DISCUSSION: SIMPLEX DIRECT MODE CONTROL

The virtue of simplicity [23] is not lost on the complex FBW systems due to extremely stringent numerical and non-numerical safety requirements and considerations of generic errors, common mode failure, and single point failure.

The 777 Primary Flight Control Modes is shown in Table 1. The Direct Control mode provides simplex control law in the event of occurrences of "known or unknown" combinations of generic errors and common mode failure, or in the event of pilot decision to engage PFC Disconnect Switch for whatever reasons.

Table 1. 777 Primary Flight Control Modes

	PITCH	ROLL	YAW
NORMAL Control	CONTROL C* Maneuver Cmd with Speed Feedback Manual Trim for Speed Variable Feel	CONTROL Surface Cmds Manual Trim Fixed Feel	CONTROL Surface Cmd Ratio Changer Wheel/Rudder Cross Tie Manual Trim Yaw Damping Fixed Feel Gust Supression
	ENVELOPE PROTECTION Stall Overspeed	ENVELOPE PROTECTION Bank Angle	ENVELOPE PROTECTION Thrust Asymmetry
	AUTOPILOT Backdrive	AUTOPILOT Backdrive	AUTOPILOT Backdrive
SECONDARY Control	CONTROL Surface Cmd (Augmented) Flaps Up/Down Gain Direct Stabilizer Trim Flaps Up/Down Feel	CONTROL Surface Cmd Manual Trim Fixed Feel	CONTROL Surface Cmds, Flaps Up/Down Gain PCU Pressure Reducer Manual Trim Yaw Rate Damper (if available)
DIRECT Control	CONTROL Surface Cmd (Augmented) Flaps Up/Down Gain Direct Stabilizer Trim Flaps Up/Down Feel	CONTROL Surface Cmd Manual Trim Fixed Feel	CONTROL Surface Cmds, Flaps Up/Down Gain PCU Pressure Reducer Manual Trim

The 777 Actuator Control Electronics Architecture is shown in Figure 2. The hardware circuitry for Direct Mode control function in ACE is designed to be as simple as possible. Further the hardware system architectures resided in all critical LRUs supporting the Normal Mode function are designed to be fail-passive so that the ISM (input signal management function) can direct/fail to the defaulted condition of Direct Mode control.

REFERENCES

[1] J.H. Wenseley et al "SIFT: Design and Analysis of a Fault Tolerant Computer for Aircraft Control" Proceeding of the IEEE, Vol. 66, No. 10, October 1978.

[2] A.L. Hopkins Jr., T.B. Smith,III, J.H. Lala, "FTMP-A Highly Reliable Fault-Tolerant Multiprocessor for Aircraft", Proceeding of the IEEE, Vol. 66, No. 10, October 1978.

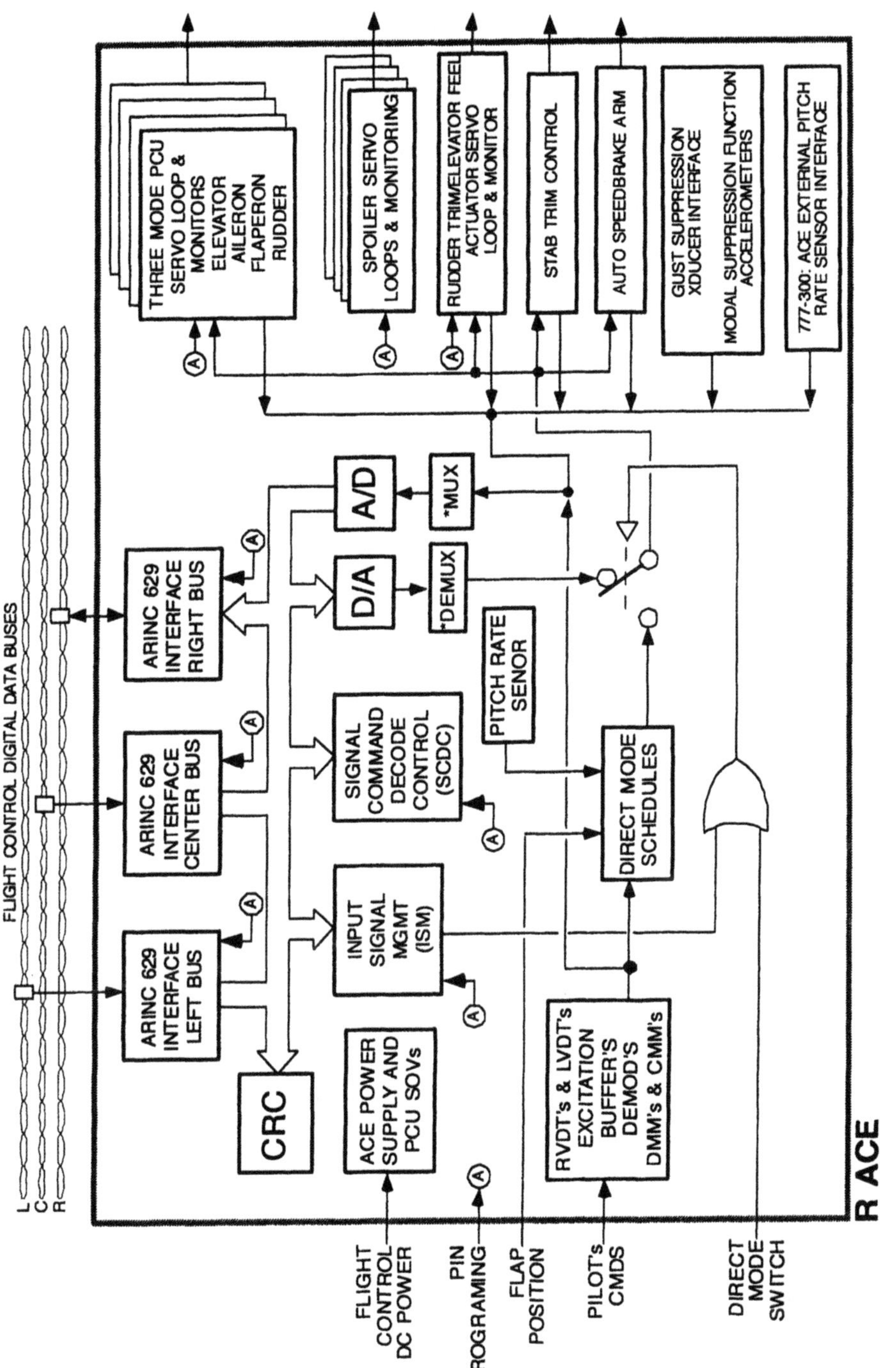

Figure 2. 777 Actuator Control Electronics Architecture

[3] L. Lamport, R. Shostak, and M. Pease, "The Byzantine Generals Problem", ACM Trans. On Programming Languages and Systems, Vol.4, No.3, July 1982.
[4] R. Kieckhafer, C. Walter, A. Finn, and P. Thambidurai, "The MAFT Architecture for Distributed Fault Tolerance", IEEE Trans. On Computers, 37(4):398-405, 1988.
[5] J.H. Watson, W.J. Yousey, A.M. Arabian, and T.M. Schindler, "Lessons learned from development of AFTI/F-16 Digital Flight Control System", 5th digital avionics systems conference, Seattle, Washington, 1983.
[6] S.S. Osder, "Generic Faults and Architecture Design Considerations in Flight-Critical Systems", AIAA Journal of Guidance, Vol.6, No.2, March-April 1983.
[7] J. McGough, "Effects of Near-Coincident Faults in Multiprocessor Systems", Fifth AIAA/IEEE Digital Avionics Conference, October 1983.
[8] A. Avizienis, "A Design Paradigm for Fault-Tolerant Systems", AIAA Computers in Aerospace Conference, October 1987, Paper 87-2764.
[9] R.J. Bleeg, "Commercial Jet Transport Fly-By-Wire Architecture Consideration", Ninth AIAA/IEEE Digital Avionics Conference, October 1988.
[10] J. McWha, "777 Systems Overview", RAeS Presentation, November 1993.
[11] Y.C. Yeh, "Design Considerations in 777 Fly-By-Wire Computers", 3rd IEEE International High-Assurance Systems Engineering Conference, Washington, DC, October 1988.
[12] A. Avizienis, J.-C. Laprie, and B. Randell, "Fundamental Concepts of Dependability", Research Report NO1145, LAAS-CNRS, April 2001.
[13] Y.C. Yeh, "Dependability of the 777 Primary Flight Control System", in Dependable Computing for Critical Applications (DCCS-5), Dependable Computing and Fault-Tolerant Systems, 10, pp.3-17, IEEE Computer Society Press, 1998.
[14] Y.C. Yeh, "Triple-Triple Redundant 777 Primary Flight Computers", 1996 IEEE Aerospace Applications Conference, February 1996.
[15] D. Briere and P. Traverse, "AIRBUS A320/A330/A340 Electrical Flight Controls – A Family of Fault-Tolerant Systems", in FTCS-23, pp.616-23, IEEE Computer Society Press, 1993.
[16] A. Avizienis, "Design Diversity – the Challenge of the Eighties", FTCS-12, pages 44-45, June 1982.
[17] A. Avizienis, and J.P.J Kelly, "Fault Tolerance by Design Diversity: Concepts and Experiments", Computer, August 1984.
[18] A. Avizienis, M.R. Lyu, and W. Schutz, "In Search of Effective Diversity: A Six-Language Study of Fault-Tolerant of Fault-Tolerant Flight Computer Software", FTCS-18, 1988.
[19] J.C. Knight, N.G. Leveson, "An Experimental Evaluation of the Assumption of Independence in Multiversion Programming", IEEE Trans. on Software Engineering, January 1986.
[20] D. Powell, J.P. Blanquart, Y. Crouzet, and J.C. Fabre, "Architecture Approaches for using COTS Components in Critical Applications", 11th European Workshop on Dependable Computing (EWDC-11), Budapest, Hungary, 2000.
[21] SAE ARP4761, "Guidelines and Methods for Conducting The Safety Assessment Process on Civil Airborne Systems and Equipment", Society of Automotive Engineers.
[22] H. Buss, et al, "777 Flight Controls Validation Process", Fourteen AIAA/IEEE Digital Avionics System Conference, November 1995.
[23] L. Sha, B. Goodenough, and B. Pollak, "Simplex Architecture: Meeting the Challenges of Using COTS in High-Reliability Systems", Cross Talk, The Journal of Defense Software Engineering, April 1998.

THE FAULT HYPOTHESIS FOR THE TIME-TRIGGERED ARCHITECTURE

H. Kopetz[1]

[1] *Vienna University of Technology, Austria*
hk@vmars.tuwien.ac.at

Abstract A precise fault-hypothesis is essential for the design and validation of a safety-critical computer system. The fault-hypothesis must specify the fault-containment regions (FCRs), the assumed failure modes of the FCRs with their respective failure frequencies, the error detection latency and the time-interval that is required in order that an FCR can repair the state corruption that has occurred as a consequence of a transient fault. After a general discussion of the detailed contents of the fault-hypothesis document, this paper presents the fault-hypothesis that has formed the basis for the design of the time-triggered architecture. The time-triggered architecture is a distributed architecture that has been developed for the control of safety-critical embedded applications.

Keywords: Safety-Critical Systems, Fault-Hypothesis, Error Detection, Fault-tolerance, Error-Containment, State Repair

1. Introduction

Ultra-dependable computer systems that are deployed in safety-critical applications are expected to exhibit a mean-time-to-failure (MTTF) of better than 10^9 hours [Walter et al., 1995], i.e. more than 100 000 years. Although this number has its origin in the dependability requirements of a *fly-by-wire system*, it is applicable to the automotive domain as well. It has been stipulated that the dependability requirements for a *drive-by-wire* system are even more stringent than the dependability requirements for fly-by-wire systems, since the number of exposed hours of humans is higher in the automotive domain.

It is *impossible* to gain confidence about a system reliability of 100 000 years by testing [Littlewood and Strigini, 1993]. A consequence of the *untestability* of 10^{-9} systems is the need to analyze critical algorithms by formal methods in order to convince certification authorities of the correctness of the algorithms within the specified operational envelop. Since the observed *mean-time to fail* of hardware components is two orders of magnitude below the aimed-for reliability at the system level, the safety argument must be based on experimental data about the component reliability and analytical arguments taking into account the redundancy in the fault-tolerant system structure. Even a very low correlation in the failure probabilities of replicated subsystems has a significant effect on the system reliability of ultra-dependable systems. The system design must thus assure that replicated subsystems of an architecture for ultra-dependability systems *fail independently* of each other.

It is the objective of this paper to present the fault hypothesis of the time-triggered architecture (TTA). In the following section we argue why a precise fault-hypothesis is essential for the design of a safety critical system and outline the contents of such a precise fault hypothesis. Section three gives a short overview of the time-triggered architecture. Section four presents the fault hypothesis of the TTA with respect to hardware faults, while Section five is devoted to the discussion of the fault-hypothesis with respect to software faults. The paper finishes with a conclusion in Section six.

2. The Fault Hypothesis

The fault hypothesis is a statement about the assumptions made concerning the types and number of faults that a fault-tolerant system is expected to tolerate [Laprie, 1992]. The fault hypothesis divides the fault space into two disjoint partitions: the partition of *covered faults* and the partition of *uncovered faults*. The covered faults are those faults that are contained in the fault-hypothesis and are addressed during the system design. The occurrence of a covered fault during system operation should not have an adverse effect on the availability of the *safety-critical* system functions. The occurrence of an uncovered fault can lead to critical system failure, since no mechanisms are provided to protect against uncovered faults. During system validation it must be shown that uncovered faults are *rare events*.

2.1 Why do we need a precise Fault Hypothesis?

Before the design of a safety-critical system can commence, a precise fault hypothesis is needed for the following reasons:

1 **Design of the Fault-Tolerance Algorithms:** Without a precise fault-hypothesis it is not known which fault-classes must be addressed during the system design [Avizienis, 1997].

2 **Assumption Coverage:** There is a probability that the assumptions that are contained in the fault hypothesis are not met by reality. This probability is called the assumption coverage [Powell, 1992]. The *assumption coverage* predicts the probability of failure of a *perfectly designed* fault-tolerant system. Without a precise fault-hypothesis, the probability for

the occurrence of uncovered faults cannot be predicted. The assumptions that form the fault-hypothesis must be carefully scrutinized and in a safety-critical system it must be demonstrated that the assumption coverage is significantly better than 10^{-9}/hour.

3 **Validation:** The implementation of the fault-tolerance mechanisms can only be validated, if it is precisely known which faults must be tolerated by the given system and which faults are not expected to be tolerated, since they are outside the scope of the given implementation.

4 **Certification:** Without a precise fault hypothesis it is impossible to certify the correct operation of a fault-tolerant system.

5 **Design of the Never-Give-Up (NGU) Strategy:** In a safety-critical application, the control system should never *give up*, even if the fault-hypothesis is violated by reality. In a properly designed fault-tolerant system chances are high that a violation of the fault hypothesis is caused by a correlated shower of *external transient faults* or by a *Heisenbug* and that a fast restart of the system will be successful. The activation of the restart mechanism must be activated by an NGU algorithm. Such an NGU algorithm can only be designed if a precise fault hypothesis is available.

2.2 Contents of the Fault Hypothesis

In the following Section we elaborate on the required contents of a fault hypothesis w.r.t. hardware faults of a distributed real-time control system that is intended for safety-critical applications. A safety critical distributed real-time system consists of a set of node computers that are interconnected by replicated communication channels (see Figure 1).

Specification of the Fault Containment Regions (FCR). The notion of a *fault-containment region (FCR)* is introduced in order to delimit the immediate impact of a single fault to a defined subsystem of the overall system. A fault-containment region is defined as a part of the system that may be affected by a *single fault*. The probability of failure of two different FCRs failing at the same time should be independent, i.e. there should not be any correlation of the failure probabilities of different FCRs, Since the immediate consequences of a fault in any one of the shared resources in an FCR may impact all subsystems of the FCR, the subsystems of an FCR cannot be considered to be independent of each other and cannot be considered to form their own FCRs [Kaufmann and Johnson, 2000]. In the context of this paper the following shared hardware resources that can be impacted by a fault are considered:

- Computing Hardware

- Power Supply
- Timing Source
- Cock Synchronization Service
- Physical Space

For example, if two subsystems depend on a single timing source, e.g., a single oscillator, then these two subsystems are not considered to be independent and therefore belong to the same FCR. Since this definition of independence allows that two FCRs can share the same design, e.g., the same software, design faults in the software or the hardware are not part of this fault-model.

In a distributed real-time system consisting of a set of SoCs (System on a Chip) node computers, a complete node computer must be considered to form a single FCR, since all correlated failures of two subsystems residing on the same silicon die cannot be eliminated: the subsystems residing on a single die share the same physical space, the same silicon substrate, the same manufacturing mask and manufacturing process, the same ground and power supply, probably the same timing source etc. There is a non-negligible probability that a fault in any one of these resources will affect both subsystems simultaneously.

A communication channel connecting the nodes of the distributed system can be formed by a bus, a ring, a star or any other interconnection structure. From the point of view of fault-containment, such a channel forms also a single FCR in a safety-critical environment.

Failure Modes. A failure mode specifies the type of failure that may occur if an FCR is impacted by a fault. In the literature different failure modes of an FCR are introduced from *restricted* to *unrestricted* [Laprie, 1992]. The most restricted failure mode is a fail-silent failure, i.e. where the assumption is made that an FCR either operates correctly or is silent. The most unrestricted failure mode is a Byzantine failure, where no assumptions is made about the behavior of a faulty component. Every restriction in the failure mode, i.e. every assumption about the behavior of a faulty component must be scrutinized w.r.t. the assumption coverage. It follows that a system that can tolerate an unrestricted failure mode of an FCR will lead to a better assumption coverage than a system with restricted failure modes.

Temporal Properties of Faults. Another classification considers the temporal properties of faults. We distinguish between the following five types of faults in the temporal domain:

1 **Transient fault:** A transient fault is caused by some random event. An example for a transient is a SEU (single event upset caused by a radioactive particle) [Constantinescu, 2002].

2 **Intermittent fault:** An intermittent fault is considered to be a *correlated sequence of transient faults* that is caused by some single physical degradation of a component. An example of an intermittent fault is the partial degradation of the junction of a transistor on a chip (e.g., caused by oxidation) that causes sporadic load dependent or data dependent errors. Experimental data show that an intermittent fault is likely to eventually produce a permanent fault [Normand, 1996].

3 **Soft permanent fault:** A soft permanent fault is a corruption of the h-state or of the i-state within a component [Kopetz, 1997] without causing any permanent damage to the component. For example, a corruption can be caused by a single-even-upset (SRU) [Kaufmann and Johnson, 2000]. The repair of the erroneous data structure eliminates the soft-permanent fault without any further effect on the hardware.

4 **Permanent fault:** A permanent fault occurs, if the hardware of an FCR brakes down permanently. An example for a permanent fault is a broken wire.

5 **Massive transient disturbance:** A massive transient disturbance is a transient an external occurrence (e.g., a powerful imission of electromagnetic radiation) that results in the correlated failure of two or more communication channels and possibly some of the nodes. Whereas failure mode 1 to 4 relate to *internal* faults, failure mode 5 is concerned with an *external* fault. The probability for the occurrence of an external fault depends on the characteristics of the system environment, not on the design of the system per se.

Failure Frequency. The third part of the fault-hypothesis is concerned with the frequency of failures of the identified failure modes. Whereas failure rate data of electronic components w.r.t. permanent failures are available in the literature [Pauli et al., 1998], it is much more difficult to get consistent failures for intermittent and transient faults. One reason for this difficulty lies in the fact that transient failures often depend an physical location or on a particular geometry which is difficult to reproduce. For example, the SEU soft error rate caused by high-energy particles originating from the space depends on the altitude and the geographical location [Kaufmann and Johnson, 2000].

Error Detection Latency. The consequence of a *fault* is an *error* in the system state [Laprie, 1992]. The time it takes to detect the error is called the error detection latency. The *error detection latency* should be very short in order to be able to process the error before it propagates to a failure that impacts parts of the system that have not been disturbed by the original fault. *Knowing* *that **a failure has occurred** is more important than the actual failure* [Rechtin and Maier, 2002, p. 276].

Recovery Intervals. From the point of view of reliability modeling is important to know the time it takes the system to recover from a transient fault. For a permanent fault that has not caused spare exhaustion it is important to know the time it takes until all correct FCRs have a consistent view of the faulty FCR. For a transient fault there are thee intervals of importance:

- **Transient fault duration:** The time interval between the start of the transient fault and the instant when all communicating partners recognize that the transient fault has disappeared.

- **Protocol recovery interval:** The time it takes until the protocol has recovered and established a consistent view among all communicating partners (e.g., w.r.t. clock synchronization).

- **State repair interval:** The time it takes until an application has recovered from the transient fault and repaired the damage to its h-state (history state).

3. The Time-Triggered Architecture

The Time-Triggered Architecture (TTA) is a distributed architecture for the implementation of safety-critical applications [Kopetz and Bauer, 2003]. A large TTA system can be decomposed into a set of clusters. The structure of a typical single-cluster TTA system is depicted in Figure 1. Such a cluster consists of a *backbone core architecture* of node computers that are interconnected by two replicated communication channels. The media access to the communication channels is controlled by a time-division-multiple-access (TDMA) protocol. All correct nodes of a TTA system have synchronized clocks that are used to construct a fault-tolerant global *sparse time lattice* [Kopetz, 1992]. The guardians in the communication channels of Fig. 1 are needed in order to transform an *arbitrary timing failure* of a node into a *fail-silent failure.*

It is a goal of the TTA to reach–in a properly configured system–a service reliability at the system level of better than 10^{-9} failures/hour. This is achieved by

- structuring the system into a set of independent fault-containment regions (FCRs)

- Provide replica-deterministic operation of the node computers that can operate concurrently in a TMR (triple-modular-redundancy) mode.

- Tolerate an unrestricted (arbitrary) failure each FCR.

- Establish error-detection regions (EDR) such that the consequences of a fault, the ensuing errors, are detected before they corrupt the state of any other independent FCR [Kopetz, 2003]

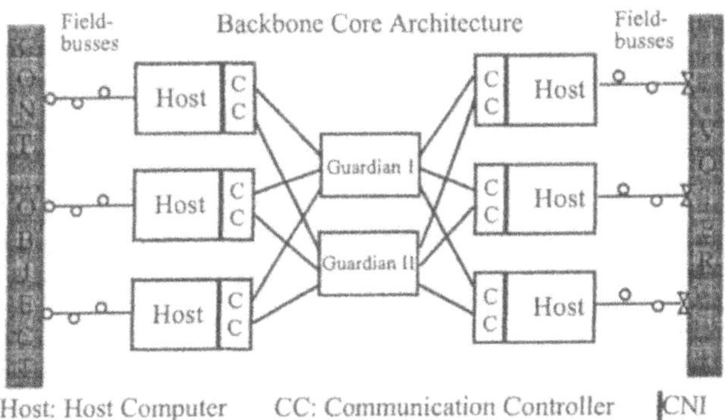

Figure 1. Structure of the Time-Triggered Architecture

A TTA node is supposed to be a *system-on-a-chip (SOC)*. From the hardware point of view, an SOC forms a single fault-containment region that can fail in an arbitrary failure mode. Each node computer contains a Time-Triggered Communication Controller (CC) and a host computer. The interface between the Communication Controller and the host computer is called the Communication Network Interface (CNI). A host computer can support local field-busses (e.g., CAN, LIN, or TTP/A) for the interconnection of the intelligent transducers (sensors and actuators) in the controlled object. The internal structure of a node is depicted in Fig. 2.

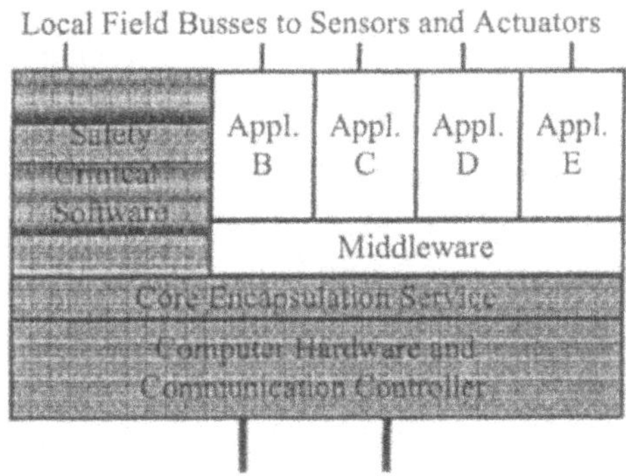

Figure 2. Structure of a TTA Node

The node of Figure 2 comprises five partitions: the upper leftmost partition provides a safety-critical service, while the other four partitions (B,C,D,E) provide non-safety critical services. Each partition has access to its local sensors and actuators via a local field bus. Given that the node hardware functions correctly and the shaded area is free of design faults, the core encapsulation service ensures that there cannot be any error propagation from the non-critical partitions to the critical partition. The certification for the safety-critical services is thus reduced to the shaded area of Figure 2.

The *middleware partition* in of Figure 2 establishes and monitors the encapsulated execution environments of the non-safety-critical jobs. In addition to a state message interface it provides event messages interfaces to the non-safety critical jobs and emulates legacy interfaces (e.g., a CAN controller interface) such that existing legacy software can be ported with minimal modifications.

The application software which resides within a partition is called a *job*. A set of cooperating jobs, each one possibly at a different node, forms a distributed application subsystem (DAS). The jobs of a DAS communicate via an encapsulated communication service with guaranteed temporal properties. If required, jobs of a DAS may be replicated at different nodes in order that the system provides a required level of fault tolerance in case a node fails. A TTA system may support many different encapsulated DASes that can interact via virtual gateways [Kopetz et al., 2004].

4. Fault Hypothesis w.r.t. Hardware Faults

With respect to hardware faults, the fault hypothesis of the the TTA consists of the following assumptions:

1 A node computer forms a single fault-containment region (FCR). From the point of view of hardware faults, a node is thus considered to be an atomic unit.

2 A physical communication channel including the central guardian forms a single FCR. All virtual channels that are implemented on a physical channel form a single unit of failure

3 A node computer can fail in an arbitrary failure mode. As long as only a single node computer fails, it is not relevant whether the failure is caused by a hardware fault or a software fault.

4 A central guardian distributes the messages received from the node computers. It can fail to distribute the messages, but cannot generate messages on its own (this is called the *distribution assumption*).

5 The permanent failure rate of a node computer or a central guardian is in the order of 100 FIT [Pauli et al., 1998] i.e. about 1000 years.

6 The transient failure rate of a node computer is in the order of 100 000 FIT, i.e, about 1 year. One important mechanism that causes transient failure is an SEU [Kaufmann and Johnson, 2000].

7 One out of about fifty failures of a node computer is *non-fail silent*. The relation of *silent* to *non-silent failures* of a node has been derived from fault injection experiments [Karlsson et al., 1995].

8 The central guardian transforms the non-fail-silent and the slightly-out-of-specification (SOS) failures of the node computers in the temporal domain to fail-silent failures in the temporal domain [Ademaj et al., 2003] (this is called the *SOS assumption*).

9 The detection of a single error is performed by a membership algorithm. The error detection latency is less then two TDMA rounds.

10 The detection of multiple errors is performed by a clique avoidance algorithm. The detection latency is less than two TDMA rounds.

11 The system can recover from a single transient fault within two TDMA rounds.

12 The system can recover from a massive transient that destroys the clock synchronization within 8 TDMA rounds [Steiner et al., 2003] after the transient has disappeared.

13 The state repair time of an application takes an application specific amount of time which must be derived from knowledge about the application software.

There are two important assumptions in this fault hypothesis that must be further investigated the *distribution assumption* and the *SOS assumption*.

The distribution assumption states that the central guardian cannot distribute valid messages without having received a valid message. If the central guardian has no knowledge about how to generate a CRC of a message, the probability that a random fault will produce a random message that is syntactically correct, is generated at the proper time, is of the proper length and contains a proper CRC is far below the 10^{-9} limit.

The validity of the *SOS assumption* has been established by extensive fault-injection experiments [Ademaj et al., 2003]. In more than twenty thousand experiments that resulted in a node failure because of the radiation of the TTA node with α particles, no error propagation has been observed when the system was equipped with a central guardian. In contrast to this, a number of error propagations have been observed when the nodes where protected by a local guardian. Considering the low failure rate for permanent node errors and the results of these experiments it can be concluded that the SOS assumption is valid within the 10^{-9} limit if the system contains a central guardian.

A correctly configured TTA system will recover from a massive external transient that causes correlated transient faults in the worst case *within 8 TDMA rounds* after the transient has disappeared. This scenario has been investigated by model checking [Steiner et al., 2004].

Considering the failure rates that have been presented above, the probability that a second independent failure will happen before the recovery from the first failure has been completed is below the 10^{-9} limit.

To summarize, a properly configured TTA system tolerates a single arbitrary hardware failure of any one of its nodes within the 10^{-9} limit. At the moment the TTA implementation of TTTech [TTTech, 1998] is in the process of being certified by the FAA (Federal Aviation Authority) for aerospace applications that are in the highest criticality class.

5. Fault Hypothesis w.r.t. Design Faults

5.1 Bohrbugs versus Heisenbugs

In his classical paper [Gray, 1986], Jim Gray proposed to distinguish between two types of software design errors, *Bohrbugs* and *Heisenbugs*. Bohrbugs are design errors in the software that cause reproducible failures. An example for a Bohrbug is a logic error in a program that causes the program to always take an unintended branch if the same computation is repeated. *Heisenbugs* are design errors in the software that seem to generate quasi-random failures. An example for a Heisenbug is a synchronization error that will cause the violation of an integrity condition (e.g., only one process is active in its critical section) if the temporal relationship of two concurrent processes happens to cause a race condition. A minor change in the temporal interleaving of the two concurrent processes will eliminate this race condition and thus the manifestation of the software error. From a phenomenological point of view, a transient failure that is caused by a Heisenbug cannot be distinguished from a failure caused by transient hardware malfunction.

In a system with state, a Heisenbug can cause a permanent state error [Kopetz, 1997]. The correct operation of the node will resume, as soon as this state error has been eliminated (e.g., by voting over the state in a TMR triade).

Experience has shown that it is much more difficult to find and eliminate Heisenbugs than it is to eliminate the Bohrbugs from a large software system [Eisenstadt, 1997].

5.2 Safety-Critical Design

We assume that the *hardware design*, the *core encapsulation service* and the *safety-critical software* (the *safety-critical design*–see Fig. 2) is free of design errors. In order to justify this strong assumption, this *safety critical* design must be made as small and simple as possible in order that it can be analyzed formally. In order to reduce the probability of Heisenbugs, the safety critical design should be time-triggered. The control signals are derived from the progression of the *sparse global time base* which guarantees that all replicated components will visit the same state at about the same physical time.

Concerning Heisenbugs, the above assumption is more stringent than needed. If there would be a Heisenbug in the safety-critical design that manifests itself as an *uncorrelated failure* with a failure rate that is in the same magnitude as the failure rate for failures caused by transient hardware faults then a properly configured TTA architecture would mask such a failure.

5.3 Non-Safety-Critical Software

The non-safety-critical software of a node is encapsulated by the *encapsulation service* such that even a malicious fault in the non-safety critical software will have no effect on the correct function of the safety-critical software.

6. Conclusions

The fault hypothesis states the assumptions about the types and number of faults that a fault-tolerant system must tolerate. The fault-hypothesis must be established at the beginning of the design process, since it has a profound influence on the architecture of the emerging fault-tolerant system. It is thus one of the most important documents for the design process. Without a precise fault hypothesis it is impossible to decide which faults are covered and which faults are *uncovered* by a given design. In order to achieve a high *assumption coverage* the fault hypothesis should make minimal assumptions about the *behavior of faulty nodes*. These minimal assumptions must be carefully documented and scrutinized in order to establish that the *assumption coverage* is in agreement with the overall dependability objective of the intended system.

The fault-hypothesis for the TTA states that a faulty node may fail in any failure mode, irrespective of whether the faulty behavior is caused by a physical fault in the hardware or a design fault in the hardware/software system. However, in the fault hypothesis of the TTA it is assumed that the failures of any two nodes are not correlated.

Acknowledgements

This work has been supported, in part by the European IST project NEXT TTA and the IST network of excellence ARTIST.

References

Ademaj, A., Sivencrona, H., Bauer, G., and Torin, J. (2003). Evaluation of fault handling of the time-triggered architecture with bus and star topology. In *Proceedings of the 2003 International Conference on Dependable Systems and Networks*, pages 123–132.

Avizienis, A. (1997). Toward systematic design of fault-tolerant systems. *Computer*, 30(4):51–58.

Constantinescu, C. (2002). Impact of deep submicron technology on dependability of VLSI circuits. In *Proceedings of the International Conference on Dependable Systems and Networks*, pages 205–209. IEEE.

Eisenstadt, M. (1997). My hairiest bug war stories. *Commun. ACM*, 40(4):30–37.

Gray, J. (1986). Why do computers stop and what can be done about it? In *Proceedings of the 5th Symposium on Reliablity in Distributed Software and Database Systems*.

Karlsson, J., Folkesson, P., Arlat, J., Crouzet, Y., and Leber, G. (1995). Integration and comparison of three physical fault injection techniques. In Randell, B., Laprie, J., Kopetz, H., and Littlewood, B., editors, *Predictably Dependable Computing Systems*, pages 309–327. Springer Verlag, heidelberg edition.

Kaufmann, L.F. and Johnson, B.W. (2000). Modeling of common-mode failures in digital embedded systems. In *Proc. of the Reliability and Maintainability Symposium*, Los Angeles, Cal.

Kopetz, H. (1992). Sparse time versus dense time in distributed real-time systems. In *Proceedings of 12th International Conference on Distributed Computing Systems*, Japan.

Kopetz, H. (1997). *Real-Time Systems, Design Principles for Distributed Embedded Applications*. Kluwer Academic Publishers, Boston, Dordrecht, London.

Kopetz, H. (2003). Fault containment and error detection in the time-triggered architecture. In *Proceedings of the Sixth International Symposium on Autonomous Decentralized Systems*.

Kopetz, H. and Bauer, G. (2003). The time-triggered architecture. *IEEE Special Issue on Modeling and Design of Embedded Software*.

Kopetz, H., Obermaisser, R., Peti, P., and Suri, N. (2004). From a federated to an integrated architecture for dependable embedded systems. Research Report 22/2004, Technische Universitat Wien, Institut fur Technische Informatik, Treitlstr. 1-3/182-1, 1040 Vienna, Austria.

Laprie, J.C. (1992). *Dependability: Basic Concepts and Terminology*. Springer Verlag, Vienna, Austria.

Littlewood, B. and Strigini, L. (1993). Validation of ultrahigh dependability for software-based systems. *Commun. ACM*, 36(11):69–80.

Normand, E. (1996). Single event upset at ground level. *IEEE Transactions on Nuclear Science*, 43(6):2742–2750.

Pauli, B., Meyna, A., and Heitmann, P. (1998). Reliability of electronic components and control units in motor vehicle applications. In *VDI Berichte 1415, Electronic Systems for Vehicles*, pages 1009–1024. Verein Deutscher Ingenieure.

Powell, D. (1992). Failure mode assumptions and assumption coverage. In *Proceedings of the 22nd IEEE Annual International Symposium on Fault-Tolerant Computing (FTCS-22)*, pages 386–395, Boston, USA.

Rechtin, E. and Maier, M.W. (2002). *The Art of Systems Architecting*. CRC Press, Boca Raton, USA.

Steiner, W., Paulitsch, M., and Kopetz, H. (2003). Multiple failure correction in the time-triggered architecture. In *Proc. of the IEEE WORDS 2003 Conference*, CAPRI, Italy.

Steiner, W., Rushby, J., Sorea, M., and Pfeifer, H. (2004). Model checking a fault-tolerant startup algorithm: From design exploration to exhaustive fault simulation. *The International Conference on Dependable Systems and Networks (DSN 2004)*.

TTTech (1998). homepage of TTTech at `www.tttech.com`.

Walter, C. J., Hugue, M. M., and Suri, Neeraj (1995). *Advances in Ultra-Dependable Distributed Systems*. IEEE Computer Society, 10662 Los Vaqueros Circle, Los Alamitos, CA 90720.

COMMUNICATIONS DEPENDABILITY EVOLUTION

Between Convergence and Competition

Michele Morganti

Siemens Mobile Communications, Italy — michele.morganti@siemens.com

Abstract: The high dependability standards that once characterized telecommunications networks were largely the consequence of the monopolistic regimes under which they were built and operated. With the progressive liberalization and deregulation of telecommunication markets this situation has dramatically changed and dependability, once a self imposed obligation, has now become a product differentiator that needs to be justified in terms of higher value for the customers and lower costs of ownership for the network operator.

Key words: Communications, Dependability, Convergence, Liberalization, Deregulation

1. ONCE UPON A TIME ...

Telecommunications were synonymous of public telephone networks, were almost anywhere a state monopoly, and their dependability was almost legendary.

The association of these three elements (telephony, monopoly and dependability) is definitely not accidental.

The fact, for example, that telephony was the only service officially to be delivered by the network meant a very specific and consistent set of Quality of Service (QoS) requirements and, as a direct consequence, a rather limited variance in network architectures and technological solutions.

Monopoly, on its side, meant that in each country there was only one network infrastructure, only one network operator and, obviously, only a few accredited suppliers, all of whom were willingly collaborating (among themselves and with operators) to defend their shares of an essentially closed and captive market.

Monopoly also meant only one source for services that were essential for the economical development of the country and for the welfare of its citizens and, at the same time, no real need to match offer and demand, with social costs usually charged to the high (and supposedly wealthy) consumers.

In this situation, dependability was perceived almost as an obligation to the country, in exchange for the privilege of monopoly, and the very high standards set for it were usually self imposed.

2. A LONG WAY FORWARD

Over time, many different and important events have contributed to determine an almost complete upturn of the above situation, some of them technological, some cultural, and some directly related to evolving market conditions and new regulations.

Historically, the first of these changes was the digitalization of telephone networks, and the most recent one the diffusion of public wireless access.

2.1 Digitalization

Digitalization initiated almost 40 years ago, and was initially aimed at improving the efficiency of long haul transmission, at the time one of the most expensive components of telecommunications networks. From there it quickly extended to all other network elements (although even today it cannot be said complete, as many analog local loops still exist in most countries). Digitalization contributed to the evolution of dependability in several different ways.

First of all it forced engineers to transpose requirements and objectives originally set for electromechanical equipment managing single circuits to computer controlled systems managing several thousand circuits at one time. Furthermore, computers and electronics in general were at the time fairly new, unreliable, and also very expensive objects, that needed to be used with parsimony. The challenge was in itself so big that the result was a large variety of architectural solutions, all of them embedding sophisticated fault tolerance techniques and various levels of hardware redundancy.

Another major consequence of digitalization was that by changing voice into a stream of bits it made it undistinguishable from data as well as from any other digitalized content. This fact did not produce an immediate effect on the architecture of telecommunications networks, but opened the way to another important historical period that went under the name of convergence.

2.2 Convergence

Convergence is in itself a fuzzy concept and, therefore, also a term that is easily abused and misused. Whether applied to technology, infrastructures, services or even market segments, it has often been invoked to assert one thing and the contrary at the same time.

Its first appearance in telecommunications referred to the theoretical possibility that, through digitalization, the same (first circuit, then packet based) infrastructure could be used to deliver all services and contents.

Eventually, everybody had to acknowledge that requirements were in most cases so different and conflicting that a single network could never satisfy them all, both technically and economically. Hence, the most evident effect of convergence on communications was a sort of creative divergence that fostered many new technologies, new network architectures, and even entirely new communication paradigms, like the Internet.

Eventually, some solutions proved to be intrinsically more pervasive and general purpose than others. However, convergence days demonstrated that there is always value in diversity, that one size does not always fit all, and that communications are there to satisfy people needs and not to create them.

2.3 The Internet

Talking dependability, the main lesson that came from the Internet is that reliable communications can be built on top of relatively unreliable network elements. Until then it had been common belief in the telecommunications community that this could only be done by purpose design, and that circuit based networks were intrinsically more dependable than packet ones just because their behavior was easier to predict and to engineer.

The Internet also proved that distributed control can be as (or even more) effective than centralized one, and that best results are achieved when there is intelligence both inside and outside of the network. At the time, the typical architecture of public telecommunications networks was strictly hierarchical, with most of the intelligence concentrated in the network core. Terminals were generally assumed to be dumb and, therefore, unable to contribute to the overall performance of the network or to dynamically adapt its status.

Finally, the Internet community showed to the telecommunications world that there could be forms of governance much simpler, faster and effective than those provided by official standardization bodies, and that, especially in a fast changing world, it was unwise to set standards as broad, detailed and rigid as it had been the case until then. Although it took quite some time for the Internet lessons to be fully understood and accepted, success stories like GSM, MPEG and WiFi could never have happened without them.

2.4 Privatization, Liberalization and Deregulation

Liberalization of telecommunications initiated almost a decade ago and quickly became a global phenomenon.

By introducing competition and by forcing formerly public operators to justify all of their operational costs to private investors, liberalization also obliged them to reassess all of their business practices, including those relevant to the realization of network infrastructures. Furthermore, many regulators decided to relax a number of previous obligations (also in term of minimum QoS requirements) in order to reduce entry barriers for the new operators.

In this context, the previous high network dependability standards, which in most cases implied massive hardware redundancy without clear evidence of a corresponding market benefit, became an easy target for CAPEX cutting measures.

The new cell based ATM switches and cross connects (which were at the time under development by a number of leading manufacturers worldwide) were the first and most illustrious victims of the new era. Their extremely demanding specifications had in fact become too expensive for those same operators who had originally imposed them.

This also caused a definitive rupture in the previously intimate relationships between operators and manufacturers. From there on operators took a strictly opportunistic behavior (take no commitment and buy what is available when you really need it), while manufacturers were obliged to assume full risk and responsibility for all new product developments.

2.5 Mobile Communications

The QoS of mobile communications is intrinsically lower than that of fixed ones. The radio resource is scarce and there are numerous constraints, interferences and physical obstacles that further reduce its efficiency of use. Nevertheless, the exceptional market response they got demonstrated that people are willing to accept all of these limitations and still pay a premium for the several other advantages they get. In short, they represent the outstanding proof that dependability and QoS are, to a large extent, options that need, as everything else, to be justified in terms of additional market share and value recognition.

They also demonstrated that steady state availability (until then the main design goal of telecommunications engineers) is only one of the many components of network dependability that need to be taken care of, and not necessarily the most important one. As a matter of fact, unavailability in mobile networks is more frequently due to poor coverage or to access congestion than to equipment failures.

On the other hand, mobile networks require considerable intelligence in the perifery, and this implies that their operational costs are much more influenced by equipment reliability than those of fixed ones. Terminals too are orders of magnitude more complicated, and still they must provide continuous fault free operation for several years.

Mobile handsets also include a number of specific dependability features that allow them to deal with the many adverse situations that they can meet in a hostile mobile environment. For example, most of them can deal with multiple networks and network technologies at the same time and then choose the best one (e.g., 3G terminals automatically switch to 2G service if signal quality drops below a certain level). Further, they dynamically adapt their transmit power and rate to actual transmission conditions.

Other dependability aspects that require special attention in designing mobile networks are data security and integrity, customer localization and tracking, and, consequently, customer data privacy. It is common knowledge that, in recent years, several criminals have been captured thanks to their incautious use of mobile phones, and with the introduction of A-GPS, location accuracy will further improve to within just a few meters.

2.6 Wireless Ubiquity

Public WiFi Hot-Spots made their appearance a couple of years ago, and immediately caught public attention.

Conceived for private usage in confined indoor environments, WiFi is a relatively unreliable and rather insecure technology that operates in a very crowded and noisy portion of unlicensed spectrum: totally unsuitable, one would say, for public usage and definitely unable, in this context, to guarantee any significant level of QoS. That it was immediately regarded as a concrete threat to mobile communications, and more specifically to 3G, is a clear indication of the fact that even operators had no clear understanding of how customers would react to the new offer, however unreliable.

Eventually public Hot-Spots disappointed the unrealistic expectations of some financial analysts. However, this was due more to coverage limitations than to their lack of QoS guarantees, including dependability related ones.

Technicians are now working to complement WiFi through WiMAX. Conceived for outdoor usage, WiMAX is definitely more robust that WiFi, will be operated in both licensed and unlicensed spectrum and will offer 70Mb/s access over cells that are the same size of mobile ones. In the new versions of the standard, WiMAX could also support some limited mobility.

Although WiMAX is IP native (and therefore intrinsically unable to guarantee certain QoS classes) wireline operators (especially alternative ones) see it as a perfectly viable alternative to xDSL over copper pairs while mobile operators are seriously considering it as an inexpensive solution for their back-hauling networks.

At the same time, silicon and terminal manufacturers are committed to embed WiFi and WiMAX capabilities directly into Lap-Tops, PDA's and even handsets. Further, almost everybody already agrees that 4G will not be a single new network but many different ones, each with its own specificity, to be used in alternative or in combination depending on instantaneous availability and needs.

3. IN CONCLUSION

Some ten years ago communications dependability had become a sort of routine work: on the one side there was a set of networks elements with precise functionalities and requirements; on the other, a matching set of design alternatives that could be used to implement them. Both sets had been consolidated through almost thirty years of experience, and it was common understanding that there was little more left to invent and no real motivation to justify the effort.

Liberalization and mobility completely upturned this situation and forced network operators and their suppliers to completely reassess, in terms of real market value, their traditional design practices and architectural choices. They had to recognize, for example, that IP backbones, although less predictable than SDH ones, could indeed provide, through over-sizing, a still adequate and much less expensive alternative. Similarly, in most cases a temporary roaming agreement with a competitor could prove more effective and less expensive than extensive redundancy to ensure continuity of service in case of mobile access equipment failures.

In this fast evolving business context, manufacturers are obliged to make their own choices and to take their own risks. Operators, on their part, need to justify all of their investments in terms of additional market opportunities and higher margins.

Dependability too, once simply a must, has become an option that needs to be tuned, on a case by case basis, to actual needs and opportunities. Terms like QoS and redundancy scalability have become commonplace in product descriptions. At the same time, however, the scope of dependability has much broadened to include once disregarded aspects like security and safety.

Looking to the future, the main challenge is no more how to build highly dependable networks, but how to get the best out of many unreliable ones.

INTRUSION TOLERANCE FOR INTERNET APPLICATIONS

Yves Deswarte and David Powell
LAAS-CNRS, 7 avenue du Colonel Roche, 31077 Toulouse Cedex 4, France
yves.deswarte@laas.fr, david.powell@laas.fr

Abstract: The Internet has become essential to most enterprises and many private individuals. However, both the network and computer systems connected to it are still too vulnerable and attacks are becoming evermore frequent. To face this situation, traditional security techniques are insufficient and fault tolerance techniques are becoming increasingly cost-effective. Nevertheless, intrusions are very special faults, and this has to be taken into account when selecting the fault tolerance techniques.

Key words: security, intrusion-tolerance, Internet, dependability, fault-tolerance

1. INTRODUCTION

Arpanet, the experimental network that was to give rise to the Internet, was created by a small group of researchers and computer scientists who wanted to improve communication between themselves and to share some rare and expensive resources such as processors, mass storage and inter-computer communication lines. The protocols and services that they developed were aimed primarily at achieving the best possible availability, despite the use of relatively unreliable components (communication lines, routers, computers). They did not envisage any malicious use of the network since it was only accessible to a small group of pioneers who had a common aim: making the network work. None of them would have had the crazy idea of experimenting with attacks endangering this common aim, since that would probably have led to them being immediately expelled from the group. It is thus natural that the developed protocols and services only took into account transmission errors and accidental faults affecting hardware and software, without worrying about malicious attacks and intrusions. For example, in those protocols, nothing guarantees the authenticity of addresses, which facilitates spoofing attacks and session hijacking. Furthermore, the protocols include network maintenance functions, such as source routing (a technique whereby the sender of a packet can specify the route that a packet should take through the network), which can easily be exploited to bypass protection mechanisms such as firewalls.

Today, the same protocols are used in the Internet, which has become a totally open system, i.e., one to which anybody can have access. The current users of the Internet are very different to those forming the small closely-knit community of the original Arpanet. There are interactions between many different user-categories: business-to-business (B2B), business-to-consumer (B2C), citizen-to-administration (C2A) or government (e-Government), or simply among private citizens, who create their own virtual communities. The Internet is used for commercial, administrative, democratic, social, and cultural reasons, or simply for recreation. Most uses of the Internet are perfectly legitimate. No single group has the right to exclude another group under the pretext that the latter could prevent the former from achieving its objectives. Indeed, there would be no interest in doing so since it is the very diversity of uses to which the Internet is put that enables it to exist at a reasonable cost. Since the objectives are different, it is quite normal that the security requirements are also different, and it would be unreasonable to expect a schoolchild to manage his personal computer with as much care and attention to security as would the administrator of a bank server, for example. There are many more schoolchildren than banks, so it is not surprising that many systems connected to the Internet are not well administered. Such machines are very vulnerable to attack from malicious persons or agents, who might attempt to take control of them to further propagate their attacks. It is thus possible for attackers not only to increase their firing power in order to perpetrate attacks targeted at well-protected sites, but also to hide their tracks and make it more difficult to find clues enabling them to be identified.

Attacks are very common, which is not really surprising: the users of the Internet are more or less representative of the populations of developed countries, and among the hundreds of millions of Internet users, there must be a non-negligible proportion of individuals who are potential attackers. The most frequent types of attacks, and also the easiest ones, are those aimed against availability, by "denial of service": the attacker aims simply to prevent the targeted system from being used. Other attacks are aimed against confidentiality: the attacker aims to obtain sensitive information such as commercial, industrial, political, or even military secrets, but also personal data whose disclosure may endanger people's privacy. Yet other types of attacks are aimed against the integrity of information: destruction or modification of sensitive data, spreading of false information, manipulation of published data, etc. Thus, one of the "sports" currently popular among hackers is to "deface" Web servers, i.e., to alter (or deviate the access route to) legitimate web pages so as to replace the displayed information by humoristic, polemic or pornographic parodies.

Attackers have various motivations. They may act out of sport or by curiosity (to carry out experiments), by vanity (to show off their competence), by vandalism (for the pleasure of destruction or damage), by vengeance (to hurt people they don't like or to punish those who do not consider them for their "merit"), by greed (blackmail, extortion), or even for political, strategic or terrorist reasons. Attackers thus vary in degrees of tenacity and competency, and are able to deploy different levels of resources, according to whether they are disturbed adolescents, more-or-less structured groups of hackers, simple thieves, criminal or terrorist organizations, or government services specialized in electronic warfare.

There are also many ways to carry out attacks. They may exploit vulnerabilities in networks or their protocols: eavesdropping (or "sniffing"), interception (message destruction, insertion, modification or replay), address falsification, injection of counterfeit network control messages (e.g., for routing), and denial of service (e.g., by network jamming). Routers are also becoming evermore-frequent targets. Attacks can also exploit flaws in operating systems and application software, such as buffer or stack overflows. It should also be noted that the Internet is also a medium for spreading information about security vulnerabilities, both for hackers, and for system administrators and developers. The former use this information to develop and publish new "exploits" (i.e., methods for carrying out successful attacks) or even scripts to carry them out automatically. The latter use the same information to develop and publish remedies and patches. Like Aesop's tongue, the distribution of such security information over the Internet can be both the best and the worst of things.

2. SHORTCOMINGS OF CONVENTIONAL SECURITY TECHNIQUES

Computer and communication security relies mostly on user authentication and authorization, i.e., control of access rights. Authentication is necessary to identify each user with sufficient confidence, in order to assign him adequate privileges and to make him responsible and liable for his actions. Authorization aims to allow the user to perform only legitimate actions. As much as possible, authorization should obey the *least privilege principle*: at any given instant, a user can only perform the actions needed to carry out the task duly assigned to him. Authorization is implemented through protection mechanisms, which aim to detect and block any attempt by a user to exceed his privileges. Security officers can then detect such attempts and initiate legal actions, which in turn constitute deterrence against further attempts. Authentication, authorization, detection, retaliation and deterrence constitute the arsenal of security defenders.

Unfortunately, these weapons are of little efficiency in the context of the Internet:

- Any Internet user, even anonymous users, has some rights on connected machines: e.g., the capacity to know their existence and to identify them by their name or address, the ability to read pages on public Web servers, etc.
- Many systems connected to the Internet are accessible by the public at large, making strong authentication infeasible. Weak mechanisms such as password authentication are often used carelessly, e.g., password lending, which makes it possible for one user to masquerade as another. Even without the cooperation of a user, it is often easy to guess passwords.
- COTS operating systems and application software contain many design flaws that can be exploited by attackers to circumvent protection mechanisms; when software companies develop and distribute patches to correct such flaws, relatively few system administrators apply the patches either because this would require more time or competence than available, or because the patches may disable certain features needed by other legitimate software.
- As mentioned in the introduction, most Internet protocols were designed thirty years ago, at a time when computing and communication resources were expensive and unreliable, and when intrusions were unlikely; so communication availability was the primary objective. Many facilities developed for that purpose can be diverted by malicious agents to perform denial of service attacks (e.g., by SYN flooding) or to multiply their efficiency (e.g., by "smurfing"), to by-pass protection mechanisms such as firewalls (e.g., by source routing), to hide their tracks (e.g., by IP address spoofing), etc.
- Due to harsh economic pressures, many Internet Service Providers and telecommunication operators do not implement ingress filtering and trace-back facilities, which would help to locate and identify attackers.

3. A DIFFERENT ANGLE ON SECURITY METHODS

Almost twenty years ago, a few pioneering researchers contended that a "tolerance" approach to security could be defined using concepts borrowed from the area of dependable computing and fault-tolerance. Notable work of this period includes that done by Laprie et al. [11, 17], Dobson and Randell [15], Joseph and Avizienis [16]. More recently, institutionally-financed research efforts such as the DARPA Organically Assured and Survivable Information System (OASIS) program[1] and the European IST project on Malicious and Accidental Fault Tolerance for Internet Applications (MAFTIA)[2] have given new credence to the basic tenets of this early work.

Here, we briefly introduce and discuss two particularly-relevant key ideas from the field of dependable computing and fault tolerance [3, 4, 18].

The first key concept is that three causally-related impairments to system dependability need to be considered: fault, error and failure. A system *failure* is an event that occurs when the service delivered by the system deviates from correct service. An *error* is that part of the system state that may cause a subsequent failure, whereas a *fault* is the adjudged or hypothesized cause of an error. The notion is recursive in that a failure at one level can be viewed as a fault at the next higher level (e.g., a component failure is a fault seen from the containing system).

The labels given to these concepts conform to standard usage within the dependability community, but the important point we would like to stress is not the words but the fact that there are *three* concepts.

First, it is essential to be able to distinguish the internally observable phenomenon (error) from the externally observable one (failure), which tolerance techniques aim to avert. Indeed, any tolerance technique must be based on some form of detection and recovery acting on internal perturbations before they reach the system's interface to the outside world. The alternative viewpoint, in which any detectable anomaly is deemed to make the system "insecure" in some sense, would make intrusion-*tolerance* an unattainable objective.

Second, the distinction between the internally observable phenomenon (error) and its root cause (fault) is vital since it emphasizes the fact that there may be various plausible causes for the same observed anomaly, including an atypical usage profile, an accidental fault or an intentionally malicious fault.

[1] http://www.tolerantsystems.org/

[2] http://www.research.ec.org/maftia/

The type of intentionally malicious fault of particular concern here is an *intrusion*, which is a deliberate software-domain[3] operational[4] fault. An intrusion occurs when an *attack* is able to successfully exploit a *vulnerability*. Attacks may be viewed either at the level of human activity (of the attacker), or at that of the resulting technical activity that is observable within the considered computer system. Attacks (in the technical sense) are malicious faults that attempt to exploit one or more vulnerabilities (e.g., email viruses, malicious Java applets or ActiveX controls). The intrusion resulting from the successful exploitation of a vulnerability by an attack may be considered as an internal fault, which can cause errors that may provoke a system security failure, i.e., a violation of the system's security policy.

The second key concept from dependable computing is that methods for designing and validating dependable systems can be broadly classified into four broad categories:

- *fault prevention*: how to prevent the occurrence or introduction of faults,
- *fault tolerance*: how to deliver correct service in the presence of faults,
- *fault removal*: how to reduce the number or severity of faults,
- *fault forecasting*: how to estimate the present number, the future incidence, and the likely consequences of faults.

Fault prevention and fault removal are sometimes grouped together as *fault avoidance*; fault tolerance and fault forecasting constitute *fault acceptance*. Note that avoidance and acceptance should be considered as complementary rather than alternative strategies.

It is enlightening to equate "fault" in these definitions with the notions of attack, vulnerability and intrusion defined earlier. Taking "attack" in both its human and technical senses leads to ten distinct security-building methods out of a total of sixteen (see Table 1).

As discussed earlier, it would be illusory to imagine that all attacks over the Internet might be prevented. Similarly, it is impossible to eliminate all possible vulnerabilities. For example, the very fact that a system is connected to the Internet is in itself a vulnerability, but what use would a Web server be if it were not connected to the net? The focus in this paper is therefore on intrusion-*tolerance* techniques, which should be seen as an additional defense mechanism rather than an alternative to the classic set of techniques grouped under the heading intrusion-*prevention* on Table 1. Before addressing intrusion-tolerance per se, we first present some background material on fault tolerance in the traditional sense of dependable computing.

[3] As opposed to faults in the hardware domain, e.g., physical sabotage.
[4] As opposed to faults introduced during system development, e.g., trapdoors.

Table 1. Classification of Security Methods

Method Category	Attack (human sense)	Attack (technical sense)	Vulnerability	Intrusion
Prevention (how to prevent occurrence or introduction of...)	deterrence, laws, social pressure, secret service...	firewalls, authentication, authorization...	semi-formal & formal specification, rigorous design & management...	= attack & vulnerability prevention & removal
Tolerance (how to deliver correct service in the presence of...)	= vulnerability prevention & removal, intrusion tolerance		= attack prevention & removal, intrusion tolerance	error detection & recovery, fault masking, intrusion detection & response, fault handling
Removal (how to reduce number or severity of...)	physical counter-measures, capture of attacker	preventive & corrective maintenance aimed at removal of attack agents	1. formal proof, model-checking, inspection, test... 2. preventive & corrective maintenance, including security patches	⊆ attack & vulnerability removal, i.e., preventive & corrective maintenance
Forecasting (how to estimate present number, future incidence, likely consequences of...)	intelligence gathering, threat assessment...	assessment of presence of latent attack agents, potential consequences of their activation	assessment of: presence of vulnerabilities, exploitation difficulty, potential consequences...	= vulnerability & attack forecasting

4. FAULT TOLERANCE

Fault tolerance [1] is a technique that has proven to be efficient to implement computing systems able to provide a correct service despite accidental phenomena such as environmental perturbations (external faults), failures of hardware components (internal physical faults), or even design faults such as software bugs.

As outlined in Section 3, *faults* are causes of errors, errors are abnormal parts of the computing system state, and *failures* happen when errors propagate through the system-to-user interface, i.e., when the service provided by the system is incorrect. When faults are accidental and sufficiently rare, they can be tolerated. To do so, errors must be *detected* before they lead to failure, and then corrected or *recovered*: this is the role of *error handling*. It is also necessary to diagnose the underlying faults (i.e., to identify and locate the faulty components), so as to be able to isolate them, and then replace or repair them, and finally to re-establish the system in its nominal configuration: fault diagnosis, isolation, repair and reconfiguration together constitute *fault handling*.

There are various techniques for detecting errors. For simplicity, we categorize these as being either property-checks or comparison-checks.

Property-checks consist in observing the system state, in particular certain values or events, and verifying they satisfy certain properties or rules.

This usually imposes only a small hardware or software overhead (*redundancy*). Among hardware property-checks, let us note that most microprocessors detect non-existing or unauthorized instructions and commands, non-existing addresses and unauthorized access modes, and that watchdogs can detect excessive execution durations. Software-based property-checks include likelihood tests inserted into programs to check the values of certain variables, or the instants or sequences of certain events (*defensive programming*). Error detecting codes and run-time model checking can also be viewed as property-checks.

Comparison-checks consist in comparing several executions, carried out either sequentially on the same hardware, or on different hardware units. This requires more redundancy than the first class of error detection techniques, but it also assumes that a single fault would not produce the same effect (i.e., identical errors) on the different executions. If only internal physical faults are considered, the same computation can be run on identical hardware units, since it is very unlikely that each hardware unit would suffer an identical internal fault at the same execution instant to produce the same error. On the contrary, design faults would produce the same errors if the same process is run on identical hardware units, and thus the comparison of the executions would not detect discrepancies. In that case, it is necessary to diversify the underlying execution support (hardware and/or software), so that a single design fault would affect only one execution, or at least would affect differently the different executions [2, 7, 13].

To correct errors, one approach it to take the system back to a state that it had occupied prior to the detection of errors, i.e., to carry out rollback recovery. To be able to do that, it is necessary to have created and saved copies of the system state, known as recovery points or checkpoints. Another error correction technique is called forward recovery, which consists of replacing the erroneous system state by a new, healthy state, and then continuing execution. This is possible, for example, in certain real-time control systems in which the system can be re-initialized and input data re-read from sensors before continuing execution. Finally, a third technique consists in "masking" errors; This is possible when there is enough redundant state information for a correct state to be built from the erroneous state, e.g., by a majority vote on three (or more) executions.

In most cases, the efficacy of fault tolerance techniques relies on the fact that faults are rare phenomena that occur at random points in time. It is thus possible, for example in a triple modular redundant architecture, to suppose that is unlikely for a second unit to fail while a failed unit is being repaired. This hypothesis is unfortunately not valid when intrusions are considered. An attacker that succeeds in penetrating one system can pursue his attack on that system, and also simultaneously attack other similar systems.

5. INTRUSION TOLERANCE

Intrusion tolerance aims to organize and manage a system such that an intrusion in one part of the system has no consequence on its overall security. To do that, we can use techniques developed in the traditional field of fault tolerance. However, there are two main problems:

- It should be made very difficult for the same type of attack to succeed in different parts of the system. This means that each "part" of the system must be sufficiently protected in its own right (so that there are no trivial attacks), and should ideally be diversified.
- An intrusion into a part of the system should not allow the attacker to obtain confidential data. This is especially important in that redundancy, which is necessary for fault tolerance, may result in more alternative targets for hackers to attack.

If these problems can be solved, we can apply to intrusions the techniques that have been developed for traditional fault tolerance: error handling (detection and recovery) and fault handling (diagnosis, isolation, repair, reconfiguration).

5.1 Tolerance based on Intrusion Detection

In the context of intrusions, specific detection techniques have been developed. These have been named "intrusion detection" techniques, but it should be noted that they do not directly detect intrusions, but only their effects, i.e., the errors due to intrusions (or even due to attacks which did not successfully cause intrusions).

The so-called intrusion detection techniques may be divided into two categories: anomaly detection and misuse detection (see Figure 1). Anomaly detection consists in comparing the observed activity (for example, of a given user) with a reference "normal activity" (for the considered user). Any deviation between the two activities raises an alert.

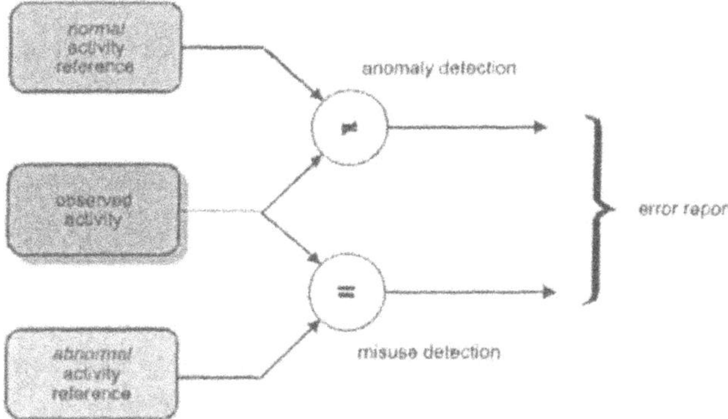

Figure 1. Intrusion Detection Paradigms

Conversely, misuse detection consists in comparing the observed activity with a reference defining known attack scenarios. Both types of detection techniques are characterized by their proportions of false alarms (known as false positives) and of undetected intrusive activities (known as false negatives). In the case of anomaly detection, one can generally adjust the "threshold" or, by analogy with radar systems, the "gain" of the detector, to choose a point of operation that offers the best compromise between the proportions of false positives and false negatives. On the other hand, misuse detection techniques have the advantage of identifying specific attacks, with few false positives. However, they only enable the detection of known attack symptoms. In both cases, it should be noted that detection is based on property-checks.

To correct the damage caused by the intrusion, one may, like in traditional fault tolerance, carry out backward recovery (if one has taken the precaution of maintaining up-to-date backups) or forward recovery (if one can rebuild a healthy state), but it is often easier and more efficient to mask errors, using some form of active (or modular) redundancy.

5.2 Fragmentation-Redundancy-Scattering

Several years ago, we developed an error masking technique, called "fragmentation, redundancy and scattering, or FRS", aimed at protecting sensitive data and computations [12]. This technique exploits distribution of a computing system to ensure that intrusion into part of the system cannot compromise the confidentiality, integrity and availability of the system. Fragmentation consists of splitting the sensitive data into fragments such that a single isolated fragment does not contain any significant information (confidentiality). The fragments are then replicated so that the modification or the destruction of fragment replicas does not impede the reconstruction of correct data (integrity and availability). Finally, scattering aims to ensure that an intrusion only gives access to isolated fragments. Scattering may be: *topological*, by using different data storage sites or by transmitting data over independent communication channels, or *temporal*, by transmitting fragments in a random order and possibly adding false padding fragments. Scattering can also be applied to privileges, by requiring the cooperation of several persons with different privileges in order to carry out some critical operation (separation of duty).

The FRS technique was originally developed in the Delta-4 project [19] for file storage, security management and data processing (see Figure 2). For file storage, fragmentation is carried out using simple cryptographic techniques and fragment naming employs a secret key one-way function. The fragments are sent over the network in a random order, which means that one of the hardest tasks for an intruder would be to sort all the fragments

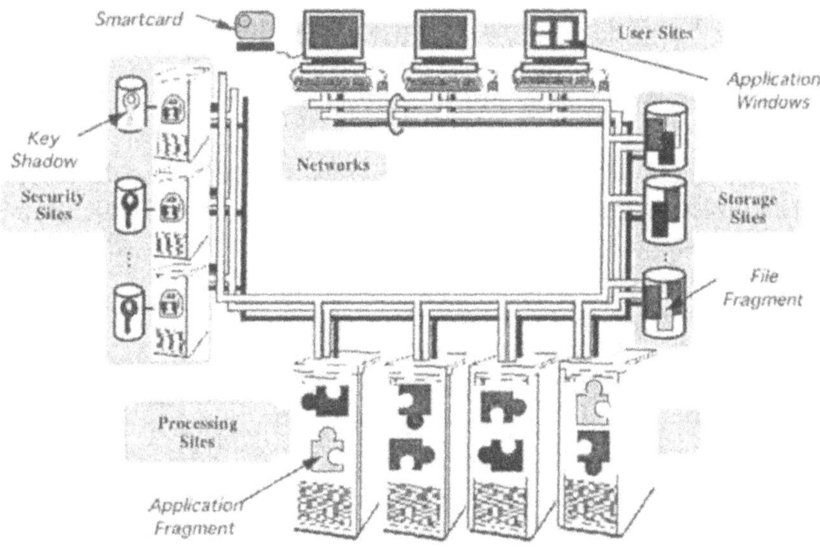

Figure 2. Fragmentation-Redundancy-Scattering in Delta-4

into the right order before being able to carry out cryptanalysis. For security management, the principle resides in the distribution of the authentication and authorization functions between a set of sites administered by different people so that failure of a few sites or misfeasance by a small number of administrators do not endanger the security functions. On these sites, non-sensitive data is replicated, whereas secret data is fragmented using threshold cryptographic functions. Finally, for data processing, two data types are considered: a) numerical and logical data, whose semantics are defined by the application, (b) contextual data (e.g., character strings) that is subjected only to simple operations (input, display, concatenation, etc.). In this scheme, contextual data is ciphered and deciphered only on a user site during input and display. In contrast, context data is subjected to successively finer fragmentation until the fragments do not contain any significant information. This is achieved using an object-oriented decomposition method.

6. THE INTERNET CONTEXT

The techniques developed in Delta-4 are well adapted to predominately homogeneous applications that are distributed over a LAN. However, they are not directly transposable to the Internet, especially when the concerned applications involve mutually suspicious companies or organizations. In this case, it is no longer possible to manage security in a homogeneous way.

Here, we briefly outline two projects were the tolerance approach has been adapted to account for the inherent heterogeneity of the Internet.

6.1 The MAFTIA Project

The European project MAFTIA was directly aimed at the development of intrusion-tolerant Internet applications [20]. Protocols and middleware were developed to facilitate the management of fault-tolerant group communications (including tolerance of Byzantine faults), possibly with real-time, confidentiality and/or integrity constraints [5, 8, 9, 21]. In particular, the developed protocols and middleware enabled the implementation of trusted third parties or TTPs (e.g., a certification authority) that tolerate intrusions (including administrator misfeasance) [6] through error masking.

Particular attention was also paid to intrusion detection techniques distributed over Internet, since intrusion detection not only contributes to intrusion tolerance, but is itself an attractive target for attack. It is thus necessary to organize the intrusion detection mechanisms in such a way as to make them intrusion-tolerant [10].

Furthermore, the project developed an authorization scheme for multiparty transactions involving mutually suspicious organizations (see Figure 3) [14].

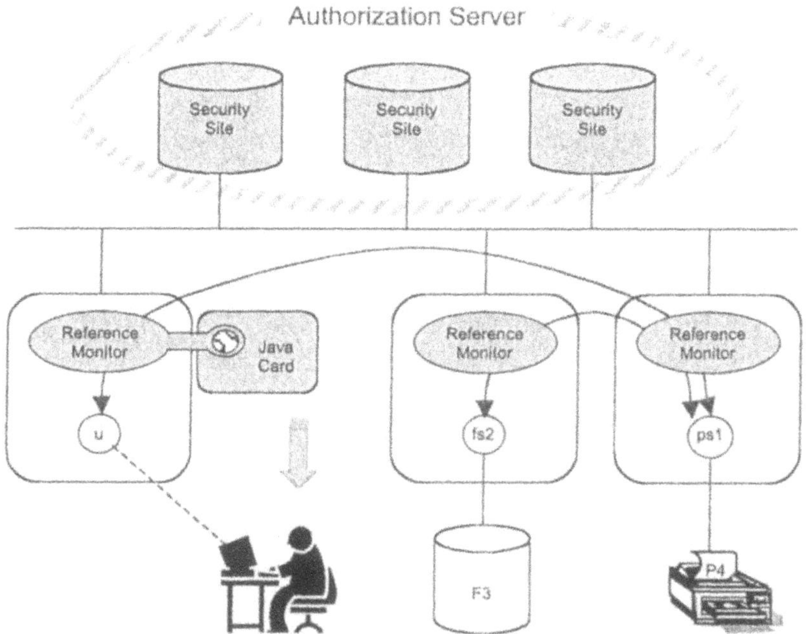

Figure 3. MAFTIA Authorization Scheme

An authorization server, implemented as an intrusion-tolerant TTP, checks whether each multiparty transaction is authorized. If that is so, the server generates the authorization proofs that are necessary for the execution of each component of the transaction (invocations on elementary objects). On each of the sites participating in the authorization scheme, a reference monitor, implemented on a JavaCard, checks that each method invocation is accompanied by a valid authorization proof. The scheme is intrusion-tolerant in the sense that the corruption of a participating site does not allow the intruder to obtain any additional privileges regarding objects residing on other sites.

6.2 The DIT Project

In cooperation with SRI International, we are participating in the development of the DIT (Dependable Intrusion Tolerance) architecture [22]. The objective is to be able to build Web servers that continue to provide correct service in the presence of attacks. For this type of application, confidentiality is not essential, but integrity and availability must be ensured, even if the system is under attack from competent attackers. It is thus essential that a successful attack on one component of the system should not facilitate attacks on other components. The architecture design is thus centered on a diversification approach (Figure 4).

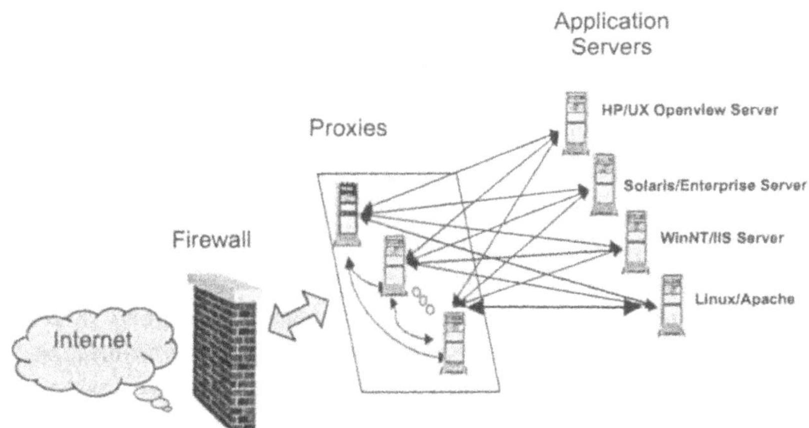

Figure 4. DIT Architecture

The architecture is composed of a pool of ordinary Web servers, using as much diversification as possible at the hardware level (Sparc, Pentium, PowerPC, etc.), the operating system level (Solaris, Microsoft Windows, Linux, MacOS, etc.) and Web application software level (Apache, IIS, Enterprise Server, Openview Server, etc.). Only the content of the Web pages is identical on each server. There are sufficient application servers at a given redundancy level (see below) to ensure an adequate response time for the nominal request rate. The servers are isolated from the Internet by *proxies*, which are implemented by purpose-built software executed on diversified hardware. Requests from the Internet, filtered by a firewall, are taken into account by one of the proxies acting as a *leader*. The leader distributes the requests to multiple Web servers and checks the corresponding responses before returning them to the request initiator. The back-up proxies monitor the behavior of the leader by observing the firewall/proxy and proxy/server networks. If they detect a failure of the leader, they elect a new leader from among themselves. The proxies also process alarms from intrusion detection sensors placed on the Web servers and on both networks.

Depending on the current level of alert, the leader sends each request to one server (simplex mode), two servers (duplex mode), three servers (triplex mode) or to all available servers. Each server prepares its response, then computes an MD5 cryptographic checksum of this response and sends it to the leader. In simplex mode, the server also sends its response to the leader, which recomputes the checksum and compares it to the one sent by the server. In duplex mode, the leader compares the two checksums from the servers and, if they concur, requests one the responses, which is verified by recomputing the checksum. In triplex or all-available modes, the checksums are subjected to a majority vote, and the response is requested from one of the majority servers.

The alert level is defined as either a function of recent alarms triggered by the intrusion detection mechanisms or other error detection mechanisms (result cross-checking, integrity tests, etc.), or by information sent by external sources (CERTs, other trusted centers, etc.). The redundancy level is raised towards a more severe mode as soon as alarms are received, but is lowered to a less severe mode when failed components have been diagnosed and repaired, and when the alarm rate has decreased. This adaptation of the redundancy level is thus tightly related to the detection, diagnosis, reconfiguration and repair mechanisms. In the case of read-only data servers, such as passive Web servers, repair involves just a simple re-initialization of the server from a back-up (an authenticated copy on read-only storage).

Diversification renders the task of the attacker as difficult as possible: when an attacker sends a Web page request (the only means for him to access the application servers), he does not know towards which servers his request will be forwarded and thus which hardware or software will process it. Even if he were able to design an attack that would be effective on all server types (except maybe for denial-of-service attacks, which are easy to detect), it would be very difficult to cause redundant servers (in duplex mode and above) to reply in exactly the same incorrect way.

7. CONCLUSION

Given the current rate of attacks on Internet, and the large number of vulnerabilities in contemporary computing systems, intrusion tolerance appears to be a promising technique to implement more secure applications, particularly with diversified hardware and software platforms. There is of course a price to pay, since it is expensive to support multiple heterogeneous systems. However, this is probably the price that must be paid for security in an open, and therefore, uncertain world.

REFERENCES

[1] J. Arlat, Y. Crouzet, Y. Deswarte, J.-C. Laprie, D. Powell, P. David, J.-L. Dega, C. Rabéjac, H. Schindler, and J.-F. Soucailles, "Fault Tolerant Computing", in *Encyclopedia of Electrical and Electronic Engineering*, vol. 7, J. G. Webster, Ed., Wiley-Interscience, 1999, pp. 285-313.

[2] A. Avizienis and L. Chen, "On the implementation of N-version programming for software fault tolerance during execution", in *First IEEE-CS International Computer Software and Applications Conference (COMPSAC 77)*, Chicago, IL, USA, November 1977, IEEE CS Press, pp. 149-55.

[3] A. Avizienis, J.-C. Laprie, and B. Randell, "Fundamental Concepts of Dependability", in *3rd Information Survivability Workshop*, Boston, MA, USA, 24-26 October 2000, IEEE CS Press, pp. 7-12.

[4] A. Avizienis, J.-C. Laprie, and B. Randell, "Dependability and its Threats: A Taxonomy", in *Fault Tolerance for Trustworthy and Dependable Information Infrastructures, IFIP World Computer Congress*, Toulouse, France, August 2004, Kluwer Academic Publishers (these proceedings).

[5] M. Backes and C. Cachin, "Reliable Broadcast in a Computational Hybrid Model with Byzantine Faults, Crashes, and Recoveries", in *Proc. of the 2003 Int. Conf. on Dependable Systems and Networks (DSN'2003)*, Washington, D.C., USA, 22-25 June 2003, IEEE CS Press, pp. 37-46.

[6] C. Cachin, "Distributing Trust on the Internet", in *Int. Conf. on Dependable Systems and Networks (DSN-2001)*, Goteborg, Sweden, 1-4 July 2001, IEEE CS Press.

[7] L. Chen and A. Avizienis, "N-Version-Programming: A Fault-Tolerance Approach to Reliability of Software Operation", in *8th IEEE Int. Symp. on Fault-Tolerant Computing (FTCS-8)*, Toulouse, France, June 1978, IEEE CS Press, pp. 3-9.

[8] M. Correia, L. C. Lung, N. F. Neves, and P. Verissimo, "Efficient Byzantine-Resilient Reliable Multicast on a Hybrid Failure Model", in *21st IEEE Symp. on Reliable Distributed Systems (SRDS'2002)*, Suita, Japan, 13-16 October 2002, IEEE CS Press.

[9] M. Correia, P. Verissimo, and N. F. Neves, "The Design of a COTS Real-Time Distributed Security Kernel", in *4th European Dependable Computing Conference (EDCC-4)*, Toulouse, France, October 2002, Springer, pp. 234-52.

[10] H. Debar and A. Wespi, "Aggregation and Correlation of Intrusion-Detection Alerts", in *Recent Advances in Intrusion Detection (RAID 2001)*, Davis, CA, USA, 10-12 October 2001, Springer, pp. 85-103.

[11] Y. Deswarte, J.-C. Fabre, J. da Silva Fraga, J.-C. Laprie, and D. Powell, "The SATURNE Project. A Fault- and Intrusion-Tolerant Distributed System", *IEEE Computer Architecture Technical Committee Newsletter*, pp. 4-22, 1985.

[12] Y. Deswarte, L. Blain, and J.-C. Fabre, "Intrusion Tolerance in Distributed Systems", in *IEEE Symp. on Security and Privacy*, Oakland, CA, USA, May 1991, IEEE CS Press, pp. 110-21.

[13] Y. Deswarte, K. Kanoun, and J.-C. Laprie, "Diversity against Accidental and Deliberate Faults", in *Computer Security, Dependability and Assurance: From Needs to Solutions*, P. Amman, B. H. Barnes, S. Jajodia, and E. H. Sibley, Eds., IEEE CS Press, 1999, pp. 171-82.

[14] Y. Deswarte, N. Abghour, V. Nicomette, and D. Powell, "An Intrusion-Tolerant Authorization Scheme for Internet Applications", in *Supplement of the IEEE/IFIP Int. Conf. on Dependable Systems and Networks (DSN'2002)*, Washngton, D.C., USA, 23-26 June 2002, pp. C.1.1-C.1.6.

[15] J. E. Dobson and B. Randell, "Building Reliable Secure Systems out of Unreliable Insecure Components", in *IEEE Symp. on Security and Privacy*, Oakland, CA, USA1986, IEEE CS Press, pp. 187-93.

[16] M. K. Joseph and A. Avizienis, "A Fault Tolerance Approach to Computer Viruses", in *IEEE Symp. on Security and Privacy*, Oakland, CA, USA, April 1988, IEEE CS Press, pp. 52-58.

[17] J.-C. Laprie, "Dependable Computing and Fault Tolerance: Concepts and Terminology", in *15th IEEE Int. Symp. on Fault Tolerant Computing (FTCS-15)*, Ann Arbor, MI, USA, June 1985, IEEE CS Press, pp. 2-11.

[18] J.-C. Laprie, "Dependability: Basic Concepts and Terminology", in *Dependable Computing and Fault-Tolerance*, vol. 5, A. Avizienis, H. Kopetz, and J.-C. Laprie, Eds. Vienna, Austria: Springer-Verlag, 1992, pp. 265.

[19] D. Powell, G. Bonn, D. Seaton, P. Veríssimo, and F. Waeselynck, "The Delta-4 Approach to Dependability in Open Distributed Computing Systems", in *18th IEEE Int. Symp. on Fault-Tolerant Computing Systems (FTCS-18)*, Tokyo, Japan, June 1988, IEEE CS Press, pp. 246-51.

[20] D. Powell, A. Adelsbach, C. Cachin, S. Creese, M. Dacier, Y. Deswarte, T. McCutcheon, N. Neves, B. Pfitzmann, B. Randell, R. Stroud, P. Veríssimo, and M. Waidner, "MAFTIA (Malicious- and Accidental-Fault Tolerance for Internet Applications)", in *Supplement of the IEEE/IFIP Int. Conf. on Dependable Systems and Networks (DSN'2001)*, Göteborg, Sweden, 1-4 July 2001, pp. D32-D35.

[21] R. Stroud, I. Welch, J. Warne, and P. Ryan, "A Qualititative Analysis of the Intrusion-Tolerant Capabilities of the MAFTIA Architecture", in *Int. Conf. on Dependable Systems and Networks (DSN 2004)*, Florence, Italy, 28 June - 1 July 2004, IEEE CS Press.

[22] A. Valdes, M. Almgren, S. Cheung, Y. Deswarte, B. Dutertre, J. Levy, H. Saidi, V. Stavridou, and T. E. Uribe, "An Architecture for an Adaptive Intrusion-Tolerant Server", in *10th International Workshop on Security Protocols (2002), Lecture Notes in Computer Science*, 2845 ed, Cambridge, UK: Springer, 2004, pp. 158-78.

STATIC PROGRAM TRANSFORMATIONS FOR EFFICIENT SOFTWARE MODEL CHECKING

Shobha Vasudevan
Computer Engineering Research Center
The University of Texas at Austin
Austin, Texas, U.S.A.
shobha@cerc.utexas.edu

Jacob A. Abraham
Computer Engineering Research Center
The University of Texas at Austin
Austin, Texas, U.S.A.
jaa@cerc.utexas.edu

Abstract

Ensuring correctness of software by formal methods is a very relevant and widely studied problem. Automatic verification of software using model checking suffers from the state space explosion problem. *Abstraction* is emerging as the key candidate for making the model checking problem tractable, and a large body of research exists on *abstraction based verification*. Many useful abstractions are performed at the syntactic and semantic levels of programs and their representations.

In this paper, we explore abstraction based verification techniques that have been used at the program source code level. We provide a brief survey of these *program transformation* techniques. We also examine, in some detail, *Program Slicing*, an abstraction technique that holds great promise when dealing with complex software. We introduce the idea of using more specialized forms of slicing, *Conditioned Slicing* and *Amorphous Slicing*, as program transformation based abstractions for model checking. Experimental results using conditioned slicing for verifying safety properties written in temporal logic show the promise of these techniques.

Keywords: Formal verification, Model checking, Abstraction, Data abstractions, Abstract interpretation, Counterexample based refinement, Program slicing, Conditioned slicing, Amorphous slicing, Strong/Weak property preservation

1. Introduction

Designing a dependable complex system is a difficult problem and techniques for dealing with faults in a system have been studied widely by many researchers. A pioneer in this field is Dr. Algirdas Avizienis who developed the basic concepts, including the need for diversity in order to achieve fault tolerance [Avizienis and Kelly, 1984], [Avizenis and Laprie, 1986]. He also developed systematic approaches for designing fault-tolerant systems [Avizienis, 1997]. Reducing the number of design faults in the components is a necessary step in the design of a highly dependable system. This paper focuses on techniques to verify the correct operation of the software in the system.

As software begins to occupy a larger fraction of the overall system, faults in the software have a greater impact on system dependability, and ensuring dependability of the software portion of a system is becoming a leading concern. Toward this goal, software testing and debugging techniques as well as formal verification techniques are being explored as candidate solutions.

Among these, formal verification inspires the highest confidence due to the completeness of its approaches in ensuring correctness.

Model checking is an automatic technique used to formally verify programs [Clarke et al., 1986]. Temporal logic model checking typically requires a formal description of the model whose correctness needs to be established and a property specified in temporal logic. The main temporal logics used to specify properties are LTL [Manna and Pnueli, 1992], [Lichtenstein and Pnueli, 1985] CTL and CTL* [Clarke et al., 1986]. Complicated programs like hardware controllers and communication protocols have very large state spaces. In these cases, model checking techniques can suffer from state space explosion problems.

Since the number of states in the model grows exponentially with the number of variables and components of the system, model checking present day programs that have many hundreds of thousands of lines of code is computationally intractable.

In order to make model checking practically feasible, it is necessary to reduce the sizes of these models so that the computations have reasonable time and space requirements. It is also essential that the reduced models retain sufficient information to produce the same results as the original models, with respect to the properties being checked. These two requirements need to be balanced while creating these reduced models, i.e., while generating the *abstract* models from the original or *concrete* models. The process of constructing the abstract model from the concrete one is called *abstraction*. Abstractions are emerging as the key candidates for program verification using model checking.

Abstractions can be performed on the Kripke structure (state-transition model) of a program as well as on the program's source code. Abstraction techniques on Kripke structures are symmetry reduction [Emerson and Sistla, 1996], partial order reduction [Chou and Peled, 1996], cone of influence reduction [Kurshan, 1994], parameterization, compositionality etc. Since the state space of even small programs can be extremely large, it may not be possible to build the Kripke structure for any reasonably sized program. In contrast, abstractions formed by static program analysis will scale well with program size, and are of high economic interest. We focus on these abstraction techniques based on *program transformations* in the rest of the paper.

This paper consists of three main parts. In the first, we give an overview of the abstraction techniques employed in the prior art for software model checking. We provide an extensive literature survey and also give a classification of the types of abstractions and their applicability. We then give an overview of *Program Slicing*, a program analysis technique that has been used for various software applications [Weiser, 1979]. We give some prior applications that use Weiser's *static* program slicing for creating abstractions for verification. In the third part, we explore more sophisticated slicing techniques, *Amorphous Slicing* and *Conditioned Slicing*. Our contribution to the state-of-the-art is to introduce the use of conditioned slicing as a new abstraction for software model checking. We provide some promising preliminary results on sample programs using the SPIN model checker.

2. Abstractions in Model Checking

Abstractions have been used extensively to reduce the computational complexity of model checking. The abstractions are *property preserving* [Loiseaux et al., 1995].

This implies that given a program and a property to be verified, the In this paper, we will mostly deal with abstractions that are created from t satisfaction of the property in the abstract program implies the satisfaction of the property in the concrete program. Property preservation can be *weak* or *strong* . Weak property preservation can be defined using the branching time μ-calculus defined in [Kozen, 1998]. Weak property preservation preserves the truth of properties from the abstraction to its concrete model.

A function α from the powerset of states of a state transition system S_1 to the powerset of states of another system S_2 is said to weakly preserve a property f, if for any state of S_1 that satisfies f, the states in S_2 also satisfy f.

If the converse is also true, then α is said to strongly preserve f. As a result, both truth and falsehood of properties are preserved from the abstraction to its concrete model. Diagnostic counter-examples are "carried over" to the concrete model.

Strong property preservation puts a lower bound on the size of suitable abstractions. Abstractions that result in strong property preservations are typically difficult to construct.

There exist two closely related frameworks for developing abstractions and proving their correctness. Simulation, [Milner, 1971], [Park, 1981] is about structural relation between abstract and concrete transition systems, representing the step relation of programs by means of an abstraction relation between abstract and concrete sets of states. Each concrete transition must be simulatable by an abstract transition.

Abstract interpretation [Cousot and Cousot, 1977] is the relation between concrete and abstract states by an abstraction function α from concrete sets of states to the smallest element of some abstract property lattice, which represents all the elements of the concrete sets. With α is associated γ, a concretization function, which associates with each abstract element the set of all concrete states represented by it, such that (α, γ) makes a Galois connection.

A difference between these two frameworks is that in the abstract interpretation framework, the computation of the abstract property is given emphasis. The theory of abstract interpretation formalizes the notion of *approximations*. The computation of abstract systems in simulation, however, does not lay emphasis on the precision of abstractions. In fact, simulation was proposed only in the context of strong preservation of properties.

Abstraction techniques are methods that can be used to construct abstractions from the concrete models. The decision as to which details need to be included in the abstraction (for the verification task) can be made manually or automatically.

Manual techniques include user chosen abstract interpretations. The manual construction of safe abstractions trades automation for generality, in the sense that no restrictions are imposed on the class of large (infinite) state systems amenable to the method. The abstractions considered are usually weakly preserving, which means that properties are preserved only from the abstraction to its concrete model. As a result, only the truth of properties is guaranteed to be preserved. The weak requirement guarantees the existence (at least for universal properties) of finite-state and arbitrarily small weakly preserving abstractions for any concrete model. Users are free to use their 'intuition' for the behavior of the concrete system to come up with an abstraction that they find suitable. There is no *a priori* guarantee regarding the number or the type of properties that can be verified using the abstraction. The appropriateness of the abstractions must be investigated by trial and error. The obligation of proving the safety of the abstraction, in general cannot be automated. Instead, the proof is done manually or with support from theorem provers.

Automatic construction of abstraction systems is more ambitious. Finite-state strongly preserving abstractions (which are small enough for model checking) can only be automatically constructed for restricted kinds of large (infinite) state models. One such well-studied restricted domain is real-time systems, where continuous time gives rise to an infinite state space [Alur et al., 1993]. Only the systems whose behavior is guarded by certain linear constraint systems on the 'clock' variables are guaranteed to have finite-state strongly preserving abstractions that can be constructed automatically. Almost all existing model checkers for dense reactive systems (real time or hybrid) are based on automatically constructed strongly preserving abstractions. The idea is to let the abstract states be equivalence classes of concrete states, with respect to some behavioral equivalence or equivalence with respect to a property.

An abstraction technique is said to be *sound* if the abstract program is always guaranteed to be a conservative approximation of (*i.e.,* simulates) the original with respect to a set of specification properties. This means that a property holds in the original program if it holds in the abstraction. An algorithm is said to be *exact,* if the abstraction it constructs is bisimilar to the original program. This means that a property holds in the original program if it holds in the abstraction, and the converse is also true. An abstraction technique is *complete* if the algorithm will always find a finite state abstract program for the original program, if one exists. In terms of simulation, if the state-transition graph of the original program has a finite simulation quotient, then the algorithm can produce a finite simulation equivalent abstract program.

Abstractions can be organized broadly into data, control, configuration or communication abstractions. Data abstractions operate on data values and operations on the data. Control abstractions operate on the order of the operations within a process. Configuration and communication abstractions operate on the order of processes in a program as well on as the communication between programs.

Data Abstractions

Data abstractions abstract away some of the data information for creating smaller models. The abstract model can be derived from some high level description of the program like the program text. Data abstractions are typically manual abstractions. In [Clarke et al., 1994], the abstract transition systems are obtained by computing the abstractions of primitive operators as defined previously.

The programs are modeled as transition systems where states are n-tuples of variable values. The set of all program states is expressed as $D_1 \times D_2 \times \ldots D_n$. A surjective function h maps each D_i onto a set of abstract values. The surjection then maps program states to abstract states. The resulting abstraction (called minimal abstraction by the authors) is approximated by statically analyzing the text of the program. These abstractions show weak property preservation. The approximated abstract model may demonstrate more behaviors than the concrete model, but it is easier to build and verify. The abstractions proposed in this work include arithmetic operation abstractions (such as congruence modulo an integer), single bit abstractions for dealing with bitwise logical operations, product abstractions for combining the effect of abstractions, and symbolic abstractions.

For verifying programs involving arithmetic operations, congruence modulo a specific integer may be a useful abstraction. Thus, for any $h(i)$, i is replaced by $i \, mod \, m$. The values of an expression are, therefore, constrained to a smaller range, depending on m. When comparing the orders of magnitude of some quantities, the logarithmic representation is used instead of the actual data value. For programs that have bitwise logical operations, a large bit vector is abstracted to a single bit value, according to some function such as a parity generator. Symbolic abstractions can be used in situations where the enumeration of the data values is cumbersome. If the data value is changed to a symbolic parameter, there can be significant savings.

Kurshan [Kurshan, 1990] uses a similar framework for data abstractions for finite state system verification. The abstractions in this case, however, are not approximated by static analysis of the program text. Instead, they are computed as language homomorphisms in the algebra. The homomorphisms are specified by the user between the actual and the abstract processes, but are checked automatically.

In all the above abstractions, the infinite behavior of the system, resulting from the presence of variables with infinite domains, is abstracted. The abstractions are computed by means of abstract data types. For each variable to be abstracted, the abstract domain and the operations on the sets representable in the abstract domain are defined. An abstract model is then obtained by replacing each variable by one in the abstract domain and each operation by an abstract one. These are general predefined abstractions that are not aimed at specific properties.

Some variations to the above data abstraction techniques are found in [Bharadwaj and Heitmeyer, 1999]. Here, the focus is on properties of single states or transition state-pairs rather than execution sequences. The abstractions use *variable restriction* that eliminates certain variables. The data types of each eliminated variable are abstracted to a single value. This work also constructs abstractions with respect to a single property, as opposed to the generic abstractions constructed by other methods.

Data independent systems are those where the data values do not affect the control flow of the computation. In these cases, the datapath can be abstracted away entirely [P.Wolfer and V.Lovinfosse, 1990].

In hardware verification, important abstraction techniques use data abstractions [Moundanos et al., 1998] and uninterpreted function symbols [Bryant et al., 2001].

Abstract interpretation based abstractions

Many abstraction techniques can be viewed as applications of the abstract interpretation framework [Sifakis, 1983], [Cousot and Cousot, 1999], [Cousot, 2003].

The abstract interpretation framework establishes a methodology based on rigorous semantics for constructing abstractions that overapproximate the behavior of the program, so that every behavior in the program is covered by a corresponding abstract execution. Thus, the abstract behaviors can be exhaustively checked for an invariant in temporal logic. In abstract interpretation, abstractions are usually defined *a priori* for a particular type of analysis. The abstract version of the language semantics is constructed once with manual assistance. Producing a new abstract semantics for on-the-fly verification is a non-trivial task. Some tools such as Cospan [Kurshan, 1994], [Kurshan, 1990] and Bandera [Corbett et al., 2000], [Dwyer et al., 2001] try to do this task automatically.

Although data abstractions can be included in the realm of abstract interpretations, they form only a part of the possible abstract interpretations. Also, they may not hold over all of the system's execution semantics. Informally, abstract interpretation has a domain of abstract values, an abstraction function mapping concrete program values to abstract values and a set of abstract operations.

Some common abstract interpretations are briefly described for providing a flavor of the technique. *Sign abstraction* consists of replacing integers by their sign and ignoring their actual value. Such abstractions may be useful if there is a proposition like $x = 0$ for some integer x. Since all the information about x is not required, the sign abstraction may be applied, which keeps track of whether x is greater than (`gt`), less than (`lt`) or equal to zero (`eq`). The powerset of the abstract domain is now {`gt, lt, 0`}. Now, all the primitive operations are defined over this abstract domain, such that they satisfy every program execution.

Another common abstraction is *interval abstraction*, that approximates a set of integers by its maximal and minimal values. Thus, if a counter variable appears in a property, the counter can be replaced by the lower and upper limits of the counter.

Relational abstractions retain the relationship between a set of data values. For instance, a set of integers can be approximated by its convex hull. Abstract interpretations of functions is done by maintaining the parameter and the result (signature) of the function in the abstract domain. Fixpoint iteration can also be thought of as an abstraction. A detailed treatment of these abstract interpretations can be found in [Cousot, 2001]. Abstract interpretation for μ-calculus is shown in [Dams, 1996], [Dams et al., 1997].

Since abstract interpretations are not specific to any given property or for any given program, they have the power of generality. The technique considers predefined specifications for all possible programs of a given language. However, this results in the practical problem of computing these abstract interpretations during static analysis, before the verification task begins. The theory of abstract interpretation is mainly concerned with soundness, and not completeness.

Counterexample Guided Refinement

A highly researched field is abstraction refinement techniques for model checking [Lee et al., 1996], [Pardo, 1997], [Pardo and Hachtel, 1998]. These techniques are typically automatic abstraction techniques. Counterexample guided abstraction refinement techniques have been widely studied. An approximation of the set of states that lie on a path from the initial state to a bad state is successively refined. The refinement is done by forward or backward passes, where each pass uses (or refines) the approximation computed by the previous pass. This process is repeated until a fixpoint is reached. If the resulting set of states is empty, the property is proven, since no bad state is reachable. Otherwise, the method does not guarantee that the counterexample trace found is genuine. In other words, the counterexample could be spurious due to the overapproximations. A heuristic is used to find a subset of the reachable states from the initial states. If there is a match, the error is genuine and can be reported as a bug.

Cho *et al.* [H.Cho et al., 1996] propose symbolic forward reachability algorithms that induce an overapproximation. The state bits are partitioned into mutually disjoint subsets and do a symbolic forward propagation on individual subsets. Some approaches also use symbolic backward reachability analysis [Cabodi et al., 1994]. Govindaraju and Dill [Govindaraju and Dill, 2000], [Govindaraju and Dill, 1998] allow for overlapping subsets as opposed to the mutually disjoint ones, and present a more refined approximation as compared to earlier schemes.

A model checker that uses upper and lower approximations to verify properties in temporal logic was proposed in [Lind-Nielsen and Andersen, 1999]. These approximation techniques guarantee completeness without rechecking the model after each refinement. A similar approach has been described in [Balarin and Sangiovanni-Vincentelli, 1993], and in Kurshan's localization reduction [Kurshan, 1994]. These are iterative techniques that are based on the *variable dependency graph*. The localization reduction either leaves a variable unchanged, or replaces it by a non-deterministic assignment.

Predicate Abstraction. This technique was first introduced by Graf and Saidi [Graf and Saidi, 1997]. The predicates are related to the property that is being verified and are automatically extracted from the program text. Das and Dill [Das et al., 1999] use this technique with some variation to formally verify complex systems. While Graf and Saidi used monomials to represent the abstract state space, this work uses Binary Decision Diagrams (BDDs) as the representation. Clarke et al describe a related technique in [Clarke et al., 2000]. This work is based on *atomic formulas* that correspond to the predicates, but are used to construct an abstraction function. The abstraction function maintains a relationship between the formulas instead of treating them as individual propositions. The authors also introduce symbolic algorithms to determine if the abstract counterexamples are spurious. If a counterexample is spurious, the shortest prefix of the abstract counterexample that does not correspond to an actual trace in the concrete model is identified. The last abstract state in this prefix (the failure state) needs to be split into fewer abstract states by refining the equivalence classes in such a way that the spurious counterexample is eliminated. The extension of these forward algorithms for analyzing counterexamples to backward algorithms that do the same, are found in [Bensalem et al., 2003]. This can lead to completely different abstractions. This technique can also handle loop unfolding.

A related approach that performs predicate abstractions by syntactic program transformations automatically is presented in [Namjoshi and Kurshan, 2000]. The algorithm starts from the predicates in the specification formula. Predicates of the original boolean program are represented by Boolean variables in the abstraction. To preserve the correspondence between the predicate and the Boolean variables, the weakest precondition is calculated syntactically, and the Boolean variables are updated iteratively. This method of constructing abstractions is sound and complete. For programs with bounded non-determinacy, the algorithm does not need manual intervention using theorem provers to compute the abstract program, as other predicate abstraction based methods do.

Lazy Abstraction. A more efficient method to compute abstractions in this paradigm is *Lazy Abstraction*, presented in [Henzinger et al., 2002],[Henzinger et al., 2003]. Intuitively, lazy abstraction proceeds as follows. The abstract state in which the abstract counterexample fails to have a concrete counterpart is called the pivot state. The pivot state suggests which predicates should be used to refine the abstract model. However, instead of building an entire new abstract model, the refinement of the abstract model is done "from the pivot state on".

Abstraction is done on-the-fly, and only up to the precision necessary to rule out spurious counterexamples. On-the-fly construction of an abstract transition system eliminates an often wasteful and expensive model construction phase. Model checking only the "current" portion of the abstract transition system saves the cost of unnecessary exploration in parts of the state space that are already known to be free of errors. The lazy abstraction algorithm terminates under a customary condition on the predicate theory (no infinite ascending chains of predicates) and an abstract condition on the program (finite trace equivalence), which has been established for many interesting classes of infinite-state systems.

Lazy abstraction is sound, since the counterexample refinement phase rules out false positives. In case an error is found, the model checker also provides a counterexample trace in the program showing how the property is violated. Automatic abstraction allows running the analysis directly on an implementation, rather than constructing an abstract model that may or may not be a correct abstraction of the system. The authors show that by always maintaining the minimal necessary information to validate or invalidate the property, lazy abstraction scales to large systems.

Earlier applications of the predicate abstraction type of the abstract interpretation approach [S. Graf and H. Saidi, 1997], [Bensalem et al., 1998], [Colon and Uribe, 1998] were dependent on the user identifying the set of predicates that influence the verification property and used general-purpose theorem proving to compute the abstract program. The user-driven discovery of relevant predicates makes them less effective for large programs. Recently, various decision procedures have been proposed to compute the set of predicates for the abstraction. The most common approach is to use error traces to guide the discovery of predicates. In [Clarke et al., 2000], the algorithm is based on BDD representations of the program. This is a draw back for large programs, where transition relation BDDs are commonly too large for efficient manipulation.

In [Ball and Rajamani, 2001], the SLAM toolkit is introduced, that generates an abstract *Boolean program* from a C program and a set of predicates. The SLAM tools can be used to find loop invariants expressible as Boolean functions over a given set of predicates. The loop invariant is computed by the model checker Bebop [Ball and Rajamani, 2000] using a fixpoint computation on the abstraction. Boolean programs are programs with the usual control flow constructs of an imperative language such as C, but in which all variables are of Boolean type. Boolean programs contain procedures with call-by-value parameter passing and recursion, and a restricted form of control nondeterminism. Since the amount of storage a Boolean program can access at any point is finite, questions of reachability and termination are decidable in the realm of

Boolean programs. The generation of the Boolean program is done by calling a theorem prover for each potential assignment to the current and next state predicates. The number of theorem prover calls could be very high. Several heuristics are used to reduce this number. Existing tools stop the computation after a user-specified number of calls, and add all remaining transitions for which the theorem prover call was skipped. This is a safe over-approximation, but will yield a potentially large number of unnecessary spurious counterexamples.

Other abstraction techniques

Some abstraction techniques that are highly automatic, but very specific to the program and the property being verified, are *variable hiding* [Dams et al.,] and program slicing [Weiser, 1984].

Variable Hiding. Variable hiding is a powerful program transformation technique that was used in [Dams et al.,], [Holzmann and Smith, 2000] for verifying C programs. This is an iterative refinement technique that creates overapproximations. In the first iteration, all assignments and function calls that are irrelevant to the property being verified are replaced with a no-op. All conditional choices that refer to irrelevant statements in the program are replaced by *nondeterministic choices*. The use of nondeterminism is a standard reduction technique that can be used to make a model more general. The nondeterminism tells the model checker that instead one specific computation, all possible outcomes of a choice should be considered equally possible. The original computation of the system is preserved as one of the possible abstracted computations, and the scope of the verification is therefore not restricted. If no property violation exists in the reduced system, we can safely conclude that no property violation can exist in the original application.

The resulting abstraction has weak property preservation. It is possible, for instance, that the full expansion of an error trace for a property violation detected in the abstraction does not correspond to a valid execution of the original application. If this happens, it constitutes a proof that the abstraction was too coarse. In that case, the counterexample generated provides clues for including some more statements to make the abstraction less coarse. Typically a few iterations of this type suffice to converge on a stable definition of an abstraction that can be used to extract a verifiable model from a program text.

An example of variable hiding is illustrated. A piece of code and the program transformations that are generated by variable hiding are given below.

```
h = A[i];
r = r + (++A[i]);
res = r + h;
```

```
if (r > MAX)
        {
        m++;
        r = 0;
        }
```

If the property involves m or h, we obtain the following abstraction after variable hiding. The non-determinism is introduced in the conditional statement, where the variables r or MAX are not present in the property.

```
h = A[i];
if (NONDET)
        {
        m++;
        }
```

An important abstraction paradigm is *program slicing* [Weiser, 1984],[Weiser, 1979]. We explore this technique in some detail in the next section, in the context of program verification.

3. Static Program Slicing

Slicing, in a general sense, is a program transformation which preserves some projection of the semantics of the original program. A particular approach to slicing is defined by describing the aspect of the program to be preserved and the nature of the transformations to be performed upon the program to construct the slice. The aspect of the program that must be preserved is captured by the slicing criterion. The published work on slicing is concerned with a very simple transformation: statement deletion. Therefore, slicing is the process of deleting commands from a program, while preserving some aspects of the behavior as captured by the slicing criterion. The original definition of a program slice was presented by Weiser [Weiser, 1979]. Only statically available information is used for computing slices; hence this type of slice is referred to as a *static slice.* Since then, various slightly different notions of slicing have been proposed, as well as a number of methods to compute them. Program slicing has been used in several tasks including testing, debugging, maintainence, complexity analysis, comprehension, reverse engineering, reengineering and reuse. Recently, slicing has also been used as an abstraction for verification. We present here, some results on slicing for verification.

DEFINITION 1 *Static slicing criterion*
A slicing criterion of a program P with an input alphabet Σ, is a pair $\langle i, V\rangle$ such that i is a statement in P and $V \subseteq \Sigma$. A set of statements I_s is said to *affect* the values of V at i in a given slicing criterion $\langle i, V\rangle$, if I_s defines a subset of V that is used in i.

DEFINITION 2 *Static slice for programs*
A slice S of a program P on a slicing criterion $\langle i, V \rangle$ is a subset of the statements of P that might affect the values of V at i.

An alternative method for computing static slices was suggested by Ottenstein and Ottenstein, [Ottenstein and Ottenstein, 1984] who restate the problem of static slicing in terms of a reachability problem in a program dependence graph (PDG). A PDG is a directed graph with vertices corresponding to statements and control predicates, and edges corresponding to data and control dependences. The slicing criterion is identified with a vertex in the PDG, and a slice corresponds to all the PDG vertices from which the vertex under consideration can be reached.

Static Program Slicing for Verification

Static slicing has been used as a program transformation for software model checking. [Hatcliff et al., 2000], [Millett and Teitelbaum, 1998]. Slicing allows for strong preservation of properties. The primary advantage of slicing in verification is that the construction of the abstraction (slice) is completely automatic. State-of-the-art verification tools incorporate program slicing as a feature [Corbett et al., 2000]. Slicing is a very simple program transformation that only effects the syntax of the original program. Therefore, slicing can be used in conjunction with all the partial evaluation based abstraction techniques. The software can be preprocessed using slicing before applying the abstraction techniques. Slicing provides a safe approximation of the relevant portions of code and enables the scaling of abstraction based techniques and tools to more complicated systems. All other abstraction techniques, can thus be seen as complements to slicing. The property being verified is written in temporal logic, and the propositions within the temporal logic property form the variables in the slicing criterion.

Slicing is different from other abstraction techniques that sacrifice completeness for tractability and generality. While other techniques preserve correctness with respect to a generic class of properties, slicing preserves correctness with respect to a specific property. The abstractions created by slicing are sound and complete with respect to the property being checked.

Static slicing can be likened to the cone-of-influence reductions done by model checkers, since both these transformations have the same semantics. However, slicing is done at the source code level, as opposed to the cone-of-influence reduction. Slicing, therefore, is a pre-encoding mechanism, that does not build the state transition graphs. Hence, despite being the same type of abstraction as the cone-of-influence reductions, it still shows a benefit in performance.

In [Hatcliff et al., 2000], an interesting application of program slicing to verification has been illustrated. Slicing is used to assist the creation of relevant abstract interpretations for abstraction based verification. Selecting appropriate abstract interpretations can be a non-trivial task for the user. The methodology of finding the variables in a program that can influence the program's execution, (relative to a property's propositions) is essentially based on heuristics. When a variable is determined to be potentially influential, its abstraction is refined to strengthen the resulting system model. If the variable is not found to be potentially influential, it is modeled with a point abstraction that ignores any effect it may have, until there is a case where the variable needs to be refined. The authors show that the information produced by pre-processing the program with slicing is exactly what they need to provide automated support for selecting appropriate abstract interpretations. Specifically, slicing identifies relevant variables, eliminates irrelevant program variables from consideration in the abstraction selection process, and reduces the size of the software (and thereby the size of the transition system) analyzed.

4. Specialized Slicing Techniques

We introduce the idea of using some specialized types of program slicing for verification. These slicing techniques have been used for a number of applications. However, to the best of our knowledge, this is the first application of these techniques for verification. Traditional static slicing produces very large slices [Korel and Laski, 1990]. Since these specialized slicing techniques are used to create smaller slices, we can also extend their use to verification, by exploiting the reduction in verification state space. Also, the sophisticated slicing techniques we employ for verification are not semantically equivalent to cone-of-influence reductions. We present some of our ideas on slicing based verification, and preliminary experimental results on some sample programs.

Amorphous Slicing

A variation of traditional program slicing called *amorphous slicing* [Harman et al., 2003], can produce smaller slices by abandoning the traditional requirement of syntax-preservation. Traditional, syntax-preserving program slicing simplifies a program by removing program components (i.e., statements and predicates) that do no affect a computation of interest. The resulting slice captures a projection of the semantics of the original program. In addition, traditional slicing requires that a subset of the original program's syntax be maintained. This syntactic requirement is important when slicing is applied to cohesion measurement, algorithmic debugging and program integration. However, for applications such as re-engineering, program comprehension and testing, it is primarily the semantic property of a slice that is of interest.

DEFINITION 3 *Amorphous Slicing for programs*

An amorphous slice for a program P with respect to a slicing criterion (i, V) is a program q, such that starting from the same initial state, the same state is reached with respect to the variables in V at point i in both P and q.

An example of amorphous slicing, as explained in [Harman et al., 2003] is given below.

```
for(i=0,sum=a[0],biggest=sum;i<19;sum=a[++i])
   if (a[i+1] > biggest)
   {
      biggest = a[i+1];
      average = sum/20;
   }
```

The fragment was written with the intention that the variable `biggest` would be assigned the largest value in the 20-element array `a`, and that the variable `average` would be assigned the average of the elements of `a`. However, the fragment contains a bug which affects the variables `sum` and `average`, but not the variable `biggest`. To illustrate amorphous slicing, the variables `biggest` and `average` will be analyzed using both traditional syntax-preserving slicing and amorphous slicing. The static slice is given below.

```
for(i=0,sum=a[0],biggest=sum;i<19;sum=a[++i])
   if (a[i+1] > biggest)
   {
      biggest = a[i+1];
   }
```

However, the amorphous slice, constructed using transformations such as a loop unrolling (which has changed the loop bounds) is the following.

```
for(i=1, biggest=a[0]; i<20; ++i)
   if (a[i] > biggest)
   {
      biggest = a[i];
   }
```

The amorphous slice for the variable `average` is given below.

```
average=a[19]/20;
```

It can be seen that there is a bug in the program, from the amorphous slice.

Amorphous Slicing for Verification. We propose the idea of using amorphous slicing for verification. Since abstraction based verification does not require syntactic preservation of the program behavior, this slicing technique can be exploited to form meaningful abstractions in this context. A program can be sliced with respect to a slicing criterion (i, V), where V is a part of a property written in temporal logic. The resulting amorphous slice is an abstraction, that can now be model checked.

We give an example of how amorphous slicing could be used for verification. Consider the following piece of code

```
begin
   i = start;
   while (i <= (start + num))
   {
      result = K + f(i);
      sum = sum + result;
      i = i + 1;
   }
end
```

Consider the LTL property $G(sum > K)$. This property checks if the value of `f(i)` is greater than 0. The slicing criterion derived from the property is $(end, \{sum, K\})$. The program transformations that can be applied on the code for amorphous slicing correspond to a couple of rules presented in [Harman et al., 2003]. The induction variable elimination rule is applied as a transformation. It replaces qualifying loops with two assignments that capture the requirements on array safety. The second assignment is the value of `i` in the final iteration of the loop. In cases where the loop variables are very large numbers, such a transformation would yield useful savings. The dependent assignment removal rule is applied for eliminating redundant assignment statements. The resulting amorphous slice is shown below

```
begin
   sum = sum + K + f(start);
   sum = sum + K + f(start + num);
end
```

We notice that the amorphous slice is a reduced program. When executed, the amorphous slice takes a fraction of the time taken to verify the original code on the SPIN model checker.

Amorphous slicing can be viewed as a type of term rewriting, that has been used by theorem provers for deductive verification. The difference is, however, in the fact that theorem provers and rewriters try to prove a property, entirely by rewriting. In the method that we propose, the rewriting is done only on a part of the program, that is decided by the slicing criterion. After the program has been reduced to a certain desired state, model checking can be used. The advantage in this methodology is that the manual component of rewriting, as well as the task of proving the transformations correct, is now vastly reduced. We expect this approach to yield beneficial results.

Amorphous slicing does not guarantee that the resulting slice has the same signature (variables and functions) as the original program. Since amorphous slicing can allow any transformation to the program, and does not require any faithfulness to the original program, proving the correctness of the transformations is very important.

In order to prove these transformations correct, two approaches can be taken. The set of transformations or rules can be collected to form a rule base. The transformations in this rule base will then be proved correct separately. This rule base will be incomplete, but will have a high efficiency, due to fewer program states. Another procedure could be to prove the program transformations correct in an abstract interpretation framework, for a given concrete operational semantics of the language. Transformations can be control-based as well as data-based in amorphous slicing. Whenever slicing results in the elimination of the nodes in the control flow graph, it is possible to visualize this slicing as a form of rewriting. Whenever the slicing includes data transformations, the technique is better expressed in the abstract interpretation framework. An example of the rewriting rule base has been given in [Harman et al., 2003].

Conditioned Slicing

Canfora et al [Canfora et al., 1998] introduced the notion of *conditioned slicing*, that forms a theoretical bridge between static and dynamic slicing [Korel and Laski, 1988]. Conditioned slices are constructed with respect to a set of possible input states, characterized by a first order predicate logic formula. Conditioned slicing augments static slicing by introducing a condition that specifies the initial set of states in the criterion. This slicing technique, therefore allows slicing with respect to the initial states of interest, or initial constraints in the program. We present some basic definitions of conditioned slicing that appear in the literature.

DEFINITION 4 *Conditioned Slicing criterion*
Let Σ be the set of input variables to the program P. Let C be a first order predicate logical formula on the variables in Σ. A conditioned slicing criterion is a triple $\langle C, i, V \rangle$, where i is a statement in the program, and $V \subseteq \Sigma$.

DEFINITION 5 *Conditioned Slicing for programs*
A conditioned slice of a program P on a conditioned slicing criterion $\langle C, i, V \rangle$ consists of all the statements and predicates of P that might affect the values of the variables in V at i, when the condition C holds true.

Tip [Tip, 1995] introduced a more restricted form of conditioned slicing called constraint based slicing. In all these cases, the *condition* that specifies the set of initial states, and is used for slicing is a first order predicate logic formula. We will refer to this condition as the *conditional predicate*, or simply *predicate*. We will use the term *conditioning* to mean the process of obtaining a conditioned slice with respect to a given conditional predicate C.

Conditioned slicing is a significant improvement over static, dynamic or quasi-static [Venkatesh, 1991] slicing, since it subsumes all of these as special cases [Canfora et al., 1998].

The static slicing criterion is captured by conditioned slicing, when the conditional predicate is always *true*. The slicing criterion then captures program behavior, regardless of initial state.

In situations where the initial set of constraints for the program analysis are known, this technique can be employed to get much smaller slices than those produced by static slicing. This technique can therefore be used to simplify the code, before applying a traditional static slicing algorithm. Conditioned slicing has been automated with significant success on C and WSL code [Daoudi et al., 2002], [Danicic et al., 2000].

Conditioned Slicing for Verification. Our technique aims at reducing state space of the program, by slicing away the part of the program irrelevant to the property being verified. We focus on safety properties that can be specified as temporal logic formulae of the form, $antecedent \implies consequent$. For these properties, we can use the antecedent to specify the set of initial states that we are interested in. *The antecedent therefore, forms the condition in the slicing criterion.* All the statements that would get executed when the antecedent is true (or the condition is satisfied) are retained in the slice. The statements on the paths that cannot get executed when the antecedent is false, are removed. The reduced program still preserves its behavior *with respect to the property being checked.* We therefore create property preserving abstractions using conditioned slicing.

All prior art in verification using program slicing uses static program slicing techniques. While slicing property specifications of the form $antecedent \implies consequent$, these techniques retain the set of all statements of the program where the antecedent is true, *as well as those where it is not.* This is because static slicing retains all possible executions of the relevant variables.

However, in property based verification, *we do not need to check the states where the antecedent is false.* In these cases, 'static slices might be too large and include statements that are not of interest. We introduce a precise abstraction on the basis of conditioned slicing, *Antecedent Conditioned Slices*. We present an example to show how conditioned slicing can be performed for a given property. Let the property that needs to be verified be $G((N < 0) \Rightarrow (B = f(A)))$. The slicing criterion for all slicing techniques will be extracted from this property. The static slice for the code in Figure 1 for the slicing criterion

```
        begin
1:              read(N);
2:              A = 1;
3:              if (N < 0)
                    {
4:                  B = f(A);
5:                  C = g(A);
                    }
                else
6:                      if (N > 0)
                            {
7:                          B = f'(A);
8:                          C = g'(A);
                            }
                        else
                            {
9:                          B = f''(A);
10:                         C = g''(A);
                            }
11:             print(B);
12:             print(C);
        end
```

Figure 1. Example Program written in psuedocode

$\langle 11, B \rangle$ would be as shown in Figure 2. The conditioned slice for the same code, with respect to the slicing criterion $\langle C, 11, B \rangle$, where C corresponds to the predicate $(N < 0)$ would be as shown in Figure 3. This shows that the conditioned slice is much smaller in size than the static slice.

Preliminary Results. We provide experimental results of conditioned slicing using the SPIN model checker on the Group Address Registration Protocol and the X.509 Authentication Protocol. The Group Address Registration Protocol (GARP) is a datalink-level protocol for dynamically joining and leaving multicast groups on a bridged LAN. The X.509 is a CITT recommendation for an authentication protocol. It gives details of a method of allowing a user agent to send a password to a system agent in a safe manner that is not vulnerable to interception or replay. The source code and the properties can be found in [Lafuente, 2002].

All experiments were performed using a 450 MHz Pentium dual processor with 512 MB RAM. A memory limit of 512 MB was given for running these properties, with a max search depth of 2^{20} steps. The time taken to

```
        begin
1:                  read(N);
2:                  A = 1;

3:                  if (N < 0)
                        {
4:                      B = f(A);

                        }
                    else
6:                          if (N > 0)
                                {
7:                              B = f'(A);

                                }
                            else
                                {
9:                              B = f''(A);

                                }
11:                 print(B);

        end
```

Figure 2. Static Slice of program

```
        begin
1:                  read(N);
2:                  A = 1;
3:                  if (N < 0)
                        {
4:                      B = f(A);
                        }
        end
```

Figure 3. Conditioned Slice of program

check the properties, in seconds, is given in Table 1. The conditioned slicing of the source code was based on the properties that were written in the form $antecedent \Longrightarrow consequent$.

Property P1 is from the assertions present in the source code of the GARP. Property P4 is from the assertions that find the protocol errors in the X.509

Table 1. Performance of conditioned slicing over regular model checking

Property	Unsliced	Conditioned Sliced	Property Proved
P1	91.65	1.72	Yes
P2	145.78	8.44	Yes
P3	145.36	8.41	Yes
P4	154.96	1.95	Yes
P5	117.81	10.23	Yes

source code. In these cases, the conditionals in the code presented the antecedent, while the consequents were the assertions themselves. Properties P2, P3 and P5 were written as LTL properties.

P2 corresponds to the LTL property $G((p \wedge (\neg(m))) \implies (\neg(q) \wedge \neg(r)))$, and P3 corresponds to the LTL property $G((p \wedge (\neg(m))) \implies (\neg(r)))$ where

```
p = empty(llc_to_regist[i])
m = (leavetimer != true)
q = (r_state != lv_imm)
r = (r_state != out_reg)
```

P5 corresponds to the LTL property$G((p) \implies (q))$ where

```
p = (macuser1[pid]@user1_end)
q = (r_state != out_reg)
```

Thus, conditioned slicing yields very promising results, as is evident from the table.

5. Conclusion

Abstraction techniques are necessary for the analysis of complex systems with very large state spaces. The table below gives a comparison of all the abstraction techniques we have mentioned in this paper. The comparison criteria are the degree of automation, the generic nature and applicability of the technique, the amount of dependence of the technique on individual properties for verification and finally the type of abstraction that we obtain by the technique.

The various program transformation techniques that we have discussed in this paper are steps toward building dependable computing systems. State-of-the-art tools must incorporate many of these techniques to deal with design faults in software. Effective analysis of programs entails that the techniques be applied compositionally. "A verification methodology is judged on the basis of how well it conciliates *correctness, automation, precision, scaling up and performance efficiency*" [Cousot, 2003]. "Software reliability is the grand

Table 2. Comparison of program transformation techniques

Technique	Automation	Generality	Property Dependence	Type of Abstraction
Data Abstractions	Low	High	Low	Overapproximation
Abstract Interpretation	Low	High	Low	Overapproximation
Counterexample guided refinement	Medium	Medium	High	Overapproximation
Predicate Abstraction	Medium	Medium	High	Overapproximation
LazyAbstraction	Medium	Medium	High	Overapproximation
Variable Hiding	Medium	Low	High	Overapproximation
Amorphous Slicing	Low	High	High	Depends on type of rewrite
Static Slicing	High	Low	High	Exact
Conditioned Slicing	Medium	Low	High	Exact

challenge of the next decade" [Cousot, 2001]. It is thus the great challenge of the computer science community to analyze these factors for all abstraction based verification techniques and integrate these techniques optimally into a framework, such that the correctness and robustness of the system is ensured for all programming paradigms.

References

Alur, Rajeev, Henzinger, Thomas A., and Ho, Pei-Hsin (1993). Automatic symbolic verification of embedded systems. In *IEEE Real-Time Systems Symposium*, pages 2–11.

Avizenis, A. and Laprie, J. (1986). Dependable computing: From concepts to design diversity. *Proceedings of the IEEE*, 74:629–638.

Avizienis, A. (1997). Toward systematic design of fault-tolerant systems. *Computer*, 30(4):51–58.

Avizienis, A. and Kelly, J. P. J. (1984). Fault tolerance by design diversity: Concepts and experiments. pages 67–80.

Balarin, F. and Sangiovanni-Vincentelli, A. L. (1993). An iterative approach to language containment. In *Proceedings of the 5th International Conference on Computer Aided Verification*, pages 29–40.

Ball, Thomas and Rajamani, Sriram K. (2000). Bebop: A symbolic model checker for boolean programs. In *SPIN*, pages 113–130.

Ball, Thomas and Rajamani, Sriram K. (2001). Automatically validating temporal safety properties of interfaces. *Lecture Notes in Computer Science*, 2057:103–122.

Bensalem, Saddek, Graf, Susanne, and Lakhnech, Yassine (2003). Abstraction as the key for invariant verification. In *Symposium on Verification celebrating Zohar Manna's 64th Birthday*.

Bensalem, Saddek, Lakhnech, Yassine, and Owre, Sam (1998). Computing abstractions of infinite state systems compositionally and automatically. In *Computer-Aided Verification, CAV '98*, volume 1427, pages 319–331.

Bharadwaj, R. and Heitmeyer, C. L. (1999). Model checking complete requirements specifications using abstraction. *Automated Software Engineering: An International Journal*, 6(1):37–68.

Bryant, R. E., German, S., and Velev, M. N. (2001). Processor verification using efficient reductions of the logic of uninterpreted functions to propositional logic. *ACM Trans. Comput. Logic*, 2(1):93–134.

Cabodi, G., Camurati, P., and Quer, S. (1994). Symbolic exploration of large circuits with enhanced forward/backward traversals. In *Proceedings of the conference on European design automation*, pages 22–27.

Canfora, G., Cimitile, A., and Lucia, A. De (1998). Conditioned program slicing. *Information and Software Technology Special Issue on Program Slicing*, 40:595–607.

Chou, C. and Peled, D. (1996). Formal verification of a partial-order reduction technique for model checking. In *Tools and Algorithms for Construction and Analysis of Systems*, pages 241–257.

Clarke, E. M., Emerson, E. A., and Sistla, A. P. (1986). Automatic verification of finite state concurrent system using temporal logic specifications: a practical approach. *ACM Trans. Program. Lang. Syst.*, 8(2):244–263.

Clarke, E. M., Grumberg, O., Jha, S., Lu, Y., and Veith, H. (2000). Counterexample-guided abstraction refinement. In *Computer Aided Verification*, pages 154–169.

Clarke, Edmund M., Grumberg, Orna, and Long, David E. (1994). Model checking and abstraction. *ACM Transactions on Programming Languages and Systems*, 16(5):1512–1542.

Colon, Michael and Uribe, Tomas E. (1998). Generating finite-state abstractions of reactive systems using decision procedures. In *Computer Aided Verification*, pages 293–304.

Corbett, James C., Dwyer, Matthew B., Hatcliff, John, Laubach, Shawn, Păsăreanu, Corina S., Robby, and Zheng, Hongjun (2000). Bandera: extracting finite-state models from java source code. In *International Conference on Software Engineering*, pages 439–448.

Cousot, P. (2001). Abstract interpretation based formal methods and future challenges, invited paper. In *Informatics — 10 Years Back, 10 Years Ahead*, volume 2000 of *Lecture Notes in Computer Science*, pages 138–156.

Cousot, P. (2003). Automatic verification by abstract interpretation, invited tutorial. In *Proceedings of the Fourth International Conference on Verification, Model Checking and Abstract Interpretation (VMCAI 2003)*, pages 20–24.

Cousot, P. and Cousot, R. (1977). Abstract interpretation: a unified lattice model for static analysis of programs by construction or approximation of fixpoints. In *Proceedings of the 4th ACM SIGACT-SIGPLAN symposium on Principles of programming languages*, pages 238–252.

Cousot, P. and Cousot, R. (1999). Refining model checking by abstract interpretation. *Automated Software Engineering*, 6(1):69–95.

Dams, D. (1996). *Abstract Interpretation and Partition Refinement for Model Checking*. PhD thesis, Eindhoven University of Technology.

Dams, D., Gerth, R., and Grumberg, O. (1997). Abstract interpretation of reactive systems. *ACM Trans. Program. Lang. Syst.*, 19(2):253–291.

Dams, D., Hesse, W., and Holzmann, G. J. Abstracting C with abC. pages 515–520.

Danicic, S., Fox, C., Harman, M., and Hierons, R. (2000). Consit: A conditioned program slicer. pages 216–226.

Daoudi, M., Ouarbya, L., Howroyd, J., Danicic, S., Marman, Mark, Fox, Chris, and Ward, M. P. (2002). Consus: A scalable approach to conditional slicing. In *IEEE Proceedings of the Working Conference on Reverse Engineering*, pages 181–189.

Das, S., Dill, D., and Park, S. (1999). Experience with predicate abstraction. In *Computer Aided Verification*, pages 160–171.

Dwyer, M. B., Hatcliff, J., Joehanes, R., Laubach, S., Pasareanu, C. S., Robby, Zheng, H., and Visser, W. (2001). Tool-supported program abstraction for finite-state verification. In *International Conference on Software Engineering*, pages 177–187.

Emerson, E. Allen and Sistla, A. Prasad (1996). Symmetry and model checking. *Formal Methods in System Design: An International Journal*, 9(1/2):105–131.

Govindaraju, S. G. and Dill, D. L. (1998). Verification by approximate forward and backward reachability. In *Proceedings of the 1998 IEEE/ACM international conference on Computer-aided design*, pages 366–370. ACM Press.

Govindaraju, Shankar G. and Dill, David L. (2000). Counterexample-guided choice of projections in approximate symbolic model checking. In *Proceedings of the 2000 IEEE/ACM international conference on Computer-aided design*, pages 115–119.

Graf, S. and Saidi, H. (1997). Construction of abstract state graphs with pvs. In *Proceedings of the 9th International Conference on Computer Aided Verification*, pages 72–83.

Harman, M., Binkley, D., and Danicic, S. (2003). Amorphous program slicing. *Journal of Systems and Software*, 68(1):45–64.

Hatcliff, J., Dwyer, M. B., and Zheng, H. (2000). Slicing software for model construction. *Higher-Order and Symbolic Computation*, 13(4):315–353.

H.Cho, G.Hachtel, E.Macii, B.Pleisser, and F.Somenzi (1996). Algorithms for approximate fsm traversal based on state space decomposition. *IEEE TCAD*, 15(12):1465–1478.

Henzinger, T. A., Jhala, R., Majumdar, R., and Sutre, G. (2002). Lazy abstraction. In *Symposium on Principles of Programming Languages*, pages 58–70.

Henzinger, T. A., Jhala, R., Majumdar, R., and Sutre, G. (2003). Software verification with blast. In *Proceedings of the Tenth International Workshop on Model Checking of Software (SPIN)*, pages 235–239. Lecture Notes in Computer Science 2648, Springer-Verlag.

Holzmann, G. J. and Smith, M. H. (2000). Automating software feature verification. *Bell Labs Technical Journal*, 5(2):72–87.

Korel, B. and Laski, J. (1988). Dynamic program slicing. *Inf. Process. Lett.*, 29(3):155–163.

Korel, B. and Laski, J. (1990). Dynamic slicing of computer programs. *Journal of Systems and Software*, 13(3):187–195.

Kozen, D. (1998). Results on the propositional mu-calculus. In *Theoretical Computer Science*, volume 27, pages 333–354.

Kurshan, R. P. (1990). Analysis of discrete event coordination. In *Proceedings on Stepwise refinement of distributed systems: models, formalisms, correctness*, pages 414–453.

Kurshan, R. P. (1994). *Computer-aided verification of coordinating processes: the automata-theoretic approach*. Princeton University Press.

Lafuente, Alberto Lluch (2002). Database of promela models. *http://www.informatik.uni-freiburg.de/~lafuente/models/models.html*.

Lee, W., Pardo, A., Jang, J., Hachtel, G., and Somenzi, F. (1996). Tearing based automatic abstraction for ctl model checking. In *Proceedings of the 1996 IEEE/ACM international conference on Computer-aided design*, pages 76–81.

Lichtenstein, O. and Pnueli, A. (1985). Checking that finite state concurrent programs satisfy their linear specification. In *Proceedings of the 12th ACM SIGACT-SIGPLAN symposium on Principles of programming languages*, pages 97–107.

Lind-Nielsen, J. and Andersen, H. (1999). Stepwise CTL model checking of state/event systems. In *CAV'99: Computer Aided Verification* .

Loiseaux, C., Graf, S., Sifakis, J., Bouajjani, A., and Bensalem, S. (1995). Property preserving abstractions for the verification of concurrent systems. *Formal Methods in System Design*, 6(1):11–44.

Manna, Z. and Pnueli, A. (1992). *The Temporal Logic of Reactive and Concurrent Systems: Specification*. Springer-Verlag.

Millett, L. and Teitelbaum, T. (1998). Slicing promela and its applications to model checking.

Milner, R. (1971). An algebraic definition of simulation between programs. In *Proceedings of the 2nd International Joint Conference on Artificial Intelligence.*, pages 481–489.

Moundanos, Dinos, Abraham, Jacob A., and Hoskote, Yatin V. (1998). Abstraction techniques for validation coverage analysis and test generation. *IEEE Trans. Comput.*, 47(1):2–14.

Namjoshi, K. S. and Kurshan, R. P. (2000). Syntactic program transformations for automatic abstraction. In *Computer Aided Verification*, pages 435–449.

Ottenstein, K. J. and Ottenstein, L.M. (1984). The program dependence graph in software development environments. *SIGPLAN Notices*, 19(5):177–184.

Pardo, A. and Hachtel, G. (1998). Incremental CTL model checking using BDD subsetting. In *Proceedings of the Design Automation Conference.*

Pardo, Abelardo (1997). *Automatic Abstraction Techniques for Formal Verification of Digital Systems*. PhD thesis, University of Colorado at Boulder.

Park, D. (1981). Concurrency and automata on infinite sequences. In *Proceedings of the 5th GI-Conference on Theoretical Computer Science*, pages 167–183. Springer-Verlag.

P.Wolfer and V.Lovinfosse (1990). Verifying properties of large sets of processes with network invariants. 407:68–80.

S. Graf and H. Saidi (1997). Construction of abstract state graphs with PVS. In *Proc. 9th INternational Conference on Computer Aided Verification (CAV'97)*, volume 1254, pages 72–83.

Sifakis, J. (1983). Property preserving homomorphisms of transition systems. *Lecture Notes in Computer Science*, 164:458–473.

Tip, F. (1995). *Generation of Program Analysis Tools*. PhD thesis.

Venkatesh, G. A. (1991). The semantic approach to program slicing. *ACM SIGPLAN Conf. on Programming Language Design and Implementation*, 26(6):107–119.

Weiser, M. (1979). *Program slices: formal, psychological, and practical investigations of an automatic program abstraction method*. PhD thesis.

Weiser, M. (1984). Program slicing. *IEEE Transactions on Software Engineering*, 10(4):352–357.

ARCHITECTURAL CHALLENGES FOR A DEPENDABLE INFORMATION SOCIETY

Luca Simoncini
University of Pisa and PDCC, Italy
luca.simoncini@iet.unipi.it

Felicita Di Giandomenico
ISTI-CNR and PDCC, Pisa, Italy
felicita.digiandomenico@isti.cnr.it

Andrea Bondavalli
University of Florence and PDCC, Italy
a.bondavalli@dsi.unifi.it

Silvano Chiaradonna
ISTI-CNR and PDCC, Pisa, Italy
silvano.chiaradonna@isti.cnr.it

Abstract This paper is two-fold. In the first part it tries to raise awareness on the level of complexity of future computer-based interconnected systems/infrastructures, at least as they are envisioned, and on the level of dependability we are today able to justify with confidence. It tries to motivate that fundamental methods and methodologies must be reconsidered, studied, exploited, assessed and applied to move towards an utopia that can be called "ambient dependability", a global view of the concept of dependability [Laprie, 1992], which encompasses not only the technological aspects but includes inter and multi disciplinary fields, which span over ergonomics, usability, education, sociology, law and government. The second part of the paper provides the authors views, based on their experience, on future directions and architectural challenges to be tackled for approaching, as a first step towards ambient dependability, at least an Information Society which we can depend on.

Introduction

Our society is heavily dependent on computerized interconnected systems and services for which the computer plays a central role in controlling communications, databases and infrastructures. In addition, the use of PCs, home appliances, PDAs, wireless phones and all sort of everyday life objects increases of order of magnitudes the number of networked users, who want to use such objects with low, if any, knowledge of the technicalities behind or embedded in them, and worse by blindly relying on the myth of "infallibility" associated to computers and services controlled by computers [Ducatel et al., 2001; ISTAG, 2002; AMSD, 2003].

In Europe, starting with the March 2000 Lisbon Summit [European Presidency, 2000], EU is stressing the strategic relevance of Europe being the most advanced part of the world based on ICT, by making many sensitive components of our society (finance, banking, insurance, health, commerce, business, government, etc.) dependent on computers, computer-controlled services, networks or infrastructures. The statement that European citizens will be able to rely and depend on "Ambient Intelligence" by using dependable computers or computerized systems is true only for a very limited part. Instead it must be clear that an ICT-based society will need a very large societal reorganization, which should be able to manage the global nature of the envisioned services and infrastructures, which are not limited by national borders or legislations.

Despite significant advances have been achieved in the topic of dependable computing systems over the past ten years or so much further research is required when considering the future landscape. In February 2001 the IST Advisory Group published a number of scenarios for Ambient Intelligence (AmI) in 2010 [Ducatel et al., 2001]. In AmI space, and in these scenarios in particular, dependability in general, and privacy and security in particular, emerge as central socio-technical challenges to be addressed. Devices are ubiquitous, and interact with pervasive networked infrastructures; information assets flow over open information and communications infrastructures, exposed to accidental and deliberate threats. The ISTAG scenarios envision new kinds of human relationships and interactions, and powerful technologies to support them. Important perspectives on the dependability of socio-technical systems arise from detailed ethnographic and human-computer interaction analyses of their actual use.

For sake of understanding, one of the ISTAG scenarios is described in the Appendix, with the discussion on dependability implications reported in the AMSD Roadmap [AMSD, 2003]. This description tries to highlight the threats to AmI scenarios, thus pointing out that research in dependability beyond the current state-of-the-art is essential.

The way towards the landscape envisioned by the ISTAG scenarios has to cope with the actual evolution towards more complex services and infrastructures. They are usually based on the layering of different systems (legacy systems), designed in different times, with different technologies and components and difficult to integrate, and a dependable ICT-based society will have to cope not only with accidental and non-malicious human-made faults, but also with malicious faults of different severity up to the possibility of terrorist attacks against infrastructures or through infrastructures. In addition to these faults, taking into account the commercial strategies of large industries - Microsoft has just announced and will soon commercialize very powerful communication gadgets, which will make ubiquitous computing a reality [Microsoft Research, 2003]-, a new type of subtle fault will become evident in the near future. They will be mainly generated by the combination of: 1) a very large number of computer-controlled systems of common usage, and 2) a large number of non-trained users operating such systems. Envisioning a type of "common mode operational fault" with unpredictable social consequences is no more futuristic.

This landscape needs a "global" view of the concept of "dependability", which has to start from the basic intrinsic characteristics of the components (of a computer, of a network, of an infrastructure, of a set of services, of the interested managing and user bodies, of the society) to grow up and reach reliance in "ambient dependability", which encompasses not only the technological aspects but includes inter and multi disciplinary fields, which span over ergonomics, usability, education, sociology, law and government.

A first step towards ambient dependability is achieving a dependable Information Society that requires a harmonized effort from a large set of actors, and need to consider many challenging points:

- New threats have to be analyzed, studied and modeled.
- New fault types have to be analyzed, studied and modeled.
- Design methodologies have to be studied for designing under uncertainty.
- A user-centered design approach, like design for usability, has to be applied.
- The concepts of "architecture" and "system" have to be rethought and redefined.
- Architectural frameworks are needed for adapting functional and non-functional properties while at least providing guarantees on how dependably they are adapting.
- A move is needed towards the definition of extended dependability attributes, like "acceptable availability under attack".

- New modeling and simulation means and tools are needed for complex interdependencies, for system evolution, evaluation of combined measures, evaluation of vulnerabilities related to security to mention some of challenges.

1.1 Where are we today?

We are facing such a huge problem that it is important to understand what level of trustworthiness we may pose on our present (theoretic) knowledge and industrial practice. Some data:

- In 1995, The Standish Group [The Standish Group] reported that the average US software project overran its budgeted time by 190%, its budgeted costs by 222%, and delivered only 60% of the planned functionality. Only 16% of projects were delivered at the estimated time and cost, and 31% of projects were cancelled before delivery, with larger companies performing much worse than smaller ones. Later Standish Group surveys show an improving trend, but success rates are still low.

- A UK survey, published in the 2001 Annual Review of the British Computer Society [British Computer Society 2001] showed a similar picture. Of more than 500 development projects, only three met the survey's criteria for success. In 2002, the annual cost of poor quality software to the US economy was estimated at $60B [NIST, 2002].

While recognizing that much advancement has been made in dependability methods, tools and processes, still a great gulf remains between what is known and what is done. It appears evident that many industrial engineering designs are still based on best effort processes with limited, if any, application of the theories developed so far. This implies a relevant educational issue, addressed later.

Current research in dependability covers a wide spectrum of critical systems, going from embedded real-time systems, to large open networked architectures. The vision of research and technology development in Dependable Computing has been summarized by the dependability community involved in the IST-2000-25088 CaberNet Network of Excellence (`http://www.newcastle.research.ec.org/cabernet/research/projects`), where a considerable number of pointers to relevant research activities is also provided. A brief recall of this vision document is reported in the following.

Fault Prevention

Fault prevention aims to prevent the occurrence or the introduction of faults. It consists in developing systems in such a way as to prevent the introduction of design and implementation faults, and to prevent faults from occurring during operation. In this context, any general engineering technique aimed at introducing rigor into the design process can be considered as constituting fault prevention. At level of *specifications*, the assumption that a complex software-based system may have a fixed specification is wrong. Today systems have in their requirements, and therefore in the specifications, assumptions related to human processes, from their interactions to the way they report their results. Such processes change as normal evolutionary processes. Thus software engineering methods must support these changes, but this is not the actual situation. The relevant issues to be considered are related to the *form* of the specifications (read it as the need to use proper abstractions) and to the *notation* of the specification (read it as the need to use formal mathematical notations, able to manage the changes). If in the specification process requirements are dealt with approximate or ambiguous notations, not able to provide manageability of abstractions, it is difficult, if not impossible, to know what it is tried to be achieved. Particularly challenging appear: i) the formal definition of security policies in order to prevent the introduction of vulnerabilities, and ii) the human factors issues in critical "socio-technical" systems.

Fault Tolerance

Fault-tolerance techniques aim to ensure that a system fulfils its function despite faults. Current research is centred on *distributed* fault-tolerance techniques, *wrapping* and *reflection* technologies for facilitating the implementation of fault-tolerance, and the generalization of the tolerance paradigm to include deliberately malicious faults, i.e., *intrusion-tolerance*.

Distributed fault-tolerance techniques aim to implement redundancy techniques using software, usually through a message-passing paradigm. Much of the research in the area is concerned with: i) the definition of distributed algorithms for fault-tolerance; ii) facilities for group communications and consensus; iii) automatic recovering and re-integration of failed replicas; iv) fault-tolerance techniques for embedded systems (tailored to both the synchronous and asynchronous models); v) tolerance to intrusion and intruders.

Other areas of active research concern fault-tolerance in large, complex distributed applications. Of special note in this area are techniques aimed at the coordinated handling of multiple exceptions in environments where multiple concurrent threads of execution act on persistent data; fault-tolerance in peer-to-peer systems; recursive structuring of complex cooperative applications to provide for systematic error confinement and recovery and mechanisms for dealing with errors that arise from architectural mismatches.

The implementation of distributed fault-tolerance techniques is notoriously difficult and error-prone, especially when using COTS (off-the-shelf components) that typically (a) have ill-defined failure modes and (b) offer opaque interfaces that do not allow access to internal data without which fault-tolerance cannot be implemented. There is thus considerable interest in addressing these difficulties using wrapping technologies to improve robustness and reflective technologies to allow introspection and intercession.

Fault Removal

Fault removal, through verification and validation techniques such as inspection, model-checking, theorem proving, simulation and testing, aims to reduce the number or the severity of faults. Among the most recent research activities in this field, there are:

i) *probabilistic verification*, an approach with strong links to fault forecasting that aims to provide stochastic guarantees of correctness by neglecting systems states whose probability of occupation is considered negligible;

ii) *statistical testing*, an approach to software testing which is based on the notion of a test quality measured in terms of the coverage of structural or functional criteria;

iii) assessment of the correlation between software complexity, as measured by object-oriented metrics, and fault proneness;

iv) *robustness testing*, aiming to assess how well a (software) component protects itself against erroneous inputs. Fault tolerant mechanisms can be tested for their robustness through classical *fault injection*;

v) testing the use of the reflective technologies considered earlier as a means for simplifying the implementation of fault-tolerance;

vi) support to verification and validation, for analyzing the impact of changes and for ensuring that the design and all its documentation remain consistent.

Fault Forecasting

Fault forecasting is concerned with the estimation of the presence, the creation and the consequences of faults. This is a very active and prolific field of research within the dependability community. Analytical and experimental evaluation techniques are considered, as well as simulation.

Analytical evaluation of system dependability is based on a stochastic model of the system's behaviour in the presence of fault and (possibly) repair events. For realistic systems, two major issues are that of: (a) establishing a faithful and tractable model of the system's behaviour, and (b) analysis procedures that allow the (possibly very large) model to be processed.

Ideally, the analytical evaluation process should start as early as possible during development in order to make motivated design decisions between alternative approaches. Specific areas of research in analytical evaluation include: systems with multiple phases of operation, and large Internet-based applications requiring a hierarchical modelling approach. In the area of software-fault tolerance, specific attention must be paid to modelling dependencies when assessing the dependability achieved by diversification techniques for tolerating design faults.

Experimental evaluation of system dependability relies on the collection of dependability data on real systems. The data of relevance concerns the times of or between dependability-relevant events such as failures and repairs. Data may be collected either during the test phase or during normal operation. The observation of a system in the presence of faults can be accelerated by means of fault-injection techniques, which constitute a very popular subject for recent and ongoing research. Currently, there has been research into using fault injection techniques to build dependability *benchmarks* for comparing competing systems/solutions on an equitable basis.

1.2 System Dependability and Education

System dependability is "per se" very challenging, but there is the feeling that a methodological approach and a methodic attitude are lacking. No system developer yet knows what is the appropriate blend of methods for fault prevention, fault removal, fault tolerance and fault forecasting. Also, the choices of dependability cases appear to be rather difficult: a meaningful case should contain all the evidence that is needed to argue that the system is adequately dependable. This evidence is made of the dependability targets and related failure rates, hazard analysis, arguments based on the architecture and design just to mention few of them. The lack of such methodic approach is the hardest point to take into account. The situation is even worse considering that a gap exists between theoretical knowledge and what is done in practice.

This open a very relevant educational issue: there is a gap between what is *known* and what is *done*. A point that should be raised, when shaping any system design course is the ratio of fundamentals and principles, which should be taught, and the part of teaching related to the status of the art in techniques and technologies. A student, who in the future will become part of a team of system developers should be taught all fundamentals and principles which will remain invariant in the years to come. This is the only way to reduce the gap between what is *known* and what is *done*.

There is the need of a careful re-visitation of several methodologies and design methods that have been largely studied when computer science had to be credited as a science, and then quickly abandoned when under the pressure of the market a trend has started towards more and more functionally rich and sophisticated artifacts.

Relevant keywords, which may drive towards new architectural frameworks for a dependable Information Society, are:

- Abstraction
- Composition
- Recursion
- Integration
- Usability

They can be used to get the required level of genericity, openness, adaptability and re-use for different architectural/infrastructural layers:

- For designing dependable architectures/infrastructures at component level.
- For designing architectures/infrastructures for dependability.
- For obtaining dependable architectures/infrastructures from user perspective.

Design of dependable components for architectures/infrastructures

Table 1 identifies requirements, enabling technologies and instruments that are well suited for dependable architectures made of components.

Modelling, designing and using **generic, composable, open source, and reusable components** appear from this table very helpful towards the goal of building systems of systems that can be easily validated and assessed.

Designing architectures/infrastructures for dependability

Another perspective is related to coping with "how to?" (Table 2). Here multiple facets of dependability raise many issues.

We can deduce that **abstraction, recursion, and incremental verification** will definitely help in designing and structuring multi-layers architectures up to the level of complex infrastructures.

Dependable architectures/infrastructures from user perspective

A final perspective is the architectural level that includes the user. Actually the user is the one who has the final word on system dependability. The types of user requests, which can be used for driving this level, are in Table 3.

Table 1.

	Rigorous design (i.e. fault prevention)	*Verification and validation (i.e. fault removal)*	*Fault Tolerance (accidental and malicious faults)*	*System evaluation (i.e. fault forecasting)*
Requirements	- Composable components - Secure components - Separation of concern - Invariance	- Early prototyping - Test cases generation	- Adaptable components	- Testable components - Coverage evaluation - Early prototyping
Enabling technologies	- Formal methods - Design for V&V	- State observability - Testing - Supports to validation and verification - Formal methods	- Redundancy - Functional diversity - Middleware	- Analytical modeling - Fault injection
Instruments	- Specs languages - Modeling	- Tools	- Function placement	- Tools

Table 2.

Rigorous design (i.e. fault prevention)	*Verification and validation (i.e. fault removal)*	*Fault Tolerance (accidental and malicious faults)*	*System evaluation (i.e. fault forecasting)*
- How to compose: - Interfaces - Legacy systems - How to guarantee integrity - How to guarantee security - How to guarantee survivability - How to guarantee predictable timing	- How to assess risks - How to trust the tools - How to test	- How to cope with new fault types - How to reach survivability - How to coordinate adaptability - How to get good usability	- How to deal with uncertainty - How to build meaningful models and simulations - How to evaluate coverage - How to perform experimental verification and testing

Table 3.

Rigorous design (i.e. fault prevention)	*Verification and validation (i.e. fault removal)*	*Fault Tolerance (accidental and malicious faults)*	*System evaluation (i.e. fault forecasting)*
- Is the system compliant with specifications? - Is the system able to adapt to changes	- Do I have the knowledge of possible residual faults?	- Is the system able to provide meaningful service in presence of accidental and malicious faults?	- Has the system sufficient performance to satisfy my needs? - Is system usability sufficiently good to reduce the probability of human errors? - Does the system protect my privacy, integrity of my data and security? - Is the cost/dependability ratio optimal for my needs?

The final rating for a system or infrastructure or service being perceived as dependable comes from a statement like **"I think the system/infrastructure/ service has an adequate dependability, obtained in an efficient way!"**. And this is the real judgment that counts.

Reaching this level of trust and confidence is a very challenging goal. It needs to consider any system/infrastructure/service from different perspectives and distilling from them the very special aspects that contribute to overall dependability.

1.3 Future Directions

The discussion carried on in the previous sections has analysed and pointed out many requirements for dependability in the future AmI landscape, which encompass different key aspects of the future generation computing systems. Here, some challenging research directions, as envisioned by the authors, are discussed.

Generic, COTS-based architectures for dependable systems

The natural evolution towards more complex services and infrastructures impose an enhancement on how an "architecture" is designed, as the supporting element for the system and the services, and what it is supposed to offer in terms of different x-abilities.

Most of the large-scale infrastructures have been developed connecting previously stand-alone systems usually developed from proprietary architectures, where ad hoc solutions were chosen and several electronic components were developed independently.

A basic property in such a context was that the components were designed having in mind the entire structure of the system, and this type of approach had pros and cons.

Positive aspects were:

- The design and implementation of ad hoc components makes easier the validation of the system.
- The knowledge of the system is completely under control of the designer and parts do not exist which are protected by third party intellectual property rights, again making easier validation and procuring, which are mandatory for safety critical systems.
- Re-design and updating the system does not depend on third parties.

Negative aspects were:

- Components and implementation technologies changes and evolutes very quickly, so that several of them may be obsolete when a design is completed and the system can be put in operation.
- Upgrading of components may be required if the operational life of the system is rather extended.
- The strict dependence between components and the system (through the design) makes the system rather inflexible and not adaptable to different contexts or to be interfaced to other systems, that is configurability may be very hard if not impossibe.
- Any new system or major revision needs to be revalidated ex-novo.

Moreover, with respect to interactions, for the integration of large-scale infrastructures, or simply aiming at interoperability between different systems negative aspects of such architectural approaches are:

- Systems with even slightly different requirements and specifications cannot reuse components used in previous designs, so that new systems require, in general, a complete redesign, and experience gained from the operation of older systems cannot be used.
- Interoperability is hard to achieve because of different projects specifications (different dependability properties offered, different communication protocols or media etc.), and the integration of two or more different systems must consider this.

For being able to follow the trend which demands the usage of COTS (components off-the-shelf) and to avoid the negative points previously listed, thus reducing development and operational costs, a strategic R&D activity towards the definition, prototyping and partial verification and validation of a generic, dependable, and real-time architecture is required. Such an effort would aim at the definition and construction of an architectural framework such:

- To reduce the design and development costs.
- To reduce the number of components used in the several subsystems.
- To simplify the evolution process of the products and reduce the associated costs.
- To simplify the validation (and certification) of the products through an incremental approach based on reuse.

The proposed infrastructure should have the following characteristics:

- Use of generic components (possibly COTS) which can be substituted, following technological evolution, without redesign or revalidation of the system.
- Reliability/availability and safety properties should be associated to the architectural design and not only to intrinsic properties of its components, so that techniques for error detection, diagnosis and error recovery be as most as possible independent from the specific components, be they hardware or software.
- Use of a hierarchical approach for functional and non functional properties, so to ease validation.
- Use of early evaluation methods to support design refinements. An early validation of the concepts and architectural choices is essential to save on money and on the time to market for a final product. The feedback of such evaluation is highly beneficial to highlight problems within the design, to identify bottlenecks and to allow comparing different solutions so as to select the most suitable one.
- Openness of the system, in the sense that it should be able to interface and communicate with other systems through different communication systems and to adapt itself to the different kind of architectures it has to interact with.

Developing dependable systems requires also an open utility program framework which may be easily and dynamically enriched to cope with new needs which may arise during system lifetime. On-line support for administration, operation, maintenance and provisioning is needed. Examples of key areas are: error/fault diagnosis, QoS analysis to trigger appropriate reconfiguration actions in faulty situations, on-line software upgrades without loss of service.

A large body of activities has been performed in this direction by the international dependability community. The main contributions of our group are [Bondavalli et al., 2000; Bondavalli et al., 2001a; Porcarelli et al., 2004].

Model-based dynamic reconfiguration in complex critical systems

Information infrastructures, especially as foreseen by the AmI vision, are very complex networked systems where interdependencies among the several components play a relevant role in the quality of services they provide. In such system organization, the failure of a core node may induce either saturation on other parts of the infrastructure or a cascading effect which puts out of work large part of the infrastructure, with consequent loss of service and connectivity with lengthy recovery times. Therefore, adaptivity of the system architecture with respect to unforeseen changes that can occur at run-time becomes one of the most challenging aspects. Apart from natural system's evolution, many other sources of variability are possible, such as the occurrence of fault patterns different from those foreseen at design time, or the change of application's dependability requirements during the operational lifetime. To cope with unpredictability of events, approaches based on on-line system reconfiguration are necessary/desirable.

A simplified solution to cope with such a dynamic framework would be to pre-plan (through off-line activities) the "best" reaction to system and/or environment conditions, and to utilize the appropriate pre-planned answer when a specific event occurs at run-time. However, such a solution would be practically feasible only in presence of a limited and well defined in advance number of situations requiring the application of a new reconfiguration policy in the system. Unfortunately, especially in complex systems, such a complete knowledge is not available, and situations may occur for which a satisfactory reaction has not been foreseen in advance.

Therefore, it raises up the need of dynamically devising an appropriate answer to variations of the system and/or environment characteristics in order to achieve the desired dependability level. To this purpose, a general dependability manager would be very useful, which continuously supervises the controlled system and environment, ready to identify and apply reconfiguration policies at run-time.

The architectural definition of such a general dependability manager includes an evaluation subsystem to provide quantitative comparison among several possible reconfiguration strategies. Model-based evaluation approaches are very suited to this purpose. The idea is to build simplified (but still meaningful) models of the system to be controlled. The model simplicity in such a context is dictated by the need to solve the model dynamically as quickly as possible, in order to take appropriate decisions online. Too complex systems, in fact, would require too high computation time, thus defeating the effectiveness of the solution itself. In a logical view, monitoring entities have to be inserted in the framework, able to catch exceptional system/environment conditions and to report appropriate signals to the dependability manager. Issues of distributed observation and control are involved in this process. Simple but yet effective indicators have to be defined, as a synthesis of a set of "alarming symptoms" (such as fault occurrence, different applications' request, traffic conditions, detection of attacks, ...). Based on critical values assumed by such indicators, a reconfiguration action is triggered. Of course, because resources are precious for assuring satisfactory levels of service accomplishments, the triggering of reconfiguration/isolation procedures have to be carefully handled.

As soon as a system reconfiguration is required, the model solution helps to devise the most appropriate configuration and behavior to face the actual situation. For example, through the model solution it can be evaluated the dependability of a new architecture of the system obtained by rearranging the remaining resources after a fault, or some performability indicator to carry out cost-benefit tradeoff choices. Therefore, the output provided by the dependability manager is a new system configuration; of course, it is expected to be the best reconfiguration in order to satisfy the dependability requirements. Different modeling techniques and models solution can be considered and integrated to reach the goal. Already evaluated reconfiguration actions can be maintained in a database accessible by the dependability manager, to be easily retrieved when the same "alarming pattern" will be subsequently raised in the system.

A general framework should be pursued, not tied to a specific application but flexible enough to be easily adapted to different problems. In particular, a methodology has to be defined, allowing to identify systematically the input parameters of the manager, the metrics of interest and the criteria to base the decision on. These are very challenging issues, especially the last one, which is an instance of the well known and long studied problem of multiple-criteria decision making.

Also in this area there is a noteworthy body of research. The main contributions of our group are [Porcarelli et al., 2004; Bondavalli et al., 1999].

Enhancing methods for dependability evaluation

System evaluation is a key activity of fault forecasting, aimed at providing statistically well-founded quantitative measures of how much we can rely on a system. In particular, system evaluation achieved through modelling supports the prediction of how much we will be able to rely on a system before incurring the costs of building it. It is therefore a very profitable evaluation approach to be employed since the very beginning of a system development activity.

However, a number of new issues are raised by the relevant characteristics of the future systems, that are not satisfactorily dealt with by current modelling methodologies. Most of the new challenges in dependability modelling are connected with the increasing complexity and dynamicity of the systems under analysis. Such complexity need to be attacked both from the point of view of system representation and of the underlying model solution. A few issues and directions to go are discussed in the following.

State-space explosion and ways to cope with it. The state space explosion is a well known problem in model-based dependability analysis, which strongly limits the applicability of this method to large complex systems, or heavily impacts on the accuracy of the evaluation results when simplifying assumptions are made as a remedy to this problem. Modular and hierarchical approaches have been identified as effective directions; however, modularity of the modelling approach alone cannot be truly effective without a *modular solution* of the defined models.

Hierarchical approaches. Resorting to a hierarchical approach brings benefits under several aspects, among which: i) facilitating the construction of models; ii) speeding up their solution; iii) favoring scalability; iv) mastering complexity (by handling smaller models through hiding, at one hierarchical level, some modeling details of the lower one).

At each level, details of the architecture and of the status of lower level components are not meaningfull, and only aggregated information should be used. Therefore, information of the detailed models at one level should be aggregated in an abstract model at a higher level. Important issues are how to abstract all the relevant information of one level to the upper one and how to compose the derived abstract models.

Composability. To be as general as possible, the overall model (at each level of the hierarchy) is achieved as the integration of small pieces of models (building blocks) to favour their composability. We define composability as the capability to select and assemble models of components in various combinations into a model of the whole system to satisfy specific application requirements.

For the sake of model composability, we are pursuing the following goals:

- to have different building block models for the different types of components in the system. All these building blocks can be used as a pool of templates,
- to automatically instantiate an appropriate model, one for each component, from these templates, and
- at a given hierarchical level, to automatically link them together (by means of a set of rules which are application dependent), thus defining the overall model.

The international dependability community is very active on topics related with methods and tools for dependability evaluation and a massive production exists on the several involved aspects. The main contributions of our group on the above discussed issues are [Mura and Bondavalli, 1999; Bondavalli et al., 2001b; Mura and Bondavalli, 2001].

On-line evaluation as a component/mechanism for dynamic architectures. Dependability evaluation is typically an off-line activity. However, because of the unpredictability of events, both external and internal to the system, on-line evaluation would be desirable in a number of circumstances. In fact, when the topology of the architecture changes significantly along time, accounting for too many configurations may become a prohibitive activity when done off-line. Of course, although appealing, the online solution shows a number of challenging problems requiring substantial investigations. Models of components have to be derived online and combined to get the model of the whole system. Thus, compositional rules and the resulting complexity of the combined model solution appear to be the most critical problems to be properly tackled to promote the applicability of this dynamic approach to reconfiguration.

The main contributions of our group on this research direction are [Porcarelli et al., 2004; Bondavalli et al., 1999; Chohra et al., 2001].

Integration of experimental and model-based evaluation. Moreover, synergistic collaboration between model-based and measurement approaches throughout the system life cycle is more and more pressed by the future landscape. This calls for *benchmarking for dependability*, to provide a uniform, repeatable, and cost-effective way of performing the evaluation of dependability and security attributes, either as stand-alone assessment or, more often, for comparative evaluation across systems and components. The shift from system evaluation techniques based on measurements to the standardized approaches required by benchmarking touches all the fundamental problems of current measurement approaches (representativeness, portability, intrusion, scalability, cost, etc.) and needs a comprehensive research approach, with a special attention to COTS and middleware aspects.

The main contributions of our group in this area are [Bondavalli et al., 2002; Bondavalli et al., 2003].

Appendix: ISTAG scenario: Maria - The Road Warrior

After a tiring long haul flight Maria passes through the arrivals hall of an airport in a Far Eastern country. She is traveling light, hand baggage only. When she comes to this particular country she knows that she can travel much lighter than less than a decade ago, when she had to carry a collection of different so-called personal computing devices (laptop PC, mobile phone, electronic organizers and sometimes beamers and printers). Her computing system for this trip is reduced to one highly personalized communications device, her 'P-Com' that she wears on her wrist. A particular feature of this trip is that the country that Maria is visiting has since the previous year embarked on an ambitious ambient intelligence infrastructure program. Thus her visa for the trip was self-arranged and she is able to stroll through immigration without stopping because her P-Com is dealing with the ID checks as she walks. A rented car has been reserved for her and is waiting in an earmarked bay. The car opens as she approaches. It starts at the press of a button: she doesn't need a key. She still has to drive the car but she is supported in her journey downtown to the conference center-hotel by the traffic guidance system that had been launched by the city government as part of the 'AmI-Nation' initiative two years earlier. Downtown traffic has been a legendary nightmare in this city for many years, and draconian steps were taken to limit access to the city center. But Maria has priority access rights into the central cordon because she has a reservation in the car park of the hotel. Central access however comes at a premium price; in Maria's case it is embedded in a deal negotiated between her personal agent and the transaction agents of the car-rental and hotel chains. Her firm operates centralized billing for these expenses and uses its purchasing power to gain access at attractive rates. Such preferential treatment for affluent foreigners was highly contentious at the time of the introduction of the route pricing system and the government was forced to hypothecate funds from the tolling system to the public transport infrastructure in return. In the car Maria's teenage daughter comes through on the audio system. Amanda has detected from 'En Casa' system at home that her mother is in a place that supports direct voice contact. However, even with all the route guidance support Maria wants to concentrate on her driving and says that she will call back from the hotel. Maria is directed to a parking slot in the underground garage of the newly constructed building of the Smar-tel Chain. The porter - the first contact with a real human so far! - meets her in the garage. He helps her with her luggage to her room. Her room adopts her 'personality' as she enters. The room temperature, default lighting and a range of video and music choices are displayed on the video wall. She needs to make some changes to her presentation - a sales pitch that will be used as the basis for a negotiation later in the day. Using voice commands she adjusts the light levels and commands a bath. Then she calls up her daughter on the video wall, while talking she uses a traditional remote control system to browse through a set of webcast local news bulletins from back home that her daughter tells her about. They watch them together. Later on she 'localizes' her presentation with the help of an agent that is specialized in advising on local preferences (color schemes, the use of language). She stores the presentation on the secure server at headquarters back in Europe. In the hotel's seminar room where the sales pitch is take place, she will be able to call down an encrypted version of the presentation and give it a post presentation decrypt life of 1.5 minutes. She goes downstairs to make her presentation... this for her is a high stress event. Not only is she performing alone for the first time, the clients concerned are well known to be tough players. Still, she doesn't actually have to close the deal this time. As she enters the meeting she raises communications access thresholds to block out anything but red-level 'emergency' messages. The meeting is rough, but she feels it was a success. Coming out of the meeting she lowers the communication barriers again and picks up a number of amber level communications including one from her cardio-monitor warning her to take some rest now. The day has been long and stressing. She needs to chill out with a little meditation and medication. For Maria the meditation is a concert on the video wall and the medication... a large gin and tonic from her room's minibar.

Plots elements

WHO: Maria, Devices: P-Com, Cardio monitor; AmI service providers: Immigration control system, Rent-a-car, Car, Traffic management, Hotel Smart-tel, Hotel room, Seminar room, Maria's Company remote access, "En casa" system.

WHERE: Airport, City roads, Hotel, Home.

WHEN: Arrival to airport and immigration control; Car rental and trip through city; Arrival to hotel; Communication to/from "En casa" system; Access to room and adaptation; Communication with company; Presentation delivery; Relaxing.

WHAT:

- Maria: Interacts with P-Com through screen/voice interfaces. P-Com works as Personal data holder, Communications device, Negotiation tool; Holds a Cardio monitor that monitors and transmits signals
- Immigration control system: Carries out an ID check.
- Rent-a-car system: Automates the renting process by means of transaction agents.
- Car: Manages the access to the car, supports driving in the city traffic, offers telecommunications.
- Traffic management system: Manages access rights to the city streets.
- Hotel (Smart-tel): Manages parking reservation, provides local information, activates transaction agents and local preferences agents.
- Hotel Room: Manages temperature/light controls, Video/music adaptive systems, commanded bath, communications systems, provides facilitates for editing documents.
- Seminar room: Provides communications, and document life manager.
- Company remote access: Provides remote billing, negotiation agents, Remote access to servers.
- "En casa" communications system: Provides Multimedia communication capabilities.

ASSETS: Personal data, business data, infrastructure.

Scenario characteristic: Degrees of Comfort

Maria in this scenario moves through different public and private spaces, which she characterizes according to specific values that determine the information she will exchange and the type of interactions she will engage in. She starts her journey at the airport, she moves in a public space and a public invidualized profile seems convenient and comfortable at this stage as her P-Com helps her clear passport controls quickly and to be instantly contactable and recognizable. In the car from the airport to the hotel, she is in a semi-public space and maybe she desires to concentrate on her thoughts and be disturbed only by a select group of people, maybe her family and work associates - En Casa is recognized as a cyberspace object in her select group. In the Smar-tel hotel she is in semi-private space, as it is offered in temporary privacy to successive individuals. She may want the room therefore to behave like a trusted private space or she may feel more comfortable switching her AmI space off.

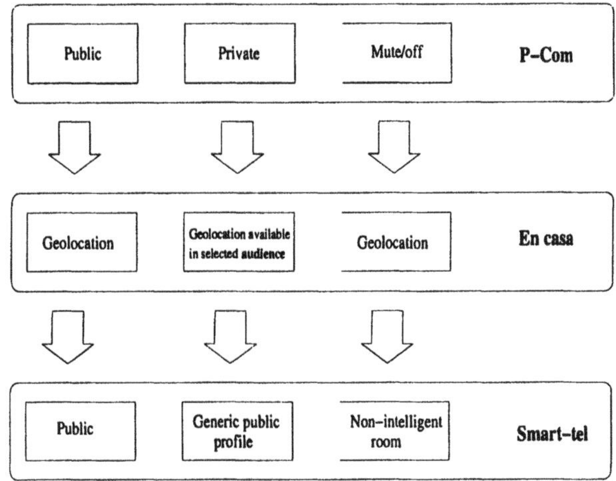

Figure A.1. Maria - Degrees of comfort.

The scenario continues: what goes wrong and how it works out...

The P-com (support for critical personal information) that Maria wears around her wrist sometimes fails causing her to get stranded at airports and wherever she needs to identify herself. A broken P-com is reason enough for the security system at her office to alert the authorities and refuse access to the office building that she wants to enter. To minimize delays in case of trouble with her P-com, Maria always carries her passport and some other documents describing her identity and containing passwords, user ID's and other kinds of codes. Malfunctioning of her P-com not only makes Maria lose her digital identity (single point of failure), it can also make her invisible to the tracking systems that keep an eye on her whereabouts for her daughter, the company she works for and her friends. For this reason Maria still carries a mobile phone. P-Com's rarely get stolen. However, high tech devices are frequently the target of "crackers" that try to gain access to the digital identity of the owner and their assets. For this reason Maria demonstrates some lack of trust in the hotel system although it claims to deploy strong encryption. This sometimes motivates a constant level of alert, as prevention of nuisances and inconvenience: some while ago Maria was stopped while trying to pass through an airport as suspected owner of a stolen identity.

The role of AmI and potential threats

Privacy. AmI understands context, and its spatial awareness adapts to the socially accepted natural modes of interaction between people. In Maria's case, her P-Com enables her to be public to the authorities but not to the crowd in general, although some degree of surprise and unexpected meeting might be welcome by her. In the taxi her P-Com enables her to retain a moment of reflection and contemplation by respecting some privacy, which fits well to the occasion. At the hotel, she would feel better to switch it off altogether, or to make it selectively public depending on her mood. Digital ID theft is a major concern, and the main menace to trust in AmI. As Maria comes to rely more on the P-Com and its support to her digital identity, its loss is likely to be increasingly traumatic. Tolerability to this risk will be similar to the fervent social debates society has conducted concerning risks in the area of personal safety. Countering ID theft requires a combination of different social engineering and technical counter-mechanisms. Prevention is likely to be a continuous competition between defense and attack techniques in a form of "arms race". The attitude to risk is likely to vary widely between social and national groups. There may be P-Com product families that allow the user to choose on the basis of (informal) risk assessments, in a trade off among style, functionality and robustness. To this end there would need to be clear methods for assessing the probability of digital ID loss, its duration, and the potential consequences and liabilities. In addition to the violation of the confidentiality of the digital ID, there is also the problem of partial loss of personal data (which could have effects such as erosion of privileges, counterfeiting of personal security policies, ...). As users will manage multiple identifies for their different social roles (citizen, employee, mother, ...), this could lead to inappropriate behavior of P-Com in certain contexts - a failure that could be much more difficult to detect.

Trust and confidence. AmI acts as Maria's invisible assistant. It efficiently provides Maria the necessary resources to enable her to successfully complete her mission. AmI is unobtrusive; it silently and discreetly acts for her in the background. It has to be robust, pro-actively correcting any failures that may occur. AmI increases Maria's capabilities: she can act, while her environment takes care of her needs. The other side of Maria's trust and confidence on the P-Com is the need to make provision for when it fails. The severity of the failure and its duration depend on the extent to which there are methods for rapid recovery and what alternative methods are in place e.g. how practicable is it to revert to a passport and a mobile phone to replace P-Com. The medical advice given by the cardio-monitor has serious safety implications. If it really behaves as an active e-health device integrated into AmI, there should be serious evidence of its dependability. Most users would feel comfortable with isolated devices that provide some assistance, without interacting with public open systems. Trust and confidence have to be also developed on AmI infrastructure support systems. Maria has also done some type of informal risk assessment to judge that the hotel digital security may not be adequate for the sensitive content of her presentation. In a future she might ask for some security certification and third-party evaluation. Maria seems to have placed complete trust in the navigation and travel support that she accesses through the P-com. The dependability requirements of AmI are very influenced by the performance, capability and dependability offered by alternative applications. Is the ordinary taxi system still functioning so that it will be only a mild inconvenience if the automatic traffic control system is not available? What would happen should she get lost? There may be longer-term negative consequences of AmI related to the development of strong dependence on AmI. Any unavailability or incorrect response by AmI might provoke the blockage of Maria's personal, social and professional lives. She has incorporated AmI into her existence, and now she cannot survive without it.

Interdependencies. This AmI scenario makes very apparent the interdependence of systems deriving from the pervasive deployment of ICT-based systems. Studying each dependability attribute in isolation might be misleading. The propagation and cascading effects that can derive from the failure of single elements might cause effects that are unforeseeable at first sight. The interconnectivity among systems requires different levels for the analysis of the potential threats to dependability. Faults that might not affect a local system might distress the more general application, and trigger a distant failure. For instance, a rather small diminution in the bandwidth of the network supporting the traffic system might in the long run cause an accumulation of delays and problems in the management of parking places. A significant problem is the widespread presence of single failure points. Any disturbance of the immigration control could affect a great quantity of people and of other services. It is also important to emphasize that most of the services depend on mobile code and agents, who are in charge of representing the different actors, perform negotiations and transactions, and to take crucial decisions for their owners. The dependability of these agents appears as one of the weakest points of AmI. In the Road Warrior scenario privacy can be managed in a linear way, by establishing profiles that are pre-configured by the user, by context, audience/communication group, time or day, location, etc. Private, semi-private, public, semi-public and mute profiles with all the possible nuances in-between may be identified or 'learnt' by use and pattern. Maria would feel more comfortable setting her P-com intentionally in the degree of comfort that she would require in each situation or teaching it to understand her personal social protocol of what is comfortably public and what is safely private.

Additional dependability issues. The assets at risk are of very different nature. They range from Maria's personal data to business data of Maria's company and of the hotel, and even other infrastructures such as the city traffic management system. Personal data can be the object of different critical faults:

- If P-Com has an internal accidental failure in the airport or when accessing the car or when entering into the hotel (for instance, availability of data, or integrity of data) Maria will be unable to benefit from these AmI services.
- More importantly, P-Com can be subject to malicious attack when acting in open environments (e.g. in the airport, in the car, in the hotel), putting the confidentiality of her personal data at risk. Business data is exposed at each dialogue between AmI business systems and personal and social-wide systems. When dealing with potential customers, any AmI has to send and accept information that can be the source of faults.
- Accidental faults can affect mainly the availability of the service and the integrity of the data managed.
- Malicious failures can provoke an attack to the confidentiality of data, and to the availability of the service. A third type of risks is related to AmI services that are deployed as societal infrastructures, for instance the traffic management system. Here, any fault might cause not just nuisances but potentially critical accidents. The dependability attributes of all hardware and software components, and of the data processed and stored by the system are relevant for the whole of society, giving rise to a new type of Critical Infrastructure.

References

AMSD (2003). A dependability roadmap for the information society in Europe. Deliverable D1.1, Accompanying Measure on System Dependability (AMSD). IST-2001-37553 - Workpackage 1: Overall Dependability Road-mapping, `http://www.am-sd.org`.

Bondavalli, A., Chiaradonna, S., Cotroneo, D., and Romano, L. (2003). A fault-tolerant distributed legacy-based system and its evaluation. In *LADC2003 - First Latin-American Symposium on Dependable Computing*, Sao Paulo, Brazil. to be published.

Bondavalli, A., Chiaradonna, S., Di Giandomenico, F., and Grandoni, F. (2000). Threshold-based mechanisms to discriminate transient from intermittent faults. *IEEE Transactions on Computers*, 49(3):230–245.

Bondavalli, A., Chiaradonna, S., Di Giandomenico, F., Grandoni, F., Powell, D., and Rabejac, C. (2001a). Error processing and fault treatment. In Powell, D., editor, *A Generic Fault-Tolerant Architecture for Real-Time Dependable Systems*, pages 71–86. ISBN 0-7923-7295-6, Kluwer Academic Publishers, Boston.

Bondavalli, A., Coccoli, A., and Di Giandomenico, F. (2002). Qos analysis of group communication protocols in wireless environment. In Ezhilchelvan, P. and Romanovsky, A., editors, *Concurrency in Dependable Computing*, pages 169–188. Kluwer Academic Publishers.

Bondavalli, A., Di Giandomenico, F., and Mura, I. (1999). An optimal value-based admission policy and its reflective use in real-time dependable systems. *Real-Time Systems Journal, Kluwer Academic Publishers*, 16(1):5–30.

Bondavalli, A., Nelli, M., Simoncini, L., and Mongardi, G. (2001b). Hierarchical modelling of complex control systems: Dependability analysis of a railway interlocking. *Journal of Computer Systems Science and Engineering, CRL Publishing*, 16(4):249–261.

British Computer Society 2001. `http://www.bcs.org.uk`.

Chohra, A., Di Giandomenico, F., Porcarelli, S., and Bondavalli, A. (2001). Towards optimal database maintenance in wireless communication systems. In Callaos, N., Da Silva, N. I., and Molero, J., editors, *The 5th World Multi-Conference on Systemics, Cybernetics and Informatics, ISAS-SCI 2001, Volume I: Information Systems Development*, pages 571–576, Orlando, Florida, USA. IIIS.

Ducatel, K., Bogdanowicz, M., Scapolo, F., Leijten, J., and Burgelman, J-C. (2001). Scenarios for ambient intelligence in 2010. Final report, IST Advisory Group (ISTAG), European Commission. IST. European Communities. `http://www.cordis.lu/ist/istag-reports.htm`.

European Presidency (2000). Presidency conclusions. Lisbon European Council. 23 and 24 March 2000. `http://ue.eu.int/en/Info/eurocouncil/index.htm`, Council of the European Union.

ISTAG (2002). Trust, dependability, security and privacy for IST in FP6. Ist advisory group report, IST Programme, EC. `http://www.cordis.lu/ist/istag-reports.htm`.

Laprie, J. C., editor (1992). *Dependability: Basic Concepts and Associated Terminology*, volume 5 of *Dependable Computing and Fault-Tolerant Systems*. Springer-Verlag.

Microsoft Research (2003). Microsoft research faculty summit 2003, Cambridge, UK. `http://research.microsoft.com/collaboration/university/europe/Events/FacultySummit/2003`.

Mura, I. and Bondavalli, A. (1999). Hierarchical modelling and evaluation of phased-mission systems. *IEEE Transactions on Reliability*, 48(4):360–368.

Mura, I. and Bondavalli, A. (2001). Markov regenerative stochastic Petri nets to model and evaluate the dependability of phased missions. *IEEE Transactions on Computers*, 50(12):1337–1351.

NIST (2002). The economic impacts of inadequate infrastructure for software testing. Final report RTI Project Number 7007.011, US National Institute of Standards and Technology.

Porcarelli, S., Castaldi, M., Di Giandomenico, F., Bondavalli, A., and Inverardi, P. (2004). A framework for reconfiguration-based fault-tolerance in distributed systems. In De Lemos, R., Gacek, c., and Romanovsky, A., editors, *Architecting Dependable Systems*, LNCS. Springer-Verlag. To appear, also ICSE-WADS2003, Post-Proceeding of ICSE-WADS2003.

The Standish Group. `http://www.standishgroup.com/chaos`.

EXPERIMENTAL RESEARCH IN DEPENDABLE COMPUTING AT CARNEGIE MELLON UNIVERSITY

From Faults to Manifestations

Daniel P. Siewiorek*◊, Roy A. Maxion* and Priya Narasimhan◊

**Department of Computer Science, ◊Department of Electrical and Computer Engineering, Carnegie Mellon University, Pittsburgh, PA 15213, USA — {dps, maxion, priya}@cs.cmu.edu*

Abstract: This paper aims to capture the decades of experimental research, results and impact in the field of dependable computing and systems at Carnegie Mellon University (CMU), starting from the 1970's to the present day. This research has spanned a diverse array of topics, such as modeling, abstractions, testing, anomaly detection, trend analysis and distributed systems. We also present the current state of our dependability research at CMU, outlining the potential directions for our work in the decade to come.

Key words: Abstractions, anomaly detection, fault-model, fault-injection, fault-tolerant middleware, trend analysis

1. INTRODUCTION

In 1945, the Carnegie Plan for higher education was evolved. The basic philosophy of the plan was "learning by doing". The strong emphasis on experimental research at Carnegie Mellon University (CMU) is one example of the Carnegie plan in operation. In particular, research in reliable computing at CMU has spanned five decades of researchers and students.

In the early 1960's, the Westinghouse Corporation in Pittsburgh had an active research program in the use of redundancy to enhance system reliability; William Mann, who had been associated with CMU, was one of the researchers involved in this effort. In 1962, a symposium on redundancy techniques was held in Washington, D.C., and led to the first comprehensive book [57], co-authored by Mann, on the topic of redundancy and reliability.

	1970's	1980's	1990's	2000's
Monitoring	Crash Dumps (1975)	Error Logs (1980)	Natural Workloads (1990)	Distributed, Asynchronous
Fault Model	Gate Level	Register Transfer	Design, User Errors, Reactive	Attacks, Proactive (2004)
Fault Injection	Stuck-At	Memory Level (1985)	API-Level (1995)	Security (2000), Resource Exhaustion
Abstractions	Stuck-At	Error Logs ⇨ Clustering ⇨ Space/DFT (1986)	Gate ⇨ RT, Message ⇨ Fault feature vector, Memory ⇨ Crash (1995)	Multi-Dimensional
Modeling	Event, Mathematical Distribution/Parameters (1975)	Fault and Workload Interaction (1985)	Event Clustering, Trend Analysis, Prediction (1995)	Machine Learning

Figure 1. The depth, breadth and chronology of dependability research at Carnegie Mellon University

CMU's Professor William H. Pierce wrote a paper on adaptive voting [40] that formed a part of this book. Pierce also published one of the first textbooks on redundancy [41].

During the next four decades, a large number of experimental hardware and software systems were designed, implemented, and made operational, at CMU. These systems covered a range of computer architectures, from uniprocessors, to multiprocessors, to networked systems. Each system represented a unique opportunity to include, and to quantify the results of incorporating, reliability features in the design of the system. This paper surveys the monitoring, measurement, and evaluation of those systems. A common theme has been to understand the natural occurrence of faults, to develop mathematical models for prediction, and to raise the level of abstraction of fault-models in order to monitor and design dependability mechanisms more easily. Figure 1 illustrates the breadth, diversity, depth and chronological progress of the dependability research at CMU, over the past few decades up until the present day.

2. MULTIPROCESSOR ARCHITECTURES

In 1969, Gordon Bell headed up a research seminar whose goal was to design an architecture that would be particularly suited for artificial intelligence applications. The result of the seminar was a paper study outlining *C.ai* [4]. One subunit of the C.ai architecture was a multiprocessor employing a crossbar switch. Ultimately, the multiprocessor portion of C.ai evolved into *C.mmp* (Computer.multi-mini-processor). The DARPA-funded C.mmp project started in 1971, became operational in mid-1975, and was

Figure 2. The "H" shaped configuration of C.mmp with crossbar switch and memory in the center, surrounded by banks of four processors

decommissioned in March 1980. C.mmp (see Figure 2) was comprised of sixteen PDP-11 processors communicating with 16 memories through a crossbar switch C.mmp [58] added a minimal amount of error-detection in its hardware. The natural redundancy in its replicated processors and memory provided opportunities for substantial software error-detection and reconfiguration techniques [25].

In 1972, Professors Samuel Fuller and Daniel Siewiorek joined CMU. During that time, the hardware design for C.mmp was in full swing. It was a fruitful period for developing analytical models of its performance [5] and reliability [49]. The major results of the C.mmp project are described in [59].

In the fall of 1972, a seminar was launched at CMU to explore the architectural possibilities of using microprocessors in a large-scale multiprocessor whose cost grew linearly in the number of processors employed. Architectural specifications for the computer module project were developed and reported [3], and a detailed architectural design was undertaken, culminating in the *Cm*.* architecture (see Figure 3) [52].

Cm*. was extensively studied with performance and reliability models during the design process. A ten-processor system became operational in 1977. Cm*. was extensively studied with performance and reliability models during the design process. A ten-processor system became operational in 1977. As a result, Cm*. had incorporated many more performance and reliability features than C.mmp [49], and grew into a fifty-processor

Figure 3. Two of the five clusters of Cm*.; the open cluster has four computer modules on the top backplane; K.map is on the bottom

experimental system, complete with two independent operating systems, that became operational in 1979. Further details on Cm*. can be found in [17].

Cm*. was extensively studied with performance and reliability models during the design process. A ten-processor system became operational in 1977. As a result, Cm*. had incorporated many more performance and reliability features than C.mmp [49], and grew into a fifty-processor experimental system, complete with two independent operating systems, that became operational in 1979. Further details on Cm*. can be found in [17].

Dan Siewiorek spent the summer of 1975 with the Research and Development group at Digital Equipment Corporation. The goal of the summer project was to study issues of testing and reliability in computer structures. The work culminated in an architectural specification for *C.vmp* (Computer.voted multi-processor). C.vmp employed off-the-shelf components with little or no modification to achieve hard and transient fault survivability [51]; furthermore, C.vmp executed an unmodified operating system. In addition to a voting mode, the bus-level voter also allowed a non-replicated device (such as a console terminal) to broadcast results to all three processors, or it allowed the system to divide into three independent computers intercommunicating through parallel interfaces. C.vmp could switch between independent-mode and voting-mode operation, thereby permitting the user to dynamically trade performance for reliability [47].

C.vmp became operational in the fall of 1976, and was operational for five years. Experience indicated that C.vmp was about six times more reliable for transient faults than the single LSI-ll systems employed in Cm* [3]. Performance degradation due to the voter was theoretically predicted and experimentally measured [45]; the voter was found to reduce the system-level performance by about 15%. The voter design was generalized to include both asynchronous and synchronous bus protocols [32][33].

At the time of C.vmp's inception, engineers and designers were becoming aware of the predominance of transient errors over hard failures. A major goal of the C.vmp project was to use C.vmp as a transient meter whereby the sources of transients could be measured in much the same way that a voltmeter can measure sources and magnitudes of voltages. A statistics board was added to the C.vmp design [43] in order to compare the three buses for disagreements and to store the contents of all three buses (including a unique time-stamp) into a shift register when a disagreement was observed.

There exist a wide variety of applications where data availability must be continuous, that is, where the system is never taken off-line and any interruption in the accessibility of stored data causes significant disruption in the service provided by the application. Examples of such systems include on-line transaction processing systems such as airline reservation systems and automated teller networks in banking systems. In addition, there exist many applications for which a high degree of data availability is important, but continuous operation might not be required. An example is a research and development environment, where access to a centrally stored CAD system is often necessary to make progress on a design project. These applications and many others mandate both high performance and high availability from their storage subsystems.

Redundant disk-arrays are systems in which a high level of I/O performance is obtained by grouping together a large number of small disks, rather than by building one large, expensive drive. The high component-count of such systems leads to unacceptably high rates of data-loss due to component failure; thus, such systems typically incorporate redundancy to achieve fault-tolerance. This redundancy takes one of two forms: replication or encoding. In replication, the system maintains one or more duplicate copies of all data. In the encoding approach, the system maintains an error-correcting code (ECC) computed over the data. The latter category of systems is very attractive because it offers both low cost per megabyte and high data reliability; unfortunately, such systems exhibit poor performance in the presence of a disk failure. Our research at CMU addressed the problem of ECC-based redundant disk-arrays [14] that offer dramatically higher levels of performance in the presence of failure, as compared to systems comprising the current state-of-the-art, without significantly affecting the performance, cost, or reliability of these systems.

The first aspect of the problem considered the organization of data and redundant information in the disk-array. Our research demonstrated techniques for distributing the workload induced by a disk failure across a large set of disks, thereby reducing the impact of the failure recovery process on the system as a whole. Once the organization of data and redundancy had been specified, additional improvements in performance during failure recovery could be obtained through the careful design of the algorithms used to recover lost data from redundant information. The research showed that structuring the recovery algorithm so as to assign one recovery process to each disk in the array, as opposed to the traditional approach of structuring it so as to assign a process to each unit within a set of data units to be concurrently recovered, provided significant advantages.

Finally, the research developed a design for a redundant disk-array targeted at extremely high availability through extremely fast failure-recovery. This development also demonstrated the generality of the technique.

3. HARD AND TRANSIENT FAULT DISTRIBUTIONS

Often, designers must make tradeoffs between alternative reliability techniques with inadequate knowledge about how systems fail during operation. In 1977, Dan Siewiorek took a one-semester leave of absence from CMU and spent eight months working with the VAX-II /750 design team on the issues of reliability, availability, and maintainability. To answer questions about modeling hard failures, the research focused on collecting data from Cm*. Several different module types were utilized in Cm*.; a chip count for each module was tabulated, followed by the modules of that type in the system, the total number of hours that these modules were utilized, and the total number of failures. The data was found to follow an exponential distribution with the failure-rate as predicted by the Military Handbook 217 [56] suitably modified to take into account the time-rate of the change of technology [49].

While substantial progress had been made in the area of understanding hard failures, transient faults posed a much harder problem. Once a hard failure had occurred, it was possible to isolate the faulty component uniquely. On the other hand, by the time a transient fault manifested itself (perhaps in the form of a system-software crash), all traces of its nature and location were long gone. Thus, research was started on the data collection and the modeling of transient faults. Data was collected from various systems – four time-sharing systems, an experimental multiprocessor, and an experimental fault-tolerant system – that ranged in size from microprocessors to large ECL mainframes. The method of detecting transient-induced errors varied widely. For the PDP-I0 time-sharing systems, internally detected errors were reported in a system event-log file. For the experimental multiprocessor, Cm*., a program was written (under the guidance of Sam Fuller) that automatically loaded diagnostics into idle processors, initiated the diagnostics, and periodically queried the diagnostics as to their state. For the triply- redundant C.vmp, a manually generated crash-log was kept. Transient faults were seen to be approximately twenty times more prevalent than hard failures [34]. Gross attributes of observed transients were recorded [49]. The data from C.mmp illustrated that the manifestation of transient faults was significantly different from the traditional permanent fault-models of stuck-at-l and stuck-at-0[1].

4. TREND ANALYSIS

During the summer of 1978, Dan Siewiorek worked at DEC on a project whose goals were to improve the reliability, availability, and maintainability of DEC systems. The VAX cluster concept was evolving and one offshoot of the summer's activity was a diagnosis and maintenance plan for VAX clusters. Some of the advocated concepts included increased numbers of user-mode diagnostics (up until that time, the majority of DEC diagnostics executed in either stand-alone mode or under a separate diagnostic supervisor), and on-line analysis of system event-logs to determine trends and to advise the operating system of desirable reconfigurations prior to catastrophic failure. Subsequently, three separate internal DEC groups started projects in the off-line analysis of system event-logs. The extra user-mode diagnostics were used to exercise suspected system components in order to gather more evidence in the system event-log.

Back at CMU, research continued in understanding system event-logs. The first step was to analyze the inter-arrival times of transient errors. Studies of these times indicated that the probability of crashes decreased with time, *i.e.*, a decreasing failure-rate Weibull function (and not an exponential distribution) was the best fit for the data.

[1] Examples included incorrect time-out indications, incorrect number of arguments pushed into or popped out of a slack, loss of interrupts, and incorrect selection of a register from a register file.

Because experimental data supported the decreasing failure-rate model, a natural question was "How far could you stray if you assumed an exponential function with a constant, instead of a decreasing, failure-rate?" The difference in reliability – as a function of time between an exponential and a Weibull function with the same parameters – was examined. Reliability differences of up to 0.25 were found; because the reliability function can range only between 0 and 1, this error is indeed substantial [8][31]. Another area of modeling involved the relationship between the system load and the system error-rate. Software was developed to analyze system event-log entries and to statistically sample load [6][7]. From those data, a model of the system was developed which predicted failures involving hardware and software errors. Starting from first principles,[2] a new model – the *cyclostationary* model – was derived; this model was an excellent match to the measured data, and also exhibited the property of a decreasing failure-rate. A physical test demonstrated that, for the cost of some modeling accuracy, the Weibull function was a reasonable approximation to the cyclostationary model, with the advantage of less mathematical complexity.

A natural extension of our work with system event-logs was to analyze log entries to discover trends [55]. From a theoretical perspective, the trend analysis of event-logs was based on the common observation that a hardware module exhibits a period of (potentially) increasing unreliability before final failure. Trend analysis developed a model of normal system behavior, and watched for a shift that signifies abnormal behavior. Trend-analysis techniques based on data from normal system workloads were better suited for pointing out failure mechanisms than specification-based diagnostics are. This was because normal system workloads tended to stress systems in ways different than specification-based diagnostic programs did. Moreover, trend analysis could learn the normal behavior of individual computer installations. By discovering these behaviors and trends, it was possible to predict certain hard failures (and even discern hardware/software design-errors) prior to the occurrence of catastrophic failure.

One trend-analysis method employed a data-grouping or clustering technique called *tupling* [54]. Tuples were clusters, or groups, of event-log entries exhibiting temporal or spatial patterns of features. The tuple approach was based on the observation that, because computers have mechanisms for both hardware and software detection of faults, single-error events could

[2] It was assumed the system has two modes of operation: user and kernel. The probability of being in kernel mode was a random event with measurable statistics. A second random event was the occurrence of a system fault. It was assumed that the system is much more susceptible to crashing if a fault occurred while in kernel mode than if a fault occurred in user mode. Thus, a doubly stochastic process was set up between the probability of being in kernel mode and the probability of the occurrence of a system fault.

propagate through a system, causing multiple entries in an event-log. Tupling formed clusters of machine events whose logical grouping was based primarily on proximity and time in hardware space. A single tuple could contain from one to several hundred event-log entries.

5. AUTOMATED MONITORING AND DIAGNOSIS

The research at CMU was slowly progressing toward the online diagnosis of trends in systems. The work gained critical mass with the addition of Professor Roy Maxion in the summer of 1984. Roy had built a system at Xerox [28] wherein a network of host workstations was automatically monitored and diagnosed by a diagnostic server that employed system event-logs in making diagnostic decisions.

There were three basic parts to the monitoring and diagnostic process, and correspondingly, three basic requirements for building a system to implement the process.

- **Gathering data/sensors**. Sensors must be provided to detect, store, and forward performance and error information (*e.g.*, event-log data) to a diagnostic server whose task it is to interpret the information.
- **Interpreting data/analyzers**. Once the system performance and error data have been accumulated, they must be interpreted or analyzed. This interpretation is done under the auspices of expert problem-solving modules embedded in the diagnostic server. The diagnostic server provides profiles of normal system behavior as well as hypotheses about behavior exceptions.
- **Confirming interpretation/effectors**. After the diagnostic server interprets the system performance and error information, a hypothesis must be confirmed (or denied) before issuing warning messages to users or operators. For this purpose, there must be effectors for stimulating the hypothesized condition in the system. Effectors can take the form of diagnostics or exercisers that are down-line loaded to the suspected portion of the system, and then run under special conditions to confirm the fault hypothesis or to narrow its range.

Several on-line monitoring and diagnosis projects have evolved. The first involved CMU's Andrew System, a distributed personal computing environment based upon a message-oriented operating system. The monitoring and diagnostic system for the Andrew File System, one of the first distributed, networked file systems ever developed, was a passive one because it did not actively communicate with network devices for the purposes of hypothesis confirmation or loading and running test-suites. Data collection was done with an Auto-Logging tool embedded in the operating-system kernel. When a fault was exercised, error events propagated from the lowest hardware error-detectors, through the microcode level, to the highest level of the operating system. Event-log analysis in a distributed computing environment exhibited some fundamental differences from the uniprocessor environment. The workstations, and indeed the diagnostic server, went through cycles of power-on and power-off. Yet, it was still possible to piece together a consistent view of system activity through a coordinated analysis of the individual workstations' views of the entire system. In addition, the utilization of workstation resources was highly individualized. Thus, the law of large numbers did not apply, and there was no "average" behavior, as there might have existed on a large, multi-user mainframe. The error dispersion index – the occurrence count of related error events – was developed to identify the presence of clustered error-events that might have caused permanent failure in a short period of time [23].

Data collected from the file servers over twenty-two months was analyzed; twenty-nine permanent faults were identified in the operator's log, and were shown to follow an exponential failure distribution. The error log was shown to contain events that were caused by a mixture of transient and intermittent faults. The failure distribution of the transient faults could be characterized by the Weibull function with a decreasing error-rate, whereas that of the intermittent faults exhibited an increasing error rate. The failure distribution of the entire error-log also followed a Weibull distribution with a decreasing error-rate. The parameters of the entire error-log distribution were a function of the relationship between transient and intermittent faults, as summarized by the ratios of the shape parameters and the relative frequency of error occurrences (Nt/Ni). Simulation was used to study the mixing of the two error functions and the sensitivity of the overall parameters to varying shape parameters and Nt/Ni ratios. The simulation result was subsequently used to verify the process that was used for isolating the intermittent faults from the transient faults in the actual file-server's error-log.

It was shown that twenty-five faults were typically required for statistical techniques to estimate the Weibull parameters satisfying the Chi-Square Goodness-of-Fit Test requirements. Studying the average number of faults before repair activities showed that users would not tolerate such a large number of errors and subsequent system crashes prior to an attempted repair. Hence, the *Dispersion Frame Technique (DFT)* [24] was developed from the observation that electromechanical devices experienced a period of deteriorating performance, usually in the form of increasing error-rate, prior to catastrophic failure. DFT provided a methodology to effectively extract error-log entries (which were caused by individual intermittent faults) and a set of rules that could be used for fault-prediction. Once error-log entries associated with individual fault sources had been extracted, rules that used at most five data points were employed to predict failure. Mathematical analysis of the rules indicated that they captured the same trends deduced by the statistical analysis, supporting their validity as fault-prediction tools. Five rules were derived from the data collected on the SPICE and ANDREW networks and, in the latter case, these rules were able to predict 93% of the physical failures with recorded error-log symptoms including both electromechanical and electronic devices. The predictions ranged from one to over seven hundred hours prior to actual repair actions, with a false-alarm rate of 17%. The automatic data analysis feature is currently on-line and automatically producing warnings for maintenance personnel.

A portable version of the DFT was implemented in *Dmod* [42], an on-line system dependability measurement and prediction module. The Dmod architecture defines an API (Application Program Interface) between system monitoring functions and an analysis module; a second API defines the interface between user programs and the analysis module. Dmod continuously interprets system data to generate estimates of current and projected resource capabilities. Dmod incurs an overhead of less than 0.1% CPU usage and less than 0.1% memory usage in Unix systems, with about 1% memory usage in Windows NT systems.

In an Ethernet network, a common type of failure is the temporary or extended loss of bandwidth, also categorized as "soft failures" in the literature. Although the causes of soft failures vary, to the network user, such failures are perceived as noticeably degraded or anomalous performance. A second project at CMU involved a system for the active, on-line diagnostic monitoring of Andrew, the CMU campus-computing network. The monitoring system is termed "active" because it has the ability to initiate tests to confirm or deny its own hypotheses of failing network nodes or devices. The CMU/Andrew network currently supports about 600 workstations, servers, and gateways/routers. The number of nodes on the network grew from 1000 in the fall of 1986 and to over 5000 by the end of 1987. The research project, as a whole, monitored eight network routers, as well as the Computer Science Department's entire Ethernet network, for traffic and diagnostic information. Examples of monitored traffic parameters included transmitted and received packets, network load, and network collisions. Examples of monitored diagnostic parameters were CRC errors, packet-alignment errors, router-resource errors due to buffer limitations, and router-overrun errors due to throughput limitations [26].

The project used anomaly detection [29][30] as a means to signal to performance degradations that are indicative of network faults. In addition, a paradigm called the *fault feature vector* was used to describe the anomalous conditions particular to a fault. This paradigm can be used to detect instances of specific faults by determining when anomalous conditions in the network match the feature vector description. In a two-year study of the CMU Computer Science Network, the fault feature vector mechanism proved to be effective in detecting failures and in discriminating between failure types. This mechanism was also effective at abstracting large amounts of network data to only those events that warranted operator attention; in this two-year study, over 32 million points were reduced to fewer than two hundred event-matches.

A third research project concerned fault-tolerance at the user-system interface. Roughly 30% of all system failures are due to human error [52]. Any diagnostic system eventually involves people, either to perform certain tests, or to make physical repairs or system adjustments. Rather than considering the human as a mere peripheral element, we consider the human to be a component of the overall system. This requires that care be taken to ensure fault-tolerance or fault-avoidance for human-related activities. A study was done to identify the cognitive sources of human error at the user-system interface [27]. A new interface architecture was developed to account for the cognitive limitations of users. An interface based on that architecture was built and user-tested against a pre-existing program that performed the same task, but with a traditional interface design. The interface based on the new architecture was effective in reducing user error to almost zero, and in facilitating a task speedup by a factor of four. Error reduction and task speedup are of particular importance in critical applications such as air traffic control and nuclear plant monitors.

6. TOOLS AND TECHNIQUES FOR RELIABILITY ANALYSIS

Even with the current interest in reliability, designers have had to use intuition and *ad-hoc* techniques to evaluate design trade-offs because there have been few, if any, reliability-oriented computer-aided design tools. If such a tool existed, it usually would be a stand-alone entity (*i.e.*, would not be integrated in the CAD database), and would require a reliability expert to operate it. Starting with the VAX-11/750 in 1977, through the design of the VAX 8600 and 8800, Dan Siewiorek was involved in the design and evaluation of the reliability, availability, and maintainability features of VAX CPU design and other major DEC projects. During that time, a design methodology [18] with supporting CAD tools for reliable design was developed. The experiences gained have been documented [44][45] in the literature and in a textbook.

7. EXPERIMENTAL EVALUATION OF FAULT-TOLERANT SYSTEMS

Once a fault-tolerant architecture has been designed, modeled, and built, there remains the question of whether the system meets its original specifications. Two fault-tolerant multiprocessors, FTMP and SIFT were developed and delivered to the Air-Lab facility at the NASA Langley Research Center. In 1979, a weekend workshop was held at the Research Triangle Institute to develop a suite of experiments for these fault-tolerant systems [36][37]. Starting in 1981, CMU performed a series of experiments to validate the fault-free and faulty performance of FTMP and SIFT. The methodology was developed initially from Cm*., and later transferred to FTMP. The same experiments were then conducted on SIFT to demonstrate that the methodology was robust, and that it transcended individual architectures [9][10][11][12][15].

Subsequently, the methodology has been used to assist the Federal Aviation Administration in the design of the next-generation air traffic control system. The methodology consists of a set of base-line measurements meant to characterize the performance of the system. A synthetic workload generator (SWG) was developed which allowed experimental parameters to vary at run-time. The synthetic workload generator drastically reduced the turnaround time for experimentation by eliminating the edit/compile/downlink-load portion of the experimental cycle. The avionic workload was developed, and the results of the baseline experiments were reproduced through appropriate settings of the synthetic workload generator's runtime parameters. The synthetic workload generator was modified to include software fault insertion.

8. RAISING THE LEVEL OF ABSTRACTION OF FAULTS

A number of simulators were also developed at CMU. The Instruction Set Processor (ISP) was extended to describe arbitrary digital systems from a functional level, down to and including, the gate level [1][2]. The ISP compiler and companion simulator are in use by over eighty government, university, and industrial organizations. The simulator has the ability to insert faults into memories, registers, and control logic. These faults can be permanent, intermittent, or transient. The ISP simulator and fault inserter has been used by Bendix to explore, at the gate level, the fault-tolerant properties of the SIFT computer.

Another topic of interest was generation of tests [46]. A program was written to generate functional diagnostics automatically from an ISP-like description of a digital system [21][22]. To calibrate the quality of the automatically generated functional diagnostics, a comparison was made between the manufacturer's diagnostics and the automatically generated diagnostics for a PDP-8. Using the ISP fault inserter, almost 1500 faults were inserted into the PDP-8 description, after which the respective diagnostics were simulated. The results showed that the automatically generated diagnostics had a higher detection percentage (95.57% *vs.* 85.5%), and required a factor-of-twenty fewer instruction executions.

The problem of assuring that the design goals were achieved required the observation and measurement of fault-behavior parameters under various input conditions. The measures included fault coverage, fault latency, and error recovery operation, while the input conditions included the applications' inputs and faults that were likely to occur during system operation. One means to characterize systems was fault injection, but the injection of internal faults was difficult due to the complexity and level of integration of contemporary VLSI implementations of the time. Other fault injection methods and models, which allowed observability and controllability of the system, regardless of system implementation, needed to be developed and validated based on the manifestation of low-level or actual faults. This research explored the effects of gate-level faults on system operation as a basis for fault-models at the program level.

A simulation model of the IBM RT PC was developed and injected with gate-level transient faults. Transient faults were selected because their behavior closely resembled actual faults occurring during system operation. To further the ties between normal operation and the simulation model, several applications or workloads were executed to observe and model the dependency on workload characteristics. Moreover, faults were injected at each cycle of the workload execution to imitate the temporary and random occurrence of transient faults.

A prediction model for fault manifestation was developed based on the instruction execution. The expected prediction coverage for the model was between 60% and 80% of all fault locations and instructions within the RT PC processor under study, thereby yielding a reduction of the fault space, by a factor up to eight, for fault-injection analysis. Prediction models of fault behavior at the system level, based on workload execution, showed that behavior was more dependent on workload structure rather than on the general instruction mix of the workload. This dependency could potentially allow applications to be modified to utilize specific error-detection mechanisms. Models for fault-injection through software were explored, with an analysis of the RT PC model showing that a subset of faults within all components was capable of being emulated by *software-implemented fault injection (SWIFI)*, with total coverage of faults in the data path.

Overall, the use of SWIFI, coupled with simulation and prediction modeling, showed a factor-of-eight reduction of effort for fault-injection studies.

In summary, a general fault-prediction model based on instruction execution was developed, along with a model of fault manifestations that were injectable through software. These models coupled to reduce the fault space required during fault-injection studies. Moreover, these results aided in understanding the effects of transient gate-level faults on program behavior and allowed for the further generation and validation of new fault-models, fault-injection methods, and error-detection mechanisms.

A new fault-model for processors, based on a register-transfer-level (RTL) description, was subsequently created. This model addressed the time, cost, and accuracy limitations imposed by existing fault-injection techniques at the time. It was designed to be used with existing software-implemented fault-injection (SWIFI) tools, but the error patterns that it generated were designed to be more representative of actual transient hardware faults than the ad-hoc patterns injected via SWIFI.

The fault-model was developed by abstracting the effects of low-level faults to the RTL level. This process attempted to be independent of processor implementation details while obtaining a high coverage and a low overhead. The coverage was the proportion of errors that were generated by gate-level faults that were successfully reproduced by the RTL fault-model. The overhead was the proportion of errors that were produced by the RTL fault-model, but not by gate-level faults. A prototype tool, *ASPHALT* [60], was developed to automate the process of generating the error patterns. As a paradigm for future fault-injection studies, the IBM RISC-Oriented Micro-Processor (ROMP) was used as a basis for several experiments. The experiments injected over 1.5 million faults and varied initial machine states, operand values, opcodes, and other parameters. Our results showed that ASPHALT was capable of producing an average coverage of over 97% with an average overhead of about 20%, as compared to a gate-level model of the ROMP. In addition, ASPHALT generated these errors over 500 times faster than the gate-level model. If additional coverage was required, methods were proposed to use a combination of RTL and gate-level simulations. If less coverage was allowed, the RTL fault-model could be abbreviated, reducing overhead further.

Traditional functional test methods were inadequate for pipelined computer implementations. We studied a design error-log, with the resulting conclusion that errors associated with pipelining were not negligible. A new methodology was developed based upon a systematic approach to generate functional test programs for pipelined computer implementations. Using information about the pipelined implementation and the target computer architecture definitions, this new methodology generated *pipeline functional test (PFT)* programs specifically designed to detect errors associated with pipeline design. These PFT programs were in machine assembly language form, and could be executed by the pipelined implementation.

Our research progressed to develop an instruction execution trace model for pipelined implementations. This model could determine the correctness of the concurrently executed instructions in a pipelined implementation. The basis for PFT program generation, the dependency graph, was a three-stage pipelined implementation of a von Neumann style computer architecture that was used to illustrate how to construct a dependency graph. A quantitative analysis approach for the number of dependency arcs exercised by a given instruction stream was presented. The determination of the total number of dependency arcs for a dependency graph was performed both for the example computer architecture and a three-stage pipelined implementation. Techniques were investigated to reduce the complexity of the analysis. A methodology for generating PFT programs, consisting of PFT modules, from the dependency graph for a pipelined computer implementation was developed. Each PFT module exercised some dependency arc in the dependency graph and automatically checked the correctness of the execution.

Application of the PFT methodology to two different pipelined implementations of a standard computer architecture, the MIL-STD-1750A, was described. Automatic tools, using an instruction database that conveyed computer architecture information, were developed to generate the PFT programs.

The dependency-arc coverage analysis was applied to the standard architectural verification program of the MIL-STD-1750A architecture and the PFT programs. The results showed that the PFT programs covered more than 60% of all dependency arcs for the two pipelined implementations. Coverage of the standard architectural verification program was less than 1% for both implementations. Furthermore, the total length of the PFT programs was about half that of the standard architectural verification program. Finally, the PFT reported any violation of the dependency arc automatically, while the standard architectural verification program was not designed to check specifically for dependency violations. Actual design errors uncovered by the PFT programs have been described.

Research on automatic diagnosis adopted one of two philosophies. The engineering school of thought developed practical diagnostic systems that are usually specific to a device. The diagnostic theory school strived to understand the concept of diagnosis by developing general engines that diagnosed classes of simple devices.

We developed the design of practical mechanisms to diagnose a class of complex devices. The theory work developed a vocabulary of general mechanisms. This is extended to *x-diagnosis*. The engineering school determined that x-diagnosis, if feasible, would be useful for the test and repair of circuit boards in computer manufacturing. A number of issues needed to be addressed. The first difficulty was modeling – a device representation needed to be developed to reflect the high generality and high complexity of x-diagnosis. For example, the representation needed to account for dynamic behavior and feedback. To be practical, device models had to be acquired efficiently. It was shown that circuit simulation models developed by designers could be automatically transformed to device models that were useful for diagnosis.

Next, a task representation had to be developed for diagnosis. The questions to be answered included: In the face of dynamic behavior, feedback and incomplete device-models how should fault localization be done? For instance, fault-localization techniques were usually based on a fault-model. If a fault occurred that was outside this class, the technique would err. The number of different faults that a processor board could manifest was very large, making fault modeling a serious issue. Optimization was another concern. Traditionally, there had been much interest in minimizing the cost of diagnostic procedures. Was this practical for x-diagnosis? Finally, fault localization began with a known symptom, *i.e.*, a measurement at a point that was different from its expected value. For complex devices, this might not be a valid assumption. More likely was the discovery of symptoms that aggregate information about many points on the device. For example, test programs that exercised circuit boards reported error messages that aggregated information about the signal values and presented it in a concise form. How should we perform diagnosis when dealing with aggregate symptoms? Diagnostic techniques that addressed these issues were presented. The new results were used to sustain several theses:

1. Model-based diagnosis - which had been successfully used for gate-level circuits - could be scaled up to system-level circuits.
2. X-diagnosis for computer manufacturing was feasible. Specifically, the automation of test program execution - a methodology to test circuits in which diagnosis is currently done manually - was feasible.
3. A framework for researching and building x-diagnostic systems was presented.

Besides the theoretical development, the results were validated by an implementation that diagnosed digital circuits whose Verilog simulation models had 10-600 Kbytes of information. These circuits included likenesses of the VAX 8800 datapath, an Intel 386-based workstation board, *etc.* Furthermore, the techniques were shown to be applicable to devices other than digital circuits, provided that they were diagnosed in a manufacturing environment.

9. ROBUSTNESS TESTING

Benchmarks exist for performance measuring, software robustness testing, and security probing. Benchmarks are one way of evaluating COTS (Commercial Off The Shelf) components as well as monitoring network end-to-end capabilities. Synthetic workloads can also be used to inject workload during exercises to see how doctrines work when network resources are strained.

COTS (Commercial Off The Shelf) and legacy software components may be used in a system design in order to reduce development time and cost. However, using these components may result in a less dependable mission-critical system because of problems with exception handling. COTS software is typically tested only for correct functionality, not for graceful handling of exceptions, yet some studies indicate that more than half of software defects and system failures may be attributed to problems with exception handling. Even mission-critical legacy software may not be robust to exceptions that were not expected to occur in the original application (this was a primary cause of the loss of the Ariane 5 rocket initial flight in June 1996).

Because a primary objective of using COTS or legacy software is cost savings, any method of improving robustness must be automated to be cost-effective. Furthermore, machine-parseable software specifications are unlikely to be available in most cases, and for COTS software, it is possible that source code will be unavailable as well. While it can be hoped that a COTS vendor will fix any bugs reported by users, the small number of copies purchased by a defense developer might not grant enough leverage to ensure that this is the case. Finally, new versions of COTS software may be continually released, causing quick obsolescence of any manually created software modifications.

The success of many products depends on the robustness of not only the product software, but also operating systems and third party component libraries. But, until the inception of *Ballista* [13], there was no way to quantitatively measure robustness. Ballista provided a simple, repeatable way to directly measure software robustness without requiring source code or behavioral specifications. As a result, product developers could use robustness metrics to compare off-the-shelf software components, and component developers could measure their effectiveness at exception handling.

The Ballista automated robustness testing methodology characterizes the exception handling effectiveness of software modules. For example, Ballista testing can find ways to make operating systems crash in response to exceptional parameters used for system calls, and can find ways to make other software packages suffer abnormal termination instead of gracefully returning error indications. The Ballista testing server enables users to test the robustness of their own and third-party software via the Internet. Ballista is a "black box" software-testing tool, and works well on testing the APIs of COTS software.

When a software module is tested with many different inputs, the response of that module typically falls into a number of "response regions". For example, for many inputs the module will work correctly, but for some other related input sets it may crash or hang. In one set of experiments, Ballista results [20] for fifteen operating systems tested indicated that the large majority of robustness failures were caused by single parameter values, independent of other parameter values. This means that a hardening wrapper could test just one parameter value, instead of many combinations of parameters, and still achieve significant hardening, yielding significant performance benefits. As an example, checking for null pointers in an operating system interface could reduce the measured robustness failure-rate by a third.

By associating test cases with data types rather than with module functions, specific test cases could be created and applied to newly submitted modules with minimal effort. For example, once test cases for a "pointer" data type were created, re-using the object-oriented pointer test case library could test any module that takes a pointer as an input. The net result was that the amount of work required to create test cases was sub-linear with the number of functions being tested. For example, 233 operating system functions were successfully tested with only 20 sets of test cases (one set of approximately 10 tests for each of the 20 data types required).

Each of the fifteen different operating systems' respective robustness was measured by automatically testing up to 233 POSIX functions and system calls with exceptional parameter values. The work identified repeatable ways to crash operating systems with a single call, ways to cause task hangs within OS code, ways to cause task core dumps within OS code, failures to implement defined POSIX functionality for exceptional conditions, and false indications of successful completion in response to exceptional input parameter values. Overall, only 55% to 76% of tests performed were handled robustly, depending on the operating system being tested.

Hardening can be accomplished by first probing a software module for responses to exceptional inputs that cause "crashes" or "hangs". When these robustness bugs have been identified, a software wrapper can be automatically created to filter out dangerous inputs, thus hardening the software module.

Many classifications of attacks have been tendered, often in taxonomic form. A common basis of these taxonomies is that they have been framed from the perspective of an attacker – they organize attacks with respect to the attacker's goals, such as privilege elevation from user to root (from the well known Lincoln taxonomy). Taxonomies based on goals are attack-centric; those based on defender goals are defense-centric. Defenders need a way of determining whether or not their detectors will detect a given attack. It is suggested that a defense-centric taxonomy would suit this role more effectively than an attack-centric taxonomy. Research at CMU has led to a new, defense-centric attack taxonomy [19], based on the way that attacks manifest as anomalies in monitored sensor data. Unique manifestations, drawn from 25 attacks, were used to organize the taxonomy, which was validated through exposure to an intrusion-detection system, confirming attack detectability. The taxonomy's predictive utility was compared against that of a well-known extant attack-centric taxonomy. The defense-centric taxonomy was shown to be a more effective predictor of a detector's ability to detect specific attacks, hence informing a defender that a given detector is competent against an entire class of attacks.

10. FAULT-TOLERANCE FOR DISTRIBUTED SYSTEMS

The research on dependability gained additional emphasis in distributed fault-tolerance with the addition of Professor Priya Narasimhan in the fall of 2001. Priya had been instrumental in helping to establish an industrial standard for dependability, *i.e.*, the Fault-Tolerant CORBA standard [38], based on her research [35] on the development of the Eternal and Immune systems that aimed to provide transparent fault-tolerance and survivability, respectively, to middleware applications. The new research at CMU focused on integrating other properties, such as real-time, into fault-tolerant systems, and on examining the trade-offs in such a composition.

The *MEAD* system, born out of lessons learned and experiences [16] with other distributed fault-tolerant systems, focuses on proactive (rather than the traditionally reactive) fault-tolerance [39], which examines pre-fault symptoms and trend analysis in distributed systems, in order to compensate for faults before they happen. Proactive fault-tolerance yields reduced jitter in the presence of certain kinds of faults, and also mitigates the adverse impact of faults in a real-time distributed system. Other novel aspects, currently being emphasized as a part of this research effort, include: (i) the resource-aware trade-offs between real-time and fault-tolerance, (ii) sanitizing various kinds of nondeterminism and heterogeneity in replicated systems, (iii) mode-driven fault-tolerance for mission-critical applications, and (iv) development-time and run-time advice on the appropriate configuration and settings for the parameters (*e.g.*, number of replicas, checkpointing frequency, fault-detection frequency) that affect the fault-tolerance of applications. The approach aims to involve the use of machine learning techniques and feedback in distributed fault-tolerant systems in order to improve (and adapt) the response of the systems and their hosted applications to resource changes, faults and other dynamic behavior.

11. CONCLUSION

Fault-tolerant computing research at CMU spans researchers and students in both the Computer Science Department and the Department of Electrical and Computer Engineering. The three axes of integration that characterize the CMU research philosophy are:

- **Integration of Theory and Practice.** CMU research has had a strong and balanced emphasis on both the development of theoretical concepts and the application of these concepts to practical systems. Experimental approaches have been a key element in our fault-tolerance research. Currently, there is a plan to establish a laboratory for the study of machine and human diagnosis of complex systems from both theoretical and experimental perspectives. The main objective of the laboratory is the exploration, definition, and implementation of advanced systems for intelligent diagnostic problem solving.
- **Integration of Hardware and Software**. Traditional fault-tolerant techniques have been directed primarily at hardware systems. As systems become more complex and software engineering costs increase, an approach involving synergistic integration of hardware and software techniques will be essential. Most traditional techniques can be labeled as system/structure-based. One direction of our future research is algorithm-based/behavior-based fault-tolerance.
- **Integration of Space/Defense and Commercial.** While most early research in reliable systems was geared for space and defense applications, in recent years, we have seen fault-tolerance concepts being applied in many commercial applications. We believe that research in both sectors can – and should be – mutually benefiting. There has been substantial research effort in fault-tolerant computing at CMU, and there is strong indication that this research area will continue to grow in both scope and visibility at Carnegie Mellon University.

ACKNOWLEDGEMENTS

The authors would like to acknowledge the graduate students and the multiple funding sources that, through the years, have made this research possible. These funding sources include BMD, DARPA, DEC, IBM, NASA, NSF, ONR, and Xerox. We also thank Laura Forsyth for her help in preparing this paper.

REFERENCES

[1] Barbacci, M., Instruction Set Processor Specifications (ISPS): The notation and its application. In *IEEE Transactions on Computers*, vol. 30, no. 1, pp. 24-40, January 1981.

[2] Barbacci, M., Barnes, G., Cattell, R. and Siewiorek, D. P., The ISPS computer description language, Carnegie Mellon University, Department of Computer Science Technical Report, 1978.

[3] Bell, C. G., Chen, R. C., Fuller, S. H., Grason, J., Rege, S. and Siewiorek, D. P., The architecture and applications of computer modules: A set of components for digital systems design, In *Proceedings of the COMPCON Conference*, pp. 177-180, San Francisco, CA, February 1973.

[4] Bell, C. G. and Freeman, P., C.ai – a computer architecture of AI research, In *Fall Joint Computer Conference Proceedings*, December 1972.

[5] Bhandarkar, D.P., *Analytic Models for Memory Interference in Multiprocess Computer Systems*, PhD thesis, Carnegie Mellon University, Pittsburgh, Pennsylvania, September, 1972.

[6] Castillo, X., *A Compatible Hardware/Software Reliability Prediction Model*, PhD thesis, Carnegie Mellon University, July 1981, Also Department of Computer Science Technical Report.

[7] Castillo, X. and Siewiorek, D. P., A workload dependent software reliability prediction model, In *International Fault Tolerant Computing Symposium*, pp. 279-286, June 1982.

[8] Castillo, X., McConnel, S. R. and Siewiorek, D. P., Derivation and calibration of a transient error reliability model, *IEEE Transactions on Computers*, vol. 31, no. 7, pp. 658-671, July 1982.

[9] Clune, F., Segall Z. and Siewiorek, D. P., Validation of fault-free behavior of a reliable multiprocessor system, FTMP: A case study, In *International Conference on Automation and Computer Control*, San Diego, CA, June 6-8, 1984,

[10] Clune, E., Segall, Z., and Siewiorek, D. P., Fault-free behavior of reliable multiprocessor systems: FTMP experiments in AIR-LAB, NASA Contractor Report 177967, Grant NAG 1-190, Carnegie Mellon University, August 1985.

[11] Czeck, E. W., Feather, F. E., Grizzaffi, A. M., Finelli, G. M., Segall, Z. and Siewiorek, D. P., Fault-free performance validation of avionic multiprocessors, In *Digital Avionic Systems Conference*, October 1986, Dallas, Texas.

[12] Czeck, E. W., Siewiorek, D. P. and Segall, Z., Validation of a fault-tolerant multiprocessor: Baseline and synthetic workload measurements, Technical Report CMU-CS-85-177, Carnegie Mellon University, November 1985.

[13] DeVale, J., Koopman, P. J. and Guttendorf, D., The Ballista software robustness testing service, In *Testing Computer Software Conference*, June 1999.

[14] Elkind, S. and Siewiorek, D. P., Reliability and performance of error-correcting memory and register arrays, In *IEEE Transactions on Computers*, vol. 29, no. 10, pp. 920-927, October 1980.

[15] Feather, F., Siewiorek, D. P. and Segall, Z., Validation of a fault-tolerant multiprocessor: Baseline experiments and workload implementation, Technical Report CMU-CS-85-145, Carnegie Mellon University, July 1985.

[16] Felber, P. and Narasimhan, P., Experiences, strategies and challenges in building fault-tolerant CORBA systems, In *IEEE Transactions on Computers*, vol. 53, no. 5, pp. 497-511, May 2004.

[17] Gehringer, E. F., Siewiorek, D. P. and Segall, Z., *Parallel Processing: The Cm*. Experience*, Digital Press, Bedford MA, 1987.

[18] Guise, D., Siewiorek, D. P. and Birmingham, W. P., Demeter: A design methodology and environment, In *IEEE International Conference on Computer Design/VLSI in Computers*, October 1983.

[19] Killourhy, K. S., Maxion, R. A. and Tan, K. M. C., A defense-centric taxonomy based on attack manifestations, In *International Conference on Dependable Systems & Networks*, Florence, Italy, June-July 2004.

[20] Koopman, P. J. and DeVale, J., Comparing the robustness of POSIX operating systems, In *International Conference on Dependable Systems & Networks*, Madison, WI, June 1999, pp. 30-37.

[21] Lai, K. W, *Functional Testing of Digital Systems*, PhD thesis, Carnegie Mellon University, Department of Computer Science, 1981.

[22] Lai, K. W. and Siewiorek, D. P., Functional testing of digital systems, In *Design Automation Conference*, Miami Beach, FL, June 1983.

[23] Lin, T.-T. Y. and Siewiorek, D. P., Architectural issues for on-line diagnostics in a distributed environment, In *IEEE International Conference on Computer Design*, Port Chester, NY, October 1986.

[24] Lin, T.-T. Y. and Siewiorek, D. P., Error log analysis statistical modeling and heuristic trend analysis, *IEEE Transactions on Reliability*, vol.39, no.4, p.419-32, October 1990.

[25] Mashburn, H. H., The C.mmp/Hydra project: An architectural overview, In Siewiorek. D. P., Bell, C. G. and Newell, A., *Computer Structures: Principles and Examples*, pp. 350-370, McGraw-Hill. New York 1982.

[26] Maxion, R. A., Distributed diagnostic performance reporting and analysis. In *IEEE International Conference on Computer Design*. Port Chester NY, October 1986.

[27] Maxion, R. A., Toward fault-tolerant user interfaces, In *IFAC International Conference on Achieving Safe Real-Time Computing Systems (SAFECOMP-86)*, Sarlat, France, October 1986.

[28] Maxion, R. A., Human and machine diagnosis of computer hardware faults. *IEEE Computer Society Workshop on Reliability of Local Area Networks*, South Padre Island, Texas, February 1982.

[29] Maxion, Roy A. and Tan, K. M. C., Anomaly detection in embedded systems, *IEEE Transactions on Computers*, vol. 51, no. 2, pp. 108-120, February 2002.

[30] Maxion, Roy A. and Tan, K. M. C., Benchmarking anomaly-based detection systems." In *International Conference on Dependable Systems and Networks*, pp. 623-630, New York, NY, June 2000.

[31] McConnel, S.R., *Analysis and Modeling of Transient Errors in Digital Computers*, PhD thesis, Carnegie Mellon University, Department of Electrical Engineering, June 1981, also Department of Computer Science Technical Report.

[32] McConnel S.R. and Siewiorek, D. P., The CMU voter chip, Technical Report, Carnegie Mellon University, Department of Computer Science, 1980.

[33] McConnel. S.R. and Siewiorek, D. P., Synchronization and voting. In *IEEE Transactions on Computers*, vol. 30, no. 2, pp.161-164, February 1981.

[34] McConnel. S.R., Siewiorek D. P. and Tsao, M. M., Transient error data analysis, Technical Report, Carnegie Mellon University. Department of Computer Science. May 1979.

[35] Narasimhan, P., *Transparent Fault-Tolerance for CORBA*, PhD thesis, Department of Electrical and Computer Engineering, University of California, Santa Barbara, December 1999.

[36] NASA-Langley Research Center, *Validation Methods for Fault-Tolerant Avionics and Control Systems - Working Group Meeting I*, NASA Conference Publication 2114, Research Triangle Institute, 1979.

[37] NASA-Langley Research Center, *Validation Methods for Fault-Tolerant Avionics and Control Systems - Working Group Meeting 11*, NASA Conference Publication 2130, Research Triangle Institute, 1979.

[38] Object Management Group, *Fault-Tolerant CORBA Standard (Final Adopted Specification)*, OMG Technical Committee Document formal/01-12-29, December 2001.

[39] Pertet, S. and Narasimhan, P., Proactive recovery for distributed CORBA applications, *IEEE Conference on Dependable Systems and Networks*, Florence, Italy, June 2004.

[40] Pierce, W.H., Adaptive vote-takers improve the use of redundancy, In Wilcox R.H. and W.C. Mann, *Redundancy Techniques for Computing Systems*. pp. 229-250, Spartan Books, Washington. D.C. 1962.

[41] Pierce, W.H., *Failure Tolerant Design*, Academic Press, New York 1965.

[42] Shi, Y., A portable, self hosting system dependability measurement and prediction module, Electrical and Computer Engineering Department, Carnegie Mellon University.

[43] Shombert. L., *The C.vmp Statistics Board Experiment*, Master's thesis, Carnegie Mellon University, Department of Electrical Engineering, 1981.

[44] Siewiorek, D.P., Architecture of fault-tolerant computers, In *IEEE Computer*, vol. 17, no. 8, pp. 9-18, August 1984.

[45] Siewiorek, D. P., Architecture of fault-tolerant computers, In D.K. Pradhan, *Fault-Tolerant Computing: Theory and Techniques*, Vol. II, pp. 417-466, Prentice-Hall, Englewood Cliffs, N.J., 1986.

[46] Siewiorek, D.P. and Lai, K. W., Testing of digital systems, In *Proceedings of the IEEE*, pp. 1321-1333, October 1981.

[47] Siewiorek, D. P. and McConnel, S. R., C.vmp: The implementation, performance, and reliability of a fault- tolerant multiprocessor, In *Third US-Japan Computer Conference*, October 1978.

[48] Siewiorek, D.P. and Swarz, R. S., *The Theory and Practice of Reliable System Design*, Digital Press, Bedford MA, 1982.

[49] Siewiorek, D. P., Kini, V., Mashburn, H., McConnel, S. and Tsao, M., A case study of C.mmp, Cm*, and C.vmp, Part I: Experiences with fault tolerance in multiprocessor systems, In *Proceedings of the IEEE*, vol. 66, no. 10, pp. 1178-1199, October 1978.

[50] Siewiorek, D. P., Kini, V., Mashburn, H. and Joobbani, R., A case study of C.mmp, Cm*, and C.vmp, Part II: Predicting and calibrating reliability of multiprocessor systems, In *Proceedings of the IEEE*, vol. 66, no. 10, pp. 1200-1220, October 1978.

[51] Siewiorek, D. P., Canepa, M. and Clark, S., C.vmp: The architecture and implementation of a fault-tolerant multiprocessor, In *International Symposium on Fault-Tolerant Computing*, Los Angeles CA, pp. 37-43, June 1977.

[52] Swan, R. J., Fuller, S. H., Siewiorek, D. P., Cm*: A modular, multi-microprocessor. In *AFIPS: Proceedings of the National Computer Conference*, pp. 637-644, June 1977.

[53] Toy, W. N., Fault-tolerant design of local ESS processors, In *Proceedings of the IEEE*, vol. 66, no. 10, pp. 1126-1145, October 1978.

[54] Tsao, M.M., *Transient Error and Fault Prediction*, PhD thesis, Carnegie Mellon University, Department of Electrical Engineering, January 1981.

[55] Tsao, M. M. and Siewiorek, D. P., Trend analysis on system error files, In *International Fault Tolerant Computing Symposium*, pp. 116-119, June 1983, Milan, Italy.

[56] U.S. Department of Defense, *Military Standardization Handbook: Reliability Prediction of Electronic Equipment*, MIL-STD-HDBK-217B, Notice 1, 1976.

[57] Wilcox, R.C. and W.C. Mann, *Redundancy Techniques for Computer Systems*, Spartan Books, Washington, D.C., 1962,

[58] Wulf, W.A. and Bell, C.G., C.mmp: A multi-mini-processor, In *AFIPS Conference*, vol. 41, pp. 765-777, Montvale, NJ, 1972.

[59] Wulf, W.A., Levin, R. and Harbison, S., *Hydra/C.mmp: An Experimental Computer System*, McGraw-Hill. New York, New York, 1980.

[60] Yount, C. and Siewiorek, D. P., The automatic generation of instruction-level error manifestations of hardware faults, In *IEEE Transactions on Computers*, vol. 45, no. 8, pp. 881-891, August 1996.

SYSTEMS APPROACH TO COMPUTING DEPENDABILITY IN AND OUT OF HITACHI

Concept, Applications and Perspective

Hirokazu Ihara* and Motohisa Funabashi**

** Hiro Systems Laboratory, ihara@coral.ocn.ne.jp*

*** Systems Development Laboratory, Hitachi, Ltd., funa@sdl.hitachi.co.jp*

Abstract: Authors and their colleagues have been contributing to dependable computing for the wide lines of Hitachi products since 1960. Fault-tolerance concept was not permitted under the company motto that no fault by fault-avoidance technology was one of engineering achievements. Suppose the bullet train system "Shinkansen" would have a failure, no need to explain social damage. Nowadays dependability concept seems accepted but failures are never permitted to keep our society safe and comfortable. In order to meet it, we took systems architecture and intelligence approaches chasing property of creatures from architectural and intellectual viewpoints though we never gave up fault-avoidance. Autonomous Decentralization Concept (ADC) was extracted in late 1970s. The basic principle is that the system state with no faulty part is only one of numerous states. Intelligent behavior is necessary to play autonomy and decentralization. We started AI technology around 1980. Hitachi Group has applied autonomous decentralization systems technology and AI technology to its computing systems and enjoyed their business with good reputation. The authors present their R&D activities namely at Systems Development Laboratory and practices in and out of the group. Finely future R&D horizon for dependable information systems is presented as the extension of the past and the present R&D.

Key words: fault-tolerance, dependability, autonomous decentralization, artificial intelligence, assurance

1. INTRODUCTION

Hitachi, Ltd. has had two major computer groups, that is, the computer systems business group which corresponds to business process and the control systems business group which corresponds to control process. The former supplies the computer systems itself and, for the latter group, the computer system is only the attachments of industrial plants or apparatuses. The critical items of the computer control area compared to other as follows,

(a) The faults of the control equipments or apparatuses cause large damage or disaster to the society or the business while they control on line and in real-time. They are mission-critical real-time systems with long MTBF. Thus, the reliability of the control systems is prior to its performance and cost.

(b) The environment conditions such as ambient temperature, humidity, vibration, dust, etc. are very rigorous compared to those in normal environment.

(c) The control functions are triggered by event-driven or data-driven means from the machines of processes. Therefore response time and processing time have to be within the limitation even if many tasks occurred at once. They can be the time-critical systems. In addition, both on-line and offline tasks exist together under one OS.

(d) Manufacturers have to deliver the systems that are designed, implemented, tested, installed, and validated according to the approved specifications by the buyer. This business model may be designated as, so-called, those of the turnkey or the solution.

(e) The systems used periodically to adapt their functions by changing demands and to metamorphose their hardware and software. Even various tests should be done without any interruption while the systems are working.

Therefore, we started our development on our own terms in 1960 and have developed many types of the computer control systems and delivered them to national infrastructure industries from our independent systems' approach standpoint.

Systems Development Laboratory of Hitachi, Ltd. has been taking the leadership in R&D of both business and control computer systems since its establishment in 1973. Here, we will namely describe on R&D activities with practical reality and its surrounding engineering of system dependability from its beginning and the coming perspectives regarding dependability. Dr. Ihara of System Development Laboratory had first acquaintance with Prof. Avižienis at UCLA in 1978. IFIP WG 10.4 was started after the working conference in 1979 in London [Ih 79]. At that time, Japanese had not accepted fault-tolerance approach since they had chased fault-avoidance in component level and get good product reputation as its result. Furthermore, the dependability concept published by the Working Group in 1992 took long time for Japanese industry, as well academia, to take in instead of reliability, until late 1990s [La 85] [La. 92].

2. FOOTPRINTS OF HITACHI'S CONTRIBUTIONS TO DEPENDABLE COMPUTING

We have more than 40 years of research and development activity chasing dependable computing and supplied dependable systems to the market with high reputation.

2.1 Before 1970s

The beginning of 1960s was when transistor as well as digital computers was rapidly introduced into business. Automation and systems engineering were the key words as advanced business. Several introduction of computer to real-time control were attempted in leading industries, such as iron and steel making process, electricity generation, electricity dispatching, chemical process, manufacturing automation, and so on. The digital computer control development at Hitachi started with development of the data logger from the beginning of 1960s after analog control apparatuses widely in industry. The reliability of the computer could not afford to industrial requirements, such as its ambient temperature, humidity, vibration, and shock as well as to its cost.

Semi-conductor as logics was in the rapid change to LSI. Hitachi developed three mini-computer systems named HIDIC according to the advent and applied them as infant systems to heavy industries, oxygen steel furnaces, slab mills, blast furnaces, thermal turbines, hot strip mills, chemical plants, electric dispatches, subway train dispatches, and so on. They realized fairly accepted reliability by fault avoidance technologies, for examples, selection of component, less components and connections, reduction of rate, and accelerated aging. However the reliability of computer was insufficient for critical applications. The system was single and stand-alone with centralized architecture with limited functions because of balance of hardware cost and reliability. It is gradually recognized that fault-avoidance could never achieve 100% operation.

2.2 In 1970s

In 1970s, mini-computer systems were widely introduced in to the market. Mainstream of computer introduction to industry was still single architecture systems with manual back-up. However customers were gradually apt to accept redundant system architecture for critical system management and control. Software development cost emerged as one of constraints. The requirements of limited functions were strictly decided and the complete verification was claimed before commercial operations although high-level languages and software engineering were presented.

As one of social systems, we succeeded in commercial operation of the train dispatching systems of Sapporo city subway in 1971, which was the first try as life-critical systems in Japan.

Computer Aided Traffic Control systems (COMTRAC) for Shinkansen have opened the leading system technology in critical dependable computing by Hitachi and Japanese National Railways. Fig.1 shows the Shinkansen network now in operation over Japan islands. The first system was for the Tokaido Line between Tokyo and Okayama in 1972 in operation. The second was for the Sanyo Line extended from Okayama to Hakata in Kyushu Island in 1975 [IhFu 78]. In 1983, the Tohoku Line was inaugurated from Tokyo to Morioka in northern part of Main Island and branched off at Takasaki toward Niigata in 1985. In northern Japan, the Shinkansen Lines were branched at Fukushima to Yamagata in 1992 and at Morioka to Akita, at Takasaki to Nagano in 1997, at Yamagata to Shinjyo in 1999, at Morioka to Hachinohe in 2002. The Kyushu Line has opened between Kumamoto and Kagoshima in 2004.

Figure 1. Extension of Shinkansen

One example of the functional distributed systems was the image data processing systems for NASDA with cooperative development with TRW Inc., USA. It arranged the remote sensing data sent down every 90 minutes all day from satellites such as LANDSAT or EOS and corrected its geometric and radiometric distortions within next 90 minutes. The systems consisted of two subsystems, an image processing and an image generation connected in line by the high density digital tape. The image generation system consisted of a HIDIC and an array processor with mass storage. The array computer had a two-stage pipeline floating computing architecture, which devoted to image correction by FFT, IFFT and re-sampling. The system was not on-line but in-line in time-critical. This image processing technology was applied to X-CT and MRI in medicine later on.

2.3 In 1980s

In 1980s, the mini-computer steeply improved its size, number of component, performance, and cost in addition to reliability. The rapid advent of minicomputers made the systems widely available to be distributed as well as multiplex. The same and/or different functions were run respectively in assigned processors. The property of centralized and distributed architecture alike was namely fit to the needs from system manufactures. They could choose and connect their subsystems to meet their variety of product lines. The rigid communication protocol was standardized for local and wide area networks. The hierarchical and functional distributed architectures were widely applied to various industries. Hitachi delivered their unique architecture of HIDIC with global memory, task synchronization, and buss control for the dual or duplex architecture systems to life critical applications [Ka78].

Japanese economy rocketed up and the increasing mass production needed computerized lines. The larger and more complicated the system grew, the more difficult it became to construct and to isolate its faulty portions, which made service undependable and partially shut down. Sometimes the fault caused the domino effect. In addition, expandability and extensibility during on-line operation became necessary instead of replacement. The information systems of multi-national enterprises over the world introduced non-stop computer architecture. Advanced HIDIC were introduced to the transaction processing for its non-stop property and extensibility.

In order to break through these difficulties, we proposed new idea "Autonomous Decentralization Concept (ADC)" analogous to bio-structure. The first introduction as Autonomous Decentralized Systems (ADS) was the subway control mid 1980s when subways or new transportation systems were appearing in many major cities. Thereafter almost all subway control systems as well as suburban railways adopted ADS in addition to industrial applications [MiMo 84] [MoMi 84]. We proposed new measurement index, "Functionability" that shows the probability of functions working in real time [MoIh 82] [OrKa 84] [OrMo 92] [KeBe 01]. That is to say, it is a product of summation of the working durations of invoked tasks divided by their summarized mission time.

Multiplex architecture consisted of three off-the-shelf M-68000 bare microchips, produced by Hitachi, with stepwise-negotiating-voting (SNV) method was developed for aerospace [KaMa 89]. It was launched in January 1990 as the communication system on MUSES (HITEN) satellite to play moon-swing-by and attained healthy operation over three mission years and eight swing-bys. It was furnished the spatiotemporal design diversity and the autonomous decentralized architecture both in hardware and software. Bare chips, a BPU, memories, controllers were mounted on a printed multilayer ceramic plate, 3 x 3 x 0.5 inches in size, three of which contained in anti-radiation metal. During its mission time, the system worked successfully despite 665 soft errors in three CMOS 64MB memories by cosmic rays.

We started research of artificial intelligence, knowledge engineering and fuzzy logics prior to national project "Fifth Generation Project" in 1980. Knowledge engineering was practically applied to nuclear power plant control, CMOS memory fabrication process and project management as the trials within the company. Fuzzy logics were applied to operation of the trains of Sendai municipal subway, which was the first commercial success in the world [YaMi 83]. Neural network technology was also in the scope of our research. It was applied to the crown control of cold strip rolling mills.

2.4 In 1990s

In early 1990, Japanese society turned to new era due to collapse of bubble economy and rapid inclination to the aging and information society as well as world wide environmental conservation. There came big innovational wave of business models by the computer networks and the personal computer. People's needs diversified for their favorites, by which the product lines were encountered multiple–type and small lots instead of mass production. In addition, there occurred many disasters as well as failures by human-made faults in business, industrial, social and aerospace area, where dependability of human intelligence and behavior in computerized environment was taken up for discussion. User engineering was one solution to avoid human error and to develop huge systems including human being, either professional or nonprofessional.

Production cost threat forced for us to use PC as real-time control though the system nucleus still consisted of our original HIDIC. Programmable logic controllers (PLC) also controlled widely various machineries in production lines through LAN. We internationally proposed the interface of LAN by ADC to prevent domino effect and maintain assurance in operation, and legislated in 1996 by Open DeviceNet Association (OVDA) [ToSh 99]. All the efforts were integrated into an ADS product series named NX.

According to diffusion of Internet services, application of ADC was extended to the Internet service systems named Autonomous Decentralized Service Systems (ADSS). The essence of ADSS was an abstract model of Internet services comprising with three players; service requesters that request and use services, service providers that provide services, and service mediators that mediate services among requesters and providers. In ADSS, service mediators played a role of the data field in ADS with intelligent brokerage functions that permit frequent joining and leaving of the system participants. The model was adopted into the OMG (Object Management Group) standard as TSAS (Telecommunication Service Access and Subscription), and was applied to Japanese and German Government Information Service Systems [KoAg 99][FuTo 01][ToFu 01].

We had initiative establishment of the international symposium of ADS (ISADS) of IEEE in 1993. One hundred and fourteen researchers of systems Science in academia set up the basic research project supported by Ministry of Education & Science for three years from 1990.

We can pick up COSMOS and ATOS for train management and control systems as our excellent results [SaKa 97].

According to the socio-economical change, COSMOS system based on Autonomous Decentralization Concept was developed as the descendant of COMTRAC for the Tohoku and the Jyoetsu Lines in 1995. The name stands for Computerized Safety, Maintenance and Operation System. The systems, HIDIC based, set up at each station and offices were connected through high speed transmission line played the leading part together with the station staffs provided with PC. The station systems took in safety function and other operations widely.

Autonomous Decentralized Transport Operation control and information System (ATOS) was introduced to phase in for the general management and control of high-density traffic railway transport in Tokyo metropolitan area [KiKa 99] [KeBe 00] [KeBe 03]. The experience of COMTRAC development considerably influenced ATOS.

ATOS has been continuously expanding since the first station started in operation in July 1993. The Chuo Line firstly began using this system in December 1996. The Yamanote Line and the Keihin Tohoku Line began using this system in July 1998, and the Sobu Line between Ochanomizu and Chiba began in May, 1999. The system installation is phasing in year by year, as shown in Fig.2.

Welfare and healthcare that had been out of the engineering became social big concerns. Dependability of medical treatment (radiation therapy, fiber scope, and so on) and advanced medical imaging apparatuses (X-CT, MRI, and USI) were closed up as life–critical systems [Ih 95].

Hospital Information Systems (HIS) and Radiology Information Systems (RIS) as business process, Picture Archiving and Communication System (PACS) as the medical image database became in real-time at sophisticated hospitals. Hitachi has delivered them based on ADC.

Intelligent Transport System (ITS) emerged as the means of environment conservation and safety. We proposed ADC applying to ad hoc grouping control of cars on the roads in the systems and experimental trial was done as a part of the national project [ShSa 03].

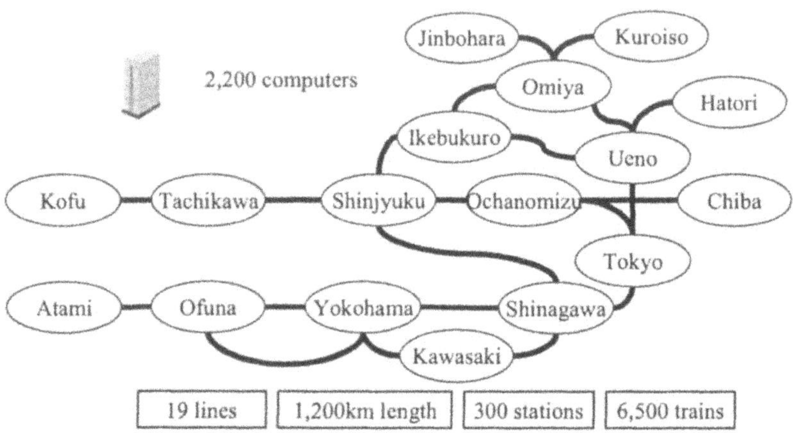

Figure 2. Managing area of ATOS

Progress of Artificial Intelligence in 1990s includes hybridization of fuzzy logics and neural networks as well as data mining technology for reducing cost for knowledge acquisition that was one of the most serious issues in developing intelligent systems. These knowledge acquisition methodologies significantly extended the application opportunity of intelligent systems such as public utility systems, financial dealing systems, CRM systems in telecommunication industries, and so on.

2.5 After 2000

After 2000, ADC has stridden to ubiquitous information environment [We 93] named Autonomous Super Distributed Objects or simply SDO (Super Distributed Objects) [FuKa 02]. The SDO are characterized two distinct features given by wireless technologies as well as micro-electronic device technologies such as Radio Frequency Identification (RFID), namely, (1) frequent and quick joining and leaving of the entities, (2) non-deterministic nature of services provided by relevant entities. These SDO features call for automatic services delivery according to the contexts of the system users with the constraints that come from the degree of trusts among the entities [KaSa 03][ToFu 03]. In contrast to ADC of which metaphor is biological cells constituting organs of life systems, the metaphor of SDO is placed on human society with multiple relationship that is characterized the following facts, (1) human belongs to multiple communities, (2) human recognizes identities of others by the degrees of belonging to the communities, (3) human interacts with others based on the recognition.

A model of SDO is developed that abstracts and wraps existing diversified application oriented standards such as UPnP, HAVi, ECHONET, etc. The SDO model permits inter-operability among the existing technologies and is standardized by the OMG [SaKa 01] [KaSa 04].

The ADS product, NX series, is continuously spreading over social and industrial infrastructural systems. Among them, remarkable topic is that COMTRAC for Taiwan Shinkansen based on the NX series is scheduled in operation in 2005.

3. DEPENDABLE SYSTEMS APPROACH

We present two approaches to realize dependable computer systems in this chapter. One is systems architecture technology as system basis and the other is artificial intelligence technology as for information processing.

3.1 Fault Tolerance and Assurance Architecture of Real time Systems

We classify the real systems to four domains from point of view of the system architecture in Fig.3. The vertical axis shows fault tolerance-fault avoidance and the horizontal centralization-distribution.

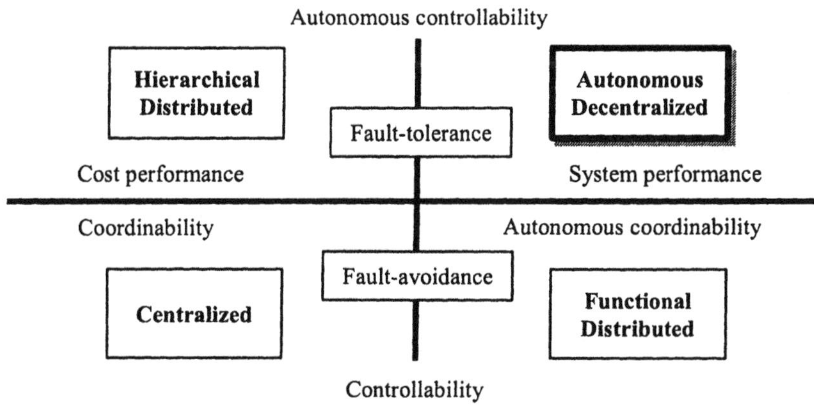

Figure 3. System architecture

As we describe in the previous chapter, it also shows the paradigm shift of system perception from centralization in 1970s to decentralization in 1990s with need shifts from the manufacture or technology to the user or demands. The centralized system structure, which was characterized by time-sharing process and fixed protocol for attaining best efficiency, had unacceptable weakness of flexibility and extensibility. The distributed structure took over the centralized one to realize flexibility and extensibility. However this does not satisfy critical requirement from system dependability in on-line real-time operation. And high-assurance during system expansion became necessary since the total system is not defined in advance. The conventional centralized system is in the third quadrant and the distributed in the second and the fourth. All of subsystems forming Autonomous Decentralized System, placed in the first quadrant, upper right, have to satisfy autonomous controllability and autonomous coordinability as well as fault-tolerance and life cycle cost performance as the total system. Here we describe R&D and practices by Hitachi.

3.1.1 Centralized systems and distributed systems

The computer control and management systems for the railway are suitable to explain for fine examples.

The first COMTRAC for the Tokaido Line in 1972 had the dual system structure, which runs programs synchronously in two computers shown in Fig.4. Specially tailored hardware compares two computed results, which are route control information selected as critical for safety. When some disagree arises between them, the comparator, Dual System Controller (DSC), cuts off both outputs and activates check programs in two computers. Then the results of check programs are compared to some pattern pre-stored in the ROM of the comparator. The either computer that produces its result, which meets with the pattern, is recognized as healthy one and its output is transferred as the right route control command. Therefore, when one of the dual computers is failed, the survival can run as single. The single system is not dependable from safety as well as reliability points of view.

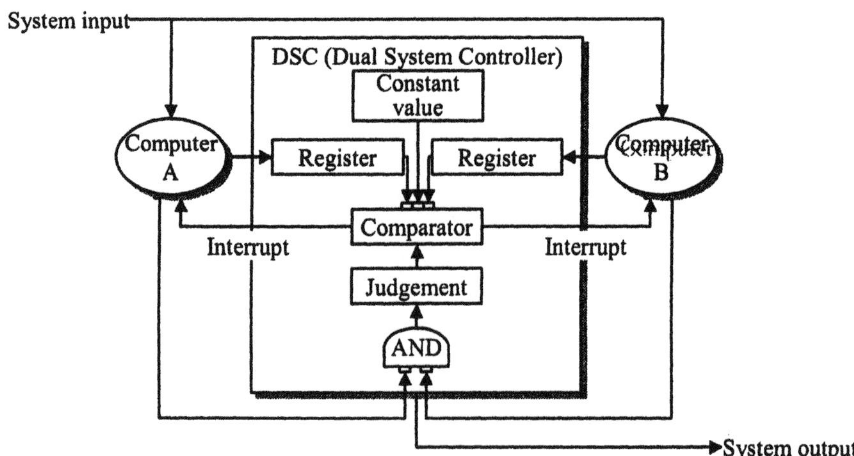

Figure 4. Dual system

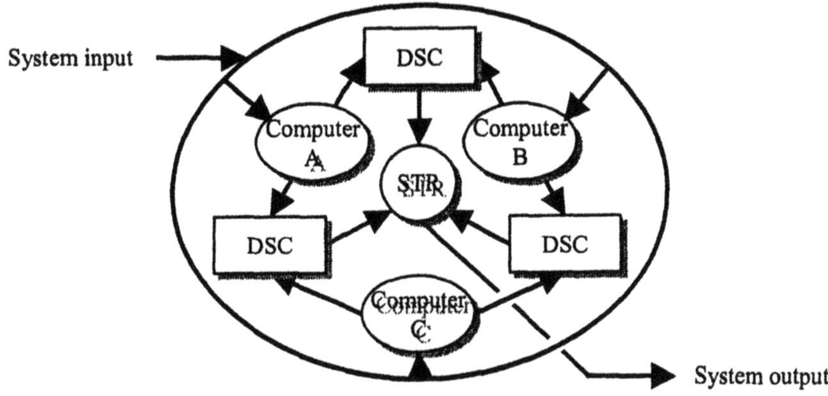

Figure 5. Dual-Duplex architecture

The next COMTRAC, shown in Fig.5 had a stand-by computer by the lessons learnt from the above [IhFu 78]. When the dual operation moves to single operation, the third one is connected to the surviving computer automatically. That is, the system is restructured again to dual operation. The command output is stopped about 2.5 seconds during reconfiguration to new dual system since the train control can permit time delay of three seconds. It may be called the system structure as symmetrical dual-duplex. It is reported more than 99.999% availability for 24-hour operation and no unsafe output in its operation life. This COMTRAC had the hierarchical system structure connected to another two main frame computers, so-called the duplex configuration, as the upper level system for planning schedule of train operation.

The same system structure was applied to the Tohouku and the Joetsu Lines later on. Of course, additional new functions were included according to economic-social demand for railway transportation.

The systems of the Tokaido and the Sanyo Lines were replaced by the up-dated hardware in 1988. The front-end computers for communicating with other computer systems, single, and message transfer computer for passenger, and duplex were separately added to the main processors of which structure was the same as its predecessor. Computers and 53 operator's consoles were connected with the main computers by double loop reliable network.

Although COMTRAC hardware systems structure has been changed according to social demand-pull and technology-push described in chapter 2.3, the system concept, that is, centralization, and fundamental program structure, that is, time sharing processing, were not changed. And the safety function for prevention of collision still remained in the traditional signal system assembled special components. This structure has great difficulties on reliability, construction, extension and replacement of the systems in commercial operation from assurance viewpoint. We had to find out new paradigm for huge large real time computer control systems.

3.1.2 Autonomous Decentralized Systems [IhMo 84] [IhMo 87]

We grasped biological organism as a system with the following attributes,

(a) It always includes inactive (temporary faulty, complementary or spare) parts
(b) It always changes its conditions and states among operation, metabolism, generation and growth (plus or minus)
(c) It always changes its objectives to the goal by alternatives selection, optimization and adaptation
(d) It keeps accomplishing its objectives almost completely

This observation was opposite recognition against that system should be complete and stable.

Living thing is the integration of organs that are also integration of cells. We could consider that cell has uniformity of structure, equality of function and locality of information as cell level. Each cell has the same embedded programs as genes or DNA chain. Each cell has its autonomy, which means cell can live and function by itself following its environment. Organs or individuals are the integration of numerous cells, which have their autonomy with coordination around them. The system always survives despite it is not stable because of metabolism, growth, aging, and so on. Therefore, the system including faulty subsystem is quite normal. In other word, the system without any fault is only in one state of the system. This is our basic perception on systems.

Initially subsystems autonomously exist, and a system is defined as the result of the coalition assembly of subsystems when a certain objectives appear. Two attributes are applicable to not only the hardware system but also the software system with the following definition. [MoSa 81]

(a) **Autonomous controllability**: if any subsystem fails, the other subsystems can manage themselves.
(b) **Autonomous coordinability**: if any subsystem fails, the other subsystems can coordinate their individual objectives among themselves.

It is clear that these two properties assure not only the fault tolerance but also the expandability and the maintainability of the system. They suggest that every subsystem requires an intelligence to manage itself and to coordinate with other sub-systems. That is, the subsystem consists of not only the application modules but also its own management module.

Moreover, these properties do not permit a common resource in order to isolate from the connected subsystems. Hence, a common file in the systems is not acceptable in the autonomous decentralized software structure. For communicating and coordinating among the software subsystems without using the common file, the virtual data field (VDF) concept is proposed in Fig.6. All data is sent out to all other subsystems as soon as the subsystems originate the data. The subsystem does not continue to store the data without broadcasting it. The subsystem can access the data in the VDF when it passes over the subsystems. The data is removed after it transmitted through the VDF. The identical function of VDF is autonomously distributed in the subsystems though they have different control missions. [MoMi 85]

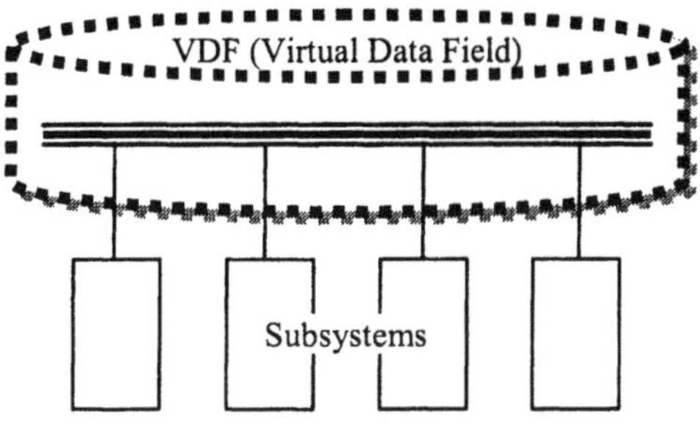

Figure 6. Virtual data field

Under this idea of VDF, the following conditions are required to satisfy the properties of the ADC.

(a) **Uniformity**: Each subsystem must be self-contained and independent of others, so that it can continue to operate even if others fail. That is, every structure is uniform to join VDF.

(b) **Equality**: Any subsystem could behave correctly because of the receiver initiative protocol. Therefore, it is not permitted for each subsystem to direct any others. That is, all subsystems are equal in VDF.

(c) **Locality**: Failure of one subsystem could mean a breakdown in communication and a failure to collect global information from other subsystems. Hence, every subsystem must be able to control itself and to coordinate with the other subsystems on a local-information basis only. That is, subsystem can access the dada in VDF.

In order to realize these properties technically, asynchronous daisy chain broadcast communication with Content Code (CC) and data field (DF) scheme are invented. The subsystem generates some information broadcasts it with assigned code as the tag that means content of the information to all other subsystems. Any of them takes the broadcasted information selected by referring CC if it needs. There is not any special communication control process between sender and receiver. The receiver takes initiative in communication. Each subsystem is connected each other by Autonomous Control Processor (ACP) in duplex architecture. Thus, the database, named

DF, consists virtually of distributed data in the subsystems. The subsystems can access immediately their data accumulated in their memory when other subsystems that generate original transactions are out of order. Therefore the transaction rate of the connection lines remains on average even if any subsystem fails. In other words, the bottleneck of the communication does not emerge in the system.

The uniformity and the equality conditions mean that every subsystem has the same ACP and there is no master-slave relationship among them. The locality condition indicates that the subsystems must communicate synchronously only with neighboring ACPs without using the destination addresses. In a conventional system, as the exchange protocol is decided by hand-shake procedure, the destination address is a must since the sender subsystem recognizes in advance how the total system is structured and which subsystem must receive the data. Hence, the destination address restricts the autonomy of the subsystems to judge whether or not to receive the data. In the autonomous decentralized system, the packet with the content code protocol is used shown in Fig.7.

Flag	CC	Sender ID	Control code	Data or Command	CRC	Flag

Figure 7. Content code

Every item of data attaching its corresponding CC is broadcasted into the DF and the ACP that selects only the necessary data by CC receives it. No data in the DF has priority. Each ACP judges autonomously how to process the data without being dependent on any priority and drives a corresponding software module when all the necessary input data, with which CC is previously specified within the ACP, is received from the DF and arranged by time stamp or serial number in the received data if necessary.

CC can include not only online information but also offline information such as test data and maintenance procedure. Thus, both online and offline functions are simultaneously carried on in the same hardware. It realizes easy modification, expansion and extension of the systems. This largely contributes to phase in implementation and operation [MoMi 84].

Systems Development Laboratory made up two types of the systems, loosely-coupled networks (Autonomous Decentralized Loop network: namely ADL) as the analogy of neural systems [MoIh 82] [IhMo 82] and tightly-coupled systems (Fault-tolerant Multi-micro Processor system by ADC, namely FMPA) as the analogy of the cerebellum [MiNo 83] to show by means of evidence. [MiMo 84] A NCP of ADL has two outlets and two inlets respectively to make the ladder loop DF shown in Fig.8.

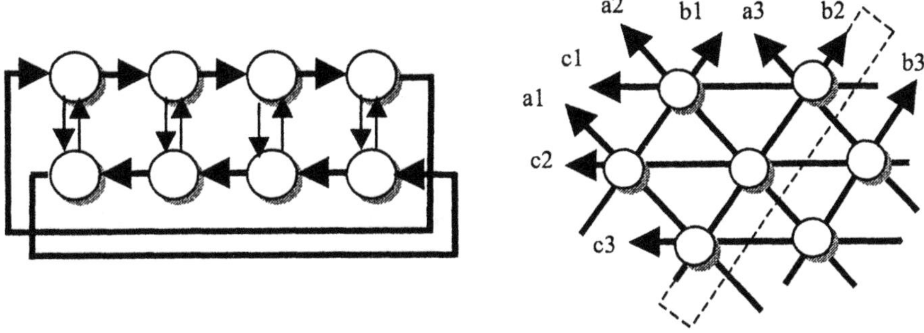

Figure 8. ADL and FMPA

Photo couplers isolated cells against electrical disturbance. FMPA consists of homogeneous cells. Each Cell has a microprocessor and three symmetrical pairs of bi-directional bus ports (FTB) and its controller, which make the hexagonal array structure shown in Fig.8.

Each cell was connected with the adjacent six cells. FMPA has dynamic addressing and threshold voting for dependability. Two systems were connected and used to develop the control program for NCP in the laboratory. Pluralism easily form complex systems; dual, duplex and majority voting through DF. They showed high reliability by means of evidence and applied widely to the commercial systems by De-fact Standards [KaSa 99].

We have proved the property of high assurance of ADS by ATOS. ATOS is a large-scale system involving 19 train lines, 300 stations, and a total track length of 1,200 kilometers. It has been developed with the goal of improving safe and stable transport, passenger service, and management efficiency. First installation of ATOS was in 1993. Since then, the expansion of the service area and the functions of ATOS have been expanded by phase in installation procedure month by month. ATOS shows high assurance through the whole installation.[KeBe 00][KeBe 01][KeBe 03]

The station systems take charge of route control, passenger guidance, etc.; the central system notes the running status of trains and takes charge of general operation control work. A trunk network (100 Mbps) connects both systems. Ethernet as a branch LAN connects the railway-side equipments. For the hardware, general-purpose computers (WSs, PCs, PLCs, controllers, and real-time control servers namely RCSs) are used as open system architecture. The main sections of the station systems and central system are duplicated to secure reliability. Nowadays ATOS consists of more than 2,200 computers.

3.2 Artificial Intelligence

It is generally accepted that the computer program is following human problem solving procedure, that is, algorithm. We have to make computer programs by concept originally given by Von Neumann after deciding rigorously their boundary conditions.

Here we tried to clarify the step from human thinking way to the stored programming to justify our R&D target in artificial intelligent system for dependability of decision-making.

Fig.9 shows our understanding of intelligent activity [IhMo 87]. We choose two axes, the vertical one is structuring degree of problem and the other horizontal one is the extent of knowledge domain. We can assign the present programming technology in the first quadrant, and actual human thinking ability is assigned in the third quadrant. Human being has broad and emergent ways of subjective consideration and common sense. The problem in the second is universal and well structured. Knowledge is written deterministically and objectively in numerical expression and the structure of the problems is combinations of numerical formula. Non-liner problem and combinatorial problem are examples. The second area includes mathematics, result search, gaming, FFT, and so on. They have been investigated from ancient times as well as general problem solver (GPS) in early AI research. Fuzzy set and neural network are also placed in the second. The forth has deductive reasoning in specific knowledge domains. Knowledge is written in the character trains. Its structure is non-deterministic. It is rather difficult to examine reasoning results that greatly depend on accumulated volume of the knowledge and on vagueness of necessary knowledge. The written knowledge itself is power.

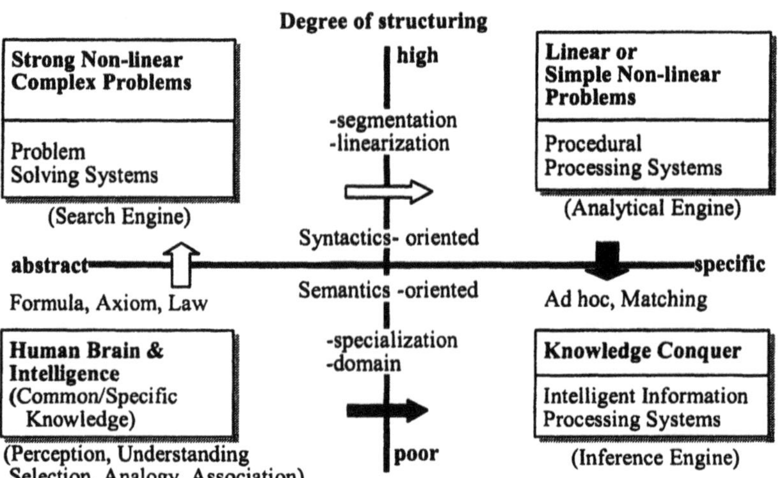

Figure 9. AI domains

Some of intellectual activity of human beings is transferred the third quadrant to the second by being distilled to axioms, natural laws and abstraction. Linearization and segmentation transform the problems in the second to the first. On the other hand, the forth cuts the expert knowledge of a selected domain out of the third. Knowledge Engineering begun by the Stanford Heuristic Programming Project (HPP). Knowledge Engineering aims to deduct the problem that is characterized by undefined structure and less-arithmetic knowledge. The combination of knowledge is dynamically varies by the contents of accumulated knowledge. In order to extract expertise, knowledge engineers and support environments were proposed. Stored program system in the first is made use with interpreting instead of compiling. We, having a lot of experiences in the first and the second went in the forth as the remained area in 1980.

Our first attempts to utilize linguistic knowledge targeted computerization of shallow expertise that consisted of pairs of situations and actions to be taken for higher level of goal attainments. The attempts covered diagnosis of nuclear power plants, quality control of semiconductor manufacturing [KuKo 89], project management for construction of fossil power plants [NiSa 84], and so on. It was found that applications in physical process should incorporate with existing mathematical models in addition to experts' linguistic knowledge. In parallel with these trials, a couple of AI development systems were developed including EUREKA that combined production and object oriented programming, LONLI that was based on Prolog, and KRIT for design and diagnosis of dynamic systems.

After number of trials, we formulated knowledge engineering approach for practical situations, but we needed powerful inference engines for the practices in real-time environment. We developed a fast pattern matching algorithm that permitted operation guidance by mini-computers in real-time situations. One of the most successful applications was a guidance system for blast furnace operation. The inference engine named EUREKA II was so powerful that enjoyed diversified applications including operation guidance of public utility plants, generation assistance of train diagrams, construction planning and project management support, financial investment assessment, and so on [TaMa 87][TsMa 88][TsKa 92][TsEg 96][TsEg 99].

Rich experiences of knowledge engineering provided further advancement of knowledge utilization. The guiding framework was predictive control where predictive simulation based on the knowledge of the controlled objects was conducted so as to select the best control alternative. Train operation control in the Sendai subway succeeded first commercial use of fuzzy logics in the world where fuzzy logics were used in evaluating control alternatives even though train dynamics were described by a set of traditional differential equations [YaMi 83]. The application based on the train control idea was extended to controlling cranes that were definitely difficult for the traditional control theory. Much more thorough use of linguistic knowledge was realized in tunnel ventilation control where pollutant, air, and traffic dynamics in the tunnel were described by linguistic fuzzy knowledge that were used for prediction of the air quality in the tunnel with state filtering mechanism [FuAo 91].

Fuzzy logics were very effective in computerizing expertise knowledge, because the grade of fuzziness can be used for tuning outcome of the fuzzy logic inferences in contrast to the crisp logic inferences that require acquiring complete rigorous knowledge. However the adjustment of the grade values was not easy task for the system developers. In order to automate the adjustment of the grade values, the back propagation algorithm, namely chained algorithm for calculating partial derivatives, in neural network technologies was successfully introduced to the fuzzy logic network that was a network representation of fuzzy logics [MaSo 91][IcMa 93][MaIc 93]. The development significantly reduced the burden in developing intelligent systems that resulted in expanding application domains that covered control systems for public utility plants as well as financial trading systems [FuMa 95].

In the late of 1990s, IT was becoming pervasive for human more and more so that capturing data that representing human behavior in IT could be simply realized. However it was not easy for systems analysts to utilize large amount of data in obtaining models of user behavior that were the determinants for delivering cost-effective superior services to the users. In order to cope with this problem, data mining technology was developed that permitted extracting knowledge on user behavior from large amount of data. Traditional statistical modeling technology was based on liner analysis, but extraction of knowledge from data mostly was assumed requiring nonlinear analysis. In order to deal with nonlinearity, categorizations for the continuous values were adopted and a powerful algorithm conscious to frequency in reading data from storage was developed that finds dependency among the data items. The technology was packaged as a software product named DATAFRONT and applied to customer relationship management systems in telecommunication operators and quality control systems in LSI manufacturers [MaMa 98][MoSa 98][AsMo 99][MaMa 99].

4. PERSPECTIVE AND THE OFFERING FOR NEW HORIZONS

In this chapter, we will try to write down several perspectives of dependable systems from our experiences and Japanese market demands.

4.1 Extended Autonomous Decentralization Concept [Ih 98] [Ih 99]

We have been doing research and development activities of ADC since 1980 as one of long term program at Hitachi and academia. Meanwhile, as described in previous chapters, the evolution of technology is greatly changing and renewing our society with information and visa versa. Rapid transition of the society requires the information systems must correspond to it.

Although neural system of living creatures looks as if the cerebral activity controls other organs, the normal cerebral functions are not generally ignited spontaneously without any stimuli from other organs or sensors. The organs are isolated from each other and permitted only to communicate with the brain neural cells in principle. Body system can consequently attain its survival objectives by the stimuli from sense organs. In addition, sensory subsystems change themselves according to their environmental conditions. Here we can recognize the hierarchical relation between the brain system and sensory subsystems.

Autonomous Decentralization Concept has put assumption that cell belongs to one layer with uniformity, equality and locality as subsystem level. An assembly of the cells that have a same object makes an organ. An assembly of the organs makes a human. A human makes family and so on. Each layer generally fulfills uniformity, equality and locality. And we can observe the hierarchy from the cell to the United Nations shown in Fig. 10.

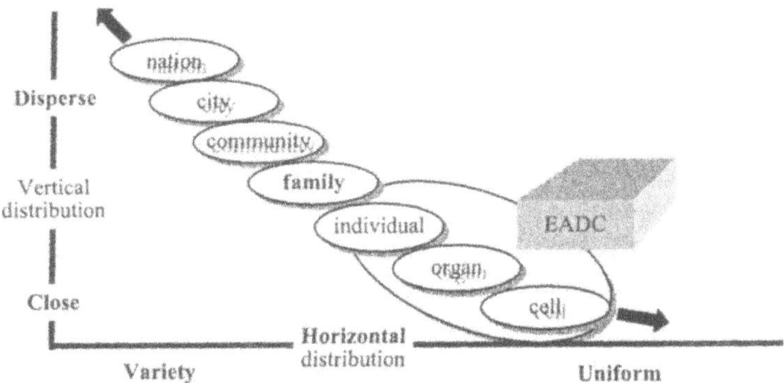

Figure 10. Hierarchical layer of EADC

Then we have to introduce the hierarchical layers in ADC. This hierarchy is adequate enough to attain the specific object of each layer. However, we have to recognize that each layer is not subjected to upper layer level although each layer consists of the lower level components, which are subsystems, from structure point of view. The subsystems of each layer coordinate each other within their layers to achieve their objectives as ADC described in Chapter 3.1.

When we recognize the hierarchy of subsystem level, the upper level members are mostly influenced by the lower level members, their belonging level ones and their own conditions. We must notice that there are not certain master-slave relations between the layers.

After above observations, we proposed the extension of ADC (EADC) adding Autonomous Observability as the third attribute shown in Fig.11.

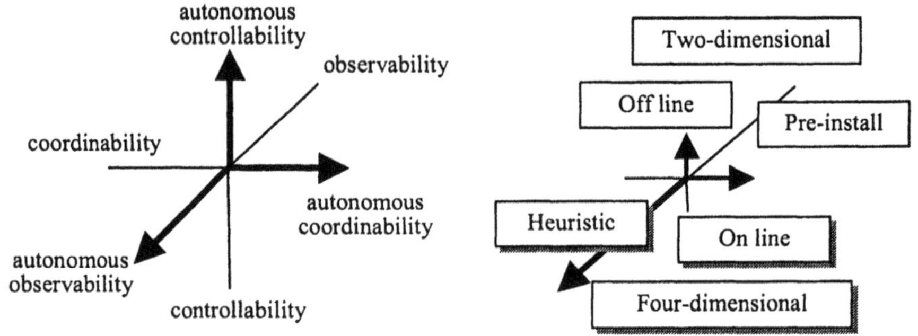

Figure 11. EADC

Autonomous Observability: if any change occurs in the surrounding of the subsystem, it can be observed immediately.

It aims at more dependable systems structure enhanced by our experiences until now and rapid advent of recent technologies. Though it is still infant level, the concept is now under R&D. One of the leading examples is the ad hoc grouping in ITS [ShSa 03] and entertainment robotics.

The definition of Autonomous Observability means that the system can autonomously observe its surrounding, recognize four dimensional changes (space and time), and report to the upper level of VDF.

It also includes a kind of the firewall against harmful interaction and malicious attack from the outside just like immunity. As for Autonomous Controllability previously defined, the subsystems have additionally the ability to change their control regions. And Autonomous Coordinability is added the ability of changing of information exchange for coordination. EADC implies autonomous adaptation of the structure and functions of the system to its environment fluctuation. In other words, the systems based on EADC will be built up by the demand sides oriented from quality of services instead of the supply sides oriented from quality of product. The boundaries and the conditions of large and complicated systems are getting hard for the supplier side to strictly decide prior to tailoring the systems. Proto-typing method or user engineering method will be introduced.

Autonomous observability can be assumedly intelligent sensor subsystems. We have already developed various smart sensor systems such as vision, hearing, touch and etc. for signal detection and processing. Radio wave watches, global positioning systems (GPS), gyrocompass, and RFID (μ-chips) will be used to identify the accurate location and time of information source. Technologies of artificial intelligence and robotics make the observation intelligently autonomous.

The system structure with EADC dynamically expects the systems more flexible, dependable and secure than ever against environment changes.

4.2 Open Development and Operation Infrastructure

Recently fatal failures and disasters often occurred in our daily life, for example transportation, public utility, production, medicine, administration and etc. The faults are often human-made by ignorance, careless mistakes and unskillful ness. Furthermore, it will be more difficult to call experienced experts and well-qualified project leaders together and to detain them for certain term in a project team. Lessons learnt from previous failures have not been reflected to the successive programs. Participating organizations or persons cannot be responsible for the system totally and have organized their peer group against criticisms outside. Project is still based on old-fashioned project management, not recursive one introducing rapid advent of information technologies [Ih 04].

Engineering and designing by IT seems getting important because the systems consist of tremendous number of the components, either hardware or software, is becoming difficult to develop and operate. The activities need deep specific knowledge and experience as well as ability of analysis and synthesis. Further more, know-how form human experience should be reserved in documentation or multimedia before the experts retire or remembrance diminishes.

In making information systems dependable for these 40 years, we have considerable experiences that the authors presented in the previous chapters.

From above observations, Open Development and Operation Infrastructure (ODOI) will be required for design and operation of sophisticated systems that furnish high dependability [TsUe 04]. The environment is opened to people who are especially interested in the applicable systems. They, including volunteers, can offer their knowledge, opinion, advice, verification, validation, criticism and work to the project through Internet. ODOI could serve:

(a) The project members means to retrieve, accumulate, suggest, simulate, validate and synthesize comprehensive information and knowledge using suitable intelligent models for the phases of plan, design, validation and operation.

(b) The outer project members and the experts outside opportunities to communicate, exchange, discuss, and interact with recursively among them.
(c) The people interested in including citizens opportunities to watch recursively the on-going process and propose new idea or suggestion.
(d) The target systems necessary dependability which is supported throughout their life cycles by sophisticated engineering systems.

The ODOI that the project teams maintain accumulation of necessary information in its database and knowledge base in addition to running project management, necessary analysis and synthesis with system technologies [KaTs 04]. The systems will gather the chronological multimedia record of the whole activity through the life cycle of development and operation, by which investigation of failures will make the target systems more dependable as defined Autonomous Observability in EADC.

The Emergent Synthetic Environment (ESE) for space development has been proposed since 2000, with the support of the National Space Development Agency, to acquire by advanced IT all information on development, design, verification, validation and operation of spacecrafts, in order to avoid human-made faults. It is a trial proposal of ODOI for the future [TsUe 04].

4.3 The Yaoyorozu Project: Marriage of Social Science and Information Technology

4.3.1 Emerging technology affecting our social life

M. Weiser advocated ubiquitous computing in 1988 where a lot of computers surrounding human help him/her to work without noticing their existences. Experiment of the ubiquitous computing by M. Weiser were conducted with 3 layered computer systems, namely the tab of Intel 8051 with 128KB, the pad of Motorola 68302 with 4MB, and the board of Sun workstation [We 93]. Nowadays our electronic surroundings are far different from those in the beginning of 1990s. For example, we might be surrounded by embedded controllers in many home appliances, mobile phones with a camera as well as a positioning sensor, and so on. In future, we will be surrounded a lot of intelligent devices based on nano-technology that function for monitoring and controlling our physical conditions, augmenting our sensing and memorizing capabilities, and information control systems interacting our environment where everything is equipped with smart tags.

This future picture suggests that we will be surrounded heterogeneous powerful intelligent devices based on the advanced super distributed objects

(SDO) technology which deals with dynamically forming trusted parties and their chains. In classical Japanese, the word "Yaoyorozu" (literally "eight million") was used to refer to something that was countless in number, particularly in the phrase "Yaoyorozu no Kami-gami," or "eight million gods." The belief was that gods lived not only in the many old temples throughout Japan, but in the trees and the stones, in the sky and the water, constantly surrounding and protecting us. For this reason, we use "Yaoyorozu" for our coming heterogeneneous information soceity in stead of ubiquitous.

The emerging technology as described in the above has great potential for changing our life style as well as our way of thinking about others and society. We have to be prepared for the new technological paradigm so that in 2002 an interdisciplinary research activity named Yaoyorozu Project formed under the sponsorship by Ministry of Education, Culture, Sports, Science and Technology, Japan.

4.3.2 Yaoyorozu approach based on the trans-disciplinary science and technology

Collaboration of humanity, sociological, and engineering knowledge is strongly required for attaining the Project goal, however this type of multi-disciplinary collaboration has been seldom realized so far. Some sophisticated mechanism shall be introduced for the collaboration. M. Gibbons et al. [GiLi 94] advocated so called Mode 2 knowledge production model that best utilizes IT for collaborations among multi-disciplines. For the efficient collaboration, Mode 2 claims (1) restoring interests in individual ordered knowledge, (2) emphasizing on design knowledge, and (3) modeling based on computer technology. H. Shimizu who conducts the social technology is proposing co-creation through sharing future vision among participants.

In the Yaoyorozu Project, the trans-disciplinary science and technology is the guiding principle for integrating knowledge diversified over multiple disciplines. Even though definition of the trans-disciplinary science and technology is not commonly agreed so far, but we assume that systems technology provides basic functions for integrating knowledge as well as producing new ideas. Many traditional disciplines have mainly been focusing on cognition of the internal and external entities but the trans-disciplinary science and technology calls for design of science in addition to traditional science and technology. This is the distinctive requirement to the trans-disciplinary science and technology. The systems technology including scenario generation, collective discussion over diversified disciplines, multi-agent simulation, and so on are expected respond to this synthetic requirement of our future [FuHo 03].

5. SUMMARY

We, Hitachi group, have been chasing dependability as the company highest motto since it established in 1910. The motto seems considerably similar to the concept of "Dependability" though we did not recognized the word till IFIP WG 10.4 published firstly the book edited by J-C Laprie in 1991 including Japanese version by Y. Koga [La 92]. In the book, he did not describe Japanese word for dependability. Hence we have used phonetic spelling by Japanese Kana characters "dhi-pe-n-da-bi-ri-thi."

Hitachi group has a wide product lines across from the semiconductor to the nuclear plant. Information technology is one of its important business area including dependable computer control systems. Here we described the activities concerning computer system dependability focusing on Systems Research Laboratory and its outskirts. In addition, we proposed new R&D horizon for dependable information systems.

We, researchers of Hitachi groups, have been greatly influenced the phrase "Although our lifetime may not span a hundred years, we have concerns of a thousand years (from an ancient Chinese poem)." Dependability of information systems is based on the phrase.

6. ACKNOWLEDGEMENTS

We express our sincere appreciation to Algirdas Avižienis for his valuable support for 25 years. Special thanks go to Prof. Alain Costes, Prof.Yoshihiro Tohma and the colleagues of IFIP WG 10.4 for their friendship.

The original suggestion on analogy of biology for ADC came from Prof. Takemochi Ishii during his talks and discussions. Prof. Atsunobu Ichikawa organized, and the late Prof. Masami Itoh promoted, the ADC research group in Japanese academia. Prof. Edward Feigenbaum gave us valuable suggestions and encouragements on AI research, Prof. Lotfi Zadeh on fuzzy control, Prof. Takeo Kanade on image understanding and Mr. Daniel Goldin on R/D management. We would like to put the late Mr. Arne O. Berglund of Sweden and the late Prof. Tohru Tanabe on record for their comprehension on ADC. Dr. Takeo Miura supported us with great patience from the beginning through the R&D mentioned here. We thank Dr. Michitaka Kosaka, General Manager of Systems Development Laboratory for his assistance too.

It is too hard for us to line up all of numerous excellent researchers, engineers and managers in and out of Hitachi, to whom we want to give our best regards and gratitude.

REFERENCES

We referred mostly to the papers that were made only in English by the acquaintances of authors.

[AsMo 99]Ashida,H. Morita,T. 1999: Architecture of Data Mining Server: DATAFRONT/Server, Proc. IEEE SMC'99, pp.882-887.

[FuAo 91]Funabashi,M. Aoki,I. Yahiro,M. Inoue,H. 1991: A Fuzzy Model Based Control Scheme and its Application to a Road Tunnel Ventilation System, Proc. IECON '91, pp.1596-1601.

[FuHo 03]Funabashi,M. Homma,K. Sasaki,T. 2003: Introduction to the Yaoyorozu Project, Proc. SICE 2003, pp.1332-1335.

[FuKa 02]Funabashi,M. Kawano,K. Sameshima,S. Kato,H. 2002: Middleware technology for ubiquitous computing: AYA(context-Aware and Yet Another service) that permits autonomous collaboration on super distributed objects, Proc. 2002 IEEE SMC, pp.623-628.

[FuMa 95]Funabashi,M Maeda,M. Morooka,Y. Mori,K 1995: Fuzzy and Neural Hybrid Expert Systems-Synergetic AI-, IEEE Expert, Vol.10, No.4, pp.32-40.

[FuTo 01]Funabashi,M. Toyouchi,J. Kanai,A. Uchihashi,T. Kobayashi,T. Hakomori,S Yoshida,E. Strick,L. Born,M 2001: Development of Open Service Collaborative Platform for Coming ECs by International Joint Efforts, in Chin,W. Patricelli,F. Milutinovic,V. (eds.), "Electronic Business and Education: Recent Advances in the Internet Infrastructure," Kluwer Academic Publishers, pp.284-299.

[GiLi 94]Gibbons,M. Limoges,C. Nowotny,H. Schwartzman,S. Scott,P. Trow,M. 1994: The New Production of Knowledge, Sage Publications of London.

[IcMa 93]Ichimori,T. Maeda,A. Funabashi,M. Ohmori,K. Kometani,N. 1993: Improving Fuzzy Knowledge Using a Network Representation of Fuzzy Logic Inference Procedures, Proc. IEEE International Workshop on Neuro-Fuzzy Control, pp.102-106.

[Ih 04]Ihara,H. 2004: What do Fatal Failures in Japanese Space Programs Suggest Us?, Proc. PRDC-10, pp.343-352.

[Ih 79]Ihara,H. 1979: Fault-Tolerance Through Autonomous Decentralized Systems, IFIP Working Conference on "Reliable Computing and Fault-Tolerance in 1980s', London.

[Ih 95]Ihara,H. 1995: Dependable medical systems, Proc. FTCS-25 Silver Jubilee, pp.76-84.

[Ih 98]Ihara,H. 1998: More Dependable Systems in Computing –Autonomous Decentralized Systems, Proc. IFIP-DCIA 98, pp.127-135.

[Ih 99]Ihara,H. 1999: Proposal of Extended Autonomous Decentralization Concept and Dependable Medical Home Care System, Technical Report (R999-9) of IEICE, pp.1-6.

[IhFu 78]Ihara,H. Fukuoka,K. Kubo,Y. Yokota,S. 1978: Fault-tolerant Computer System with Three Symmetric Computers, Proc. IEEE, Vol.66, No.10, pp.1160-1177.

[IhMo 82]Ihara,H. Mori,K. 1982: Highly Reliable Loop Computer Network System on Fault-tolerant Decentralization Concept, Proc. FTCS-12, pp.187-194 .

[IhMo 84]Ihara,H. Mori,K. 1984: Autonomous decentralized computer control systems, IEEE Computer, Vol.17, No.8, pp.57-66.

[IhMo 87]Ihara,H Mori,K. Miyamoto,S. 1987 : Evolution of Reliable Computing in Hitachi and Autonomous Decentralized System, in Avizienis,A. Kopetz,H. Laprie,J.(eds.) "Dependable Computing and Fault–Tolerant Systems Vol.1," The Evolution of Fault-Tolerant Computing, pp.77-99, Springer-Verlag Wien NewYork .

[IhMo 87]Ihara,H. Mohri,S. Kawai,S. 1987: On Dependable Intelligent Systems in Space, Space Technol., Vol., No.3, pp.233-240, Maxell Pergamon Macmillan (38th IAF-82-32,1987).

[Ka 78]Kamiuchi,T. et al 1978: A Load Sharing, N:1 Backup Multisystem, COMPCON Spring '78, pp.261-264.

[KaMa 89]Kanekawa,N, Maejima,H. Kato,H. Ihara,H. 1989: Dependable Onboard computer Systems with a New Method: Stepwise Negotiating Voting, Proc. FTCS-19, pp.13-19.

[KaSa 03]Kato,H. Sato,Y. Fukumoto,T. Homma,K. Sasaki,T. Funabashi,M: Trust Network-Based Filtering to Retrieve Trustworthy Word-of-Mouth Information, The 2nd Workshop on Security in Ubiquitous Computing, Ubicomp 2003.

[KaSa 04]Kawakami,K. Sameshima,S. Kawano,K. Suzuki,J. Suda,T. Steglich,S. Shin,S. 2004: SDO model and its standardization activity, Proc. SAINT 2004 Workshops, pp.315-320.

[KaSa 99]Kawano,K. Sameshima,S. Adachi,Y. 1999: An autonomous decentralized manufacturing system architecture and its trends for de-facto standards, Proc. IEEE SMC'99, pp422 - 427.

[KaTs 04]Kanuf,R. Tsuruta,S. Gonzalez,A Kurbad,T Ihara,H. 2004: Improving AI Systems' Dependability by Utilizing Historical Knowledge, Proc.PRDC-10 pp.343-352.

[KeBe 00]Kera,K Bekki,K Fujiwara,K. Kitahara,F Kamijyo,K. 2000: Assurance System Technologies based on Autonomous Decentralized System for Large Scale Transport Operation Control System,IEICE Trans.COMMUN.Vol.E83-B NO5.

[KeBe 01] Kera,K. Bekki,K Fujiwara,K. Kitahara,F. Kamijyo,K. 2001: Assurance Technology for Growing System and Its Application to Tokyo Metropolitan Railway Network, IEICE Trans. Vol. E-84-D No.10.

[KeBe 03]Kera,K. Bekki,K. Mori,K. 2003: High Assurance Autonomous step-by-step System Construction Technique based on Assurance Evaluation IFICE Trans. VOL.E86-D NO.10.

[KiKa 99] Kitahara,F. Kamljou,K. Kakurai,Y. Bekki,K. Kera,K. Kawano,K. 1999: Phased-in construction method of ATOS, Proc. Integration of Heterogeneous Systems, pp.415- 424.

[KoAg 99]Korner,A. Aghoutane,N. Ercan,G. Strick,R. Wunderlich,W. Funabashi,M. Kawano,S. Toyouchi,J. 1999: Efficient Brokerage in a CORBA-based Service Mediation Platform, Proc. ISADS 99, pp. 284-291.

[Ku 97]Kuwahara,H. 1997: Experiences teach us the future of autonomous decentralized systems, Proc. ISADS 97, pp.169-175.

[KuKo 89]Kurihara,K. Kobayashi,T. Akashi,K. 1989: Knowledge Based Process Diagnosis Expert System for LSI Manufacturing, IPSJ Journal, Vol.30, No.7, pp.918-921.

[La 85] Laprie, Jean-Claude 1985: Dependable Computing and Fault Tolerance: Concept and Terminology, Proc.FTCS-15, pp.2-11.

[La 92]Laprie,J-C. 1992: Dependable Computing and Fault –Tolerant Systems, in Laprie,J-C. (eds.) "Dependability: Basic Concepts and Terminology," Vol.5, Springer-Verlag, Wien NewYork.

[MaIc 93]MaedaA. Ichimori,T. Funabashi,M. 1993: FLIP-net: A Network Representation of Fuzzy Inference Procedure and its Application to Fuzzy Rule Structure Analysis, Proc. of 2nd IEEE International Conference on Fuzzy Systems, pp.391-395.

[MaMa 98]Maeda,A. Maki,H. Akimori,H. 1998: Characteristic Rule Induction Algorithm for Data Mining, Proc. PAKDD-98.

[MaMa 99]Maki,H. Maeda,A. Morita,T. Akimori,H. 1999: Applying data mining to data analysis in manufacturing, APMS'99, pp.324-331.

[MaSo 91]Maeda,A. Someya,R. Yasunobu,S. Funabashi,M 1991: A Fuzzy-based Expert System Building Tool with Self-tuning Capability for Membership Functions, Proc. the World Congress on Expert Systems, pp.639-647.

[MiMo 84]Miyamoto,S. Mori,K Ihara,H. Matsumaru,H. 1984: Autonomous Decentralized Control and its Application to the Rapid Transit System, Computer in Industry, vol.5 no.2 pp.115-124, Elsevier Science Publishers BV.

[MiNo 83]Miyamoto,S. Nohmi,M. Mori,K. Ihara,H. 1983: FMPA: Fault Tolerant Multi-Microcomputer System based on Autonomous Decentralization Concept, Proc. FTCS-13, pp.4-9.

[MoIh 82]Mori,K. Ihara,H. 1982: Autonomous Decentralized Network, Proc.COMPCON SPRING 1982, pp.192-195.

[MoMi 84]Mori,K. Miyamoto,S. Matsumaru,H. Ohshima,H. Hattori,A. 1984: Autonomous Decentralized Loop Network and its Application to Train Traffic Control System, Proc. IECON'84, pp.663-666.

[MoMi 84]Mori,K. Miyamoto,S. Nohmi,M. Ihara,H. 1984: Online Maintenance in Autonomous Decentralized Loop Network ADL, Proc. COMPCON FALL'84, pp.323-332.

[MoMi 85]Mori,K. Miyamoto,S. Ihara,H 1985: Autonomous Decentralized computer system and software structure, Computer Systems Science and Engineering, Vol.1, No.1, pp.17-22, Butterworths.

[MoSa 81]Mori,K. Sano,K. Ihara,H. 1981: Autonomous Controllability of Decentralized System Aiming a at Fault-Tolerance, 8th IFAC-World Congress, pp.183-189.

[MoSa 98]Morita,T. Sato,Y. Maeda,A. Yamanaka,Y. Miller,R.M. Takeda,H. 1998: Techniques for Time-Series Data Processing in Plant Data Warehouse, PADD98, pp.177-182.

[NiSa 84]Niwa,K. Sasaki,K. Ihara.H 1984: An Experimental Comparison of Knowledge Representation Schemes, The AI Magazine, Vol.5, No.2, pp.29-36.

[OrKa 84]Orimo,M. Kawano,K. Mori,K 1984: Functional Reliability and its Utilizaion for Evaluating the Decomposition of System, Proc. IECON, pp.1197-1202.

[OrMo 92]Orimo M. Mori,K. Ihara,H, 1992: Evaluation of System Division Based on Functional Reliability, Proc. the Automatic Control Conference, Vol. 28, No. 2,.

[SaKa 01]Sameshima,S. Kawano,K. Funabashi,M. 2001: A trend to super distributed system and standardization activity in OMG, Proc. SAINT 2001 Workshops, pp.5-8 .

[SaKa 97]Sameshima,S. Kawano,K. Kumayama,J. Ito,T. Inoue,K. Fujishiro,S. 1997: An autonomous decentralized system architecture and techniques for on-line development and maintenance, Proc. ISADS 97, pp.121-128 .

[ShSa 03]Shimura,A. Sakaibara,T. Hiraiwa,M. Aizono,T. 2003: Proposal of an autonomous group-management model and its application to intelligent transport system, Proc. ISADS 2003, pp.71-79 .

[TaMa 87]Tano,S. Masui,S. Sakaguchi,S. Funabashi,M. 1987: A Fast Pattern Match Algorithm for a Knowledge Based Systems Building Tool-EUREKA, IPSJ Journal, Vol.28, No.12, pp.1255-1268.

[ToFu 01]Toyouchi,J. Funabashi,M. Kanai,A. Uchihashi,T. Hakomori,S. Yoshida,E. Strick,L. Born,M. 2001, Development of Service Integration Platform for One-stop Service Applications, Proc. WECWIS 2001, pp.123-125.

[ToFu 03]Toyouchi,J. Funabashi,M. Honjo,S. Komoda,N. 2003: Web Service Integration Platform with Privacy Preferences for One-stop Application, ICWS'03.

[ToSh 99] Tomita,N. Shibao,S. Omura,M. Oku,M. 1999 : Flow oriented approach for human-centered agile manufacturing systems, Proc. Integration of Heterogeneous Systems, pp.98-106.

[TsEg 96]Tsuruta,S Eguchi,T Yanai, S. Ooshima, T. 1996:DGCAI: Dynamic Goal centered Coordination AI technology –For flexible computation solving real-time large-scale complex problems, Proc. AAAI-96, pp.490-495.

[TsEg 99]Tsuruta, S. Eguchi,T. Yanai,S Ooshima,T 1999:A Coordination Technique in A Highly Automated Train Rescheduling System, Proc. IEEE SMC'99, pp.601-606.

[TsKa 92]Tsuruta,S. Kakumoto, Y. 1992: Development of a Highly-Automated Train-Scheduling System using an Advanced AI Technology for Creating Very-High-Speed, Very-High-density Train-Schedules, Proc. OMPRAIL92, pp.155-166.

[TsMa 88]Tsuruta, S. Matsumoto, K. 1988: A Knowledge-based Interactive Train Scheduling System-- Aiming at Large-Scale Complex Planning Expert Systems, Proc. of IEEE Workshop on AIIA 88, pp.490-495.

[TsUe 04]Tsuruta,S. Uehara,K. Ihara,H. Tohma,Y Ooba,H. Oota,Y 2004: Design and Application of Emergent Synthesis Environment for Developing Dependable System, Proc. CITSTA 2004 (to appear in July, 2004).

[We 93]Weiser,M. 1993: Some Computer Science Issues in Ubiquitous Computing, Communications of the ACM, Vol.36, Vol.7, pp.75-84.

[YaMi 83]Yasunobu,S. Miyamoto,S. Ihara,H. 1983: Fuzzy Control for Automatic Train Operation System, Proc. 4th IFAC/IFIP/IFORS Conference, pp.33-39.

[YaMi 85]Yasunobu,S. Miyamoto,S. 1985: Automatic Train Operation by Predictive Fuzzy Control," in M. Sugeno (ed.): "Industrial Applications of Fuzzy Control," Elsevier Science Publisher.

Topic 4

Abstract Interpretation

Organiser:

Patrick Cousot
École Normale Supérieure, Paris, France
Patrick.Cousot@ens.fr

Abstract Interpretation is a theory of approximation of mathematical structures, in particular those involved in the semantic models of computer systems. Abstract interpretation can be applied to the systematic construction of methods and effective algorithms to approximate undecidable or very complex problems in computer science such that the semantics, the proof, the static analysis, the verification, the safety and the security of software or hardware computer systems. In particular, the *static analysis by abstract interpretation,* which automatically infers dynamic properties of computer systems, has been very successful these last years to automatically verify complex properties of real-time, safety critical, embedded systems.

The topical day is a vertical presentation of abstract interpretation from theory to practice, including an informal introduction to abstract interpretation, the presentation of static analysis tools and the assessment of their use in an industrial context at Airbus France.

BASIC CONCEPTS OF ABSTRACT INTERPRETATION

Patrick Cousot
École Normale Supérieure
45 rue d'Ulm
75230 Paris cedex 05, France
Patrick.Cousot@ens.fr

Radhia Cousot
CNRS & École Polytechnique
91128 Palaiseau cedex, France
Radhia.Cousot@polytechnique.fr

Abstract A brief introduction to the theory of Abstract Interpretation, examplified by constructing a hierarchy of partial traces, reflexive transitive closure, reachable states and intervals abstract semantics of transition systems.

Keywords: Abstract Interpretation, Safety, Specification, Static Analysis, Verification.

1. Introduction

Abstract Interpretation [Cousot, 1978] is a theory of approximation of mathematical structures, in particular those involved in the semantic models of computer systems. Abstract interpretation can be applied to the systematic construction of methods and effective algorithms to approximate undecidable or very complex problems in computer science such that the semantics, the proof, the static analysis, the verification, the safety and the security of software or hardware computer systems. In particular, static analysis by abstract interpretation, which automatically infers dynamic properties of computer systems, has been very successful these last years to automatically verify complex properties of real-time, safety-critical embedded systems.

All applications presented in the WCC 2004 topical day on Abstract Interpretation compute an overapproximation of the program reachable states. Hence, we consisely develop the elementary example of reachability static analysis [Cousot and Cousot, 1977]. We limit the necessary mathematical concepts to naïve set theory. A more complete presentation is [Cousot, 2000a] while [Cousot, 1981; Cousot and Cousot, 1992b] can be recommended as first readings and [Cousot and Cousot, 1992a] for a basic exposition to the theory.

2. Transition systems

Programs are often formalized as graphs or transition systems $\tau = \langle \Sigma, \Sigma_i, t \rangle$ where Σ is a set of states, $\Sigma_i \subseteq \Sigma$ is the set of initial states and $t \subseteq \Sigma \times \Sigma$ is a transition relation between a state and its possible successors [Cousot, 1978; Cousot, 1981]. For example the program `x := 0; while x < 100 do x := x + 1` can be formalized as $\langle \mathbb{Z}, \{0\}, \{\langle x, x' \rangle \mid x < 100 \wedge x' = x + 1\}\rangle$ where $\mathbb{Z}$ is the set of integers.

3. Partial trace semantics

A finite partial execution trace $s_0 s_1 \ldots s_n$ starts from any state $s_0 \in \Sigma$ and then moves on through transitions from one state s_i, $i < n$, to a possible successor s_{i+1} such that $\langle s_i, s_{i+1} \rangle \in t$. The set of all such finite partial execution traces will be called the *collecting semantics* $\Sigma_\tau^{\vec{*}}$ of the transition system in that it is the strongest program property of interest (in this paper).

There is no partial trace of length 0 so the set Σ_τ^0 of partial traces of length 0 is simply the empty set $\emptyset$. A partial trace of length 1 is s where $s \in \Sigma$ is any state. So the set Σ_τ^1 of partial traces of length 1 is simply $\{s \mid s \in \Sigma\}$. By recurrence, a trace of length $n + 1$ is the concatenation $\sigma s s'$ of a trace σs of length n with a partial trace s' of length 1 such that the pair $\langle s, s' \rangle \in t$ is a possible state transition. So if Σ_τ^n is the set of partial traces of length n then $\Sigma_\tau^{n+1} = \{\sigma s s' \mid \sigma s \in \Sigma_\tau^n \wedge \langle s, s' \rangle \in t\}$. Then the collecting semantics of τ is the set $\Sigma_\tau^{\vec{*}} = \bigcup_{n \geq 0} \Sigma_\tau^n$ of all partial traces of all finite lengths.

4. Partial trace semantics in fixpoint form

Observe that $\Sigma_\tau^1 \cup \Sigma_\tau^{n+1} = \mathcal{F}_\tau^{\vec{*}}(\Sigma_\tau^n)$ where:

$$\mathcal{F}_\tau^{\vec{*}}(X) \quad = \quad \{s \mid s \in \Sigma\} \cup \{\sigma s s' \mid \sigma s \in X \wedge \langle s, s' \rangle \in t\}$$

so that $\Sigma_\tau^{\vec{*}}$ is a *fixpoint* of $\mathcal{F}_\tau^{\vec{*}}$ in that $\mathcal{F}_\tau^{\vec{*}}(\Sigma_\tau^{\vec{*}}) = \Sigma_\tau^{\vec{*}}$ [Cousot and Cousot, 1979]. The proof is as follows:

$$\begin{aligned}
\mathcal{F}_\tau^{\vec{*}}(\Sigma_\tau^{\vec{*}}) &= \mathcal{F}_\tau^{\vec{*}}(\bigcup_{n \geq 0} \Sigma_\tau^n) && \text{(by def. } \Sigma_\tau^{\vec{*}}\text{)} \\
&= \{s \mid s \in \Sigma\} \cup \{\sigma s s' \mid \sigma s \in (\bigcup_{n \geq 0} \Sigma_\tau^n) \wedge \langle s, s' \rangle \in t\} && \text{(def. } \mathcal{F}_\tau^{\vec{*}}\text{)} \\
&= \{s \mid s \in \Sigma\} \cup \bigcup_{n \geq 0} \{\sigma s s' \mid \sigma s \in \Sigma_\tau^n \wedge \langle s, s' \rangle \in t\} && \text{(set theory)} \\
&= \Sigma_\tau^1 \cup \bigcup_{n \geq 0} \Sigma_\tau^{n+1} && \text{(by def. } \Sigma_\tau^1 \text{ and } \Sigma_\tau^{n+1}\text{)} \\
&= \bigcup_{n' \geq 1} \Sigma_\tau^{n'} = \bigcup_{n \geq 0} \Sigma_\tau^n && \text{(by letting } n' = n+1 \text{ and since } \Sigma_\tau^n = \emptyset.\text{)}
\end{aligned}$$

Now assume that $\vec{\mathcal{F}_\tau^*}(X) = X$ is another fixpoint of $\vec{\mathcal{F}_\tau^*}$. We prove by recurrence that $\forall n \geq 0 : \Sigma_\tau^n \subseteq X$. Obviously $\Sigma_\tau^0 = \emptyset \subseteq X$. $\Sigma_\tau^1 = \{s \mid s \in \Sigma\} \subseteq \vec{\mathcal{F}_\tau^*}(X) = X$. Assume by recurrence hypothesis that $\Sigma_\tau^n \subseteq X$. Then $\sigma s \in \Sigma_\tau^n$ implies $\sigma s \in X$ so $\{\sigma s s' \mid \sigma s \in \Sigma_\tau^n \wedge \langle s,\ s'\rangle \in t\} \subseteq \{\sigma s s' \mid \sigma s \in X \wedge \langle s,\ s'\rangle \in t\}$ whence $\Sigma_\tau^{n+1} \subseteq \vec{\mathcal{F}_\tau^*}(\Sigma_\tau^n) \subseteq \vec{\mathcal{F}_\tau^*}(X) = X$. By recurrence $\forall n \geq 0 : \Sigma_\tau^n \subseteq X$ whence $\vec{\Sigma_\tau^*}$ is the *least fixpoint* of $\vec{\mathcal{F}_\tau^*}$, written:

$$\vec{\Sigma_\tau^*} \;=\; \operatorname{lfp}_\emptyset^\subseteq \vec{\mathcal{F}_\tau^*} \;=\; \bigcup_{n\geq 0} \vec{\mathcal{F}_\tau^*}^{\,n}(\emptyset)$$

where $f^0(x) = x$ and $f^{n+1}(x) = f(f^n(x))$ are the *iterates* of f.

5. The reflexive transitive closure as an abstraction of the partial trace semantics

Partial execution traces are too precise to express program properties that do not relate to intermediate computation steps. Considering initial and final states only is an abstraction:

$$\alpha^*(X) \;=\; \{\vec{\alpha}(\sigma) \mid \sigma \in X\} \quad \text{where} \quad \vec{\alpha}(s_0 s_1 \ldots s_n) \;=\; \langle s_0,\ s_n\rangle\,.$$

Observe that $\alpha^*(\vec{\Sigma_\tau^*})$ is the reflexive transitive closure t^* of the transition relation t viz. the set of pair $\langle s,\ s'\rangle$ such that there is a finite path in the graph $\tau = \langle \Sigma,\ \Sigma_i,\ t\rangle$ from vertex s to vertex s' through arcs of t: $\langle x,\ y\rangle \in t^*$ if and only if $\exists s_0, \ldots, s_n \in \Sigma : x = s_0 \wedge \ldots \wedge \langle s_i,\ s_{i+1}\rangle \in t \wedge \ldots \wedge s_n = y$.

Now if Y is a set of pairs of initial and final states, it describes a set of partial traces where the intermediate states are unkown :

$$\gamma^*(Y) \;=\; \{\sigma \mid \vec{\alpha}(\sigma) \in Y\} \;=\; \{s_0 s_1 \ldots s_n \mid \langle s_0,\ s_n\rangle \in Y\}$$

So if X is a set of partial traces, it is approximated from above by $\alpha^*(X)$ in the sense that $X \subseteq \gamma^*(\alpha^*(X))$.

6. Answering concrete questions in the abstract

To answer concrete questions about X one may sometimes answer it using a simpler abstract question on $\alpha^*(X)$. For example the concrete question "Is there a partial trace in X which has s, s' and s'' as initial, intermediate and final states?" can be replaced by the abstract question "Is there a pair $\langle s,\ s''\rangle$ in $\alpha^*(X)$?". If there is no such a pair in $\alpha^*(X)$ then there is no such a partial trace in $\gamma^*(\alpha^*(X))$ whence none in X since $X \subseteq \gamma^*(\alpha^*(X))$. However if there is such a pair in $\alpha^*(X)$ then we cannot conclude that there is such a trace in X since this trace might be in $\gamma^*(\alpha^*(X))$ but not in X. The abstract answer must always be sound but may sometimes be incomplete. However if the concrete question is "Is there a partial trace in X which has respectively s and s' as initial and final states?" then the abstract answer is sound and complete.

7. Galois connections

Given any set X of partial traces and Y of pair of states, we have :

$$
\begin{array}{ll}
\alpha^*(X) \subseteq Y \iff \{\vec{\alpha}(\sigma) \mid \sigma \in X\} \subseteq Y & \wr\text{by def. } \alpha^*\int \\
\iff \forall \sigma \in X : \vec{\alpha}(\sigma) \in Y \iff X \subseteq \{\sigma \mid \vec{\alpha}(\sigma) \in Y\} & \wr\text{by def. } \subseteq\int \\
\iff X \subseteq \gamma^*(Y) & \wr\text{by def. } \gamma^*\int
\end{array}
$$

So $\alpha^*(X) \subseteq Y$ if and only if $X \subseteq \gamma^*(Y)$, which is a characteristic property of *Galois connections*. Galois connections *preserve joins* in that $\alpha^*(\bigcup_{i\in\Delta} X_i)$ $= \{\vec{\alpha}(\sigma) \mid \sigma \in \bigcup_{i\in\Delta} X_i\} = \bigcup_{i\in\Delta}\{\vec{\alpha}(\sigma) \mid \sigma \in X_i\} = \bigcup_{i\in\Delta} \alpha^*(X_i)$. Equivalent formalizations involve Moore families, closure operators, etc [Cousot, 1978; Cousot and Cousot, 1979].

8. The reflexive transitive closure semantics in fixpoint form

Since the concrete (partial trace) semantics can be expressed in fixpoint form and the abstract (reflexive transitive closure) semantics is an abstraction of the concrete semantics by a Galois connection, we can also express the abstract semantics in fixpoint form. This is a general principle in Abstract Interpretation [Cousot and Cousot, 1979].

We have $\emptyset \subseteq \gamma^*(\emptyset)$ whence $\alpha^*(\emptyset) \subseteq \emptyset$ proving $\alpha^*(\emptyset) = \emptyset$ by antisymmetry.

For all sets X of partial traces, we have the *commutation property*:

$$
\begin{array}{lll}
& \alpha^*(\vec{\mathcal{F}}^*_\tau(X)) & \\
= & \alpha^*(\{s \mid s \in \Sigma\} \cup \{\sigma s s' \mid \sigma s \in X \wedge \langle s,\, s'\rangle \in t\}) & \wr\text{def. } \vec{\mathcal{F}}^*_\tau\int \\
= & \{\vec{\alpha}(s) \mid s \in \Sigma\} \cup \{\vec{\alpha}(\sigma s s') \mid \sigma s \in X \wedge \langle s,\, s'\rangle \in t\}) & \wr\text{def. } \alpha^*\int \\
= & \{\langle s,\, s\rangle \mid s \in \Sigma\} \cup \{\langle \sigma_0,\, s'\rangle \mid \exists s : \sigma s \in X \wedge \langle s,\, s'\rangle \in t\}) & \wr\text{def. } \vec{\alpha}\int \\
= & \mathbb{1}_\Sigma \cup \{\langle \sigma_0,\, s'\rangle \mid \exists s : \langle \sigma_0,\, s\rangle \in \alpha^*(X) \wedge \langle s,\, s'\rangle \in t\}) & \\
& & \wr\text{def. } \mathbb{1}_S = \{\langle x,\, x\rangle \mid x \in S\} \text{ and } \alpha^*\int \\
= & \mathbb{1}_\Sigma \cup \alpha^*(X) \circ t & \wr\text{def. composition } \circ \text{ of relations}\int \\
= & \mathcal{F}^*_\tau(\alpha^*(X)) & \wr\text{by defining } \mathcal{F}^*_\tau(Y) = \mathbb{1}_\Sigma \cup Y \circ t\int
\end{array}
$$

If follows, by recurrence, that the iterates $\vec{\mathcal{F}}^{*\,n}_\tau(\emptyset)$ of $\vec{\mathcal{F}}^*_\tau$ and those $\mathcal{F}^{*\,n}_\tau(\emptyset)$ of $\mathcal{F}^*_\tau$ are related by α^*. For the basis, $\alpha^*(\vec{\mathcal{F}}^{*\,0}_\tau(\emptyset)) = \emptyset = \mathcal{F}^{*\,0}_\tau(\emptyset)$. For the induction step, if $\alpha^*(\vec{\mathcal{F}}^{*\,n}_\tau(\emptyset)) = \mathcal{F}^{*\,n}_\tau(\emptyset)$ then $\alpha^*(\vec{\mathcal{F}}^{*\,n+1}_\tau(\emptyset)) = \alpha^*(\vec{\mathcal{F}}^*_\tau(\vec{\mathcal{F}}^{*\,n}_\tau(\emptyset)))$ $= \mathcal{F}^*_\tau(\alpha^*(\vec{\mathcal{F}}^{*\,n}_\tau(\emptyset))) = \mathcal{F}^*_\tau(\mathcal{F}^{*\,n}_\tau(\emptyset)) = \mathcal{F}^{*\,n+1}_\tau(\emptyset)$. It follows that $\alpha^*(\vec{\Sigma}^*_\tau) =$ $\alpha^*(\mathrm{lfp}^{\subseteq}_{\emptyset}\, \vec{\mathcal{F}}^*_\tau()) = \alpha^*(\bigcup_{n\geq 0} \vec{\mathcal{F}}^{*\,n}_\tau(\emptyset)) = \bigcup_{n\geq 0} \alpha^*(\vec{\mathcal{F}}^{*\,n}_\tau(\emptyset)) = \bigcup_{n\geq 0} \mathcal{F}^{*\,n}_\tau(\emptyset) =$

$\mathrm{lfp}_{\emptyset}^{\subseteq}\, \mathcal{F}_{\tau}^{*}$. This can be easily generalized to order theory [Cousot, 1978; Cousot and Cousot, 1979] and is known as the *fixpoint transfer* theorem.

Observe that if Σ is finite then the fixpoint definition provides an iterative algorithm for computing the reflexive transitive closure of a relation as $X^0 = \emptyset, \ldots, X^{i+1} = \mathcal{F}_{\tau}^{*}(X^i), \ldots,$ until $X^{n+1} = X^n = \mathrm{lfp}_{\emptyset}^{\subseteq}\, \mathcal{F}_{\tau}^{*} = t^*$.

9. The reachability semantics as an abstraction of the reflexive transitive closure semantics

The reachability semantics of the transition system $\tau = \langle \Sigma,\ \Sigma_i,\ t \rangle$ is the set $\{s' \mid \exists s \in \Sigma_i : \langle s,\ s' \rangle \in t^*\}$ of states which are reachable from the initial states Σ_i. This is an abstraction $\alpha^{\bullet}(t^*)$ of the reflexive transtive closure semantics t^* by defining the right-image $\mathrm{post}[r]Z = \{s' \mid \exists s \in Z : \langle s,\ s' \rangle \in r\}$ of the set Z by the relation r and

$$\alpha^{\bullet}(Y) \quad = \quad \mathrm{post}[Y]\Sigma_i \quad = \quad \{s' \mid \exists s \in \Sigma_i : \langle s,\ s' \rangle \in Y\}\,.$$

Let $\gamma^{\bullet}(Z) = \{\langle s,\ s' \rangle \mid s \in \Sigma_i \Longrightarrow s' \in Z\}$. We have the Galois connection:

$$\begin{array}{ll}
\alpha^{\bullet}(Y) \subseteq Z \iff \{s' \mid \exists s \in \Sigma_i : \langle s,\ s' \rangle \in Y\} \subseteq Z & \wr \text{def. } \alpha^{\bullet} \wr \\
\iff \forall s' : \forall s \in \Sigma_i : \langle s,\ s' \rangle \in Y \Longrightarrow s' \in Z & \wr \text{def. inclusion } \subseteq \wr \\
\iff \forall \langle s,\ s' \rangle \in Y : s \in \Sigma_i \Longrightarrow s' \in Z\} & \wr \text{def. implication } \Longrightarrow \wr \\
\iff Y \subseteq \{\langle s,\ s' \rangle \mid s \in \Sigma_i \Longrightarrow s' \in Z\} \iff Y \subseteq \gamma^{\bullet}(Z) & \wr \text{def. } \subseteq, \gamma^{\bullet}. \wr
\end{array}$$

10. The reachability semantics in fixpoint form

To establish the commutation property, we prove that

$$\begin{array}{lll}
& \alpha^{\bullet}(\mathcal{F}_{\tau}^{*}(Y)) & \\
= & \{s' \mid \exists s \in \Sigma_i : \langle s,\ s' \rangle \in (\mathbb{1}_{\Sigma} \cup Y \circ t)\} & \wr \text{by def. } \alpha^{\bullet} \ \&\ \mathcal{F}_{\tau}^{*} \wr \\
= & \{s' \mid \exists s \in \Sigma_i : s' = s\} \cup \{s' \mid \exists s \in \Sigma_i : \exists s'' : \langle s,\ s'' \rangle \in Y \wedge \langle s'',\ s' \rangle \in t)\} & \\
& & \wr \text{by def. } \mathbb{1}_{\Sigma} \ \&\ \text{function composition} \circ \wr \\
= & \Sigma_i \cup \{s' \mid \exists s'' \in \alpha^{\bullet}(Y) \wedge \langle s'',\ s' \rangle \in t)\} & \wr \text{by def. } \alpha^{\bullet} \wr \\
= & \mathcal{F}_{\tau}^{\bullet}(\alpha^{\bullet}(Y)) & \wr \text{by defining } \mathcal{F}_{\tau}^{\bullet}(Z) = \Sigma_i \cup \mathrm{post}[t]Z. \wr
\end{array}$$

By the fixpoint transfer theorem, it follows that $\alpha^{\bullet}(t^*) = \alpha^{\bullet}(\mathrm{lfp}_{\emptyset}^{\subseteq}\, \mathcal{F}_{\tau}^{*}) = \mathrm{lfp}_{\emptyset}^{\subseteq}\, \mathcal{F}_{\tau}^{\bullet}$.

Observe that if Σ is finite, we have a forward reachability iterative algorithm (since $\mathrm{lfp}_{\emptyset}^{\subseteq}\, \mathcal{F}_{\tau}^{\bullet} = \bigcup_{n \geq 0} \mathcal{F}_{\tau}^{\bullet\, n}(\emptyset)$) which can be used to check e.g. that all reachable states satisfy a given safety specification S: $\alpha^{\bullet}(t^*) \subseteq S \iff \forall n : \mathcal{F}_{\tau}^{\bullet\, n}(\emptyset) \subseteq S$.

11. The interval semantics as an abstraction of the reachability semantics

In case the set of states of a transition system $\tau = \langle \Sigma, \Sigma_i, t\rangle$ is totally ordered $\langle \Sigma, <\rangle$ with extrema $-\infty$ and $+\infty$[1], the interval semantics $\alpha^{\text{H}}(\alpha^{\bullet}(t^*))$ of τ provides bounds on its reachable states $\alpha^{\bullet}(t^*)$:

$$\alpha^{\text{H}}(Z) \quad = \quad [\min Z, \max Z]$$

where $\min Z$ ($\max Z$) is the infimum (resp. supremum) of the set Z and $\min \emptyset = +\infty$ (resp. $\max \emptyset = -\infty$). All empty intervals $[\ell, h]$ with $h < \ell$ are identified to $[+\infty, -\infty]$. By defining the concretization $\gamma^{\text{H}}([\ell, h]) = \{s \in \Sigma \mid \ell \leq s \leq h\}$, we can define the abstract implication $[\ell, h] \sqsubseteq [\ell', h']$ as $\gamma^{\text{H}}([\ell, h]) \subseteq \gamma^{\text{H}}([\ell', h'])$ or equivalently $(\ell' \leq \ell \wedge h \leq h')$. We have a Galois connection:

$$\begin{aligned}
& \alpha^{\text{H}}(Z) \sqsubseteq [\ell, h] \iff [\min Z, \max Z] \sqsubseteq [\ell, h] && \wr\text{def. } \alpha^{\text{H}}\wr \\
\iff & \ell \leq \min Z \wedge \max Z \leq h && \wr\text{def. } \sqsubseteq\wr \\
\iff & Z \subseteq \{s \in \Sigma \mid \ell \leq s \leq h\} && \wr\text{def. min \& max}\wr \\
\iff & Z \subseteq \gamma^{\text{H}}([\ell, h]) && \wr\text{def. } \gamma^{\text{H}}\wr
\end{aligned}$$

By defining $\bigsqcup_{i\in\Delta}[\ell_i, h_i] = [\min_{i\in\Delta} \ell_i, \max_{i\in\Delta} h_i]$, the characteristic property that Galois connections preserves least upper bounds is now $\alpha^{\text{H}}(\bigcup_{i\in\Delta} Z_i) = \bigsqcup_{i\in\Delta} \alpha^{\text{H}}(Z_i)$.

12. The interval semantics in fixpoint form

Obviously, $\alpha^{\text{H}}(\emptyset) = [+\infty, -\infty]$. Moreover:

$$\begin{aligned}
& \alpha^{\text{H}}(\mathcal{F}^{\bullet}_{\tau}(Z)) \; = \; \alpha^{\text{H}}(\Sigma_i \cup \text{post}[t]Z) && \wr\text{def. } \mathcal{F}^{\bullet}_{\tau}\wr \\
= \; & \alpha^{\text{H}}(\Sigma_i) \sqcup \alpha^{\text{H}}(\text{post}[t]Z) && \wr\text{Galois connection}\wr \\
\sqsubseteq \; & [\min \Sigma_i, \max \Sigma_i] \sqcup \alpha^{\text{H}}(\text{post}[t](\gamma^{\text{H}}(\alpha^{\text{H}}(Z)))) && \wr\text{def.}
\end{aligned}$$

α^{H} and since $Z \subseteq \gamma^{\text{H}}(\alpha^{\text{H}}(Z))$ so $\text{post}[t]Z \subseteq \text{post}[t](\gamma^{\text{H}}(\alpha^{\text{H}}(Z)))$ whence $\alpha^{\text{H}}(\text{post}[t]Z) \sqsubseteq \alpha^{\text{H}}(\text{post}[t](\gamma^{\text{H}}(\alpha^{\text{H}}(Z))))\wr$

$\sqsubseteq \mathcal{F}^{\text{H}}_{\tau}(\alpha^{\text{H}}(Z))$ $\wr$by defining $\mathcal{F}^{\text{H}}_{\tau}$ such that $[\min \Sigma_i, \max \Sigma_i] \sqcup \alpha^{\text{H}} \circ \text{post}[t] \circ \gamma^{\text{H}}(I) \sqsubseteq \mathcal{F}^{\text{H}}_{\tau}(I)\wr$

We only have *semi-commutation* $\alpha^{\text{H}}(\mathcal{F}^{\bullet}_{\tau}(Z)) \sqsubseteq \mathcal{F}^{\text{H}}_{\tau}(\alpha^{\text{H}}(Z))$ hence a *fixpoint approximation* [Cousot and Cousot, 1979]: $\alpha^{\text{H}}(\alpha^{\bullet}(t^*)) = \alpha^{\text{H}}(\text{lfp}^{\subseteq}_{\emptyset}\, \mathcal{F}^{\bullet}_{\tau}) \sqsubseteq \text{lfp}^{\sqsubseteq}_{[+\infty,-\infty]}\, \mathcal{F}^{\text{H}}_{\tau}$. So questions $\alpha^{\bullet}(t^*) \subseteq \gamma^{\text{H}}(S)$ have sound answers $\text{lfp}^{\sqsubseteq}_{[+\infty,-\infty]}\, \mathcal{F}^{\text{H}}_{\tau} \sqsubseteq S$ in the abstract.

[1] or, more generally, form a complete lattice.

13. Convergence acceleration

In general, the iterates $\mathrm{lfp}^{\sqsubseteq}_{[+\infty,-\infty]} \mathcal{F}^{\mathrm{H}}_{\tau} = \bigsqcup_{n\geq 0} \mathcal{F}^{\mathrm{H}\,n}_{\tau}([+\infty,-\infty])$ diverge.

For example for the transition system $\langle \mathbb{Z}, \{0\}, \{\langle x, x'\rangle \mid x' = x+1\}\rangle$ of program `x := 0; while true do x := x + 1`, we get $\mathcal{F}^{\mathrm{H}}_{\tau}([\ell,h]) = [0,0] \sqcup [\ell+1, h+1]$ with diverging iterates $[+\infty,-\infty]$, $[0,0]$, $[0,1]$, ..., $[0,n]$, ... which least upper bound is $[0,+\infty]$.

14. Widening

Therefore, to accelerate convergence, we introduce a *widening* ∇ [Cousot and Cousot, 1977] such that $I \sqsubseteq I \nabla J$, $J \sqsubseteq I \nabla J$ and the *iterates with widening* defined as $I^0 = [+\infty,-\infty]$, $I^{n+1} = I^n$ if $\mathcal{F}^{\mathrm{H}}_{\tau}(I^n) \sqsubseteq I^n$ while $I^{n+1} = I^n \nabla \mathcal{F}^{\mathrm{H}}_{\tau}(I^n)$ otherwise do converge. Then their limit I^λ is finite ($\lambda \in \mathbb{N}$) and is a *fixpoint overapproximation* $\mathrm{lfp}^{\sqsubseteq}_{[+\infty,-\infty]} \mathcal{F}^{\mathrm{H}}_{\tau} \sqsubseteq I^\lambda$.

An example of interval widening consists in choosing a finite ramp $-\infty = r_0 < r_1 < \ldots < r_k = +\infty$, $k \geq 1$ and $[+\infty,-\infty] \nabla [\ell',h'] = [\ell',h']$ while, otherwise, $[\ell,h] \nabla [\ell',h'] = [$if $\ell' < \ell$ then $\max\{r_i \mid r_i \leq \ell'\}$ else ℓ, if $h' > h$ then $\min\{r_i \mid h' \leq r_i\}$ else $h]$.

For the transition system $\langle \mathbb{Z}, \{0\}, \{\langle x, x'\rangle \mid x < 100 \wedge x' = x+1\}\rangle$ of program `x := 0; while x < 100 do x := x + 1` and ramp $-\infty < -1 < 0 < 1 < +\infty$, we have $\mathcal{F}^{\mathrm{H}}_{\tau}([\ell,h]) = [0,0] \sqcup [\ell+1, \min(99,h)+1]$ and the iterates with widening $I^0 = [+\infty,-\infty]$, $I^1 = I^0 \nabla \mathcal{F}^{\mathrm{H}}_{\tau}(I^0) = \mathcal{F}^{\mathrm{H}}_{\tau}(I^0) = [0,0] \sqcup [1,1] = [0,1]$, $I^2 = I^1 \nabla \mathcal{F}^{\mathrm{H}}_{\tau}(I^1) = [0,1] \nabla [0,2] = [0,+\infty]$. This is the limit of these iterates with widening since $\mathcal{F}^{\mathrm{H}}_{\tau}([0,+\infty]) = [0,100] \sqsubseteq [0,+\infty]$.

15. Narrowing

The limit of an iteration with widening can be improved by a *narrowing* Δ [Cousot and Cousot, 1977] such that $J \sqsubseteq I$ implies $J \sqsubseteq I \Delta J \sqsubseteq I$. All terms in the *iterates with narrowing* $J^0 = I^\lambda, \ldots, J^{n+1} = J^n \Delta \mathcal{F}^{\mathrm{H}}_{\tau}(J^0)$ improve the result obtained by widening since $\mathrm{lfp}^{\sqsubseteq}_{[+\infty,-\infty]} \mathcal{F}^{\mathrm{H}}_{\tau} \sqsubseteq J^n \sqsubseteq I^\lambda$.

An example of interval narrowing is $[\ell,h] \Delta [\ell',h'] = [$if $\exists i : \ell = r_i$ then ℓ' else ℓ, if $\exists j : h = r_j$ then h' else $h]$.

For the program `x := 0; while x < 100 do x := x + 1`, we have $J^0 = [0,+\infty]$, $J^1 = [0,+\infty] \Delta \mathcal{F}^{\mathrm{H}}_{\tau}([0,+\infty]) = [0,+\infty] \Delta [0,100] = [0,100]$ and so $J^n = [0,100]$ for $n \geq 1$ since $\mathcal{F}^{\mathrm{H}}_{\tau}([0,100]) = [0,100]$.

16. Composition of abstractions

We have defined three abstractions of the partial trace semantics $\Sigma^{\vec{*}}_{\tau}$ of a transition system τ. The design was compositional in that the composition

$\langle \alpha^{\mathrm{H}} \circ \alpha^{\bullet} \circ \alpha^{*}, \gamma^{*} \circ \gamma^{\bullet} \circ \gamma^{\mathrm{H}} \rangle$ of Galois connections is a Galois connection so the successive arguments on sound approximations do compose nicely.

17. Hierarchy of semantics

The four semantics of a transition system $\tau = \langle \Sigma, \Sigma_i, t \rangle$ that we have considered form a hierarchy from the partial traces $\Sigma_\tau^{\vec{*}}$, to the reflexive transitive closure $\alpha^*(\Sigma_\tau^{\vec{*}})$, reachability $\alpha^\bullet \circ \alpha^*(\Sigma_\tau^{\vec{*}})$ and interval semantics $\alpha^{\mathrm{H}} \circ \alpha^\bullet \circ \alpha^*(\Sigma_\tau^{\vec{*}})$, in abstraction order. The complete range of other possible abstract semantics include all classical ones for programming languages [Cousot, 2002]. By undecidability, none is computable, but effective widening/narrowing iterations can be used to compute approximations (which are more precise than resorting to finite abstractions, as in abstract model checking [Cousot and Cousot, 1992b]). More abstract semantics can answer less questions precisely than more concrete semantics but are cheaper to compute or approximate. This covers all static analysis, including dataflow analysis [Cousot and Cousot, 1979], abstract model checking [Cousot, 2000b], typing [Cousot, 1997], etc. In practice the right balance between precision and cost can lead to precise and efficient abstractions, as for example in *Astrée* [Blanchet et al., 2003].

References

Blanchet, B., Cousot, P., Cousot, R., Feret, J., Mauborgne, L., Miné, A., Monniaux, D., and Rival, X. (2003). A static analyzer for large safety-critical software. *PLDI'2003*, 196–207, ACM.

Cousot, P. (1978). Méthodes itératives de construction et d'approximation de points fixes d'opérateurs monotones sur un treillis, analyse sémantique de programmes. Thèse d'État ès sciences mathématiques, Grenoble University, 21 March 1978.

Cousot, P. (1981). Semantic foundations of program analysis. In Muchnick, S.S. and Jones, N.D., editors, *Program Flow Analysis: Theory and Applications*, ch. 10, 303–342. Prentice-Hall.

Cousot, P. (1997). Types as abstract interpretations. *24th POPL*, 316–331, ACM.

Cousot, P. (2000a). Abstract interpretation based formal methods and future challenges. *« Informatics — 10 Years Back, 10 Years Ahead »*, LNCS 2000, 138–156, Springer.

Cousot, P. (2000b). Partial completeness of abstract fixpoint checking. *SARA'2000*, LNAI 1864, 1–25, Springer.

Cousot, P. (2002). Constructive design of a hierarchy of semantics of a transition system by abstract interpretation. *Theoret. Comput. Sci.*, 277(1—2):47–103.

Cousot, P. and Cousot, R. (1977). Abstract interpretation: a unified lattice model for static analysis of programs by construction or approximation of fixpoints. *4th POPL*, 238–252, ACM.

Cousot, P. and Cousot, R. (1979). Systematic design of program analysis frameworks. *6th POPL*, 269–282, ACM.

Cousot, P. and Cousot, R. (1992a). Abstract interpretation frameworks. *J. Logic and Comp.*, 2(4):511–547.

Cousot, P. and Cousot, R. (1992b). Comparing the Galois connection and widening/narrowing approaches to abstract interpretation. *PLILP'92*, LNCS 631, 269–295, Springer.

TVLA: A SYSTEM FOR GENERATING ABSTRACT INTERPRETERS*

Tal Lev-Ami, Roman Manevich, and Mooly Sagiv
Tel Aviv University
{tla@trivnet.com, {rumster,msagiv}@post.tau.ac.il}

Abstract TVLA (Three-Valued-Logic Analyzer) is a "YACC"-like framework for automatically constructing abstract interpreters from an operational semantics. The operational semantics is specified as a generic transition system based on first-order logic. TVLA was implemented in Java and successfully used to prove interesting properties of (concurrent) Java programs manipulating dynamically allocated linked data structures.

1. Introduction

The abstract-interpretation technique of [Cousot and Cousot, 1979] for static analysis allows one to summarize the behavior of a statement on an infinite set of possible program states. This is sometimes called an *abstract semantics* for the statement. With this methodology it is necessary to show that the abstract semantics is *conservative*, i.e., it summarizes the *(concrete) operational semantics* of the statement for every possible program state. Intuitively speaking, the operational semantics of a statement is a formal definition of an interpreter for this statement. This operational semantics is usually quite natural. However, designing and implementing sound and reasonably precise abstract semantics is quite cumbersome (the best induced abstract semantics defined in [Cousot and Cousot, 1979] is usually not computable). This is particularly true in problems like shape analysis and pointer analysis (e.g., see [Sagiv et al., 1998; Sagiv et al., 2002]), where the operational semantics involves destructive memory updates.

*Supported, in part, by a grant from the Academy of Science, Israel.

1.1 An Overview of the TVLA System

In this paper, we review TVLA (Three-Valued-Logic Analyzer), a system for automatically generating a static-analysis implementation from the operational semantics of a given program ([Lev-Ami and Sagiv, 2000]). The small-step structural operational semantics is written in a meta-language based on first-order predicate logic with transitive closure. The main idea is that program states are represented as logical structures and the program transition system is defined using first-order logical formulas. TVLA automatically generates the abstract semantics, and, for each program point, produces a conservative abstract representation of the program states at that point. The idea of automatically generating abstract semantics from concrete semantics was proposed in [Cousot, 1997].

TVLA is intended as a proof of concept for abstract interpreters. It is a test-bed in which it is quite easy to try out new ideas. The theory behind TVLA is based on [Sagiv et al., 2002].

Static Analysis Using TVLA A front-end `J2TVLA` converts a Java program into `tvp`, the input meta-language of TVLA. This front-end is available separately and is not further described in this document. A typical input of TVLA consists of four text files: (i) The type of concrete states of the analyzed programs is defined in the file `pred.tvp`. This file defines predicates (relation symbols) which hold concrete values of variables and program stores. (ii) The meaning of atomic program statements and conditions is defined in the action file `acts.tvp`. Actions allow to naturally model program conditions and mutations of stores. They are defined using first-order logical formulas. TVLA actions can also produce error messages when safety violations occur. Both actions and predicates are usually defined once for a given analysis. They are parameterized by information specific to the analyzed program, such as the names of program variables, types, fields, and classes. (iii) A file `fots.tvp` defines the transition system of the analyzed program. It is basically a control flow graph with edges annotated by actions from the action file, and can be automatically generated by `J2TVLA` for Java programs. (iv) The `tvs` file `init.tvs` describes the abstract value at the program entry. It can be used to allow modular TVLA analysis of a separate program component, which does not start with an empty store.

The core of the TVLA engine is a standard chaotic iteration procedure, where actions are conservatively interpreted over an abstract domain of 3-*valued structures*. This means that the system guarantees that no safety violation is missed but it may produce "false alarms", i.e., warnings about violations that can never occur in any concrete execution. Finally, TVLA allows to investigate the output 3-valued structures, which can either be displayed in `Postscript` format or as a `tvs` file `out.tvs` to be read by other tools.

Table 1. Predicates used to verify the running example.

Predicates	Intended Meaning
$x(v)$	reference variable x points to the object v
$t(v)$	reference variable t points to the object v
$root(v)$	reference variable $root$ points to the object v
$\texttt{left}(v_1, v_2)$	field `left` of the object v_1 points to the object v_2
$\texttt{right}(v_1, v_2)$	field `right` of the object v_1 points to the object v_2
$set[marked](v)$	object v is a member of the $marked$ set
$set[pending](v)$	object v is a member of the $pending$ set
$r[root](v)$	object v is heap-reachable from reference variable $root$

The unique part of TVLA is the automatic generation of the abstract interpretation of actions in a way that is: (i) guaranteed to be sound, and (ii) rather precise—the number of false alarms in our applications is very small.

Outline The rest of this tutorial is organized as follows: In Sect. 2 we describe the TVLA meta-language for constructing concrete semantics; In Sect. 3 we provide an overview of 3-valued logical based static analysis; In Sect. 4 we describe several enhancements and applications of the system; and in Sect. 5 we give concluding remarks.

2. First-Order Transition Systems

We now present an overview of *first order transition systems* (FOTS). In FOTS, program statements are modelled by *actions* that specify how the statement transforms an incoming logical structure into an outgoing logical structure.

A Running Example Fig. 2 shows our running example—a method implementing the Mark phase of a mark-and-sweep garbage collector and its transition system. The challenge here is to show that this method is partially correct, i.e., to establish that "upon termination, an element is marked if and only if it is reachable from the root." TVLA successfully verifies this correctness property in 5 CPU seconds.

2.1 Concrete Program States

In FOTS, program states are represented using 2-valued logical structures.

In the context of heap analysis, a logical structure represents the memory state (heap) of a program, with each individual corresponding to a heap-allocated object and predicates of the structure corresponding to properties of heap-allocated objects.

```
//@Ensures marked == REACH(root)
void mark(Node root, NodeSet marked){
  Node x, t;
  if (root != null) {
     NodeSet pending = new NodeSet();
     pending.add(root);
     marked = new NodeSet();
     while (!pending.isEmpty()) {
       x = pending.selectAndRemove();
       marked.add(x);
       t = x.left;
       if (t != null)
          if (!marked.contains(t))
             pending.add(t);
          x = x.right;
          if (t != null)
             if (!marked.contains(t)
                pending.add(t);
     }
  }
}
```

```
n0  IsNotNull(root)                  n1
n1  AssignEmpty(pending)             n2
n2  Add(pending,root)                n3
n3  AssignEmpty(marked)              n4
n4  NotIsEmpty(pending)              n5
n4  IsEmpty(pending)                 n17
n5  SelectAndRemove(pending,x)       n6
n6  Add(marked,x)                    n7
n7  Load(t,x,left)                   n8
n8  IsNotNull(t)                     n9
n8  IsNull(t)                        n12
n9  NotContains(marked,t)            n11
n9  Contains(marked,t)               n12
n11 Add(pending,t)                   n12
n12 Load(t,x,right)                  n13
n13 IsNotNull(t)                     n14
n13 IsNull(t)                        n4
n14 NotContains(marked,t)            n16
n14 Contains(marked,t)               n4
n16 Add(pending,t)                   n4
n17 NotEqualReach(marked,root)       error
n17 EqualReach(marked,root)          exit
```

Figure 1. A simple Java-like implementation of the mark phase of a mark-and-sweep garbage collector and its transition system.

Table 1 shows the predicates we use to record properties of individuals for the analysis of our running example. A unary predicate $x(v)$ holds when the reference (or pointer) variable x points to the object v. Similarly, a binary predicate $fld(v_1, v_2)$ records the value of a reference (or pointer-valued) field `fld`; in our example `fld` $\in$ {`left`, `right`}. A unary predicate $set[s](v)$ holds when the object v belongs to the set s; in our example $s \in \{marked, pending\}$. The predicate $r[root](v)$ is a special kind of predicate, used to record reachability information. It is not needed to define the concrete semantics, but is needed to refine the abstraction. Here, it is used to distinguish between individuals that are reachable from the root variable and individuals that are garbage. Predicates of this kind are called "instrumentation predicates".

In this paper, program states (i.e., 2-valued logical structures) are depicted as directed graphs. Each individual of the universe is drawn as a node. A unary predicate $p(o)$, which holds for a node u, is drawn inside the node u. If a unary predicate represents a reference variable it is shown by having an arrow drawn from its name to the node pointed by the variable. A binary predicate $p(u_1, u_2)$ that evaluates to 1 is drawn as a directed edge from u_1 to u_2 labelled with the predicate symbol.

Fig. 2(a) shows an example of a concrete program state arising before the statement `t = x.left`.

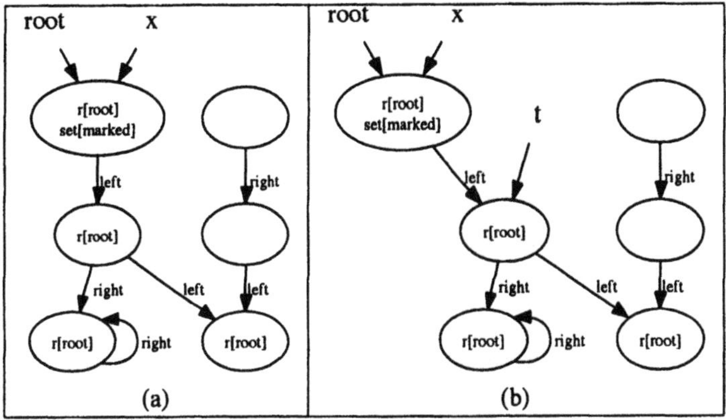

Figure 2. (a) A concrete program state arising before the statement `t = x.left`; (b) A concrete program state arising after the statement `t = x.left`.

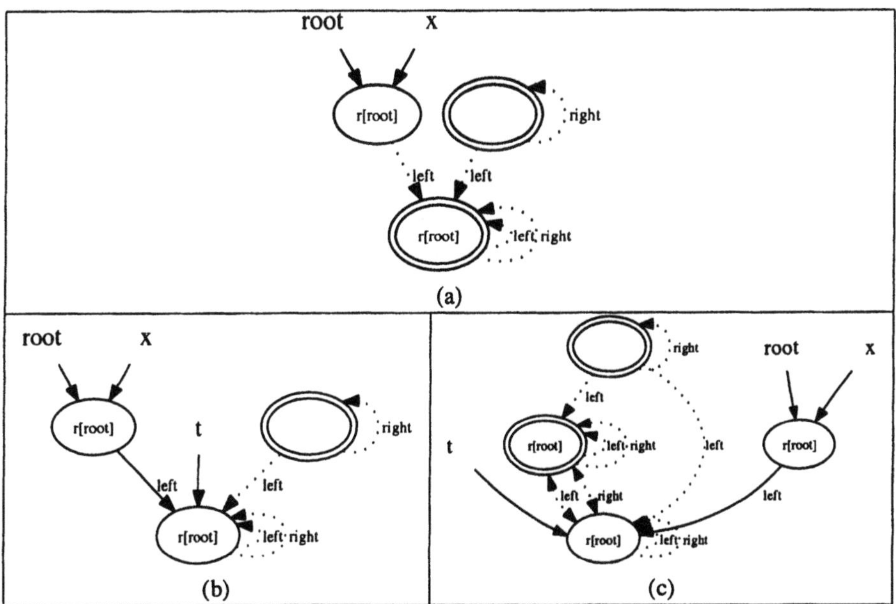

Figure 3. (a) An abstract program state approximating the concrete program state shown in Fig. 2(a); (b) and (c) are the abstract program states resulting from the abstract interpretation of the action `Load(t,x,left)`.

3. 3-Valued-Logic-Based Analysis

We now describe the abstraction used to create a finite (bounded) representation of a potentially unbounded set of 2-valued structures of potentially unbounded size. The abstraction is based on 3-valued logic, which extends boolean logic by introducing a third value $1/2$ denoting values that may be 0 or 1.

A 3-valued logical structure can be used as an abstraction of a larger 2-valued logical structure. This is achieved by letting an abstract state (i.e., a 3-valued logical structure) to include *summary nodes*, i.e., individuals that correspond to one or more individuals in a concrete state represented by that abstract state. During the sequel of this paper, we will assume that the set of predicates P includes a distinguished unary predicate *sm* to indicate if an individual is a summary node.

In this paper, 3-valued logical structures are also depicted as directed graphs, where binary predicates with $1/2$ values are shown as dotted edges and summary individuals are shown as double-circled nodes.

TVLA relies on a fundamental abstraction operation for converting a potentially unbounded structure into a bounded 3-valued structure. This abstraction operation is parameterized by a special set of unary predicates A referred to as the *abstraction* predicates.

Let A be a set of unary predicates. Individuals u_1 and u_2 in a structure S are said to be A-equivalent iff for every predicate $p \in A$, $p^S(u_1) = p^S(u_2)$. A 3-valued structure is said to be A-bounded if no two different individuals in its universe are A-equivalent.

Informally, an A-bounded structure can be obtained from any structure by merging all pairs of A-compatible nodes, resulting in a structure with at most $2^{|A|}$ individuals that approximates the original (non-bounded) structure.

Fig. 3(a) shows an A-bounded structure obtained from the structure in Fig. 2(a) with $A = \{x, t, root, r[root], set[marked], set[pending]\}$.

3.1 Abstract Semantics

TVLA automatically produces an implementation of an abstract transformer for every action, which is guaranteed to be a conservative approximation of that action. Users can tune the transformer to achieve a high degree of precision. For example, in Fig. 3, the application of the transformer of the action `Load(t,x,left)` to the structure in (a) results in the structures shown in (b) and (c). In this case, the result is identical to the result of the best (most precise) transformer.

4. TVLA Enhancements and Applications

In this section we sketch several TVLA enhancements that were implemented in order to increase applicability, and mention some applications.

Algorithm Explanation by Shape Analysis In [Bieber, 2001], TVLA is extended with visualization capabilities to allow re-playing changes in abstract states along different control-flow paths.

Finite Differencing In [Reps et al., 2003], an algorithm for generating predicate-update formulas for instrumentation predicates is described. This technique is applied to generate predicate-update formulas for intricate procedures manipulating tree data structures.

Automatic Generation of Instrumentation Predicates In [Ramalingam et al., 2002], a technique for generating instrumentation predicates based on backward weakest preconditions is described. This technique is applied to verify the absence of concurrent modification exceptions in Java. In [Loginov et al., 2004], orthogonal techniques for (forward) generation of instrumentation predicates are applied to prove the correctness and stability of sorting algorithms.

Compactly Representing 3-Valued Structures In [Manevich et al., 2002], the space cost of TVLA is reduced by representing 3-valued structures with data structures that share equivalent sub-parts.

Partially Disjunctive Abstractions In [Manevich et al., 2004], the cost of TVLA analyses is reduced by applying more aggressive abstractions. The running time of the running example is reduced from 579 CPU seconds to 5 CPU seconds.

Numeric Abstractions In [Gopan et al., 2004] it is shown how to handle numeric properties for an unbounded number of elements. This allows more precise and more automatic analyses using existing numeric abstractions. The method is applied to show absence of array bound violations in a program implementing sparse matrix multiplications using double indirections (i.e., `a[b[j]]`).

Best Transformers In [Yorsh et al., 2004], theorem-provers are harnessed to compute the best (induced) transformers for 3-valued structures. This can be applied for modular assume-guarantee abstract interpretation in order to handle large programs with partial specifications.

Heterogenous Abstractions In [Yahav and Ramalingam, 2004], a framework for *heterogeneous abstraction* is proposed, allowing different parts of the heap to be abstracted with different degrees of precision at different points during the analysis. The framework is applied to prove correct usage of JDBC objects and I/O streams, and absence of concurrent modifications in Java collections and iterators.

Interprocedural Analysis In [Rinetzky and Sagiv, 2001], TVLA is applied to handle procedures by explicitly representing activation records as a linked list, allowing rather precise analysis of recursive procedures.

Concurrent Java Programs [Yahav, 2001] presents a general framework for proving safety properties of concurrent Java programs with unbounded number of objects and threads. In [Yahav and Sagiv, 2003] it is applied to verify partial correctness of a two-lock queue implementation.

Temporal Properties [Yahav et al., 2003] proposes a general framework for proving temporal properties by representing program traces as logical structures. A more efficient technique for proving local temporal properties is presented in [Shaham et al., 2003] and applied for compile-time garbage collection in Javacard programs.

5. Conclusion

TVLA is a system for generating implementations of static analysis algorithms, successfully used for a wide range of applications. Several aspects contributed to the usefulness of the system:

Firm theoretical background TVLA is based on the theoretical framework of [Sagiv et al., 2002], which provides a proof of soundness via the embedding theorem. This relieves users from having to prove the soundness of the analysis.

Powerful meta-language The language of first-order logic with transitive closure is highly expressive. Users can specify different verification properties, and model semantics of different programming languages and different programming paradigms.

Automation and flexibility TVLA generates several ingredients that are essential for a precise static analysis. Users can tune the precision and control the cost of the generated algorithm.

Although TVLA is useful for solving different problems, it has certain limitations. The cost of the generated algorithm can be quite prohibitive, preventing analysis of large programs. Some of the costs can be reduced by better engineering certain components and other costs can be reduced by developing more efficient abstract transformers. The problem of generating more precise algorithms deserves further research.

References

Bieber, R. (2001). Alexsa—algorithm explanation by shape analysis—extensions to the TVLA system. Diplomarbeit, Universitat des Saarlandes, Saarbrucken, Germany.

Cousot, P. (1997). Abstract interpretation based static analysis parameterized by semantics. In *Static Analysis Symp.*, pages 388–394.

Cousot, P. and Cousot, R. (1979). Systematic design of program analysis frameworks. In *Symp. on Princ. of Prog. Lang.*, pages 269–282, New York, NY. ACM Press.

Gopan, D., DiMaio, F., Dor, N., Reps, T., and Sagiv, M. (2004). Numeric domains with summarized dimensions. In *Int. Conf. on Tools and Algs. for the Construction and Analysis of Systems*, pages 512–529.

Lev-Ami, T. and Sagiv, M. (2000). TVLA: A system for implementing static analyses. In *Static Analysis Symp.*, pages 280–301.

Loginov, A., Reps, T., and Sagiv, M. (2004). Abstraction refinement for 3-valued-logic analysis. Tech. Rep. 1504, Comp. Sci. Dept., Univ. of Wisconsin.

Manevich, R., Ramalingam, G., Field, J., Goyal, D., and Sagiv, M. (2002). Compactly representing first-order structures for static analysis. In *Static Analysis Symp.*, pages 196–212.

Manevich, R., Sagiv, M., G.Ramalingam, and J.Field (2004). Partially disjunctive heap abstraction. In *Static Analysis Symp.* To appear.

Ramalingam, G., Warshavsky, A., Field, J., Goyal, D., and Sagiv, M. (2002). Deriving specialized program analyses for certifying component-client conformance. In *SIGPLAN Conf. on Prog. Lang. Design and Impl.*, pages 83–94.

Reps, T., Sagiv, M., and Loginov, A. (2003). Finite differencing of logical formulas for static analysis. In *European Symp. on Programming*, pages 380–398.

Rinetzky, N. and Sagiv, M. (2001). Interprocedural shape analysis for recursive programs. In Wilhelm, R., editor, *Proc. of CC 2001*, volume 2027 of *LNCS*, pages 133–149. Springer.

Sagiv, M., Reps, T., and Wilhelm, R. (1998). Solving shape-analysis problems in languages with destructive updating. *Trans. on Prog. Lang. and Syst.*, 20(1):1–50.

Sagiv, M., Reps, T., and Wilhelm, R. (2002). Parametric shape analysis via 3-valued logic. *Trans. on Prog. Lang. and Syst.*

Shaham, R., Yahav, E., Kolodner, E., and Sagiv, M. (2003). Establishing local temporal heap safety properties with applications to compile-time memory management. In *Proc. of SAS'03*, volume 2694 of *LNCS*, pages 483–503.

Yahav, E. (2001). Verifying safety properties of concurrent Java programs using 3-valued logic. In *Symp. on Princ. of Prog. Lang.*, pages 27–40.

Yahav, E. and Ramalingam, G. (2004). Verifying safety properties using separation and heterogeneous abstractions. In *SIGPLAN Conf. on Prog. Lang. Design and Impl.* To appear.

Yahav, E., Reps, T., Sagiv, M., and Wilhelm, R. (2003). Verifying temporal heap properties specified via evolution logic. In *European Symp. on Programming*, volume 2618 of *LNCS*.

Yahav, E. and Sagiv, M. (2003). Automatically verifying concurrent queue algorithms. In *Workshop on Software Model Checking*.

Yorsh, G., Reps, T., and Sagiv, M. (2004). Symbolically computing most-precise abstract operations for shape analysis. In *Int. Conf. on Tools and Algs. for the Construction and Analysis of Systems*, pages 530–545.

aiT:
WORST-CASE EXECUTION TIME PREDICTION BY STATIC PROGRAM ANALYSIS

Christian Ferdinand and Reinhold Heckmann
AbsInt Angewandte Informatik GmbH,
Stuhlsatzenhausweg 69, D-66123 Saarbrucken, Germany
info@absint.com http://www.absint.com

1. Introduction

Many tasks in safety-critical embedded systems have hard real-time characteristics. Failure to meet deadlines may result in the loss of life or in large damages. Utmost carefulness and state-of-the-art machinery have to be applied to make sure that all requirements are met. To do so lies in the responsibility of the system designer(s). Fortunately, the state of the art in deriving run-time guarantees for real-time systems has progressed so much that tools based on sound methods are commercially available and have proved their usability in industrial practice.

AbsInt's WCET Analyzer **aiT** (`http://www.absint.de/wcet.htm`) is the first automatic tool for checking the correct timing behavior of software in safety-critical embedded systems as found in the aeronautics and automotive industries. To compute automatically upper bounds for the worst-case execution time (WCET), **aiT** first derives safe upper bounds for the execution times of basic blocks and then computes, by integer linear programming, an upper bound on the execution times over all possible paths of the program. These upper bounds are *valid* for all inputs and each task execution, and usually *tight*, i.e. the overestimation of the WCET is small.

2. Challenges of Modern Processor Architecture

In modern microprocessor architectures caches, pipelines, and all kinds of speculation are key features for improving performance. Caches are used to bridge the gap between processor speed and the access time of main memory. Pipelines enable acceleration by overlapping the executions of different instructions. The consequence is that the execution times of individual instructions, and thus the contribution of one execution of an instruction to the

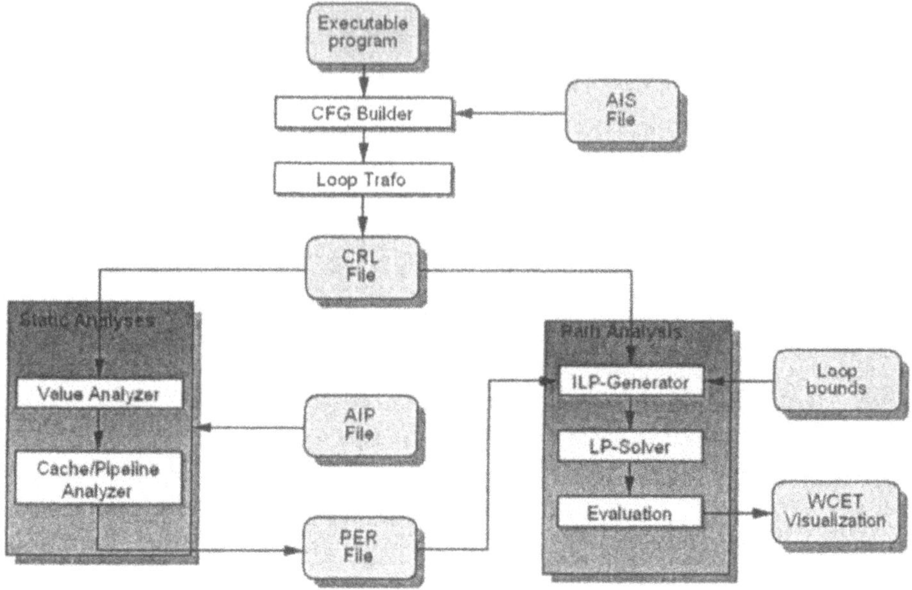

Figure 1. Phases of WCET computation

program's execution time can vary widely. The timing difference between the minimal case (when execution of an instruction goes smoothly through pipeline and cache) and a timing accident (when everything goes wrong) can be in the order of several hundred processor cycles. Since the execution time of an instruction depends on the execution state, e.g., the contents of the cache(s), the occupancy of other resources, and thus on the execution history, the execution time cannot be determined in isolation from the execution history.

3. Phases of WCET Computation

AbsInt's WCET tool **aiT** determines the WCET of a program task in several phases [Ferdinand et al., 2001] (see Figure 1):

- **CFG Building** decodes, i.e. identifies instructions, and reconstructs the control-flow graph (CFG) from a binary program;
- **Value Analysis** computes value ranges for registers and address ranges for instructions accessing memory;
- **Loop Bound Analysis** determines upper bounds for the number of iterations of simple loops;
- **Cache Analysis** classifies memory references as cache misses or hits [Ferdinand, 1997];

- **Pipeline Analysis** predicts the behavior of the program on the processor pipeline [Langenbach et al., 2002];
- **Path Analysis** determines a worst-case execution path of the program [Theiling and Ferdinand, 1998].

Cache Analysis uses the results of value analysis to predict the behavior of the (data) cache. The results of cache analysis are used within pipeline analysis allowing the prediction of pipeline stalls due to cache misses. The combined results of the cache and pipeline analyses are the basis for computing the execution times of program paths. Separating WCET determination into several phases makes it possible to use different methods tailored to the subtasks [Theiling and Ferdinand, 1998]. Value analysis, cache analysis, and pipeline analysis are done by abstract interpretation [Cousot and Cousot, 1977]. Integer linear programming is used for path analysis.

Value Analysis

Value analysis tries to determine the values in the processor registers for every program point and execution context. Often it cannot determine these values exactly, but only finds safe lower and upper bounds, i.e. intervals that are guaranteed to contain the exact values. The results of value analysis are used to determine loop bounds and possible addresses of indirect memory accesses (important for cache analysis).

Value analysis uses the framework of abstract interpretation: an abstract state maps registers to intervals of possible values. Each machine instruction is modeled by a transfer function mapping input states to output states in a way that is compatible with the semantics of the instruction. At control-flow joins, the incoming abstract states are combined into a single outgoing state using a combination function. Because of the presence of loops, transfer and combination functions must be applied repeatedly until the system of abstract states stabilizes. Termination of this fixed-point iteration is ensured on a theoretical level by the monotonicity of transfer and combination functions and the fact that a register can only hold finitely many different values. Practically, value analysis becomes only efficient by applying suitable widening and narrowing operators as proposed in [Cousot and Cousot, 1977]. The results of value analysis are usually so good that only a few indirect accesses cannot be determined exactly. Address ranges for these accesses may be provided by user annotations.

Pipeline Analysis

Pipeline analysis models the pipeline behavior to determine execution times for sequential flows (basic blocks) of instructions, as done in [Schneider and

Ferdinand, 1999]. It takes into account the current pipeline state(s), in particular resource occupancies, contents of prefetch queues, grouping of instructions, and classification of memory references by cache analysis. The result is an execution time for each basic block in each distinguished execution context.

Like value and cache analysis, pipeline analysis is based on the framework of abstract interpretation. Pipeline analysis of a basic block starts with a set of pipeline states determined by the predecessors of the block and lets this set evolve from instruction to instruction by a kind of cycle-wise simulation of machine instructions. In contrast to a real simulation, the abstract execution on the instruction level is in general non-deterministic since information determining the evolution of the execution state is missing, e.g., due to non-predictable cache contents. Therefore, the abstract execution of an instruction may cause a state to split into several successor states. All the states computed in such tree-like structures form the set of entry states for the successor instruction. At the end of the basic block, the final set of states is propagated to the successor blocks. The described evolution of state sets is repeated for all basic blocks until it stabilizes, i.e. the state sets do not change any more.

The output of pipeline analysis is the number of cycles a basic block takes to execute, for each context, obtained by taking the upper bound of the number of simulation cycles for the sequence of instructions for this basic block. These results are then fed into path analysis to obtain the WCET for the entire task.

4. Usage of aiT

aiT reads an executable, user annotations, a description of the (external) memories and buses (i.e. a list of memory areas with minimal and maximal access times), and a task (identified by a start address). A task denotes a sequentially executed piece of code (no threads, no parallelism, and no waiting for external events). This should not be confused with a task in an operating system that might include code for synchronization or communication.

aiT computes an upper bound of the running time of the task (assuming no interference from the outside). Effects of interrupts, IO and timer (co-) processors are not reflected in the predicted running time and have to be considered separately (e.g., by a quantitative analysis).

In addition to the raw information about the WCET, detailed information delivered by the analysis can be visualized by **AbsInt's aiSee** tool (`http://www.aisee.com`). Figure 2 shows the graphical representation of the call graph for some small example. The calls (edges) that contribute to the worst-case running time are marked by the color red. The computed WCET is given in CPU cycles and in microseconds.

Figure 3 shows the basic block graph of a loop. The number `max #` describes the maximal number of traversals of an edge in the worst case, while

Worst Case Execution Time: 2389 cycles = 53.089 us

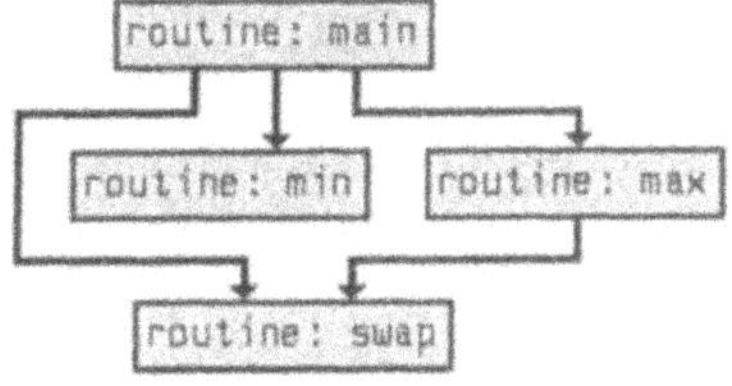

Figure 2. Call graph with WCET results

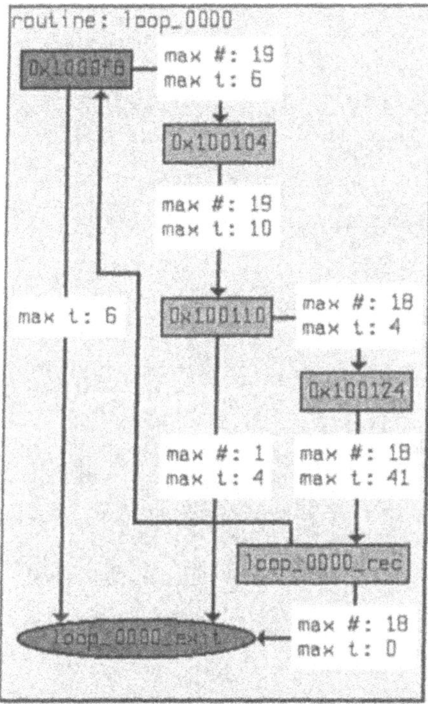

Figure 3. Basic block graph in a loop, with timing information

`max t` describes the maximal execution time of the basic block from which the edge originates (taking into account that the basic block is left via the edge). The worst-case path, the iteration numbers and timings are determined automatically by **aiT**.

Figure 4 shows the development of possible pipeline states for a basic block in this example. Such pictures are shown by **aiT** upon special demand. The grey boxes correspond to the instructions of the basic block, and the smaller

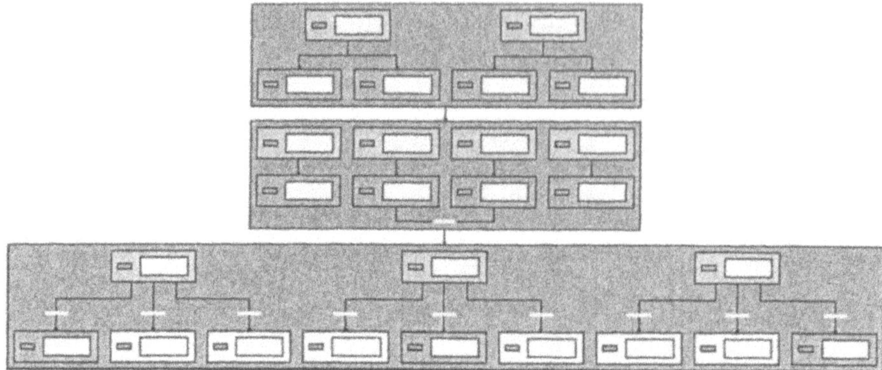

Figure 4. Possible pipeline states in a basic block

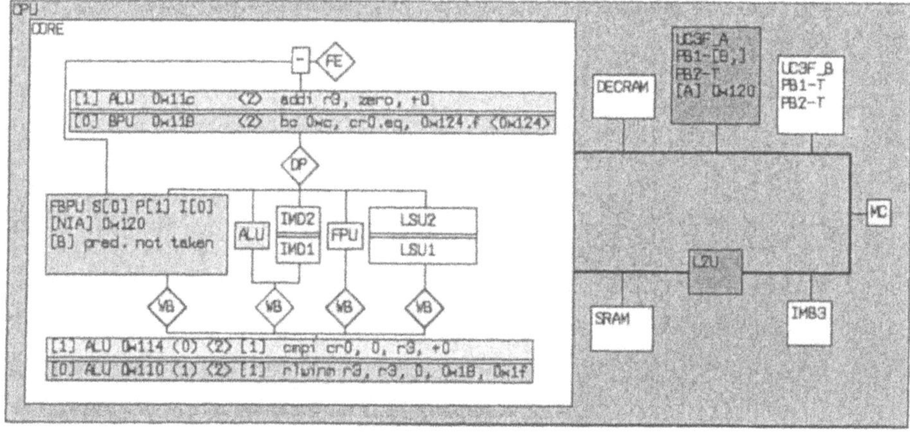

Figure 5. Individual pipeline state

rectangles are individual pipeline states. Their cycle-wise evolution is indicated by the edges connecting them. Each layer in the trees corresponds to one CPU cycle. Branches in the trees are caused by conditions that could not be statically evaluated, e.g., a memory access with unknown address in presence of memory areas with different access times. On the other hand, two pipeline states fall together when the details they differ in leave the pipeline. This happened for instance at the end of the second instruction.

Figure 5 shows part of the top left pipeline state from Figure 4 in greater magnification. It displays a diagram of the architecture of the CPU (in this case a PowerPC 555) showing the occupancy of the various pipeline stages with the instructions currently being executed.

5. Conclusion

aiT enables one to develop complex hard real-time systems on state-of-the-art hardware, increases safety, and saves development time. It has been applied to real-life benchmark programs containing realistically sized code modules. Precise timing predictions make it possible to choose the most cost-efficient hardware. Tools like **aiT** are of high importance as recent trends, e.g., X-by-wire, require the knowledge of the WCET of tasks.

References

Cousot, Patrick and Cousot, Radhia (1977). Abstract Interpretation: A Unified Lattice Model for Static Analysis of Programs by Construction or Approximation of Fixpoints. In *Proceedings of the 4th ACM Symposium on Principles of Programming Languages*, Los Angeles, California.

Ferdinand, Christian (1997). *Cache Behavior Prediction for Real-Time Systems*. PhD thesis, Saarland University.

Ferdinand, Christian, Heckmann, Reinhold, Langenbach, Marc, Martin, Florian, Schmidt, Michael, Theiling, Henrik, Thesing, Stephan, and Wilhelm, Reinhard (2001). Reliable and precise WCET determination for a real-life processor. In *Proceedings of EMSOFT 2001, First Workshop on Embedded Software*, volume 2211 of *Lecture Notes in Computer Science*, pages 469–485. Springer-Verlag.

Langenbach, Marc, Thesing, Stephan, and Heckmann, Reinhold (2002). Pipeline modeling for timing analysis. In *Proceedings of the 9th International Static Analysis Symposium SAS 2002*, volume 2477 of *Lecture Notes in Computer Science*, pages 294–309. Springer-Verlag.

Schneider, Jørn and Ferdinand, Christian (1999). Pipeline Behavior Prediction for Superscalar Processors by Abstract Interpretation. In *Proceedings of the ACM SIGPLAN Workshop on Languages, Compilers and Tools for Embedded Systems*, volume 34, pages 35–44.

Theiling, Henrik and Ferdinand, Christian (1998). Combining abstract interpretation and ILP for microarchitecture modelling and program path analysis. In *Proceedings of the 19th IEEE Real-Time Systems Symposium*, pages 144–153, Madrid, Spain.

ASTRÉE: VERIFICATION OF ABSENCE OF RUN-TIME ERROR*

Laurent Mauborgne
École Normale Supérieure
Paris, France
astree@ens.fr
http://www.astree.ens.fr

Keywords: Static analysis, abstract interpretation, verification, critical software.

1. Introduction

Everybody knows about failure problems in software: it is an admitted fact that most large software do contain bugs. The cost of such bugs can be very high for our society and many methods have been proposed to try to reduce these failures. While merely reducing the number of bugs may be economically sound in many areas, in critical software (such as found in power plants or aeronautics), no failure can be accepted.

In order to achieve an unfailing critical software, industrials follow very strict production patterns and must also certify the absence of errors through state-of-the-art verification. When old verification methodologies became intractable in time and cost due to the growth of code size, the Abstract Interpretation Team[2] of École Normale Supérieure started developing Astrée [Blanchet et al., 2002]. The object of Astrée is the automatic discovery of all potential errors of a certain class for critical software. As most critical software don't (or won't) have any error, the main challenge was to be exhaustive and very selective, that is yielding few or no false alarms on the software, so as to reduce the cost of verifying those alarms.

In this paper, we show how Astrée is based on sound approximations of the semantics of C programs, tailored to be very accurate on a class of embedded

*Work supported in part by the Réseau National de recherche et d'innovation en Technologies Logicielles (RNTL) exploratory 2002 project ASTRÉE.

[2]The team that developed Astrée is composed of Bruno Blanchet, Patrick Cousot, Radhia Cousot, Jérôme Feret, Laurent Mauborgne, Antoine Miné, David Monniaux and Xavier Rival. They are supported by CNRS, École Normale Supérieure and École Polytechnique.

synchronous critical software. In section 5, we describe how these abstractions can also be applied or augmented to deal with a wider class of critical software.

2. Related Work

The first method which was used to try and give some confidence in the absence of errors in programs was testing. It consists in running a program on a set of inputs and checking that it behaves as intended. For critical software, the coverage of the tested inputs should be very high in order to achieve a high confidence. The number of possible inputs for real time embedded systems is nearly infinite, so testing is at the same time very expensive (hundreds of man years) and not fully satisfying as some unwanted behaviors may have escaped detection by testing.

Because testing is so expensive, one can use bug finders which will detect some common programming mistakes or report on suspicious codes. Such programs are usually fully automatic, so their cost is very low. They do find bugs in many codes, but they don't give good results on critical softwares: they report too many false alarms and they may overlook some unpredicted bugs.

Formal methods on the other hand can give exhaustive results. Some of them can prove very complex properties of the software, but usually at the cost of heavy human interaction and expertise. This is the case for proof assistants, which may be useful on small parts of the code but cannot scale to full systems. Other formal methods can be more automated, such as software model checkers.

The main problem of many formal methods based tools is that they perform the proof on a model of the code. In order to be tractable, this model cannot be too big, so either they are restricted to a small part of the code or they are restricted to some aspects of the semantics of the code. In general, models concentrate on the logical design and forget about abstruse machine implementation aspects of the software. In the case of critical software, where the logical design is well-mastered, potential errors are more likely to lurk in the machine implementation (such as the rounding errors introduced by floating-point arithmetics).

The theory of abstract interpretation [Cousot, 1978] makes it possible to analyze the actual semantics of real programs while performing sound abstractions to give correct results. Some industrial code analyzers are based on this theory and they give exhaustive results. So far, they discovered bugs in some applications, but they have not been precise enough on critical software: they yield too many false alarms to be useful. The cost of formally proving that all these alarms are indeed false is way too high even for a selection rate[3] of 1%.

[3]The selection rate is the ratio (number of lines with alarms)/(total number of lines).

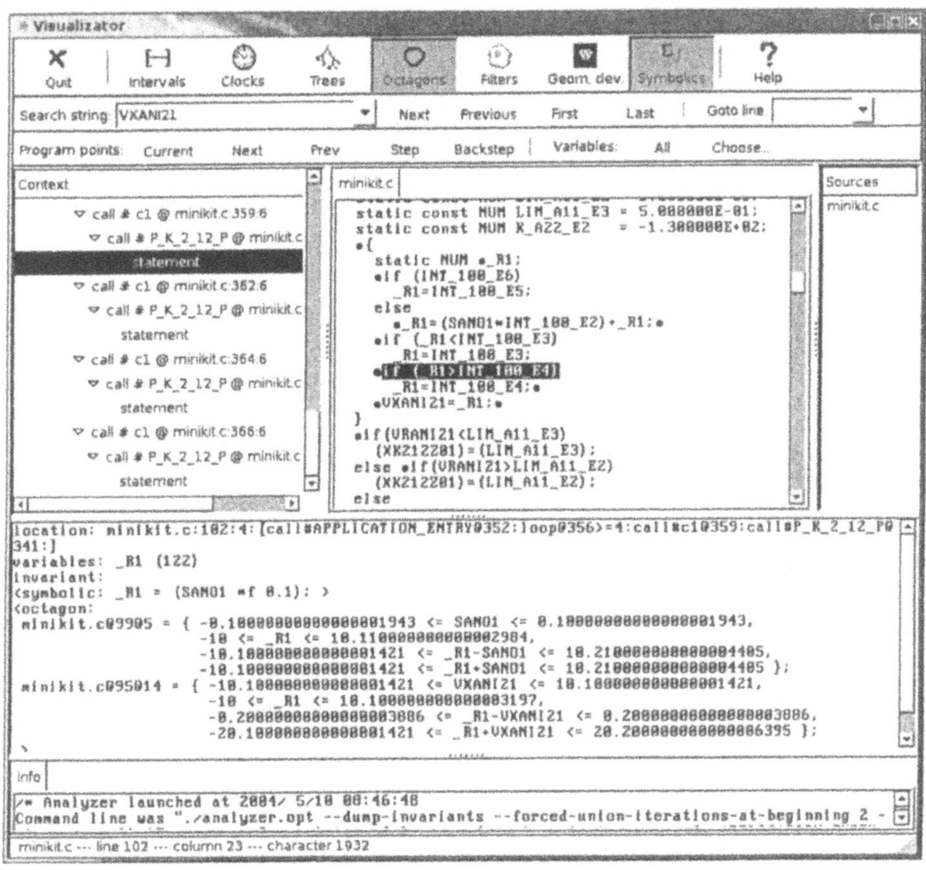

Figure 1. An example visualization of the results of Astrée.

3. What Astrée Does

Astrée is a static analyzer that automatically computes supersets of the possible values in synchronous C programs at every program points. Thus, if Astrée does not report any bad behavior, it proves that no such behavior can happen whatever the inputs of the C program.

Errors detected by Astrée

Once having a superset of the possible values of all program variables at each program point, Astrée can automatically report on a number of errors. The kind of errors which are currently reported by Astrée stems from the first end-user requirements. They wanted to see what could be proved without going through the expensive process of producing formal specifications. The least one can expect from a critical software is that the code never produces fatal errors, such as divisions by zero. Another common requirement is that the language is never used in cases where the result is stated as "undefined" in the norm of the language [JTC 1/SC 22, 1999]. For example, this is the case of out-of-bound array accesses, or integer overflows.

The errors which are currently reported are:

- out-of-bound array accesses,
- integer division by zero,
- floating point operations overflows and invalid operations (resulting in IEEE floating values Inf and NaN),
- integer arithmetics wrap around behavior (occurring mainly in overflows),
- casts that result in wrap around operations (when the target type is too small to contain a value).

In addition, Astrée can use some user-defined known facts and report on arbitrary user defined assertions (written in C) on the software.

Some Characteristics of Astrée

Astrée was developed to prove the absence of run-time errors for a specific class of synchronous C programs. As expected, it will be quite efficient and precise on the difficulties raised by this class of programs and may be weak on other aspects of the language.

One restriction of the class of C programs for which Astrée was originally designed is that it does not contain any dynamic memory allocation, string manipulation and very restricted pointers. That allows for a fast and precise memory analysis which would not be possible otherwise.

On the other hand, the class of analyzed C programs contains large programs (hundreds of thousands of lines of code), with a huge number of global interdependent variables (about 10 000 for a 100 000 lines program). This makes it hard to be efficient and precise, and specific algorithms and heuristics have been developed to keep the complexity of Astrée low (not far above linear in the number of lines of codes and the number of global variables).

As is necessary for many critical software, Astrée deals well with complex control using thousands of boolean variables. In addition, Astrée makes a sound analysis of floating values computations (as described in [IEEE Computer Society, 1985]), taking into account all possible rounding errors [Miné, 2004]. Astrée is even able to prove tight invariants for a variety of numerical filters implemented with floating numbers [Feret, 2004].

4. Inside Astrée

In order to understand what Astrée proves and how to use it, we describe the basic techniques used in the analyzer.

How Sets of Values can be Approximated

Astrée is a static analyzer based on abstract interpretation [Cousot and Cousot, 1979]. Following this theory, Astrée will proceed by approximating the set of all possible inputs into a symbolic representation. Then the program to analyze will be interpreted on this set of values, approximating each basic instruction when necessary to keep the sets of values representable. Approximation mechanisms are also necessary to find the sets of all possible values at a given point inside a loop, as the problem of finding the exact set is in general undecidable. The main mechanism is the so-called widening which allows extrapolating this set.

There is usually a balance between precision and efficiency in abstract interpretation. This balance can be tuned in two main categories: the widening strategy and the symbolic representation of sets of values. Thanks to the abstract interpretation theory, the symbolic representation can be split into a number of so-called abstract domains, each abstract domain being specialized on certain shapes of sets of values, and all abstract domains communicating to obtain as precise information as possible. Knowing which abstract domains are used in a static analyzer, one can have an idea of its potential precision.

Basic Abstract Domains. The less expensive abstract domain for numerical values is the domain of intervals, as described in [Cousot and Cousot, 1976]. In Astrée, an interval is associated with each variable, with a possibility of distinguishing each cell in arrays, or only the union of all cell values if the array is too big.

Octagon Abstract Domain. This domain, described in [Miné, 2001], will capture relational sets of values. The shape of these relations is of the form $X \pm Y \in$ interval. The complexity of manipulating groups of variables linked through an octagon is cubic in the number of variables. Although it is the relational domain with the best complexity, we cannot afford the complexity of one big octagon relating all pairs of variables in the program. Instead, variables are grouped into small octagons according to user directives or pattern matching of predefined program schemata.

Digital Filters Abstract Domains. Linear filters are widely used in control software. The problem is that although their ideal versions (on real numbers) are well studied, the effect of computing on IEEE floating numbers may change the stability of the filters. Also, with many filters, it is not possible to bound the output stream in the presence of retroactions by using classical linear abstract domains (even the more powerful polyhedra of [Cousot and Halbwachs, 1978]). [Feret, 2004] developed for Astrée a way of designing very precise and efficient abstract domains to deal with linear filters on floating point numbers.

Decision Trees Abstract Domain. In order to represent precisely the effect of complex control based on boolean variables, Astrée uses decision trees such that the decisions are based on the boolean variables, and the leaves of the trees are numerical abstract domains. This gives very precise informations about booleans, but the complexity is exponential in the number of boolean variables. So we group some boolean variables and some numerical ones in the same way as for octagons: either through user directives or pattern matching.

Unions. Unions of sets of possible values must be performed each time we merge the two branches of an `if` or each time we loop when computing the invariants of `while` loops. In addition to being a costly operation, for all the abstract domains used in Astrée unions imply a loss of precision. In order to keep more precision, at least locally, it is possible to delay the unions. The effect is to partition the traces of executions. Such partitioning, which can be extremely costly if the unions are too much delayed, can be introduced by the user or automatically through pattern matched program schemata.

Choosing Parameters for the Analysis

If Astrée always used all its most precise abstract domains and strategies on all program points and variables, the time and memory consumption of the analysis would be intractable. Luckily, no critical software required that much precision to prove their absence of run-time error so far. Astrée provides a lot of opportunities for the end-user to tune different parameters, so that the analyzer will be precise where it matters. As tuning the analyzer might be difficult for a non-expert, Astrée comes with a number of automatic decision procedures to compute default parameters. Still, it can be useful to know where these parameters can be taken into account.

The different phases of Astrée, after parsing, are:

Preprocessing. Preprocessing is decomposed in three passes. In the first one, the code is simplified, computing constant expressions (in a sound way with respect to floating point computations) and removing unused variables. Then the analyzer uses various pattern matched program schemata to determine where to put partitioning directives, in addition to those specified by the user in the source code. In the third phase, some variables are put together to be later incorporated into octagons or decision trees. The end-user can choose to put some packs or influence the parameterization, choosing for exemple the maximum number of boolean variables in a decision tree.

Iterator. The actual abstract interpretation of the program starts from a user supplied entry point in the program, such as the `main` function. This interpretation follows the directives (relational packs and partitioning) introduced in the preprocessing phases. For each instruction, the iterator asks the abstract domains to compute a sound approximation of the result of the instruction (the abstract transfer function). The difficult point is then the analysis of the loops, where other parameters must be taken into account. For example, the end-user can choose the number of loop unrollings performed by the iterator, or the stages which will be used in the widening process [Blanchet et al., 2003].

5. Different Uses for Astrée

Although Astrée was designed to answer the specific needs of one end-user, many more end-users might find the analyzer useful.

The primary use of Astrée is the proof of absence of run-time errors. Because Astrée can also use known facts and report on violated assertions inserted in the source code to analyze, it is possible to prove complex user-defined properties. In the near future, we plan to add the possibility of specifying complex temporal properties, such as often required by critical, real-time software specifications.

In addition to reporting potential errors, Astrée can also output the possible sets of values of the variables which were computed to check for those potential errors. On the class of programs for which Astrée was developed, the analysis time is quite low: about one hour per 100 000 lines of program on a 2GHz PC. That makes it possible for using Astrée at the earlier stages of software development. Its high precision makes it likely to discover bugs, and to find their origin by inspecting the sets of possible values leading to that bug. This task will be eased in the future, when Astrée will incorporate some backward analysis which will allow to discover an approximation of the values which led to a failure.

6. Conclusion

Astrée is a static analyzer aiming at proving the absence of run-time errors of synchronous C programs. It is already successful on a class of large embedded programs, where the analysis time is as low as a few hours for hundreds of thousands of lines of code. As Astrée was developed for that class of programs, the Astrée team (B. Blanchet, P. Cousot, R.Cousot, J. Feret, L. Mauborgne, A. Miné, D. Monniaux and X. Rival) expects that some adjustments could be necessary to apply that tool to other families of programs. Our hope is that it will be possible in a near future to prove the safety of all critical softwares at a reasonable cost.

In addition to analyzing more synchronous programs, we plan the evolution of Astrée in three directions. First, Astrée will propose the automatic proof that the compiled codes of the C programs are also correct by transferring automatically the analysis from source code to compiled code. Second we will add in the analyzer the possibility to perform a backward analysis. This will help to determine if an alarm is due to the imprecision of the analysis or if it is a true bug, and in both cases, it will help finding the source of the imprecision or cause of the bug. Finally, Astrée will be extended to analyze precisely asynchronous programs.

Acknowledgments. Thank you to Radhia Cousot, Antoine Miné and Patrick Cousot who helped me with useful comments and technical support.

References

Blanchet, B., Cousot, P., Cousot, R., Feret, J., Mauborgne, L., Miné, A., Monniaux, D., and Rival, X. (2002). Design and implementation of a special-purpose static program analyzer for safety-critical real-time embedded software. In Mogensen, T., Schmidt, D.A., and Sudborough, I.H., editors, *The Essence of Computation: Complexity, Analysis, Transformation. Essays Dedicated to Neil D. Jones*, LNCS 2566, pages 85–108. Springer.

Blanchet, B., Cousot, P., Cousot, R., Feret, J., Mauborgne, L., Miné, A., Monniaux, D., and Rival, X. (2003). A static analyzer for large safety-critical software. In *Proceedings of the ACM SIGPLAN 2003 Conference on Programming Language Design and Implementation (PLDI'03)*, pages 196–207, San Diego, California, USA. ACM Press.

Cousot, P. (1978). *Méthodes itératives de construction et d'approximation de points fixes d'opérateurs monotones sur un treillis, analyse sémantique de programmes*. Thèse d'état ès sciences mathématiques, Université scientifique et médicale de Grenoble, Grenoble, France.

Cousot, P. and Cousot, R. (1976). Static determination of dynamic properties of programs. In *Proc. of the Second Int. Symp. on Programming*, pages 106–130. Dunod, Paris, France.

Cousot, P. and Cousot, R. (1977). Abstract interpretation: a unified lattice model for static analysis of programs by construction or approximation of fixpoints. In 4th *ACM POPL*, pages 238–252.

Cousot, P. and Cousot, R. (1979). Systematic design of program analysis frameworks. In 6th *ACM POPL*, pages 269–282.

Cousot, P. and Halbwachs, N. (1978). Automatic discovery of linear restraints among variables of a program. In 5th *ACM POPL*, pages 84–97.

Feret, J. (2004). Static analysis of digital filters. In *European Symposium on Programming (ESOP'04)*, LNCS 2986. Springer.

IEEE Computer Society (1985). IEEE standard for binary floating-point arithmetic.

JTC 1/SC 22 (1999). Programming languages – C. Technical Report ISO/IEC 9899:1999.

Miné, A. (2001). The octagon abstract domain. In *IEEE AST in WCRE*, pages 310–319.

Miné, A. (2004). Relational abstract domains for the detection of floating-point run-time errors. In *European Symposium on Programming (ESOP'04)*, LNCS 2986, pages 3–17. Springer.

INDUSTRIAL EXPERIENCE OF ABSTRACT INTERPRETATION-BASED STATIC ANALYZERS

Jean Souyris
Airbus France
jean.souyris@airbus.com

Abstract This paper presents two Abstract Interpretation-based static analysers used by Airbus on safety-critical avionics programs: aiT [Thesing et al., 2003], a Worst case Execution Time analyzer developed by AbsInt, and ASTRÉE [Blanchet et al., 2003], aiming at the proof of absence of Run Time Errors and developed by the École normale supérieure.

Keywords: Abstract Interpretation, Worst Case Execution Time, Run Time errors, Product Based Assurance.

1. Introduction

The current verification process of an avionics program is almost exclusively based on tests. Testing has the great advantage of producing results by real executions of the program being verified but, unfortunately, this kind of verification has the major disadvantage of covering a tiny subset of the huge (very often considered as infinite) set of all possible executions. Moreover, if one takes into account the rate at which avionics program size is increasing from one aircraft development to the next one, maintaining the coverage of tests at the same level than it is today is increasingly expensive.

In this context, complementary tool-aided verification techniques must be used, which must compensate the disadvantages just mentioned. That is why Airbus makes a significant R&D effort, in collaboration with fundamental research laboratories and toolmakers, on static analyzers based on Abstract Interpretation [Cousot, 2000]. Such tools must satisfy the following constraints: they must analyze real code (source, assembly or binary) automatically, be usable by "normal" engineers and lead to results that can be used without heavy human effort.

The experimentations presented in this WCC 2004 Topical Session on Abstract Interpretation are an essential part of the process, which will allow using Abstract Interpretation-based static analyzers massively.

Two Abstract Interpretation-based static analyzers are presented in this paper: aiT from AbsInt, which computes Worst Case Execution Times by analysis of the binary of a program, and ASTRÉE, which proves the absence of Run Time Errors (division by zero, numerical overflows, array overflow, etc), both analyzing synchronous programs.

The paper is organized as follows: section 2 presents Airbus' R&D effort around Abstract Interpretation-based static analyzers, section 3 gives an idea of what the introduction of these kind of tools and techniques in the verification Workbench is, section 4 is about aiT, section 5 is about ASTRÉE , section 6 presents the Product Based Assurance, beyond the use of aiT or ASTRÉE, section 7 concludes.

2. An R&D Effort for Getting Industrial Static Analyzers

Abstract Interpretation-based static analyzers are specialized. The first specialization is due to the class of properties they prove, e.g., Run Time Errors. As Airbus' motivation is the proof, not only debugging, and because Abstract Interpretation means approximation (most of the time over-approximation), consequently "false alarms", a second specialization is required: the "per family of program" specialization. This is mandatory for limiting false alarms to the minimum (the "zero false alarm" objective), in the case of an analyzer of RTEs, or for obtaining a tight Worst Case Execution Time, in the case of aiT.

These specializations must be done by the tool makers with a close interaction with the End-User (here: Airbus) this is the R&D effort presented here.

This effort aims at obtaining static analyzers for solving industrial verification problems and introducing them into the development process of avionics programs. This cannot be achieved without fulfilling the following acceptance criteria:

- a static analyzer must constitute a *sound application of theoretical principles* (Abstract Interpretation framework),
- it must analyze *non modified programs ("the ones which fly")*,
- *"normal" engineers* can use it, on *normal machines*,
- it must be possible to *integrate it into the existing DO178B conforming process and verification workbench*,
- it must be fully *accepted by the developers*,
- and, from an industrial point of view, it must *reduce the cost of the verification significantly.*

The R&D maturation process for achieving the fulfillment of the acceptance criteria, for a particular static analyzer, consists in assessing the tool on real programs, while defining the associated method of use, reporting problems to the tool maker, assessing again, and so on till the analyzer and the associated method are ready for an industrial use.

This process requires the following enabling conditions: close interaction with development teams and tool makers; and trainings, even on the theoretical framework, i.e., Abstract Interpretation.

The tools on which this process is currently applied, or has been applied on are: Caveat [Randimbivololona et al., 1999] (Program proof – Commissariat à l'énergie atomique – Caveat is used in A380 program development); AbsInt's Stackanalyzer; AbsInt's aiT [Thesing et al., 2003] (Worst Case Execution Time Analyzer); ASTRÉE [Blanchet et al., 2003] (École normale supérieure); Fluctuat [Goubault et al., 2002] (CEA - Floating-point calculus analysis).

3. Introduction to the Verification Workbench

DO178B conforming aspects

In its section 6.3.4. "Reviews and Analyses" paragraph f: "accuracy and consistency", DO178B [Randimbivololona et al., 1999] mentions a subset of the RTEs treated by ASTRÉE and the necessity of computing the WCET, but this standard does not impose a way to perform the relevant demonstrations.

More generally, Abstract Interpretation-based static analyzers are of great interest with respect to the fundamental objective of DO178B: *dependability*.

Industrial aspects

The major industrial characteristic of the avionic program verification workbench is to be as automated as possible. In fact, all phases of the development process are strongly integrated under the control of a configuration and process management tool. Static analyzers must be automatically controllable from this tool.

4. aiT (ABSINT – Worst Wase Execution Time Analyzer)

R&D effort

The collaboration between AbsInt and Airbus on WCET analysis started during the EU project DAEDALUS (on Abstract Interpretation, research and applications). The first aiT was developed for Coldfire 5307 micro-processor, which was used in a fly-by-wire avionics computer.

Why is computing WCET a challenge?

There are two main reasons: firstly, finding the inputs leading to the worst case is most of the time impossible, particularly by executing the program, or by intellectual analyses; Secondly, capturing the subtle effects on the accelerating mechanisms of modern processors is also a challenge.

Legacy method

On safety-critical avionics programs like fly-by-wire programs, a measurement-based method exists, which deals with the above mentioned difficulties. The structure of the program allows reducing the problem of the identification of the inputs leading to the worse case of the complete program to such an identification at the level of very simple elementary operators the whole program is built with. In this context, the WCET of each basic operator is measured safely. The WCET of the whole program is computed by applying a formula deduced from the structure of the program and whose inputs are the WCET of the basic operators.

Limitation of the legacy method

The limitation of this method is mainly due to the conditions in which the measurements of the basic WCETs are preformed. Indeed, since the measurements are performed on basic operators individually, the initial state of the execution must be the worst possible: something like empty caches and pipeline. For some processors, this is sound but might lead to a very pessimistic WCET (waste of available CPU power), for others like the PowerPC 755, it is almost impossible to find the worst initial state (e.g., Pseudo LRU cache line replacement strategy).

Ait

Ait is an application of the theory of Abstract Interpretation. This basically allows to safely compute the WCET of a superset of all possible executions of the analyzed program. What is analyzed is the binary of the program. AiT embeds a model of the micro-processor and peripheral components in which characteristics having no impact on the timings have been abstracted away. Thanks to this model, the effects of the computation history based accelerating mechanisms are precisely captured. One can notice that even when a quite deterministic processor is used, aiT is worthwhile because fully automatic.

Targets

Safety-critical avionics program embedded into the A330/340 and A380 aircrafts, and using the following processors: PowerPC 755, Texas TMS320C33 and Coldfire 5307.

Status on the fulfillment of the acceptance criteria (sect. 2)

All criteria are fulfilled; the next step is the qualification of aiT and the associated method in the operational contexts in which they will be used, as required by DO178B.

Results

Two aiT have already been used in real industrial context: aiT for Coldfire 5307 and aiT for PowerPC 755.

AiT Coldfire 5307. When the aiT was available, the WCET of the fly-by-wire program running on a Coldfire 5307 board was already computed by the legacy method. Indeed the traditional approach can be applied to this processor. In fact, the pre-existence of timing figures allowed us to compare them with the ones produced by aiT. These comparisons were made for each basic operator, each module and each task. The conclusion was a completely deterministic behavior of aiT, and WCETs of tasks (which are relevant for the schedulability analysis) less pessimistic than the ones obtained by the legacy method.

Ait PowerPC 755. The legacy method is not reliable with this processor any more. So aiT is the only solution. Like for aiT Coldfire 5307, current status is aiT's capability to compute a tight WCET, and a deterministic behavior, even if less comparisons than for the other application could be made. Current Airbus' effort is on the user-validation of the tool on two safety-critical avionics programs, in order to be used for the temporal aspects of these program's certification process.

5. ASTRÉE (ENS – Proof of Absence of RTE)

R&D effort

This Abstract Interpretation-based static analyzer is developed by the École normale supérieure with the support of the French RNTL (Réseau national des technologies du logiciel) via the ASTRÉE project. Airbus also participates in this project as an End-User. The first class of program ASTRÉE is specialized for is safety-critical avionics synchronous programs (Fly-by-Wire programs).

Proving the absence of RTE "by hand"

Absence of RTE is impossible to prove by hand for real life programs and testing cannot be considered as a proof. The question is "how to be confident" (and the 20 year service history of RTE-free operations is a strong indication) in the behaviors of a safety-critical avionics program with respect to RTE?

Legacy method

Precise answer to the above question must be made "per RTE type" and three kinds of requirements must be considered. First requirement: safety; if a runtime mechanism, like some exceptions of the processor (ex: floating-point overflow), is available then it is used. Since such an exception forces the computer to a no-return failure mode, the second requirement is for the availability of the avionics function. It states that RTEs must be detected during program development, as soon as possible. Last requirement: design and coding rules must be defined and well applied in order to avoid situations in which RTEs might occur.

ASTRÉE

This analyzer attempts to prove the absence of a Run Time Error in a synchronous program. Its maximum precision (zero false alarm) is obtained on code controlling servo-loops. In this case, if an alarm is raised by ASTRÉE, it is either a real problem or it is due to an imprecision of the description of the execution environment of the analyzed program (assertions on the inputs). With respect to the requirements mentioned just above, ASTRÉE is suitable for being sure of the absence of RTE as soon as the code is available, which is a lot better than getting a partial confidence after the heavy campaign of tests of the program.

Targets

Safety-critical avionics C programs embedded into A330/340 and A380 aircrafts.

Status on the fulfillment of the acceptance criteria (sect. 2)

OK for the A330/340 application. ASTRÉE is currently improved by ENS for being able to accept a wider class of programs, including A380 programs.

Results

Zero false alarm is a reality on the first family of programs ASTRÉE has been tuned for. The main computational characteristics of these programs are: about 100,000 lines of code, synchronous behavior, intensive numerical computations using the floating-point representation of real numbers, control-flow often "encoded" into boolean variables, type of calculus: digital filtering, servo-loop control.

The experimentations of ASTRÉE particularly revealed its ability to cope with the subtle effects of floating-point operations, specially when these computations are performed during hours, 10 hour typical flight duration for an A340, at a 10ms rate.

6. Towards the Product Based Assurance

AiT, ASTRÉE and the other Abstract Interpretation-based static analyzers are a first step towards the effective application Product Based Assurance concept. It should be noticed that this first set of static analyzers, e.g., WCET analyzers (aiT), RTE analyzers (ASTRÉE), and stack analyzers, share the following characteristic: the properties they prove are defined in their specification, i.e., they are not user-defined. The next step in the application of the Product Based Assurance will be supported by static analyzers that will allow to prove user-specified properties.

7. Conclusion

The main goal of this paper was to show how promising Abstract Interpretation is, for the verification of safety-critical avionics programs. Two successful applications of this theory were presented for illustrating this point of view.

With respect to Airbus' needs, the development of industrial applications of the Abstract Interpretation theory really started in 2000. To conclude, a lot of work is still needed for concretizing all the potentialities of the theory, and, for that, Abstract Interpretation must leave the state of confidentiality in which it currently is.

References

Randimbivololona, F., Souyris, J., Baudin, P., Pacalet, A., Raguideau, J., and Schoen, D. (1999). Applying formal proof techniques to avionics software: A pragmatic approach. In Wing, J.M., Woodcock, J., and Davies, J., editors, *Proceedings of the World Congress on Formal Methods in the Development of Computing Systems, FM '99*, volume II of *Toulouse, France, Lecture Notes in Computer Science 1709*, pages 1798–1815. Springer.

Thesing, S., Souyris, J., Heckmann, R., Randimbivololona, F., Langenbach, M., Wilhelm, R., and Ferdinand, C. (2003). Abstract interpretation-based timing validation of hard real-time avionics software. In *Proceedings of the International Conference on Dependable Systems and Networks (DSN 2003)*, San Francisco, California, United States, pages 625–634. IEEE Computer Society Press, Los Alamitos, California.

Cousot, P. (2000). Interprétation abstraite. *Technique et science informatique*, 19(1-2-3):155–164.

Blanchet, B., Cousot, P., Cousot, R., Feret, J., Mauborgne, L., Miné, A., Monniaux, D., and Rival, X. (2003). A static analyzer for large safety-critical software. In *Proceedings of the ACM SIGPLAN '2003 Conference on Programming Language Design and Implementation (PLDI)*, pages 196–207, San Diego, California, United States. ACM Press.

Goubault, É., Martel, M., and Putot, S. (2002). Asserting the precision of floating-point computations: A simple abstract interpreter. In Le Métayer, D., editor, *Proceedings of the Eleventh European Symposium on Programming Languages and Systems, ESOP '2002*, Grenoble, France, Lecture Notes in Computer Science 2305, pages 209–212. Springer.

Topic 5

Multimodal Interaction

Organiser:

Laurence NIGAY
University of Grenoble, CLIPS-IMAG Laboratory, France
Laurence.Nigay@imag.fr

The use of multiple modalities such as speech, gesture, sound and graphics opens a vast world of possibilities for human-machine interaction. By extending the sensory-motor capabilities of computer systems to better mach the natural communications means of human beings, multimodal interfaces enhance interaction between users and systems in several ways.

The topical day is geared towards researchers, engineers, developers and practitioners interested in the ergonomic design, software development, usability evaluation of multimodal systems and in their future applications. Multimodal user interfaces imply a vast range of theories, studies, interaction paradigms and application domains. For the topical day, we therefore decided to provide a review of theories and generic results for the design and development of robust and efficient multimodal systems and then focus on some specific major applications of multimodality. The day is structured into two parts: i) design and development of multimodal user interfaces and ii) domains of multimodality.

DESIGN SPACE FOR MULTIMODAL INTERACTION

Laurence Nigay
CLIPS-IMAG, Université de Grenoble 1 38000 Grenoble, France
Email Laurence.Nigay@imag.fr

Abstract: One trend in Human Computer Interaction is to extend the sensory-motor capabilities of computer systems to better match the natural communication means of humans. Although the multiplicity of modalities opens a vast world of experience, our understanding of how they relate to each other is still unclear and the terminology is unstable. In this paper we present our definitions and existing frameworks useful for the design of multimodal interaction.

Key words: Multimodal UI, I/O devices, Interaction Languages, Combination.

1. INTRODUCTION

The area of multimodal interaction has expanded rapidly and since the seminal "Put that there" demonstrator (Bolt 1980) that combines speech, gesture and eye tracking, significant achievements have been made in terms of both modalities and real multimodal systems. Indeed, in addition to more and more robust modalities, conceptual and empirical work on the usage of multiple modalities is now available for guiding the design of efficient and usable multimodal interfaces. As a result, real multimodal systems are now being built in various application domains including medicine (Oviatt et al. 2000) and education.

Recent progress achieved in the miniaturization of microprocessors and in wireless networks make it possible to foresee the disappearance of the "grey box" that is the personal computer, or at least to understand that it is no longer the only place of interaction between people and the numerical world. This development is driven by the recent concepts of Ubiquitous Computing and Disappearing Computer and from the evolution occurring in the field of interaction modeling. Indeed the research is now gradually directed towards models of interaction in which the data-processing resources are distributed in a multitude of everyday objects with which users interact in explicit (active modalities) and implicit ways (passive modalities). This has given rise to several recent interaction paradigms (i.e., Augmented Reality, Ubiquitous/Pervasive Computing, Tangible Bits, and Embodied Multi-surfaces) that increase the set of possibilities for multimodal interaction. A good example of a recent type of modality is provided by the "phicons" (Physical Icons) that define new input modalities based on the manipulation of physical objects or physical surfaces such as a table or a wall that can be used for displaying information (output modality) in an ubiquitous computing scenario.

Although the multiplicity of modalities opens a vast world of experience, our understanding of how they relate to each other is still unclear and the terminology is unstable.

2. DEFINITION: MODALITY

2.1 Device and Language

In his theory of action, Norman structures the execution and evaluation gulfs in terms of semantic and articulatory distances that the user needs to cover in order to reach a particular goal (Norman 86). This user-centered approach pays little attention to the processing steps that occur within the computer system. Our Pipe-lines model makes these stages explicit (Nigay 1994). By so doing, we extend Norman's theory in a symmetric way within the computer system. Two relevant concepts emerge from this model: the notion of physical device and that of interaction language. Interestingly, these concepts cover the semantic and articulatory distances of Norman's theory.

A physical device is an artifact of the system that acquires (input device) or delivers (output device) information. Examples include keyboard, loudspeaker, head-mounted display and GPS. Although this notion of device is acceptable for an overall analysis of an interactive multimodal system, it is not satisfactory when one needs to characterize the system at a finer grain of interaction. The design spaces of input devices such as that of Mackinlay et al. (Mackinlay et al., 1990) and of Foley et al. (Foley et al., 1994) are frameworks that valuably refine a physical device. A review of these taxonomies are presented in (Nigay et al., 1996).

An interaction language is a language used by the user or the system to exchange information. A language defines the set of all possible well-formed expressions, i.e., the conventional assembly of symbols, that convey meaning. Examples include pseudo-natural language, direct manipulation language. Three properties of an interaction language are introduced in the theory of output modalities (Bernsen et al., 1994): (1) Linguistic or non-linguistic (2) Analogue or non-analogue (3) Arbitrary or non-arbitrary.

The generation of a symbol or a set of symbols, results from a physical action. A physical action is an action performed either by the system or the user on a physical device. Examples include highlighting information (system physical actions), pushing a mouse button or uttering a sentence (physical actions performed by the user). The physical actions performed by the user can be either explicitly performed for conveying information to the system (explicit actions of the user towards the interactive system) or can be part of the user's tasks and is a source of information that is not explicitly expressed to the computer but is useful for the interaction ("perceptual user interfaces" (Turk et al., 2000)).

If we adopt Hemjslev's terminology (Hemjslev 1947), the physical device determines the substance (i.e., the unanalyzed raw material) of an expression whereas the interaction language denotes its form or structure.

2.2 Interaction Modality and Multimodality

In the literature, interaction modality is discussed at multiple levels of abstraction from both the user and the system perspectives. At the lowest level, a modality may refer to a human sensory capability or to a computer physical device such as a microphone, a camera, or a screen. At a higher level of abstraction, a modality is viewed as a representational system, such as a pseudo-natural language that the user and the system might share. Whereas the device level is related to the human sensory capabilities, the representational level calls upon cognitive resources. Clearly, the physical and the representational computer models are tightly coupled to the sensory and cognitive dimensions of human behavior. For this reason, in (Nigay et al., 95) we define a modality as the coupling of an interaction language L with a physical device d: <d, L>. Examples of input modalities while using a

PDA (Zouinar et al., 2003) include: <microphone, pseudo natural language>, <camera, 3D gesture>, <stylus, direct manipulation> and <PDA, 3D gesture> (Embodied user interface (Harrison et al. 1998)).

Within the vast world of possibilities for modalities, we distinguish two types of modalities: the active and passive modalities. For inputs, active modalities are used by the user to issue a command to the computer (e.g., a voice command or a gesture recognized by a camera). Passive modalities refer to information that is not explicitly expressed by the user, but automatically captured for enhancing the execution of a task. For example, in the "Put that there" seminal multimodal demonstrator of R. Bolt (Bolt 1980), eye tracking was used for detecting which object on screen the user is looking at. Similarly, in our MEMO system (Bouchet et al. 2004), "orientation" and "location" of the mobile user are two passive input modalities. The modality "orientation" is represented by the magnetometer (device) and the three orientation angles in radians (language), the other modality "localization" by the pair <Localization sensor, 3D location>. MEMO allows users to annotate physical locations with digital notes which have a physical location and are then read/removed by other mobile users.

In the literature, multimodality is mainly used for inputs (from user to system) and multimedia for outputs (from system to user), showing that the terminology is still ambiguous. In the general sense, a multimodal system supports communication with the user through different interaction modalities. Literally, "multi" means "more than one".

Our definition of modality and therefore of multimodality is system-oriented. A user-centered perspective may lead to a different definition. For instance, according to our system-centered view, electronic voice mail is not multimodal. It constitutes a multimedia user interface only. Indeed, it allows the user to send mail that may contain graphics, text and voice messages. It does not however extract meaning from the information it carries. In particular, voice messages are recorded and replayed but not interpreted. On the other hand, from the user's point of view, this system is perceived as being multimodal: The user employs different modalities (referring to the human senses) to interpret mail messages.

In addition our definition enables us to extend the range of possibilities for multimodality. Indeed a system can be multimodal without having several input or output devices. For example, a system using the screen as the unique output device is multimodal whenever it employs several output interaction languages. In (Vernier et al. 2000), we claim that using one device and multiple interaction languages raises the same design and engineering issues as using multiple modalities based on different devices.

3. COMBINATION OF MODALITIES

Although each modality can be used independently within a multimodal system, the availability of several modalities in a system naturally leads to the issue of their combined usage. The combined usage of multiple modalities opens a vastly augmented world of possibilities in user interface design. Several frameworks addressed the issue of relationships between modalities. In the seminal TYCOON framework (Martin 1997) six types of cooperation between modalities are defined:

1. Equivalence involves the option of choosing between several modalities that can all equally well convey a particular chunk of information.
2. Specialization implies that specific kinds of information are always conveyed by the same modality.
3. Redundancy indicates that the same piece of information is conveyed by several modalities.
4. Complementarity denotes several modalities that convey complementary chunks of information.
5. Transfer implies that a chunk of information processed by one modality is then treated by another modality.
6. Concurrency describes the case of several modalities conveying independent information in parallel.

The CARE properties (Coutaz et al., 1995) define another framework for reasoning about multimodal interaction from the perspectives of both the user and the system: These properties are the Complementarity, Assignment, Redundancy, and Equivalence that may occur between the modalities available in a multimodal user interface. We define these four notions as relationships between devices and interaction languages and between interaction languages and tasks. In addition, in our multifeature system design space (Nigay et al., 1995) we emphasized the temporal aspects of the combination, a dimension orthogonal to the CARE properties. Finally in (Vernier et al., 2000), we present a combination framework that encompasses and extends the existing design spaces for multimodality. The combination framework is comprised of schemas and aspects: While the combination schemas (Allen's relationships) define how to combine several modalities, the combination aspects determine what to combine (temporal, spatial, syntactic and semantic).

4. CONCLUSION

In this article, we have provided an overview of a number of definitions and frameworks useful for the design of multimodal user interfaces. To do so we have focused on the definition of a modality and then on the composition of modalities.

ACKNOWLEDGEMENTS

This work is partly funded by French DGA under contract #00.70.624.00.470.75.96. The author also acknowledges the support of the SIMILAR European FP6 network of excellence (http://www.similar.cc).

REFERENCES

Bolt, R., (1980), Put-that-there: Voice and gesture at the graphics interface, in Proceedings of the 7th annual conference on Computer graphics and interactive techniques, pp. 262-270.

Bouchet, J., Nigay, L., 2004, ICARE: A Component-Based Approach for the Design and Development of Multimodal Interfaces, *in Proceedings of CHI'2004*, ACM Press.

Bernsen, N., (1994), A revised generation of the taxonomy of output modalities, *Esprit Project AMODEUS Working Paper RP5-TM-WP11.*

Coutaz, J., et al., 1995, Four easy pieces for assessing the usability of multimodal interaction: The CARE properties, in Proceedings of Interact'95, Chapman&Hall, pp. 115-120

Foley, J., Wallace, V., Chan, P., (1984), The Human Factors of computer Graphics interactiontechniques, *IEEE computer Graphics and Applications*, 4(11), pp. 13-48.

Harrison, B., et al., 1998, Squeeze me, Hold me, Tilt Me ! An exploration of Manipulative User Interface, in Proceedings of CHI'98, ACM Press, pp. 17-24.

Hemjslev, L., 1947, Structural Analysis of language, *Studia Phonetica*, Vol. 1, pp. 69-78.

Mackinlay, J., Card, S., Robertson, G., (1990), A Semantic Analysis of the Design Space of Input Devices, *Human Computer Interaction*, Lawrence Erlbaum, 5(2,3), pp. 145-190.

Martin, J. C., 1997, TYCOON: Theoretical Framework and Software Tools for Multimodal Interfaces. Intelligence and Multimodality in Multimedia Interfaces, AAAI Press.

Norman, D. A., 1986, Cognitive Engineering, *User Centered System Design, New Perspectives on Computer Interaction*, Lawrence Erlbaum Associates, pp. 31-61.

Nigay, L., 1994, Conception et modélisation logicielles des systèmes interactifs : application aux interfaces multimodales, *PhD dissertation University of Grenoble 1*, 315 pages.

Nigay, L., Coutaz, J., 1995, A Generic Platform for Addressing the Multimodal Challenge, *in Proceedings of CHI'95*, ACM Press, pp. 98-105.

Nigay, L., Coutaz, J., 1996, Espaces conceptuels pour l'interaction multimédia et multimodale, *TSI*, 15(9), AFCET&Hermes Publ, pp. 1195-1225.

Oviatt, S. et al., 2000, Designing the user interface for multimodal speech and gesture applications, *Human Computer Interaction*, Lawrence Erlbaum, 15(4), pp. 263-322.

Turk, M., Robertson, G., (ed.), 2000, Perceptual user Interfaces, *Communications of the ACM*, 43(3), ACM Press, pp. 32-70.

Vernier, F., Nigay, L., 2000, A Framework for the Combination and Characterization of Output Modalities, *in Proceedings of DSV-IS2000*, LNCS, Springer-Verlag., pp. 32-48.

Zouinar, M., et al. , 2003, Multimodal Interaction on Mobile Artefacts, *Communicating with smart objects-developing technology for usable pervasive computing systems*, Hermes Penton Science, ISBN 1-9039-9636-8.

SOFTWARE DESIGN AND DEVELOPMENT OF MUTIMODAL INTERACTION

Marie-Luce Bourguet
Queen Mary University of London

Abstract: The multimodal dimension of a user interface raises numerous problems that are not present in more traditional interfaces. In this paper, we briefly review the current approaches in software design and modality integration techniques for multimodal interaction. We then propose a simple framework for describing multimodal interaction designs and for combining sets of user inputs of different modalities. We show that the proposed framework can help designers in reasoning about synchronization patterns problems and testing interaction robustness.

Key words: multimodal software architectures; integration techniques; finite state machines; synchronization patterns; recognition errors.

1. INTRODUCTION

Recent developments in recognition-based interaction technologies (e.g. speech and gesture recognition) have opened a myriad of new possibilities for the design and implementation of multimodal interfaces. However, designing and implementing systems that take advantage of these new interaction techniques is difficult. On one hand, our lack of understanding of how different modes of interaction can be best combined in the user interface often leads to interface designs with poor usability. On the other hand, developers still face major technical challenges for the implementation of multimodality, as indeed, the multimodal dimension of a user interface raises numerous challenges that are not present in more traditional interfaces. These new challenges include: the need to process inputs from different and heterogeneous streams; the co-ordination and integration of several communication channels that operate in parallel (*modality fusion*); the partition of information sets for the generation of efficient multimodal presentations (*modality fission*); dealing with uncertainty and recognition errors; and implementing distributed interfaces over networks (e.g. when speech and gesture recognition are performed on different processors).

One of the main multimodal challenges lays in the implementation of adapted software architectures that enable modality fusion mechanisms. In this paper, we briefly review the current approaches in software design and modality integration techniques (section 2). Then in section 3, we propose a simple framework for describing multimodal interaction designs and for combining sets of user inputs of different modalities. In particular, we show that the proposed framework can help designers in reasoning about synchronization patterns problems and testing interaction robustness.

2. SOFTWARE ARCHITECTURES AND MODALITY FUSION TECHNIQUES

When implementing a multimodal system, several design and architectural decisions have to be made. The interdependency of input modalities and therefore the need for their integration in the system architecture can take several forms and fulfill different roles: redundancy (e.g. speech and lip movements), complementarity (e.g. "delete this" with a pointing gesture), disambiguation, support (e.g. speech and iconic hand gestures), modulation (e.g. speech and facial expressions), etc. Depending on the type of interdependency, a developer must try answering the following questions:

- At which level of granularity should data be processed on each input stream?
- How should heterogeneous information be represented?
- According to what criteria should modality integration be attempted?

Modality integration is usually attempted at either the feature (low) or the semantics (high) level, in two fundamentally different types of software architectures. Feature level architectures are generally considered appropriate for tightly related and synchronized modalities, such as speech and lip movements (Duchnowski et al, 1994). In this type of architecture, connectionist models can be used for processing single modalities because of their good performance as pattern classifiers, and because they can easily integrate heterogeneous features (Waibel et al, 1994). However, a truly multimodal connectionist approach is dependent on the availability of multimodal training data and such data is not currently available.

When the interdependency between modalities implies complementarity or disambiguation (e.g. speech and gesture inputs), information is typically integrated at the syntactic or semantic levels (Nigay et al, 1995). In this type of architecture, current approaches for modality integration include frame-based methods, multimodal grammars and agent-based frameworks. In frame-based methods, data structures called frames (Minsky, 1975) are used to represent meaning and knowledge and to merge information that results from different modality streams (Johnston, 1998). The use of grammars to parse multimodal inputs takes its inspiration from previous work in speech and natural language understanding (Shimazu et al, 1995). Grammars are sets of rules that describe all possible inputs. The main advantage of the grammatical approach is its generality, as grammars can be declared outside the core of a mutimodal system. Its main drawback lies in the difficulty of declaring the grammar without imposing constraints on users' behavior since a grammar must encompass all legal multimodal messages that a system will find acceptable. Finally, The agent based framework approach employs multiple agents to co-ordinate distributed information sources. In Martin et al (1999) for example, the framework is based on the Open Agent Architecture (OOA), a complex and general-purpose infrastructure for constructing systems composed of multiple software components. Agent based architectures are flexible and able to exploit parallelism.

3. PROTOTYPING MULTIMODAL INTERACTION

The models of architecture and integration techniques that can be found in the literature today and that were briefly reviewed in the previous section are often too generic or complex to provide ready-made solutions for developers. To date, no toolkit is available that addresses both the design and technical challenges of multimodality. In this section, we present a simple framework to support the designers and developers of multimodal user interfaces.

3.1 Designing Multimodality

Finite State Machines (FSMs) are a well-known technique for describing and controlling dialogs in graphical user interfaces (Wasserman, 1985). We show here that FSMs are also useful for modelling multimodal interaction and constitute a good framework for combining sets of user inputs of different modalities. Figure 1 illustrates how a speech and pen "move" command can be represented by an FSM.

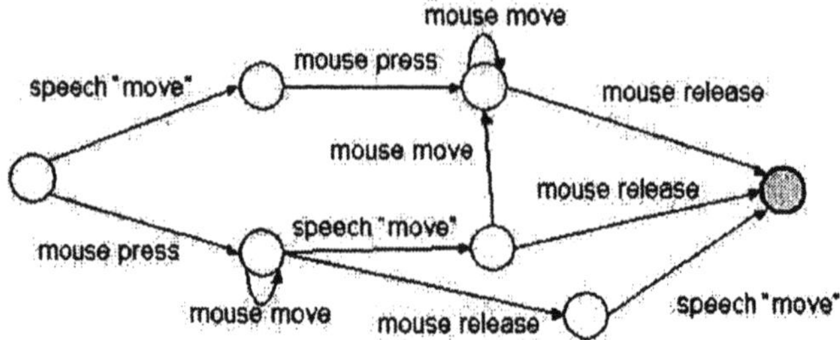

Figure 1. FSM modelling a "move" speech and pen command where many synchronisation patterns are represented.

When designing multimodal commands, one important task is the specification of the synchronization requirements. The aim is to guarantee that users will be able to activate the commands in a natural and spontaneous manner (Oviatt et al, 1997). In practice, a user can produce inputs in a sequential (e.g. with pen input completed before speech begins) or simultaneous manner (when both inputs show some temporal overlap). FSMs constitute a good framework for testing different synchronization patterns (Bourguet, 2003a). For example, Figure 1 describes a speech and pen "move" command where many different synchronisation patterns are represented. According to this representation, users are free to deliver inputs in their preferred order (sequentially or simultaneously, pen first or speech first). However, if we kept only the top branch of the FSM, users would become forced to use speech first and then the pen. Such an FSM would have for effect to constrain users in their usage of the modalities.

3.2 Testing interaction designs

Recognition-based technologies are still error-prone. Speech recognition systems, for example, are sensitive to vocabulary size, quality of audio signal and variability of voice parameters. In Oviatt (2000) it is shown that, during the process of semantic fusion, multimodal architectures can achieve automatic recovery from recognition errors and false interpretations. The phenomenon in which an input signal in one modality allows recovery from recognition error or ambiguity in a second signal in a different modality is called *mutual disambiguation* of input modes (Oviatt, 2000). However, the degree to which mutual disambiguation can operate in a given application is dependent on the design of the interaction, i.e. on the set of multimodal constructions that the system is able to interpret. In this section, we show that FSMs can help assessing the potential of different multimodal designs for mutual disambiguation of input signals (Bourguet, 2003b).

An FSM can naturally filter out erroneous recognition hypotheses because mis-recognised inputs that do not match the transition events of the current states can be ignored ("passive error handling"). The user may then choose to either repeat the input or reformulate it in order to increase the chances of good recognition. Once the input is correctly recognized, the dialog can resume. Passive error handling is a very simple technique that does not achieve error correction but is able to filter out erroneous recognition results. It is appropriate for testing the robustness of simple interaction models, where all FSMs are significantly different from each other.

When the recognition engine delivers more than one recognition hypothesis, an alternative strategy become possible. The event handler may dispatch subsequent recognition hypotheses until one is accepted by an FSM. In this case, the user does not need to repeat the input, as the recognition error has been automatically corrected. In order to work, this technique relies on the fact that the correct speech input is present in one of the recognition hypotheses.

The use of probabilistic state machines for dialog management for inputs with uncertainty has been discussed in Hudson et al (1992). This technique is relevant and applicable to multimodal interaction. The main difference between a probabilistic model and the traditional model of FSMs is that instead of having a single current state, a probabilistic FSM can have a distribution of alternative states. The probability that the machine is in any of these states is calculated based on a probability associated with each of the alternative user inputs. One potential advantage to this technique is that the probability of a state that triggered an action can be communicated to the application. The application can then combine this probability with its internal models to evaluate if an action should be executed or not, or to compare several concurrent actions.

4. CONCLUSION

The iterative design, implementation and testing of multimodal user interfaces is difficult, due to a lack of supporting tools for designers and developers. In response to this, we have developed a toolkit that aims to facilitate this process (Bourguet, 2002). In particular, modality integration, error handling and user input management are handled by the toolkit in a transparent manner. We have also developed a graphical tool that facilitates the process of declaring interaction models in the form of collections of FSMs (Bourguet, 2002). In the near future we are planning to automatically generate interaction models from experimental observations. Potential users will be asked to freely produce actions with the aim of activating specific multimodal commands. These actions will then form the basis for the automatic generation of FSMs. These automatically generated FSMs will then be tested for error robustness using the techniques that were outlined in this paper.

REFERENCES

Bourguet, M.L., 2002, A Toolkit for Creating and Testing Multimodal Interface Designs, *in companion proceedings of UIST'02*, pp. 29-30.

Bourguet, M.L., 2003a, Designing and Prototyping Multimodal Commands, *in proceedings of INTERACT'03*, pp. 717-720.

Bourguet, M.L., 2003b, How finite state machines can be used to build error free multimodal interaction systems, *in proceedings of HCI'03 volume 2*, pp. 81-84.

Duchnowski, P., Meier, U. & Waibel, A., 1994, See Me, Hear Me: Integrating Automatic Speech Recognition and Lipreading, *in proceeding of ICSLP 94*.

Hudson, S. & Newell, G., 1992, Probabilistic Sate Machines: Dialog Management for Inputs with Uncertainty, *in Proceedings of UIST'92*, pp. 199-208.

Johnston, M., 1998, Unification-based Multimodal Parsing, *in proceeding of COLING-ACL*.

Martin, D., Cheyer, A. & Moran, D., 1999, The Open Agent Architecture: A framework for building distributed software systems, Applied Artificial Intelligence, **13** (1-2), pp 91-128.

Minsky, M., 1975, A framework for presenting knowledge, *The Psychology of Computer Vision*, P.H. Winston (ed.), McGraw-Hill.

Nigay, L & Coutaz, J., 1995, A Generic Platform for Addressing the Multimodal Challenge, *in Proceedings of CHI'95*, ACM Press, pp. 98-105.

Oviatt, S., De Angeli, A. & Kuhn, K., 1997, Integration and synchronisation of input modes during multimodal human-computer interaction, *in Proceedings of CHI'97*, ACM Press, pp. 415-422.

Oviatt, S., 2000, Taming recognition errors with a multimodal interface, *in Communications of the ACM*, **43** (9), ACM Press, pp. 45-51.

Shimazu, H. & Takashima, Y., 1995, Multimodal Definite Clause Grammar, *Systems and Computers in Japan*, **26** (3).

Waibel, A. & Duchnowski, P., 1994, Connectionist models in multimodal human-computer interaction, *in proceedings of GOMAC 94*.

Wasserman, A., 1985, Extending State Transition Diagrams for the Specification of Human-Computer Interaction, *IEEE Transactions on Software Engineering*, **11** (8), pp. 699-713.

A GENERIC FORMAL SPECIFICATION OF FUSION OF MODALITIES IN A MULTIMODAL HCI

Yamine AIT AMEUR[1] and Nadjet KAMEL[1,2]

LISI/ENSMA-Université de Poitiers[1]
Site du Futuroscope. 86960 Futuroscope Cedex.
France

LRIA-USTHB[2]
BP 32. El Allia. 16111 Algiers.
Algeria

{yamine,kamel}@ensma.fr

Abstract This paper is an overview of a generic formal description allowing to encode multi-modal interactive systems, their behaviors and properties.

Keywords: Multi-modal Interaction, Formal Methods, Transition Systems.

1. Introduction

The development of computers on the one hand, and of input and output devices on the other hand allow new system interaction modes. Indeed, nowadays voice, touch, movements, etc. can be used in order to interact with a given system. The use of such interaction modes increases the usability and the ease of use of a given system. Moreover, these interaction modes are close to those used by human beings. However, handling these new interaction modes has favored the emergence of a number of problems like fusion of input interaction, fission of output interaction, modelling, describing, designing and coding of multi-modal systems, etc.

The objective of this paper is to overview a formal description technique of a multi-modal interaction system in order to help the designers to describe, design, validate and check the properties of a multi-modal interaction system using particular formal methods or techniques. We propose a formal description based on transition system, independent of any type of interaction modes and of any particular multi-modal system which helps the designers in describing either a multi-modal system or the system required properties.

2. Multi-modal HCI

Multi-modal interaction is complex since it supports complex events issued from different input channels. As a consequence, parallelism with all its difficulties is induced. Several modalities (each modality has several basic events), may be used in order to build an interaction with the system. The building process associated to the interaction is based on a composition of sub-interactions which are themselves compositions of sub-interaction tasks and so on, until basic events are reached. Composition operators are needed in order to build such multi-modal interactions.

Multi-modal interactive systems can be categorized following several criteria. According to (Nigay and Coutaz, 1993, Nigay and Coutaz, 1995, Bellik, 1995), we base our classification on three criteria: (1) production of interactions either in parallel or in sequence; (2) use of medias exclusive or simultaneous, and; (3) number of medias per interaction. The combination of these criteria leads to seven types of multi-modal interactions.

1- *Exclusive.* Only one modality is used and the interaction are produced sequentially.

2- *Alternate.* Several modalities can be used alternatively and interactions are produced sequentially.

3- *Synergistic.* Interactions are produced concurrently but events of different modalities can be fired in parallel or interleaved.

4- *Parallel exclusive.* Interactions are produced concurrently and only one event of a modality is fired.

5- *Parallel simultaneous.* Several independent interactions can be produced concurrently and only one modality is used for each interaction. The events of the modalities may be fired concurrently.

6- *Parallel alternate.* Several independent interactions can be produced concurrently and several modalities may be used to produce an interaction but only one modality is active each time.

7- *Parallel synergistic.* Several independent interactions can be produced concurrently, several modalities may be used to produce an interaction and several events may be fired each time.

Formal methods in Multi-modal HCI. As outlined in (Palanque and Schyn, 2003), only few work for applying formal methods for the development of multi-modal interactive systems have been achieved. Three main approaches may be distinguished. First the approach of (Paterno and Mezzanotte, 1994) uses interactors to model the application of the *matis* case study starting from a task model described in a user task notation (UAN). The Lotos formal technique has been used to encode these interactors and the ACTL temporal logic supported by the Lite model checker tool has been used for verifying properties expressed on these interactors. The second approach is due to (Duke and Harrison, 1993, Duke and Harrison, 1995) (MacColl and Carrington, 9908). They show how formal techniques, based on proof systems, may be used to encode a multi-modal application. Finally, the third approach of the Interactive Cooperative Objects (ICO) of (Palanque et al., 1995, Palanque and Schyn, 2003) based on Petri nets deals with fusion of modalities. These approaches have a partial coverage of the engineering of multi-modal interaction. Indeed, some of them deal with system representation, or with fusion of modalities while others address the property verification and validation.

We observe that all the previous approaches use specific formal techniques that have their own domain of efficiency. None of them supports the whole multi-modal interactive system design.

3. A generic representation of Multi-modal HCI

Our approach does not consist in the use of a formal technique in order to design a multi-modal interactive system. It suggests a formal methodology allowing to represent a multi-modal interactive system independently of any particular formal technique. This approach is based on the expression of the system and of the properties corresponding to the user requirements. Our proposal consists in describing both the system and the properties in a generic and universal formal description technique: transition systems for the system representation and logics for the properties expression. Notice, that we do not push any particular formal technique nor a particular tool. Moreover, we do not give any recommendation about the way the system is designed. Indeed, at least three scenarios can be identified (1) describe the system first and then the properties it shall satisfy; (2) describe the properties and extract a system that fulfills these properties (3) describe in parallel the system and the properties to be satisfied. The scenario is usually imposed by development practices or methods and by the chosen development technique.

System description: formal specification. The chosen representation for a multi-modal interactive system is based on the theory of interactive systems and of process algebra developed by several authors. Transition systems encoding the interactive system are used to represent formally this system. This formal description technique is universal and well understood. Moreover, several semantic aspects can be encoded using this description technique. One can encode synchrony/asynchrony, parallelism/interleaving and sequentiality. It is up to the designer to choose the semantics he/she thinks to be well adapted to his/her description of the problem. This possibility increases the description power of the system.

Finally, several composition/decomposition operations have been developed on transition systems based description. Indeed, refinement, synchronous products, abstraction, etc. operations have been formally defined. They allow to structure the development of a given system using a compositional approach providing ascending or descending developments.

Expression of properties. (Coutaz et al., 1995) have identified the properties that need to be expressed in order to assert that a multi-modal interactive system is usable. The authors have defined Complementarity, Assignment, Redundancy and Equivalence as the main properties that may be satisfied by a multi-modal system.

Properties are formal representations of intended behavior of a given system. Several representations of properties can be suggested. In our approach for the description of multi-modal interactive systems, we focus on two representations commonly available when using formal techniques. The first one consists in expressing properties, which are checked on the transition system describing the system, by logics whose semantics is given in terms of transition systems. Model checking techniques and proof based techniques are based on such an approach. The second approach for properties verification is based on behavioral descriptions of properties. Indeed, properties are described by transition systems that describe a suited behavior of the system. Language inclusion, simulation, bi-simulation relationships are used to check that the described behavior is also a possible behavior of the system. Proof based and model checking approaches may be used to establish such properties.

Methodology. Our proposal consists in a global generic model for handling multi-modal interactions. We focus on input modalities and their fusion. This approach consists in defining a formal representation for both the system and the properties to be expressed on the system. The expression of the system is based on general transition systems while properties are expressed either by transition systems expressing suited behaviors or by logical expression in a given logic. We just use basic formal description techniques and leave the choice of a formal technique to the methodology a designer wants to use.

System description. The syntax of the language describing the input multi-modal interactions is given by the following grammar issued from classical process algebra. The rule defining S generates the user task interactions at a higher level. These tasks use basic interaction events of the set $A = \bigcup_{i=1}^{n} A_{m_i}$ where A_{m_i} is the set of events e_i produced by a modality m_i. We denote by A_{Set} any subset of A.

$S ::= S[]S \mid S >> S \mid S|||S \mid S||S \mid E$	higher order multi-modal interaction.
$E ::= e; E \mid e|||E \mid e||E \mid \delta$ with $e \in A$	basic events rules

where $[]$, $>>$, $|||$, $||$ and ; stand for choice, enabling, interleaving, parallelism and sequence operators.

Formal semantics of the system. The underlying semantics of a multi-modal system with input modalities is a transition system. Let P and Q be two terms of the previous grammar and e, e_1 and e_2 be events of A, then the transition $P \xrightarrow{e} Q$ expresses that the term Q is obtained from P when the event e occurs. Using, this notation for transitions, the operational semantics is formally expressed by transition rules expressing the behavior of each operator of the previously described system. According to Plotkin, 1981, each rule of the form $\frac{premises}{conclusion}$ expresses that when the premises hold, then the conclusion holds. The formal semantics is given by the following set of rules.

δ : empty axiom	$\delta \not\longrightarrow$	
; : prefix axiom	$e; P \xrightarrow{e} P$	
$[]$: rules	$\frac{P \xrightarrow{e} P'}{P[]Q \xrightarrow{e} P'}$	$\frac{Q \xrightarrow{e} Q'}{P[]Q \xrightarrow{e} Q'}$
$>>$: sequence rules	$\frac{P \xrightarrow{e} P' \text{ and } P' \neq \delta}{P>>Q \xrightarrow{e} P'>>Q}$	$\frac{P \xrightarrow{e} P' \text{ and } P' = \delta}{P>>Q \xrightarrow{e} Q}$
$\mid\mid\mid$: interleaving rules	$\frac{P \xrightarrow{e} P'}{P\mid\mid\mid Q \xrightarrow{e} P'\mid\mid\mid Q}$	$\frac{Q \xrightarrow{e} Q'}{P\mid\mid\mid Q \xrightarrow{e} P\mid\mid\mid Q'}$
$\parallel$: parallel rules	$\frac{P \xrightarrow{e} P'}{P\parallel Q \xrightarrow{e} P'\mid\mid\mid Q}$ $\frac{P \xrightarrow{e_1} P',\, Q \xrightarrow{e_2} Q' \text{ with } e_1 \in A_{m_i}, e_2 \in A_{m_j}, A_{m_i} \neq A_{m_j}}{P\parallel Q \xrightarrow{(e_1,e_2)} P'\parallel Q'}$	$\frac{Q \xrightarrow{e} Q'}{P\parallel Q \xrightarrow{e} P\mid\mid\mid Q'}$

These rules will be encoded according to the chosen formal used technique.

Representation of multi-modal interactions. The previous model has shown a notation allowing to represent any multi-modal input interaction expressed by a user in order to fire a given action of the target system. However, usually, not all the composition operations are allowed to combine different modalities. This section shows that it is possible to extract different subsystems corresponding to particular multi-modal interaction systems. In the following we define the restricted interaction elements allowed for particular by restricting the allowed syntax.

Exclusive multi-modal interaction.

$S ::= S[]S \mid S >> S \mid E$	choice and enabling of sub-interactions.
$E ::= e; E \mid \delta$ with $e \in A_{m_i}$	events issued from one modality.

Alternate multi-modal interaction.

$S ::= S[]S \mid S >> S \mid E$	choice and enabling of sub-interactions.
$E ::= e; E \mid e\mid\mid\mid E \mid \delta$ with $e \in A_{Set}$	events are issued from different modalities.

Synergistic multi-modal interaction.

$S ::= S[]S \mid S >> S \mid E$	choice and enabling of sub-interactions.
$E ::= e; E \mid e\mid\mid\mid E \mid e\parallel E \mid \delta$ with $e \in A_{Set}$	events are issued from different modalities.

Parallel exclusive multi-modal interaction.

$S ::= S[]S \mid S >> S \mid S\mid\mid\mid S \mid E$	choice, enabling and interleaving of sub-interactions.
$E ::= e; E \mid \delta$ with $e \in A_{m_i}$	events issued from one modality.

Parallel simultaneous multi-modal interaction.

$S ::= S[]S \mid S >> S \mid S\parallel S \mid E$	choice, enabling and parallelism of sub-interactions.
$E ::= e; E \mid \delta$ with $e \in A_{m_i}$	events issued from one modality.

Parallel alternate multi-modal interaction.

$S ::= S[]S \mid S >> S \mid S\mid\mid\mid S \mid E$	choice, enabling and interleaving of sub-interactions.
$E ::= e; E \mid e\mid\mid\mid E \mid \delta$ with $e \in A_{Set}$	events are issued from different modalities.

Parallel synergistic multi-modal interaction.

$S ::= S[]S \mid S >> S \mid S|||S \mid S||S \mid E$	all operators allowed for sub-interactions.
$E ::= e; E \mid e|||E \mid e||E \mid \delta$ with $\delta \in A_{Set}$	events are issued from different modalities.

These different definitions characterize behaviors of the multi-modal system. Properties may be expressed as well. Both behaviors and properties shall be checked using the chosen formal technique.

4. Conclusion

This paper presented a generic representation of multi-modal interactive systems. The developed approach is based on the expression of the multi-modal systems using transition systems and their associated semantics. The properties are represented either by other transition systems expressing behaviors or using a logic. This representation is independent from any particular formal technique or tool. The methodology suggests to encode the system and properties description in the formal technique the designers may use.

References

Bellik, Y. (1995). *Interfaces Multimodales : concepts, modèles et architecture.* PhD thesis, LIMSI- Université d'Orsay.

Coutaz, J., Nigay, L., Salber, D., Blandford, A., May, J., and Young, R. (1995). Four easy pieces for assessing the usability of multimodal interaction: the CARE properties. In *Proceedings of Human Computer Interaction - Interact'95*, pages 115–120. Chapman and Hall.

Duke, D. and Harrison, M. D. (1993). Abstract Interaction Objects. In *Proceedings of Eurographics conference and computer graphics forum*, volume 12, pages 25–36.

Duke, D. and Harrison, M. D. (1995). Event Model of Human-System Interaction. *IEEE Software Engineering Journal*, 10(1):3–10.

MacColl and Carrington, D. (19908). *Testing MATIS: a case study on specfication based testing of interactive systems.* FAHCI ISBN 0-86339-7948.

Nigay, L. and Coutaz, J. (1993). A design space for multi-modal interfaces: concurrent processing and data fusion. In *Proceedings of INTERCHI-93 - INTERCHI-93*, pages 172–178. ACM Press.

Nigay, L. and Coutaz, J. (1995). A Generic Platform for Adressing the Multimodal Challenge. In *Proceedings of CHI-95 - CHI-95*, pages 98–105. ACM Press.

Palanque, P., Bastide, R., and Sengès, V. (1995). Validating interactive system design through the verification of formal task and system models. In Bass, L. J. and Unger, C., editors, *IFIP TC2/WG2.7 Working Conference on Engineering for Human-Computer Interaction (EHCI'95)*, pages 189–212, Grand Targhee Resort (Yellowstone Park), USA. Chapman & Hall.

Palanque, P. and Schyn, A. (2003). A Model-based for Engineering Multimodal Interactive Systems. In *9th IFIP TC13 International Conference on Human Computer Interaction (Interact'2003)*.

Paterno, F. and Mezzanotte, M. (1994). Analysing MATIS by Interactors and ACTL. Technical report, Amodeus Esprit Basic Research Project 7040, System Modelling/WP36.

Plotkin, G. (1981). A Structural Approach to Operational Semantics. Technical report, Department of of computer Science, University of Arhus DAIMI FN 19.

MULTIMOMODALITY AND MULTI-PLATFORM INTERACTIVE SYSTEMS

Fabio Paternò
ISTI-CNR, Via G.Moruzzi 1, 56124 Pisa, Italy

Abstract: This paper discusses how to take into account multimodality when designing multi-platform interactive systems. In particular, it focuses on graphical and vocal interaction and discusses how to obtain interfaces in either one modality or their combination starting with logical descriptions of the tasks to perform. It also introduces how such an approach can enable migratory interfaces exploiting various modalities.

Key words: Multimodality, Multi-platform User Interfaces, Model-based Design, Migratory Interfaces

1. INTRODUCTION

One of the current main challenges for designers and developers of interactive systems is how to address applications that can be accessed through a variety of devices that can vary in terms of interaction resources (screen size, processing power, modalities supported, ...). In order to address such challenges model-based approaches have raised a good deal of interest: the basic idea is to have concepts and languages that express aspects relevant to user interaction in a device independent manner and then to support a design process that is able to identify usable solutions taking into account the features of the devices available.

In this context many modalities can be considered. In the paper we focus on the graphical and vocal modalities and discuss their impact in the design process following a model-based approach aiming at developing multi-modal interfaces in Web environments. The approach discussed is supported by a tool, TERESA (Mori, Paternò, and Santoro, 2003) providing various transformations among different abstraction levels. The abstraction levels considered are: the task level, where the logical activities are described including the objects necessary to their accomplishment; the abstract interface level, a conceptual description of the user interface in a modality independent language; the concrete level, where the concrete design decisions are described; and lastly the user interface. The design process goes through these levels, and information regarding the target platforms and devices is considered at each level even if the approach allows designers avoid dealing with low-level implementation details. By platform we mean a class of systems that share the same characteristics in terms of interaction resources. They range from small devices, such as interactive watches to very large flat displays. Examples of platforms are the graphical desktop, PDAs, mobile phones and vocal systems. The modalities available have an important role in the definition of each platform.

Multimodality is important in this approach because of the intrinsic differences among modalities. For example, the vocal channel is more suitable for simple or short messages, for signaling events, immediate actions, to avoid visual overloading and when users are on the move, whereas the visual channel is more useful for complex or long messages, for identifying spatial relations, when multiple actions have to be performed, in noisy environments or with users stationary.

This paper discusses how multimodality can be considered when designing multi-device interfaces through an approach that takes into account the potential interactive devices since the early phases (for example, identifying the tasks suitable for each platform). The approach allows designers to avoid a plethora of low-level details related to all the potential devices by using conceptual descriptions that are automatically translated into the user interface implementation.

2. MAPPING TASKS INTO MULTIMODAL INTERFACES

Our approach exploits a number of transformations that allow designers to move through various views of interactive systems. TERESA allows designers to focus on the logical tasks to accomplish and then transform their descriptions into a user interface description, which incorporates the design decisions but is still in a format modality independent. This is then used to derive a modality-dependent interface description that is used to generate the final code of the user interface. For each logical level considered a XML-based language has been defined. While the languages for the task and the abstract interface descriptions are the same for all the platforms, each platform has its own description language for the concrete interface. The advantage of this approach is that designers can focus on logical aspects and make design decisions without having to deal with many low-level implementation details. The environment provides support to make concrete design decisions that take into account the target platforms and generate the code where all the low-level details are specified. This type of support is particularly useful when a variety of devices should support access to the interactive application. On the other hand, it is worth noting that in order to make effective decisions designers should be aware of the target platforms and modalities even since the early stages of the design process. They do not need to know the implementation details of all the targeted devices but they still should know their main features (through the platform concept).

Indeed, there are tasks that may be meaningful only when using some specific platform or modality. For example, watching a long movie makes sense only in a multimedia desktop system whereas accessing information from a car in order to know directions to avoid a traffic jam can be done only through a mobile device and if this task should be performed while driving it can be supported only through a vocal interface. The description of an object can be easily communicated through the graphical channel with the support of images whereas it can require long and less effective texts through a vocal device. It is said that "a picture is worth a thousand words" but people do not like to hear so many words. Identifying spatial relations such as how to get in a certain position can be immediately communicated through a graphical interface whereas may be difficult to explain precisely through a vocal interface.

The available modality may also have an impact on how to accomplish a task, for example a vocal interface or a graphical mobile phone interface can require to perform sequentially tasks that can be performed concurrently in a desktop graphical interface.

In TERESA a user interface is structured into a number of presentations. A presentation identifies a set of interaction techniques that are enabled at a given time. The presentation is structured into interactors (logical descriptions of interaction techniques) and composition operators that indicate how to put together such interactors. While at the abstract level such interactors and their compositions are identified in terms of their semantics in a modality independent manner, at the concrete level their description and the values of the attributes depend on the available modality.

TERESA is able to generate code in Web user interface languages for different modalities: XHTML, XHTML Mobile Profile, VoiceXML, X+V (a combination of XHTML and VoiceXML that supports multimodal interaction). In the case of both vocal and graphical support the multimodality can be exploited in different manners. The modalities can be used alternatively to perform the same interaction. They can be used synergistically within one basic interaction (for example, providing input vocally and showing the result of the interaction graphically) or within a complex interaction (for example, filling in a form partially vocally and partially graphically). Some level of redundancy can be supported as well, for example when feedback of a vocal interaction is provided both graphically and vocally.

The composition operators indicate how to put together such interactors and are associated with a communication goal. A communication goal is a type of effect that designers aim to achieve when they want to structure presentations. Grouping is an example of composition operator that aims to highlight that a group of interface elements are logically related to each other. It can be implemented in the graphical channel through one or multiple attributes (fieldset, colour, location ..) whereas in the vocal channel it is possible to group elements by inserting a sound or a pause at the beginning and the end of the grouped elements. In case of multimodal interfaces we have to consider the actual resources available for the modalities. It is different to design a multimodal interface for a desktop and one for a PDA because the graphical resources available are different. Thus, the grouping on a multimodal desktop interface should be mainly graphical and the use of the vocal channel can be limited to provide additional feedback of the selected elements whereas the grouping of a multimodal PDA interface should be mainly vocal and using the graphical channel only for important information or for supporting or explicative information.

If we consider an interactor the reasoning is similar. For example, the single selection interactor is implemented differently depending the modality and the cardinality of the potential choices. A graphical desktop has a lot of space available and so it is able to support a long list (for example a list of countries at world level), eventually providing some support to scroll it but in the case of small devices this is not possible. Thus, it is possible to consider splitting the single selection into two or more selections. The first selection is among groups of elements and the second one allows the section of the desired element within a smaller group. This can be implemented through either a graphical or a vocal mobile device. If multimodality can be supported for this type of interaction then in the case of the desktop system it can be used to provide some explanations about the purpose of the selection in order to avoid screen cluttering. In the case of the PDA it can be used to support the two resulting interaction and the associated feedback in either modality.

3. MIGRATORY MULTI-MODAL INTERFACES

Another interesting result of the model-based approach discussed is the possibility of supporting migrating interfaces: interfaces that can be transferred from one device to another one during a user session without having to restart from scratch. This type of interfaces makes sense only if the various interfaces are able to adapt to the hosting devices. This can be achieved through the approach discussed, which allows designers to obtain different versions of application interfaces tailored for each platform. Such versions should be managed by a migration server. The goal of the migration server is to maintain information of the devices available for the migration service and their characteristics, receive requests of migration, identify the target device of the migration and activate a new instance of the interface for the identified device. Such interface should already have the state of the results of the user interactions with the source device.

This implies a number of operations:

- The state of the user interactions should be stored;
- The server should be able to convert such state into the state for the target device interface;
- The server should be able to identify the specific presentation that should be activated in the target device in order to allow continuity of interaction;

These types of operations can be performed because of the logical information that is created during the model-based design process. The tasks supported by each interface device can vary or can substantially change how they are supported. The migration server knows the associations between tasks and interactors and between interactors and interface elements for each platform. Thus, for each user interaction it can identify the corresponding task and then identifies how it is supported by the target device and associate to the corresponding interface elements the state generated by the results of the user interactions in the source device. In addition, the knowledge of the last task performed on the source device is information useful also for identifying the presentation in the target device that should be activated as a result of the migration because the user expects to carry on its session from that point.

This type of approach can be exploited also in multimodal applications. It enables multimodal migrating services that, for example, allow the user to start the registration to the service through a desktop system and, in case he realizes that it is getting late, he can carry on the registration on the move using a PDA until he reaches his car where he can use a vocal interface to complete it. All this activity can be performed without having to restart the registration procedure from the beginning at each device change.

4. CONCLUSIONS

One of the main current issues for designers of interactive systems is how to address the wide variety of potential interaction platforms that can be used to access their applications. Multimodality plays an important role in characterizing such platforms.

The paper provides a description of an approach that aims to provide a solution to such issues providing support for designing multi-device, multi-modal interfaces. Such an approach exploits the semantic information associated with the potential user interfaces at run time to support dynamic migration even through various modalities. A number of tools supporting such an approach are under development in my group at ISTI-CNR. TERESA is publicly available at http://giove.isti.cnr.it/teresa.html

ACKNOWLEDGEMENTS

This work has been supported by the EU IST Project CAMELEON (http://giove.isti.cnr.it/cameleon.html) and the EU Network of Excellence SIMILAR (http://www.similar.cc). I also thank Silvia Berti for her work on supporting vocal interfaces.

REFERENCES

R.Bandelloni, S.Berti, F.Paternò, Mixed Initiative, Trans-Modal Interface Migration, Proceedings Mobile HCI 2004, Springer Verlag LNCS.

S. Berti, F. Paternò, Model-based Design of Speech Interfaces, Proceedings DSV-IS 2003, Springer Verlag, LNCS 2844, pp.231-244.

G. Mori, F. Paternò, C. Santoro, Tool Support for Designing Nomadic Applications, Proceedings ACM IUI'03, Miami, pp.141-148, ACM Press.

MULTIMODALITY AND CONTEXT-AWARE ADAPTATION

Quentin Limbourg and Jean Vanderdonckt
Université catholique de Louvain (UCL), School of Management (IAG), ISYS-BCHI
Place des Doyens, 1 – B-1348 Louvain-la-Neuve (Belgium)
Phone: +32-10 / 478525 – Fax: +32-10 / 478324
E-mail: {limbourg, vanderdonckt}@isys.ucl.ac.be
Web: http://www.isys.ucl.ac.be/bchi/members/{qli,jva}

Abstract: In principle, context-aware adaptation is assumed to bring to the end user the benefit of adapting the user interface currently being used according to significant changes of the context of use in which the user interface is manipulated. To address major shortcomings of system that hardcode the adaptation logic into the user interface or the interactive software, a mechanism is introduced to express context-aware adaptation as a set of logical production rules. These rules are gathered in graph grammars and applied on graphs representing elements subject to change and conditions imposed on the context of use. These rules can express both adaptations within the same modality of interaction (*intra-modality adaptation*) and across several modalities of interaction (*trans-modality adaptation*).

Keywords: Adaptation, Context of use, Graph grammars, Graph transformations, Intra-modality adaptation, Production rules, Trans-modality adaptation.

1. INTRODUCTION

The context of use is typically considered as a potential source of information to trigger an adaptation of the User Interface (UI) of a system according to significant changes of some properties of interest (Thevenin, 2001). The context of use is hereby defined as a triplet (*U*,*P*,*E*) where *U* represents the user and her properties (e.g., demographics attributes, skills, preferences, native language, motivations), *P* represents the computing platform and related properties (e.g., screen resolution, interaction capabilities, devices), and *E* represents the environment in which the user is carrying out the interactive task on the computing platform (Calvary *et al.*, 2003). Similarly, the environment is described by attributes like organisational structure, psychological parameters (e.g., level of stress). Any change of the current value of any of the *U*, *P*, and *E* parameters can potentially indicate a change of the context of use. However, in practice, only some of them truly represent a significant change of the context of use that should have an impact on the user interface. The adaptation logic that reacts to these significant changes of context is generally embedded in the software (i.e. hardcoded), thus resulting into little or no flexibility for changing it. In addition, the adaptation logic is rarely expressed in a formal way that is immediately executable by an automaton without requiring further modification. To address these shortcomings and to enable any person to express an adaptation rule according to the same language that can be communicated, we relied on the mechanism of graph transformations (Freund *et al.*, 1992) that is further explained in the next section. The steps of the methodology are (Limbourg & Vanderdonckt., 2004):

1. The context of use is represented by a graph (with nodes and arcs).
2. Other models that are typical of model-based approaches for multi-platform UIs (Paternò & Santoro, 2002) (e.g., presentation and dialog of the UI) are also represented by graphs.
3. The adaptation logic is expressed by transformation rules that check existing graphs for satisfying conditions of applicability and apply them consequently so as to create new specifications imposed on the adapted UI that can then be rendered.
4. The adaptation logic can be executed statically at design time or dynamically at execution time (Kawai *et al.*, 1996).

2. GRAPH TRANSFORMATION FOR CONTEXT-AWARE ADAPTATION

TOMATO consists of a general-purpose methodology that systematically applies design knowledge to produce a final UI by performing different steps based on a transformational approach. This approach enables expressing and simultaneously executing transformation of models describing UIs viewpoints. Fig. 1 illustrates the transformations steps supported in TOMATO:

- **Reification** is a transformation of a high-level requirement into a form that is appropriate for low-level analysis or design.
- **Abstraction** is a transformation of a low level the extraction of high-level requirement from a set of low-level requirements artefacts or from code (Bouillon *et al.* 2003).
- **Translation** is a transformation a UI in consequence of a context of use

change.

- **Reflection** is a transformation of the artefacts of any level onto artefacts of the same level of abstraction, but different constructs or various contents.
- **Code generation** is a process of transforming a concrete UI model into a compilable or interpretable code.
- **Code reverse engineering** is the inverse process of code generation.

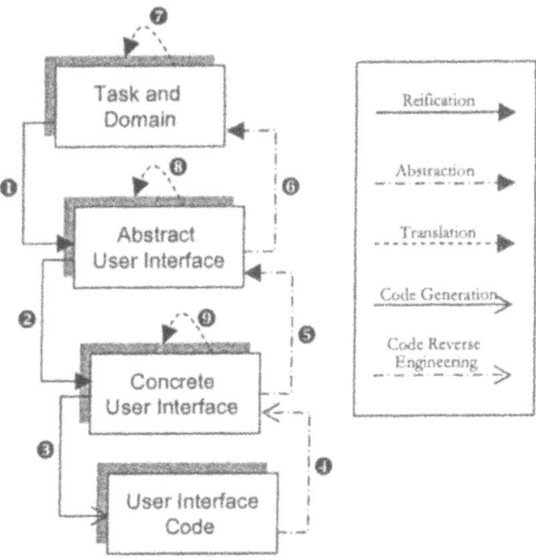

Figure 1. Transformations between viewpoints.

The different transformation types are instantiated by *development steps* (each occurrence of a numbered arrow in Fig. 1). These development steps may be combined to form *development paths*. While code generation and code reverse engineering are supported by specific techniques, we use graph transformations to perform model-to-model transformations i.e., reifications, abstractions and translations. TOMATO models have been designed with an underlying graph structure. Consequently any graph transformation rule can be applied to any TOMATO specification. Graph transformations have been shown convenient formalism for our present purpose in (Limbourg *et al.*, 2004). The main reasons of this choice are (1) an attractive graphical syntax (2) a clear execution semantic (3) an inherent declarativeness of this formalism. Development steps are realized with transformation systems. A transformation system is a set of (individual) transformation rules. A transformation rule is a graph rewriting rule equipped with negative application conditions and attribute conditions (Roszenberg, 1997).

Fig. 2 illustrates how a transformation system applies to a TOMATO specification: let G be a TOMATO specification, when 1) a Left Hand Side (LHS) matches into G and 2) a Negative Application Condition (NAC) does not matches into G (note that several NAC may be associated with a rule) 3) the LHS is replaced by a Right Hand Side (RHS). *G* is consequently transformed into *G'*, a resultant TOMATO specification. All elements of G not covered by the match are considered as unchanged. All elements contained in the LHS and not contained in the RHS are considered as deleted (i.e., rules have destructive power). To add to the expressive power of transformation rules, variables may be associated to attributes within a LHS. Theses variables are initialized in the LHS, their value can be used to assign an attribute in the expression of the RHS (e.g., LHS : button.name:=x, RHS : task.name:=x). An expression may also be defined to compare a variable declared in the LHS with a constant or with another variable. This mechanism is called 'attribute condition'.

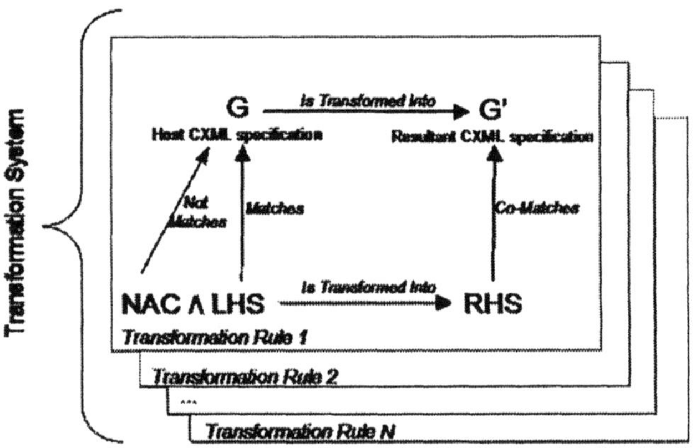

Figure 2. A transformation system in TOMATO methodology.

3. ADAPTATION TO CONTEXT CHANGE

According to the Cameleon reference framework (Calvary *et al.*, 2003), adaptation with respect to the context change can take place at three levels (Fig. 3): (1) at the "task & domain" level where one or both models are affected to reflect a change of context of use (e.g., a change in the organisational structure may move a task from one role to another one, thus resulting in deleting this task from the task set of a person); (2) at the "abstract UI" level, where the UI is described independently of any modality of interaction; (3) at the "concrete UI" level, where the UI is described with specific modalities, but still independently of any computing platform. In terms of graph transformations, context adaptation covers model transformations adapting a viewpoint to another context of use. This adaptation is performed at any of the three above levels.

Fig. 4 depicts a production rule that perform the following adaptation: for each pair of abstract individual component mapped onto concurrent tasks, transfer all facets of the abstract individual component that is mapped onto the task that is target of the concurrency relationship, to the other abstract individual component. Abstract individual components represent a sort of abstraction of interaction objects independently of their modality of interaction. As such, they are located higher than traditional Abstract Interaction Objects (Vanderdonckt & Bodart, 1993). This rule should not be applied to task that still have decomposition. In other words, the rule is applied only on leaf tasks of the task model (Paternò & Santoro, 2002).

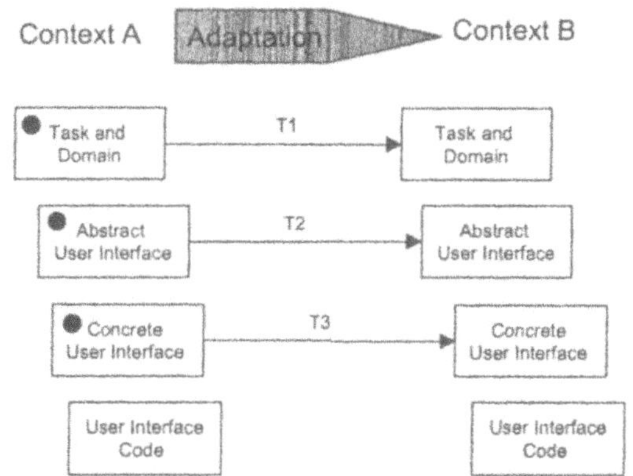

Figure 3. Context adaptation at different levels of TOMATO.

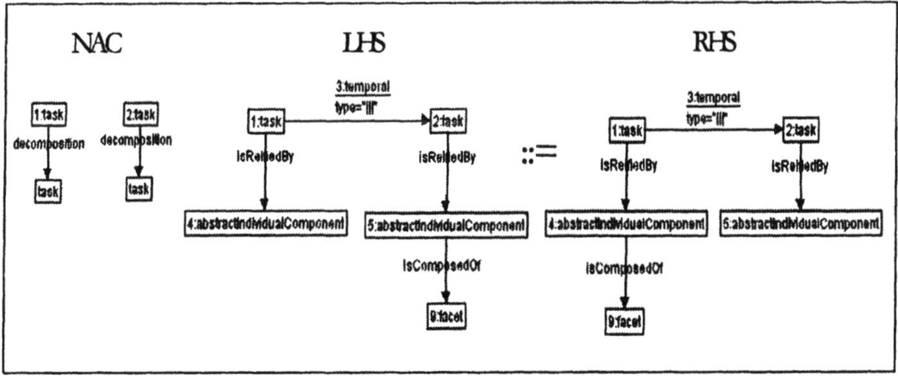

Figure 4. A merging of facets of abstract individual components

ACKNOWLEDGEMENTS

We gratefully acknowledge the support of the European IST CAMELEON research project (http://giove.cnuce.cnr.it/cameleon.html), the CAMELEON partners for fruitful exchanges and discussions, and the SIMILAR network of excellence (http://www.similar.cc), the European research task force creating human-machine interfaces similar to human-human communication of the European Sixth Framework Programme.

REFERENCES

Bouillon, L., Vanderdonckt, J., and Chow, K.C.: 2004, Flexible Re-engineering of Web Sites. In: *Proceedings of 8th ACM Int. Conf. on Intelligent User Interfaces (IUI'2004)*. Funchal, 13-16 January 2004. ACM Press, New York, pp. 132-139.

Calvary, G., Coutaz, J., Thevenin, D., Limbourg, Q., Bouillon, L., and Vanderdonckt, J.: June 2003, A Unifying Reference Framework for Multi-Target User Interfaces. *Interacting with Computers* **15**(3) 289–308.

Freund, R., Haberstroh, B., and Stary, C.: 1992, Applying Graph Grammars for Task-Oriented User Interface Development. In: Koczkodaj, W.W., Lauer, P.E., Toptsis, A.A. (eds.): *Proceedings of 4th International Conference on Computing and Information (ICCI'92)*. Toronto, May 28-30, 1992. IEEE Computer Society Press, Los Alamitos, pp. 389–392.

Kawai, S., Aida, H., Saito, T.: 1996, Designing Interface Toolkit with Dynamic Selectable Modality. In: *Proceedings of 2nd ACM International Conference on Assistive Technologies (ASSETS'96)*. Vancouver, April 11-12, 1996. ACM Press, New York, pp. 72–79.

Limbourg, Q. and Vanderdonckt, J.: 2004, Transformational Development of User Interfaces with Graph Transformations. In: *Proceedings of 5th International Conference on Computer-Aided Design of User Interfaces (CADUI'2004)*. Madeira, January 14-16, 2004. Kluwer Academics Publishers, Dordrecht.

Limbourg, Q., Vanderdonckt, J., Michotte, B., Bouillon, L., Florins, M., and Trevisan, D.: 25 May 2004, USIXML: A User Interface Description Language for Context-Sensitive User Interfaces. In: *Proceedings of the ACM AVI'2004 Workshop "Developing User Interfaces with XML: Advances on User Interface Description Languages" (UIXML'04)*

Paternò, F. and Santoro, C.: 2002, One Model, Many Interfaces. Chapter 13. In: Kolski, Ch., Vanderdonckt, J. (eds.), *Proceedings of 4th International Conference on Computer-Aided Design of User Interfaces (CA-DUI'2002)*. Valenciennes, May 15-17, 2002. Kluwer Academics Publishers, Dordrecht, pp. 143–154.

Rozenberg, G. (Ed.): 1997, *Handbook of Graph Grammars and Computing by Graph Transformation*, Volume 1: Foundations, World Scientific.

Thevenin, D.: December 2001, *Adaptation en Interaction Homme-Machine: le cas de la Plasticité*, Ph.D. thesis. Grenoble, France, 2001. On-line: http://iihm.imag.fr/publs/2001

Vanderdonckt, J. and Bodart, F.: 1993, Encapsulating Knowledge for Intelligent Automatic Interaction Objects Selection. In: Ashlund, S., Mullet, K. Henderson, A., Hollnagel, E., White, T. (eds.): *Proceedings of the ACM Conference on Human Factors in Computing Systems (InterCHI'93)*. Amsterdam, April 14-19, 1993. ACM Press, New York, pp. 424–429.

TOWARDS MULTIMODAL WEB INTERACTION

Web pages you can speak to and gesture at

Dave Raggett (W3C/Canon), Max Froumentin (W3C), Philipp Hoschka (W3C)

1. INTRODUCTION

W3C is developing standards for a new class of devices that support multiple modes of interaction.

1.1 The Dream

The Multimodal Interaction Activity is focused on developing open standards that enable the following vision:

- Extending the Web to allow multiple modes of interaction: GUI, Speech, Vision, Pen, Gestures, Haptic interfaces, ...
- Augmenting human to computer and human to human interaction: Communication services involving multiple devices and multiple people
- Anywhere, Any device, Any time: Services that adapt to the device, user preferences and environmental conditions
- Accessible to all

The Multimodal Interaction Activity is extending the Web user interface to allow multiple modes of interaction—aural, visual and tactile—offering users the means to provide input using their voice or their hands via a key pad, keyboard, mouse, or stylus. For output, users will be able to listen to spoken prompts and audio, and to view information on graphical displays. The specifications developed by the Multimodal Interaction Working Group should be implementable on a royalty-free basis.

1.2 Application Areas

The Multimodal Interaction Working Group should be of interest to a range of organizations in different industry sectors.

1.2.1 Mobile

Multimodal applications are of particular interest for mobile devices. Speech offers a welcome means to interact with smaller devices, allowing one-handed and hands-free operation. Users benefit from being able to choose which modalities they find convenient in any situation. The Working Group should be of interest to companies developing smart phones and personal digital assistants or who are interested in providing tools and technology to support the delivery of multimodal services to such devices.

1.2.2 Automotive and Telematics

With the emergence of dashboard integrated high resolution color displays for navigation, communication and entertainment services, W3C's work on open standards for multimodal interaction should be of interest to companies working on developing the next generation of in-car systems.

1.2.3 Multimodal interfaces in the office

Multimodal has benefits for desktops and wall mounted interactive displays, offering a richer user experience and the chance to use speech and pens as alternatives to the mouse and keyboard. W3C's standardization work in this area should be of interest to companies developing browsers and authoring technologies, and who wish to ensure that the resulting standards live up to their needs.

1.2.4 Multimodal interfaces in the home

In addition to desktop access to the Web, multimodal interfaces are expected to add value to remote control of home entertainment systems, as well as finding a role for other systems around the home. Companies involved in developing embedded systems and consumer electronics should be interested in W3C's work on multimodal interaction.

2. CURRENT SITUATION

The Multimodal Interaction Working Group was launched in 2002 following a joint workshop between the W3C and the WAP Forum. Relevant W3C Member contributions have been received on SALT and X+V. The Working Group's initial focus was on use cases and requirements. This led to the publication of the W3C Multimodal Interaction Framework, and in turn to work on extensible multi-modal annotations (EMMA), and InkML, an XML language for ink traces. The Working Group has also worked on integration of composite multimodal input; dynamic adaptation to device configurations, user preferences and environmental conditions; modality component interfaces; and a study of current approaches to interaction management. The Working Group is now in the process of being re-chartered for a further two years. The following organizations are currently participating in the Working Group:

Access, Alcatel, Apple, Aspect, AT&T, Avaya, BeVocal, Canon, Cisco, Comverse, EDS, Ericsson, France Telecom, Fraunhofer Institute, HP, IBM, INRIA, Intel, IWA/HWG, Kirusa, Loquendo, Microsoft, Mitsubishi Electric, NEC, Nokia, Nortel Networks, Nuance Communications, OnMobile Systems, Openstream, Opera Software, Oracle, Panasonic, ScanSoft, Siemens, SnowShore Networks, Sun Microsystems, Telera, Tellme Networks, T-Online International, Toyohashi University of Technology, V-Enable, Vocalocity, VoiceGenie Technologies, Voxeo

All participating organizations are required to make a patent disclosure statement as set out in the W3C's Current Patent Practice (CPP) Note. A separate page is being maintained for patent disclosures for the Multimodal Interaction Activity. The Working Group is obliged by its charter to produce a specification which relies only on intellectual property available on a royalty-free basis.

3. WORK IN PROGRESS

This is intended to give you a brief summary of each of the major work items under development by the Multimodal Interaction Working Group. The suite of specifications is known as the W3C Multimodal Interaction Framework.

Introduction, 6 May 2003. The Multimodal Interaction Framework introduces a general framework for multimodal interaction, and the kinds of markup languages being considered.

Use cases, 4 December 2002. Multimodal Interaction Use Cases describes several use cases that are helping us to better understand the requirements for multimodal interaction.

Core requirements, 8 January 2003. Multimodal Interaction Requirements describes fundamental requirements for the specifications under development in the W3C Multimodal Interaction Activity.

3.1 Extensible Multi-Modal Annotations (EMMA)

Requirements, 13 January 2003
Working Draft, 18 December 2003
Last Call Working Draft, Spring 2004

EMMA is being developed as a data exchange format for the interface between input processors and interaction management systems. It will define the means for recognizers to annotate application specific data with information such as confidence scores, time stamps, input mode (e.g. key strokes, speech or pen), alternative recognition hypotheses, and partial recognition results etc. EMMA is a target data format for the semantic interpretation specification being developed in the Voice Browser Activity, and which describes annotations to speech grammars for extracting application specific data as a result of speech recognition. EMMA supercedes earlier work on the natural language semantics markup language in the Voice Browser Activity.

3.2 Modality Interfaces

W3C Note expected June 2004

A common framework based upon the W3C Document Object Model (DOM) for the abstract software interfaces between user interface components for different modalities and the host environment provided by the interaction manager. The Voice Browser Working Group is expected to develop modality interfaces for Speech and DTMF. The Multimodal Interaction Working Group is tasked with defining interfaces for ink and keystrokes, enabling the use of grammars for constrained input, and the context sensitive binding of gestures to semantics. To facilitate secure end-user authentication, the framework should support the integration of bio-metric interfaces for voice, fingerprint and handwriting, etc.

3.3 Building a shared understanding of interaction management

W3C Note expected September 2004
A study of approaches to interaction management for multimodal applications from a practical and theoretical perspective, looking at standalone and distributed solutions, and at different levels of abstraction. The study will identify promising approaches for further work on standardization in collaboration with other W3C working groups.

3.4 Integration of Composite Multimodal Input

W3C Note expected June 2004
Defining the basis for an interoperable treatment of composite multimodal input, for instance, a combination of speech and pen gestures. A report is in preparation on uses cases and a range of potential approaches.

3.5 System and Environment

First Working Draft expected June 2004
A framework for enabling applications to dynamically adapt to match the current device capabilities, device configuration, user preferences and environmental conditions, such as low battery alerts or loss of network connectivity. Other possible changes include muting the microphone and disabling audio output. Dynamic configurations include snapping a camera attachment onto a cell phone or bringing devices together with Bluetooth, e.g. a camera phone and a color printer. This work is being done in collaboration with the W3C Device Independence activity.

3.6 Sessions

This work is being integrated into other deliverables.
Dynamic configurations and distributed multimodal applications present new challenges to Web developers. Sessions provide the basis for subscribing to events, synchronizing data, and hiding details of protocols and addressing mechanisms.

3.7 InkML - an XML language for ink traces

Requirements, 22 January 2003
Working Draft, 23 February 2004
Last Call Working Draft, TBD

This work item sets out to define an XML data exchange format for ink entered with an electronic pen or stylus as part of a multimodal system. This will enable the capture and server-side processing of handwriting, gestures, drawings, and specific notations for mathematics, music, chemistry and other fields, as well as supporting further research on this processing. The Ink subgroup maintains a separate public page devoted to W3C's work on pen and stylus input.

4. CONCLUSION

W3C has been active in the area of multimodal Web access for several years. Very likely, multimodal Web access will be the first widespread practical use of multimodal technology, and will have a similar impact on the adoption multimodal technology as the original Web had on the adoption of Internet technology. Industry interest in use of multimodal Web technology is increasing, and the first key specifications are being put in place at the W3C.

Acknowledgement: This work was supported by the EU FP6 project MWeb. The views are those of the authors, and do not represent the views of the funding agency.

Topic 6

Computer Aided Inventing

Organiser:

Noel León Rovira
ITESM Campus Monterrey, Mexico
noel.leon@itesm.mx

Computer Aided Innovation software has been emerging in the last decade based, among others, on the Theory of Inventive Problem Solving (TRIZ). Computer Aided Innovation is evolving to become an important component in the Product Creation Process.

The topical session Computer Aided Inventing is aimed to provide the opportunity to present the latest developments and challenges in the domain of computer tools that contribute to more effective ways of establishing innovation lines and for solving innovation and inventive problems.

TOWARDS "INVENTIVENESS-ORIENTED" CAI TOOLS

Denis CAVALLUCCI[1], Noel Leon[2]
[1]Associate professor, INSA, Strasbourg; [2] Full Professor, ITESM, Mexico

Abstract The emergence of a new category of tools baptised CAI (Computer Aided Innovation) is taking shape as industrial demand becomes more pressing. One category of tools in particular stands out as being a break from the usual trends in CAD, i.e. where the software structure is partially inspired by TRIZ. While the aim of such tools is to assist the designer in his creative act upstream of the act of designing, the link between the list of concepts these tools offer and the input required to build an object model is not ensured to date. The aim of this article is to clarify the essential factors characterising an act of designing/redesigning inspired by the fundamental aspects of TRIZ. This should help bridge the gap between the traditional knowledge (see Yoshikawa H., 1989) which contributed to the development of current CAD tools and the approach which makes TRIZ a theory totally in line with current trends in search of efficient inventiveness in terms of the design act.

Key words: inventive design, creativity, CAI, TRIZ, design

1. INTRODUCTION

Technical artefacts are becoming increasingly sophisticated as technology evolves. This logic of obeying needs, which are either latent or clearly expressed, is also evident in man's ever more impatient demands. At the same time, the buying power of households is increasing and the average cost of accessing innovations available on the market is falling. The result is that consumption of new products is continuously growing and this has a major impact on industry, where the need to rebuild design potential is strongly felt both in terms of human skills and methodological expertise.

A new situation is therefore arising, affecting the designers of these artefacts. It can be summed up as follows: are the tools and methods developed to aid the designer in his tasks still appropriate in the context briefly outlined above?

Two fundamental aspects make us think this is not the case:

1. The gap between the rate of requests for human creativity and its actual capacity;
2. The gap between the scope of knowledge required in view of the level of complexity, and the inherent ability of a collective human group within a given organisation.

Contemporary designers are faced with a two-fold dilemma – that of having to ensure design tasks in a context where:

- The tools and methods available to assist them were developed within a context of optimising quality, as imposed in the 1960s-1990s. This means they are not always adapted to meet the requirements of current design tasks which are more focussed on optimising creative potential (Shaw, M.C., 1986) leading to higher efficiency in terms of inventiveness in the design act within the company (Holtj K., 1992);
- The complexity of the artefact and the scope of knowledge required make their own creative capacity inadequate. This limitation is accentuated by the fact that a truly inventive act is often measured by the following yardstick: external knowledge (i.e. unknown at that time by the industrial sector in which the designer works) is technologically transferred to the designer's own field, thereby making the creative act inventive.

2. THE LIMITATIONS OF THE DIVERGENT APPROACHES

In this section, we would like to demonstrate that the current approaches used to deal with problems, which we shall call the divergent approaches, have the single aim of increasing the output of ideas statistically speaking. This type of approach is adopted with the aim of formalising a direction for the designing process, starting with a situation expressed as the initial problem (which is often vague or stems from a need which is more or less clearly expressed).

The creative phases situated upstream of this type of process will basically be conducted with the aim of finding a maximum number of ideas to make up a sufficient statistical population. This is then followed by a multi-stage sorting process to isolate the idea which best matches the initial specifications. Such creative acts are mainly based on brainstorming or similar sessions, or consulting databases to scan any solutions that either already exist at rival companies or are in the process of development in research laboratories. The sorting process following the creative phases are either a simple filter weeding out ideas deemed too far-fetched or eliminating ideas which cannot integrate the data given in the initial specifications. The outcome of the sorting process is to limit the number of ideas to the most relevant and to set them in a hierarchy so as to have alternative development plans which more or less break with the current state of knowledge in the company. It is then up to the decision-makers to select whichever alternative matches their own strategy.

This type of process has two obvious limitations:

- The direction chosen is necessarily induced by ideas expressed during creativity sessions and therefore depends on a random process of exploiting the knowledge of the people involved and cannot guarantee at any moment that the direction chosen is truly the optimum direction.
- The exhaustive collection of ideas depends solely on the skills and knowledge of the persons who take part in the creativity sessions. This means it is impossible to guarantee that the statistical spectrum of ideas expressed embodies the ideal solution to the problem posed.

We shall therefore summarise this section with the following postulate: adopting a divergent design process does not guarantee that the directions selected for the designing process are ideal and therefore, the costs generated through iteration on the basis of the unsatisfactory results obtained (whether it is through prototyping and tests, calculations or R&D) place the company in a trial-and-error context, which is costly for the inherent added value, as it generates significant costs in terms of man-hours.

The challenge for designers of tools and methods aimed at assisting artefact designers is therefore clear for the years to come: to enable designers to optimise their creative potential (Mars N.J.and al., 1993) through means other than brainstorming and similar processes or accessing catalogues of typical solutions in a given field.

Within the context of making CAI tools, our starting point will be the definition of the ideality of such a system in terms of TRIZ (Altshuller G.S., 1986, 1988).

The tool assisting the physical design of artefacts must enable the designer to optimise the inventive aspect of his approach by instantly giving an accurate profile of the optimum model solution for the problem posed using all the initial data.

Among existing solutions, some of which are partially based on theoretical aspects of TRIZ (see Tsourikov V., 1993) , we observe that in spite of the fact that they encompass many of the aspects linked to TRIZ databases and tools, the philosophy of how the problem is dealt with differs little from the divergent approach. The next section of our paper therefore aims to clarify the foundations required for a CAI tool to be made, by associating it with an input element and interacting with a traditional CAD architecture. Such experiments have already been carried out by the company Dassault Systems in the "Product Function Optimizer 2 (PFO)" option in version 5 of their CAD tool CATIA, but our contribution aims here to reposition this type of development in line with what makes sense in TRIZ: the convergent process.

3. TOWARDS MAKING INVENTIVENESS-ORIENTED COMPUTER TOOLS

3.1 The generic model characterising a CAD approach

The model given in figure 1 summarises the generic treatment process for a societal need for technical system design requiring a CAD tool. It should be noted that this type of model follows the divergent logic described above.

3.2 The generic model proposed in our paper

First of all, we shall attempt to base the main lines of our reflections on the theoretical approach to inventiveness-seeking as developed by Genrich Altshuller. Contrary to the divergent approach described in the previous section, this theory is based on the postulate that it is necessary to reduce the scope of research by putting a halt to investigations in fields and sectors which are irrelevant because the goals in question, the specific conditions dictated by the context and the development trends of technical systems do not indicate that this is the most logical direction to turn to for the development of the artefact. On the other hand, the picture of the solution is built up step by step by adding, as the theory unfolds (which may be associated with a method), all the elements necessary to build the profile of the solution. We are therefore adopting a guided design approach (and not random design) and an improvement can be noted compared to the two stumbling blocks apparent in the divergent approach.

- The direction selected is defined in keeping with the *laws of technical system evolution*. These laws have been developed over a period of nearly half a century following observations of the evolution of a large quantity of technical artefacts throughout their history. They have been validated by pertinent scientific analyses (Salamatov Yu.P., 1991) and regular iterations and are now presented in a synthetic form enabling the essential points of the evolutionary dynamics of a technical system to be fully understood.
- The exhaustiveness of the fields investigated is also enhanced since Altshuller's theory encompasses a set of databases which synthesise human inventive mechanisms used by inventors in all industrial sectors. These databases are models of the cognitive, technical and scientific knowledge of human inventive activity synthesised in a semantic form that can be exploited in creative contexts (as also expressed in Akman V., 1989).

Finally, the experience provided by the practical application of this theory leads us to conclude that the robustness of the outcome depends on two essential factors – the relevance of the analysis carried out and a sound knowledge and grasp of the basics highlighted by Altshuller. Designing computing products inspired by the approaches advocated by TRIZ should therefore be in keeping with the following basic points. These basic points may also be considered as a system of factors enabling the profile of the designing process to be built:

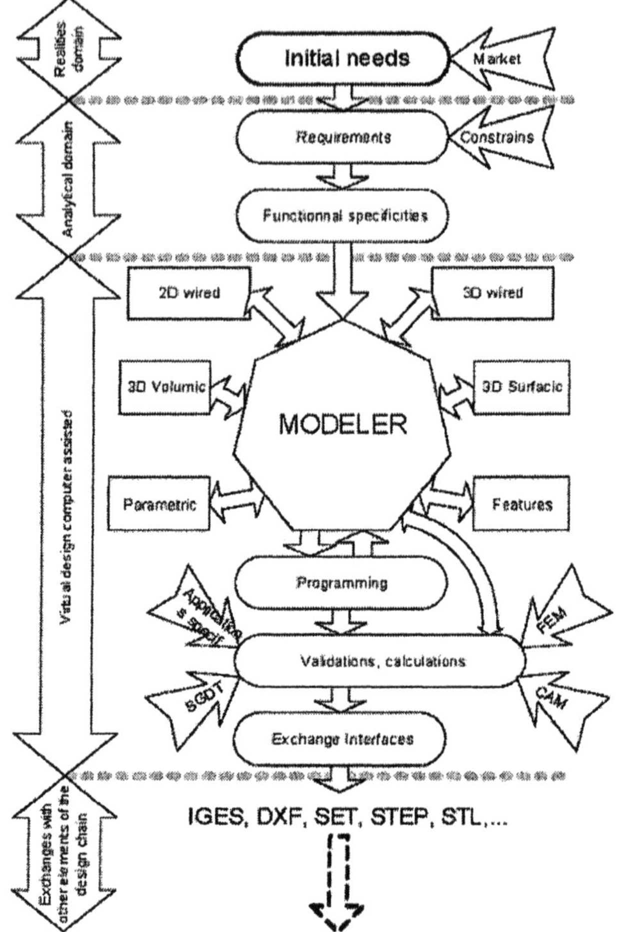

Figure 1. Generic model representing a traditional CAD approach

Definition of a final ideal objective: as the ultimate phase in the evolution of a designed artefact. In TRIZ, it is defined as minimising the material and energy resources required for its primary useful function, while maximising the functions it takes on for man. We should note that the ultimate phase is attained when the artefact becomes immaterial and its functions are automatically carried out.

- Example for CAD: Automatically designing an artefact on the basis that the alternative suggested to the designer goes in the direction of minimising the number of parts, favouring convergence and maximising the opportunities of creating new functions without increasing the level of complexity.

Relevant list of resources: They are indicated in TRIZ as being the key elements in the problem-solving process. By definition, a resource may be a substance, a physical field, a space or a time. The resources which should be focussed on are in the operating zone and are present during the operating period of producing the primary useful function.

- Example for CAD: Benefiting at all times from a balanced list of resource items available (functional surfaces, physical fields present, spaces between objects, operating times calculated by simulation, etc.) during the entire period of design so I can refer to it while systematically designing my virtual model.

Designing up a contradiction network: All design acts are carried out as cognitive acts encouraging the designer to solve a contradiction introduced by his act. This essential notion in TRIZ stipulates that the contradiction symbolises the obstacle which has to be understood and solved to enable the technical system to evolve in keeping with the laws (as expressed in Killanders A. & V. Sushkov, 1995). While cognitive reflexes often drive designers to a compromise solution, Altshuller purports that compromise does not arise from an inventive approach and that to move in the direction of inventiveness, the designer must refuse compromise despite his psychological inertia to solve the dilemma posed by the contradiction. The level of complexity involved in designing an artefact implies that a network of contradictions should be built up in order to place the designer face to face with the challenges he has to raise.

- Example for CAD: Constantly having a visual element which states contradictions of type: "The complexity of my shape must be reduced to facilitate its machinability yet significant to simplify its integration in my virtual unit". These contradictions are then collected in a coherent network modelling the complex situation the designer has to deal with.

Exploiting this network to initiate the design path: The contradiction network helps the designer to build a model of the problem in order to reduce its complexity. A set of guiding factors must then be designed for this network to enable the designer's problem-solving actions (or possibly his choices) to be directed towards an inventive approach, bearing in mind the company's strategy problems.

- Example for CAD: Having an iteration factor in the contradiction network which means links and their hierarchy can be visualised again. A contradiction may take on a different form if the objective behind the design act evolves from a desire to reduce costs to a desire to favour the inventive nature of the potential solution.

The factor of pin-pointing concordance between the directions taken and the laws: Beyond the brief introduction to the laws in the previous paragraph. As a tool for assisting the design act, the laws can constitute cartographic factors enabling the designer to situate himself in the action logic. Any approach to using a computing tool such as CAI must therefore be confronted with its coherence in relation to the laws of evolution so as to guarantee the relevance of the directions taken and possibly put the designer face to face with alternatives which may allow his action to be in line with the company's strategy.

- Example for CAD: The subordinate position of the approach compared to the laws of technical system evolution must offer the designer an overall view of his act and its impact on the evolution of the artefact. To do this, the generic breakdown of each of the laws (solid link, hinge, several hinges, flexible link, liquid link, field type link etc.) must offer the designer a choice of alternatives in which the current position of his system is located and the decision-making approach he must adopt may be conducted in keeping with the breakdown of the laws.

Access to databases and their graphic form: An important deliverable in terms of the computing tool features is also to provide access modes to TRIZ-model databases that are coherent with the typology of the designer's problem model. Links must therefore be designed between the graphic model representing the contradiction network and the databases representing inventive reflexes which inventors experienced in similar problem patterns (not moving towards compromise by definition).

Example for CAD: During the decision-making phases of contradiction-solving, the alternatives proposed by TRIZ databases will have evolved in terms of their formulation since they are associated with additional items collected during the analysis phase. These alternatives must all constitute a bolster for the thought process enabling the designer to structure his inventive response to the contradiction set by his problem model.

3.3 Method of representing a system (from the TRIZ angle)

The representational method we will use stems from Altshuller's first law of evolution: the law of the wholeness (completeness) of parts. This law stipulates that for a system to ensure its primary useful function, it must have four basic parts ideally fulfilling their role in their respective functioning so that by bringing them together we have an additional function (the Primary Useful Function) and not merely a simple combination of their respective functions.

These four major parts are:

- the driving element: The function of which is to recover the energy required to make the system come up to expectations and to transform it into an energy which can ensure the PUF.
- the transmission element: Which, through its very structure, will carry this energy towards the working factor while attempting to optimise the notion of transfer efficiency.
- the working element: Which, within the system under study, will ensure the contact between our system and the factor on which it is supposed to deliver the PUF.
- the control element: Of which the primary function is to interact and react to variations in the system's functioning by playing the role of an "orchestra conductor" by guiding one or more of the three factors quoted above (through a modification to form, structure, properties and informational output).

A graphic representation of law 1 is given in Figure 2. Its purpose is to specify the interrelations between the parts of the system and it is also used to give the physical outline of the system under study.

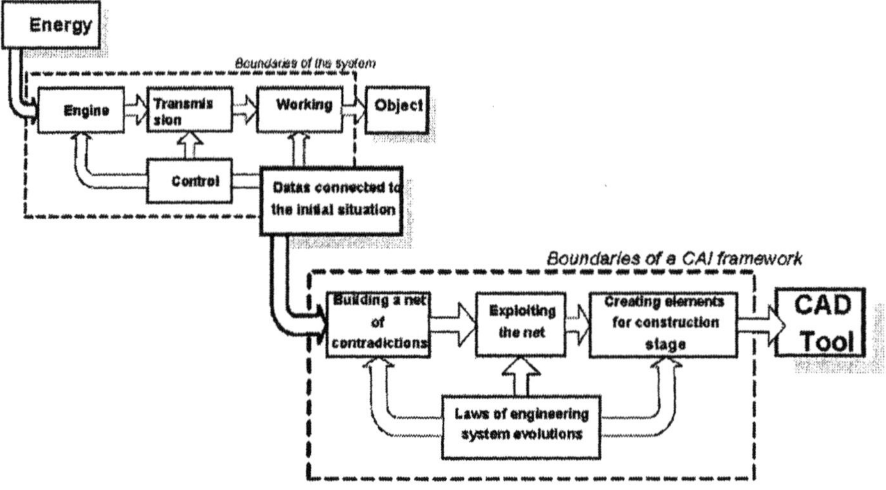

Figure 2. Representative model of the elementary architecture of a system from the TRIZ viewpoint, translated as a model for CAI

3.4 Suggested generic model

All the factors of the "CAI" system must form a coherent whole helping the designer to formalise his technical problem and come up with an inventive solution (at this stage, still in a theoretical form) on a basis which idealises the technical solution to be built. This coherence must also be in line with the corporate strategy (desire to offer new products, to promote one's position as market leader, to make profits by minimising the risks linked to innovation etc.).

3.5 Proposal for an inventive design model

The component parts of the diagram represented in Figure 3 may take the following shape so as to be integrated into the model presented in section 1:

The means of fulfilling the technical specifications for each of the entities described in the model undeniably remains to be worked on in an efficient partnership between researchers in the field of TRIZ and researchers designing fundamental structures for CAD tools. We firmly believe that the fundamentals should spring from the fruit of this cooperation leading to a relevant and long-lasting emergence of a new generation of tools that we may then entitle CAI as they will match the requirements relating to innovation in industrial environments.

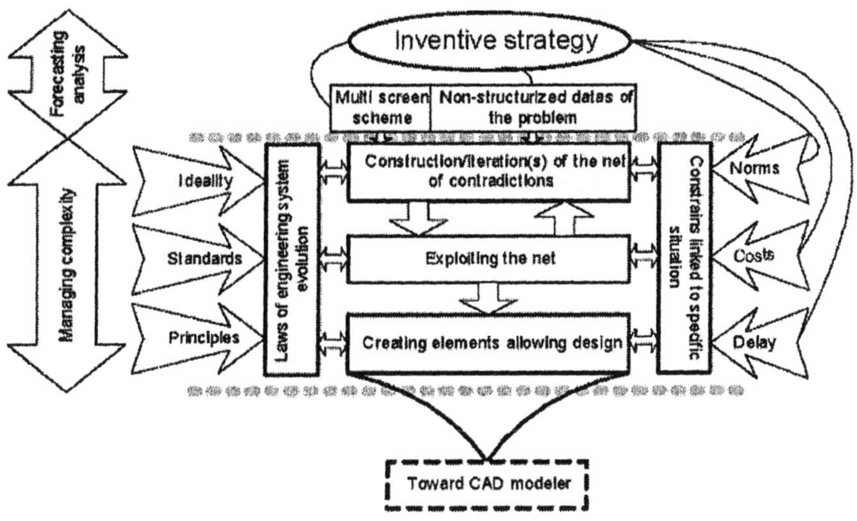

Figure 3. Proposal for a CAI model architecture

4. CONCLUSIONS

In this, our contribution aimed at designers of computing tools related to artefact-designing, we argue that the traditional reflex to move towards the compromise solution must be overcome in the search for inventive design. This design may be called inventive if it pursues an ultimate ideal objective through a dynamic process based on laws which characterise the evolution of technical systems. An essential component of these laws stipulates that a technical artefact evolves when it solves one of its contradictions, helped as far as possible by the resources present in the operating zone where the conflict between the contradictory aspects occur. Altshuller and his associates followed the aim of developing this theory for more than half a century, iterating its means decade after decade in a broad spectrum of tools and methods, teachings and algorithmisation. Today, this theory, which is emerging in our Western society, is the first to uphold the creative act of the designer by combining a synthesis of knowledge collected from human inventive activity and an objective guide to the design act based on characterising what is inventive and what is not (Cavallucci, D., 1999).

It should also be noted that our contribution is no more than a rough tree structure of the "what". In other terms, what are the key factors in a project leading to an inventive design approach? The expected and logical follow-up is now to investigate the "how" – firstly making the fundamentals coherent and then laying down links with the act of designing the artefact in a relevant way, which CAD tools already manage to do fairly well. Finally, the efficient diffusion of such tools can only occur once a large stumbling block has been overcome – that of providing a pedagogical structure so that it can be assimilated by designers whose professional reflexes have been deadened by their inertia towards the divergent approach, which is still firmly rooted anchored in our Western educational systems.

5. REFERENCES

1. Akman V., 1989, "The power of Physical Representations", AI Magazine, pp. 49-65. Altshuller G.S., 1986, "To Find an Idea: Introduction into the Theory of Inventive Problem Solving", Nauka, Novosibirsk (in Russian).
2. Altshuller G.S., 1988, "Creativity As An Exact Science", Gordon & Breach, New York, USA, ISBN 0-677-21230-5.
3. Cavallucci, D., 1999, "Contribution à la conception de nouveaux systèmes mécaniques par intégration méthodologique", Doctoral Thesis, Université Louis Pasteur, Strasbourg, France.
4. Dixon J.R., 1987, "On Research Methodology Towards a Scientific Theory of Engineering Design", Affificial Intelligence for Engineering Design, Analysis and Manufacturing, Vol. 1, No. 3, pp. 145-157.
5. Holtj K., 1992, "Computer- aided creativity in engineering design", Journal of Engineering Design, 4(4), 371-376
5. Jones J.C., 1981, "Design methods: seeds of human futures", Wiley and Son, New York. Killanders A. & V. Sushkov, 1995, "Conflict-Oriented Model of Creative Design", in Proceedings of the 3rd Int. Roundtable Conference on Computational Models of Creative Design, Queensland, Australia, 369-397.
6. Mars N.J., P.M. Wognum & V.V. Sushkov, 1993," AI and Creative Design", in Artificial Intelligence & Creativity Papers from the 1993 Spring Symposium, T. Dartnall & S. Kim, eds., Stanford, AAAI Press, 51-56.
7. Salamatov Yu.P., 1991, "A System of Laws of Engineering Evolution", in Chance for Adventure, A.B. Selutsky (ed.), Petrozavodsk, Karelia, 5-174 (in Russian).
8. Shaw, M.C., 1986, "Creative Design," CIRP Annals 35(2):461-465.
9. Tsourikov V., 1993, "Inventive Machine: second Generation", AI and Society, Vol. 7, N° 1, Springler International, UK, 1993.
10. Yoshikawa H., 1989, "Design Philosophy : The State of the Art", Annals of the CIRP, vol. 38/2.

EXPLORING THE INCLUSION OF DESIGN FACTORS IN COMPUTER AIDED INVENTING

Rosario Vidal[1], Elena Mulet[1], Belinda López-Mesa[2], M. José Bellés[1] and Graham Thompson[3]

[1] Universitat Jaume I, Castellón, Spain; [2] Luleå University of Technology, Luleå, Sweden; [3] UMIST, Manchester, U.K.

Abstract: In this paper we present three experimental research studies that examine the use of different means of expression, the methods used to obtain solutions and additional stimulation; the results of this work can affect the design of future CAI systems.

Key words: CAI, Idea generation, Design teams, Creative problem solving.

1. INTRODUCTION

Invention in the initial phases of the design process is one of the most important topics in design engineering and it becomes even more interesting when it is linked to computer systems.

We understand CAI systems to be a valuable aid to designers in creative problem solving and, like other authors, we also believe that there is still a lot to be learnt about how people actually invent. Experimental research can, therefore, provide us with the knowledge needed to design systems for the future.

In this paper we present three experimental research studies, the results of which can have repercussions on future CAI systems. This work examines the use of different means of expression (words, drawings and objects), the methods employed to obtain solutions (searches, combinations and transformations) and additional stimulation by means of methods.

2. EXPERIMENTING WITH DIFFERENT MEANS OF EXPRESSION

The means used to express ideas plays a number of different roles in the design process. Drawings, as well as acting as a way of communicating and storing the geometric shape, also contribute to other functions by expanding short-term memory, facilitating and verifying design simulation, and stimulating the imagination and creative synthesis[1,2,3]

Some studies reveal that employing the hands and drawings to aid the design process offers very important results that are better than those obtained when the search for solutions is solely a cognitive activity aided by drawings[4]. So much is this so that if the tools developed to aid creative design are to produce an environment that encourages the creativity of the designer, one of the requisites they must satisfy that of using objects during the design process [5].

In order to observe the influence exerted by the means used to express ideas, three variations of brainstorming involving different means of expression were used in an experiment carried out with Technical Engineering in Industrial Design students from Universitat Jaume I in Castellón, Spain. In all, the study involved 12 groups of 4 people.

The design problem consisted in generating solutions for a drafting table that was to take up as little space as possible when not in use. Each of the twelve groups was given a list with the same initial requirements and at the same time 3 different means of expressing ideas were established; three variations of the means of expression, namely, verbal or sentential, visual and objectual, were therefore utilised.

In the objectual variant, in addition to expressing ideas verbally, they were also constructed using the pieces and tools from 2 sets of Meccano®.

The experiments were recorded on video so that the protocol could be obtained and later analysed using the linkography method[6] but with a certain number of modifications [7].

The generated ideas were identified so as to allow the design process to be analysed. Here, "generated ideas" is taken to mean any contribution to the formation of a design solution that was communicated in the course of the design process. Ideas are aggregated on a more general level that has been called the global idea and consists in one or more ideas that belong or contribute to the same solution for the design problem.

From the analysis of the ideas obtained it can be seen that the means of expression used does not give rise to any significant difference in the total number of ideas produced. Nevertheless, significant differences are observed with regard to the type of ideas that are obtained.

The way ideas expressed by means of objects stimulate the generation of later ideas is unlike that employed by ideas that are expressed verbally or by drawings. When the design group uses objects to represent ideas, the percentage of ideas that can become feasible solutions to the problem is seen to be greater. Furthermore, the use of objects is also linked to a stronger tendency to generate subsequent ideas that are related to the most interesting ideas that arose during the design process [8].

The use of objects leads to the generation of more ideas that are centred on particular aspects of the problem. Moreover, there is a continuous stream of new ideas that build on and improve the previous ones concerning this same aspect. When verbal means are employed the ideas that arise are not clearly focused on any particular aspect of the problem, they are more abstract, the analysis of the problem is less intense or in-depth, and they co-evolve with the solution to a lesser degree than is the case when objects are used.

Findings indicate that an interesting approach is to use a system of representation based on 3D manipulation in order to boost the stimulation of invention based on representation by objects. Invention that is stimulated by this means will exert an influence and allow the designer to conduct a more thorough analysis and to gain a deeper understanding of the problem. At the same time co-evolution of the invention process will be greater and it will become easier to obtain possible solutions to the problem.

3. ANALYSING THE METHODS OF OBTAINING SOLUTIONS

One of the factors that influence the design process is the method employed to synthesise or to obtain solutions. Computer systems for synthesising or obtaining solutions make use of different techniques to generate solutions to a problem.

Boden sets out two groups of computational models of artificial intelligence for creativity, which is understood to mean the generation of ideas that are both new and valuable [9]. One of them is that of combinational creativity, where the idea that is obtained consists of an unusual combination or association between other familiar ideas. The other one is the exploratory-transformational creativity group, which is based on a vast structured conceptual space. The exploratory creativity models define a conceptual space and a set of procedures for moving inside that space and reaching locations in which suitable solutions exist, as is the case of models based on heuristic searches and discovery models. Transformational creativity applications can modify their own rules and include, for example, models based on evolutionary techniques.

Chakrabarti classified the development of computer systems for synthesis in two categories: compositional synthesis and the retrieval of existing designs for them to be modified to fit the requirements[10]. Applying both compositional methods of obtaining solutions and those based on the retrieval and adaptation of cases in a joint or hybrid manner has been proposed as a way of expanding the possibilities offered by these systems[11].

In order to analyse the effect exerted by applying each method of obtaining solutions, we examined how the design process evolved by analysing the methods employed to obtain solutions during the formation of potential solutions.

One of the methods for studying the evolution of the design is the FBS method, which derives from the design protocol and is used to identify the elements of design by means of functions (F), operation or behaviour (B) and structures (S) at each stage of the design process[12,13]. Function describes the goal of the design, whereas structure describes the solution, and behaviour describes the operation and the change of state of the structure; hence, the design process is expressed as the step from function to structure via its behaviour.

The protocol for the experiment described in the section above was analysed again using the FBS method in order to examine the methods for obtaining solutions. Experimental analysis of the ideas generated in a brainstorming session revealed that the group of designers applied more than one method during the formation of different potential solutions to the problem. For example, they started by conducting one or several isolated searches, these were then combined with one another, then a modification was introduced, and so on. That is to say, each of the potential solutions was obtained by applying the different methods for obtaining solutions in succession and not by utilising just one [8], which coincides with Chakrabarti's proposal concerning hybrid methods.

The analysis that was conducted showed that obtaining so many and such diverse ideas in such a short time was partly due to the diversity of the methods of synthesis that were applied. The more heterogeneous the methods are, the more potential the solutions will have to resolve problems. These observations imply that the simultaneous use of methods of synthesis based on search techniques, combinations and transformations helps to obtain solutions that resolve the problem.

4. EXPERIMENTING WITH ADDITIONAL STIMULI

The stimulation that arouses the creativity of the designer or the design group is a core issue in current methods of generating ideas. In some approaches this stimulation is essentially achieved using stimuli generated within the actual group itself by means of brainstorming and its variants, and the ideas that are generated play two fundamental roles: they can either be a solution or they can also act as a stimulus in the generation of new ideas. In other methods, such as SCAMPER, Direct Analogy and so on, additional stimuli are provided that arouse individual creativity.

In order to study what happens when additional stimuli are introduced into design groups during the phase in which ideas are generated for a product, an experiment was carried out as part of a joint research study with Luleå University of Technology (Sweden), Universitat Jaume I (Spain) and UMIST (England). The experiment was conducted by Design Engineering PhD students. Five groups of three people were set up, four of which are discussed in this chapter. The analysis of the results is based on two theories: the innovative-adaptive characteristic theory of methods and the reflective practice theory. This analysis is used here to study the implications they have in the creation of Computer Aided Inventing systems.

To be able to draw conclusions about the effect produced by the additional stimuli that were introduced in the experiment, first we had to identify and catalogue the other stimuli that could affect the way the creative activity progressed. These other stimuli were those that were generated spontaneously within the group and included drawings, sentences, gestures, and so on.

The 17 possible participants met for approximately 40 minutes and were given the initial requirements of the problem together with technical and market data. During this time they read the problem individually and used two different models of the object that was to be redesigned, namely, a tubular map case. Any doubts regarding the initial requirements of the problem were discussed and settled. The goal was to design a tubular map case that allows for one by one extraction and introduction of maps. Each group then went to a different room where they were given precise instructions on how to proceed. The first 5 minutes of the idea creation session had no additional stimuli, but then seven additional stimuli were introduced by means of a computer display every 5 minutes. Two groups were exposed to visual images obtained from the Internet by introducing words related to characteristics linked to the shape and use of the object to be designed. The other two groups were exposed to questions from the

SCAMPER method. Each visual stimulus contained three images or questions.

Once the protocols have been analysed, one remark that can immediately be applied to the design of CAI systems is that while they are being developed thought must be given as to whether they encourage or hinder the natural mechanisms that designers use to express themselves and what consequences this can have on their creative activity. A particular system could, for example, make it more difficult to perform the gestures required to explain the ideas, and this would hold up the expansion of ideas within the same perspective. Different stimuli bring about different effects in the designer's creative activity and these effects must be taken into account in order to decide what kind of additional stimulus is best suited to a particular situation, if indeed any of them are. The findings from the experiment presented above show that stimuli have an important effect on the design activity, which is comparable to the person's innovative-adaptive characteristic, and that there are stimuli that exert a greater and lesser influence. We also know the types of action (naming, framing, moving and reflecting) that are favoured by the visual stimuli introduced in the experiment and the questions. The stimuli that were measured can be introduced as computer-aided methods, or parts of methods or methodologies, and can also be generated by the computer itself. A stimulus that is not predefined (like that of the images) can be sought automatically on the Internet by the computer. Depending on the type of stimulus we wish to obtain, the computer will need to interact with the designers to a greater or lesser extent before being able to generate those stimuli. For example, in the case of the images that were used to stimulate ideas for the tubular map case, the computer would have to ask the designers for words that describe the shape of the case and how it will be used. Once the words (such as tube, cylinder, tubes, classifier, organiser and so on) have been introduced by the designers, the computer searches for images.

Detailed knowledge of the effects of the stimuli collected in a computer system can substitute the role of a facilitator. The facilitator adapts his or her own experience to each situation and the experience accumulated over the years about design methods enables them to make decisions about the most suitable way of facilitating the group. A thorough study of how the methods affect the design activity is required to make up for the facilitator's adaptability. A good knowledge of the effect of the method and the situation in which that effect is suitable enables the design group to choose the most appropriate stimulus [14,15,16].

5. CONCLUSION

Experimental research can provide interesting findings that can help to improve CAI systems for the future. From the three experiments that have been commented above we could conclude that it would be advisable to incorporate systems of representation in three dimensions, to apply different methods of synthesis and to include various forms of additional stimuli.

REFERENCES

1. Ullman, D., Wood, S., et al., 1990, The importance of drawing in the mechanical design process, *Computational Graphics.* **14**(2): 263 - 274.
2. Purcell, A., and Gero, J., 1998, Drawings and the design process, *Design Studies* **19**(4): 389 - 430.
3. Schütze, M., Sache, P., et al., 2003, Support value of sketching in the design process, *Research in Engineering Design.* **14**: 89 - 97.
4. Candy, L., and Edmonds, E., 1996, Creativity design of the lotus bicycle: implications for knowledge support system research, *Design Studies* **17**(1): 71 - 90.
5. Candy, L., 1997. Computers and creativity support: knowledge, visualization and collaboration. *Knowledge -Based Systems.* **10**(1): 3 - 13.
6. Goldschmidt, G., 1992, Criteria for design evaluation: a process-oriented paradigm, in: *Evaluating and Predicting Design Performance.* Y. Kalay, ed, John Wiley & Sons, pp. 67 - 79.
7. Van der Lugt, R., 2000, Devoloping a graphic tool for creative problem solving in design groups, *Design Studies* **21**(5): 505-522.
8. Vidal, R., Mulet, E. and Gómez-Senent, E., 2004, Effectiveness of the Means of Expression in Creative Problem Solving in Design Groups, *Journal of Engineering Design* **15**(3): 285-297
9. Boden, M., 1999, Computer models of creativity, in Handbook of Cretivity, R. Sternberg, Cambridge University Press, pp. 351-372
10. Chakrabarti, A., 2002, *Engineering Design Synthesis. Understanding, Approaches and Tools,* Springer-Verlag, London.
11. Chakrabarti, A., 2001, Towards hybrid methods for synthesis, *ICED'01 13th International Conference on Engineering Design*, Imeche, Glasgow
12. Gero, J., 1990, Design prototypes: a knowledge representation schema for design, *AI magazine* **11**(4): 26 - 36
13. Umeda, Y., Takeda, H., et al., 1990, Function, behaviour, and structure, in: *Applications of Artificial Intelligence in Engineering,*. J. Gero. Berlin, Springer. **1**: 177-194
14. López-Mesa, B., 2002, *Selection and Use of Engineering Design Methods Using Creative Problem Solving Principles*, licentiate thesis, Luleå University of Technology, Luleå, Sweden.
15. Mulet, E., R. Vidal, et al., 2003, Influences of representations on designing and implications for computer-based design synthesis, *ICED'03 14th International Conference on Engineering Design*, Design Society, Stokholm
16. Mulet, E., 2003, *Análisis Experimental y Modelización Descriptiva Del Proceso de Diseño,* PhD thesis, Politechnical of Valencia, Valencia

STATE-OF-THE-ART AND TRENDS OF COMPUTER-AIDED INNOVATION TOOLS

Towards the integration within the Product Development Cycle

Gaetano Cascini

Dipartimento di Meccanica e Tecnologie Industriali, Università degli Studi di Firenze, via S. Marta, 3 – 50139 Florence, Italy

Abstract: The design of competitive products requires meeting several market demands often contradictory, or at least very hard to achieve due to the hard time constrains imposed by the competitors. For example, from a structural point of view, mechanical parts must be light-weighted as well as stiff and strong according to the application requirements. The integration of CAE tools is the basic step towards the fulfillment of these demands, but it must be observed that such integration involves just detailed design phases, while only stand alone tools are available to support the designer during the preliminary product development activities. In facts, nowadays, the market offers several tools to improve designer creativity and problem solving capabilities with a systematic approach. Nevertheless, it is worth to notice that current Computer-Aided Inventing (CAI) applications cannot be integrated with other product development systems. In this paper, a survey of CAI systems is presented with a set of hints about their future development towards the integration with Product Lifecycle Management (PLM) applications.

Key words: Computer-Aided Inventing, Systematic Innovation, Product Development Cycle, PLM

1. INTRODUCTION

The increasing demand for being competitive on the market has driven companies to drastically reduce product development cycles. At the same time, the growing of CAD/CAE and virtual prototyping systems of the last decade has deeply modified the approach to design: the possibility to test varying technical solutions maintaining low costs and time has increased the level of confidence with which designers can propose "extreme" solutions. At the same time, the preliminary phases of product development cycle have been cut down in favor of testing solutions reached following a "trial and error" approach rather than adopting a systematic innovation process.

The combination of these issues has led to an unstable situation for companies that do not hold the monopoly in a specific industrial sector. The study presented by Miller and Morris[1] shows that:

1. 10% only of North American companies has put on the market a new product in the last decade of XX century;
2. 90% of new products put on the market fail within four years from their appearance;
3. less than 1% of patents fully pay back the people who took on the investments;
4. 80% of successful innovation is proposed by customers instead of being developed by producers.

In order to improve the product development process and more specifically the innovation capabilities of a company, a systematic approach and suitable tools are needed also for the conceptual design phase. Nowadays, the market offers several tools to improve designer creativity and problem solving capabilities; among these, according to the author's experience, the most effective are methods and tools supporting the systematic transferring of innovative solutions among different technical areas by means of an abstraction of the process, i.e. the TRIZ theory and tools.

During the last years, major efforts have been dedicated to the integration of TRIZ with other methodologies. Among others: the criteria to adopt in order to combine TRIZ and Theory of Constraints benefits have been presented by several authors[2,3]. Innovative product development processes are being presented, which systematically integrate QFD with TRIZ and enable the effective and systematic creation of technical innovation for new products[4,5]. It is known that the former is focused on the identification and the improvement of the most critical components of a mechanical system, and the latter is dedicated to the definition of a direct link between customer requirements and the most suitable inventive principles pointing at the solution of the corresponding technical problems. The synergy between QFD and TRIZ is extended also to Taguchi method with the goal of determining the design specifications for a product insensitive to uncontrolled influences[6]. Finally, still aiming at robust design practices, TRIZ and Axiomatic Design have been adopted in a pilot project by General Motors[7] and the guidelines to combine TRIZ and Axiomatic Design in a Design for Six Sigma development process[8].

It is clear that all the above examples, as well as other published works, are focused on the integration of tools and methods for conceptual design. Besides, there's a lack of links with the product embodiment phases, even if some preliminary experiences have been approached[9-11].

In this preliminary paper the main limits and opportunities for integrating existing Computer-Aided Inventing (CAI) tools with other Product Lifecycle Management (PLM) applications are surveyed; therefore the author's vision about the next generation of Product Development systems is presented, focusing on expected features and technology sore points. The full-length manuscript will be enriched with examples and explanations that are more detailed.

2. PLM SYSTEMS BACKGROUND

The evolution of Product Development tools has been characterized by different trends; the analysis of these trends offers useful hints for the prediction of next generation systems.

2.1 Product Modeling Trend

First, let's take into account CAD systems evolution (Fig. 1): the first generation was dedicated to explicit geometrical modeling with the transition from wireframe to canvas and solid modeling. These tools aimed at speeding-up technical representation tasks, but they didn't provide a useful support for designer, due to the big efforts required to revise geometry.

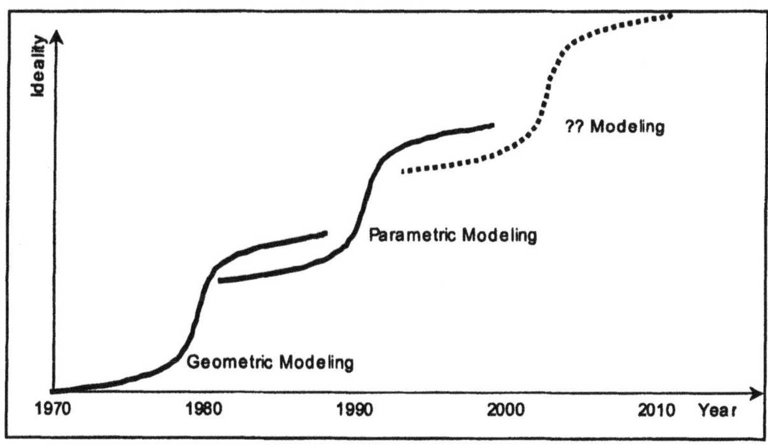

Figure 1. Product modeling evolution

The step toward was given by CSG (Constructive Solid Geometry) representation, i.e. using solid primitives combined by means of Boolean operators. The model is stored in a tree with all the information about primitives and the way they are combined. The ability to edit the tree, i.e. the transition to parametric modeling, is a fundamental step to support the typical iterative process of design activity. The introduction of Boundary representation (B-rep), consisting in a description of solid geometry by means of its skin, mathematically expressed through NURBS, allowed the definition of complex shapes even with limited computation efforts.

From the user interface point of view, feature-based modeling changed the approach to CAD models definition, from geometry to technology-centric: geometric entities are now grouped according to the technological meaning of the shape element.

2.2 Task-to-Process trend

A second relevant trend is the transition from task-oriented applications to process-oriented systems: the former CAE tools were able to speed-up and sometimes automate several engineering tasks, but the integration was limited to product data exchange formats. Such a heterogeneous and fragmented system led to the introduction of Product Data Management (PDM) systems, i.e. tools for the management of any kind of product related information and their corresponding workflow. The main limit is here represented by the poor integration with Computer-Aided-tools apart from CAD systems.

As a consequence, PLM systems have emerged as a "strategic business approach that applies a consistent set of business solutions in support of the collaborative creation, management, dissemination, and use of product definition information across the extended enterprise from concept to end of life - integrating people, processes, business systems and information"[12].

It should be observed that actual PLM systems are effectively integrated just with CAD-CAE applications; therefore, their efficiency is still poor for the preliminary design phases. One of the purposes of the present work is evaluating the perspective of linking PLM with CAI systems, as depicted in Fig. 2.

2.3 Knowledge integration trend

A third pattern of evolution that can be observed is related to the TRIZ Law of Shortening of Energy Flow Path: technological systems evolve in the direction of shortening the energy passage through the system.

A complete system is usually constituted by four components: Working Tool, Transmission, Energy Source, and Control. During the first stages of CAD evolution, major efforts have been dedicated to the Working Tool, i.e. the geometric kernel; then, the information flow (Transmission) has been improved in terms of Modeling Features capabilities, making CAD systems closer to the "Energy Source" (Knowledge).

Even the evolution of Engineering Knowledge Management (EKM) systems can be attested at the third generation[13]: starting from Content Management tools, whose intent was to support structured information management without any direct connection to product data, the following generation was focused on Design Automation, by means of tools capable of automating specific design tasks. Actually the third generation is at its infancy stage: EKM systems play the role of knowledge based automation systems capable of guiding different kind of product development tools (i.e.: CAD, FEM, PDM etc.) to create *ad hoc* automatic applications. Such an objective is approached by storing parameters and rules in relational databases and capturing others' systems functions directly. Once more the integration of EKM systems with Conceptual Design and Systematic Innovation tools is quite poor and further developments are needed (Fig. 2).

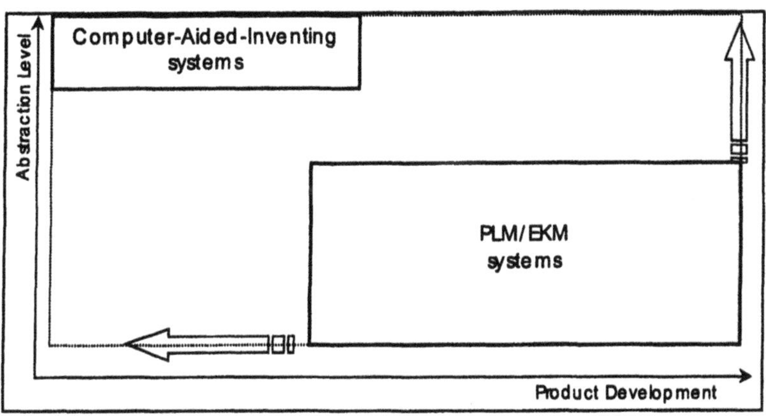

Figure 2. Toward the integration of product development systems

3. CAI-PLM SYSTEMS EXPECTED EVOLUTION

The goal of integrating CAI and PLM systems requires the development of a common platform for product data exchange: in other words all these tools must share the same product model.

A first attempt toward the integration fulfillment has just been approached by the author together with several Italian universities through the research project "From systematic innovation to integrated product development". The integration objective of the above-mentioned tools is based on the introduction of Topological Optimization systems as a bridge capable of generating optimal geometrical solutions.

Therefore, the project concerns two main tasks, as depicted in Fig. 3:

1. systematize the translation of the functional model of a system and of its design requirements into an optimization problem; that means identifying design variables, defining an objective function, defining design constraints;
2. Define a Best Practice for the integrated use of topological optimization tools together with current PLM systems; that implies the definition of procedures for translating the topological optimization results into a geometry defined by "technological" features.

Since optimization techniques look for the "optimal" solution to a suitably coded problem, a critical aspect of the research is represented by the rigorous definition of the system to be optimized: if such a task is not properly accomplished the achievement of satisfactory results can be definitely compromised. The problem formulation of an optimization task is actually demanded to designer experience and very often, the underlying criteria are not elicited. Therefore, the main purpose of the author work is defining a set of criteria to formulate with a systematic and rigorous approach an optimization problem. In other words, it is necessary to define how to translate the functional architecture of a machine and its requirements into an optimization problem, i.e. identifying design variables and defining an objective function and design constraints.

A useful contribution is provided by the techniques for establishing which components or subassemblies of a system are more critical from functional, safety, reliability, and cost viewpoints where Axiomatic Design and FMEA analyses are combined in order to identify the components requiring an optimization process[14].

With this perspective, axiomatic design tools efficiently aid the designer in capturing, analyzing, and decomposing requirements to be adopted for the optimization problem formulation. Moreover, the adoption of TRIZ based tools leads the designer to the definition of an ideal system architecture and consequently to the formulation of the objectives for each component and subassembly[15].

The above presented objectives answer to requirements that are today not yet satisfied in product development processes, and they might bring advantages in terms of design time, cost and errors reduction, improvement in product quality, etc. Nevertheless, such an approach will not provide a full integration between CAI and PLM systems, since its top-down approach does not admit the use of CAI tools in specific design tasks with a direct link.

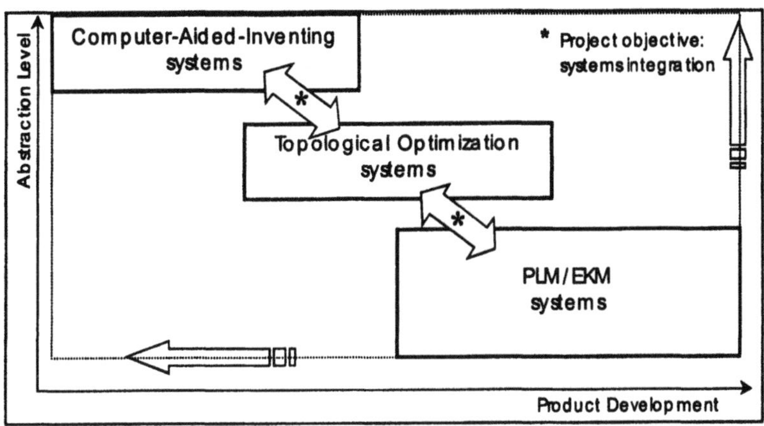

Figure 3. A proposal for the integration of product development systems

On the basis of the trends followed by Product Development tools described in the previous section, it is possible to anticipate the next generation of integrated engineering systems, according to the patterns described below.

The product modeling approach (Fig. 1) must shift to a higher abstraction level, in order to establish a direct link between product data at the conceptual design stage and detailed design; the most suitable is functional modeling for several matters:

- several CAI tools have already adopted such a technique for product modeling; hopefully they will enrich their capabilities in order to manage more complex hierarchies of functional models as well as relationships among the functions, i.e. decomposed-into, conditioned-by, enhanced-by and described-as relations[16];
- functional modeling is history independent, which means that design elements added, subtracted, and modified in any sequence will always generate the same product model, therefore effectively providing useful means for simultaneous engineering, as already implemented by ImpactXoft[17];
- functional modeling is much more powerful in capturing designer's intent, therefore codifying his implicit knowledge;
- the explicit association of geometrical features and functions allows automating the abstraction process from a specific technical system to a generic model of the problem to be solved, therefore ensuring a bi-directional integration between CAI and other PLM systems.

Further advantages deriving from the adoption of functional modeling as the product representation technique are related to the knowledge integration trend presented in section 2. In facts, semantic processing technology is already used for enriching the knowledge base of CAI systems, by extracting from technical documents the solutions capable to accomplish a given function[18]. Moreover, the semantic analysis of technical documents and patents can be pushed to the automatic extraction of functional models of a technical system[19,20].

According to the aforementioned knowledge integration trend, such a path can lead to the full "encapsulation" of the Energy Source (Knowledge) into the PLM environment. The ideal final result of such a trend is a self-operating design system, while the user should perform just "control" tasks, by selecting and not defining the most suitable solution.

It is worth to notice that in the recent past several approaches have been proposed for building Intelligent CAD systems; nevertheless, they are affected by severe limitation, mainly due to the formalism rigidity of symbolic approaches and the quest for full design automation rather than a realistic active support to the design process[21].

Therefore, it is useful to distinguish between routine and inventive design tasks, the former class constituted by any engineering activity with all the parameters and variables known *a priori* or related by strictly defined rules.

While the automation of routine design tasks is already accomplished by the state of the art EKM technologies, trying to automate inventive tasks is a wrong objective; in other words, software systems can help inventing, but not invent! The characteristic of a design thought process to be something vague, fluid, amorphous cannot be constrained by rigid formalisms.

According to this statement, a conflicting requirement is requested to the next generation of CAI systems: they must embody a formalized Knowledge Base in order to suggest a set of solutions to the designer, but they must leave the maximum freedom to his way of thinking, even if pointing to a reliable direction, as operated by standard TRIZ tools.

This means enlarging the domain of routine design tasks, by linking functional requirements with sets of geometric features capable of maintaining the consistency of their functionality when assembled in a specific embodiment. This goal can be supported by the emerging technology for managing digital CAD libraries[22] and 3D shapes searches[23], so that discarding non-matching geometries can reduce the number of candidate shapes for accomplishing a given function.

On the other side, when approaching a real inventive problem, it is necessary to leave to the designer as much freedom as he was working with a pencil and a blank sheet. During the design process, a person needs to create a visual representation, even for abstract and verbal ideas, and then respond to it perceptually to discover new arrangements and shapes representing new ideas[9]. This requirement is still more urgent for team working. In a previous paper[11], the author suggested the introduction of "CAD storming" practices: work together on a same geometrical model with the ability of applying deep changes to the geometry in absolute freedom. Such a cooperative work is actually limited by the slowness of modeling activity that counteracts brainstorming agility. Since changing easily and quickly, the model geometry is still not possible a "partial action" is proposed: by means of a common speech recognition module, the comments of the design team could be automatically translated into 3D primitive shapes to store in a more effective way the proposed solutions to be evaluated. Such a practice could be used also to track the thought process and effectively capture the design intent by linking verbal expressions with the developed geometry.

4. CONCLUSIONS

The role of CAI systems in the Product Development process will rapidly grow since product innovation has become the focus of any company's strategy.

Nevertheless state of the art CAI systems are still structured as stand-alone tools, while the need for reaching the objective in the shortest possible time (time-to-market) and with the maximum user perceived value (time to value) requires the full integration of Product Development systems.

In this paper, a survey of PLM tools evolution is presented and the opportunities to integrate CAI and PLM systems are evaluated with some hints about directions for their development.

An extended version of the paper will be presented at the IFIP World Computer Congress 2004, with further details and some examples about the proposed concepts.

REFERENCES

1. Miller, W. L., Morris, L., *4th Generation R&D : Managing Knowledge, Technology, and Innovation* (John Wiley & Sons, 1999).
2. Stratton, R., Warburton, R.D.H., The strategic integration of agile and lean supply, *International Journal of Production Economics*, v85, n2, 183-198 (2003).
3. Rantanen, K., Domb, E., *Simplified TRIZ – New Problem-Solving Applications for Engineers and Manufacturing Professionals* (St. Lucie Press, 2002).
4. Yamashina, H., Ito, T., Kawada H., Innovative product development process by integrating QFD and TRIZ", *International Journal of Production Research*, v40, n5, 1031-1050 (2002).

5. Tan, R., Kraft, D., A conceptual design methodology for variety using TRIZ and QFD, *Proceedings of the ASME 14th International Conference on Design Theory and Methodology Integrated Systems Design*, , Sep 29-Oct 2 2002, Montreal, Canada.
6. Terninko, J., The QFD, TRIZ and Taguchi Connection: Customer-Driven Robust Innovation, *Transactions of Ninth Symposium on Quality Function Deployment*, Novi, MI QFD Institute (1997).
7. Hu, M., Yang, K., Taguchi, S., Enhancing Robust Design with the Aid of TRIZ and Axiomatic Design, Part I and Part II, *The TRIZ Journal* (October-November 2000).
8. Kai Y., Basem S. E. , *Design for Six Sigma: A Roadmap for Product Development* (McGraw-Hill Professional, 2003).
9. Leon, N., A proposal to integrate TRIZ and CAD (Computer Aided TRIZ-based Design), *Proceedings of TRIZCON 2001.*
10. Cascini, G., Pieroni, N., Rissone, P., Plastics design: integrating TRIZ creativity and semantic knowledge portals, *Journal of Engineering Design*, v15, n3, (2004).
11. Abate, V., Cascini, G., CAD for Conceptual Design: Forecasted Evolution, *The TRIZ Journal* (May 2003); http://triz-journal.com.
12. CIMdata, *PLM Market Analysis Report* (2002); http://www.cimdata.com/index.htm.
13. Pulli, M., *Engineering Knowledge Management Systems evolution*, PhD Thesis, University of Parma (2004).
14. Arcidiacono, G., Delogu, M., The integration of reliability techniques as an aid to the design optimisation of an earth moving machine, *Proceedings of the 2001 ASME International Mechanical Engineering Congress and Exposition*, v112, 157-164 (2001).
15. Cavallucci, D., Lutz, P., Kucharavy, D., Converging in problem formulation: A different path in design, *Proceedings of the 14th ASME International Conference on Design Theory and Methodology Integrated Systems Design*, Montreal, Canada, Sep 29-Oct 2 (2002).
16. Shimomura, Y., Yoshioka, M., Takeda, H., Umeda, Y., Tomiyama, T., Representation of Design Object Based on the Functional Evolution Process Mode, *Journal of Mechanical Design* (ASME), Vol. 120 (June 1998).
17. Krouse, J., *Simultaneous Product Development*, ImpactXoft White Paper (2002); http://www.impactxoft.com.
18. Verbitsky, M., Semantic TRIZ, *The TRIZ Journal* (February 2004); http://triz-journal.com.
19. Cascini, G., Rissone, P., PAT-Analyzer: a tool to speed-up patent analyses with a TRIZ perspective, *Proceedings of the ETRIA World Conference: TRIZ Future 2003*, Aachen, Germany, November 12-14 (2003).
20. Cascini, G., Fantechi, A., Spinicci, E., Natural Language Processing of Patents and Technical Documentation, submitted for publication to the *IAPR Workshop on Document Analysis Systems* - University of Florence, Italy, September 8-10 (2004).
21. Bento, J., Feijó, B., An-agent based paradigm for building intelligent CAD systems, *Artificial Intelligence in Engineering*, v11, 231-244 (1997).
22. Regli1, W.C., Cicirello, V.A., Managing digital libraries for computer-aided design, *Computer-Aided Design*, v32, 119-132 (2000).
23. Iyer, N., Kalyanaraman, Y., Lou, K., Jayanti, S., Ramani, K., A reconfigurable 3D engineering shape search system - Part I: shape representation, *Proceedings of DETC' 03 ASME 2003 Design Engineering Technical Conferences and Computers and Information in Engineering Conference*, Chicago, Illinois, USA, September 2-6 (2003).

COMPUTER AIDED COMPREHENSIVE DESIGN FOR SIX SIGMA (DFSS) AND AXIOMATIC DESIGN (AD):
COMPUTER AIDED PERFORMANCE EXCELLENCE (CAPE)

Michael S. Slocum
Vice President of Research and Design, Breakthrough Management Group, 2101 Ken Pratt Boulevard, Longmont, CO, USA

Abstract: The purpose of this paper is to outline the place of computer aid in development and design. Computer aid will be discussed as it applies specifically to Design for Six Sigma and Axiomatic Design. The integration of various methodologies in a comprehensive format will be described as will the possibility of computer aid to augment and support this integration.

Key words: Axiomatic Design (AD), Computer Aided, Computer Aided Performance Excellence (CAPE), Design for Six Sigma (DFSS), DMAIC, Integration, Lean, Quality Function Deployment (QFD), Six Sigma, Theory of Constraints (TOC), Theory of Inventive Problem Solving (TRIZ)

1. INTRODUCTION

As the number of methodologies that provide benefit increases, it becomes difficult at best to control their proper integration and utilization. The advent of advances in existing methods is causing a revitalization of many systems that appeared to be mature to the point of assimilation and disappearance. The revitalization is causing the number of complementary and competing systems to increase causing significant complexity in their utilization, integration, and management. This provides an excellent opportunity for the application of computer aid to resolve these three issues.

2. METHODOLOGIES

Six Sigma has pervaded corporate society as the lead method for reducing the number of defects in a system. Lean is the method for the elimination of waste in a system. Lean also provides just-in-time strategies and a method for level loading. Quality Function Deployment provides a method for capturing, structuring, and the flow-down of the voice of the customer through the entire developmental process. Axiomatic Design has yielded a set of axioms to structure and govern the design process (attempting to apply more science to what has been considered an art). Design for Six Sigma is the method for creating a new product or process. The Theory of Inventive Problem Solving is the structured application of scientific and heuristic observations to problem solving (tactically) and the generation of concepts and their respective evolution (strategically). Theory of Constraints provides a means of identifying the barrier constraining the entire system and the application of techniques to remove the barrier allowing the system to evolve to the next constraint. Each of these methods has a complex structure and algorithms delineating the steps and application parameters necessary for their application. Even within each single method, there are "dialects". This causes considerable consternation and confusion among potential users. Sometimes the complementary nature of these methods (and others omitted for simplicity) is hidden by particular features that compete. These issues provide the fertile ground in which a homogenous poly-system may be created in which the use of a computer aided structure may resolve all difficulties (of course creating a new set).

3. INTEGRATION AND EVOLUTION

These aforementioned methodologies are each an incomplete but valid perspective of Total Performance Excellence. As the needs of a corporation are considered from the development of a concept from mind-to-market, a list of competencies is created. If the capabilities of the aforementioned methods are mapped to this need assessment, you will find the fact that each method must be used in order to augment and support each corporate need. The fact that each method competes for a portion of a finite set of resources means that the most powerful piece(s) of each method must be combined to form a hybrid structure. This hybrid structure's complex heterogeneous nature would be supported by the development of a computer program that automated and provided a meta-structure to the integrated meta-method. The complexity of the new method would be mitigated as well as the logistical flow through each method and their respective tools through product / process development. A partial set of those skills necessary is represented in Figure 1.

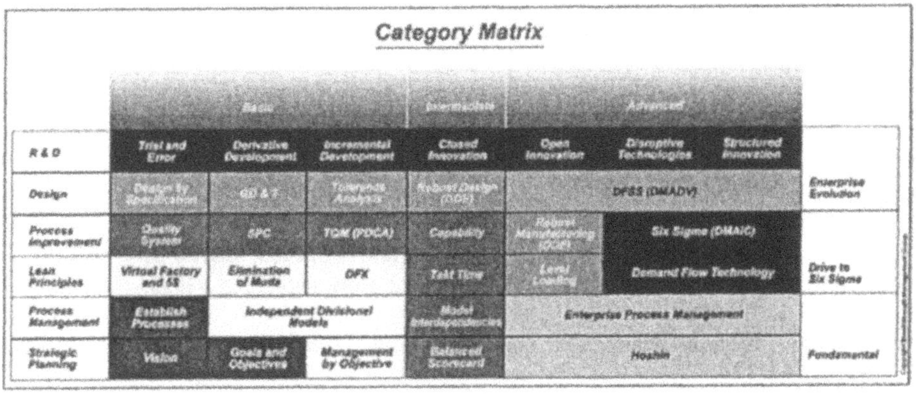

Figure 1. Total Performance Improvement Model (TPIM) indicating the evolution of necessary skills from the fundamental to enterprise evolution. Computer Aided Performance Excellence (CAPE) would provide a structure containing the methods and tools to support all of these functions.

As Six Sigma is the evolution and integration of Deming's work, Juran's work, Fischer's work, Shewhart's work, and Feigenbaum's work (not exhaustive) so to shall Total Performance Improvement be the integration of TRIZ, DFSS, TOC, Lean, and the other useful methodologies. Also, as MINITAB and Six Sigma project tracking software complement Six Sigma so to will CAPE complement Performance Excellence.

4. CONCLUSION

An excellent opportunity exists for the software development community to introduce Computer Aided Performance Excellence to society. This product should contain a meta-methodology that governs the entire developmental process from mind-to-market. This product would (at a minimum):

1. automate voice-of-the-customer (VOC) capture,
2. assist the application of QFD and preservation critical-to-customer requirement flow-down,
3. assist the application of TRIZ to resolve contradictions identified by QFD,
4. assist the application of Axiomatic Design to the design process,
5. integrate existing DMAIC and DMADV (DFSS) tools and processes,
6. integrate TOC and Lean in product and process maturation, and
7. involve TRIZ for the resolution of any secondary problems.

CAPE will revolutionize the Performance Excellence industry and help to reduce excellence to a ubiquitous core competency for the evolving organization.

5. REFERENCES

1. The Six Sigma Handbook, Thomas Pyzdek, McGraw-Hill, 2003, ISBN 0-07-141015-5
2. The Principles of Design, Nam P. Suh, Oxford University Press, 1990, ISBN 0-19-504345-6
3. Quality Function Deployment, Yoji Akao, Editor, Productivity Press, 1988, ISBN 0-915299-41-0
4. TRIZ: The Right Solution at the Right Time, Yuri Salamatov, Edited by Valeri Souchkov and Michael S. Slocum, Insytec, 1999, ISBN 90-804680-1-0
5. Goldratt's Theory of Constraints, H William Dettmer, ASQ Quality Press, 1997, ISBN 0-87389-370-0
6. Juran's Quality Handbook: Fifth Edition, Joseph M .Juran and A. Blanton Godfrey, McGraw-Hill, 1998, ISBN 0-07-034003-X

TRIZ AND COMPUTER AIDED INVENTING

Sergei Ikovenko
Professor Adjunctis (MIT, Cambridge, USA), International TRIZ Association (MA TRIZ)

Abstract: TRIZ (Theory for Inventive Problem Solving) being one of the most powerful inventing methodologies is sophisticated and requires considerable time and efforts to master. There have been and are multiple projects on developing various software packages that would make TRIZ usage and applications more user-friendly and shorten the TRIZ learning curve. Software packages that address this issue are one of the first computer aided inventing tools known. This direction of CAI has become much more active when TRIZ started its integration with other engineering methods – Value Engineering Analysis (VEA), Root-Cause Analysis (RCA), Lean Thinking, Six Sigma, Functional Analysis and others. Several software packages assist engineers with documenting data, building component and function models, and automatically calculating function rank of the components of the system. Performing a function-based information search is one of the tasks where computerized support is helping if finding new functions for improving complex systems. The next step is to identify other systems in which similar functions are performed better. The principles used to achieve similar functions in other fields can then be adapted to improve the system at hand. Developing powerful tools for Function Based Information Search to enable the substitution of inventing problems with adaptation problems is predicted to be one of major directions of CAI development

Key words: Computer-Aided Inventing, TRIZ, TRIZ++, Root-Cause Analysis, Evolutionary Analysis.

1. INTRODUCTION

TRIZ (Theory for Inventive Problem Solving) being one of the most powerful inventing methodologies is sophisticated and requires considerable time and efforts to master.

There have been and are multiple projects on developing various software packages that would make TRIZ usage and applications more user-friendly and shorten the TRIZ learning curve.

This direction of CAI has become much more active when TRIZ started its integration with other engineering methods – Value Engineering Analysis (VEA), Root-Cause Analysis (RCA), Lean Thinking, Six Sigma and others.

TRIZ is a scientifically-based and empirically-derived method that originated for the analysis of the world patent collection. Its strongest side is in the Conceptual Stage of design, while the Analytical Stage is not completely covered by TRIZ.

VEA and RCN, for example, on the contrary are extremely effective for the analysis, but lack the heuristic power of TRIZ. That is why the combination of analytical and concept generating methods is leading to increasing effectiveness and higher quality of engineering solutions.

An inevitable stumbling block, a contradiction on this path is continually growing complexity and sophistication of the combined methods. CAI looks like that magic bridge that will allow getting the benefits of both worlds – the effectiveness of the combined methods and relatively short learning curve and ease of their usage.

Merging TRIZ with other methods gave birth to several integrated methodologies based on TRIZ: ITD, I-TRIZ, TRIZ++, etc. It opens new horizons for CAI development to cover all the parts of those methods, both analytical and concept generating. As an example, this direction of CAI is illustrated on "TRIZ++" methodology.

2. TRIZ++ PROBLEM SOLVING APPROACH

The TRIZ++ methodology offers a powerful and systematic approach for solving technical problems and improving engineering systems and manufacturing processes. Furthermore, when a problem is solved or a system is improved, the value of the engineering system or process is always increased when the TRIZ++ methodology is used. Value is defined as benefits (for example, improved functional performance, increased productivity, accuracy, consumer acceptance, etc.) divided by generalized costs.1 One of the most important goals of TRIZ++ is to develop breakthrough solutions that significantly improve the value of a system, as opposed to offering compromise solutions.

The TRIZ++ approach is based upon clearly defining and understanding the main and supporting functions of a system and the underlying problems that must be solved to improve the system. If the functions of a system are clearly understood, harmful and non-useful functions can be eliminated and engineering contradictions within the system can be identified and resolved more easily. The goals of a project can be achieved with much less effort. One of the biggest traps that problem solvers often fall into is that they attempt to solve the wrong problem, often trying to eliminate the symptoms instead of the underlying root problems. Applying a functional approach to problem solving helps to avoid this pitfall.

In addition to its function-oriented approach, the TRIZ++ methodology is based on two other important principles. The first is that many engineering problems have already been solved elsewhere, but in fields that are remote from the one at hand. A function-based understanding of a system makes it much easier to search other fields for possible solutions. This approach also allows problem solvers to overcome psychological inertia and to formulate creative and unexpected solutions.

The second important principle is that future directions of development of an engineering system or a process can be predicted from predetermined trends. The Russian scientist Genrich Altshuller[1] and his followers identified these Trends of Engineering System Evolution (TESE) after analysis of more than three million patents. With knowledge of these Trends, the problem solver knows where to search and how to develop solutions that correspond to the natural evolutionary development of the system to be improved.

The TRIZ++ methodology can be divided into two basic phases: the Analysis and Problem Statement Phase and the Conceptual Phase. The purpose of the Analysis and Problem Statement Phase is to identify key/root problems that must be solved to improve the system and achieve the goals of the project. The purpose of the Conceptual Phase is to develop and substantiate concepts that solve the key/root problems identified in the Analysis Phase. These phases are described in greater detail below.

1 Generalized costs include not only the dollar value assigned to the elements that execute a given function, but also the qualitative "costs" of implementing the function, for example, problems associated with implementation. The following three paths can be used alone or in combination to increase value: (1) improved efficiency in functional performance; (2) introduction of new functions; and, (3) cost reduction.

3. ANALYTICAL AND PROBLEM STATEMENT PHASE

During the Analysis and Problem Statement Phase (see below), a set of TRIZ++ tools is systematically applied to analyze the system functions. This allows the problem solver to identify the key/root problems that must be solved to achieve the goals of the project and to increase the value of the system. These tools include Benchmarking, Function Analysis, Trimming Technique, Substance and Energy Flows Analysis, Cause-Effect Chains Analysis, a function-based information search, and S-Curve Analysis.

The power of these tools lies in their ability to help identify the key/root problems of the system, as opposed to perceived problems or superficial symptoms. Many problem solvers make the common mistake of trying to solve the wrong problem or trying to eliminate symptoms without addressing fundamental underlying problems. Upon completion of this phase, a set of clearly defined problem statements is articulated (Fig 1). These are the key problems that must be solved to achieve the goals of the project. These problem statements are specifically formulated so the TRIZ++ problem solution tools can be effectively applied during the Conceptual Phase.

3.1 Function Analysis

The purpose of Function Analysis is to build a function model of the system. The first step is to determine and to represent the main and the supporting functions of the system. Next, functions are identified as harmful or useful. Useful functions are further defined as normal, excessive, or insufficient. The important parameters of the useful functions are also defined. Finally, functions are ranked according to their importance.

Several software packages assist engineers with documenting data, building component and function models, and automatically calculating function rank of the components of the system.

3.2 Substance and Energy Flows Analysis

Substance and Energy Flows Analysis is used to identify areas in the system where substances and/or energy are lost, not used efficiently, or have harmful effects. The result of this analysis is a list of disadvantages in the system associated with substance and energy flows.

There have been some attempts, but for the time being, that part of the analysis is a challenge for CAI.

3.3 Cause-Effect Chains Analysis

Our intuition usually tells us that the larger the number of problems associated with an engineering system or a process, the harder it will be to eliminate them all and to improve the system. However, this is often not the case. One problem can create another problem, which creates another problem and so on. If the root problems are identified and eliminated, then all the associated problems, or a significant number of them, will disappear. Furthermore, breakthrough solutions often occur when root problems are solved. Cause-Effect Chains Analysis is one of the tools used to identify root problems.

Cause-effect chains are built from the disadvantages identified during Function Analysis, Trimming, and Substance and Energy Flow Analysis. These chains may branch and/or intersect. They end with known disadvantages associated with high costs, low productive capacity, poor quality, and other shortcomings. If a key disadvantage is eliminated, all subsequent disadvantages in its specific chain will be eliminated. Key disadvantages are usually found at the beginning of a cause-effect chain or at the intersection of two or more chains.

RCA-based software packages and modules have been developed and are being used both independently and a part of VEA/RCA/TRIZ software suites.

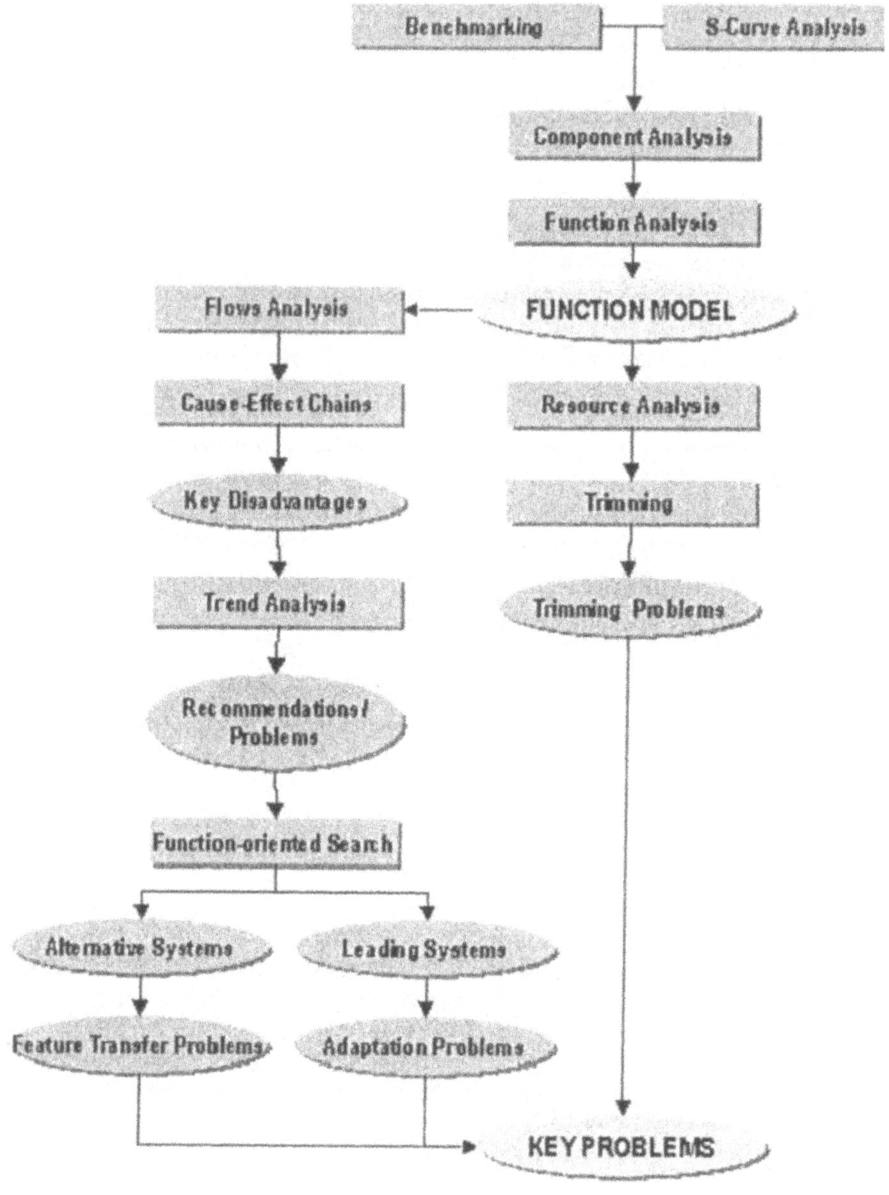

Figure 1. Flow Diagram for Key Problem Solving

3.4 Trimming

The purpose of Trimming is to improve the system by eliminating harmful and low-ranked functions. The result of Trimming is a set of newly formulated problem statements. These statements identify the problems that must be solved to eliminate the harmful and low-ranked functions and their associated components. The key is to preserve the important useful functions associated with the components that are eliminated.

Several CAI products cover this part of the method.

3.5 Function-Based Information Search

The purpose of a function-based information search is to identify solutions to problems in areas of science and engineering that are far-removed from the system at hand. Borrowing ideas or practical solutions from other fields of knowledge can be very effective. Often scientists or engineers who are experts in the field where a problem lies have little or no knowledge of the field(s) where solutions lie. Consequently, finding successful solutions is usually a haphazard process.

The key to performing a function-based information search is first to identify specific functions in the system that should be improved or modified. The next step is to identify other systems in which similar functions are performed better. The principles used to achieve similar functions in other fields can then be adapted to improve the system at hand.

Software packages that address this issue are effective web search and information procession tools. The most advance direction of Function-Based Information Search is Semantic Technologies.

3.6 Feature Transfer

In addition to TRIZ, Feature Transfer is used to help develop concepts. This tool is designed to formulate ways of combining the advantages and best features of competing engineering systems (products and processes) into a single system. The power of Feature Transfer is not that the specific elements of one engineering system are "mechanistically" transferred to another system, but rather, that the underlying reasons why a specific feature works well are analyzed and applied to the system under development.

Feature Transfer™ approach is a further development of a technique known among design methods as Pugh Concept. A number of software packages allow using this approach.

3.7 Evolutionary Analysis

Evolutionary Analysis is used to determine the general direction in which a system will naturally evolve to become an ideal system. This information is used to help determine the best directions and concepts for improving the system. In particular, Evolutionary Analysis will help to determine if a system can be substantially improved based on the current principle(s) of operation or if fundamentally, new principle(s) of operation are required to achieve substantial improvements.

Evolutionary Analysis is based upon the Trends of Engineering System Evolution. According to the Trends of Engineering System Evolution, an engineering system passes through four consecutive stages as it evolves: (1) slow development; (2) rapid growth; (3) stabilization; and (4) decline. This evolution over time can be represented as an S-shaped curve. Once a system has reached the fourth stage of decline, fundamentally new principles of operation are required to substantially improve the system.

CAI development in this direction is rudimentary and has had a merely visualization objective.

3.8 Results of the Analysis and Problem Statement Phase

The primary result of the Analysis and Problem Statement Phase is a set of key problems that must be solved in order to achieve the goals of the project. Very often, the results of the Analysis and Problem Statement Phase also include a redefinition of the goals of the project and fundamental changes to the initially proposed methods of achieving these goals. This is because the initial problem statements are significantly better understood as a result of the analysis.

4. CONCEPTUAL PHASE

The purpose of the Conceptual and Substantiation Phases (see diagram below) is to develop feasible concepts that will solve the key problems identified in the Analysis and Problem Statement Phase. A conceptual idea is an idea that is supported by references to scientific or technological sources, expert opinions, and/or known experimental results.

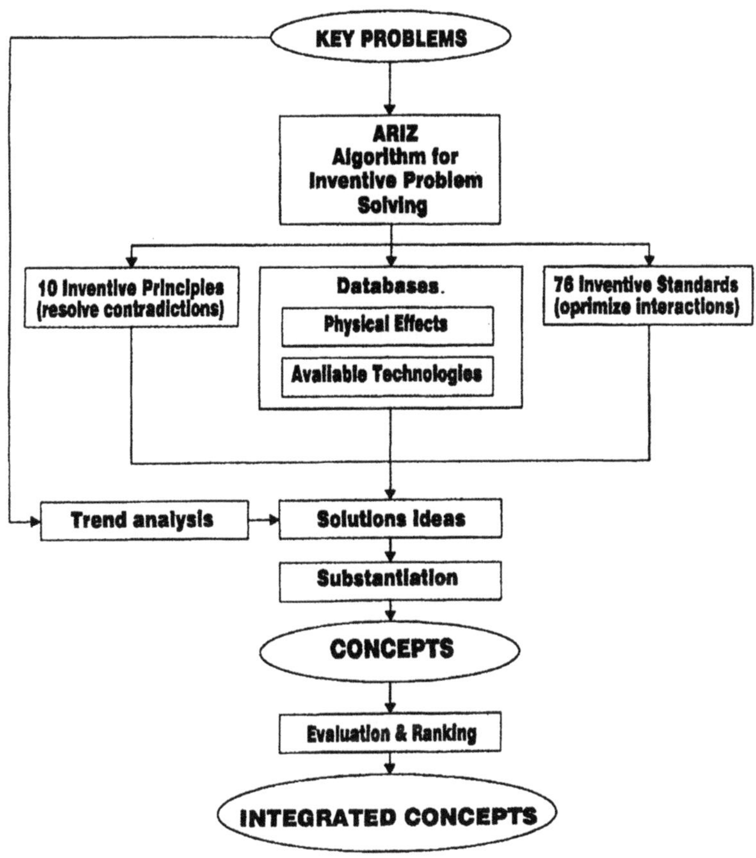

Figure 2. Flow Diagram for Key Problem Solving

Conceptual Phase includes all the types of problem modeling in TRIZ: engineering contradictions, Substance-Field Modeling, Physical Contradictions, and all the TRIZ

Tools to work with these models: Contradiction Matrix, the System of Standard Inventive Solutions and a database of scientific and engineering effects.

This part of the design process has been extensively covered by multiple software packages, although there are challenges still.

4.1 Concept Ranking and Compatibility

Some of the final concepts will be better at achieving certain results than others. However, cost, time, difficulty of implementation, and resource availability must be taken into account when assigning value to the concepts. Concepts are ranked based on a set of project-dependent criteria.

Some concepts may be implemented in combination and others may not be. In certain cases, the combined implementation of two or more concepts may offer extremely powerful solutions. A matrix of possible combinations in which the individual concepts could be implemented is also developed.

Multiple software packages address this part of the design.

5. CONCLUSIONS

The above-described TRIZ++ Methodology shows that there are a lot of gaps that CAI has not covered. I-TRIZ Methodology has some of its parts supported by the software while some parts are simply manual.

A new approach in TRIZ application and CAI has become obvious. Inventive solutions though being powerful always require proof of concept, substantiation, verification, tests. It makes the Implementation Stage long or the inventive solution can be abandoned altogether. TRIZ++ address this issue in a pretty elegant way. Using very effective Function Based Information Search, they find an existing technology that would solve problems identified in the Analysis Phase. As a rule, the technology comes from a totally different area and requires adaptation. However, the proof of concept is unnecessary and the verification stage is much shorter for solving an INVENTIVE problem is substituted with solving a VERYFICATION problem. To make this happen powerful tools for Function Based Information Tools are crucial.

Therefore, it is possible to predict two major directions of CAI development:

Computerizing "gaps" of classical TRIZ and integrated suites of TRIZ and other methods

Developing powerful tools for Function Based Information Search, to enable the substitution of inventing problems with adaptation problems. A most probable technology for such a tool is semantic technology

6. REFERENCES

1. Altshuller, G.S. Creativity as an exact science: the theory of the solution of inventive problems / New *York : Gordon and Breach, 1995*
2. S. Litvin. TRIZ++ - an Advanced Approach to TRIZ. ENITechnologie Conference Proceerings, Milan, 2003. S. Ikovenko. TRIZ and Semantic Technologies in Innovation and Knowledge Management. CROInfo2004, Zagreb, 2004.

OPTIMIZATION VS INNOVATION IN A CAE ENVIRONMENT

Towards a "Computer Aided Inventing" Environment

Noel Leon[1], Jorge Gutierrez[1], Oscar Martinez[2], Carlos Castillo[1]
[1]Center for Product Innovation and Development; [2]Department of Mechanical Engineering, ITESM, Campus Monterrey, Ave. Eugenio Garza Sada # 2501, Colonia Tecnológico, Monterrey, CP 64841, Monterrey, México

Abstract: At the kernel of TRIZ are the concepts of technical and physical contradictions and its "elimination" through inventive principles revealed by Altshuller[1]. Altshuller used the contradiction as one of the ways of identifying analogy between two different inventive problems. Recently Mann recognized that the contradiction "elimination" means rather more an improvement of the scenario but leading to new contradictions in an endless chain. Diverse authors have been analyzing the role of contradiction in product development and innovation. In this paper, a product development approach is presented where product performance enhancement is first achieved through quantitative changes in parametric design (optimization) and later through paradigm shift (innovation). The approach is based on the concept of changing the design scenario to "eliminate" technical or physical contradictions, which avoid achieving higher performance goals. Based on these results, product innovation is presented as "optimization" not restricted to parametric variation but extended to "concept variation." The role of "concept variation" in product innovation and its similarity and relationships to parametric optimization is analyzed in this paper, based on identifying contradictions that may be overcome through "constrained concept variations."

Key words: Computer-Aided Inventing, Systematic Innovation, TRIZ, Product Development, Product Optimization.

1. INTRODUCTION

Although the philosophers had discovered the role of contradictions and conflicts in empirical knowledge and in its resolution by synthesis of new systems, this knowledge had not been applied to empirical solutions of technical or scientific problems until Altshuller[1] used the contradiction as one of the ways of identifying analogy between two different inventive problems. At the kernel of TRIZ are the concepts of technical and physical contradictions and its "elimination" through inventive principles and other tools revealed by Altshuller.

In the 19th century, Hegel[2] deployed the dialectic method based on the concept of advancing contradictory arguments of thesis and antithesis and seeking the resolution by synthesis. Kant studied the contradictions in empirical knowledge leading to principles of reasoning. Marx studied the dialectic from the view point of contradictions as conflicts inherent in systems that give rise to the emergence of another more inclusive systems influenced by the quantitative development of the conflicts. These German philosophers recognize three basic laws of dialectics:

- The law of the negation of negation, which conveys the direction of development.
- The law of the mutual transformation of quantitative and qualitative changes, which demonstrates the mechanism of development.
- The law of unity and struggle of opposites, which demonstrates the source of development

It is also stated that of those three, the third law is the nucleus of dialectics and the first two laws may be considered as particular cases.

Recently Mann[3] recognized that the contradiction "elimination" means rather more an improvement of the scenario but leading to new contradictions in an endless chain. This recognition resembles the first law of dialectics, negation of negation.

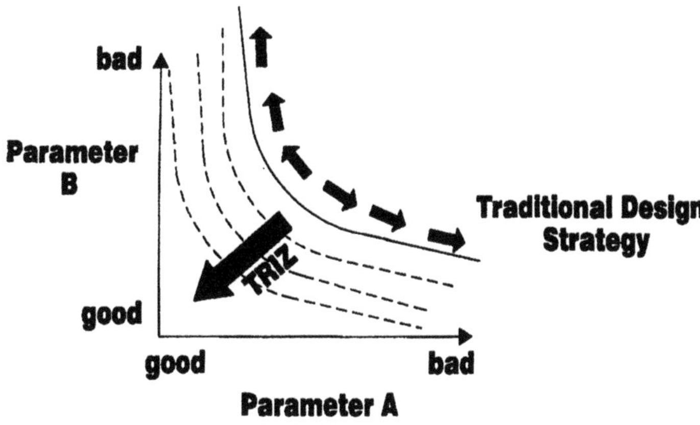

Figure 1. Traditional design vs. TRIZ

In the present paper the relationship between the second law, mutual transformation of quantitative and qualitative changes, and the third law, unity and struggle of opposites are judged against to the role of optimization and innovation in technical systems. It is known that commonly product performance enhancement is first achieved through quantitative changes in parametric design (optimization) and later, as the performance enhancement through optimization is exhausted, new searches are performed through paradigm shift or qualitative changes (innovation). Innovation allows then the removal of technical or physical contradictions, which were avoiding achieving enhanced performance goals (negation of negation). Darrell Mann represents this behavior diagrammatically in Fig. 1. Moving along the hyperboles means optimizing conflicting performance parameters (quantitative changes), while moving among the hyperboles means changing the function principle (qualitative changes).

The role of "concept variation" in product innovation and its similarity and relationships to extended parametric optimization is analyzed in this paper, based on identifying contradictions that may be overcome through "constrained concept variations."

This paper continues a series of papers about the research work that is being undertaken at the Center for Product Design and Innovation of the

Monterrey Institute of Technology in Monterrey, Mexico, looking for the integration of different design tools and methodologies.

2. OPTIMIZATION SYSTEMS BACKGROUND

The evolution of Product Development tools has been characterized by different trends; the analysis of these trends offers useful hints for the prediction of next generation systems. The optimization of products and processes has been studied by many authors, especially since the widespread of computers as an aid for looking for "optimal" combination of product or process parameters[4].

Especially the introduction of new techniques for Design of Experiments (DOE) in product or process improvement allowed reducing the number of experiments needed to identify the influence of different parameters in the performance objectives[5]. DOE also facilitated obtaining empirical mathematical models of the products and/or processes leading to the application of multi-objective optimization methods[6]. Furthermore, evolutionary and genetic algorithms[7] in engineering optimization have contributed to the achievement of higher performance goals with multi objective optimization. Nevertheless, these techniques have been restricted to the search of product or process performance enhancement through the variation of numerical product or process parameters.

2.1 Parametric optimization

Parametric optimization is perhaps the most effective approach for many industrial solutions, as commonly parametric changes in products and process are easier to achieve and to implement than innovative concepts, where shape, topology, or physical principles are changed. However, parametric optimization alone could lead to stagnation in product or process development as compromise is inherent in parametric optimization, especially when multiple optimization objectives are targeted.

Multi objective optimization requires that "priorities" be defined among conflicting performance objectives, therefore leading to compromises in conflicting goals. The conflicting performance goals appear in any product or process development process avoiding achieving further enhancements through parametric multi objective optimization.

2.2 Shape and Topological Optimization

When an absolute optimum is achieved through parametric optimization methods, the only way of achieving further performance enhancements is through innovative changes as shape or topological variations or as changing the physical functional principles. These changes often lead to better performance by overcoming the conflicting parameters. This is known as the "elimination" of the technical contradictions. However, achieving such changes requires commonly the inventive capabilities of designers and engineers.

The rapid development of the finite element method in recent years has also conduced to the introduction of the concepts of shape and topological optimization in engineering design in simulation software, which allow reducing the shape variation and topology variation to parametric changes in the product model while simulating its performance. Especially interesting are the trends of evolutionary algorithms to aerodynamic design optimization, in particular to turbine blade optimization using computational fluid dynamics packages. In this case, shape variations are achieved by fitting a spline to a target structure[8]. This approach is a special case as it actually reduces shape optimization to a parametric optimization of spline's parameters describing the airfoil section. A similar case study is performed by Obayashi, et. al.[9] applying direct numerical optimization methods by coupling aerodynamic analysis methods with numerical optimization algorithms. They used multi objective genetic algorithms to minimize (or maximize) a given aerodynamic objective function by iterating directly on the geometry. In this case, aerodynamic design of a compressor blade shape is described by B-spline polygons from the leading edge to the trailing edge of the airfoil.

Another example comprise a numerical study of the thermal performance of an impingement heat sink - fin shape optimization[10] varying the heat sink's shape. In this case, fin shapes were all parallel plate fins, with material removed from the region near the center of the heat sink.

An interesting case studying mechanisms performance by applying a systematic synthesis formulation is carried out by Sridhar et. al.[11]. They design compliant transmissions in micro electromechanical systems starting with desired force–displacement characteristics along specified directions and culminating in an "optimized design." In these cases, functional design that generates the desired output motion when subjected to prescribed input forces is searched by topological synthesis. Once a feasible topology is established, quantitative performance constraints can be imposed during the next stage in which size and shape optimization are performed using the energy formulation.

A case study where parametric vs. shape, optimization was used to further enhance the performance; leading to an innovative evolution of the product is reported by Leon and Martinez [12, 13, 14]. A railroad brake beam was subject of improvement looking for reducing manufacturing costs as also structural weight and stress. It is easily recognized that these objective parameters conflict among each other. First, a parametric optimization of the existing brake beam design was developed by means of FEM analysis and optimization techniques. After that further improvement were achieved by changing the sectional shape of some brake beam components and performing a new parametric optimization procedure afterwards.

Heuristic, knowledge-based algorithms (e.g., expert systems) have been applied for searching the design space when shape and/or topology are "variables" of the product or process design. However, such expert systems have a very limited scope. Expert systems commonly require capturing expert knowledge before its introduction into software packages at a commonly very high cost, which not always pays for the performance enhancement achievable through them.

3. INNOVATION AS CONCEPT OPTIMIZATION FOR COMPUTER AIDED INVENTING

Based on former analysis, it may be stated that product innovation may also be implicit as "optimization not restricted to parametric variation" but extended to "constrained concept variation." As has been shown in several case studies, an extended parametric optimization is achieved by adding shape and topology as possible search directions. This extended optimization has been achieved by reducing the shape variation to a parametric variation of shapes represented by spline curves or by eliminating finite elements from a meshed structure[15] to reduce it to a new shape or by considering predefined alternative shapes.

Extended shape generators in tree-structured CAD systems are under development [16,17,18]. These are able to produce variations of 3D-CAD shapes, which allow an "automatic" control of the shape variation not only when shapes are represented by parametric curves but also when represented as 3D shapes in 3D parametric CAD packages This symbolize a further step toward adding "concept variation" to optimization procedures.

The main problem for computer aided inventing algorithms resides in the fact that the possible concept variations of any product or process are infinite even inside of constrained spaces.

The computer aided optimization concept has to be based on techniques that reduce the search space by "sensing" the effect of variations of a reduced number of parameters involved. This means that an inherent contradiction is present at the widening of the search space to non parametric variations: the universe of possible solutions increases enormously to the extent that no computer aided methods are available for thoroughly searching the existing possibilities.

This inherent contradiction in computer aided inventing concept may be expressed as follows: the universe of possible variations should be widened as to not be constrained to only the parameters of the object's original functional principle but should be constrained as to reduce the search space to be affordable to existing optimization methods[19].

This idea is inherent in the Algorithm for Solving Inventive Problems (ARIZ) proposed by Altshuller, as it is intended to guide inventors in the main direction for solving inventive problems without useless random search. Some "inventive principles" disclosed by Altshuller are of geometric nature and therefore they may be implemented to be performed in a CAD/CAE system when modeling or analyzing parts.

Other inventive principles are of rather topological nature and therefore may be implemented in CAD systems' assembly modules.

In other cases, the principles are of mechanical or physical nature, which also involves the effect of time and other physical parameters as velocity, force, acceleration, temperature, etc. and may be implemented using multibody systems.

4. CONCLUSIONS

Further research work is necessary to implement the "automatic" variation of shape, topology, and physical principles involved in a product development process following the recommendations derived from the simulation of the product performance parameters in a CAD/CAE environment.

Continuing advancing towards computer aided inventing tools requires further formalization of the interpretation of the Altshuller inventive principles in a CAD/CAE environment. Shape generators, which allow automated variations of existing 3D-CAD shapes, will allow designers use "search algorithms" for "optimal shapes" that enhance product performance beyond the results achievable through pure parametric optimization.

As the patterns of product evolution are useful in selecting the directions of possible variations to the functional principles further research work is also required looking for the possible selection of alternative functional principles in a computer aided inventing environment.

An extended version of the paper will be presented at the Topical Session Top 6 Computer Aided Inventing of the IFIP World Computer Congress 2004, with further details and some examples about the proposed concepts.

5. REFERENCES

1. Altshuller, G.S. Creativity as an exact science: the theory of the solution of inventive problems / New *York: Gordon and Breach, 1995*
2. Hegel, G. W. F., Hauptwerke. In sechs Bänden". Band 6. Enzyklopädie der philosophischen Wissenschaften im Grundrisse *(1830). Hamburg, Meiner, 1999.*
3. Mann, D., Contradiction Chains, The TRIZ-Journal, January 2001, *http://www.trizjournal.com/archives/2000/01/a/index.htm*
4. Fox, R. L, Optimization methods for engineering design, *Addison-Wesley series in mechanics and thermodynamics, Reading, Mass.: Addison-Wesley Pub. Co., 1971*
5. Box, G. E. and Draper, N. R., Evolutionary operation; a statistical method for process improvement, *New York, Wiley, 1969, ISBN 047109305X*
6. Deb, K., Multi-Objective Optimization Using Evolutionary Algorithms, Chichester: *John Wiley & Sons (Sd), 2001, ISBN 0471873397*
7. Gen, M., Genetic algorithms and engineering optimization, *A Wiley-Interscience publication, New York: Wiley, 2000, ISBN 0471315311.*
8. Olhofer, M., Yaochu, J., Sendhoff, B., Adaptive encoding for aerodynamic shape optimization using evolution strategies, *Evolutionary Computation, 2001. Proceedings of the 2001 Congress on , Volume: 1 , 2001 Page(s): 576 -583 vol. 1*
9. Obayashi, S., Tsukahara, T.; Nakamura, T. , Multiobjective genetic algorithm applied to aerodynamic design of cascade airfoils, *Industrial Electronics, IEEE Transactions on , Volume: 47 Issue: 1 , Feb. 2000 Page(s): 211 -216*
10. Amit S., Sammakia, B., Srihari, H., Ramakrishna, K., A numerical study of the thermal performance of an impingement heat sink - fin shape optimization, *Thermal and Thermomechanical Phenomena in Electronic Systems, 2002. ITHERM 2002. The Eighth Intersociety Conference on , 2002 , Pages: 298 -306*
11. Sridhar K., Hetrick, J., et al., Tailoring Unconventional Actuators Using Compliant Transmissions: *Design Methods and Applications, IEEE/ASME TRANSACTIONS ON MECHATRONICS, VOL. 4, NO. 4, DECEMBER 1999, Pages 396-408*
12. Patrick N. K., et. Al, Interdigitation For Effective Design Space Exploration Using ISIGHT, *Journal of Structural and Multidisciplinary Optimization*
13. Martinez, O, Leon, N. et. Al,. Comparación entre optimización paramétrica e innovación conceptual para el desarrollo de una viga óptima de frenado de ferrocarril, Memorias del *Congreso de Investigación y Extensión del Sistema ITESM, 1998, January 1998,Pages 246-255,Vol. 1, Monterrey, Mexico.*
14. Martinez, O, Integración de metodologías de diseño innovativo y de optimización paramétrica aplicadas en el diseño de una guía de frenado de ferrocarril , *Master Degree Thesis, ITESM, 1999 (unpublished)*
15. Treviño, R., Revisión de técnicas de optimización de diseño y aplicación optimización topológica a eje frontal *Master Degree Thesis, ITESM, 2001*
16. Leon, N., A proposal to integrate TRIZ into the Product Design Process, *Proceedings of TRIZCON2002., Conference Proceedings Pages 24-1 to 24-11, The 4th Annual Conference of the Altshuller Institute for TRIZ Studies, St. Louis, Missour, USA, April 30-May 2, 2002*

17. Leon, N., Product Optimization vs. Innovation, Steps Toward a "Comuter Aided Inventing Environment, *Proceedings of TRIZCON200e., Conference Proceedings Pages 2-1 to 2-12, The Fifth Annual Conference of the Altshuller Institute for TRIZ Studies,* March 16-18, 2993, Philadelphia, Pennsylvania, USA
18. Abate, V., Cascini, G., CAD for Conceptual Design: Forecasted Evolution, *The TRIZ Journal (May 2003); http://triz-journal.com.*
19. Cavallucci, D., Lutz, P., Kucharavy, D., Converging in problem formulation: A different path in design, *Proceedings of the 14th ASME International Conference on Design Theory and Methodology Integrated Systems Design*, Montreal, Canada, Sep 29-Oct 2 (2002).

Topic 7

Emerging tools and Techniques for Avionics Certification

Organisers:

Virginie Wiels
ONERA, France
Virginie.Wiels@cert.fr

Mats Heimdahl
University of Minnesota, USA
heimdahl@cs.umn.edu

Embedded critical systems need to be validated very thoroughly. It usually results in very long and onerous test phases. New techniques and tools are emerging that could be an advantageous alternative, or at least a good complement to classical approaches and allow a significant reduction of test phases. However, for these techniques to be used in practice, one issue to consider is their efficiency on complex industrial systems.

This topical day will include presentations on experiences in using new techniques (model checking, test case generation, abstract interpretation for example) for V&V and safety analyses of critical embedded systems (at the specification and code levels).

The issue of the use of such techniques for certification purposes will be raised during some of the talks and will be the subject of the panel that will close this topical day.

FORMAL PROOF AND TEST CASE GENERATION FOR CRITICAL EMBEDDED SYSTEMS USING SCADE

Guy Durrieu[2], Odile Laurent[1], Christel Seguin[2] and Virginie Wiels[2]
[1]Airbus, 316 route de Bayonne 31000 Toulouse cedex 03, France; [2]ONERA/DTIM, 2 avenue Edouard Belin, BP 4025, 31055 Toulouse cedex, France

Abstract: This paper presents the work done within two research projects on the capability to use formal proof techniques for verifying properties and on the feasibility of automatic test generation for operational avionics systems.

Key words: formal techniques, verification, test generation, critical embedded systems.

1. INTRODUCTION

Airbus has used formal methods for several years to specify avionics systems. Thanks to these techniques, development cycles have been shortened significantly; automatic code generation from formal specification played an essential role in this improvement. A first research project conducted by Airbus and ONERA showed that the use of formal techniques for specification of avionics systems allowed the use of formal proof techniques for the validation of these systems[1]. Formal specifications that were studied are based on the SCADE language and a tool called SCADE Design Verifier was developed. Nowadays, SCADE Design Verifier is a commercial tool to verify properties of a formal SCADE specification and starts to be used at Airbus. Static validation techniques can thus be used in an operational way and this constitutes a first breakthrough with respect to the classical verification and validation process, which is usually based on dynamic techniques such as simulation and test. However, static analysis of the SCADE specifications cannot take into account all details of operational conditions and some dynamic tests such as flight tests will remain mandatory. This industrial fact and the high cost of tests definition lead us to look for assistance in the generation of test cases using automatic test generation from formal specification. This was the subject of a second research project.

This paper briefly presents the work done within these two projects (financed by DPAC, French Program Direction for Civil Aviation) on the capability to use formal proof techniques for verifying properties and on the feasibility of automatic test generation for operational avionics systems.

2. AIRBUS SPECIFICATION WITH SCADE

SCADE is an environment developed by Esterel Technologies (http://www.esterel-technologies.com), based on a graphical dataflow synchronous language. In this language, time is divided into discrete instants defined by a global clock. At instant *t* the synchronous program reads inputs from external environment and computes outputs. The synchrony hypothesis states that the computation of the outputs is made at the same instant *t*. It means that for periodic systems like control/command systems, all outputs are computed at each cycle.

A SCADE specification is a set of nodes. A SCADE node is made up of constants, variables and operators. An operator may be

- a basic operator:
  usual arithmetic and logical operators,
  temporal operators: *pre* and → (*fby*). *Pre(x)* represents the value of x at the previous instant. *Fby*, called "*followed by*", is used to assign initial values to expressions.
- a compound operator is made up of basic operators and SCADE nodes. Within Airbus, skill oriented nodes that are very often used are called symbols. Typical symbols are: filters, triggers, integrators.

3. CURRENT VERIFICATION AND VALIDATION MEANS

Currently, the main verification and validation activities done at Airbus based on dynamic techniques (execution of code generated from formal specifications) are the following:

- System level simulation: the considered system is validated in a simulated environment. The designer validates the software specification on real time computers providing a panel of commands representing possible pilot actions.
- Aircraft level simulation: several systems are validated in a simulated environment.
- System benches: first tests with real equipments, on a single system.
- Multi-systems benches: at this stage, real equipments exist for the different systems, the goal is to be sure they are correct with respect to their specification.
- General bench: last tests before the tests on the real aircraft, they are done on real equipments and with a good representation of the aircraft environment.

All the above verification and validation activities necessitate the definition of pertinent test vectors. The definition of these test cases is not easy because they have to ensure that all the functions of the system are tested and that dangerous configurations are not forgotten.

Civil airworthiness authorities require, for systems of level A, B or C, functional verification and validation activities to ensure correct operation in normal and abnormal conditions. Criteria for the termination of these functional V&V activities are also to be defined. In order to meet these requirements, Airbus defines tests by identifying:

- Equivalence classes: partitioning of inputs such as a test of a given class is functionally equivalent to any other test of the same class,
- Singular points (specific behaviour),
- Limit values of inputs domains,

Structural coverage criteria, based on the structure of the specifications, chosen as termination criteria (enough tests were executed). The structural coverage criterion used is called "symbols coverage". A symbol is considered covered when a relation between inputs and outputs is set to true at least once when executing tests. This relation depends on the symbol. (Example: for a symbol A (i1:bool, i2:bool,o1:bool); a structural criterion may be the logical expression: i1 and o1). The specification is covered when all symbols coverage criteria are met.

Currently, functional test cases are described manually in test plans. The objective of our two projects was to study whether static formal techniques could improve this V&V process, by replacing some test by formal verification of properties and automating part of the test generation activity.

4. FORMAL VERIFICATION OF PROPERTIES

To be able to achieve formal verification, a first necessary step is the expression of properties. These properties must be derived from system requirements and formalized. The properties we considered were invariants expressing relationships between inputs and outputs of the system. They are expressed in SCADE using the synchronous observer technique.

The observed system S is considered as a black box and only its interface (i.e. the input and output variables) can be involved in the expression of a property P. In order to prove that a property P is satisfied by a system S under a set of hypotheses H, we build a system S' by composition of S, P, H as shown on the figure below:

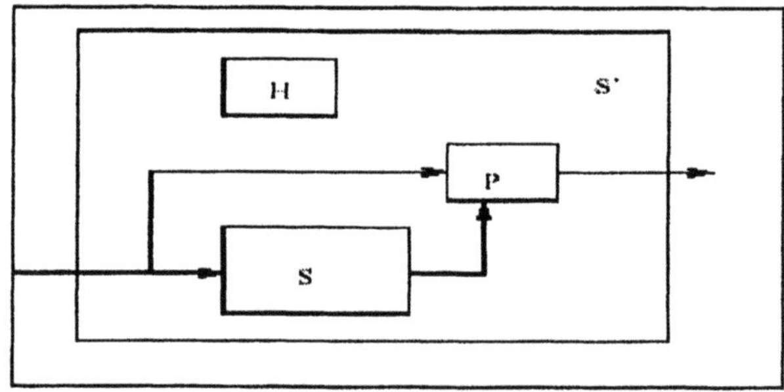

Figure 1. Obsever technique

The only output of S' is P. The verification then consists in checking that the output of system S' is always true.

SCADE Design Verifier is a tool developed by Prover Technologies (http://www.prover.com) based on a proof kernel. A verification can give three results:

- Valid: the property is proved.
- Falsifiable: a counter-example that falsifies the property is provided.
- Indeterminate: the tool did not succeed in proving the property that may be true or false.

We have experimented this tool on large operational systems and have had quite good results. However, we encountered difficulties with systems involving real numbers.

5. AUTOMATIC TEST GENERATION

As we do not want to modify the way of working of system designers, generated tests shall be defined in a very close way to the one used today at

Airbus. So, a first issue is to find for test vectors the appropriate equivalence classes, limit values and singular points. A second issue is to evaluate the structural coverage obtained by a set of test cases. This is possible only if a pertinent structural coverage criterion is defined at the specification level. Our project thus focussed on three objectives:

Is it feasible to generate tests from a detailed specification in SCADE using formal techniques? Is it possible to identify equivalence classes?

Which coverage criterion is pertinent at the specification level?

How can a coverage analysis be implemented at the specification level?

Approach

For a given system, a set of functional test objectives is defined. Functional Test Objectives (FTO) can be defined as properties expressed in SCADE. At first, only one test case is defined for each FTO, but this is not sufficient. The behaviour class defined by the FTO has to be refined to generate several test cases for each FTO. A structural coverage criterion is then used to decide whether a sufficient refinement level has been obtained. Next paragraph describes the structural coverage criterion that has been defined for SCADE specifications. This criterion is based on the structure of the specification. It allows us to define Structural Test Objectives (STO) for each operator of the language, and a STO is a boolean condition that must be set to true at least once by a test case for the STO to be covered. Thanks to these STOs, the coverage obtained by test cases generated with respect to the FTOs can be evaluated. STOs may also be used to guide the generation of test cases or to generate new test cases if it is necessary.

Structural coverage criterion

In addition to the symbols coverage criterion already used at Airbus, we have chosen a structural coverage criterion at the specification level (adapted to SCADE specifications). The criterion has been defined by LSR-IMAG. We do not give here the detailed definition of this criterion[2] but try to describe its objective in terms of coverage: for each node and for each output variable of this node, all possible values of each input variable must be exercised in a context where its value has an influence on the value of the output variable.

This criterion is very close to the constraints imposed by MC/DC (Modified Condition/Decision Coverage), the main difference is that MC/DC is defined at the code level while we are interested in a criterion at the specification level. To precisely compare both criteria, it would be necessary to study the transformations introduced by automatic code generation.

TCG

TCG (Test Case Generator) is a tool developed by Prover Technology (http://www.prover.com) based on a proof kernel. It allows to generate test cases for a given functional test objective while trying at the same time to cover as many structural test objectives as possible.

The tool was experimented on two main systems: the flight control secondary computer and the flight warning system. TCG has been able to generate interesting test cases and its good performances allowed us to deal with real size examples. Moreover, the tools can be parameterised to take into account the coverage criteria we have defined (symbols coverage and LSR-IMAG criterion). Nevertheless, TCG does not deliver its test cases as equivalence classes. Another tool called GATEL[3] providing this essential feature was experimented, but it is not yet operational in an industrial environment.

6. CONCLUSION AND FUTURE WORK

The main result of both projects is to show that formal proof and automatic test generation from SCADE specification are feasible in practice. Tools exist and are able to handle real industrial examples.

Concerning automatic test generation, more work still needs to be done in two directions. Firstly, a few experimentations have been conducted to compare automatically generated tests with tests obtained with the current manual approach, but they are not sufficient. It would be interesting to fully compare both approaches by applying them in parallel on a given system with functional test objectives. Secondly, at the methodological level, the proposed approach is compliant with the certification standards. However, the proposed approach is different from the classical coverage analysis at the code level, so we think it is necessary to study more thoroughly the possible substitution of the coverage analysis at the code level by a coverage analysis at the specification level. This reflection should be part of a more global study of the integration of this approach to the actual verification and validation process. This global study should also address the complementarity of proof and test generation techniques.

REFERENCES

1. O. Laurent, P. Michel, V. Wiels. *Using formal verification techniques to reduce simulation and test effort.* FME 2001. LNCS 2021, Jose Nuno Oliveira and Pamela Zave eds. Springer Verlag.
2. A. Lakehal, I. Parissis, L. du Bousquet. *Critères de couverture structurelle de programmes Lustre*. Proceedings of AFADL 04. .
3. B. Marre, A. Arnould. *Test Sequence Generation from Lustre Descriptions: GATEL.* 15th international conference on Automated Software Engineering (ASE) 2000.

SAFETY ASSESSMENT WITH ALTARICA

Lessons learnt based on two aircraft system studies

Pierre Bieber[2], Christian Bougnol[1], Charles Castel[2], Jean-Pierre Heckmann Christophe Kehren[2], Sylvain Metge[1] and Christel Seguin[2]
[1]AIRBUS, 316 route de Bayonne 3100 Toulouse cedex 03 France; [2]ONERA, 2 avenue E. Belin 31055 Toulouse cedex 04 France

Abstract: AIRBUS and ONERA used the AltaRica formal language and associated tools to perform safety assessments. Lessons learnt during the study of an electrical and hydraulic system are presented.

Key words: dependability, aircraft, formal methods

AIRBUS and ONERA were recently involved in the ESACS (Enhanced Safety Assessment for Complex Systems) European project. This project aimed at developing safety assessment techniques based on the use of formal specification languages and associated tools. We used the AltaRica (Arnold et al. 2000) formal language that is supported by Cecilia OCAS workshop developed by Dassault Aviation. Two case-studies based on AIRBUS aircraft electrical and hydraulic systems were used to validate the approach (Kehren et al. 2004b). In this paper we present lessons we learnt during ESACS. Lessons are sorted in three categories: **Advantages** are situations where the use of AltaRica was clearly positive, **Difficulties** are situations where the use of AltaRica was not directly positive but we found out how to circumvent the difficulties and the remaining situations are considered to be **Limitations**.

1. SYSTEM AND REQUIREMENT MODELLING

1.1 System Modelling

The first step of ESACS approach (Bozzano et al. 2003) is to obtain a formal model that is suitable to perform safety assessment of the system under study. We followed the modeling approach defined in (Fenelon et al. 1994) that abstracts nominal physical details of components and focuses on failure propagation. We defined libraries of (electrical, hydraulic, computer, ...) component models and used them to build the safety model.

Advantages: Each system component is modelled by an Altarica node that can be regarded as a mode automaton (see Rauzy 2002). In Cecilia OCAS workshop, each node is associated to an icon and belongs to a library. Once the component library created, the system is modelled easily and quickly. Components are dragged and dropped from the library to the system architecture sheet and then linked graphically. The whole hydraulic system model is made of about 15 component classes and the electrical system model uses about 20 classes of components. Furthermore, hierarchy of nodes can be used to build complex components and structure the system model. We were able to combine in a common model both models of the electrical and hydraulic systems in order to assess whether interface safety requirements were met.

Difficulties: It can be difficult to adequately model physical system failure propagation. If we consider a hydraulic circuit pipe, a leakage cannot be modelled only by considering the absence or the presence of fluid in the pipe. Indeed, the real consequence of a leakage is a quick pressure decrease for all the components located downwards the leaking component and, at last, an absence of fluid in the circuit. As a result, a pipe must transmit the pair (fluid, pressure) in order to propagate correctly the leakage information throughout the model. Moreover as all the components (i.e. downwards but also upwards) have to be informed of such a failure, the (fluid, pressure) signal has to be bidirectional.

Limitations: As explained above, components are linked with bidirectional flows. The actual topology of the electrical and hydraulic systems includes several loops that lead to potentially circular definitions in the formal models. Altarica and other data flow languages reject models that include syntactical circular definitions. This is rather pessimistic, because our models were rejected although all the loops include valves or contactors such that there is no cycle in the failure propagation. We applied the usual solution that consists in adding a time delay in the loops. One consequence is that failure propagation is not instantanneous, it needs several time steps to reach a correct state.

1.2 Formal Safety Requirements

The second step in the ESACS methodology is to formalize the safety requirements. We limited our study to qualitative safety requirements of the form "*if up to N individual failures occur then the loss of N+1 power channels shall not occur*" with N = 0,1,2. To observe situations such as the loss of several channels, special AltaRica nodes called observers are added to the model.

Difficulties: AltaRica observers do not make the difference between and instantaneous loss of power that allows power to be recovered later due to a reconfiguration and a permanent loss of power that does not allow any recovery. We used Linear Temporal Logic operators to model the several temporal flavors of the loss of channels. By now, Safety Engineers are not familiar with temporal logic operators and they might need some training in order to be able to formalize safety requirements. To limit this difficulty, we proposed to define a library of useful safety requirement formulae. When we studied the Electrical system we reused the safety requirement formulae developed for the hydraulic system study.

2. SAFETY ASSESSMENT TECHNIQUES

2.1 Graphical Interactive Simulation

A Safety Engineer can check the effect of failure occurrences on the system architecture using Cecilia OCAS graphical interactive simulator. The safety engineer chooses an event and the resulting state is computed by the simulator. As failures are events in the AltaRica model, the safety engineer can inject in the model a number of failure events in order to observe whether a failure condition is reached (such as loss of one or several power channels).

Advantages: Several icons can be associated with a component of the model depending on its state. For instance, a green box is displayed if the observer receives power and a red box is displayed otherwise. These icons help to rapidly assess if a failure condition occurs.

2.2 Fault Tree generation

Fault tree analysis is a well established technique among safety engineers. Cecilia OCAS includes a fault tree generator. This tool efficiently produces a Boolean formula (a fault tree) that describes all the sequences of failure events of the Altarica model that lead to a given observer state.

Advantages: Thanks to fault tree analysis packages the Safety Engineer can compute minimal cut sets of a failure condition and investigate what is the minimal number of failure events that lead to it. If failure occurrence rates are associated with the failure events of the AltaRica model, quantitative analysis (probabilistic computations) can be performed as well.

Limitations: The current algorithm has strong limitations on the form of the AltaRica model that can be taken into account: the order of occurrence of events in the model should not make any difference on the state of the system. So we cannot apply this tool to our models because, for a given sequence of failure events, some combinations with time delay events (that we had to add in order to avoid circular definitions) are not equivalent due to incorrect failure propagations. To overcome this limitation, Cecilia OCAS also includes a sequence generator tool that explores the state space of the model in order to find bounded length sequences that lead to a given failure conditions.

2.3 Model-checking

A model-checker as Cadence Labs SMV (McMillan 1993) performs symbolically an exhaustive simulation of a finite-state model. The model-checker can test whether the qualitative requirements stated as temporal logic formulae are valid in any state of the model. Whenever a formula is not valid, the model-checker produces a counter-example that describes a sequence of states that lead to a violation of the safety requirement. We developed tools to translate a model written in Altarica into a finite-state SMV model.

Advantages: We were able to check that both system models enforced their qualitative safety requirements. All requirements were verified in less than ten seconds although the truth value of some formulae depended in each state on as much as 100 boolean variables. The model checker was very useful to debug a preliminary version of the electrical system model where the control of contactors was not properly defined. We extracted from the counter-example generated by the model-checker a sequence of events and then simulated it with OCAS Altarica simulator. We found several scenarios with one or two failure events and several (six or seven) time delay transitions that would lead to a counter-example that we never found by ourselves when we used the interactive simulator to explore the electrical system behavior.

Limitations: The model-checking tools we used was unable to produce the set of all counter-examples with a given number of failure events.

3. CONCLUDING REMARKS: SAFETY ARCHITECTURE PATTERNS

During ESACS we found out that libraries of components and safety requirement formulae were very useful at the modeling stage. We proposed to apply a similar approach at the validation stage by using a library of safety architecture patterns. A safety architecture pattern (Kehren et al. 2004a) describes a typical safety architecture as a triplication or a primary/backup. These pieces of architecture contain intrinsic safety properties and can be used to demonstrate the fulfillment of aircraft system safety requirements. We applied this approach to check the safety requirements of the electrical system. We compared the results with the classical approach. Nevertheless this new approach does not have the purpose to compete with the classical one but to bring more methods in some aircraft system development phases, especially the preliminary ones, for supporting the engineering judgement.

The certification process of the civil aircraft is supported by guidance and recommended practices provided in ARP4754 "Certification Considerations for Highly-Integrated or Complex Aircraft Systems". Amongst different guidelines, one of them is associated to the assignment of the Development Assurance Level (DAL) to items of an aircraft system architecture. The DAL assignment takes under consideration the safety repercussion of item failure scenarios (failure conditions) and different architecture features, such as redundancy, monitoring, or partitioning to eliminate or contain the degree to which an item contributes to a specific failure condition. Depending on these considerations, a DAL level is assigned to an item from E to A, reflecting the necessary quality effort during the aircraft/system/item development. The guidance is summarized under a table format that sorts the DAL assignment by different architecture features.

In particular, it is in a big interest to formalize the DAL assignment concern by using the safety pattern concept. By this way, model checking techniques can confirm automatically the full independence of item failures within an aircraft system architecture and bring at early aircraft design steps a model to guide the DAL assignment.

ACKNOWLEDGEMENT

The work described in this paper has been developed within the ESACS Project, a European sponsored project, G4RD-CT-2000-00361.

REFERENCES

A. Arnold, A. Griffault, G. Point, A. Rauzy. The AltaRica formalism for describing concurrent systems. Fundamenta Informaticae n°40, p109-124, 2000.

M. Bozzano et alter, ESACS: an integrated methodology for design and safety analysis of complex systems. ESREL 2003 European Safety and Reliability Conference, 2003.

P. Fenelon, J.A. McDermid, M. Nicholson, D.J. Pumfrey, Towards Integrated Safety Analysis and Design, ACM Computing Reviews, Vol. 2, No. 1, p. 21-32, 1994.

K.L. MacMillan. *Symbolic Model Checking.* Kluwer Academic Publishers, 1993, ISBN 0-7923-9380-5.

C. Kehren et alter, Architecture patterns for safe design, in proceedings of the first AAAF Conference on Complex and Safe System Engineering, 2004.

C. Kehren et alter, Advanced Multi-System Simulation Capabilities with AltaRica, in proceedings of the International System Safety Conference, 2004.

A. Rauzy. Mode automata and their compilation into fault trees. Reliability Engineering and System Safety, 2002.

IMPROVING CERTIFICATION CAPABILITY THROUGH AUTOMATIC CODE GENERATION

Neil Audsley, Iain Bate, Steven Crook-Dawkins, John McDermid

Department of Computer Science, University of York, York, UK

{neil | iain.bate | steve | john.mcdermid}@cs.york.ac.uk

Abstract: Automatic code generation is a process of deriving programs directly from a design representation. Recent initiatives such as Model Driven Architectures mean they are becoming an essential component of software engineering and many commercial tools now provide this capability. Whilst these tools provide greater flexibility and responsiveness in design, they are also largely unqualified with respect to extant safety standards. This paper presents a summary of investigations into the issues in using autocode generators in critical systems, primarily avionic systems.

Key words: autocode generators, safety, MDA

1. INTRODUCTION

Recent initiatives such as Model Driven Architectures mean they are becoming an essential component of software engineering and many commercial tools now provide this capability. However these are largely unqualified with respect to the safety domain. The obvious response to the use of unqualified tools such as code generators in high integrity development is to perform extended verification, yet for this to be effective, much of the complexity of the coding process that the tool has automated would re-appear within the verification stage. Such verification may require a detailed knowledge of the design of the tool and this is often not available with commercial tools. More crucially, the costs of verification would be repeated for each instance of code production eroding many of the benefits of automatic code generation. If a model of the automatic code generation process could be constructed, greater understanding of the process could be built up allowing arguments about safe translation to be constructed and evidence to be recovered. Given such a model, individual tools could be assessed on a one off basis for their ability to uphold the requirements of the model, or new tools could be developed to conform to the model. The contribution of this paper is to build up a framework for such models that would discharge the requirements for dependable code generation put forward by other authors:

In (1) Whalen and Heimdahl established five requirements for high integrity code generation, we will assess our model against these requirements:

1. Source and Target languages must be formally well-defined syntax and semantics.
2. The translation between a specification expressed in a source language and a program expressed in a target language must be formal and proven to uphold meaning of the specification.
3. Rigorous arguments must be provided to validate the translator and/or the generated code.
4. The implementation of the translator must be rigorously tested and treated as high assurance software.
5. Generated code must be well-structured, documented and traceable to the specification.

In this paper, the term Autocode refers to any piece of code generated from a tool rather than a hand coding process. The tools themselves are referred to as Autocode Generators or AGs.

2. OUTLINE OF APPROACH

There appears to be two ways to address the problem of arguing about the behaviour of an autocode generator:

1. Show that the AG itself can be verified to some definition of high integrity *across all instances* of its use as a one off argument, or
2. Verify the output of the AG *for each instance* of its use against a stable definition of performance.

The important difference between the two strategies is that the first would require an understanding of the internal structure of the AG, whereas the second would not. O'Halloran (2) argues that verifying an automated code generator is unlikely to be commercially viable.

Rather than attempting to formulate complex, fragile arguments that are directly related to individual, specific tool design or architecture, it would make more sense to reason formally about the mapping from a design notation to the corresponding program code.

A set of mappings is used to argue about the behaviour of the AG, rather than attempting to argue about its internal structure. The rationale behind this approach is that a guarantee (or specification, definition, etc.) of a component's behaviour can be expressed at least an order of magnitude simpler than the implemented device. This approach would also provide a rigourous basis on which to discharge Whalen and Heimdahl's requirements for high integrity code generation.

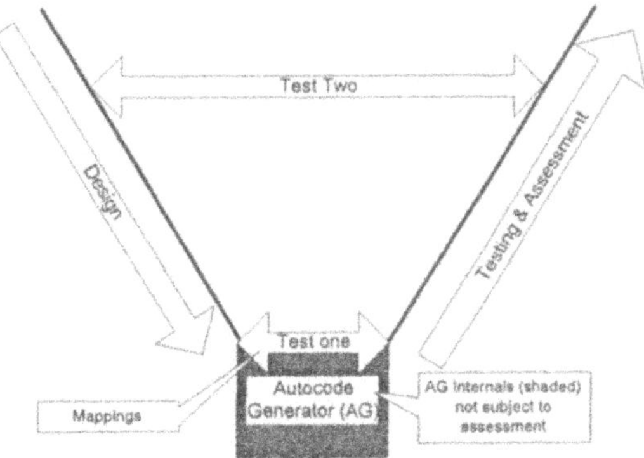

Figure 1. Isolating the Auto-code Generator

This mapping from design to code could be deployed through a two stage verification process. The first stage (Test one in Figure 1) is about the correctness of construction of the code by the AG as a refinement of the design. This test can be carried out by breaking down the input notation into basic components that map directly onto coding templates.

This approach also breaks down the proof into a set of arguments about each mapping, showing how the semantic meaning of the input construct is preserved in the corresponding code template. We believe this inductive or divide & conquer approach helps to alleviate O'Halloran's (2) concerns about the difficulty of verification through proof, by constraining each individual proof to only a single semantic concept.

It would be more cost effective to perform validation tests for safety requirements at a higher level of abstraction, as these tests can address performance and safety requirements directly (under test two). This separates the general problems of verifying of the AG from the specific problems of validating a given system against its requirements. This separation is important for (at least) three reasons:

1. Verification of the AG requires a different set of skills and tools to validation of the resulting code against performance and safety requirements.

2. Combining arguments about AG performance and System performance would make it impossible to disengage performance and safety claims from specific AG technologies. This would frustrate efforts to improve general capability for using AG tools, making AG use a project concern rather than a common concern across all developments.

3. Certification bodies will require evidence that the AG (and other similar development tools) have not introduced faults. This is in addition to a system level argument showing that overall risk is acceptable. The two issues are distinct, and arguments will be more compelling if they are addressed explicitly.

Considering the difference between safety and correctness reinforces these points. The concept of safety is concerned with risks of deploying a system within the context of specific environment (3). The mappings in Figure 1 only provide information about how the AG operates they do not present any claims that it is safe to use the AG or its output in context. Referring back to Figure 1, test one is about correctness; test two about safety.

It is not possible to make a **safety** argument for an AG out of context, as there is no way to gain a full understanding of the system hazards without this context. It would only be possible to verify the use of the AG against a common coding standard for a given design notation outside of a specific system context.

For AGs provided as COTS[1] tools by a third party supplier there may be limited information available to construct a set of mappings that define the coding standard. It may be possible to construct the mappings based on the anticipated behaviour of the AG then observe actual performance relative to these mappings. If the AG fails to uphold all the mappings, then the limitations of this AG in a specific context can be recorded and perhaps addressed elsewhere in the development process.

The offer made by some tool vendors of certification kits for the use of some AG tools may help in this regard. Such kits amount to a certificate from a standards-setting body showing conformance to specific standards and often permit access to specific evidence. However such kits provide little improvement in the capability of the development process to accommodate automatic code generation. As part of a study undertaken by Praxis and QinetiQ on COTS software, certificates for Real Time Operating Systems were described as usually insufficient due to the absence of any evidence from the design process (4). Rather than attempting to specify a

[1] COTS=Commercial off the Shelf - tools provided on a commercial basis not normally intended for safety critical development.

perfect AG, suitable for safety critical use, it is necessary to verify the performance of an AG in context.

Having defined our basic approach, the next section considers how feasible this approach is in the context of tools that must provide a useful service.

3. PROBLEMS WITH EXISTING TOOLS

The need to ensure a predictable process would motivate the use of mappings that are as simple and straightforward as possible - resulting in the use of a design language very similar to programming code. Yet such pseudo code would offer little to enable or encourage systems level safety analysis. Therefore any AG would need to trade off the need to generate correct code with the need to accommodate an appropriate design metaphor or language. This trade off is illustrated in Figure 2

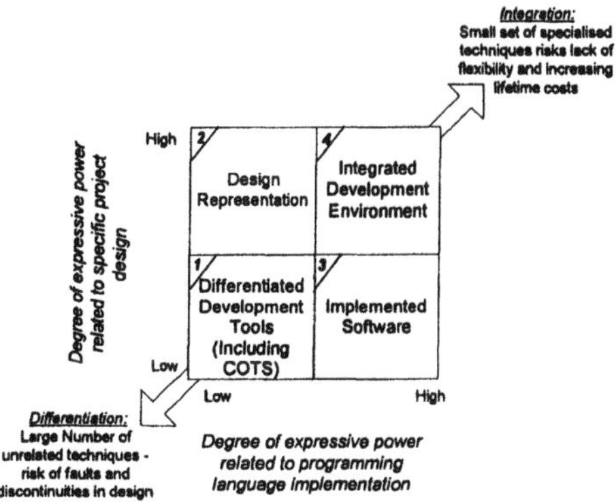

Figure 2. Trade off between different types of expressive power

There are four broad classes of trade off for the AG:

3.1 Differentiated Development Tools: Many of the tools are designed around a specific design methodology, such as UML or statecharts that are general modeling approaches. Whilst there is support for proofs of correctness and behavioural analysis through animation, these methodologies don't necessarily lend themselves to more investigative safety analysis techniques. They may require the support of additional tools to generate code, and are usually black box devices that are difficult to customize to specific requirements.

3.2 Design Representation: Within this group would be tools and techniques that are primarily concerned with modeling the project or system to be implemented. Examples would include the use of HAZOPS[2] on piping diagrams in the chemical industry. These tools help to influence safe design, but provide little to guide code generation.

3.3 Implemented Software: These are tools are techniques primarily associated with supporting implementation of software. Tools such as software fault trees (SFTA) would fall into this category. They offer limited facilities for manipulation of the design, their focus being on the construction of the code itself.

3.4 Integrated Development Environments: These devices provide a total translation solution for a small range of applications, such as aircraft cockpit systems. If each application area used different tools and methodologies, then our ability to construct a safety argument across several systems would be compromised by the need for a different argument pattern for each area.

Whilst it would be possible to develop a process for automatic generation of code using any of these tool types, none would represent a general approach to provide sufficient design expression whilst generating verifiable code. This is because they tend to specialize in a particular approach or technology rather than addressing the whole problem of translating across the matrix from project and design concerns to implementation concerns.

Relating this back to Whalen and Heimdhal's original five requirements, the table below provides (at a very broad level) the suitability of each tool to high integrity code generation:

	R1	R2	R3	R4	R5	R6*
Differentiated Tools	😐	😐	☹	☹	😐	☺
Design Representations	☺	😐	😐	☹	☹	☹
Implemented software	☺	☺	☺	😐	😐	☹
Development Environment	😐	☹	😐	☹	😐	☺

Table 1: Broad assessment of suitability using Whalen & Heimdahl's requirements

* *Additional requirement added - see point (2) below*

Where:

☺: This type of translator is ideally suited to discharge the requirement

😐: This type of translator could be specialized to discharge the requirement

☹: Discharging this requirement with this type of translator may not be feasible, either economically or technically.

The key points from this analysis are:

(1) Design representations may emphasize syntax and semantics of a design representation (R1), but economic viability may prevent rigorous

[2] HAZOPS – HAZard and OPerability Studies. This is a systematic method for assessing models against a number of anticipated failure modes, and was first described by Trevor Kletz (5)

analysis (R3, R4) and code quality (R5) would be a secondary concern for such tools

(2) Implemented software would (unsurprisingly) meet many of the requirements, but the rigour (R3,R4) of tools (such as compilers) that manipulate code remains difficult to reason about, and doesn't guarantee well structured code. The other obvious problem is that these tools offer little advantage because they do not support a design method to help derive code, and therefore offer little advantage over conventional technology. To address this, an additional requirement (R6) is suggested for AG's such that they must provide sufficient expressive power to make the translation useful.

(3) Finally, the development environment would perform many complex translations that would be difficult to reason about (R2). This additional complexity making rigourous testing (R4) infeasible.

The implication of this is that no single type of tool addresses all six requirements. A more general approach is required which takes on board all six requirements within the architecture of the AG. The next section provides discussion of the possible architectures that could be used, and the pros and cons of each.

4. REVIEW OF ARCHITECTURES

Three alternative approaches to a basic architecture for an AG have been put forward in (8). In Table 2 these approaches are identified and fitted into the general groups of tools proposed earlier.

Type of Mappings	**Type of Tool supported (from Figure 2)**
Black Box	Differentiated tools or development environment
Mapping Driven, Single Pass	Design Representations **or** Implemented Software
Mapping driven; Multiple Pass	Both design representation **and** implemented software

Table 2: Comparison between architectures and tool types

The black box AGs can only provide a specific solution to the translation and therefore would be restricted to differentiated tools or development environments, neither provides the insight required to formalize the translation rigorously as required by Whalen and Heimdhal (see table 1) and aren't adaptable to specific development requirements or coding standards.

The mapping driven, single pass (MDSP) AG breaks down the complexity of translation in one dimension by addressing the *breath* of the conversion process. With this white box approach it does not matter how many constructs are in the input or output languages – as each will have its own mapping. However, tools based on this architecture cannot unpack complex (or deep) structures. The multiple pass architecture (MDMP) takes the next step, breaking down the *depth* as well as the *breadth* of the conversion process. The multiple passes allow the conversion of expressive power from project design concerns to implementation concerns to be controlled in a number of stages, each of which can be defined and verified. It therefore provides the only architecture to meet both the formal rigour required by Whalen and Heimdahl, whilst retaining the expressive power required for a useful AG tool.

Figure 3 illustrates the approach, showing how three passes (or, tiers) of mappings could be used to achieve translation, each set of mappings achieving a separate aspect of the process.

The different passes provide a way to combine the design representation tools with the implemented software tools, by reasoning about each tool as implementing as a separate set of mappings, which can be directly verified. This means that the translation problem is broken into meaningful steps instead attempting to describe the entire translation from design to code in one single, large, step.

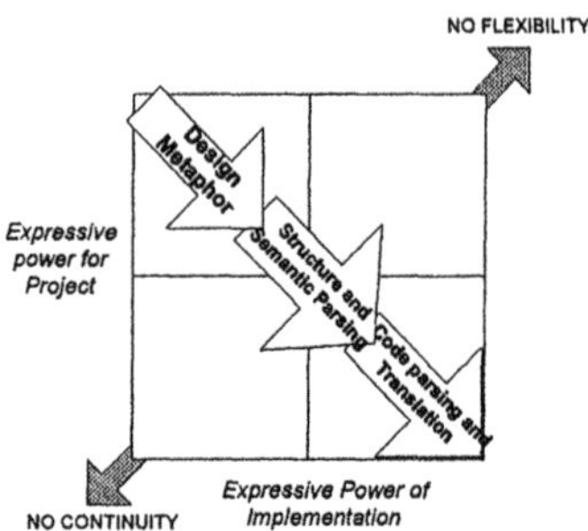

Figure 3. Controlling the change in emphasis from design focus to implementation focus

This builds a tool chain able to deliver on the six requirements without being compromised by the need for one tool to perform the whole job. This approach also has the benefit that the intermediate representation passed between each tool is a model of the system that can be stored in a standard recognized form, such as UML, or XML - preventing the need to lock in to specific tools or specific versions of those tools. One final point is that the application of mappings to refine the model from one stage to the next permits faults to be identified as soon as they occur, setting the code generator to a fail safe state that prevent anomalies propagating.

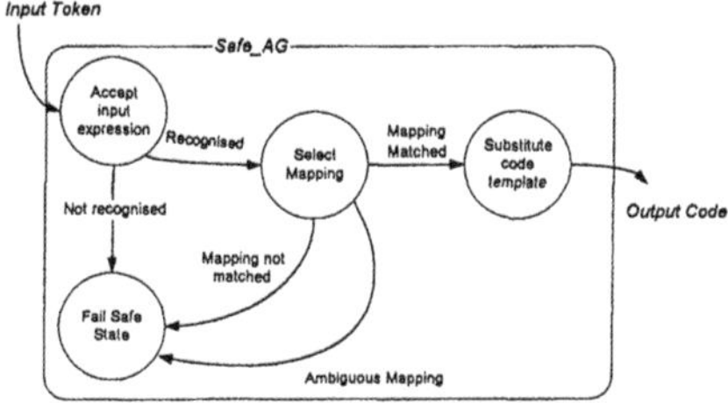

Figure 4. Simple fail safe approach to implementing mappings

This is a structured approach and is amenable to structured argument and/or proof. Using the Goal Structuring Notation or GSN (6) we have been able to argue about a simple AG. GSN allows arguments to be built up by systemically decomposing claims down to a level at which the lower level claims can be discharged by direct reference to evidence. This method of constructing arguments parallels directly the decomposition of the translation process into a set of mappings that can be verified directly. Note however, this is not a safety argument, as this can only be constructed in the specific deployment context. It is merely a argument that the AG has meet the requirements of a given coding standard defined by the tiers of mappings. Putting this another way, it is an argument that discharges test 1 in Figure 1, but only provides support for the broader safety argument required to discharge test 2. Other work performed by the authors has presented the arguments generated and considered how the resulting evidence needed can be generated (7).

5. CONCLUSIONS

The traditional arguments against the use of AGs in high integrity developments are mainly relevant to one specific type of AG, the black box, popularised by the use of COTS products with autocode facilities. We concur with Whalen and Heimdahl that rigorous arguments and formal definitions will be required in any dependable autocode technology.

A useful AG must have the ability to manage the shift in expressive power from design-centered tools to implementation tools. Design tools must have the flexibility to elicit system design issues, whilst the implementation tool must be a predictable model of a defined language or a specific platform. We identified four different types of tool that are available and discovered that no single tool architecture meets the dual requirements of facilitating rigorous proof whilst providing a translation powerful enough to be useful.

A mapping driven, multiple pass AG was suggested that systematically decomposes the translation process in both the *breadth of the language* through the use of mappings and *depth* through the use of multiple passes. The approach was recognized as being the most appropriate for use in critical systems. This decomposition approach mirrors very closely the approach taken to build up safety arguments, and makes the architecture amenable to rigorous analysis. Most crucially, it allows a code generation to be seen as the refinement of a model, using a tool chain which can be specified by mappings, and rigorously analysed and assessed.

6. REFERENCES

(1) Whalen M W, Heimdhal Mats P.E., On the Requirements of High-Integrity Code Generation, Proceedings of the Fourth High Assurance in Systems Engineering Workshop, Washington DC, November 1999

(2) O'Halloran C Issues for the automatic generation of safety critical software, Proceedings of the Fifteenth International IEEE Conference on Automated Software Engineering (ASE 2000), France, September 2000

(3) RTCA and EUROCAE, Software Considerations in Airborne Systems and Equipment Certification, Radio Technical Commission for Aeronautics RTCA DO178B/EUROCAE ED 12B, 1993

(4) Murray T, Simpson A COTS Software for High Integrity Applications, 36th Seminar of the Safety Critical Systems Club COTS & SOUP: Current thinking and Work In Progress , IEE London, April 5th 2001.

(5) Kletz, T. *Hazop and Hazan : Identifying and Assessing Process Industry Hazards*, Institute of Chemical Engineers, 3rd Edition, 1992.

(6) Kelly, T. P. Arguing Safety - A Systematic Approach to Managing Safety Cases, DPhil Thesis, Department of Computer Science, University of York, UK, YCST 99/05, September 1998

(7) Bate I, Audsley N, Crook-Dawkins S, Automatic Code Generation for Airborne Systems – the Next Generation of Software Productivity Tools, Proceedings of IEEE Aerospace Conference, 11-19, 2003.

EARLY VALIDATION OF REQUIREMENTS

A Case Study Using Formal Methods

Steven P. Miller
Rockwell Collins, Inc.
spmiller@rockwellcollins.com

Mats P. E. Heimdahl
Department of Computer Science & Engineering, University of Minnesota
heimdahl@cs.umn.edu

Abstract This paper describes a case study conducted to determine if formal methods could be used to validate system requirements early in the lifecycle at reasonable cost. Several hundred requirements for the mode logic of a typical Flight Guidance System were captured as natural language "shall" statements. A formal model of the mode logic was written in the RSML^{-e} language and translated into the NuSMV model checker and the PVS theorem prover using translators developed as part of the project. Each "shall" statement was manually translated into a NuSMV or PVS property and proven using these tools.

1. Introduction

Incomplete, inaccurate, ambiguous, and volatile requirements have plagued the software industry since its inception. The avionics industry has long recognized the need for better requirements, and has spearheaded the development of several methodologies for requirements specification, including SCR [6], CoRE [4], RSML [7], and even Statecharts [5]. Despite this legacy, the requirements for most avionics systems are still specified using a combination of natural language and informal diagrams.

This paper describes a case study conducted by the Advanced Technology Center of Rockwell Collins, the Critical Systems Research Group at the University of Minnesota, and the NASA Langley Research Center to determine

This project was partially funded by the NASA Langley Research Center under contract NCC-01001 of the Aviation Safety Program how far formal analysis could be pushed in an industrial example [9]. In this study, a model of the mode logic of a Flight Guidance System [1] was specified in the RSML^{-e} notation [11]. Translators were developed from RSML^{-e} to the NuSMV model checker [1] and the PVS theorem prover [10, 2]. These tools were then used to verify several hundred properties of the RSML^{-e} model. In the process, several errors were discovered and corrected in the original RSML^{-e} model.

The results of this study demonstrate that formal models can be written for real problems using notations acceptable to practicing engineers, and that formal analysis tools have matured to the point where they can be efficiently used to find errors before implementation.

2. Requirements Modeling

One of our first steps was to create a formal model of the black box behavior of our representative Flight Guidance System (FGS). The internal structure of a FGS can be broken down into the mode logic and the flight control laws. The flight control laws accept information about the aircraft's current and desired state and compute the pitch and roll guidance commands. The mode logic determines which lateral and vertical modes are armed and active at any given time and which flight control laws are generating guidance commands.

The formal model of the FGS was written in the RSML^{-e} language. When completed, it consisted of 41 input variables, 16 small, tightly synchronized hierarchical finite state machines, 122 macro or function definitions, 29 output values, and was roughly 160 pages long. A detailed description of the model and its simulation environment is available in [8].

In the course of building the RSML^{-e} model, we found ourselves going back and modifying the original shall statements. Sometimes, they were just wrong. More often, their organization needed to be changed to provide clear traceability to the model. Gradually, we realized that as we revised and reorganized the shall statements we produced clearer and improved description of the system. Maintaining even a coarse mapping between the shall statements and the RSML^{-e} model forced us to be more precise in writing down the shall statements.

3. Model Checking

While the FGS model could be directly translated to NuSMV using the translator developed for this project [3], the translated specification was not immediately suitable for model-checking with NuSMV due to the presence of

[1]While representative of the complexity of a typical system, this example did not desribed an actual fielded product.

a small number of integer variables. To deal with this, we abstracted the model by hand by moving comparisons involving these variables (e.g., $Altitude > PreSelectAlt + AltCapBias$) into a different part of the specification and inputting the Boolean results directly into the model. Since there were only a few such computations, this took only a few hours to implement and did not significantly alter the specification. These changes reduced the state space enough that we could check almost any property of the mode logic with the NuSMV model checker in a matter of minutes.

At first, we focused on showing that our model satisfied the safety properties we had identified through a hazard analysis and fault tree analysis [12]. However, it quickly became apparent that all of the original requirements, not just the safety properties, could be stated in CTL. As a result, we extended our verification to include all the shall statements captured during elicitation.

Our approach was to state each requirement as a CTL property over the translated model. Since there was a close correspondence between names in the RSML^{-e} model and the NuSMV model, this quickly became routine and most of the requirements could be translated by hand into CTL in a few minutes. All of the requirements could be specified with only two CTL formats. The first was simply a safety constraint that had to be maintained by all reachable states. The second was a constraint over a state and all possible next states. For example, the requirement *If the onside FD cues are off, the onside FD cues shall be displayed when the AP is engaged* was translated into the CTL property `AG((!Onside_FD_On & !Is_AP_Engaged)-> AX(Is_AP_Engaged -> Onside_FD_On))`.

Only these two formats were needed, largely because RSML^{-e} is a synchronous language in which each transition to the next system state is computed in a single atomic step. All the properties we were interested in could be stated as simple safety properties over a single state, or as a relationship describing how the system changed in a single step. If we had wanted to verify liveness properties, or if portions of the model had been allowed to evolve asynchronously, other temporal operators would have also have been needed.

Ultimately, all 281 properties originally stated informally in English were translated into CTL and checked using the NuSMV model checker. All 281 properties could be verified on a 2GHz Pentium 4 processor running Linux in less than an hour.

4. Errors Found Through Model Checking

Use of the model checker produced counter examples revealing several errors in the RSML^{-e} model of the mode logic that had not been discovered through simulation. One entire class of errors was discovered that involved more than one input event arriving at the same time. This could occur for a variety of reasons. For example, the pilot might press a switch at the same time the system captured a navigation source. Occasionally, these combinations would drive the model into an unsafe state.

To deal with this issue, we chose to define a prioritization on the input events so that higher priority events would supercede lower priority events. In course of developing this prioritization, we realized that it was possible for some combinations of events to be processed in the same step. For example, an input that changed the active lateral mode could often (but not always) be processed in the same step as an input that changed the active vertical mode. In other words, a partial rather than a total order of the input events was acceptable. Since we could check both the safety and functional properties of the specification with NuSMV, we felt confident that the specified behavior was correct. However, without the power of formal verification, we would never have been able to convince ourselves that the safety properties of the system were still met when such multiple input events were allowed.

5. Theorem Proving

We had also developed a translator to the PVS theorem prover and wanted to determine the extent of its usefulness. In contrast to model checkers, theorem provers apply rules of inference to a specification in order to derive new properties of interest. Theorem provers are generally considered harder to use than model checkers, requiring more expertise on the part of the user. However, theorem provers are not limited by the size of the state space. This makes them useful for problem domains that are not amenable to verification by model checking.

We started by using PVS to verify some of the properties already confirmed using NuSMV. In the course of completing the proofs, it became clear that we needed to define and prove many simple properties of the FGS that could be used as automatic rewrite rules by PVS. This automated and simplified the more complex proofs we were interested in. As these libraries evolved, we realized that many of these properties, as well as several useful PVS strategies (scripts defining sequences of prover commands) could have been automatically produced by the translator. These were identified as enhancements for future versions of the translator.

With this infrastructure in place, some proofs could be constructed in less than an hour. Others took several hours or even days, usually because they involved proving many other properties as intermediate lemmas. One surprise was that users proficient in PVS but unfamiliar with the FGS could usually complete a proof as quickly as someone familiar with the FGS. In fact, most of the proofs were completed by a graduate student with no avionics experience. The general process was to break the desired property down by case splits until a simple ASSERT or GRIND command could complete that branch of the proof tree. The structure of the proofs naturally reversed the dependency ordering defined in the RSML^{-e} specification. Many of the proofs could be simplified by introducing lemmas describing how intermediate values in the dependency graph changed, but identifying such lemmas seemed to require a sound understanding the FGS mode logic. As we gained experience, we started using the dependency map produced by the RSML^{-e} toolset to guide us in identifying these lemmas.

Another surprise was that while the proofs might take hours to construct, they usually executed in less than twenty seconds. This was significant since the time taken to prove similar properties using the NuSMV model checker had grown steadily with the size of the model. If the model had grown much larger, it is possible that the time to verify a property using model checking might have become prohibitive. The time required to run the PVS proofs seemed much less sensitive to the size of the model.

6. Conclusions and Future Directions

We have described how a model of the requirements for the mode logic of a Flight Guidance System was created in the RSML^{-e} language from an initial set of requirements stated as shall statements written in English. Translators were used to automatically generate equivalent models of the mode logic in the NuSMV model checker and the PVS theorem prover. The original shall statements were then hand translated into properties over these models and proven to hold over these models.

The process of creating the RSML^{-e} model improved the informal requirements, and the process of proving the formal properties found errors in both the original requirements and the RSML^{-e} model. The ease with which these properties were verified leads us to conclude that formal methods tools are finally maturing to the point where they can be profitably used on industrial sized problems.

Several directions exist for further work. Stronger abstraction techniques are needed to increase the classes of problems that can be verified using model checkers. Better libraries and proof strategies are needed to make theorem proving less labor intensive. More work also needs to be done to identify proof strategies and properties that can be automatically generated from the model. Since many systems consist of synchronous components connected by asynchronous buses, work needs to be done to determine how properties that span models connected by asynchronous channels can be verified. Perhaps most important, these formal verification tools need to used on real problems with commercially supported modeling tools such as SCADE, Esterel, and Simulink.

Acknowledgments

The authors wish to acknowledge the ongoing support of this work by Ricky Butler, Kelly Hayhurst, and Celeste Bellcastro of the NASA Langley Research Center, and the efforts of Alan Tribble and Michael Whalen of Rockwell Collins and Anjali Joshi, Yunja Choi, Sanjai Rayadurgam, George Devaraj, and Dan O'Brien of the University of Minnesota for their efforts in developing this technology.

References

[1] Anonymous. NuSMV: A New Symbolic Model Checking, 2004. http://nusmv.irst.itc.it/.

[2] Anonymous. PVS home page, 2004. http://www.csl.sri.com/projects/pvs.

[3] Yunja Choi and Mats Heimdahl. Model checking RSML^{-e} requirements. In *Proceedings of the 7th IEEE/IEICE International Symposium on High Assurance Systems Engineering*, October 2002.

[4] S. Faulk, J. Brackett, P. Ward, and J Kirby, Jr. The CoRE method for real-time requirements. *IEEE Software*, 9(5):22–33, September 1992.

[5] David Harel and Amnon Naamad. The STATEMATE semantics of statecharts. *ACM Transactions of Software Engineering and Methodology*, 5(4):293 – 333, October 1996.

[6] C.L. Heitmeyer, R.D. Jeffords, and B.G. Labaw. Automated consistency checking of requirements specifications. *ACM Transactions on Software Engineering and Methodology*, 5(3):231–261, July 1996.

[7] N.G. Leveson, M.P.E. Heimdahl, H. Hildreth, and J.D. Reese. Requirements Specification for Process-Control Systems. *IEEE Transactions on Software Engineering*, 20(9):684–706, September 1994.

[8] S. Miller, A. Tribble, T. Carlson, and E. Danielson. Flight guidance system requirements specification. Technical Report CR-2003-212426, NASA Langley Research Center, June 2003. Available at http://techreports.larc.nasa.gov/ltrs/refer/2003/cr/NASA-2003-cr212426.refer.html.

[9] Steven P. Miller, Alan C. Tribble, and Mats Per Erik Heimdahl. Proving the shalls. In Keijiro Araki, Stefania Gnesi, and Dino Mandrioli, editors, *Proceedigns of the International Symposium of Formal Methods Europe (FME 2003)*, volume 2805 of *Lecture Notes in Computer Science*, pages 75–93, Pisa, Italy, September 2003. Springer.

[10] S. Owre, J. Rushby, N. Shankar, and F. von Henke. Formal verification for fault-tolerant architectures: Prolegomena to the design of PVS. *IEEE Transactions on Software Engineering*, 21(2), February 1995.

[11] Jeffrey M. Thompson, Mats P.E. Heimdahl, and Steven P. Miller. Specification based prototyping for embedded systems. In *Seventh ACM SIGSOFT Symposium on the Foundations on Software Engineering*, number 1687 in LNCS, pages 163–179, September 1999.

[12] A. Tribble, D. Lempia, and S. Miller. Software safety analysis of a flight guidance system. In *Proceedings of the 21st Digital Avionics Systems Conference (DASC'02)*, Irvine, CA, October 2002.

PROOF OF PROPERTIES IN AVIONICS.

Jean Souyris (jean.souyris@airbus.com)

Denis Favre-Félix (denis.favre-felix@airbus.com)
Airbus France

Abstract: This paper presents the industrial use of a program proof method based on CAVEAT (C program prover developed by the commissariat à l'énergie atomique) in the verification process of a safety critical avionics program.

Key words: Proof of properties – Avionics program – Formal method - Unit Verification – Unit Testing – DO 178B

1. INTRODUCTION

Avionics programs size and complexity ever increase. This affects the most critical ones, like flight control programs, as well. Avionics programs must conform DO178B standard, leading to spend about 60 % of the development time in verification, for the most critical of them (level A). Verification activities consist of readings, intellectual (human) analyses and test.

In the 'ever increasing' context mentioned above, the cost of all kinds of verification tends to get higher, in order to keep the dependability of the programs at the same (high) level.

The main concern is about tests. Indeed, most of the verification time is spent in testing and one can predict a dramatic augmentation of the test effort if nothing is done, specially for critical avionics programs. The main concern, here, is about the coverage of the tests: how to face the augmentation of complexity by this non exhaustive verification technique?

For at least partially compensate the above drawbacks, Airbus decided to introduce tool-aided static analysis techniques into its avionics verification workbench. The objective is the availability of static analyzers for an effective industrial usage, via the participation in R&D projects together with academic laboratories and tool makers.

Examples of static analyzers ready for an industrial usage or actually used are: AbsInt's Stackanalyzers ; AbsInt's aiT (Worst Case Execution Time) analyzers, ASTREE (proof of absence of Run Time Errors) from Ecole normale supérieure (Paris, rue d'Ulm) and CAVEAT from the Commissariat à l'énergie atomique, the latter being the topic of the rest of this chapter.

Indeed, this chapter reports the industrial usage of a program proof method based on CAVEAT, from the CEA. It is structured as follows: section 2. briefly describes CAVEAT; section 3. presents the development process before using CAVEAT and shows where CAVEAT has been introduced; section 4. describes the method of using CAVEAT; section 5. is the actual experience report; section 6. concludes.

2. CAVEAT

2.1 Features

Caveat is a static analyzer which aims at automatically deriving properties (property synthesis) from a C program and proving properties on this program. These properties are expressed in a first order predicate language.

Caveat is developed by the Commissariat à l'énergie atomique (CEA) partly with the financial support of Airbus France via R&D funding (French or EU).

Airbus France's effort on Caveat has consisted in making Caveat able to analyze the targeted avionics applications. As these applications, like most of embedded real time programs, have peculiar characteristics like hardware handling, some extensions of the subset of the C language accepted by Caveat have been developed. On another hand, Caveat's automatic proof capabilities have been extended for at least giving good "automaticity rate" on the targeted applications.

Caveat takes C source files as inputs and first automatically computes properties relative to control and data flows. In particular, caveat computes the **data dependencies** at C function level. The result of this computation is the actual interface of each C routine, which is something not obvious from the C prototype of a function. Amongst the information automatically extracted from the sources during the data dependencies analysis one finds, for each C function encountered in the source files the list all the operands of the function: implicit operands, i.e. global variables, and explicit operands, i.e., those declared in the function prototypes; for each operand, the way it is used: In, Out or In/Out, respectively for read only, write only and read/write operands; the dependences between the operands: it is, for each Out or In/Out operand, the list of In and In/Out operand it depends on.

Proof of user-specified properties. Once the initial automatic analysis is completed (see section 2.1.1), Caveat is ready for input of properties by the user. Most of these properties are to be proved by the tool, in particular the *Post* property. *Post* stands for 'Post-condition', which means that the user wants the property of that type to hold at the end of a particular C function. Then Caveat is asked to prove the Post-condition. A success of this attempt to prove the Post-condition means that the latter holds, a failure have two possible reasons: first it might be that Caveat failed to prove a correct property; on the other hand, Caveat failed two prove a property which does not hold. In both cases, the user must analyze the first order predicate Caveat returns. Now it is up to the user to complete the proof process by using the Interactive Predicate Transformer feature of Caveat This feature allows the user to process the result predicate either to complete the proof or to find the reason why the proof is impossible to make, i.e., the property does not hold.

C language Restrictions: Caveat complains when, in the source code it analyses, it finds things like recursion, backward goto statements, pointers on functions, and other situations which are usually not allowed in critical avionics applications. It is the case of the industrial usage of Caveat reported in this paper.

Possible applications of Caveat. Basically, Caveat may be used to the following usual verification of avionics programs: Control and data flow verification, Unit Verification, Integration Verification and safety analyses.

2.2 First industrial application: Unit Proving

First target. For a first application of Caveat Airbus chose the safety test part of the program of the Flight Control and Guidance Unit of the A380. This onboard computer embeds the primary function of the Fly-by-wire system.

The interest of getting started with the industrial use of Caveat on this safety test program is twofold: firstly, this about 40,000 lines of code program is representative of a certain number of safety critical avionics programs; secondly, the (existing) verification process of its predecessors (previous safety test programs) was best suited for the substitution of Unit Testing by Unit Proving.

First way of using Caveat. Section 2.1 listed the different kinds of verification possibly addressable by Caveat.

As the main goal of applying formal verification techniques is to reduce the cost of the verification without reducing its quality, Airbus France chose to apply Caveat to the Data flow and Unit Verification activities.

Indeed, in the traditional approach, Data flow analysis is mostly an intellectual activity, whereas Unit Testing, in spite of being partially automated, is costly in terms of time spent in identifying and programming the test cases. About the costs of Unit Testing, one must also consider the specialized hardware means (Unit test must be realistic).

In this context the choice of Unit Proving, among the different potential usages of Caveat is motivated by:

- the high degree of automation of the proofs if the analysis is performed per function;
- the fact that this replacement, i.e., Unit Testing by Unit Proving, does not affect the DO178B conforming verification process (DO178B (1992) does not really know about program proofs).

3. FROM UNIT TESTING TO UNIT PROVING

3.1 DO178B conforming development process (briefly)

The development of an avionics program must conform to DO178B. All aspects of the development are constrained by this standard.

Amongst all the activities defined by DO178B, the ones directly involved in the production of the program are: specification, design and coding. Each of them must be verified by activities also impacted by DO 178B. The kind of verification activities promoted/accepted explicitly by DO178B are: readings for checking that rules are actually applied, intellectual analyses and tests. Program proofs are only mentioned.

From the specification of the program, called High Level Requirements, the architecture (dynamic and static) and the Low Level Requirements are derived. The dynamic architecture deals with the temporal behavior of the program and static architecture consist of the decomposition of the entities defined previously into a set of modules/routines whose interaction implements the High Level Requirements. The per routine requirements (for coding of the routine) are then produced, there are called: Low Level Requirements (LLR).

Then the code of each module/routine is written, it is the implementation of the Low Level Requirements.

A first important – sometimes the major – verification activity of safety critical avionics programs consist in checking the code of a routine against its Low Level Requirements.

3.2 Verification of the LLR by Unit Testing.

In the development process of the predecessors of the program chosen for the first application of Caveat, i.e., the safety test program of a Fly-by-Wire application) the legacy technique for verifying the Low Level Requirements is: Unit Testing. This technique consists in finding the best possible test cases (for a maximum coverage), writing test programs in the test specification language of a test automation tool, executing the tests on representative hardware and exploiting the results. The art of "finding the best possible test cases" is strongly constrained by DO178B.

3.3 Unit Proving LLR in a DO178B conforming process

The advantages of using Caveat for Unit Verification have been stated in section 2.3.2.

On the other hand, using a proof technique has some drawbacks with respect to the test-by-execution. The main concern is the fact that during a proof campaign, the actual binary code of a routine is not executed on representative - or, better, real - avionics hardware. Moreover, the proofs by Caveat are performed at source level, i.e., before compilation.

Consequently, complementary analyses and/or verifications are mandatory for demonstrating that the underlying verification objectives of the DO178B are fulfilled.

Nevertheless, the advantages of the Caveat-based proof method in terms of coverage as well as from the industrial point of view (the Low Level Requirements are directly used in the proof process whereas testing requires a costly identification of test cases and test program writing) are superior to the above mentioned drawbacks.

4. A DEDICATED METHOD

Unit Proving mainly impacts two DO178B conforming activities significantly: the production of the Low Level Requirements and the verification of these LLR.

At design time, once the static architecture has been defined, one gets a set of modules and routines whose interfaces are precisely specified. Next step is to write the LLR for each routine. These LLR mainly specify all possible behaviors of each routine. With Unit Proving, these LLR are formalized in the first order predicate language of Caveat. The properties to be produced must specify all possible input/output relations, the control flow within the routine and the interface with the called routines.

In order to write complete Low Level Requirements with respect to the High Level Requirements as well as properties which allow control flow verification, categories of properties have been defined: they are the main features of the guideline property writers must follow when they write the Low Level requirements of each routine. One of these categories is made of the so called "execution conditions" which defines relations on the inputs of a routine. These relations are the complete set of conditions which distinguish the different behaviors of the routine. A direct consequence is that the union of the subsets of all combinations of input values defined by these "execution conditions" must be the set of all possible combinations of input values.

Proof activity: Beyond the notion of exhaustivity of the verification compared to testing, a great advantage of "à la Caveat" Unit Proving is the high degree of automation of the proof activity, once the properties have been written. If algorithms have the – reduced - complexity generally admitted in safety critical avionics programs, most of the properties are proved automatically, possibly after correction of bugs in the code. Some of the properties which are not basically proved by Caveat automatically, are actually proved thanks to user-heuristics written in the script language of Caveat . The remaining properties are proved interactively under control of the Interactive Predicate Transformer of Caveat.

5. EXPERIENCE REPORT

5.1 Formalized Low Level Requirements production

The use of a formal method has great positive impact on the software design development. First of all, the property writing leads to more precise and non-ambiguous Low Level Requirements thanks to the use of a formal language.

Besides, the design guideline clearly identifies the different characteristics of a function, which should be covered by a set of properties. This categorization makes easier the way to reach the completeness of a design. In particular, some properties have to check the completeness of the execution conditions defined for a function. These properties increases in great proportion the confident we have in the completeness of the decision tree of a function.

The number of properties and the complexity of each property (in terms of writing efforts and number of operands) are a well-confident criteria in the "testability" of a function : as the properties represent the "proof plan" of the function, we can determine earlier in the software lifecycle if a function is provable or not.

Since this is the first time a formal language is used for designing functions, it was decided to keep on writing pseudo-code description of the function behaviors in order to make easier the coding phase.

Current statistics :
152 functions designed
2489 properties written
=> 16 properties per function

5.2 Proof process

One of the main objectives relative to the proof process was to automate the process as far as possible. Scripts have been developed in order to automate :

- the creation of a CAVEAT project (which include C-source file to be proved and C-source files simulating the called functions),
- the insertion of the properties,
- the addition of user-heuristics (in order to terminate automatically certain properties)
- the proof of the properties,

- the generation of a result file,
- the generation of a dataflow control file from the CAVEAT analysis of the C-source file.

User heuristics have been developed in order to automate actions under the Caveat Interactive Predicate Transformer and make easier the proof of properties. These heuristics are adapted to very specific situations, which often concern loop processing. For instance, :

- particularization of a high level quantifier into all the following low-level quantifiers
- decomposition of a quantifier in a (Min:Max) enumeration

From an industrial point of view, another advantage of the formal verification method consists in the fact that no specific hardware material is required. No test panel needs to be immobilized during the proof process.

5.3 Proofs

Current statistics :
2489 properties written
89% properties proved :

- 60 properties proved by means of heuristics or interactive manipulations (3%)

11% properties not proved :

- Syntaxes errors not yet corrected
- CAVEAT tools to be improved
- Interactive proof termination to be done
- Tools limitations

5.4 Conclusion

In comparison with a traditional software design development, the use of a formal proof method implies greater effort during the design phase. But this "waste of time" is largely compensated during the verification phase. A gain of 10 to 15 % is finally reached over the design/coding/unitary verification phases.

Furthermore, the exhaustivity of the proof verification increases the confidence in the coverage of the unitary verification.

6. CONCLUSION

This paper presented how the potentialities mentioned in [Randimbivololona et al., 1999] became effective in practice.

In the future, the use of Caveat will be extended to other avionics programs as well as the way of using it will go beyond Unit Verification: towards Integration Verification.

7. REFERENCES

Randimbivololona, F., Souyris, J., Baudin, P., Pacalet, A., Raguideau, J., and Schoen, D., (1999). Applying formal proof techniques to avionics software : A pragmatic approach. In Wing, J.M, Woodcock, J., and Davies, J., editors, *Proceedings of the World Congress on Formal Methods in the Development of Computing Systems*, FM'99, volume II of *Toulouse, France, Lecture Notes in Computer Science 1709*, pages 1798-1815. Springer.

Topic 8

The Convergence of Bio-Info-Nano-Technologies

Organiser:

Alain Costes
INPT, France
costes@laas.fr

At this time there is a widespread agreement that the Convergence of biotechnology, information technology, and nanotechnology will be a key driver for technological innovation, economic growth, and improvement on our quality of life.

Examples of on-going research are: bio-informatics, bio-chips, nano-sensors, bio-electronics, molecular nano-electronics, nano-bio-technology, bio-info-nano-medications, nano-robotics, bio-mimetic systems, nano-imaging, etc.

Examples of application domains impacted by the convergence are: aeronautics, space, food processes, medicine, medical imaging, oncology, diagnoses, sensors and environment, embedded systems, defense, etc.

The large benefits expected from the Convergence will only be obtained if the induced scientific and technologic challenges are taken up. This topical day will explore the opportunities offered by the Convergence, as well the difficulties that come across.

[Final papers for this Topical Session were not available at press time. Please contact the session organizers noted above for further information.]

Topic 9

E-Learning

Organiser:

Christian Ernst
U Social Sciences, Toulouse, France
ch.ernst@numericable.fr

This session is focused on two issues on e-learning projects: methodological issues, which are presented jointly by the Polytechnic Foundation of Calalonia and ITACA Company (Barcelona, Spain), and technological issues concerning the implementation of learning contents on heterogeneous content management systems, particularly questions around interoperability. The latter issue is addressed, in ARIADNE European project, by authors from Universities of Leuven (Belgium) and Toulouse 3 (France) Universities. Both methological and technological developments will be illustrated by two case-studies, namely a cyberdegree in law (University of Toulouse 1 in partnership with ANDIL Corp., France), and International e-Miage (IEM), an on-line professional degree in information systems engineering (Universities of Picardy and Toulouse 3, France).

RUNNING AN E-LEARNING PROJECT : TECHNOLOGY, EXPERTISE, PEDAGOGY

Xavier Delgado[1], Marie-Christine Jené[2]

[1]*Polytechnic U. Catalonia, Barcelona, Spain*
[2]*ITACA, Spain*

Abstract: this paper is focused on methodological issues of an e-learning project: components, coordination tasks, actors role, design and implementation steps

Key words: learning project, technology, expertise, pedagogy

1. THE DIFFERENT COMPONENTS IN AN E-LEARNING PROJECT

Any e-learning project, either within a company or a training centre, contains three differentiated and complementary facets: a technological facet, an expertise facet and a pedagogical facet. In this part of the talk, each of them will be analysed, as well as the way they have to be co-ordinated in order to guaranty the optimal set-up of the e-learning project within the organization.

1.1 The three facets of an e-learning project

We shall describe each of the facets, and who is involved in each.

1.1.1 Technological facet

In any e-learning project, the technical aspects within the company will have to be taken into account, in terms of infrastructure. Technical limitations should always be considered in order to evaluate the project possibilities implementations. The following points should be analyzed:

- Whether the company has got or not an e-learning platform or Learning Management system (LMS).
- Whether the company can use the corporate Intranet in order to distribute courses towards the whole employees.
- Which are the final users' computer resources (PCs, equipped classrooms, Internet connexions, modems, available bandwidth ...).

Who is involved?

Normally the technology manager (Systems Manager or Technology Officer), is directly responsible of this facet. He however must be very co-ordinated with the Project Manager. In fact any technological choice should be conditioned by the whole project objectives, but sometimes the technological complexity creates some communication problems, especially if general and pedagogic requirements are not clearly specified. Then decisions are taken only through a technological viewpoint, and that may suppose that the project will not perform in the way the Project Manager wishes.

1.1.2 Expertise facet

The experts are responsible for the project contents. Contents quality and availability are major issues in any e-learning project. In corporate e-learning projects, experts use to be senior engineers or consultants who have got a great amount of experience in the company. In this case relevant information which should be used for e-learning purposes uses to be either in seniors minds, or in disseminated printed or digital supports. In any case finding this information and putting it in a homogeneous and organized support becomes a major issue for knowledge management purposes.

In this situation, either for conception of academic and university courses or for corporate e-earning purposes, experts who elaborate the material have to be very involved in the project, from the conception to the final validation and further updating process.

Subject-matter experts can also play an important role as on-line tutors once the courses are performing. The added value they can bring as specialists, who know their matter, can be a very good contribution to the e-learning project. Not all the experts, however, are good on-line tutors. Before the learning process they should receive training and their competences as trainers should be validated before implicating them in the e-learning implementation.

During the Project implementation, in order to evaluate adequately the delays, the subject matter expert will have to take into account the following elements:

- Available multimedia resources (text files documents, audio and video files, graphics, photographs and illustrations…).
- Material which has to be modified (videos which have to be transformed into shorter sequences, graphics which have to be modified, images that have to be optimized, …)
- Non existing material: sometimes new material needs to be produced, that supposes the evaluation of different possible external providers: (multimedia designers, video recording, and audio studio recording …).

Which kind of support has to be developed: (interactive training course, instructions guide, simulations exercises …)

Who is involved?

The expert responsible for the whole contents (Contents Manager) will have to deal with several professionals:

- Project Manager
- Multimedia Editors
- video and audio Studios
- Experts responsible for part of the contents
- Graphical designer
- Illustrator
- Final testers

1.1.3 Pedagogic facet

This one is probably the most critical one, because it requires both traditional pedagogic and instructional design competences, and a few persons have got a wide and profound experience in this matter. Transforming written contents into multimedia format and making the course quite motivating and performing from a learning viewpoint, is often quite a challenge. Even thought contents are very good and the technological aspects (authoring tool, LMS, global communications infrastructure) are excellent, the e-learning project will fail if a good instructional design has not been realized.

Normally instructional design experts are either persons in huge companies e-learning departments, with a wide experience in creating training material with authoring tools, or professors who have been involved in e-learning material creation in universities (case of FESTO in Germany, who is using EasyProf technology at a corporate level, and of UPC –Universitat Politècnica de Catalunya- who has created an e-learning factory). There also some multimedia free-lance specialists, or multimedia companies specialized in custom content creation).

That requires the following specific tasks:

- Learning profiles determination
- Associated learning itinerary establishment
- Pedagogic design of the material: (course architecture definition, level of interactivity, global information structuring into general modules, and specific structuring of the training modules into didactic units)
- Evaluations method design
- Student tracking determination

Who is involved?

- Project Manager
- Pedagogic expert(s)
- Contents experts
- On-line tutors
- Training Supervisor

1.2 How to co-ordinate the whole e-learning process

The global project Manager will have a difficult task in co-ordinating the whole facets. Let's take some examples of what may happen:

- If the technologic considerations get a higher importance with respect to the other ones, selected Learning Management Systems will probably allow running very powerful e-learning projects but … what about contents? What about final users motivation and final training result?

There are unfortunately too many examples of very important companies that have invested in very expensive and powerful Learning Management Systems, and after a long process implementation they realize that no content is available for being distributed through the LMS, and no pedagogical analysis have been done on the real training needs according to the employees profiles. Then simple PDF or Power Point contents are hanged in Internet and final conclusion is that nobody is really following the course. And the ultimate result is that there is a general acceptance that e-learning does not work. But can we call those kinds of experiences e-learning?

- If the whole project responsibility relies on the Contents Experts and no specific instructions have been transmitted to them, there is a risk that delays are not respected, because the subject matter expert uses to add new contents and new chapters, being motivated by the contents quality and extension. A strict delay in contents delivery has to be established, and moreover an easy to use methodology on how information has to be delivered. Instructional designers have to transmit this methodology, but technical multimedia editors must specify the authors which kind of multimedia file has to be incorporated, and its technical characteristics (weight, format, resolution, size ...).

Probably the most important issue, that must condition the other ones, relies on the pedagogic design also called instructional design. Technological considerations as well as Experts considerations must be defined according to pedagogic objectives. Probably e-learning sector would be much more consolidated if most of companies had acted this way. We can expect that the e-learning sector in the following years will move towards more interactive and pedagogic contents, an increasing presence of easy to use authoring tools, and a decreasing presence of LMS.

2. THE ACTORS IN AN E-LEARNING PROJECT

In a multimedia project several persons have to take part and a significant number of tasks have to be performed, therefore the team members' co-ordination becomes quite an essential aspect.

We will distinguish between the contents elaboration process and the multimedia production itself.

2.1 CONTENT ACTORS

General co-ordinator:

He represents the interests of the educational centre. He controls final results in terms of quality, timing and productivity. He must be the edition team contact.

Authors:

They must write and elaborate the contents. Normally they are the subject matter experts.

Information officer:

He is responsible for searching and organizing the necessary information required for the project. He must organize multimedia digital archives that will represent the main content resources for the project.

Pedagogues

They have to define the way the information will reach the final user in a didactic and understandable manner. They must be, together with the general co-ordinator, in contact with the edition team.

Scientific experts

They will guarantee the technical and terminological validity of the created content.

2.2 EDITION ACTORS

Project Manager:

He is the maximum project responsible. He will have to forecast the required human and technical resources, he will be responsible for the product final quality and of time schedule.

Editor:

He realizes contents structuring and introduction of multimedia elements as well as interactivity. Senior Editor and Project Manager use to be the same person. The ideal situation is this same person is also an instructional design expert.

Graphical designer:

He is responsible for the course graphical design. Graphical interface quality relies on him.

Illustrator:

He will elaborate the graphical original material that is included in the application screens. He is not always necessary, but illustrations can contribute to the course originality, provided they strengthen the pedagogic aspects.

Tester

He is the final actor of the process. It is recommended to assign this task to a new person, someone who is not involved in the other tasks. Naturally a contents revision has to be realized by the authors, but this final tester has to consider all aspects: technical, orthographical, global coherence ...).

2.3 TRAINING PROCESS ACTORS

Training Manager:

He supervises the training process implementation. He has to look for the technological resources allocated to the project, and also the training resources which have to be implemented before the e-learning process launching (on-line tutors selection and training, training supervision, training feed-back and quality control).

On-line tutors:

They are responsible of part or the whole course management. They must make the student tracking, by means of the technological available tools.

Administrator:*He uses to control the courses administration: number of students, number of tutors, global communications to the students, final delivery of diplomas.*

3. THE DIFFERENT STEPS IN AN E-LEARNING PROJECT

Any e-learning project must be organized according to the following steps:

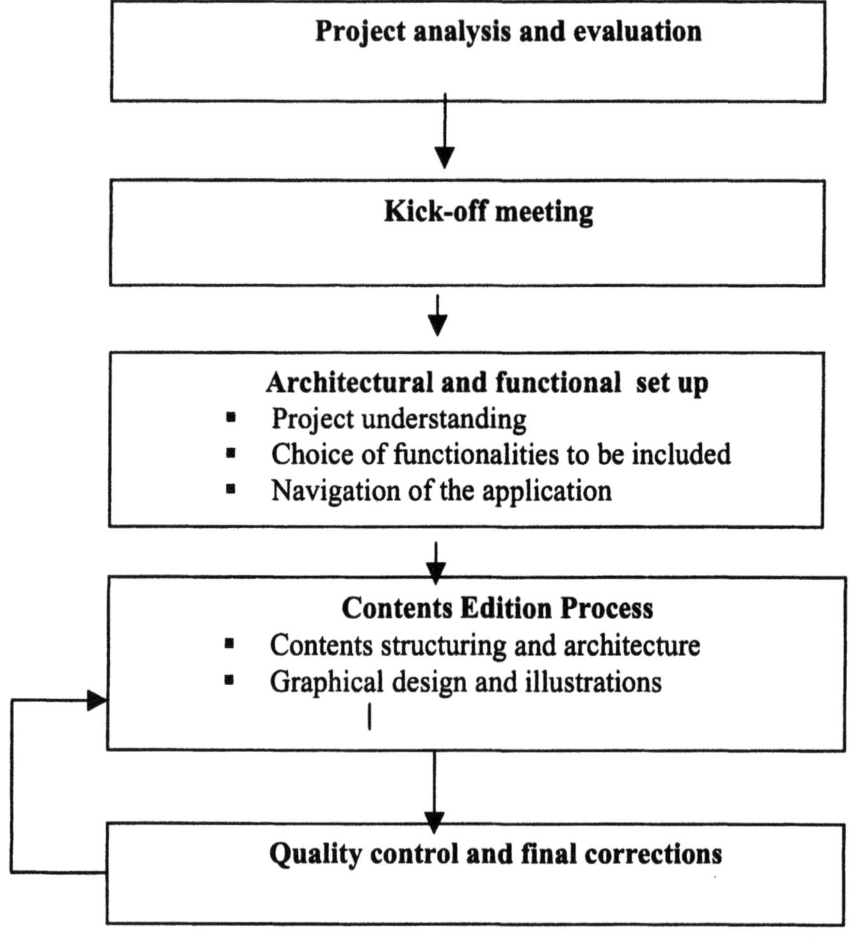
CONTENTS PRODUCTION
Project analysis and evaluation
Kick-off meeting
Architectural and functional set up
Project understanding
Choice of functionalities to be included
Navigation of the application
Contents Edition Process
Contents structuring and architecture
Graphical design and illustrations
Quality control and final corrections

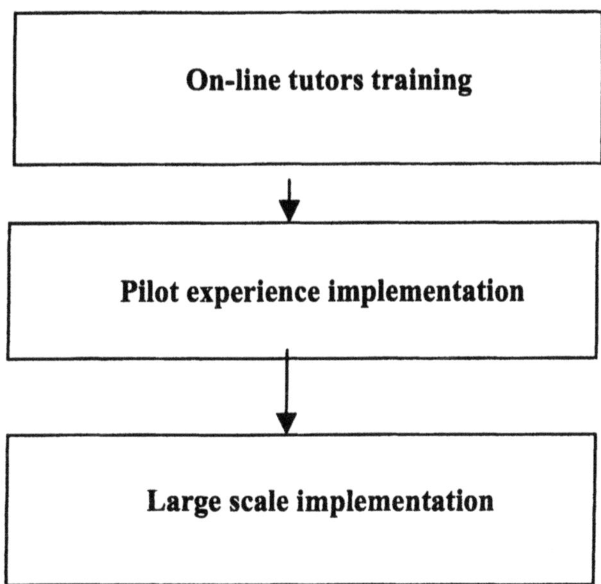

4. THE E-LEARNING PROJECT CONSOLIDATION

Beyond the projects set up it is convenient to reach the project consolidation, so that project passes from being a pilot experience to a consolidated reality within the organization.

That will suppose getting a very complete feed-back from the pilot experience implementation that has to take into account the following elements:

- Contents adaptations to the project needs. It is very important to have a flexible authoring tool that allows changing and updating contents according to the pedagogic and organizational needs.
- Tutors profile adaptation to the learning objectives: tutors that have not performed adequately the learning process should be strengthened in their weaker points. Experience exchanges and meetings have to be organized between them.

- Technological resources must be adapted according to the e-learning program detected weaknesses.

LEARNING OBJECTS INTEROPERABILITY: THE ARIADNE EXPERIENCE

Philippe Vidal[1], Julien Broisin[1], Erick Duval[2], and Stefaan Ternier[2]
[1]Université Paul Sabatier, Institut de Recherche en Informatique de Toulouse, 118 route de Narbonne, 31062 Toulouse Cedex 4, France; [2]Katholieke Universiteit Leuven, Celestijnenlaan 200A, B-3001 Leuven, Belgium

Abstract: Currently hundreds of academic or commercial platforms are present on the e-Learning market. Most of these systems are closed and allow neither share nor re-use. In this article we focus on the problem of interoperability, based on standards (some of which are still under development), and propose a solution to allow a system to share and reuse learning objects from heterogeneous sources. These solutions are implemented in our European and National projects, respectively ARIADNE and e-Mi@ge.

Key words: e-learning; learning objects; standard; Learning Object Metadata (LOM); interoperability; Learning Object Repository (LOR); Web-Based Learning Environment (WebLE); portability.

1. INTRODUCTION

Without standards, it is nearly impossible for an organization to integrate quality products into its structure or courses (Standards and Learning Objects, 2001). E-learning standards aim to ensure :

- Repositories interoperability, in order to support federated searches and, more generally, an interoperable infrastructure of heterogeneous learning object services.
- Re-use of resources and tools so that e-learning systems are as open as possible and that data and contents are as portable as possible (Vidal *et al.*, October 2002). Indeed, various e-learning systems should be able to exploit the documents stored in a particular repository.

To this aim, metadata standardization enables us to locate and make use of the various educational resources of the Internet more effectively, since metadata facilitate learning objects re-use and portability (Simard, 2002). Today various metadata sets are being used, including the Dublin Core Metadata Set[1], or the Resource Description Framework (RDF Recommendation, 1999), or the Learning Object Metadata (LOM)[2] standard.

In this article, we study the openings proposed by an e-learning system, the ARIADNE environment, a European project which has led to a self-supportive association. This system is compatible with the LOM standard, itself based on early ARIADNE results. We first initiate an interoperability solution between the ARIADNE Knowledge Pool System (KPS) and two other kinds of Learning Objects Repository (LOR), before turning to the portability of Learning Objects (LO) stored in an ARIADNE LOR.

2. INTEROPERABILITY STUDY

2.1 The ARIADNE system

The ARIADNE system focuses on share and reuse of learning hypermedia documents (Vidal et al., July 2002). The heart of the ARIADNE environment is composed of a Knowledge Pool System (KPS) (Duval et al., 2001), compatible with the LOM standard that ARIADNE actively co-founded.

Two APIs (Application Program Interface) (Ternier et al., 2003), *Indexation Tool* and *Query Tool* illustrated on Figure 1, interact with the KPS. In order to be independent from the internal structure of the KPS so as to allow interoperability with third tools or other LORs, these APIs are based on Web Services, and more specifically on both the communication network protocol SOAP (Simple Object Access Protocol) and the XML (extensible Markup Language) standard.

There are many e-learning systems calling all upon different methods of storage. We now study a solution of interoperability between the ARIADNE KPS and two other systems of learning objects repository: Peer To Peer and Federated Search.

1 http://www.dublincore.org

2 http:// ltsc.ieee.org/wg12/files/LOM_1484_12_1_v1_Final_Draft.pdf

2.2 LORs interoperability

2.2.1 Peer To Peer

A P2P (Peer To Peer) (Nejdl et al., 2002) (Ternier et al., 2002) application has both the client characteristics and the server's; this property allows the re-use of the components described in the previous section. A new intermediate layer acts like a bridge between the indexing and query tools and the KPS (Figure 1) (Ternier et al., 2003).

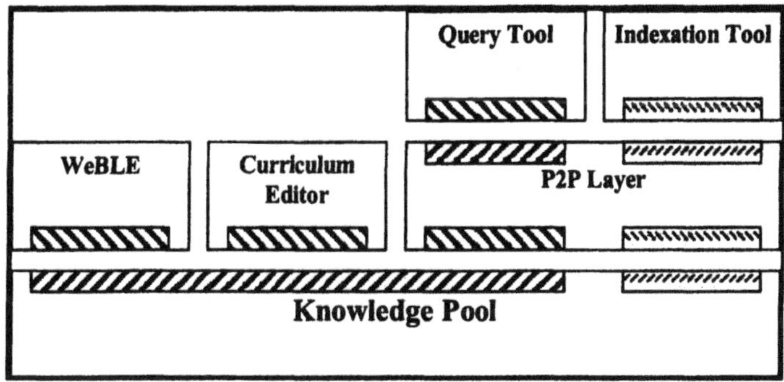

Figure 1. An intermediate P2P layer

When this layer receives a query, it locally carries out the query by using the KPS API, but also transfers the query to other actors. However, this mechanism is invisible for users; the use cases are unchanged. The local results as well as those coming from other actors are finally returned to the initiator of the query. Furthermore, the P2P layer takes care of the replication: when a user inserts a new LO from the indexing interface, the P2P layer intercepts the request and chooses the node on which the LO will be stored.

2.2.2 Federated Search

As the P2P layer, the "Federated Search" layer can be used as an intermediate layer in our architecture (Figure 2). This layer accepts the queries coming from the query tool and transmits them to the KPS as well as to the other systems. If those other systems implement the ARIADNE interface, the transmission of the query is simple (other LOR1). Otherwise, an adapter must be provided in order to convert the ARIADNE API towards the protocol used by the other LOR (other LOR2). The queries for the LOs indexing towards this "Federated Search" system are transmitted to the KPS API.

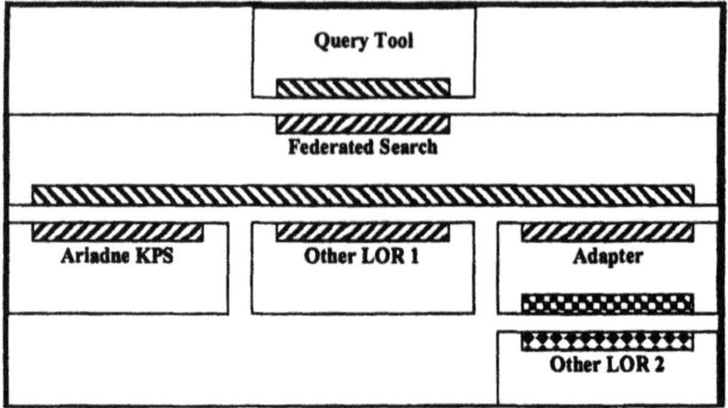

Figure 2. An intermediate Federated Search layer

After showing a possible solution to interoperability problems between heterogeneous LORs, we now discuss their interoperability with e-learning platforms.

2.3 Interoperability between LOR and WebLE

Once the resource has been described, it is inserted into the KPS and attributed a unique number (Alibert et al., 2003). The ARIADNE WeBLE (Web-Based Learning Environment), composed of a management interface and a learning interface, exploits these learning headers (Vidal et al., 2001).

In the ARIADNE environment, the system for storing LOs is independent from the e-learning platform (WebLE), which implies that any e-learning platform able to integrate LOM compatible resources can exploit all the documents contained in the ARIADNE KPS; such an example is proposed in the next section.

3. AN EXAMPLE OF PORTABILITY : DEPLOYMENT OF LOS TOWARDS THE BLACKBOARD E-LEARNING PLATFORM

The Blackboard[3] platform is a learning management system able to integrate learning objects coming from other Learning Content Management Systems (LCMS).

[3] http://www.blackboard.com

The Catholic University of Leuven has developed an extension which makes it possible for Blackboard to interact with the ARIADNE KPS (Vandepitte et al., 2003). This extension makes it possible to recopy resources stored in the ARIADNE KPS towards the Blackboard database, and to introduce some documents stored in the Blackboard system into the ARIADNE KPS. This application, or bridge, is a Web application made up of a reduced indexation tool.

4. RELATED WORK

We are currently developing a module which aims at allowing the communication between the ARIADNE KPS and the e-learning platform INES developed by the University of Picardy Jules Verne[4]. The extension's objective is to make it possible to download resources previously searched in the ARIADNE KPS and to introduce them into the INES database. The learning resources will then profit from the many functionalities this platform has. In addition, this module will propose the introduction of new learning objects into the ARIADNE KPS.

Accordingly, the "International e-Mi@ge"[5] project, an e-learning training which delivers the MIAGE diploma, plans to adopt INES for the exploitation of the whole set of modules stored in the ARIADNE KPS.

5. CONCLUSION AND PERSPECTIVES

Thus, as we have seen throughout this article, we contributed to a solution in the field of pedagogical contents portability. Our work can be used to bring a response to these problems.

We are actively looking into solving the worrying problem of interoperability between the various platforms which affects all e-learning actors. Indeed, in addition to our participation in the LOM standardization, we are implied in the PROLEARN Network of Excellence financed by the Information Society Technology (IST) program of the European Commission, whose objective – among others - is to define an interconnection architecture for the various existing specifications.

Concerning our future work, we wish to improve communication between the ARIADNE knowledge pool system and the INES platform

[4] http://www.u-picardie.fr/~cochard/e-miage

[5] http://www.e-miage.org

which provides a very complete student's learning follow-up. Our action should make it possible to solve the problem related to the learning follow-up of the student likely to sail on his own through identical learning environments.

REFERENCES

Alibert A., Vidal P., Marquié D., Baqué P., "Towards E-Learning Platforms Interoperability : an Opening Solution", *International Conference on Information Technology Based on Higher Education and Training*, Marrakech, 2003 7-9 July, Marocco.

Duval E., Forte E., Cardinaels K., Verhoeven B., Durm V., Hrndrikx K., Forte M.W., Ebel N., Macowicz M., Warkentyne K., and Haenni F., "The ARIADNE Knowledge Pool System", *Communications of the A.C.M.*, vol. 44, n° 5, 2001 May, p.73-78.

Nejdl W., Wolf B., "EDUTELLA: A P2P Networking Infrastructure Based on RDF", *Proceedings of WWW02 Conference*, Hawai, 2002 7-11 May, USA.

Ternier S., Duval E., Vandepitte P., "LOMster: Peer-to-peer Learning Object Metadata", *Proceedings of EdMedia-2002*, 2002 June, p. 1942-1943.

Ternier S., Neuven F., Duval E., Macowicz M., Ebel N. : "Web Services for Learning Object Repositories : the case of ARIADNE Knowledge Pool System"., *Proceedings of WWW03 Conference*, Budapest , 2003 20-24 May, Hungary.

Resource Description Framework (RDF) Model and Syntax Specification, W3C recommendations, 1999, www.w3c.org/TR/REC-rdf-syntax.

Simard C. : "Normalisation de la formation en ligne : Enjeux, tendances et perspectives", Prepared for the « Agence Universitaire de la Francophonie » (AUF), Bureau Amérique du Nord, 2002 February.

Standards and Learning Objects, American Journal of Distance Education, vol. 15, n° 3, 2001.

Vandepitte P., Van Rentergem L., Duval E., Ternier S., Neven F, "Bridging an LCMS and an LMS: a Blackboard Building Block for the ARIADNE Knowledge Pool System", EdMedia 2003 - World Conference on Educational Multimedia, Hypermedia & Telecommunications, 2003 27 June, Honolulu, Hawaii, USA.

Vidal P., Alibert A. : "ARIADNE : un réseau coopératif pour la conception auteur et l'apprentissage à distance", Institut de Recherche en Informatique de Toulouse, Toulouse, 2002 July.

Vidal P., Alibert A.: "Vers un enseignement à distance normalisé", SITEF 2002 Espace Forum Village de le Recherche, Toulouse, 2002 October.

Vidal P., Apcher H., Marquié D. : "Intégration de services coopératifs dans un système d'enseignement à distance", Proceedings of the ARIADNE Foundation, vol. 1, n° 1, 2001, p. 23-31.

AN E-LEARNING VERSION OF THE FRENCH HIGHER EDUCATION CURRICULUM "COMPUTER METHODS FOR THE COMPANIES MANAGEMENT"

Gérard-Michel Cochard[1] et Daniel Marquie[2]
[1]*Université de Picardie Jules Verne, DEP, 10 rue Frédéric Petit 80000 Amiens, France ;*
[2]*Université Paul Sabatier Toulouse 3 , IRIT, 118 route de Narbonne, 31062 Toulouse cedex 4, France.*

Abstract: International e-Miage International (IEM) is a program for Miage distant teaching. This Information System Engineering curriculum (to a professional end) now gathers 20 national sites which deliver fdegrees recognized by 22 universities. The IME consortium, issued from the "French Digital Campuses" proposals, regroups 18 universities. What IME program aims at is offering an e-learning version of the Miage curriculum for working computer scientists in continue training, students unable to attend face-to-face training and foreign students.

Key words: e-learning, Miage, contents, e-contents, ODL, resources deployment, virtual campus; virtual university, resource model, learning object, metadata, interoperability, development engineering.

1. THE INTERNATIONAL E-MIAGE (IEM) PROJECT

1.1 Objectives

The aim of the IEM programme tends to propose a "distance" version of the Miage curriculum

- to reach a new public
    - data processing specialists in activity in the frame of the continuing education
    - students who cannot integrate the classical training devices (handicapped people, prisoners....)
    - foreign students (from where the "international" qualifier and the possibility of a multilingualism).
- to improve the current modes of teaching, in particular by proposing online resources to in presence students "présentiels" and by the way of a sensibilisation of the academic and professional teachers with new teaching methods based on the use of the ICT.
- to place, in the domain of open and distance learning, the IUP Miage as privileged actors for the training of the companies workers in the field of data processing and information systems.
    - in dialogue with the professional and industrial environments
    - while being based on the Miage network
    - under the animation and the management of the Conference of the Directors of Miage.

The distance Miage curriculum is cut out in thematics modules of the same weight (ETCS[3]) making it possible to define learning routes (see figure 1) holding account of the personal, academic assets or professionals of the learning people. It thus anticipates, to a certain extent, the reorganization of the higher education in LMD[4] and allows a flexible application of the legal texts on the Validation of the Assets of the Experiment (2002).

The modular device makes it possible, indeed, to constitute itineraries of formation adapted to the situation of learning, people by taking into account its level of studies like its professional or personal experiment.

The Miage curriculum comprises 6 complementary fields of formation :

- Applied Mathematics

[3] ECTS : European Credit Tranfert System

[4] LMD (Licence, Master, Doctorat) concerns the new european organisation of the higher education studies ; "L" comprises 3 years of study to get the Licence diploma, "M" comprises 2 years of study to get the Master diploma (For the Miage cursus, the second year M2 of the Master cycle corresponds to a specialization year).

- Computer science
- Information systems
- Management of Organisations
- Techniques of communication
- Professionalisation

and comprises between 14 and 16 modules per year of study in e-Miage. Within the framework of the cycle Licence, e-Miage modules of prérequis are proposed with an aim of handing-over on level (L2).

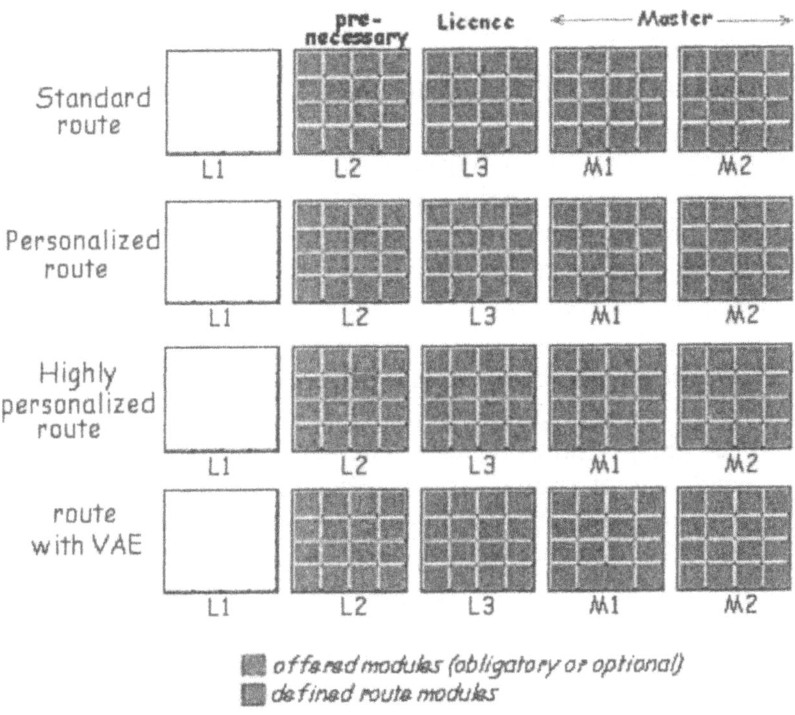

Figure 1. Examples of personnalized routes to reach the Master

A route of formation can be diplômant and lead to obtaining a national certification guaranteed by the French Ministry for National Education within the framework of enablings of the universities or simply qualifying by acquisition of thematic knowledge and practical. Modularization allows also obtaining pre-necessary to integrate a diplômant cycle.

1.2 The International e-Miage (IEM) Consortium

The IEM consortium regroups french universities[5] participating to the project either in the field of production of online resopurces or in the field of the exploitation of the learning system. University Paul Sabatier (Toulouse 3) is in charge to represent the members of the consortium.

Associated to the consortium are various and essential partners for conducting the project and to exploit it :

- Professional and industrial partners : representatives of the economic sector of computing services and engineering activities,
- Public institutional organisations : French ministry of national education, Datar, Administrative Regions,...
- Organisations for international development : Agence Universitaire Francophone
- Foreign institutions of higher education in the scope of a cooperation in the exploitation of the e-learning device.

For the project management and the decisions making a steering committee composed of representatives of members of the consortium was constituted and meet every two months approximately.

Working groups and committees were created to think of the various problems to solve and propose solutions :

- The group "Infrastructures and Functionalities" examines the conditions of pooling of the resources on line (structure, update, deployment) and the definition of the tutoring tools.
- The group "Structuring Legal and Organisational" studies the legal problems involved in the production and the exploitation of resources on line.
- The "committee of the programs" established a national program and its ventilation in thematic modules; it contributes to the more precise definition of these contents and to their actualization.
- The "editorial committee" is in charge of the evaluation of the resources on line under the scientific, pedagogical, aesthetic and ergonomic aspects.

[5] They are the universities Aix-Marseilles 3, Amiens, Bordeaux 1, Bordeaux 4, Evry, Grenoble 1, Lyon 1, Nantes, Nancy 2, Nice-Sophia Antipolis, Orleans, Paris 1, Paris 5, Paris 9, Paris 11, Rennes 1, Toulouse 1, Toulouse 3.

1.3 The learning device

It comprises the current duality (Table 1) of the formations based on the use of Internet :

- accessible online contents starting from a Web site and displayable via a Web browser .
- pêdagogical services to accompany learning people (tutoring).

Table 1. Pedagogical components]

Online contents	Pedagogical services
Informations on the cursus and modules	Mailing
Courses	Network meetings – chats
Exercices and self-evaluation tests	Modules discussion forums
Annals of examination	Physical meetings
Works or training documents submitted to correction	Evazluation and corrected documents

Each center of exploitation comprise a server of resources incorporating the components of the Table 1. Access to the server of resources can be carried out by use of a individual customer station (in residence, in company) or of a customer station placed at the disposal in a public or private numerical space (communal centers, schools, universities, cybercafés,...)

1.4 Pedagogical Model

In the field of the pedagogical organization taking into account the specificity largely "continuing education" of the public, the duration of training for a module is the six-month period (from January to June and July to December).

One or more modules of formation can be studied during the six-month period with a made up teaching accompaniment

- tutorat by electronic mailing·
- participation in the forums of modules·
- personalized correction of work ou devoirs
- suggested·meetings or chats on the network according to a definite calendar·physical
- physical regroupings.

For the practice of the tutorat, no platform of e-formation was imposed ; on the other hand the selected platforms must satisfy a schedule of conditions of minimal functionalities pointed out further.

1.5 The first experimentation

Table 1. e-Miage Candidates

Number of registered people in Licence (L3)	34
Number of registered people in Maîtrise (M1)	15

Table 2. Place of residence

Place of residence	total
Paris and suburbs	8
Rest of France	28
Dom/Tom	1
Foreign countries	12

Table 3. Age distribution

Âge (years)	total
21-25	5
26-30	19
31-35	12
36-40	4
41-45	2

Table 4. Academic level of admission

In Licence	total
Bac	1
B ac+1	0
Bac+2	24
Bac+3	3
Bac+4	1
Bac+5	

Table 5. professional situatione

Professional situatione	total
Unemployed	15
Workers of the data processing domain	26
Other workers	8

1

autres

4

In Maîtrise
total

Bac+2

2

Bac+3

6

Bac+4

1

Bac+5

6

These data, although not yet convincing because of the first experimentation, show nevertheless that it is about a public quite different from that from the students from initial formation (age, professional situation). One will also note the heterogeneity of the academic levels of admission and the already significant number of learning foreign. Since March 2004, it should be stressed that the proportion of foreign registered learners increased considerably.

2. PRODUCTION AND MANAGEMENT OF CONTENTS

2.1 Design and realization of the numerical contents

For the design and the realization of the numerical resources relating to the modules of formation, "modular" working groups were made up gathering voluntary teachers of Miage to take part in the project. There is thus, in theory, as many modular groups, therefore teaching staffs and technical, that modules in building site. Each modular group is animated by a modular head of project.

The contents are defined like a structured set including·

- a preamble : objectives of the module, pre-necessary, programs with accompanying notes, methods of training, contact tutor, bibliography and webography.·
- the strictly speaking· course under two versions : online with multimedia and to be download for printing.
- exercises of synthesis (with solution)·
- works suggested to the students·
- annals of examination (with correction).

The course is also structured in·

- Sessions: work unit of learning, the part usable on line not having to exceed 45 minutes of work. The session seems the atomic element of the device.·
- Chapters: regrouping of several sessions with an aim of better legibility or for the organization of the production of contents (division of a module between several authors).

From the beginning of the project, it has been decided that it was necessary to use the existant supplys, in particular in the form of lectures note, of presentations PowerPoint, etc... and to regard these resources as starting materials. In fact, the suggested and adopted steps are as follows (see figure 2) :

- Design includes 3 phases: definition of the contents (starting from the supplys in hand); structuring (cutting in sessions); scenarisation (setting in multimedia scene of the sessions).
- Technical realization consists of the elaboration of the documents relating to the sessions, intended to be put on line and consulted via a Web navigator; these documents are generally composite (texts, images, sounds....) and can comprise short animations or numerica vidéos l.
- Evaluation: a first evaluation of the contents is carried out by the editorial committee; after the startup of the contents approved by the editorial committee, an experimentation of these contents during one year makes it possible to collect the opinion of learning people and to proceed to the modifications, additions, final necessary improvements (Cochard, 2003c).

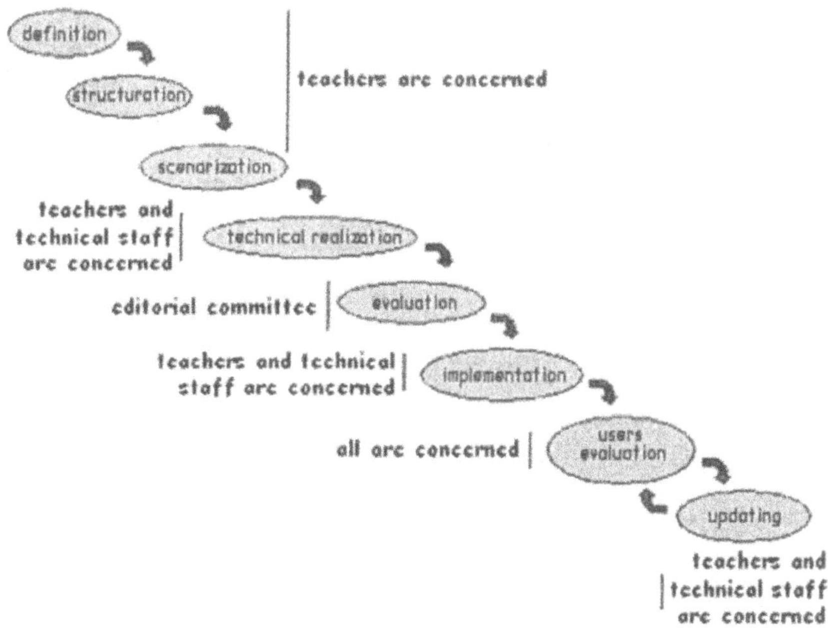

Figure 2. Prodcution chain]

2.2 Contents interoperability and distribution

Being given the structure of the consortium and its international ambitions, a standardization of the contents is necessary. The current standards (Alibert, 200á), seem insufficient or badly adapted with respect to the teaching device selected. For this reason, the working group "Infrastructures and Functionalities" produced specifications on the structure of the contents for a functional interworking, in particular to facilitate the supply contents of the exploitation centers. This work was the subject of the realization of an editor of structure (David, 2004). The structure of a module of formation IEM is described by the metadata of Table 2:

Table 6. Module structure

Level 1	Level 2	Level 3	Level 4	Level 5	Level 6
Module	Header	Identifier			
		Title			
		Module pre-necessary			
		Coordinator			
		Project manager	Name		

Level 1	Level 2	Level 3	Level 4	Level 5	Level 6
		Identifier			
			First name		
			Mail address		
			Postal address		
		Objectives	Objective		
		Programs			
		Tools	Tool		
		Methods	Method		
	Body	Chapter	Preambule		
			Session	Preambule	
				Pre-necessary	
				Course	
				Exercices	Exercice
				Tests	Test
		Exercices	Exercice		
		Bibliography	Ressource	Title	
				Author	
				Editor	
				Date	
		Works-to-do	Work-to-do	Pre-necessary	
				Statement	
				Solution	
		Annals	Annal		

This table can be supplemented by other metadata for a compatibility with the usual standards (Dublin Core, LOM, etc). Let us note that this structure is always the object of work among the members of the consortium (Heiwy, 2004)

The contents produced by the various modular groups are placed on a site of reference[6] which plays the single role of supplier of contents (Figure 3). Very new contents or all new version of contents are placed on this site.

Work is in hand (Broisin, 2004, Alibert, 2004b) for an automatic provisioning of the exploitation centers starting from the contents of the reference site and preceding metadata for an incorporation on platforms satisfying the functionalities exposed further. The first automatic deployment will relate to platform INES[7] used in the first experiments (Cochard, 2003d, Sidir, 2002).

[6] Currently established on a server at the University of Amiens, the site of reference will be transferred soon to the University of Toulouse 3.

[7] INES (Interactive E-learning System) is a platform developed by the Université de Picardie Jules Verne (Amiens), proposed free in "open source" with the university establishments.

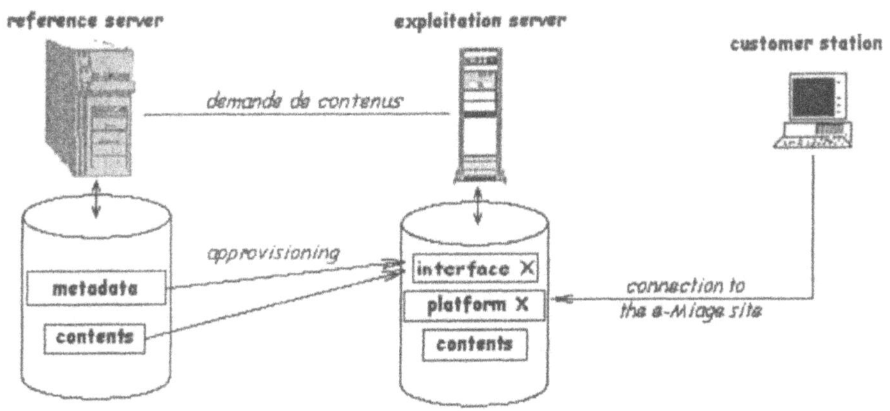

Figure 3. Contents provisioning

3. TRAINEES FOLLOW-UP AND MANAGEMENT

3.1 Tutoring actors and activities

We describe here the methods of tutoring such as they are applied and used at the Université de Picardie Jules Verne, first center of experimentation of the learning device (Cochard, 200á, 2004c, Sidir, 2004).

Each module is placed under the pedagogical reponsability of a teacher, himself tutor. Other tutors can be required according to the number of the registered students (1 tutor for a group of 25 students per module). The tutors can be university teachers, not necessarily affected to the operating university, or by doctorants specialists in the taught discipline. In the first case the service of tutorat is quantified by a specific scale; in the second case, a contract of employment fixes the tasks to be achieved and their remuneration.

The activities of tutorat include asynchronous activities and synchronous activities. The synchronous activities consist of electronic interaction with the students in the following forms:·

- Answers to the messages of the students (private correspondence tutor-learning)·

- Animation of the forums and answers to the asked questions (collective public correspondence[8])·
- Proposal for works-to-do[9] (in general 3 per module per semestre) and personalized correction of these works.

For the university teachers, the quantification of the asynchronous activities corresponds to a contractual working load of 2h by module, student, six-month period.

The synchronous activities are programmed by a semestrial calendar:·

- Network meetings or chats (4 one hour meetings in general per module and six-month period)·
- Physical regrouping (optional; a half day or a day by module and six-month period)

The general coordination is ensured by a formation organizer whose role is triple (Cochard, 2003b, Sidir, 200á):·

- to manage information spaces on the site (platform): general information, specific information, update of the calendars of events·
- to take care to identify the dysfunctions of the device (generally announced by learning) and to bring, with the adequate actors (tutors, administrative staffs or techniques) the best solutions.·
- to carry out a total evaluation of the device while basing itself on the feedbacks coming from learning like tutors.

The organizer can be a teacher or a formation engineer.

3.2 Functionalities and tools for learning follow-up

The working group "Infrastructures and Functionalities" drew up a list of the functionalities required by the adopted teaching model:·

- Accessibility to the contents; integration of external documents, management of the synopses.·
- Offer of basic teaching services: mailing, chats, forums, information spaces.·
- Actors management : students, authors, tutors, administrative staff, technical staff ; attribution of rights of access.·
- Activities management : management of the calendar of the events, management of the mailing addresses and constitution of mailing lists, procedures of update of the contents…·

[8] Learning use also the forums as tools for discussion between them and often provide answers to their own questions.

[9] In some modules, these works-to-do can be noted and to contribute to the validation.

- Learning follow-up: follow-up of the modular asset, followed connections to the contents,·
- Statistics of use: statistics of consultation.

The first experimentation was carried out with the platform INES which fills these basic functionalities in particular on management of the actors and the activities.

3.3 International dimension and cooperation

Whereas the device is reserved in metropolitan France with the students of continuing educationg, it can concern, at the international level, all types of students, the conditions of access being negotiated with foreign institutions of higher education.

The strategy of the IEM consortium is to create or contribute to the creation of relay centers in the countries where the number of students allows it. A relay center is a center partner managed by one or more schools or universities generally; they can be public structures like private. A center relay is at least

- a center of resources making it possible to use customers PC to connect itself to the teaching resources and the services of tutorat.·
- a team of "local" tutors who replace french tutors in the teaching accompaniment of local learning in the various modules proposed.·
- a center for the physical regroupings of learning.·
- a center of preparation to the diplomas of the Miage cursus and, in particular, a center of examination (the conditions of examination are identical whatever the centers).

The center relay can also lead·

- with co-operative developments of new modules·
- with the translation in the national language of the existing French modules.

It can, in the long term, become a center of open and distance learning for the considered country by putting on line local formations. Accordingly IEM consortium begins to bring all help and the necessary expertise. The modules of the e-miage can besides be used as components for local formations and be used for obtaining local diplomas.

This scheme of international co-operation lays down a certain number of training activities in the interested countries; these training courses concern, according to the cases, the teachers "authors", the teachers "tutors", the administrative and technical staffs.

Another significant characteristic of a relay center is its financial autonomy : after calculation of its running costs, the relay center fixes the local price of the formation. For the countries with low income, this provision allows a greater accessibility the formation. To obtain the French diplomas, learning them must however be registered in a French university of IEM consortium.

4. CONCLUSION

The development prospects for the device and for its implementation, in addition to the progressive assumption of responsibility by Miages and the creation of relay centers abroad relate to the following aspects :

- continuous improvement and enrichment of the contents, in particular by the addition of exercises and tests, and of course by annals of examination.·
- creation of specific tools to follow-up the students, in particular for tests on line[10].
- study and experimentation of on line practical works (definition and implementation of "servers" of practical works)·
- experimentation of co-operative work between students of different Miages (Buffa, 2004, Sidir, 2003b) and relay centers abroad[11].·
- addition of various specializations of master (M2)·
- addition of on line devices facilitating the registration, but also the procedural treatment of the Validation of the Assets of the Experience[12] (Cochard, 2004b).

The construction of the device and its first experiments, in addition, gave place to research tasks in the field of the e-learning and association, for this goal, of several groups of research within IEM consortium.

It is clear that the exploitation on a large scale, at the national and international level of the IEM programme, reveals true problems of the e-learning with real confrontation of the theory and the practice and that this situation is favorable, because of the lessons of the experiment, with great

[10] Certain tests on line are already proposed by some modular working groups

[11] while being based on already existing initiatives like the project management (Nice-Bordeaux)

[12] by benefitting from the work undertaken within the framework of the project ACT (Acquisition of Competences and Trajectories of Employment) by the universities of Versailles Saint-Quentin en Yvelines, Amiens and Toulouse 1.

progress towards a standardized and mutualized device of e-formation. The IEM programme gives also a contribution, to a certain extent, to a relative teaching restoration/innovation of the university education system and to the dissemination of knowledge.

REFERENCES

ALIBERT A., 2003a, ; "Vers l'interopérabilité des plateformes de formation ouverte et à distance" ; mémoire de DRT, Toulouse 3, juillet 2003

ALIBERT A., VIDAL Ph., MARQUIE D., BAQUE Ph., 2003b ; "Towards e-learning platforms interoperability : an opening solution" ; ITHET03, 4th International Conference on Information Technology Based Higher Education and training, Marrakech, 7-9 july 2003

BROISIN J., DEMERS B., ALIBERT A., MARQUIE D., BAQUE Ph., VIDAL Ph., SIDIR M., COCHARD G-M., 2004 ; "Serveur de contenu e-Miage pour une exploitation pédagogique distribuée" ; colloque Miage et e-Miage, Marrakech, 15-17 mars 2004. http://www.e-miage.org

BUFFA M., GRATTAROLA J-C., SANDER P., 2004 ; "Outils et Méthodes pour e-Miage" ; colloque Miage et e-Miage, Marrakech, 15-17 mars 2004. http://www.e-miage.org

COCHARD G-M., 2003a ; "La création et l'exploitation d'un dispositif de formation à distance" ; colloque "Campus Numériques et Universités Numériques en région", Montpellier 1-2 oct. 2003.

COCHARD G-M., SIDIR M., 2003b ; "Former à distance via un campus numérique : nouveaux rôles du formateur, nouveaux acteurs" ; colloque "Campus Numériques et Universités Numériques en région", Montpellier 1-2 oct. 2003

COCHARD G.M, MARQUIE.D., 2003c ; "Les enseignements de la filière Miage en accès sur Internet" ; colloque "Campus Numériques et Universités Numériques en région", Montpellier 1-2 oct. 2003

COCHARD G-M., SIDIR M., PIRES L., BAUDOUX S., 2003d ; "INES, une plateforme orientée vers la gestion des acteurs et des activités" ; colloque "Campus Numériques et Universités Numériques en région", Montpellier 1-2 oct. 2003

COCHARD G-M., 2004a ; "International e-Miage : d'un enseignement traditionnel présentiel vers un enseignement FOAD sur Internet" ; colloque Miage et e-Miage, Marrakech, 15-17 mars 2004. http://www.e-miage.org

COCHARD G-M, 2004b ; "Le projet ACTE pour la Validation des Acquis de l'expérience dans le contexte de e-formation" ; Parsi, Hermes (à paraître en mai 2004).

COCHARD G-M., SIDIR M., 2004c ; "Méthodes et Outils de gestion en e-formation". Paris, Hermes (à paraître en mai 2004).

DAVID J-P, GUILLOUX C., 2004 ; "L'outil GenModule pour éditer et mettre en ligne un module e-Miage" ; colloque Miage et e-Miage, Marrakech, 15-17 mars 2004. http://www.e-miage.org

HEIWY V., 2004 ; "Un modèle de ressources pédagogiques générique pour la FOAD" ; colloque Miage et e-Miage, Marrakech, 15-17 mars 2004. http://www.e-miage.org

SIDIR M., 2002 ; "e-formation, quel choix technique ?" ; Actes du colloque "L'enseignement à distance, théories et pratiques" ; Université Paris 8, Acte 8 (ed) p47-58. Paris 2002.

SIDIR M., COCHARD G-M.,2003a "Enseigner et apprendre autrement : nouveaux rôles du formateur, nouveaux acteur"s ; H2PTM'03, 2003, Hermes, Paris pp. 222-239.

SIDIR M., 2003b ; "La collaboration au cœur de l'enseignement à distance"; ISDM(ed) Toulon, oct. 2003.

SIDIR M.,2004 ; "Les technologies au service de la pédagogie…un mythe ou une réalité ? ; colloque Miage et e-Miage, Marrakech, 15-17 mars 2004. http://www.e-miage.org

Topic 10

Perspectives on Ambient Intelligence

Organiser:

Vijay Masurkar
Sun Microsystems, Inc., USA
Vijay.Masurkar@Sun.com

Visionary thinkers have warned time and again of how invasive technologies will increasingly affect people's lives in the coming years. Ambient Intelligence (AmI) scenarios (as mentioned in the European Commission's ISTAG Report) are examples of high sophistication, with on-demand facilities and adaptive service provisioning. We will examine some of the key technical infrastructure provider needs in comparison with the traditional computing ones. Many questions come to mind. What kinds of mechanisms are needed to establish the service objectives, and service and usage policies? How can performance be measured? Then, during or after deployment, how can these advanced technologies be governed? What are the local, regional and global community issues? Let us explore the different models of governance that maintain a balance between the managing of the advanced technologies and people's rights such as security, privacy and free will.

Ambient Intelligence (AmI) scenarios (as mentioned in the European Commission's ISTAG Report) are examples of intelligent environments with high sophistication. There is no doubt that the new, proposed and the evolving technologies will create tremendous opportunities for inventions that will improve human health and goodwill. But, certainly, not without many challenges in application delivery and ethics. What are some of the issues in increasing the utilization of advanced information and communication technologies throughout health care systems? How best to serve ethically the developers and designers of the intelligent environments when a number of technologies compete? What are the ethical principles behind the priorities to be followed when multiple tasks are opting for limited intelligent resources? In this session, we will examine some of these key societal implications in terms of health applications and ethics.

PERSPECTIVES ON COMPUTING FOR SERVICE PROVIDERS OF INTELLIGENT ENVIRONMENTS

Vijay Masurkar
Sun Microsystems, Inc., Burlington, MA, USA

Abstract; Intelligent Environments (IE) have been of interest to many modern research enterprises, particularly in advanced countries. For example, a recurring theme emerging from the European Commission regarding the Information Communication Technology (ICT) research agenda for the next 5-10 years is the notion of "Ambient Intelligence" (AmI) representative of intelligent environments and advanced services. As societies adopt such services, demands will surge on their provider infrastructures, and the environments will emerge, take shape and expand. These IEs will possess certain characteristics that will likely drive innovative operational developments in terms of dynamic policies for operations and management, service pricing structures, and infrastructure fault management and diagnosing strategies. This paper focuses, in broad terms, on these critical IE provider's infrastructure needs.

Keywords; Intelligent, ambient, environment, infrastructure, provisioning, utility, computing, service, pricing, policy, model.

1. INTRODUCTION

Intelligent devices are everywhere; yet, in the true sense, few intelligent environments exist. The ones which exist are confined within the walls of the research laboratories. In the near future, however, dependence on them will likely increase and hence will become more or less natural. In some parts of the world, wearable computing, where human activity is the central part of the user's context, is likely to be an upcoming fashion. A recurring theme emerging from the European Commission regarding the Information Communication Technology (ICT) research agenda for the next 5-10 years is the notion of "Ambient Intelligence" (AmI) representative of intelligent environments, IE. This concept describes an environment where *"people are surrounded by intelligent intuitive interfaces that are embedded in all kinds of objects and an environment that is capable of recognizing and responding to the presence of different individuals in a seamless, unobtrusive and often invisible way."* In the context of this paper, we can assume providers of IE primarily fall into two primary categories. Infrastructure providers such as vendors of network equipment or web servers, and service providers that serve travel and other end user needs with web services or back-end applications. The underlying assumption is that the latter type rely on the former one which covers the lower levels of the ISO 7-layer network protocol hierarchy.

The prominent characteristics of an IE that stand out are size, mobility, heterogeneity, complexity, knowledge and security.

1) Size: In pervasive computing, there are millions of subjects and objects, - many of them interacting with each other.
2) Mobility: Mobility introduces more vulnerability than in a static world. There is the necessity to safeguard against the danger that the physical size of a mobile unit or its ability to be location independent can be exploited by miscreants.
3) Heterogeneity: One cannot assume closed, co-designed systems in the world of IE. The permutations and combinations of interactions are countless.
4) Complexity: Both hardware and software complexity increases and the dependability matrix can become overwhelming; yet with open interfaces, the complexity must be minimized.
5) Knowledge: Distribution of knowledge, coupled with cooperating entities sharing knowledge, logarithmically increases with inter-communications between subjects and objects.
6) Security: On demand, peer-to-peer networking between objects drives requirements for secure communication that will be policy based (defined for a set of participating object types) for the duration of the communication. This will have (mutual peer level) authentication and authorization.

These characteristics, in turn, require that providers of infrastructure and various end user services take into account the constantly changing service requests of data, audio and video at different scales from static and mobile users, as well as users interacting with each other. As it is typically understood, intelligent environments are inherently attributed to be social and collaborative spaces. Consequently, users willingly subscribe to services for their social or business needs. So, behind the scenes, when large scale environments of such kind are deployed, these interactions can result in a huge number of requests that need to be translated into compute, storage or network bandwidth requirements at the infrastructure level of an "intelligent" service provider and delivered reliably and securely via subscribed services.

Grid computing is typically employed for such dynamic resources monitoring and allocation, and there are several vendors providing such solutions; N1 Grid SPS (2004) and I-Fabric (2002) from Sun, HP Utility Data Center (2001), ThinkDynamics (2003). There is also the initiative that promotes an open industry forum, OGSI Working Group (OGSI-WG, 2004), to review and refine the Grid Service Specification and others including OGSA-infrastructure-related technical specifications. Although this may form some basis for the architecture, for the IE user, there is a lacuna to be filled in terms of service provisioning where user's needs based service usage can be tracked and measured, and the pricing structure is low risk.

2. *'MARIA – ROAD WARRIOR'* SCENARIO

One scenario in the European Commission's ISTAG committee report concerns Maria who has traveled 'long-haul' to a foreign country to attend a business meeting at which she will give a presentation (Ducatel et al, 2001). The only computing system she needs to take on her trip is her 'P-Com', worn on the wrist. The P-COM interacts with external systems as Maria travels internationally, and allows her to travel unhindered by identity checks (at the airport), car rental arrangements or city-center travel restrictions.

See *Figure 1* below, which depicts P-COM's interfaces to the outside world. The device allows voice communications, both private calls and Maria's verbal instructions to nearby intelligent systems, and can store preferences and download video, on demand, at her hotel room. Maria has a biosensor within her P-COM that helps her to keep track of her own health.

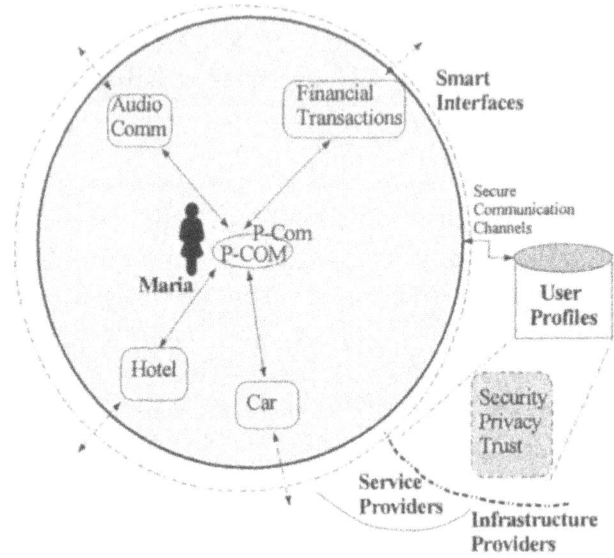

Figure 1. P-Com and Maria's Business Communication

3. IMPLICATIONS ON THE INFRASTRUCTURE ARCHTECTURE

A service provider in the above scenario may be a rental car agency or a hotel chain. Service requests could range from simple identity verification by a foreign country's immigration department to downloading of a real-time video on a hand-held device. User demands for services will be more or less random, unpredictable and will typically scale quickly up and down. Adaptive, highly available and secure computing abilities are needed. There is, of course, the traditional capacity planning model, but would it suffice?

There is the emerging utility computing (UC) model where services can be provisioned as per the needs of the consumer, and consumer's service costs can be tracked and measured in real time. In the utility computing (business) model, customers neither incur high fixed costs of purchasing system hardware and software, nor commit to long-term fixed price outsourcing contracts (Paleologo, 2004). Both are seen as threats to adoption in traditional computing. Instead, in the UC, they receive the service they need and pay for its usage just as they would pay for water or electricity.

4. USERS PAYING FOR SERVICE USAGE

Utility computing based services reduce the risk faced by the customer. This is because the costs to the customer are proportional to the volume of transactions performed during a certain service usage interval. Secondly, UC deployment comes with an advantage of economies of scale. Applying this to the IE context, as the number of services hosted onto the infrastructure increases, the hardware, software and (operational and management) labor costs grow sub-linear to the total volume of transactions. In turn, the infrastructure transfers the lower cost of running an end user service to the users. So, the critical questions that service providers face regarding pricing are: what to price, how to price and when to price. Should a single unit of service cost be fixed for a pre-determined duration? If it is designed to be variable, what specific stipulations must affect the price? Take the above specific example; should a content delivery service to Maria's P-COM include guarantees on performance such as maximum latency for the end user service provider or packet loss for the infrastructure provider?

For all the *"intelligent"* services to be delivered, payment is required from the user to the provider. When Maria downloads a video into her hotel room, that is *'on-demand'* service; notice that it's also portrayed as a location-independent service offering. The implications are significant. Her identity will have to be verified through P-COM. Is the authentication and policy database replicated in the foreign country she is visiting? Or, is there a remote query to her country of residence? Are the digital download, access and copyright laws complied with by the download-on-demand service? How is the payment method set up for the foreign money exchanges? How are the service objectives, service and usage policies, service level agreement (SLA) and payments established?

The actual mechanisms may vary depending on the type of service; however, the principles remains the same. Service providers of IE infrastructures (who are customers of the infrastructure vendors) and end users of services will primarily look for low risk and high availability, reliability, security and performance (via SLA). Pricing will be standardized as it will be public. Yet, the actual determination of the price per service needs to take into account some risk factors associated with UC; in particular, their relative short lifetimes and high initial investments such as for building the infrastructure, for example (Paliologo, 2004). Short lifetimes result from the fact that a user of the services (i.e. an end user) can switch from one service provider (or vendor) to another without much loss of investment on his or her part. Further, note that their adoption could be highly uncertain due to the pace of technological innovation in this area.

5. MEASUREMENTS FOR SLA COMPLIANCE

How can automatic measurements be done of the service level performance? This is particularly important from the perspective of the users so they can compare the actual performance of their subscribed service with the agreed level defined in the SLA with their service provider. SLAs are primarily business contracts between the provider and the user within a system or service context. For instance, certain parts of these SLAs may determine policies for the system resources that are provisioned to fulfill them. In order to make the SLAs operational, benchmarks need to be set and be based on logical entities that are "policy objects" which encapsulate their own rules.

On the overall, policy model can be useful in representing policy objects from different policies and correlating them. One such model is proposed in the IETF RFC 3060. The classes comprising the Policy Core Information Model (Moore et al, 2001), which are intended to serve as an extensible class hierarchy (through specialization) for defining policy objects. These will enable IE application (or service, comprising of several correlated applications) developers, IE infrastructure network administrators, and policy administrators to represent policies of different types. Policies can be derived for the various aspects of operations and management from the business objectives (Appleby et al , 2004). The service infrastructure (or part of it) provider needs to manage the policies (for that part) which determine how the environment is shared, costs are allocated, and so on. One important policy concerns with the diagnostic/repair servicing of the infrastructure itself; e.g. how to proceed when failure symptoms are observed. If a communications device fails between 8am and 9pm, call the system administrator; otherwise call the Help Desk.

The infrastructure provider, such as for network management services, defines the policies and parameters for its own services which will, in turn, define the parametric values of the end user service providers. Simply stated, if the mean time to repair a broken network is '*x*', the end user services relying on the routers of that network cannot be repaired and brought back as live services in less than the time '*x*'. The IE service provider should define the key parameters for the services it offers so, at any instant, status and performance can be tracked and measured. Policies that share those parameters must be linked through a relationship in a policy model (such as the one mentioned earlier).

Current service quality management products do not support SLA compliance evaluations well because of their limited support of the adjudication processes for quality measures (Sterm et al, 2002). In the UC arena, for IE, providers must proactively (a) maximize customer satisfaction with competitive service level reports, (b) minimize the exposed business impact of service level violations, and (c) lower the cost-to-quality ratio of executing service level management processes.

6. DIAGNOSTIC STRATEGIES FOR THE IE INFRASTRUCTURE

What good is an IE if its designers don't think of its diagnosing aspect? Ubiquity and large scale imposes a requirement that service provisioning infrastructure should consider some sort of an autonomous way to diagnose itself to make it cost-effective. *Faults* and downtimes are unavoidable in communication systems. *Error* is a condition that is a consequence of a fault, that deviates the service from its established behavior. It is typically visible to the end users in the traditional environments, yet is expected to remain invisible in the IE. So, designs must take into account the high availability expected out of IE, and provide for the same. *Symptoms* are external manifestations of failures (which could include service performance problem with respect to an SLA). So, the IE must detect symptoms, trace the source of possible fault and diagnose the failure while continuing to provision the service with alternative resources from its reserve pool.

An IE may needs to be managed by one or more applications, depending on its size, governance rules and other monitoring parameters. In large IEs spread over WANs, it is expected that performing fault localization process and maintaining the available knowledge base within a single management application may not be computationally feasible (Katzela et al, 1995; Wang et al, 1989; Yemini et al, 1996). Further, modern environments demand modeling of multi-layer, dynamically changing communication systems, and of representing uncertainty involved in dependencies between network objects (Steinder, 2001). This is because object relationships and policy executions between objects are dynamic and short lived as discussed by Duquenoy and Masurkar (2004) in the *'Maria – Road Warrior'* and other three scenarios of AmI.

One overall approach to take is to design automated fault localization technique that can improve performance of diagnosis not just in the lower protocol layers, but in all the the end-to-end layers, including application and service ones. In an IE functioning over a wide geographical area, service layer is realized by hop-to-hop services. So, in the *'Maria – Road Warrior'* scenario, getting a rental car which you may consider as an end-to-end service, may actually involve multiple hop-to-hop services. If a problem of a hop-to-hop service lies in the data link layer, considering that a large networked environment caters to a huge population, the number of instantiations of such hop-to-hop services could be huge. Finding the affected hop-to-hop service to be relieved, replaced or fixed is complex. This underscores the importance of diagnosing multiple layers (Gopal, 2000). Steinder et al (2001) suggest a novel technique that allows to build a fault hypothesis in an iterative and incremental fashion and base fault propagation on Pearl's work on intelligent systems (1988).

It is expected that many new technologies will interplay in the IE; for example, biotechnology. In the earlier example, Maria wears a biosensor within the P-COM that sends signals to her physician who advises her to calm down right after her presentation. This implies that in order to maintain such devices with the infrastructure, understanding is needed of their interfaces into the information and rest of the infrastructure. In addition, behavior patterns of such devices such as in terms of performance profile, failure modes and diagnosibility, to name a few critical areas.

7. CONCLUSION

Much more than traditional computing, UC facilitates strategic agility for providers of services for intelligent environments by making available computing services and business process components on a when-needed, as needed basis. As a business model, it continues to emerge in the industry, and there is potential to make it appealing to the end users of upcoming intelligent environments such as AmI.

There are many challenges, however, as mentioned in the paper. Particularly, in the areas of service pricing structures made uncertain by unpredictable market size and service adoption, dynamic policies needed for operations and management, and need for automated, intelligent fault management and diagnosis.

Diagnosing of the infrastructure to meet the high availability goals of the IEs is an aspect that needs to be thought about along with the building of the IE infrastructure itself. The size and complexity may decide, in turn, the fault and service management architecture. Certainly, there are many open questions in this area some of which are raised in the paper. These represent suggestions for further research.

In building computing models for providing services to IEs, different real life scenarios, and pros and cons of the different kinds of traditional vs. the UC models must be considered. Then it will become apparent why providers of intelligent services may have to continually evolve their businesses into an advanced type of the latter.

REFERENCES

Appleby, K., Fakhouri, S., Fong, L., Goldsmith, G., Kalantar, M., Krishnakumar, S., Pazel, D., Pershing, J., Rochwerger, B., "Oceano – SLA Based Management of a Computing Utility, Proceedings of the 7th IFIP/IEEE International Symposium on Integrated Network Management, 2001.

Appleby, K., Calo, S., Giles, J., Lee K., "Policy-based automated provisioning", IBM Systems Journal, Vol 43, No 1, 2004.

Ducatel, K., M. Bogdanowicz, F.Scapolo, J. Leijten and J-C Burgelman. "Scenarios for Ambient Intelligence in 2010", *ISTAG (Information Society Technologies Advisory Group) Final Report, February 2001*, IPTS Seville, http://cordis.lu/ist/istag.htm

Duquenoy, P., Masurkar, V., "Surrounded by Intelligence", in *Risks and Challenges of the Networked Society,* Proceedings of the 2nd IFIP Summer School, 2004 (Forthcoming).

Gopal, R., "Layered model for supporting fault isolation and recovery", in Network Operations and Management Symposium [34], 2000.

HP Utility Data Center, Technical White paper, Hewlett Packard Company, 2001.

Katzela, I., Bouloutas, A., Calo, S., "Centralized vs distributed fault localization", in IM'95 [20], pp. 250-263.

Moore, B., Ellesson, J., Strassner, J., "Policy Core Information Model, Version 1 Specification, Internet Engineering Task Force, IETF RFC 3060, ftp://ftp.rfc-editor.org/in-notes/rfc3060.txt, 2001.

N1 Grid Service Provisioning System 4.1, Sun Microsystems, Inc., http://wwws.sun.com/software/products/service_provisioning/index.html

Open Grid Services Infrastructure Working Group (OGSI-WG), Global Grid Forum, http://www.ggf.org/ogsi-wg.

Paleologo, G., "Price-at-Risk: A methodology for pricing utility computing services", IBM Systems Journal, Vol 43, No 1, 2004.

Pearl, J., "Probabilistic Reasoning in Intelligent Systems: Networks of Plausible Inference", Morgan-Kaufmann Publishers, 1988.

Rappa, M., "The utility business model and the future of computing services", IBM Systems Journal, Vol 43, No 1, 2004.

Steinder, M., Sethi, A., "The present and future of event correlation: A need for end-to-end service fault localization", Proceedings of the 5th World Conference on Systemics, Cybernetics and Informatics, 2001.

Sterm, R., Erickson-Harris, L., Onge, D., "SLM Solutions: A Buyer's Guide", Enterprise Management Associates, Boulder, CO, 2002.

Sun Microsystems, Inc., "The I-Fabric Architecture", 2002.

ThinkDynamics: On Demand Provisioning, IBM Corporation, 2003.

Wang, Z., "Model of network faults", in IM'89[17], pp. 345-352.

Yemini, S., Kilger, S., Mozes, E., Yemini, Y., Ohsie, D., "High speed and robust event correlation", IEEE Communications Magazine, 34(5):82-90, 1996.

GLOBAL GOVERNANCE OF THE TECHNOLOGICAL REVOLUTION

Emilio Mordini
Centre for Science, Society and Citizenship, Rome, IT

> *People who confuse science with technology tend to become confused about limits, they imagine that new knowledge always means new know-how, some even imagine that knowing everything would let us do anything.*
>
> - E.Drexler

Abstract; This paper discusses governance challenges of technologies emerging from the information technology (IT) and biotechnology revolutions. Of particular interest here are electronic communication and intelligent computing environments, emerging from the information revolution, and human genetic manipulation and bioinformatics, emerging from the biotechnology revolution. These technologies amplify human capabilities so significantly and profoundly that they stand to alter fundamentally the very notion of what we think of as human. How policy makers respond to the challenges these technologies pose, including the extent to which developments are supported with public research funds and whether they are regulated, is a matter of increasing concern among citizens and for governing bodies. New governance mechanisms, particularly on an international level, may be needed to address emerging issues.

Keywords; Governance, Ethics, Information, Technology, Biotechnology, Public Policies

1. INTRODUCTION

A scene in "Blade Runner", a 1980s science fiction movie, is set in the headquarters of a prosperous-looking biotechnology company. The firm makes "replicants", robots that look like humans, and the firm's boss describes how they are grown from a single cell. The replicants are genetically modified people without any legal rights. In this dystopia, it is the unaltered humans who rule. By contrast, "GATTACA", another movie set in a genetically modified future, has the modified in charge. They are beautiful, gifted and intelligent. It is those who remain untouched by modification who suffer. All this is in the realm of fiction, but the contrasting views of the potential effects of biotechnology point to an important truth about any technology. What really matters is not what is possible, but what people make of those possibilities.

Technology is the practical application of knowledge to perform some actions, to solve some practical problems, or to achieve some practical goals. Technology puts moral intuitions to the test. While knowledge has always a positive value – at least in liberal, open societies – its practical applications often need to be regulated. Policy makers should obviously be open-minded about these regulations, but be cautious and questioning as well. History has taught us that worrying much about technological change rarely stops it, it does not mean, however, that one should give up trying to govern it.

2. GOVERNANCE

Governance is the effort of human communities to try to control, direct, shape, or regulate certain kinds of activities. The governance approach implies that conventional boundaries between politics, policies and administration become less significant than the question of how the whole ensemble works (or fails to work). In this sense, governance is a broader notion referring to the act of running a government, state, regime, etc., that encompasses and transcends that of government. It is a process of management and control involving several actors, and, specifically, of interaction between formal institutions and those of civil society.

Governance may be viewed from two angles, in terms of effectiveness and of the results it aims to achieve, and from an ethical point of view, in terms of the fairness and inclusiveness of the process. From the first perspective, an effective political system – considered as any system in which supra-individual decisions must be taken and implemented – can lead to increased participation on the part of the actors involved in the decision-making process. Thus it can result in increasing the motivation on the part of citizens as active members of the "community". Thinking ethically, the idea of governance is based on the principles of fairness and transparency that should imbue any bureaucratic or political procedure in a democratic society (Koenig, 1999).

The European Commission's White Paper on European Governance lists five principles which should underpin good governance: openness, participation, accountability, effectiveness and coherence. Ideally, good governance should aim to ensure a high level of participation, and a fair, transparent and effective decision-making and implementation process, contributing to raising the level of confidence. (European Commission, 2001) This seems by and large to agree with the definition of governance provided by the World Bank, according to which "*good governance is epitomised by predictable, open and enlightened policy-making, a bureaucracy imbued with a professional ethos acting in furtherance of the public good, the rule of law, transparent processes, and a strong civil society participating in public affairs.*" (GDRC)

3. TECHNO REVOLUTION

The enormous growth of modern technology (esp., information and biotechnology) over the late 20th century has provided the basis for myriad applications in industry, agriculture, and medicine. This ever-expanding research activity is resulting in numerous discoveries that are transforming human life and societies. Technological revolution coupled with global electronic networks of exchange of capital, knowledge, commodities, and information has created a key feature of the globalisation era: a short circuit between scientific discovery and its technological application. Today, the time between new discoveries and their applications has shortened as public opinion and policy makers are often incapable to form a clear picture of what is worth worrying about. They often end up wavering between a naive enthusiasm mixed up with scientific hubris on one side and blind fear of the new on the other. This is why governance of science and technology policy is becoming increasingly important.

IT and biological technologies are post-modern technologies, in the sense that they are de-centred, dispersed and disseminated, and their control and use are largely in the hands of the individuals, citizens' groups, and small enterprises. Namely, they are network technologies. In comparison with technologies that drove the industrial revolution - which were complex, based on collective action, social infrastructure, and technical know-how - IT and biotechnologies are lighter. The governance challenge is no longer democratic control over centralized systems— as it was in the 20th century, with such technologies as nuclear weaponry and energy, telecommunications, pharmaceuticals, medicine, and airlines—but governance over decentralised, distributed systems.

The current political and legal infrastructures – shaped on "hard" technology - are inadequate for dealing with global changes in IT and biotechnology. There are three main oppositions that characterise post-modern technology: (1) global vs. local, (2) public vs. private, and, (3)use vs. misuse.

The opposition between global and local is vital to understand the particular perspective from which new technologies look at globalisation. Glocalisation is a neologism invented to describe a strategy which addresses the issues of globalisation by empowering local communities. *"In short, the word "glocalisation" is meant to point to a strategy involving a substantial reform of the different aspects of globalisation, with the goal being both to establish a link between the benefits of the global dimension - in terms of technology, information and economics – and local realities, while, at the same time, establishing a bottom-up system for the governance of globalisation, based on greater equality in the distribution of the planet's resources and on an authentic social and cultural rebirth of disadvantaged populations."* (CERFE, 2003).

New technologies are inherently "glocal" because they empower individuals and common interest groups. The fact that collective action is not required to use these technologies makes them particularly difficult to be controlled by national governments. The Internet is often cited as a promoter of *"true democracy"* because it enables the individual to interact with others directly and in real time. New technologies, such as the GRID and evolving intelligent user-oriented computing environments based upon it, hold promises to go further. The Grid refers to an infrastructure that enables the integrated, collaborative use of high-end computers, networks, databases, and scientific instruments owned and managed by multiple organizations. Grid is a system that: 1) *coordinates resources that are not subject to centralized control;* 2) *using standard, open, general-purpose protocols and interfaces* 3) *to deliver nontrivial qualities of service.* (Foster J., 2003). Distributed Computing lets people share computing power, databases, and other on-line tools securely across corporate, institutional, and geographic boundaries without sacrificing local autonomy.

Biotechnology, too, is seen as having special promise because it will tailor treatments and medicines to the individual and place emphasis of certain biological controls on processes in the hands of individuals. For example, communications in the user's context with bio-sensors (such as in intelligent human-collaborative spaces) which is not too distant. Biotechnology companies are often local in their dimensions but global in their strategies.

Agricultural biotechnology is going to lead the market. The area planted with genetically modified crops now amounts to almost 60m hectares—admittedly only 4% of the world's arable land, but a 12% increase on the year before. Where GM strains of a crop species are available, they are starting to dominate plantings of that species. Half the world's soybean crop is genetically modified. And three-quarters of those who plant GM crops are farmers in the poor world. Farmers, on the other hand, can see the virtue of paying a bit more for their seed if that allows them to use fewer chemicals and to enhance the nutritional qualities of crops.

Medical biotechnology is overturning the drug market. Genomics provides opportunities to predict responsiveness to drug interventions, since variations in these responses are often attributable to the genetic endowment of the individual. In the long term, it promises to individualise prescription practices by narrowing the target populations exclusively to those for which the medication is safe and effective. Industrial biotechnology, coupled with nanotechnology, promises to create completely new products. What is astonishing is that this revolution is happening through networks of small, medium enterprises, often localised in emerging countries.

The tension between private and public realms is the other key opposition to understand the technological revolution. IT and biotechnology participate in the post-modern tendency of a reduction of public space and regulation, in favour of private, individual or community oriented spheres. The question of the distinction between public and private is likely to be one of the main political issues of this revolution. It's a problem that it directly concerns its legal framework. The private/public distinction comes from moral and political theory. Private conduct may be seen as somewhat outside the scope of law. The private realm is the realm of morality, where actions are not judged according to the law. Liberal political theory made essential use of this category in assessing the permissible sphere of the law. In the Internet world, it is quite impossible to distinguish seriously between public and private spheres. The two spheres fade and overlap. The Internet teaches that little is *"illegal"* but that everything is possible, and even fair, from the moment that it can be found on the World Wide Web. To some extent, we support almost a growing anti-legal consideration of human actions. Through the Internet, the private sphere becomes global. The Internet has evolved into a global information network and has developed beyond its original purpose of sharing information into a global commercial trading system where everything can be purchased: human cloning, organs to be transplanted, viruses that can be weaponised. Procedures that are judged ethically or medically objectionable in one country may become available elsewhere through market mechanisms, leading to the development of foreign sites where individuals may go to avoid regulations. The development of biotechnology products requires extensive social and technical know-how but does not necessarily require a large infrastructure to be deployed. It is not clear what kind of government regulation is required to support or control biotechnology (or even whether it could be controlled), and it appears that private-sector standardisation efforts have not yet emerged in any real way.

This leads us to the third tension, which is the tension between use and misuse of new technology. Dual use technologies are those technologies that can be used both for civil and military purposes. The *"dual use"* aspect of IT and biotechnology does not only concern a few applications. The features that make these technologies different also make the effects of their abuse potentially greater than those of other technologies. Yet, the level of control that is in the hands of the individual makes social governance much more complex than for technologies that require collective action to build, use, or maintain. In principle, all of IT and biotechnology can be used both for civil and military purposes. The use of the Internet for crime and the misuse of the network by public and private groups in ways that invade personal privacy is in the limelight of the public debate. This holds true also for risks entailed by biotechnology. The knowledge needed to weaponise a germ is essentially the same that is needed to understand how that germ causes disease and how to create an effective vaccine against it. In principle, the sole guarantee against IT and biotechnology misuses would be a time gap between the new discovery and its technological applications. This time gap would allow to activate mechanisms of self-regulation and internal checks within the scientific community. But it is this gap that cannot exist any longer. As an industrial enterprise IT and biotechnology cannot afford any delay in commercialisation.

New questions will be raised as biological sciences and computer sciences converge into applications called *bioinformatics*. As science explores creating information technology that can be used as a human prosthetic, questions about when it is appropriate to use these technologies and under what conditions will arise. Science is also exploring the use of biological materials as information processors in objects, such as *"biochips"*. Technologists suggest that miniature biological sensors detecting chemical and biological information may soon be available that will be capable of providing instant feedback on individual or group activities and, further, of linking this information into ultra-scale networked computing. How can abuses of these technologies, such as surveillance and large-scale information-gathering among the population, be anticipated and regulated or countered? How can terrorist groups, mafia cartels and other *"rogue"* actors on the global stage be prevented to misuse this technology?

4. SCIENCE AND POLITICS

One characteristic of post-modern technology is the radical change of the representation, value and status of science. Science has become more of a technique, and, aptly, there is the expression *"techno-science"*. This emphasises operational ability and productivity, and the interaction of science, technology, economy and politics. The representation of science has changed so much that some people may say that: "doing science is another way for doing politics".

Government regulation and private-sector standardisation are highly active in IT and biotechnology arenas, although they have trouble keeping up with the pace of change. According to the old, elitist, model of governance, experts advise policy makers who then take decisions, while common citizens are not at all involved in decision making. It is clear that the evolution of IT and biotechnology itself has been making this old governance model inappropriate and even counterproductive. There are at least two main reasons for explaining this. First, the increasing importance of the media system – chiefly due to the information revolution - makes impracticable any form of elitist debate. Second, it has changed the public and political perception of expertise. Expert's knowledge is not available in a timely and readily useful form. Both public and policy makers perceive the scientific community as dispersed and fragmented: experts do not share the same view and any advisory committee ends up reproducing the same divisions that one can find in the society.

New governance mechanisms are needed. They should present three main features: (1) Internationality, (2) Pluralism, and, (3) Accountability.

First, it should be clear from the outset that any effort to create governance institutions for either of the two technology areas in question must be international. Modern information technology is inherently is without borders. The Internet user does not care about the physical location of any given server; so it is possible to defeat an effort by one nation or jurisdiction to control or close down a site by moving it to another nation or jurisdiction. Biotechnology is less mobile but still presents many of the same challenges: For example, if one country wants to ban cloning or genetic manipulation of offspring, people who want such things can simply obtain them in another country without such regulations. It is useless, therefore, to think about governance except in an international context.

Second, it should be clear that decision can be taken only according a pluralist model that involves a significant number of organisations and users in deciding what technologies to support with research and development funds. In addition, what technologies need governance, what the norms of use and application should be, and whether they should be regulated; and, if so, how, and at what level of formality. Researchers and policy makers cannot be the sole actors on the stage. Researchers are under increasing pressure to demonstrate the policy relevance of their findings and to deliver tangible results. In turn, policy-makers are under increasing pressure to justify their choices of technology to be developed and socio-economic goals to be pursued. Thus NGOs, consumers' associations, citizens' panels, should be directly involved in decision making through instruments such as consensus conferences, voting conferences and scenario workshops.

Third, given that NGOs, consumers' associations, citizens' panels base their authority primarily on the voluntary choices of their members, this raises issues of legitimacy. In other words, we cannot imagine to substitute democratic procedures with "survey" techniques. It means that we need to define accountable, transparent, open and effective procedures that may bring together scientific expertise, technological assessment, democratic representativeness, and policy making.

ACKNOWLEDGEMENTS

This work was funded by a grant from the European Commission - DG Research – Contract nr QLG6-CT-2002-01796 (Bioethical Implications of Globalisation Processes).

REFERENCES

CERFE, 2003 Glocalisation. Research, Study and Policy Reccomandations, Available at: http://www.glocalforum.org/New_Glocal_Website/ttank/ttank.html)

Commission of the European Communities, 2001, *European Governance: a White Paper.*

Foster, J., 2003, What is the GRID?, available at: http://www-fp.mcs.anl.gov/~foster/Articles/WhatIsTheGrid.pdf

GDRC – The Global Development Research Centre, *Understanding the concept of Governance,* online: http://www.gdrc.org.

Koenig, M. 1999, *Religion, Multiculturalism and Democracy – the contribution of international social sciences,* Opening Address, The Second Religion and Cultural Diversity Conference, London, 31st October, 1999.

e-HEALTH – MAKING HEALTHCARE BETTER FOR EUROPEAN CITIZENS: CHALLENGES AND EXPECTATIONS

Diane Whitehouse
European Commission, DG Information Society[1]

Abstract; This paper discusses e-Health and focuses on its progress in Europe. In this context, e-Health involves using information, communication and intelligent computing technologies throughout health care systems. It reports that health care systems are successfully using information, communication and intelligent computing technologies, and lists healthcare challenges that lie ahead for further progress.

Keywords; e-Health, healthcare, citizen, information, intelligent, communication, technologies

1. INTRODUCTION

e-Health matters. It can improve access to healthcare and boost the quality and effectiveness of the services offered. e-Health involves using information and communication technologies throughout health care systems. It offers benefits for both health authorities and professionals, while allowing much more personalised healthcare for patients and citizens. When combined with organisational changes and the development of new skills, e-Health can help to deliver better care for less money within citizen-centred health delivery systems. e-Health is today's tool for substantial productivity gains, while providing tomorrow's instrument for restructured, citizen-

[1] The views presented are those of the author and do not necessarily represent the official view of the European Commission on the subject.

centred health care systems and, at the same time, respecting the diversity of Europe's multi-cultural, multi-lingual health care traditions.

2. e-HEALTH PROGRESS

There are many examples of successful e-Health developments that fall within the ambit of building an Information Society characterised by ambient and intelligent technologies. These include health information networks, electronic health records, telemedicine services, wearable and portable monitoring systems, and health portals. Today, at least four out of five European doctors have an Internet connection, and a quarter of Europeans use the Internet for health information.

Many European research results have now been tested and put into practice. Europe is now in a leading position in the use of electronic health records in primary care and deployment of health (smart) cards. These developments have contributed to the emergence of a new "e-Health industry".

European Member States want to take an e-Health agenda forward. An emerging framework for concerted actions and synergies in e-Health based on an open method of coordination is envisaged that provides a favourable environment for the integration of related policies at a Community level. e-Health plays a clear role in the European Union's *e*Europe strategy of stronger growth - the vision set out by the Lisbon European Council in March 2000[2] [3]. To move ahead, action will be required within several important policy areas that range from research and the roll-out of broadband networks in telecommunications, to action in public health.

3. CHALLENGES

Healthcare systems around the globe are currently facing major challenges[4]. For the European Union, these include:

- rising demand for health and social services, due to an ageing population and higher income and educational levels;
- the increasing expectations of citizens who want the best care available, and at the same time to experience a reduction in inequalities in access to good health care;

---

[2] European Council (2000), *Presidency Conclusions*. Lisbon European Council. 23-24 March, 2000.

[3] COM(2002) 263 final. *eEurope 2005: An information society for all: An action plan to be presented in view of the Sevilla European Council, 21/22 June, 2002*. Brussels, 28.5.2000.

[4] COM (2001) 723 final *The future of health care and care for the elderly: guaranteeing accessibility, quality and financial viability*.

- increasing mobility of patients[5] and health professionals including the opening of the internal markets in services – that may result in a higher demand for reimbursable cross-border healthcare products and services[6];
- the need to reduce the so-called 'disease burden'[7], and to respond to emerging disease risks;
- the difficulties experienced by public authorities in matching investment in technology with investment in the complex organisational changes needed to exploit its potential;
- the need to limit occupational accidents and diseases, to reinforce well-being at work and to address new forms of work-related diseases[8];
- management of huge amounts of health information that need to be available securely, accessibly, and in a timely manner at the point of need, processed efficiently for administrative purposes; and , lastly,
- the need to provide the best possible health care under limited budgetary conditions.

---

[5] High level reflection process on patient mobility and healthcare developments in the EU, 2003.

[6] Regulation 1408/71 that co-ordinates social security legal schemes has recently been amended to streamline and modernise access to health care across borders, particularly when undue delays occur in the patient's home Member State. In January 2004, the Commission tabled a proposal for a directive on freedom of provision of services which lays down a framework for the provision of health care services in the internal market and for their reimbursement by the relevant health insurance institutions.

[7] The disease burden is a measure of the health of a population and quantifies the total impact of disease in terms of incidence of mortality, disability, and the cost of illness.

[8] The costs of accidents at work and occupational diseases are between 2.6% and 3.8% of national gross domestic product in the various European Member States. For further details, see Communication from the Commission on the practical implementation of the provisions of the Health and Safety at Work Directives. COM(2004) 62 final, February 2004.

INTELLIGENT ETHICS

Penny Duquenoy
School of Computing Science, Middlesex University, London, N14 4YZ.

Abstract; This paper discusses the impact of envisaged intelligent applications on the lives of the individuals who may be using them, and investigates the ethical implications of autonomous decision-making that is beyond the control of the user. In an increasingly networked world we look beyond the individual to a social picture of distributed multi-agent interaction, and in particular at the concepts of rules and negotiation between these virtual social agents. We suggest that the use of such agents in a wider social context requires an element of ethical thinking to take place at the grass roots level – that is, with the designers and developers of such systems.

Keywords; Ethics, Ambient Intelligence, intelligent agents, multi-agent systems, negotiation.

1. INTRODUCTION

Developments in technology have seen an increasing trend towards "smart" and "intelligent" applications. This trend is a natural progression from the research and work in Artificial Intelligence and the availability of enhanced computing infrastructures, combined with economic need and the marketing drive of the computer industry. The benefits of such applications are easy to see – fast and autonomous action in complex situations beyond the abilities of the human mind. As the use of technology generally has spread beyond the work environment into the lives of ordinary people the benefits are held to be increased user-friendliness - thus addressing the difficulties of the novice user - and reducing the user's cognitive load.

This trend for smart appliances has gained momentum with recent concepts in ubiquitous and pervasive computing. These terms describe the move towards computer technology operating "in the background" in an invisible and non-intrusive way[1]. The combination of smart, or "intelligent",

---

[1] Pervasive computing is described as providing a paradigm "for all the time, everywhere services" (Second IEEE International Conference on Pervasive Computing and Communications. PerCom2004.

technology with ubiquitous computing generates the notion of "Ambient intelligence" – that is, intelligent systems that operate in our surrounding environment.

Whilst fully integrated and compatible intelligent systems are still a long way off, there are some ethical concerns regarding their implementation. We can predict (based on current technologies) that issues of privacy and security will continue to prevail (cf. Petrio, 2003), but there are also deeper issues at stake. In a situation where a number of technologies are competing for bandwidth, airwaves, processing power, storage and memory, choices will need to be made. Priorities will have to be allocated, and trade-offs accepted. Who decides the rules, and makes the choices?

This short paper discusses the impact of envisaged intelligent applications on the lives of the individuals who may be using them, and investigates the ethical implications of autonomous decision-making that is beyond the control of the user. In an increasingly networked world we look beyond the individual to a social picture of distributed multi-agent interaction, and in particular at the concepts of rules and negotiation between these virtual social agents. We suggest that the use of such agents in a wider social context requires an element of ethical thinking to take place at the grass roots level – that is, with the designers and developers of such systems.

2. BACKGROUND

The background to this discussion is founded upon earlier reflections on ambient intelligence inspired by the work carried out by the European Commission Information Society Technology Advisory Group (ISTAG) in 2000/2001 (Ducatel et al. 2001). In that document four futuristic scenarios were put forward as a device for considering the future direction of research and development of intelligent systems. It is clear from these scenarios that intelligent devices will be expected to interact with others in different contexts. The devices are described as communicating systems exchanging information with each other on behalf of human individuals. Whilst the use of intelligent devices for the individual user are projected as beneficial – that is, as facilitating the management of various lifestyles (such as business, personal, and information management) – the implications of agents acting in a broader social context are not apparent.

Our previous work examined the ethical implications in the application of these devices (Duquenoy and Masurkar, 2004). This current work looks at a more fundamental issue, that is, the infrastructure of multi-agent networking. Networked agents must necessarily include decision-making procedures that deal with negotiation and priorities of operation, and in

---

The call for papers includes topics such as "Intelligent environments, wearable computers, smart devices and smart spaces" amongst others. Note also 4th International Workshop on Smart Appliances and Wearable Computing (www.unl.im.dendai.ac.jp/IWSAWC/).

situations where decisions and judgements are made by third parties (be they computer-mediated or human) there are also inherent ethical issues.

3. ETHICS, JUDGEMENT AND CHOICE

Ethics is founded upon the principle of intelligent rational agency, and is essentially about judgements and choices that lead to actions. Living a "good" life is to live a life based on good choices and actions (whatever we may determine "good" to be). Taking two of the most used ethical theories we can, in simple terms, say that actions can be good or bad in themselves, or good or bad in their consequences. That is not to say that all actions have ethical implications – but any that cause harm to others, are unjust, or take advantage of another to their detriment (exploit others), are usually considered unethical.

Making ethical decisions can be difficult - there are often competing ethical choices, and often a lack of knowledge about circumstances that may affect a judgement.

Even from this extremely simplistic picture of ethics, we can see that intelligent devices acting on our behalf will be making judgements and choices to inform actions, and that some of these actions are likely to have ethical implications. If we are to achieve the potential of ambient intelligence, and have intelligent devices operating in an "invisible and non-intrusive way" then it seems apparent that some thought should be given to the instructions we give them.

4. AGENTS, NEGOTIATIONS AND DECISIONS

It is clear that for the successful co-ordination of networked agents a co-operative system must be in place. A key element of co-operation is negotiation between participants - which necessarily implies choice. Offers are made, assessed, accepted or rejected. As a result of the negotiation a decision is reached, and appropriate action taken.

Negotiating programmes are not a new idea, and have been developed to promote ethical "good" – the World Wide Web consortium's Platform for Privacy Preferences Project (P3P) is a good example of a simple interaction[2].

A more complex "social" example of negotiation between agents is a simulation developed by Clarke and McCabe (2003). The authors demonstrate the application of the programme by setting it in the context of a "ballroom scenario" thereby allowing elements of negotiation, choice and

[2] The concept behind this is to aid user's with privacy requirements. P3P will negotiate on behalf of a user with a web site, checking the web site's privacy policy against the user's requirements, and notify of any discrepancies. A warning is given however, that this does not imply the web site will adhere to their privacy policy.

action. Their agents are able to distinguish between male and female partners, negotiate with prospective partners for dance engagements, and make choices between alternative dances and activities. By attributing attribute the concepts of belief, desire and intention to the agents, the authors can encompass "key behavioural features of agents: autonomy, adaptability and responsibility." This scenario describes a familiar context and incorporates social norms, such as male and female dance partners, the male approaching the female to request a dance, and with the alternative to dancing given as going to the bar! So, with a given set of social norms in a familiar, and fairly restricted context, negotiations can be pursued. Ethical considerations in this case could concern the application of social conventions – what happens for user's who do not conform?

5. SCARCE RESOURCES

If it is true that agents will be sharing and/or competing for finite resources such as operational space (bandwidth, signal processing, processing power, memory etc.) then some rules of precedence must be followed – some functions and operations must take priority over others. Fixed rules under these circumstances are not appropriate, as the available resources are likely to be in a continual state of flux. Negotiations in such a situation need to be on-going and adaptive. Some preliminary work in this area has been carried out by Rzevski et al. (2003) and is intended to address the changing needs of supply and demand in virtual organisations. Their guiding principle is based on "incessant negotiation between (1) internal VE resources and (2) external demands for these resources".

The above model, set as it is in a context of virtual enterprises within a global marketplace, involves an element of competition. Put simply, whilst agents within an organisation may be working as a team for the benefit of the organisation, external operators may be ignored or rejected as they become less useful. Applying this model to an individual user operating in a wider social network could be beneficial, in that the agents working for the user will always act in the user's best interests, discarding non-useful connections. We should remember though that commercial models are not always appropriate in a social context – if those who are not useful, or unsuccessful get excluded. This is not to say however, that the principles of "usefulness" cannot be changed to incorporate different values.

6. CODE AS REGULATION

Lawrence Lessig (1999) shows how programming code can, and does, act as a regulatory force. In basic terms programmes allow users to perform certain actions, and prohibit them from pursuing others. Programmes can be used to uphold laws and values – as we have seen with the W3C P3P project above. We also know that other operational programmes have preferences set – for example, browsers can be set to accept or deny cookies, and there are other security settings and levels that are optional for the user. The virtual enterprise model described above is designed to allow users to set and change priorities.

But, how many ordinary users are aware of these options? How many are aware of the rationale behind the options? Some users may say that they prefer to be left out of the loop, and not to have to make decisions. They may prefer to leave these decisions in the hands of agents.

It is also worth noting that in the field of Human Computer Interaction (HCI) the user is central to the design, that is, "users" are given a valued status. This might not necessarily be the case in some cultures and states. In answer to the question "who is the user" we might reply: governments, law enforcement agencies, commercial enterprises, illegal enterprises, etc. In other words it is equally possible to devise agents that operate out of site of the user, that exploit individuals, and cause harm. As well as "good" ethical agents we could have unethical or "rogue" agents.

7. CHALLENGES

The challenge for technologists will be to develop compatible, safe and robust multi-agent systems. These systems will be responding to given rules; negotiating; arranging tasks according to perceived worth and timeliness; matching data and profiles; and determining when tasks are complete. All of these activities clearly have an impact on the user – but consideration should be given to the extent of that impact on personal life-styles. The anticipation is that ambient intelligence will "make life better" – with some advance thought this could be the case.

The examples above illustrate the immediate impact of negotiation strategies on outcomes. In an agent-mediated environment the consequences of the negotiations are ethically relevant to the user. For example: In competing for real-time information delivery – who wins? Who (designer) or what (intelligent agent) will prioritise – will my grocery need take precedence over my medical appointment? Amongst the many likely stakeholders (individuals, commercial enterprises, social services, government) who takes priority? Will commercial interests impinge on personal management of information (as for example the current intrusions based on cookies, or spam). Will government needs override personal needs? In some cases user preferences can be set – would there be any circumstances where those preferences could, or should, be over-ridden?

The developers of such models and programmes are clearly in a position to regulate not only the operation of agents, but by default the way individuals may operate in their lives. The task is how best to serve the developers and designers, so that the considerations indicated above can be taken into account proactively in the development process – rather than trying to reactively put matters right after the event.

8. CONCLUSION

In the ambient intelligent environment we have, potentially, a number of interactions and negotiations taking place. The results of these interactions are informed by values (beliefs), motivated by need (desires), and directed by goals (intentions) - characteristics which are likely to be embedded in the early stages of development, and may not necessarily be to the benefit of users.

The examples used give some indication of the different ethical implications of the models, and the regulatory aspects of coding. Negotiations coupled with scarce resources raise a number of questions with regard to priorities, and beneficiaries. Designers and developers will be influential in determining the benefits of ambient intelligence in the future, and attending to the ethical aspects of these technologies is a vital ingredient to their success.

Intelligent devices acting as agents and pursuing negotiations with other agents and making decisions are, by definition, acting on our behalf as third parties. The decisions and judgements they make carry ethical implications. Human agents, such as lawyers, financial agents, estate agents, etc. have codes of conduct and practice to inform their practice – ethics is as important in intelligent agents, and even more important in an environment of ambient intelligence as envisaged by the EU, simply because of their implicit "invisibility".

REFERENCES

Clark, K.L. and F.G. McCabe (2003) "Go! For multi-threaded deliberative agents". Available from http://www.doc.ic.ac.uk/~klc/ Accessed: 02/03/04

Ducatel, K., M. Bogdanowicz, F.Scapolo, J. Leijten and J-C Burgelman. "Scenarios for Ambient Intelligence in 2010", *ISTAG (Information Society Technologies Advisory Group) Final Report, February 2001*, IPTS Seville. http://cordis.lu/ist/istag.htm

Duquenoy, Penny and Vijay Masurkar (2004) "Surrounded by Intelligence" in *Risks and Challenges of the Networked Society.* Proceedings of 2nd IFIP Summer School. Forthcoming.

Lessig, Lawrence (1999) *Code and other laws of cyberspace*. Basic Books.

Petrio, Roberto Di and Luigi V. Mancini. (2003) "Security and Privacy Issues of Handheld and Wearable Wireless Devices". *Communications of the ACM*, Vol.46 No. 9. Pp75-79.

Rzevski, G, Skobelev, P, Batishchev, S, Orlov, A. (2003) "A Framework for Multi-Agent Modelling of Virtual Organisations". In Camarinha-Matos, L M and Afsarmanesh, H (eds), *Processes and foundations for Virtual Organisations*, Kluwer Academic Publishers. Pp. 253-260.

World Wide Web Consortium. Platform for Privacy Preferences (P3P), http://www.w3.org/TR/P3P/ accessed 21/04/04.

Topic 11

TRain: The Railway Domain – A Grand Challenge

Organiser:
Dines Bjørner
National U. Singapore, Singapore
db@imm.dtu.dk

Software is being developed for the partial or full automation of many forms of railway planning and operation. Increasingly these software packages could benefit significantly from being interoperable - and also more properly reflecting other railway supporting technologies.

TRain stands for a worldwide consortium of computing science groups and railway engineering centers. The aim of TRain is to establish a shared, formal theory of the railway domain. A theory which can be the basis for co-design of railway solutions involving software, IT, electro-mechanics, people, etc.

The railway domain theory is to be seen as a set of co-ordinated, mathematical models of eventually all aspects of railway systems.

As physics is to mechanical, electrical, construction and chemical engineering, TRain could be to the engin- eering of railway systems. We need to establish compu- ting science (&c.) laws of railways akin to Kepler's, Newton's, etc.'s laws.

THE TRain TOPICAL DAY — A FOREWORD

Dines Bjørner*†
Department of Computer Science, School of Computing, National University of Singapore, 3 Science Drive 2, Singapore 117543
E–Mail: bjorner@comp.nus.edu.sg, URL: http://www.comp.nus.edu.sg/cs/

Prologue

Welcome to the papers presented at the first TRain presentation of its plans — as well as its scientific and technological background — for gathering a worldwide consortium of researchers and technologists "united" around an attempt to initialise focused research on an emerging domain theory for railways.

The papers are listed below and brought in this volume in the sequence they are to be, respectively were presented at the August 26, 2004 Topical Day of the IFIP World Computer Congress 2004, Toulouse, France.

The Papers

1 Dines Bjørner: TRain: *The Railway Domain — A "Grand Challenge" for Computing Science and Transportation Engineering.*

Sets the stage for the TRain effort.

2 Denis Sabatier: *Reusing Formal Models: Domain capitalization via formalization.*

A careful discussion is presented of the benefits of developing, studying and using formal models. After a careful analysis of two kinds of uses, a discussion follows of how to reuse and (thus) capitalize on formal models.

3 Alistair A. McEwan and J.C.P.Woodcock: *A calculated, refinement-based approach to building fault-tolerance into a railway signaling device.*

Exemplifies the concept of integrating formal techniques in the provably correct development of software for a railway real–time embedded system.

* On sabbatical at NUS from the Technical University of Denmark, Institute for Informatics and Mathematical Modeling, the Computer Science and Engineering Section, DK–2800 Kgs.Lyngby, Denmark
† The author acknowledges the support received from the EU 5th Framework Programme IST: The CoLogNET Computational Logic Network of Excellence.

4 Martin Penicka: *From Railway Resource Planning to Train Operation.*

Illustrates, in survey fashion, a number of railway models: From nets, via scheduling and allocation of resources (net development, time tables, rolling stock deployment, staff rostering, rail car maintenance planning, to station interlocking, line direction monitoring & control, automatic line signaling.

5 Wolfgang Reif: *Integrated Formal Methods for Safety Analysis of Train Systems.*

An approach is shown in which correct functioning, analysis of failures and their effects, and quantitative analyses of the risks of systems and subsystems, all based on formal techniques, are applied, in a coherent fashion, to a railway example.

6 Theo C. Giras and Zhongli Lin: *Stochastic Train Domain Theory Framework.*

The axiomatic safety–critical assessment process (ASCAP) is briefly analysed as a stochastic, Monte Carlo simulation model. The rail line taxonomy is thus characterised as a stochastic domain that provides for either a design–for–safety, or a risk–assessment framework — and these are seen as dual. The need for formal validation, verification and certification is presented.

7 Takahiko Ogino: *CyberRail: Information Infrastructure for New Intermodal Transport Business Model.*

Outlines dramatic new paradigms for passenger transport.

8 Dines Bjørner, Peter Chiang, Morten S.T. Jacobsen, Jens Kielsgaard Hansen, Michael P. Madsen, and Martin Penicka: *Towards a Formal Domain Model of CyberRail.*

Attempts to formalise an essence of the CyberRail idea presented in the previous paper.

Paper # 8 is currently not planned for presentation.

1. Acknowledgement

The organiser of this topical day, the current author of this Foreword, thanks his colleagues, listed above, for their perseverance, under strict deadlines and page limitations, to yet have written the following extended abstracts.

Please enjoy them. Should you think so, then please join TRain. Details are given in Paper # 1.

Dines Bjørner

TRain: The Railway Domain

A "Grand Challenge" for Computing Science & Transportation Engineering

Dines Bjørner
Department of Computer Science, School of Computing,
National University of Singapore, 3 Science Drive 2, Singapore 117543
E-Mail: bjorner@comp.nus.edu.sg, URL: http://www.comp.nus.edu.sg/cs/

Abstract We present the rationale for the TRain Grand Challenge.

Keywords: Railways, Domain Theory, Grand Challenge, Formal Methods.

1. What is the TRain Effort ?

The TRain Effort is a proposal put forward for the formation, worldwide, of an *Open, Free Consortium* of railway people and institutions (companies, industries), of academics (ie., people, researchers, scientists), and of research centres — within computer & computing science, software engineering, transportation science & engineering, reliability & safety engineering, and operations research, on the subject of exploring, creating, ie., researching, and freely propagating (publishing, on the net, etc.) *A Domain Theory for the Railway Infrastructure.*

Key points are research into the domain, not requirements, not algorithms, not software, of "all things" railways (see below). Building up a public repository of railway system models.

Of course it is unavoidable that research into domains, result also from research into and development of requirements and the design of algorithms and software. Hence the TRain effort will, obviously, see research results, ie., reports, papers, etc., that contain material on domains and requirements, or domains, requirements and algorithms, or domains, requirements and software design.

TRain is more a group of people "gathered" around joint research, reports, workshops, conferences, a railway formalisations repository, a web-based TRain newsletter, and possibly a web journal, than it is an organisation.

The organisation, ie., the TRain *Consortium,* is needed as a "mid-wife", to help secure and to help "magnify", a focused collaboration. The TRain

Working Groups are expected, in a sense, to be where "the real" work is being done (by its members) and co-ordinated (by its committee cum working group members). It is through working groups that the TRain effort will be "kick-started".

The idea is *that railways: that rail nets, their static (ie., topological) and dynamic (ie., signaling and switching) properties, net development and maintenance, etc.; that rolling stock, its maintenance, deployment, etc.; that trains, their movement along the rails, that is: Train traffic, etc.; that passenger ticketing, inquiries, ticket cancellation, etc.; that freight handling: Reception, transfer, tracing, delivery, etc.; that scheduling & allocation of timetables, rolling stock, staff, etc.: that net planning & development (construction); that entirely new forms of train service; etc.;* that is, that all aspects of railways: *Strategic, tactical and operational management as well as operations can all be both informally and formally fully adequately described* — but that such models need be developed individually, and, formally, in rather different formal specification languages, and harmonised (ie., "integration of formal methods"), as well as communicated to all stake-holders.

The idea is to call for a "human genome"-like, worldwide R&D, open and free effort among university and railway industry R&D centres to achieve the above.

2. Why the TRain Effort ?

The Railway Industry Justification, the Whys. Because IT, ie., computing systems, for all aspects of railways, and especially for integrated, cross-related tactical and operational management, monitoring and control, etc. applications, become more and more important.

Because the design of these computing systems is hard, to very hard: Often fraught with cost overruns, late deliveries, and erroneous software, etc.

Because requirements for such systems are usually badly formulated. It is claimed that a proper, widely accepted *Domain Theory for Railways* can help ameliorate the above situation.

The Software Engineering Justification, the Why. Before computing systems can be designed one must understand the requirements. Before requirements can be formulated one must understand the domain. Todays computing systems for the railway infrastructure are not developed on the basis of anywhere near a reasonable understanding of the railway domain.

The Computing Science Justification, the Why. Because we need a grand challenge project in order to gather enough momentum to make progress along the road to industrially scalable and useful, integrated formal techniques.

The Science Justification, the Whys. Because there is no domain theory for such an important domain as that of railways. The natural sciences, so reveals "their name", has domain theories: Physics (mechanics, thermodynamics, electricity, ...), biology, etc. *Is it not time for man-made structures to have their domain theories ?*

Towards a Science of Man-made Infrastructure Components, the Whys. We deploy the name 'infrastructure' - really without knowing its deeper, possible meanings. Transportation is one such infrastructure component. There are other infrastructure components: Financial service industry, health-care, public administration, etc. We must try understand the term 'infrastructure' — mathematically ! It seems high time someone started !

Sociologically and Psychologically, the Whys. Because it can be done; and because it is fun !

3. Who should Participate in the TRain Effort ?

Rail infrastructure owners, train operators, rail and train technology industries, mathematicians, operations researchers, computing scientists.

4. How to Participate in the TRain Effort ?

Individuals, interested in the TRain Effort, should either join an existing *Working Group,* or create one themselves! Working group individuals should study the railway domain, and describe parts of it, informally (but precisely) and formally, using any number of one or more formal techniques.

For characterisations of what is meant by *formal techniques* (cum 'Formal Methods') we refer to www.imm.dtu.dk/~db/colognet/train/index.php?-page=faq&subpage=fm. For a survey of *formal techniques* we refer to www.-imm.dtu.dk/~db/colognet/train/index.php?page=faq&subpage=fm-list.

Researchers of the TRain *Open Consortium* should co-ordinate their efforts across the TRain open consortium - at least by announcing: We are researching "such and such" a TRain area. Researchers of the TRain open consortium should endeavour to report, at least yearly, with one or more documents (reports or publications). Researchers of the TRain Open Consortium are expected to put their research results, that is formal models of respective aspects of the railway domain, in the open, for free consumption.

The TRain Secretariat shall endeavour to maintain a TRain Repository of as many already existing and all future such "modelisations" - free for anyone to use. Such research results are then expected to serve as "patterns" that can be used freely by anyone, in particular by the rail technology industry, when developing new technologies for the railway domain.

Possibly the TRain open consortium should, preferably in collaboration with one or more railway institutions organise special research events (seminars, workshops, symposia, conferences, congresses) where results are presented and where "open problem" challenges are identified. The TRain open consortium should encourage publication, training, education events (summer schools, courses, etc.), etc. The TRain open consortium could influence national and international rail organisations toward deployment of published domain formalisation in national and international development projects.

The TRain Open Consortium shall not advocate special technical approaches - but, and this is, of course, important: Advocate the use of carefully (informal language) narrated (annotated) formalisations.

5. What is meant by "An Open, Free Consortium"?

By an *Open Consortium* is meant a loosely knit collection of individuals: Researchers, software engineers, railway technologists, etc., and of their host institutions: Universities, railway companies, research centres, etc. The "loose knit" is the TRain consortium. At any time individuals and institutions may enter (or leave) the open consortium. Each individual (person) or institution acts individually.

There are to be no legal or financial, contractual relationship between any two distinct institutions nor individuals from distinct institutions, binding them in any other by way than their offering one another the fruits of their individual research on TRain related matters. By "acting" together, as the TRain open, free consortium", it is expected that each individual, each institution will be spurred on to a more concerted effort, including even joint efforts, towards "modelisation" of "all things" railways. By an open and free consortium of the kind proposed here is also meant that there is no central funding source, no shared or common capital from which TRain research and other TRain activities may be funded.

TRain individuals and institutions are themselves to secure any needed funding.

Although the TRain consortium will and shall not act as a funding agency, it may well decide to support identified national or international railway domain research projects. This support is not financial. Rather it could be support, say in the form of written recommendations to national or international funding agencies, of proposed research efforts.

The TRain Consortium shall be pro–active in encouraging and in helping to arrange joint research efforts. Whether the TRain Consortium can otherwise issue "blue seals" of approval of individual or joint research efforts remains to be seen. Our current "thinking" is: Rather not. We would rather like to see research efforts emerge and survive, ie., attract attention, on their own scientific merits. We would like to believe that subscribing to the TRain Consortium Charter suffices as a qualifier.

6. What is Meant by a "Grand Challenge" ?

From Tony Hoare, Journal of the ACM, Vol.50, No.1, January 2003, pp 63-69, we quote that which characterises a Grand Challenge — where the 'it's refer to the Grand Challenge being discussed:

(1) Fundamental: It relates strongly to foundations, and the nature and limits of a discipline. (2) Astonishing: It implies constructing something ambitious, heretofore not imagined. (3) Testable: It must be objectively decidable whether a grand challenge project endeavour is succeeding or failing. (4) Revolutionary: It must imply radical paradigm shifts. (5) Research-oriented: It can be achieved by methods of academic research – and is not likely to be met solely by commercial interests. (6) Inspiring: Almost the entire research community must support it, enthusiastically – even while not all may be engaged in the endeavour. (7) Understandable: Comprehensible by - and captures the imagination of - the general public. (8) Challenging: Goes beyond what is initially possible and requires insight, techniques and tools not available at the start of the project. (9) Useful: Results in scientific or other rewards - even if the project as a whole may fail. (10) International: It has international scope: Participation would increase the research profile of a nation. (11) Historical: It will eventually be said: It was formulated years ago, and will stand for years to come. (12) Feasible: Reasons for previous failures are now understood and can now be overcome. (13) Incremental: Decomposes into identified individual research goals. (14) Co-operative: Calls for loosely planned co-operation between research teams. (15) Competitive: Encourages and benefits from competition among individuals and teams - with clear criteria on who is winning, or who has won. (16) Effective: General awareness and spread of results changes attitudes and activities of scientists and engineers. (17) Risk-managed: Risks of failure are identified and means to meet will be applied.

7. Conclusion

We invite the reader to study the TRain home page: www.imm.dtu.dk/~db/-colognet/train, to consider joining TRain, and to contribute to the TRain effort. We expect to formalise the foundation of the TRain consortium by the end of 2004.

REUSING FORMAL MODELS

Domain capitalization via formalization

Denis Sabatier
ClearSy, France
E–Mail: denis.sabatier@clearsy.com

1. Introduction

Formal models of all kinds are more and more widely used in a growing number of industrial projects. In such projects, people are looking for any means to master complexity, and semi-formal or formal models seem to be the only technical option, after management and organization improvements have been pushed to their limits.

But writing useful formal models is not an easy task. So there comes the natural idea of making this task more feasible by reusing previous work; with different options:

- Building libraries of predefined models;
- Defining domain specialized formal languages;
- Defining domain specialized method or design patterns.

Which option should work best, and under what conditions? This is what I will try to guess here.

2. Two kinds of model usage

Let's examine more closely how formal models can be used in projects. There are many ways, but I think all of them fall in one of the two following categories: Detailed Component Specifications or High Level Requirements.

2.1 Detailed Component Specifications

This is what we do when use formal models to describe in an (hopefully!) non-ambiguous way all the computations done in a software module, for example. We can use sets, relationships, state diagrams, events order laws to describe the behavior of a component in any situation.

For example, in a railway system with a track divided in blocks, we can describe how each block is labeled as occupied or free by the control system. Usually, such a system will use different kinds of truck detectors on the length of the block and at its boundaries with adjacent blocks. A block gets occupied if one of these detectors detects something. It gets free only when the detector at one of the boundaries changes from "detection" to "no detection", provided that the next block's boundary detector detects something, and that all other detectors for the block say "no detection", and that no alarm conditions have occurred, etc. All these can be described using either state diagrams, booleans equations, sets and relationships.

Although such detailed models might look like programs, they are still far simpler than actual code, especially if the formal representation uses abstract enough constructs. So here is the first, and maybe the main benefit: it's possible to write such detailed formalized specifications from the global requirements with a limited risk, where writing actual code directly from these requirements would lead to catastrophic errors. Even if the formal model contains all the data to actually do the module's task, not having to be runnable gives the ability to get rid of implementation details.

The next benefit is that it should be possible to derive the actual system from such formalized detailed specification. We can use a code generator, or use a way to obtain the code in a proven way from the detailed specifications.

Successful applications of such detailed formalized specifications are numerous. A very remarkable one that I know quite well is STS's use of the B Method (STS: Siemens Transportation Systems), with in particular the METEOR automated train development. In Meteor, the code was obtained by proven successive refinements from a detailed formalized software specification, producing a system that is still now considered as completely bug free since the first version, although unit tests were bypassed. STS improved further the process by automating the lowest refinement levels: a tool named EDITHB is now used to automatically build these levels from configurable design patterns (currently used in STS's New York projects).

Components detailed formalized specification can be used even for non software parts: ClearSy uses it to describe the functional principles of PEUGEOT cars, as an input for the development of the repair tool knowledge databases.

Of course, with this kind of formal models, it is still possible that the formally described behavior might not be what the user really needs. In our previous example with free / occupied blocks, will the proposed algorithm leads to a "good", safe and available train system? Having a formalized expression of these algorithms certainly helps, but this is not a proof that the system works as it should in the most general sense.

So this "detailed component specification" use of formal methods works well when the specifications are well defined and stabilized. In projects where what each component should do is still unclear, premature detailed formalizations can be harmful. I have a personal experience for this: once I had to develop a small tool for Peugeot. Lacking the time to correctly examine the users' needs, I wrote directly a detailed specification in B language. From this specification, I was able to develop in a few days a tool that seemed bug free, but we soon discovered that its results were useless, although there were what was requested in my specification! Both the development and the formal specification work time were lost. Such an example might not transpose to large industrial projects, but most of them still suffer from lack of stabilized specifications.

2.2 Higher Level Specification

If we are unsure of what functionalities are really needed, detailed formal specification might be premature. We can then use formal models to point out what is really needed. In our previous example (free / occupied blocks), what are the true requirements? One could say:

> "block occupied" should be equivalent to the physical fact that there is some material on the block part of the track.

Such a requirement is clearly not what is done by an algorithm such as the one presented above. Firstly, it is not always possible to detect material on the track because sensors might be faulty, so the above requirement is infeasible. A better requirement would be that if all sensors are OK, block occupied represents material on the track, but if one or more sensors fail, the block is declared as occupied. Even then, alarm conditions that can stop the block release and necessary overlapping zones at block boundaries certainly exists, so this requirement shows up as a quite naive one. More, a fugitive fault of a sensor might cause a useless and dangerous emergency brake with such an "occupied if failure" naive requirement.

In fact, the block occupation and release algorithm has been carefully chosen so that the system will preserve safety with a certain amount of faulty sensors, that it will tolerate trucks with certain dimensional characteristics, that it will preserve minimum safety if a truck derails by not releasing the block... We see that finding the true requirement forces an "expansion" of the scope by always asking questions like:

- *Why* do we want this property?
- *What* can we assume on the external environment?

By recursively using these two questions, we would rapidly end up in "world level" requirements, like what is requested from any transportation system and whether we should build a train or a plane. So it is necessary to decide the limits of the scope, for example:

- Assuming that we have a control system that is certainly safe if a free block is really free of material with a certain safety gap;
- Assuming that the sensors will comply to a certain functional model and a certain failure behavior;
- Assuming that no material will never appear in the middle of the track, or be in a shape such that sensors might not detect it;
- ...
- Then the block control algorithm should be such that ...(and so on).

Trying to state formally the true requirements of a badly specified component requires the ability to expand the scope both in abstraction level and in environment knowledge, and the skill to stop this expansion at the right volume. This is not a task for beginners or newcomers in the field. Only experienced people with the proper authority on what should be assumed and what should be changed will have the best chances of success.

Generally, there is a tendency to keep the abstraction level too low and to assume too much on the environment and its stability. Things that seem so certain today become false sooner than expected... The small tool for Peugeot that I cited above as an example of too early detailed formalization was improved to satisfaction, then thrown away because a full automation was finally decided for the data generation that this tool was designed to help.

Thus, higher level models should be done with a carefully chosen larger scope. Another problem with this kind of models is that they require abstract variables: variables meant to represent physical facts but not directly measurable. For instance, the notion of detectable material in our free / occupied block example. Such variables require very precise definition, otherwise models become links between vague notions that are no longer unambiguously related to reality.

One more problem with higher level models is the omnipresence of quantitative criteria. For instance, in our block example declaring a block as occupied because of failures should be restricted to the minimum. Formalizing quantitative requirements like this one is useless, as in most cases we cannot prove a design as being the optimal one.

High skills, large scopes, abstract notions and unprovable quantitative requirements are claims against higher level formal models. Why not keep all this informal? Despite the difficulties, I still believe that higher level models are worth it, because if not we are restricted to finding proper design by trial and error and careful examination of requirements doomed to stay informal; this would be giving up the intellectual mastering of complex problems. To succeed with higher level models, let's not make them too high and let's not require them to cover all aspects.

Industrial use of higher level models is not yet common. Case studies on examples from industry show that designing a system with important high level properties formalized and proven is possible and affordable; and we use higher level "modelization" at ClearSy in real projects as internal initiatives. We believe that in the near future, we will see larger scale applications for this kind of formalization.

3. Clues for capitalization

After this examination of formal model types, let's go back to how to reuse and capitalize on formal models.

3.1 Reusing detailed models

If we consider formal models like the one that describes the algorithm used for block occupation and release, it is quite clear that such models are valuable only for what they are made for. Of course, careful study of these models will help building new ones for a different system, but as they constitute the company's know-how, it is unlikely that exchanges will go beyond the development team where models were originally written, maybe even not beyond the very person who wrote each model. Reuse always works well within a team of one person...

As a side effect of being developed from a detailed formalized specification, the obtained modules have a well known behavior. So instead of trying to reuse formal specifications as specifications, a better way would be to reuse the developed modules as COTS, claiming that their behavior is well known. Equipment manufacturers could thus sell components from their own systems as *formally defined reusable parts*. They could hope that by common use in other systems, their components and their architecture might become a standard. This could counter-balance the necessary diffusion of valuable know-how. In this idea of making components reusable thanks to formal specification, it's probably better to extract components out of real operational projects only. Specifying reusable components without the help of a real need is a very difficult challenge.

Another way of capitalization would be designing domain specific formal languages. As each domain has its specialized technical terms, each domain could have its specialized formal language. The problem is that in the same domain specialized formal languages could rapidly become different between companies, the same way technical terms often differ, and this could lead to harmful obscurantism. I feel that formal languages should remain open, at least as a necessary condition for the diffusion of formally specified reusable components.

3.2 Reusing higher level models

Are higher level models reusable? In the occupied / free block example, the higher model would be the one that says all the assumptions about sensors type and performances, rolling stock characteristics, etc, to define what the necessary occupation property should be. In other words, such a model would be a pre-digested understanding of what should be considered to design a safe and available train localisation system, with the choice of any type of rolling stock and sensors (within the assumptions limits) that the up-to-date technology can offer. This is naturally useful for any case that falls within the limits of the assumptions made on the environment. Naturally, the more abstract the models are, the more reusable they are.

Probably, the formal design between highest level models to detailed specifications might not be reusable, due to know-how confidentiality problems or simply because the next user will design differently. So the most reusable part is at the top, applicable to all analog cases in the domain. We obtain domain specific models which are pre-digested understanding of good, out of the field domain notions. This is reusable by construction.

The main difficulty for reusing higher level models is obviously that there are only few actually written. In addition to the technical difficulties depicted before, higher level models cause organisation problems: they require the collaboration of domain experts and "modelization" experts. Domain experts have a long time established view of their field, they won't easily accept any change in the way their notions are expressed: this would interfere with their very mental constructs. "Modelization" experts tend to reinvent terms and notions differently, which is a bad idea when unnecessary. To avoid these pitfalls, a common solution is trying to build a tool that would allow domain experts to become "modelization" experts as well. I'm afraid that this solution will always limit the quality of models.

If all these difficulties are overcome, let's imagine an equipment manufacturer who designs products with a first phase of higher level "modelization" gathering domain experts and formalization experts. How and why would this manufacturer propose his top level models for reuse by others? The immaterial nature of these models makes it difficult to view them as sell-able items. The only way I can think of is that certification organisms could collect these models as certification templates, a bit like the Common Criteria in the domain of IT system security. Quite often, the certification organism is the company that will use the final product; such companies gather the best possible set of domain experts. So if top level models could be created in phases where the manufacturer and the final exploitation company collaborate, these models would be certification templates from the start. The final exploitation company would naturally provide them to increase the competition between manufacturers and get better prices.

4. Who will pay for that?

Both for detailed or higher level models, there are clues for re-usability. But who will pay for that anyway? Formal models in projects are a bit like fluor in toothpaste: it costs more at the beginning and one can only see the effects after a long time.

Even if the perspective of formally specified reusable components and formally defined common certification models is nice, the first step to this is to collect data about the development and exploitation of complex systems and relate them to how much formalization was used. Only a big amount of such studies by independent organisms can prove the return over investment of formal methods. In the meantime, companies who regard the existing evidence as sufficient can use formal methods internally for the benefit of their customers, this is what we do at ClearSy. These companies can start the reuse process, probably more with reusable components than with higher level models.

5. Conclusion

There are two ways of reusing formal models that seem best promising:

- Providing components out of projects with detailed level formal specifications, claiming that the formal specifications make them reusable;
- Providing higher level formal models as certification criteria.

The development of these reuse possibilities should follow the spreading of formal methods. Let's see them as additional reasons to promote the use of formal methods.

A REFINEMENT BASED APPROACH TO CALCULATING A FAULT-TOLERANT RAILWAY SIGNAL DEVICE

Alistair A. McEwan & J. C. P. Woodcock
Computing Laboratory, University of Kent at Canterbury, UK
A.A.McEwan@kent.ac.uk, J.C.P.Woodcock@kent.ac.uk

Abstract In this extended abstract, we present a technique whereby a new, fail-safe and fault-tolerant architecture for an existing device is calculated, and verified, from an existing abstract specification. The inspiration for the architecture draws from the Byzantine Generals problem. The model is presented in Hoare's CSP, safety properties are proved using the model checker FDR, and development is guided by the laws of *Circus*. The case study is Montigel's Dwarf Signal.

Keywords: Safety, fault-tolerance, verification, CSP, *Circus*, Montigel's Dwarf Signal

1. Introduction

In this extended abstract, we show how safety critical devices employing distributed consensus approaches to compositional safety can be designed and calculated from an abstract specification, using Communicating Sequential Processes (CSP) [3, 9] and *Circus* [12]. A new implementation of an existing device is calculated from an existing abstract specification, appealing to a well-known distributed consensus algorithm. The result is an architecture that can be shown to preserve all the safety properties of the original, and offer more fault-tolerance. Proofs are conducted using a model-checking tool. The case study used is Montigel's Dwarf Signal [7], a track-side railway signalling device in use in the Austrian railway system.

We begin by presenting relevant background. Section 2 presents a CSP model of a simple distributed consensus algorithm, followed by a description in section 3 of how a new architecture can be calculated, developed, and verified; appealing to the distributed consensus algorithm. Finally, in section 4 we suggest where further improvements to the architecture may be possible, and analyse the success of the development strategy.

CSP and *Circus*

The process algebra CSP is a mathematical approach to the study of concurrency and communication. It is suited to the specification, design, and implementation of state-based system that are characterised by the events in which they participate. *Failures Divergences Refinement* (FDR) [5] is a tool for model-checking networks of CSP processes, checking the containment of processes, and allowing the proving or refuting of assertions about those processes.

The development of a Unifying Theory of Programming [4] has fuelled interest in integrating different languages and notations to obtain new formalisms. *Circus* is an integration of CSP, Z[15], the Guarded Command Language[2] and the Z Refinement Calculus[1]. The semantics of the language have been defined [13]; and a development calculus is presented in [12]. The reasons for choosing to conduct this case study in CSP and *Circus* are three-fold. Firstly, existing techniques in the area are presented in CSP. Secondly, the laws of *Circus* can be used to guide development. Thirdly, verification of each design step can be performed automatically using FDR.

[14] presents a refinement-based technique for verifying safety properties in CSP by building *safety specifications*. The technique involves a set of predicates, implemented as CSP processes, restricting observable states and transitions in a system. Furthermore, a model describing the safe/failed life cycle of a process is presented. This model is used to calculate the fault-tolerance of a system—the failures that can be tolerated before functionality is lost.

Development of the new device is done in a top-down manner. An existing abstract specification of the device is refined, guided by design decisions, into models where sections of the implementation are exposed gradually. It is our belief that, by taking an abstract specification, and refining it into a concrete model by applying a design calculus, greater confidence can be gained in the verification of the implementation, combined with the ability to experiment with design patterns.

Montigel's Dwarf Signal

Montigel's Dwarf Signal is a track-side railway signalling device produced by Alcatel, in use in the Austrian Railway system. The signal advises train drivers how to proceed on a section of track, indicating one of three options—*stop*, *go*, or *proceed with caution*. It is implemented using three lamp assemblies. A lamp assembly consists of the lamp, sensors reporting the state of the lamp, channels calculating required changes of state, actors effecting those changes and an interlock ensuring behaviour is agreed between actors. A further control system accepts commands from a signal-man—for instance, *set to go*—and translates these into concrete commands in each lamp assembly.

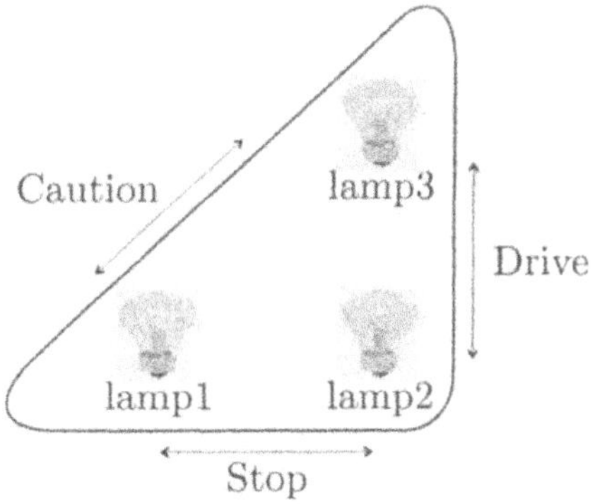

Figure 1. The Dwarf Signal

Previous work includes [11], demonstrating that CSP can be used to accurately model the Dwarf Signal. Furthermore, [14] constructs a safety specification for the device, and its behaviour is verified correct with respect to this safety specification. A further result is that it is shown that only one failure may be tolerated before all further functionality is lost, even though the device is in a safe state.

2. A CSP model of a distributed consensus algorithm

Frequently, distributed consensus algorithms are used to identify, and mitigate, failures in a system—the most general failure considered is termed a *Byzantine failure*, where a process may start to behave arbitrarily. Many authors have considered this problem, and a number of common problem areas and well understood algorithms is given in [6]. [8] introduces the constraint that a network containing unauthenticated signatures requires $3n+1$ processes to reach consensus in the presence of up to n failures, and that where messages are more reliable—i.e, authenticated, $2n + 1$ processes is sufficient. An algorithm for achieving consensus, and for identifying suspect processes is given.

The algorithm consists of two rounds of communication between participants. In the first round, each process informs every other of its intent, and in the second, informs every other process of information collected in the first round. A faulty process may lie at any stage, and the algorithm allows processes to detect this.

Previous experience of the case study permits optimisations of the algorithm. When a channel fails, it informs other channels—therefore other processes in the system may ignore it in all further negotiations. The other possibility of failure is in a sensor—in this event, a channel will observe in round one of the protocol that it disagrees with the majority, and take appropriate

$$
\begin{array}{l}
Inform_{v,a,P,Q} \mathrel{\widehat{=}} \\
\quad P \neq \emptyset \ \& \ \Box x : P \bullet \\
\qquad\qquad\qquad notify.x?y \rightarrow \textbf{if } y = v \textbf{ then } Inform_{v,a\cup\{x\},P\setminus\{x\},Q} \\
\qquad\qquad\qquad\qquad\qquad\qquad \textbf{else } Inform_{v,a,P\setminus\{x\},Q} \\
\quad \Box \\
\quad \neg\, Q \ \& \ notify.i.v \rightarrow Inform_{v,a\cup\{v\},P,true} \\
\quad \Box \\
\quad P = \emptyset \wedge Q \ \& \ \textbf{if } \#a \leq 2 \textbf{ then } Minority'_{Chan} \textbf{ else } Consent_v
\end{array}
$$

$$
\begin{array}{l}
Consent_v \mathrel{\widehat{=}} \\
\quad actuate.i.v \rightarrow Inform_{v,\{i\},Chan\setminus\{i\},false}
\end{array}
$$

$$
\begin{array}{l}
Minority_P \mathrel{\widehat{=}} \\
\quad ((|||\ x : P \setminus \{i\} \bullet notify.x?y \rightarrow SKIP) \ ||| \ notify.i.gs \rightarrow SKIP); \\
\qquad Minority'_P
\end{array}
$$

$$
\begin{array}{l}
Minority'_P \mathrel{\widehat{=}} \\
\quad (|||\ x : P \bullet confirm.x?y \rightarrow SKIP); \ actuate.i.gs \rightarrow Minority_P
\end{array}
$$

Figure 2. An optimised protocol for a channel

action. Therefore any one channel has no need to suspect that another has failed, leading to an optimised, single voting round version of the protocol, as in figure 2.

3. Development strategy

Figure 3 presents the development strategy for the new design, and compares it to a suggested strategy for the existing design. This strategy is divided into four identifiable stages, one of which is common to both designs.

In the first stage, the existing abstract specification is refined into one where a lamp, and an abstract model of the control system is revealed. In the second stage, the decision to adopt a distributed consensus algorithm is taken, and consequently, the refined abstract control system reveals interlocks and an abstraction of a four-way lane. Verification of both of these stages is performed automatically using FDR, and calculated using a test-refute cycle.

In the third stage, externally observable state in each lane is revealed, and the actions are partitioned into four concurrent processes using the laws of *Circus*. Typically, a development step such as this in a *Circus* specification involves

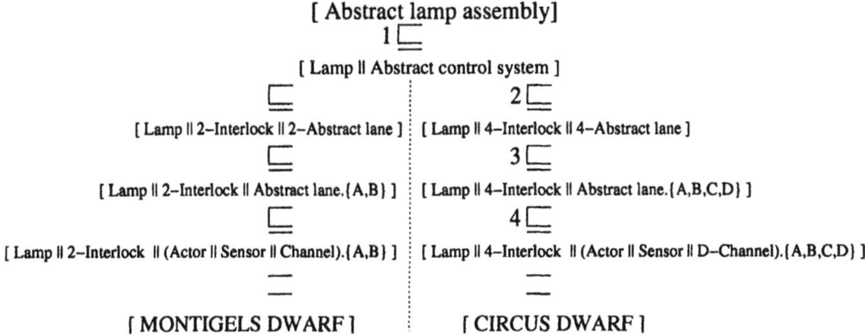

Figure 3. Development strategy for 2 and 4 lane architectures

proof obligations; however, in this case study, we verify the correctness of the design step using FDR.

The final stage is to calculate the specification of a channel from the previous phase. This is a weakest pre-specification style calculation: the behaviour sought is that of the abstract specification minus the known behaviour of the actor and sensor. The implementation of this weakest pre-specification must use the distributed consensus model, and the correctness is again verified using FDR.

Figure 4 shows the final architecture. Lamps, sensors, actors and interlocks are all taken from [11]. The interlock system consists of three interlocks, allowing four inputs. A lane consists of a sensor, an actor, and a channel. The lamp reports to all of the sensors, each of which in turn reports to its channel, which, in turn, drives its actor. Each channel is driven by the outside world through its *set* command, and communicated its intentions, or failure, via the events *inform*, and *die*. A channel drives its actor via a *change* event, which, in turn, attempts to drive its interlock via a *switch* command. Failure, negotiations, and driving the actor are internal to the lane and not externally visible.

4. Conclusions and future work

Previous work showed the abstract specification to be fail-safe; transitivity of refinement guarantees that the new architecture is also. Additionally, existing techniques may be applied to the new architecture to investigate the hypothesis that it is more fault-tolerant than the existing design.

[8] introduced the result that when messages are authenticated, $2n+1$ processes are sufficient to achieve safety in the presence of n failures. In this case study, messages are assumed authenticated and correct. If this assumption holds in the physical device, three lanes would be sufficient to tolerate the failure of a single lane; investigation of this is an item we leave for future work.

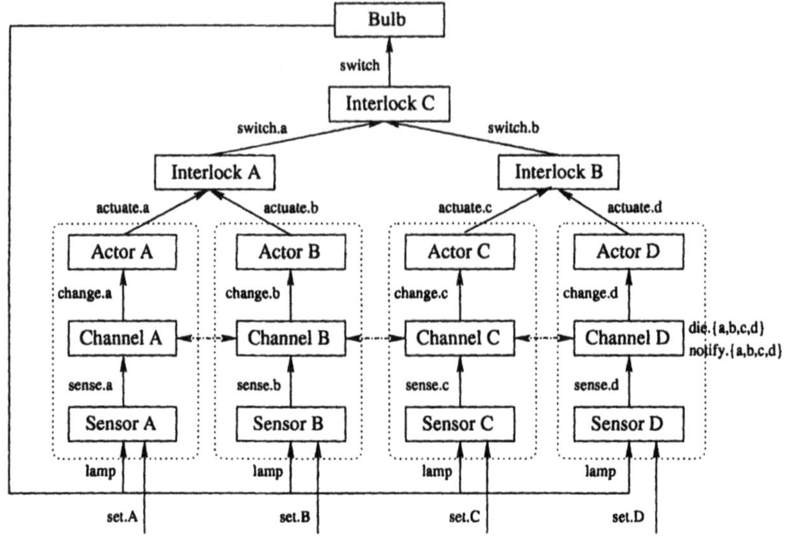

Figure 4. A 4-lane distributed consensus design

A second possible optimisation concerns the interlock. An interlock drives the lamp to ground state if any of the participants request it: this may happen in the case of a single actor failure. However, in this architecture, a channel only requests to leave ground state if it is correct to do so—so an interlock that effected a change out of ground state if *any* actor requests it may tolerate more actor failure. Design of such an interlock is an area we leave for future investigation.

A limitation of this model is the assumption that the *set* commands received by a lamp assembly are synchronous and reliable. This assumption may be too strong if the control system driving the three lamps has failure modes where this is not the case. Investigation of a more asynchronous model of driving the channels is another item we leave for future investigation.

In conclusion, in this abstract we have demonstrated how a new design for an existing device may be developed using CSP and refinement laws for *Circus*, and the development steps verified using FDR. By designing the new architecture to use existing distributed consensus results, a more fault-tolerant system has been built.

References

[1] A. L. C. Cavalcanti. *A Refinement Calculus for Z*. DPhil thesis, The University of Oxford, 1997.

[2] E. W. Dijkstra. *A Discipline of Programming*. Prentice-Hall, 1976.

[3] C. A. R. Hoare. *Communicating Sequential Processes*. Prentice-Hall International Series in Computer Science. Prentice-Hall, 1985.

[4] C. A. R. Hoare and Jifeng He. *Unifying Theories of Programming*. Prentice-Hall Series in Computer Science. Prentice-Hall, 1998.

[5] Formal Systems (Europe) Ltd. FDR: User manual and tutorial, version 2.28. Technical report, Formal Systems (Europe) Ltd., 1999.

[6] Nancy A. Lynch. *Distributed Algorithms*. Morgan-Kaufmann, 1996.

[7] Markus Montigel. Specification of the control processes for a Dwarf Signal. In *Proceedings of the 5th FMERail Workshop*, Toulouse, France, 1999.

[8] M. Pease, R. Shostak, and L. Lamport. Reaching agreement in the presence of faults. *Journal of the Association for Computing Machinery*, 27, 1980.

[9] A. W. Roscoe. *The theory and practice of concurrency*. Prentice Hall Series in Computer Science. Prentice Hall, 1998.

[10] Andrew Clive Simpson. *Safety through security*. DPhil thesis, The University of Oxford, 1996.

[11] J. C. P. Woodcock. Montigel's Dwarf, a treatment of the Dwarf Signal problem using CSP/FDR. In *Proceedings of the 5th FMERail Workshop*, Toulouse, France, 1999.

[12] J. C. P. Woodcock and A. L. C. Cavalcanti. A concurrent language for refinement. In *5th Irish Workshop on Formal Methods*, 2001.

[13] J. C. P. Woodcock and A. L. C. Cavalcanti. The semantics of Circus. In Didier Ber, Jonathan P. Bowen, Martin C. Henson, and Ken Robinson, editors, *Formal Specification and Development in Z and B*, pages 184–203. ZB 2002, Springer-Verlag, 2002.

[14] J. C. P. Woodcock and Alistair A. McEwan. Verifying the safety of a railway signalling device. In H. Ehrig, B. J. Kramer, and A. Ertas, editors, *Proceedings of IDPT 2002*, volume 1. The 6th Biennial World Conference on Integrated Design and Process Technology, Society for Design and Process Science, 2002. Winner of the best paper award.

[15] Jim Woodcock and Jim Davies. *Using Z: Specification, Refinement, and Proof*. International Series in Computer Science. Prentice-Hall, 1996.

FROM RAILWAY RESOURCE PLANNING TO TRAIN OPERATION

a brief survey of complementary formalisations

Martin Penicka*
Department of Applied Mathematics, Faculty of Transportation Sciences, Czech Technical University, Na Florenci 25, CZ-11000 Prague
penicka@fd.cvut.cz

Dines Bjørner*
Department of Computer Science, School of Computing, National University of Singapore, 3 Science Drive 2, Singapore 117543
E–Mail: bjorner@comp.nus.edu.sg, URL: http://www.comp.nus.edu.sg/cs/

Abstract From seasonal planning via day-to-day train operation to real-time monitoring and control of trains, software applications are becoming increasingly integrated. Timetabling implies train traffic. Train staff rosters and train car maintenance are initially derived from timetables and influences future timetables.

In this extended abstract we shall sketch a formal model of Railway Nets, Timetables, Rosters, Maintenance, Station Interlocking, Line Direction Agreement and Automatic Line Signaling. The last three formal models are based on four integrated formal techniques (RAISE, Petri Nets, Live Sequence Charts and State Charts). The formal sketches are all "backed-up" by either a publication or a research report.

Keywords: Railways, Planning, Timetabling, Rostering, Control, Interlocking, Signalling, RAISE, Petri Nets, Live Sequence Charts, State Charts, Technique Integration

1. Railway System

A *railway system* (Ω) can be modelled as a function from *time* (T) to states of a *railway net* (N), to states of all *rolling stock* (RS), to its *timetable* (TT), to states of all *passengers* (P) and *freight* (F).

*This paper was written while the authors were at Inst. of Informatics & Modelling, Technical University of Denmark, DK-2800 Kgs. Lyngby, Denmark. The first author gratefully acknowledges support from the EU 5FP Network of Excellence Programme: CoLogNET: Computational Logic Network

```
type
    T, N, RS, TT, P, F
    Ω' = T → (N × RS × TT × (P × F))
    Ω = {|rw:Ω' • wf_Ω(rw)|}
value
    wf_Ω: Ω' → Bool
    wf_Ω(rw) ≡ well-formedness of railway states
```

The well-formedness describes constraints that must be met by any railway system. They are laws of nature, e.g. trains move monotically, net changes states accordingly, etc.

2. Allocation & Scheduling of Resources

From Passenger Statistics to Railway Nets and Timetables

Passenger statistics (STA) express predicted number of passengers between pairs of *geographical centers* (C) (urban area were potential passengers live) in *time intervals* (TxT). From a *cartographical map* (MAP) one can observe the geographical centers and their positions.

```
type
    MAP, C, POS
    STA' = (C×C) →m ((T×T) →m Nat)
    STA = {|sta:STA' • wf_sta(sta)|}
value
    wf_sta: STA → Bool
    wf_mapsta: MAP × STA → Bool
    obs_Cs: MAP → C-set
    obs_Pos: MAP × C → POS
```

A railway net (N) is composed from stations and lines. *Lines* (T) connect stations. A *railway station* (S) is a place where trains stop to allow passengers to enter and get off a train as reflected in timetable.

A *timetable* (TT) expresses for all *planned trains* (Tn) their *journeys* (J). A train *journey* (J) is a list of line visits (departure time from a station, line, arrival time time to a station, train *capacity* (K), and possible *periodicity* (PRD) (e.g. 24hour, or 20 minutes) and *restrictions* (RST) on the days for which it applies (e.g. Mon-Fri, only or summer season only)).

Now one can define a function genNTT which from a given geographical map and passenger statistics, and according to a given set of *predicates* (P), generates all possible pairs of *nets and timetables* (NTT), such that these satisfy the map and the passenger statistics.

```
type
    N, L, S
    Tn, PRD, RST

    TT' = Tn →m J
    TT = {|tt:TT' • wf_TT(tt)|}
    NTT' = N × TT
    NTT = {|ntt:NTT' • wf_NTT(ntt)|}

    J = (T×S×L×S×T×K×PRD×RST)*
    P: N × TT → Bool
value
    p: P
    wf_TT: TT' → Bool
    wf_NTT: NTT' → Bool

    genNTT: (MAP × STA) → P → NTT-infset
    genNTT(map,sta)(p) as intts
        post ∀ ntt: NTT • ntt ∈ intts ⇒
            satisfy(n,map) ∧ satisfy(tt,sta) ∧ p(n,tt)
```

From Nets & Timetables to Operational Planning

Let us now define a usually heuristic operational planning process, `Planning`, which from a given geographical map and passenger statistics according to a given set of *predicates* (`P`), generates one possible pair of *nets and timetables* (`NTT`).

```
Planning(map, sta)(p) ≡
    let ntts = genNTT(map,sta)(p) in
    if card ntts = 1 then ntts
    else
        if ∃ p′: P • 1 ≤ card genNTT(map,sta)(p′) < card ntts in
            then let p′: P • 1 ≤ card genNTT(map,sta)(p′) < card ntts in
                Planning(map,sta)(p′) end
            else let ntt: NTT • ntt ∈ ntts in ntt end
        end
    end
    end
```

From Timetables and Rolling Stock to Vehicle Scheduling

Given a net, a timetable and an available *rolling stock* (`RS`) one is interested in computing optimal *working plans* (`VWP`) for *vehicles* (`V`) of rolling stock such that these plans honour the timetable. A set of *predicates* (`P`) on rolling stock, nets and timetables has to be satisfied (one can operate electric powered engine only on suitable lines, etc.). We model the set of predicate as one "grand" predicate.

```
type
    V, RS = V-set
    VWP = (V ⇀ (Tn × J)*) × RS

    P: N × TT × RS × RS → Bool
value
    p: P

genVWP: (N×TT×RS)→P→VWP-set
genVWP(n,tt,rs)(p) as vwps
    post ∀ (vwp,rs′):VWP • (vwp,rs′) ∈ vwps ⇒
        dom vwp ⊆ rs ∧ rs′=rs\dom vwp ∧
        honour(n,tt,vwp) ∧
        p(n,tt,rs,rs′)
```

From Timetables and Human Resources to Rostering

Given a net and a timetable one can determine the number of *human resources* (`HR`) of each type (drivers, conductors, etc.) needed to honour the timetable. We refer to [5]. Let us just show, how one can generate a set of *working plans* (`HWP`) for *railway employees* (`H`). A set of *predicates* (`P`) on human resources, nets and timetables has to be satisfied. We model the set of predicate as one "grand" predicate.

```
type
    H, HR = H-set
    HWP = (H ⇀ (Tn × J)*) × HR

    P: N × TT × VWP × HR × HR → Bool

value
    p: P
```

```
genHWP: (N×TT×VWP×HR)→P→HWP-set
genHWP(n,tt,vwp,hr)(p) as hwps
    post ∀ (hwp,hr′):HWP • (hwp,hr′) ∈ hwps ⇒
        dom hwp ⊆ hr ∧ hr′=hr\dom hwp ∧
        honour(n,tt,vwp,hwp,hr) ∧
        p(n,tt,vwp,hr,hr′)
```

From Timetables to Vehicle Maintenance

The earlier vehicle working plans did not specify that any vehicle has to undergo preventive maintenance. We now define a set of functions, which modify vehicle working plans to reflect timely maintenance. By a maintenance we understand all regular activities which must be done with rolling stock and according to some *rules* (R). Each vehicle, according to its type, has associated with it certain types of maintenance tasks to be performed with a frequency which can be expressed by elapsed number of kilometer or operating house since a previous maintenance.

Given a *railway net* (N), *vehicle working plans* (VWP), a *timetable* (TT) and a *planning period* (TxT) the job is to generate all the possible *sets of changes* (CS), necessary and sufficient to secure maintenance. Given these sets, one is selected and used for update of existing vehicle working plans.

```
type
    CS = (DayChange | NightChange | EmptyRide)-set
value
    genCS: N×TT×VWP×(T×T) ~→ CS-set

    MPlanning: N×TT×VWP×(T×T)→(VWP×CS)
    MPlanning(n,tt,vwp,(tb,te)) ≡
        let css = genCS(n,tt,vwp,(tb,te)) in
            Select(vwp,css) end

    Select: VWP×CS-set → (VWP×CS)
    Select(vwp,css) as (vwp′,cs)
        post cs ∈ css ∧ equivalent(vwp,vwp′)
```

More details about this task can be found in [4].

3. Monitoring & Control

Railway Net States. *Lines* (L) and *stations* (S) are composed from "smallest" rail parts called *units* (U) (linear, points, cross-overs, switchable cross-overs). A unit define a number of connectors (linear:2, point:3, cross-overs:4). A subset of pairs of distinct connectors of a unit define paths though the unit. By a *unit state* (Σ) we understand any such subset. A unit may change state. The state space of a unit is called Ψ. A unit is said to be closed, if it is in *path state* ($\sigma_{\{\}}$) of no paths.

A *route* (R) is a sequence of units. A route is open, if all units are in non-closed states and if the units state paths connect [1].

By *traffic* (TF) we mean a function from time to net and *train states* (TΠ). A train state contains information about train position on the net, its actual and planned velocity and acceleration, etc. Our *primed definition of traffic* (TF') defines values that do not respect laws-of-nature (there are no "ghost trains", trains do not"jump" all over the net, etc.). Also desired *railways properties* (RR) are not respected in TF' (train movements only on open routes, only one train on a open route, obeying interlocking rules and regulations, etc.). See [3].

```
type
    N, TΠ, Tn, POS, RR
    U, C, P=C×C
    Σ = P-set
    Ψ = Σ-set

    TF′ = T → (N × TP)
    TF = {|tf:TR′ • wf_TF(tf)|}
    TP = Tn ⇀ TΠ

value
    obs_Cs: U → C-set
    obs_Σ: U → Σ
    obs_Ψ: U → Ψ

    wf_TF: TF′ → Bool
    wf_TF(tf) ≡ obeyLaws(tf)

    obs_POS: TΠ → POS
    regs: TF × N × RR → Bool
```

From Timetable to Traffic

The syntactic quantity a *timetable* (TT) denotes the semantic quantity a set of possible *traffics* (TF) which satisfy the timetable. See [2].

```
type
    TR, TT, N

value
    denote: TT × N → TF-infset
    denote(tt,n) as itfs
        ∀ tf:FT • tf ∈ itfs ⇒
            regulations(tf,n) ∧ obeysTT(tf,tt,n)
```

From Traffic to Station Interlocking

The above model of dynamics of units did not show how units change states. This is what we will now consider. We will use Petri Nets to model conditions for state changes of a unit.

Interlocking has to do with setting up proper routes from station approached signal to a track (platform) in the station and from these to the lines. We shall focus on one way of constructing models for proper interlocking control scheme using Place Transmission Petri Nets. Petri Net for stations can be built up from four subparts: Petri Net for units, for switches (ie., point or switchable crossover), for signals (Fig. 1), and finally Petri Net for routes. The Petri Net of a route (Fig. 2) is then a composition of all its unit, switch and signal Petri Nets — where the composition is specified by an interlocking table. Since we do not show a specific station nor its interlocking table we refrain from showing the full Petri Net [3]. The table expresses for each interesting route the state requirements for switches (points and switchable crossovers) and the requirements for signal states.

So, on one hand we have our RSL model for nets and trains states; on the other hand we have shown Petri Nets that control state spaces. In other words we have brought two different specification techniques. Hence from RLS specification of a station one can build a interlocking table and then the Petri Net.

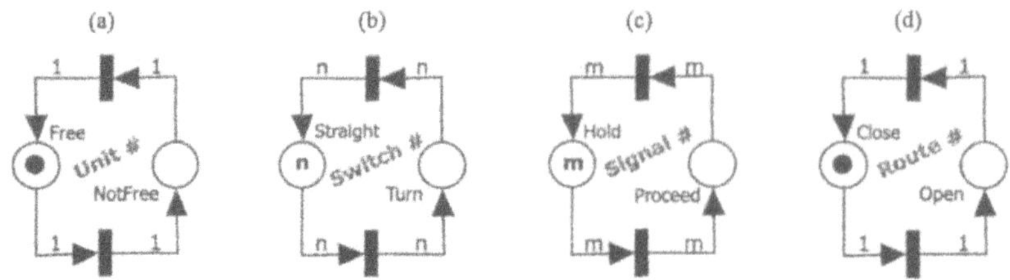

Figure 1. Petri Net for unit, switch, signal and route

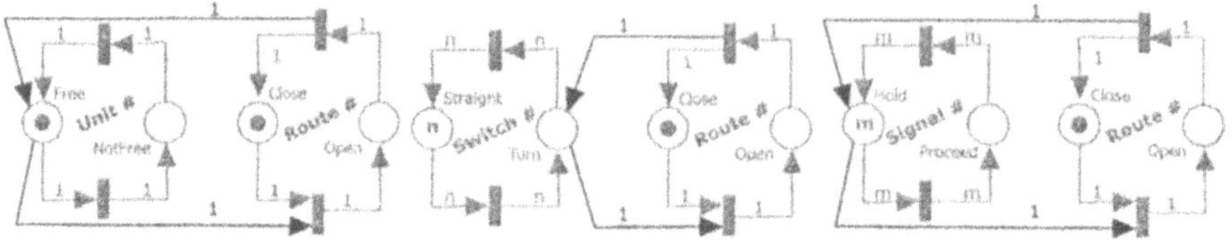

Figure 2. Adding arcs for unit|switch|signal and route

From Traffic to Line Direction Agreement

The above RSL model of traffic did not show how certain rules could be obeyed. In this section we with to show one of the important safety properties of a railway line: that two trains are not allowed to move in opposite directions on a line. One way of ensuring this is by a so called Line Direction Agreement System (LDAS).

The externally visible behavior of the LDAS can be illustrated using Live Sequence Charts. The three entities are: Station A (SA), the Line Direction Agreement System (LDAS), and Station B (SB). The charts in Figure 3 illustrate only the partial communication as seen from Station A. The mutual exclusive control of the LDAS can illustrated by a Statechart. For more details we refer to [3]. Transitions of the Statechart corresponds to messages of the LDAS.

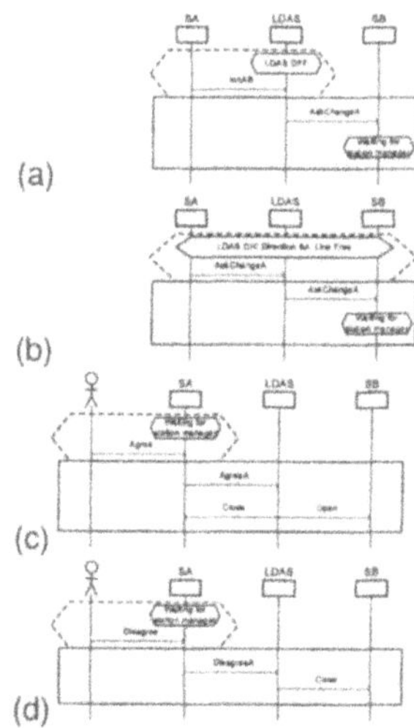

Figure 3. (a) Initial LDAS, (b) Request Direction Reversal, (c) Request Approval, (d) Request Rejection

From Traffic to Automatic Line Signalling

Again the above RSL model of traffic did not show how trains on a line can be separated. Lines connect exactly two stations and can be divided into several segments (see Fig. 4). Each segment can be either in '*Free*' state (when no train is detected in the segment) or in '*Occupied*' state. For each segment there are two signals (one in each direction of travel). With each signal we associate four possible states (*'Hold'*, *'NextHold'*, *'Proceed'* and *'Off'*).

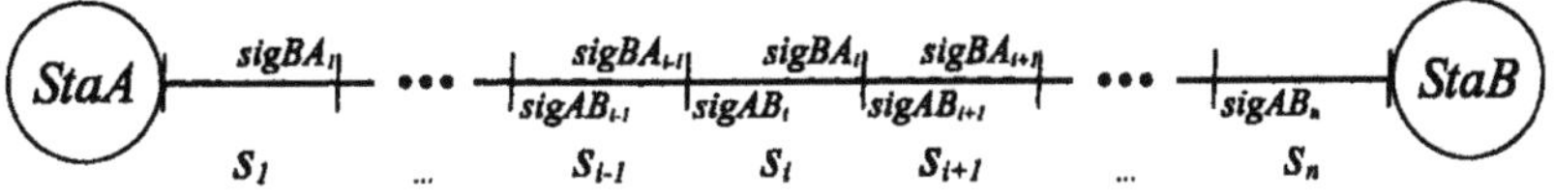

Figure 4. Signal positions on a line with n segments

```
type
    TR, N, L, S, SEG, SIG
    SegSt == Free | Occupied
    SigSt == Hold | NextHold | Proceed | Off
value
    obs_Ss: L → S-set
    obs_Segs: L → SEG*
    obs_Sigs: SEG → SIG × SIG
    obs_SegState: TR × SEG → SegSt
    obs_SigState: TR × SIG → SigSt
```

Statecharts can be used to specify requirements for pair of signals along a line including pairs including station interlocking.

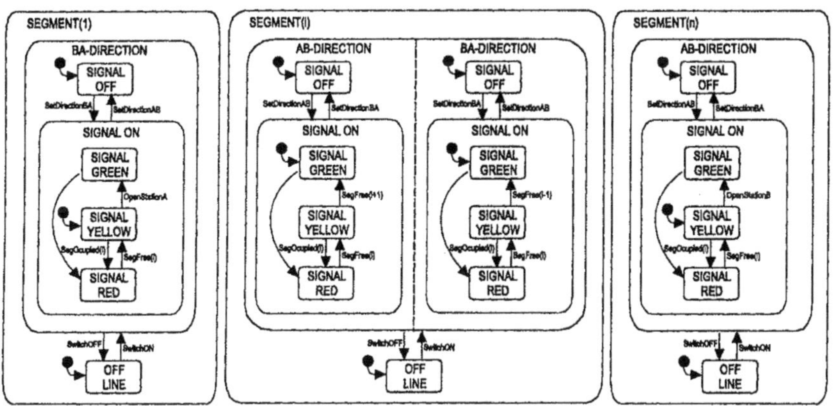

Figure 5. Sub-Statechart for Automatic signalling in lines

The Statechart for a line with three and more segments is composed from the three subparts shown on Fig. 5.

4. Conclusion

We have covered a part of the railway domain by rough sketching the synopses of several examples concerning scheduling & allocation and monitoring & control aspects of railways. Our focus has been the underlying formal models. Several different formal methods, f.e. RAISE, Petri Net, StateChart, Live Sequence Chart have been used.

References

[1] Dines Bjorner. Dynamics of Railway Nets: On an Interface between Automatic Control and Software Engineering. In *CTS2003: 10th IFAC Symposium on Control in Transportation Systems*, Oxford, UK, August 4-6 2003. Elsevier Science Ltd. Symposium held at Tokyo, Japan. Editors: S. Tsugawa and M. Aoki.

[2] Dines Bjfirner, Jakob Braad, and Karin S. Mogensen (Eds.). Models of Railway Systems: Domain. In Thierry Lecomte and Peter Gorm Larsen, editors, *FME Rail Workshop # 5*, volume # 5 of *FME Rail Workshop; Toulouse, France*. FME: Formal Methods Europe, Steria, France, September 22–24 1999. (60 pages) Dept. of IT, Techn. Univ. of Denmark.

[3] Dines Bjorner, Chris George, Anne E. Haxthausen, Christian Krog Madsen, Steffen Holmslykke, and Martin Penicka. "UML"–ising Formal Techniques. In *INT 2004: Third International Workshop on Integration of Specification Techniques for Applications in Engineering*. Institut fur Softwaretechnik und Theoretische Informatik, Sekr. FR 6-1, Techn.Univ. of Berlin, Franklinstrasse 28/29, D–10587 Berlin, Germany, 28 March 2004, ETAPS, Barcelona, Spain. To be published in INT–2004 Proceedings, Springer–Verlag.

[4] Martin Penicka, Albena Kirilova Strupchanska, and Dines Bjorner. Train Maintenance Routing. In *FORMS'2003: Symposium on Formal Methods for Railway Operation and Control Systems*. L'Harmattan Hongrie, 15–16 May 2003. Conf. held at Techn.Univ. of Budapest, Hungary. Editors: G. Tarnai and E. Schnieder, Germany.

[5] Albena Kirilova Strupchanska, Martin Penicka, and Dines Bjorner. Railway Staff Rostering. In *FORMS2003: Symposium on Formal Methods for Railway Operation and Control Systems*. L'Harmattan Hongrie, 15–16 May 2003. Conf. held at Techn.Univ. of Budapest, Hungary. Editors: G. Tarnai and E. Schnieder, Germany.

INTEGRATED FORMAL METHODS FOR SAFETY ANALYSIS OF TRAIN SYSTEMS

Wolfgang Reif, Frank Ortmeier, Andreas Thums, and Gerhard Schellhorn
Chair of Software Engineering, Department of Computer Science, University of Augsburg, Universitätsstr 14, 86135 Augsburg, Germany
E-Mail: {reif, ortmeier}@informatik.uni-augsburg.de

Abstract In many technical applications the notion of system safety covers different aspects. The first is correct functioning. This means that the system does what it is supposed to do. The second is an analysis of failures and their effects. This answers the question what happens, if components break or fail. And finally a quantitative analysis, which quantifies the risk of the system and its subsystems.

In all three dimension formal methods may help. Temporal logics and formal verification assure functional correctness. Formal safety analysis techniques give rigorous proof of cause-consequence relationships. finally statistical models and mathematical optimization help to minimize risk and give advice for design decisions.

In this paper we sketch an example and illustrate how such an integrated approach can be done and what benefits it provides.

Keywords: safety analysis, formal methods, fault tree analysis, quantitative optimization

1. Introduction

New technologies are emerging in every aspect of railways. Let it be electronic scheduling and speed control, new propulsion techniques like in the German ICE 3, where the engines are distributed among all cars of the whole train or autonomous, intelligent equipment on the track. This all results in great benefits like faster travel, less energy consumption and improved maintainability. But there is also a price to pay for it. More and more software has to be integrated into the control units, control is increasingly decentralized and the complexity of track items like track switches, signals or level crossings rises dramatically.

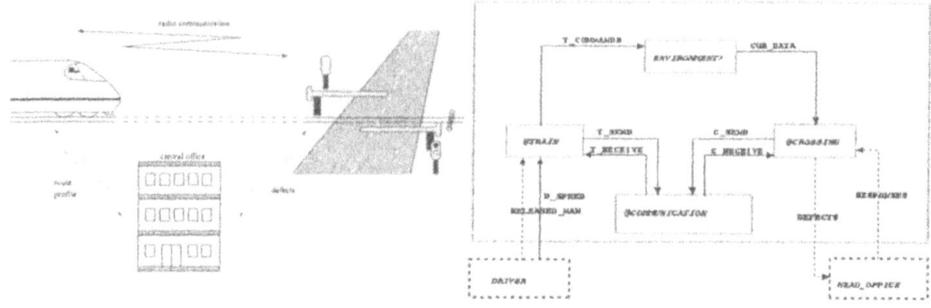

Figure 1. Overview over the Radio-Based Crossing

Figure 2. Involved subsystems for the Radio-Based Crossing

This results in an increased risk of failure. For example the U.S. Department of Transportation lists in its 2003 report on transportation [6] more fatalities involving railroads than any other form of transportation besides cars.

The most advanced techniques with respect to safety guarantees are formal methods. Systems are described as mathematical models and safety predictions can be analyzed and rigorously verified. In the following we present the ForMoSA approach for safety-critical systems [9]. It combines formal methods and safety analysis techniques covering different aspects of safety.

2. An Example

In the following example is taken from the German railway organization, Deutsche Bahn, which prepares a novel technique to control level crossings: the decentralized, radio-based level crossing control [7]. This technique aims at medium speed routes, i.e. routes with maximum speed of 160 km/h. The main difference between this technology and the traditional control of level crossings is, that there is no central control unit. Signals and sensors on the route are connected by radio communication. Software computations in the train and in the level crossing decide if the crossing can be passed safely or if an emergency stop must be triggered.

To achieve this, the train computes the position where it has to send a signal to secure the level crossing. Therefore the train has to know the position of the level crossing, the time needed to secure the level crossing, and its current speed and position, which is measured by an odometer. When the level crossing receives this command it switches on the traffic lights - first the 'yellow' light, then the 'red' light - and finally closes the barriers. When they are closed, the level crossing is 'safe' for a certain period of time. After this time the crossing opens the barriers again automatically.

The train requests the status of the level crossing, before reaching the latest point for a safety stop. Depending on the answer the train will brake or pass the crossing. The level crossing periodically performs self-diagnosis and automatically informs the central office about defects and problems. This solution is cheaper and more flexible than a centralized control, but also shifts safety critical functionality towards all involved components.

This example involves a number of complex tasks like calculations of speed, expected time of arrival at the danger zone (DZ) of the level crossing and latest point in time for a safety stop in the train, specific control sequences for the crossing to activate the lights and the bars with respect to different timing constraints and - between crossing and train - a radio based communication protocol. All these components must interact correctly to assure safety.

The main safety relevant questions, that must be answered, are:

- "Is this complex interplay correctly designed, such that the system always closes the barriers before a train passes?" (functional correctness)
- "How failure tolerant is the design? What happens if e.g. the radio communication is out of order" (failure tolerance)
- "What is an upper bound for failure? Is there a better design with less risk?" (risk calibration)

3. Modeling and Verification

First the radio-based level crossing is modeled in the formalism of state charts (of Statemate). This notation has a formal semantics [4] and is very similar to common engineering notations. Figure 2 shows the top level of the model of the example. The system is decomposed into the four parts train, crossing, communication and environment. These parts are again modeled using state charts and activity charts.

Mathematically the system model describes a set of traces over which the safety properties can be expressed in temporal logic. To express safety properties we use interval temporal logic (ITL) [3]. This logic allows to state many safety properties in a very intuitive way. The central safety property in the example - a train must not pass the crossing while the barriers are not closed - is stated in ITL as follows:

$$\Box\ (Train = DZ \rightarrow Barriers = closed)$$

This formula says: "It is always the case ($\Box$), that a passing train (Train=DZ) implies ($\rightarrow$), that the barriers are closed (Barriers=closed)." The next step is to verify or falsify the property. Depending on the system we use an interactive theorem prover - the KIV system [2] - or a suitable model checker.

In the example the first proof attempts failed and revealed a safety gap. The gap is, that the original system design had some flaws involving different timers, responsible for reopening the barriers after the train has passed the crossing. This problem could be fixed, and then the safety property could successfully be verified.

4. Formal Safety Analysis

Verification showed, that the complex interaction between all components works correctly. This means, there are no inadvertent flaws in the design of the system. The next step is to analyze, what happens if for example the brakes fail or the barriers get stuck. Cause-consequence techniques like fault tree analysis (FTA) [5] or failure modes and effects analysis (FMEA) try to answer this problem.

FTA stepwise reduces hazards to primary events that may cause the hazard. For example an unsafe crossing may be due to either a failure of the brakes **or** the barriers getting stuck.

Originally FTA and FMEA operate on informal models. In ForMoSA both techniques have been formalized [10]. FTA gates resp. the connection of the FMEA columns are expressed in interval temporal logic. Then it is possible to use the same reasoning techniques as before to verify the correctness of the analysis. So if the fault tree has the form, that a collision may only occur if either the brakes failed or the barriers got stuck, this could be translated into the (ITL) formula:

$$\Box\ (Collision \rightarrow Brakes = failure \vee Barriers = stuck)$$

If this formula is proven correct, then a universal theorem - the minimal cut set theorem - ensures, that no other causes for a potential collision have been forgotten (at least with respect to the mathematical system model).

5. Quantitative Analysis

In practical application no safety analysis is complete without a quantitative assessment on the risk. Most traditional safety analysis techniques incorporate a quantitative part as well [11]. This part may easily be adopted for formal safety analysis.

But the quantitative analysis may also be augmented. For example traditionally quantitative FTA is simply done by using static probabilities for all leaves of the fault tree. In many applications, this often not good enough. Systems frequently have free parameters, which have various effects on the system. In the example, allowed speed of the train or run-times of the timers are such parameters. This makes it necessary to give up the requirement of static probabilities but rather use continuous distribution functions. This allows a far more elaborate analysis, as the effect of free parameters on the system may be examined. It is even possible to find optimal configurations, that minimize risk [8]. Another possibility to use formal methods to improve quantitative analysis is the use of probabilistic model checkers [1]. This approach allows to analyze the difficult problem of common cause failures. But it requires more elaborate system models as input.

6. Summary

Railways is not only traditionally but also nowadays highly safety-critical. This makes an increase in R&D effort for safety necessary. Increasing complexity and more and more software in all parts of railways systems result in very difficult safety analysis tasks. This problem may be addressed using formal methods. They are very well suited to deal with software/hardware interaction. Formal methods are used for safety critical applications in three flavors. Verification is used to assure correct functioning. Formal safety analysis gives answers about qualitative safety-critical, cause-consequence relationships. Mathematical and statistical models help in finding upper bounds for risk and to calibrate antagonistic safety requirements.

Altogether, the approach helps to achieve a very high level of safety with acceptable effort.

References

[1] Christel Baier, Edmund M. Clarke, Vassili Hartonas-Garmhausen, Marta Z. Kwiatkowska, and Mark Ryan. Symbolic model checking for probabilistic processes. In *Automata, Languages and Programming*, pages 430–440, 1997.

[2] M. Balser, W. Reif, G. Schellhorn, K. Stenzel, and A. Thums. Formal system development with KIV. In T. Maibaum, editor, *Fundamental Approaches to Software Engineering*, number 1783 in LNCS, pages 363–366. Springer-Verlag, 2000.

[3] A. Cau, B. Moszkowski, and H. Zedan. *ITL – Interval Temporal Logic*. Software Technology Research Laboratory, SERCentre, De Montfort University, The Gateway, Leicester LE1 9BH, UK, 2002. www.cms.dmu.ac.uk/~cau/itlhomepage.

[4] W. Damm, B. Josko, H. Hungar, and A. Pnueli. A compositional real-time semantics of STATEMATE designs. In W.-P. de Roever, H. Langmaack, and A. Pnueli, editors, *COMPOS' 97*, volume 1536 of *LNCS*, pages 186–238. Springer-Verlag, 1998.

[5] J. Fragole J. Minarik II J. Railsback Dr. W. Vesley, Dr. Joanne Dugan. *Fault Tree Handbook with Aerospace Applications*. NASA Office of Safety and Mission Assurance, NASA Headquarters, Washington DC 20546, August 2002.

[6] Marsha Fenn, editor. *Transportation Statistics Annual Report*. U.S. Department of Transportation, Bureau of Transportation Statistics, October 2003.

[7] J. Klose and A. Thums. The STATEMATE reference model of the reference case study 'Verkehrsleittechnik'. Technical Report 2002-01, Universitat Augsburg, 2002.

[8] F. Ortmeier and W. Reif. Safety optimization: A combination of fault tree analysis and optimization techniques. Technical Report 5, Institut für Informatik, Universität Augsburg, 2004.

[9] F. Ortmeier and A. Thums. Formale Methoden und Sicherheitsanalyse. Technical Report 15, Universität Augsburg, 2002. (in German).

[10] G. Schellhorn, A. Thums, and W. Reif. Formal fault tree semantics. In *Proceedings of The Sixth World Conference on Integrated Design & Process Technology*, Pasadena, CA, 2002.

[11] W. E. Vesely, F. F. Goldberg, N. H. Roberts, and D. F. Haasl. *Fault Tree Handbook*. Washington, D.C., 1981. NUREG-0492.

STOCHASTIC TRAIN DOMAIN THEORY FRAMEWORK

Theo C. Giras, Zongli Lin
Center of Rail Safety-Critical Excellence, Department of Electrical and Computer Engineering University of Virginia, P.O. Box 400743, Charlottesville, VA 22904-4743, U.S.A.
tgiras@virginia.edu, zl5y@ee.virginia.edu

Abstract The Axiomatic Safety-Critical Assessment Process (ASCAP) is illustrated as a Stochastic Train Domain Theory Framework "Plug & Play" large-scale Monte Carlo simulation vision. The framework supports the US traditional railway system component models as generalized operational train line taxonomy. The railway domain can be Direct Traffic Control (DTC), Centralized Traffic Control (CTC), Cab Signaling, Positive Train Control (PTC) or a Maglev system. The train line taxonomy is characterized as a stochastic train domain that provides either a design for safety or a risk assessment framework. The design for safety domain is the dual of the risk assessment domain. A significant property of the stochastic vision is that it handles the stochastic quantification of safety for processor-based train systems integrated with structural and electromechanical devices.

The stochastic Train Domain Theory Framework vision is illustrated with a Maglev guideway reliability, availability, maintainability and safety (RAMS) Monte Carlo risk assessment component model. A Monte Carlo discrete event simulation method is used to illustrate and extend traditional guideway RAMS analysis beyond the traditional methods of a static Fault Tree Analysis (FTA) to a dynamic RAMS analysis that is based on the movement of all the vehicles and their intersection with unsafe guideway substructures, guideway switch conditions and/or electrical and propulsion segment "out of service" events.

The need for a formalized validation, verification and certification vision is presented that includes individual component models, the overall Monte Carlo properties of the simulation and the statistical behavior of the Design for Safety and Risk Assessment methodologies.

1. Stochastic Train Domain Taxonomy

The ASCAP train domain framework is decomposed as a set of component models that describe the detailed stochastic and deterministic operation of a railway track plan infrastructure, rolling mixed mode passenger and freight stock, processor-based signaling and train control system, train movement scheduling and train dynamic behavior to aid in the assessment of an Incident/Accident risk cost severity metric. The risk cost metric is the societal cost versus train miles traveled for all accumulated Incident/Accidents. In addition, the operational rule book of the railway is characterized as an Artificial Intelligence (AI) Blackboard that evaluates the dispatcher, train crew and road way worker human-factors compliance and non-compliance to the operational rules. Finally, extensive logging is provided for all Events of Interest (EOI's) that describe the details of the safety-critical behavior.

The stochastic framework is illustrated in Fig. 1.

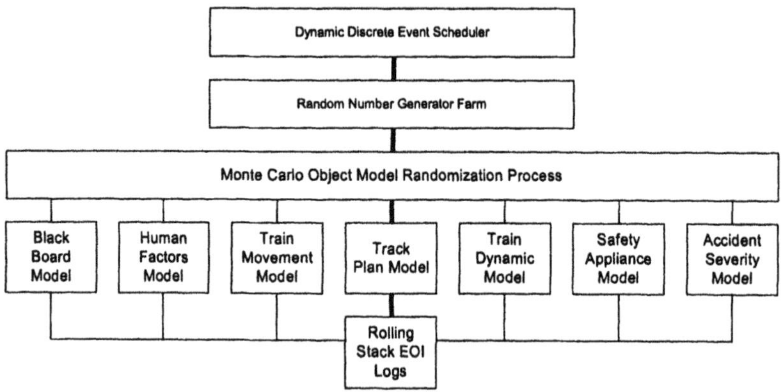

Figure 1. The Stochastic Framework of ASCAP

All the ASCAP component models are implemented with a common generalized probabilistic state mode domain: (1) operational, (2) fail-safe, (3) fail-unsafe, (4) rule book compliant and (5) rule book non-compliant. In addition, a deterministic train dynamic model is included. A fundamental axiom of ASCAP is that Incident/Accidents can only occur when a train intersects with a component unsafe state. When all the components are interconnected, they form a large-scale Monte Carlo probabilistic train dynamic behavior domain. ASCAP executes either as a hazard-free train domain that provides a proof-of-correctness of the train line operation or non hazard-free domain that provides a proof-of-the-safety level.

The basic principle of the stochastic Train Domain Framework is illustrated with a Maglev example (Fig. 2). The vehicles travel along the guideway and interest with all the component models as defined by the Maglev system guideway. At each intersection the probabilistic behavior of the intersected component model is calculated and its impact evaluated as operational, fail-safe or fail-unsafe as determined by the Maglev operational rule book. The result is that the vehicle operational modalities such as speed and acceleration are modified.

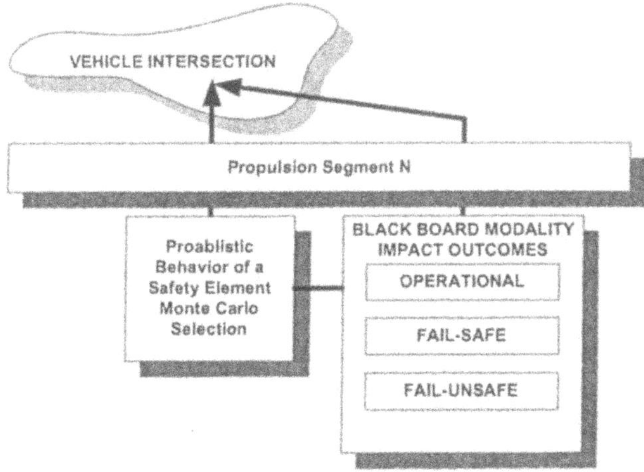

Figure 2. Train Domain Framework for a Maglev System

2. A Maglev Guideway Illustrative Example

The Maglev guideway "plug & play" component model is a dynamic risk impact model that decomposes the guideway propulsion segments into safety-critical elements. The safety-critical elements are further decomposed into individual beams and pillars. The decomposition methodology allows the guideway model to characterize four levels of structural and electrical probabilistic behavior: (1) propulsion segment behavior, (2) switch segment behavior, (3) safety element behavior and (4) the behavior of each beam and its three supporting pillars.

The electrical safety behavior of the propulsion and switch segments are considered, along with the structural behavior of the guideway construction for the guideway RAMS analysis. The beam/pillar decomposition is generalized to accommodate unique alignments as may be required for a Maglev system in the United Sates. This model is applicable to steel, concrete as well as hybrid guideway beam configurations.

The guideway RAMS structural and switch analysis simulate an eighty-year life cycle. The ASCAP RAMS risk assessment simulation estimates the risk versus millions of vehicle miles traveled as a bounded risk containment region subject to a high degree of confidence.

The ASCAP RAMS risk assessment Monte Carlo methodology extends the more traditional safety assessment conducted with a static Fault Tree Analysis (FTA) safety analysis. The ASCAP simulation extends the static FTA method with a dynamic risk assessment analysis that is based on the travel exposure of the vehicles to guideway unsafe events. The unsafe events shall be the time and position events that are coincident with the travel of the vehicle that are potential accidents. In this way, the traditional requirements of the RAMS methodology are extended to include "safety-related exposure" as determined by vehicle miles traveled over the life cycle of the guideway. In addition, the concept of guideway near term repairs to correct detected failures and a phased-interval long term maintenance policy to mitigate undetected failures is simulated to ensure real world safety risk estimates of the guideway structure.

The RAMS assessment partitions the guideway into safety-critical elements similar to a structural finite element analysis. A three state Markov probabilistic model is used to describe the safety element probabilistic behavior. A similar model is implemented for the switch segments that include the electrical motor behaviors and the redundant motor mechanism that shall provide the switch safety coverage. Each safety element consists of a set of beams and their supporting pillars. The alignment shape and the types of beams that are required determine the number of safety elements used to describe a propulsion segment. The ASCAP Monte Carlo risk assessment methodology for the Maglev system requires that the probabilistic behavior of the guideway be considered as a sequence of potential hazards to be mitigated. The ASCAP methodology quantifies the likelihood of occurrence of such potential guideway hazards along with their respective risk consequences. These consequences result in either performance degradation of the vehicle speeds, overall headway performance reduction and/or accidents.

The guideway structural plan is decomposed into N-propulsion segments (see Fig. 3), where a propulsion segment is a contiguous collection of M-safety-critical elements. Each ASCAP safety-critical element is a contiguous set of K beams, where three pillars support each beam. The number of beams per safety element is determined by the guideway alignment characteristics, which are specific to a given Maglev system. For the ASCAP simulation of the system under analysis, the number of safety elements, M, are selected to characterize the alignment curvature in the three-dimensional space.

In order to develop the risk assessment for the guideway, a series of ASCAP simulations with various propulsion segments out of service are used to identify vehicle "out of service" routing versus normal operation and the impact on system headway performance. A guideway propulsion segment is designated "out of service" due to either electrical and/or structural failures. In the event that a safety element failure takes place, the propulsion segment is placed in a degraded mode of service depending on the state of the failure: fail-safe or fail-unsafe. That is, the velocity of the vehicles traversing that particular segment may be required to travel at a lower speed or that propulsion segment may be taken out of service and no travel over the segment is allowed. Each beam that used to assemble a propulsion segment and its related three supporting pillars is described with a minimum probabilistic three state model. The safety element model is based on an exponential failure law.

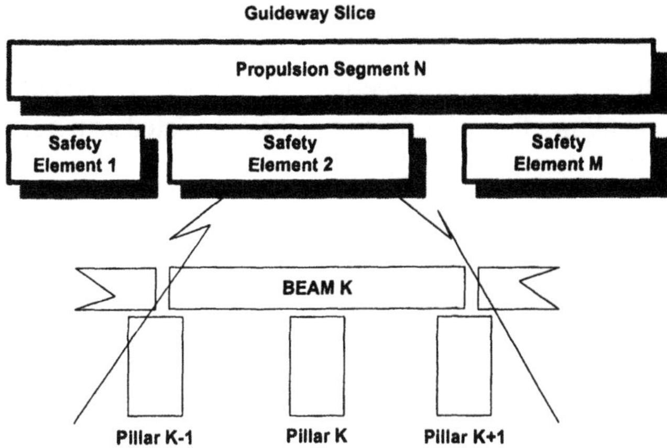

Figure 3. A Propulsion Segment of the Guideway Structure

The RAMS guideway assessment model includes the probabilistic behavior of the pillar and beam configuration identified to form a safety element. These safety elements, as shown in Fig. 3, define the guideway structure object. It is these objects with which a given vehicle intersects at a particular moment in time. The behavioral characteristics of these objects shall be obtained using a multi-state model whose state is selected using a Monte Carlo process.

Guideway Safety Element Decomposition

The guideway shall be decomposed as physical objects for the guideway RAMS ASCAP simulation as follows:

- N propulsion segments;
- M safety elements per each propulsion segment;
- K beams/pillars for each M safety element, where the alignment requirements and the types of beams for each safety element shall determine K.

The guideway is a distributed set of safety elements that describe all the attributes of the guideway, as it exists in the physical world. That is, the detailed geometry of the guideway and all the attributes of the geometry such as curves, grades and elevations shall be included to provide an accurate characterization of the guideway alignment. The ASCAP guideway risk assessment model is a set of interconnected objects, where each object describes a given safety element, with which continuously traveling vehicles intersect. At each intersection, the probabilistic behavior of each safety element is calculated. The three primary state behaviors - operational, fail-safe, and fail-unsafe - are reduced to an active state with a Monte Carlo selection method. The active state selected by the Monte Carlo method is posted as a blackboard entry, which defines the movement modality of the intersecting vehicle. This process is highlighted in the intersection of the vehicle traveling over the safety element sections of the guideway and allows the risk exposure to be calculated as required by the FRA Processor-based Regulatory Rule.

Guideway Safety Element Model

A generic three-state model, as shown in Fig. 3, is developed to represent the behavioral characteristics of the guideway safety element model. The concept of coverage is included in the model to provide the ability of hazard detection. Each safety element contains a potential hazard(s) and the probabilistic model calculates its likelihood of occurrence. Hence, the ASCAP simulation of the real-world physical guideway builds the hazards list and determines their potential consequences.

The transition probabilities that take the model from the Operational State to either the fail-safe state or the fail-unsafe state have the capability to be generalized in the ASCAP Monte Carlo simulation such that structural variations in the guideway RAMS analysis are feasible. The model has the capability to handle different failure laws, along with coverage parameters that describe the behavior of configurations such as hybrid (steel and concrete) beam, pillar and overall bridge structures. In this way, the guideway RAMS behavior has the capability to handle different deployments of the Maglev technology in the United States.

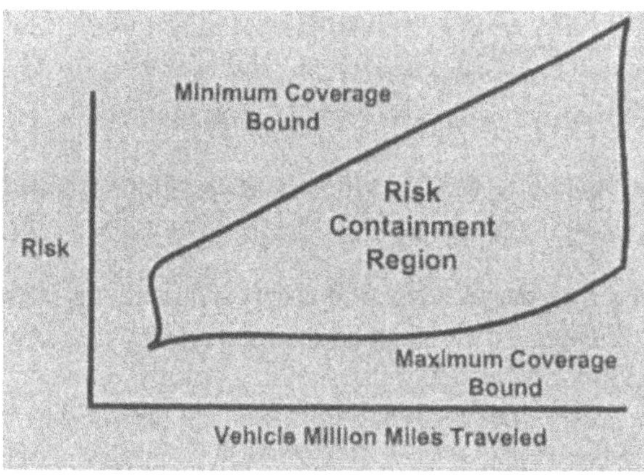

Figure 4. Risk vs Vehicle per Million Miles Traveled

3. Conclusions

ASCAP provides a large-scale Monte Carlo stochastic train domain framework that has the capability to provide a real-world design for safety or risk assessment analysis of a train system. The current limitation is the ability to validate and verify the simulation to insure that the result confirm to the real world. Current validation and verification has focused on the "Peer Review Process".

The next step in the validation and verification process is to proceed with a rigorous development of Formal Methods applied to each of the component models and the overall ASCAP simulation. In addition, the statistical performance of the simulation must be evaluated for vehicle miles traveled sufficiency to insure that all the possible incident/accidents have been revealed by the simulation.

CYBERRAIL

Information Infrastructure for New Intermodal Transport Business Model

Takahiko OGINO
Chief Researcher, Railway Technical Research Institute
ogino@rtri.or.jp

Abstract One of the achievements of the CyberRail concept is that it has proposed the fabric of the transport, which is so simple and strong that we cannot miss the future direction of the revolution towards an intermodal transport system. The second one is the creation of a tailor-made travel assistant model, that is, itinerary-based, situation-sensitive traveler information services. Considering the fast development of ubiquitous computing technology, functions of CyberRail will become more and more realistic. We have established a special interest group (SIG) on CyberRail in Japan. One of the purposes of the SIG is to make CyberRail architecture. We also proposed some of the service-oriented system packages, which are often referred to as "market packages." In addition to the system architecture development, we have developed an experimental implementation of traveler support features of CyberRail. Using this system, passengers get train transfer guidance according to their enquiry through mobile phone. Once the passengers started travel, the system continues to give information during the travel when they arrived at particular transfer points as if the passengers have assistants with them. The paper describes structure and mechanism of CyberRail.

Keywords: intermodal transport, ubiquitous computing, travel assistant, tailor-made travel

1. Introduction

Railway transport was/is like a cheap restaurant. You would be full if you could be patient with a same menu and nasty food. In the age when no other means are possible to provide transport with reasonable cost and safety, railways were one of the best. This characteristic could last, if your travel demands happen to be one of the services that the railway provides. We could replace "railways" with "public transportation" in the above context.

The emergence of automobiles, particularly private cars, destroyed this prosperity of public transport. Once people found a way to meet their travel demands with more comfortable way, a very few people would like to use public transport. The risk to drive a car is 1000 times bigger than to take a train, however, the people still prefer driving.

Are cars future transport means? Are railways out-of-date mechanisms for transport? Are railways dying as if an endangered animal? No, definitely not! CyberRail is an information infrastructure, on which a brand new transport business model can be constructed, in order to rescue this situation.

2. SCENARIO OF CYBERRAIL

Let us explain a scenario, where one of the services of CyberRail is available, and where IT is the key technology to offer railway customers a virtual assistant and/or a ubiquitous companion. A traveller explains the purpose of the journey to this virtual assistant with information including the destination, personal preference, budget, selection priorities, etc. In this example, perhaps the person would like to visit tourist resorts. The virtual assistant then accesses the records of client's travel history and personal preference for complementing the enquiry, and offers various suggestions based on preferred cost, duration and other conditions.

Travel planning is often a time-consuming process. If there are several potential destinations, the assistant will evaluate the timetables, booking conditions, overcrowding, etc., to propose suitable travel itineraries. Then the traveller can make a final decision and asks the assistant to make the necessary reservations and virtually purchase the tickets.

On the day that the journey starts, a virtual travelling companion, realized by ubiquitous computer technology, continually would sit beside the traveller and would access the travelling conditions on all the transport modes so that the passenger can enjoy even the most difficult trip. Furthermore, if the passenger becomes bored during the trip, the companion will give advice about entertainment, resorts, etc., or if the passenger wants to rest, the companion will not disturb them unless absolutely necessary.

Other services include re-bookings for missed connection, advices on shopping, restaurants, etc., and notices for special shopping sales. If there is enough number of passengers looking for a connection, extra trains may be on service, depending upon the policy of railway operators.

The service is not only for passengers - a guardian may contact the virtual assistant to locate his/her children en route. The higher level of travel safety and security will allow handicapped passengers to travel smoothly and safely, such as, elderly people, small children, and foreigners who do not speak the local language.

If this type of social infrastructure can be provided at very low cost or for free, there is little doubt that many more passengers will find public transport systems more convenient to use. This type of information business model focused on railways and based on the future growth of IT, offers benefits to both railway passengers and operators, and we believe that it is an essential component in achieving an efficient and mobile society.

3. INNOVATIVE IDEA OF CYBERRAIL

The conventional way of railway transport consists of the following acts:

- for passengers to take a train, which actually runs and roughly meets their potential travel demands;
- for railway operators to run trains as planed and to maintain railway related equipment and facilities, no matter what will happen.

One of the reasons why CyberRail is so different from an information provision and guidance system is that, extremely speaking, CyberRail aims at creation of new carrying power, depending upon the current demands from passengers, and give passengers information so as to make passengers flows optimum. This function is not only convenient for passengers, but also profitable to railway operators, because they could provide transport capacity efficiently.

Communication between passengers and railway operators is an essential part of CyberRail. If information about what is going on in the real transport is on a cyberspace, we can introduce various planning methodology to solve effective transport operation control problems. This is why information processing is useful for creating effective transport plan.

4. STRUCTURE OF CYBERRAIL

Conceptual model

To facilitate smooth use of different public transport modes, it is necessary to know transport demands and current positions of passengers. There must be a constant communications link between "tags" and the objects in cyberspace, where the moving passengers carry the former and the latter represents the transport demands. "Tag" provides continuous updates on the passenger's status.

The cyberspace that comprises CyberRail is composed of the following three basic classes:

Demand Class

The object of this class, which represents its holder, is a mapped one from "user demands" in real space. Its attributes are movement demands, current positions, profile, etc. The profile includes the preferences of the travel demands, the holder's travel history and other customer management information.

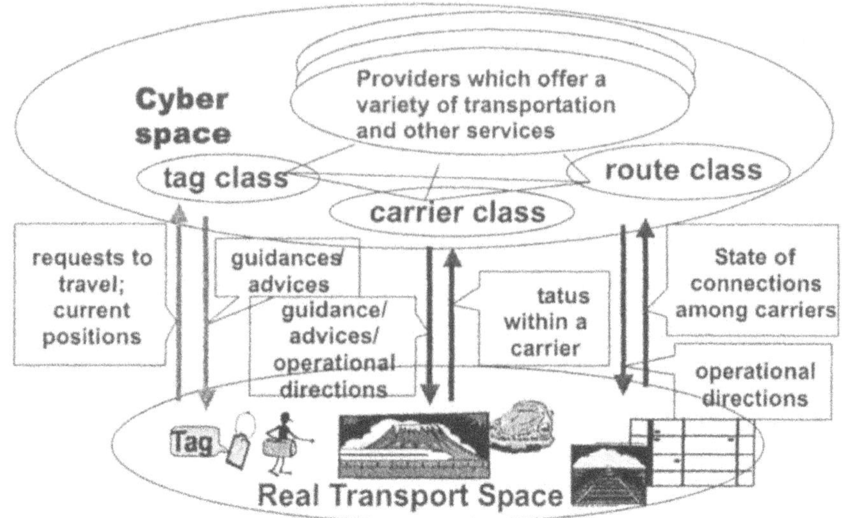

Figure 1. Conceptual Model of CyberRail

"Tag" may not be single equipment on your palm or in your pocket. It could be a combination of a season ticket and a cellular phone. A public information kiosk could become display equipment for the passengers instead of the cellular phone. We will have variety of ubiquitous equipment in the near future.

The meaning of the above sentence can be easily understood by Mark Weiser's quotation, a founder of ubiquitous computing, "A good tool is an invisible tool. By invisible, I mean that the tool does not intrude on your consciousness; you focus on the task, not the tool. ... The blind person tapping the cane feels the street, not the cane. ..." From this point of view, "tag" must be invisible and unconscious when it is used. Also it must be always beside the passengers.

Carrier class

This class represents facilities, which carry passengers in an intermodal way, that is, an abstraction of automobiles, trains and planes. Its attributes include current position, status of passengers on carriers, status and condition of vehicles, maintenance data, etc. Looking at this model, it is possible to view the current road-based ITS, as a system in which only a part of the carrier classes with an individual driver-passenger is considered, that is, carrier classes that carry plural travel demands are excluded.

Route class

This class was originally intended to represent rail tracks, roads and air routes, together with their maintenance functions. This class is important; particularly when we introduce numerical and statistical control over railway facilities. We, in Japan, sometimes, have to restrain railway traffic due to probable natural disasters, such as strong winds. If we could predict precise probability of the hazards, we could reduce the occasion of holding traffic, or make a detour plan for a train.

In addition to the physical routes, we could expand this class to logical routes, which is a graph, logically representing connections of points in four-dimensional space, x, y, z and time axes. A travel is a movement from one place to another, while being aware of time. Train timetable is a very example, though the geographical dimension is reduced. Guidance map in a station may be another good example without a time axis.

We have a problem how to represent a node in train timetable graph, which seems to be a graph recursively describing structures of a station or a station area. These graphs would be key elements for guidance of travel and movement.

5. CONCLUSION

An intermodal transport should be the mode of transport in the future, which is more environmentally friendly. For a short distance travel, railways definitely play a central role. CyberRail observations convince us the necessity of logical cooperation among three classes. We could develop an intermodal transport model upon this concept.

TOWARDS A FORMAL MODEL OF CyberRail

Dines Bjørner[1,2]
(1) *Department of Computer Science, School of Computing, National University of Singapore, 3 Science Drive 2, Singapore 117543*
E–Mail: bjorner@comp.nus.edu.sg, URL: http://www.comp.nus.edu.sg/cs/

Peter Chiang[2], Morten S.T. Jacobsen[2], Jens Kielsgaard Hansen[2], and Michael P. Madsen[2]
(2) *Section of Computer Science and Engineering, Institute of Informatics and Computer Engineering, Technical University of Denmark, DK–2800 Kgs.Lyngby, Denmark*
E–Mail: {s001402,s001693,s001842,s001700}@student.dtu.dk

Martin Penicka[1,3*]
(3) *Czech Technical University, Faculty of Transportation Sciences, Department of Applied Mathematics, Na Florenci 25, 110 00 Praha 1, Czech Republic*
E–Mail: penicka@fd.cvut.cz

Abstract Based on a number of reports and publications, primarily by Takahiko Ogino [14], [15], [16] (in these proceedings), and [17], on the emerging concept of CyberRail, we attempt to show what a formal domain model of CyberRail might look like, and what benefits one might derive from establishing and having such a formal model.

Keywords: CyberRail, Formalisation, Domain Model, RAISE, RSL, CSP, Non–determinism, Abstract Data Types

1. Background

The background for the work reported in this extended abstract is threefold: (i) Many years of actual formal specification as well as research into how to engineer such formal specifications, by the first author, of domains, including the railway domain [8] [7] [9] [10] [1] [6] [3] [2] [5] — using abstraction and

*MPs work was supported, in part, by the EU 5th IST FP Programme acttion: CoLogNET: The Computational Logic Network of Excellence.

modelling principles and techniques extensively covered in three forthcoming software engineering textbooks [4]. (ii) A term project with four MSc students. And (iii) Some fascination as whether one cold formalise an essence of the novel ideas of CyberRail. We strongly believe that we can capture one crucial essence of CyberRail — such as this paper will show.

The formalisation of CyberRail is expressed in the RAISE [12] Specification Language, RSL [11]. RAISE stands for Rigorous Approach to Industrial Software Engineering. In the current abstract model we especially make use of RSL's parallel process modeling capability. It builds on, ie., borrows from Tony Hoare's algebraic process concept of Communicating Sequential Processes, CSP [13].

2. A Rough Sketch Formal Model

2.1 An Overall CyberRail System

CyberRail consists of an index set of traveller behaviours and one cyber behaviour "running" in parallel. Each traveller behaviour is uniquely identified, p:Tx. Traveller behaviours communicate with the cyber behaviour. We abstract the communication medium as an indexed set of channels, ct[p], from the cyber behaviour to each individual traveller behaviour, and tc[p], from traveller behaviours to the cyber behaviour. Messages over channels are of respective types, CT and TC. The cyber behaviour starts in an initial state ω_i, and each traveller behaviour, p, starts in some initial state $m\sigma_i(p)$.

type
  Tx, Σ, Ω, CT, TC
  MΣ = Tx $\overrightarrow{m}$ Σ
channel
  {ct[p]:CT,tc[p]:TC|p:Tx}, cr:CR, rc:RC
value
  $m\sigma_i$:MΣ, ω_i:Ω

  cyberrail_system: **Unit** $\rightarrow$ **Unit**
  cyberrail_system() $\equiv$ || { traveller(p)($m\sigma_i$(p)) | p:Tx } || cyber(ω)

  cyber: Ω $\rightarrow$ **in** {tc[p]|p:Tx},cr **out** {ct[p]|p:Tx},rc **Unit**
  cyber(ω) $\equiv$
    cyber_as_server(ω) $\sqcap$ cyber_as_proactive(ω) $\sqcap$ cyber_as_co_director(ω)

  traveller: p:Tx $\rightarrow$ Σ $\rightarrow$ **in** ct[p] **out** tc[p] **Unit**
  traveller(p)(σ) $\equiv$ active_traveller(p)(σ) $\sqcap$ passive_traveller(p)(σ)

The cyber behaviour either acts as a server: Ready to engage in communication input from any traveller behaviour; or the cyber behaviour acts pro–actively: Ready to engage in performing output to one, or some traveller behaviours; or the cyber behaviour acts in consort with the "rest" of the transportation market (including rail infrastructure owners, train operators, etc.), in improving and changing services, and in otherwise responding to unforeseen circumstances of that market.

Similarly any traveller behaviour acts as a client: Ready to engage in performing output to the cyber behaviour; or its acts passively: Ready to accept input from the cyber behaviour.

2.2 Travellers

2.2.1 Active Travellers. Active traveller behaviours alternate internally non–deterministically, ie., at their own choice, between *start (travel) planning st_pl, select (among suggested) travel plan(s) se_pl, change (travel) planning ch_pl, begin travel be_tr, board train bo_tr, leave train lv_tr, ignore train ig_tr, cancel travel ca_tr, seeking guidance se_gu, notifying cyber no_cy, entertainment ent, deposit resource de_re* (park car, ...), *claim resource cl_re* (retreive car, ...), *get resource ge_re* (rent a car, ...), *return resource re_re* (return rent-car, ...), *going to restaurant rest* (or other), *change travel ch_tr, interrupt travel in_tr, resume travel re_tr, leave train le_tr, end travel en_tr,* and many other choices. Each of these normally entail an output communication to the cyber behaviour, and for those we can assume immediate response from the cyber behaviour, where applicable.

```
value
  active_traveller: p:Tx → Σ → out tc[p] in ct[p] Unit
  active_traveller(p)(σ) ≡
    let choice = st_pl ⌈⌉ ac_pl ⌈⌉ ch_pl ⌈⌉ en_tr ⌈⌉ ... ⌈⌉ le_tr ⌈⌉ te_tr in
    let σ′ = case choice of
                st_pl → start_planning(p)(σ),
                se_pl → select_travel_plan(p)(σ),
                ch_pl → change_trael_plan(p)(σ),
                be_tr → begin_travel(p)(σ),
                bo_tr → board_train(p )(σ),
                ... → ..,
                le_tr → leave_train(p)(σ),
                en_tr → end_travel(p)(σ),
                ... → ..
             end in
   traveller(p)(σ′) end end
```

```
    start_planning: p:Tx → Σ → out tc[p] in ct[p] Σ
    start_planning(p)(σ) ≡
        let (σ′,plan) = magic_plan(σ) in
        tc[p]!plan;
        let sps = ct[p]? in updateΣ((plan,sps))(σ′) end end
    ...
    updateΣ: Update → Σ → Σ
type
    Update == mkInPlRes(ip:InitialPlan,ps:Plan-set) | ...
```

2.2.2 Passive Travellers. When not engaging actively with the cyber behaviour, traveller behaviours are ready to accept any cyber initated action. The traveller behaviour basically "assimilates" messages received from cyber — and may make use of these in future.

```
value
    passive_traveller: p:Tx → Σ → in ct[p] out tc[p] Unit
    passive_traveller(p)(σ) ≡ let res = ct[p]? in updateΣ(res)(σ) end
```

2.2.3 Active Traveller Actions. The *active_traveller* behaviour performs either of the internally non–deterministically chosen actions: *start_planning, select_travel_plan, change_travel_plan, begin_travel, board_train, ..., leave_train,* or *end_travel.* They make use only of the "sum total state" (σ) that that traveller behaviour "is in". Each such action basically communicates either of a number of plans (or parts thereof, here simplified into plans). Let us summarise:

```
type
    Plan
    Request = Initial_Plan | Selected_Plan | Change_Plan | Begin_Travel
              | Board_Train | ... | Leave_Train | End_Travel | ...
    Initial_Plan == mkIniPl(pl:Plan)
    Selected_Plan == mkSelPl(pl:Plan)
    Change_Plan == mkChgPl(pl:Plan)
    Begin_Travel == mkBTrav(pl:Plan)
    Board_Train == mkBTrai(pl:Plan)
    ...
    Leave_Train == mkLeTr(pl:Plan)
    End_Travel == mkEnTr(pl:Plan)
value
    ∀ f: p:Tx → Σ → out tc[p] Σ
```

magic_f: $\Sigma \rightarrow \Sigma \times$ Request

f(p)(σ) $\equiv$ **let** (σ',req) = magic_f(σ) **in** tc[p]!req;σ' **end**

The magic_functions access and changes the state while otherwise yielding some request. They engage in no events with other than the traveller state. There are the possibility of literally "zillions" such functions, all fitted into the above sketched traveller behaviour.

2.3 cyber

2.3.1 cyber as Server. cyber is at any moment ready to engage in actions with any traveller behaviour. cyber is assumed here to respond immediately to "any and such".

```
value
   cyber_rail_as_server: Ω → in {tc[p]|p:Tx} out {ct[p]|p:Tx} Unit
   cyber_rail_as_server(ω) ≡
      ⌷ {let req = tc[p]? in cyber(serve_traveller(p,req)(ω)) end | p:Tx}

   serve_traveller: p:Tx × Req → Ω → in {tc[p]|p:Tx} out {ct[p]|p:Tx} Ω
   serve_traveller(p,req)(ω) ≡
      case req of
         mkIniPl(pl) →
            let (ω',pls) = sugg_pls(p,pl)(ω) in ct[p]!pls;cyberrail(ω') end
         mkSelPl(pl) →
            let (ω',res) = res_pl(p,pl)(ω) in ct[p]!book;cyberrail(ω') end
         mkChgPl(pl) →
            let (ω',pl') = chg_pl(p,pl)(ω) in ct[p]!pl';cyberrail(ω') end
         mkBTrav(pl) → ...
         mkBTrai(pl) → ...
         ...
         mkLeTr(pl) → ...
         mkEnTr(pl) → ...
      end
```

2.3.2 cyber as Pro–Active. cyber, on its own volition, may, typically based on its accumulated knowledge of traveller behaviours, engage in sending messages of one kind or another to selected groups of travellers. Section 2.3.5 rough sketch–formalises one of these.

```
type
   CR_act == gu_tr | no_tr | co_tr | wa_tr | ...
```

```
value
   cyber_as_proactive: Ω → out {ct[p]|p:Tx} Unit
   cyber_as_proactive(ω) ≡
      let cho = gu_tr ⌈⌉ no_tr ⌈⌉ co_tr ⌈⌉ wa_tr ⌈⌉ ... in
      let ω′ = case cho of gu_tr → guide_traveller(ω),
                           no_tr → notify_traveller(ω),
                           co_tr → commercial_to_travellers(ω),
                           wa_tr → warn_travellers(ω),
                           ... → ... end in
      cyber(ω′) end end
```

2.3.3 cyber as Co–Director. We do not specify this behaviour. It concerns the actions that cyber takes together with the "rest" of the transportation market. One could mention input from cyber_as_co_director to the train operators as to new traveller preferences, profiles, etc., and output from the rail (ie., net) infrastructure owners or train operators to cyber_as_co_director as to net repairs or train shortages, etc. The decomposition of CyberRail into cyber and the "rest", may — to some — be articificial, namely in countries where there is no effective privatisation and split–up into infrastructyre owners and train operators. But it is a decomposition which is relevant, structurally, in any case.

2.3.4 cyber Server Actions. We sketch:

```
value
   sugg_plans: p:Tx × Plan → Ω → Ω × Plan-set
   res_pl: p:Tx × Plan → Ω → Ω × Plan
   chg_pl: p:Tx × Plan → Ω → Ω × Plan
   ...
```

There are many other such traveller instigated cyber actions.

2.3.5 Pro–Active cyber Actions. We rough sketch just a single of the possible "dozens" of cyber inititated actions versus the travellers.

```
value
   guide_traveller: Ω → out {ct[p]|p:Tx} Ω
   guide_traveller(ω) ≡
      let (ω′,(ps,guide)) = any_guide(ω) in broadcast(ps,guide) ; ω′ end

   any_guide: Ω → Ω × (Tx-set × Guide)

   notify_traveller: Ω → out {ct[p]|p:Tx} Ω
```

commercial_to_travellers: $\Omega \rightarrow$ **out** {ct[p]|p:Tx} Ω
warn_traveller: $\Omega \rightarrow$ **out** {ct[p]|p:Tx} Ω
...

broadcast: Tx-**set** $\times$ CT $\rightarrow$ **Unit**
broadcast(ps,msg) $\equiv$
case ps **of** {}$\rightarrow$**skip**,{p}$\cup$ ps′$\rightarrow$ct[p]!msg;broadcast(ps′,msg) **end**

type
CT = Guide | Notification | Commercial | Warning | ...
Guide == mkGui(...)
Notification == mkNot(...)
Commercial == mkCom(...)
Warning == mkWar(...)
...

3. Conclusion

A formalisation of a crucial aspect of CyberRail has been sketched. Namely the interplay between the rôles of travellers and the central CyberRail system.

Next we need analyse carfully all the action functions with respect to the way in which they use and update the respective states ($\sigma : \Sigma$) of traveller behaviours and the cyber behaviour ($\omega : \Omega$). At the end of such an analysis one can then come up with precise, formal descriptions, including axioms, of what the title of [16] refers to as the *Information Infrastructure.* We look forward to report on that in a near future.

The aim of this work is to provide a foundation, a domain theory, for CyberRail. A set of models from which to "derive", in a systematic way, proposals for computing systems, including software architectures.

References

[1] Dines Bjørner. Formal Software Techniques in Railway Systems. In Eckehard Schnieder, editor, *9th IFAC Symposium on Control in Transportation Systems*, pages 1–12, Braunschweig, Germany, 13–15 June 2000. Invited talk.

[2] Dines Bjørner. Dynamics of Railway Nets: On an Interface between Automatic Control and Software Engineering. In *CTS2003: 10th IFAC Symposium on Control in Transportation Systems*, Oxford, UK, August 4-6 2003. Elsevier Science Ltd.

[3] Dines Bjørner. New Results and Trends in Formal Techniques for the Development of Software for Transportation Systems. In *FORMS2003: Symposium on Formal Methods for Railway Operation and Control Systems*. 2003. Budapest, Hungary. Editors: G. Tarnai and E. Schnieder, Germany.

[4] Dines Bjørner. *Software Engineering*, volume Vol. 1: Abstraction and Modelling, Vol. 2: Advanced Specification Techniques, Vol. 3: From Domains via Requirements to Software. Springer–Verlag, 2004–2005.

[5] Dines Bjørner, Chris George, Anne E. Haxthausen, Christian Krog Madsen, Steffen Holmslykke, and Martin Pěnička. "UML"–ising Formal Techniques. In *INT 2004: Third International Workshop on Integration of Specification Techniques for Applications in Engineering*. 28 March 2004, ETAPS, Barcelona, Spain. INT–2004 Proceedings, Springer–Verlag.

[6] Dines Bjørner, Chris W. George, and Søren Prehn. Computing Systems for Railways — A Rôle for Domain Engineering. Relations to Requirements Engineering and Software for Control Applications. In *Integrated Design and Process Technology. Editors: Bernd Kraemer and John C. Petterson*, 24–28 June 2002. Society for Design and Process Science.

[7] Dines Bjørner, C.W. George, and S. Prehn. *Scheduling and Rescheduling of Trains*, chapter 8, pages 157–184. *Industrial Strength Formal Methods in Practice,* Eds.: Michael G. Hinchey and Jonathan P. Bowen. FACIT, Springer–Verlag, London, England, 1999.

[8] Dines Bjørner, Dong Yu Lin, and S. Prehn. Domain Analyses: A Case Study of Station Management. In KICS'94: *Kunming International CASE Symposium, Yunnan Province, P.R.of China*. Software Engineering Association of Japan, 16–20 November 1994.

[9] Dines Bjørner, Søren Prehn, and Chris W. George. Formal Models of Railway Systems: Domains. FME Rail Workshop on Formal Methods in Railway Systems, FM'99 World Congress on Formal Methods, France.

[10] Dines Bjørner, Søren Prehn, and Chris W. George. Formal Models of Railway Systems: Requirements. FME Rail Workshop on Formal Methods in Railway Systems, FM'99 World Congress on Formal Methods, France.

[11] Chris George, Peter Haff, Klaus Havelund, Anne Haxthausen, Robert Milne, Claus Bendix Nielsen, Søren Prehn, and Kim Ritter Wagner. *The RAISE Specification Language*. The BCS Practitioner Series. Prentice-Hall, Hemel Hampstead, England, 1992.

[12] Chris George, Anne Haxthausen, Steven Hughes, Robert Milne, Søren Prehn, and Jan Storbank Pedersen. *The RAISE Method.* The BCS Practitioner Series. Prentice-Hall, Hemel Hampstead, England, 1995.

[13] C.A.R. Hoare. *Communicating Sequential Processes*. C.A.R. Hoare Series in Computer Science. Prentice-Hall International, 1985.

[14] Takahiko Ogino. Aiming for Passenger Interoperability. Technical report, Railway Technical Research Institute, Transport Information Technology Division, Railway Technical Research Institute, 2-8-38 Hikari-cho, Kokubunji-shi, Tokyo, 185-8540 Japan, 2003.

[15] Takahiko Ogino. CyberRail: For Urban Mobility Tomorrow. Technical report, Railway Technical Research Institute, Transport Information Technology Division, Railway Technical Research Institute, 2-8-38 Hikari-cho, Kokubunji-shi, Tokyo, 185-8540 Japan, 2004.

[16] Takahiko Ogino. CyberRail: Information Infrastructure for New Intermodal Transport Business Model. In *Topical Days @ IFIP World Computer Congress 2004*, IFIP Series. IFIP, Kluwer Academic Press, August 2004.

[17] Takahiko Ogino, Koivhi Goto, Ryuji Tsuchiya, Kiyotaka Seki, and Akihiko Matsuoka. CyberRail and its significance in the coming ubiquitous society. In , 2004.

Topic 12

Open-Source Software in Dependable Systems

Organisers:

Philippe David
ESA, The Netherlands
Philippe.David@esa.int

Hélène Waeselynck
LAAS-CNRS, France
Helene.Waeselynck@laas.fr

While Open-Source Software (OSS) is penetrating the software business at large, software-intensive applications having high dependability requirements have been little concerned so far. At a first glance, introducing OSS into such critical systems seems risky. The constraints imposed by adherence to certification standards may be deemed irreconcilable with the open-source development model. Still, the question is being taken seriously in domains like transportation, space, or nuclear energy: gaining acceptance into dependable systems might well be the new challenge for some mature OSS products.

OPEN SOURCE SOFTWARE IN CRITICAL SYSTEMS

Motivation and challenges

Philippe David[1], Hélène Waeselynck[2] and Yves Crouzet[2]
[1]ESA/ESTEC, Keplerlaan 1, 2200 AG Noordwijk, The Netherlands; [2]LAAS-CNRS, 7 av du Colonel Roche, 31077 TOULOUSE Cedex 4, France

Abstract: This paper summarizes the main conclusions and recommendations from a Working Group on "Open Source Software and Dependability". The Group was launched in the framework of a cooperative structure, a Network for Dependability Engineering, and gathered representatives of ten academic and industrial organizations.

Key words: Open source software, COTS, critical systems, certification, wrapping, validation.

1. INTRODUCTION

While Open Source Software (OSS) is penetrating the software business at large, software-intensive applications having high dependability requirements have been little concerned so far. At a first glance, introducing OSS into such critical systems seems risky. The constraints imposed by adherence to certification standards may be deemed irreconcilable with the open-source development model. Still, the question is being taken seriously in domains like transportation, space, or nuclear energy: gaining acceptance into dependable systems might well be the new challenge for some mature OSS products.

It is no longer true for the development of highly dependable systems to be solely based on dedicated, specific equipments, with cost not being a primary concern. Today, market pressure – together with the increasing complexity of applications – has led companies to consider the use of off-the-shelf components in parts of their systems. Compared to proprietary commercial off-the-shelf components (COTS)[1], OSS components may offer an interesting alternative. Availability of the source code may obviously be a strong advantage from a dependability perspective. There also are some strategic concerns, like avoiding dependence on monopolistic support, that may turn the balance in favor of OSS.

This is why a Working Group on "Open Source Software and Dependability" was launched in May 2001 by the **Network for Dependability Engineering**[2] (Réseau d'Ingénierie de la Sûreté de fonctionnement – *RIS*). The working group included representatives from ten academic and industrial organizations: Airbus, Astrium, ESA, INRETS, IRISA, LAAS-CNRS, LSV, SNCF, Technicatome, Thales. The results of the Group were concretized by the publication of a book [1] (in French) in September 2003, and by the organization of an open seminar that gathered more than 80 participants.

This paper summarizes the main conclusions and recommendations from the Group. Section 2 discusses the use of OSS as an alternative to proprietary COTS, and compares their respective advantages and drawbacks. Section 3 is concerned with certification. It is studied to what extent the use of OSS may be compatible with certification requirements. Section 4 presents architectural design principles, so as to host OSS in a dependable way. Section 5 discusses OSS validation issues. Section 6 concludes on recommendations to promote the use of OSS in critical applications.

2. OSS AS AN ALTERNATIVE TO COTS

Critical computerized systems can be life-critical (such as a fly-by-wire control system) or money-critical (such as a telecommunication satellite). Whatever the critical domain, the increasing complexity of applications has yielded more and more functions to be implemented by software. Cost constraints, as well as interoperability ones, have favored engineering practices based on software reuse and standardized interfaces. System providers were pushed to focus their software development activity on domain-specific functions, and to integrate standard off-the-shelf components for non-specific ones, such as executive support or communication protocols.

[1] Throughout this paper, the "COTS" acronym will denote *proprietary* commercial software, as opposed to open source software. This is the usual meaning of "COTS" while, strictly speaking, nothing prevents commercial software from being distributed under the terms of an open source license.

[2] http://www.ris.prd.fr

Proprietary commercial software was first considered for integration. Such COTS components are usually purchased as black boxes, with no access to the source code. A support contract is concluded with the supplier, in order to facilitate the integration of the COTS into the system and perform the maintenance actions. Unfortunately, such a solution might not be satisfactory for critical systems.

2.1 Drawbacks of Proprietary COTS

The quality of the technical support is primordial, but can largely vary depending on the supplier. Moreover, critical systems are long-living systems (e.g., from 15 to 40 years of operation for systems developed by members of the Working Group). In order to avoid re-entering a certification process, there is a need to limit the upgrades and "freeze" the components versions for long periods of time (typically five years) with only corrective maintenance actions. The need for stability may conflict with the supplier's commercial strategy, which is to release new versions at a frequent rate. The supplier may have no interest in ensuring high quality support for obsolete versions of the COTS. Also, due to the high competition in the software market, the supplier may have disappeared before the end of the system's operational life. The risk should be considered from the very beginning. If no alternative support can be found, an ultimate solution can be for the integrator to acquire technological expertise on the COTS, which cannot be achieved for black-box components.

Should the system suffer major failures due to the unreliability of the COTS, the responsibility of the supplier would be limited. This is fairly understandable: the COTS was not designed to fulfill ultra-high dependability requirements, and it is the responsibility of the integrator to control the technical risks induced on the critical system. An acute problem is then the low expertise the integrator has on the COTS. Once again, black-box usage may be unacceptable even if part of the dependability case is done with the support of the supplier.

These risks may force integrators to negotiate the purchase of the source code. This is usually obtained at a prohibitive price. When critical systems only represent a marginal part of the supplier's business, the integrator is not in strong position to conduct the negotiation.

Such problems have yielded integrators to consider the use of open source components for which, by definition, there is no restriction to access the source code.

2.2 The OSS Alternative

OSS licenses give the users the right to read, modify and redistribute the source code. OSS is generally associated with a community development model, the so-called "bazaar" [2]. But underlying practices are actually so disparate that it is not possible to refer to a single model. For many successful OSS products, the development and maintenance activities are more structured than the mythical bazaar. As for (proprietary) COTS, there are companies selling support on some OSS. Since the justification for these companies to exist is their deep expertise on the product, not the delivery of the product, the supplied support may even be of higher quality than in the case of classical COTS products.

Basically, the risks induced by the integration of off-the-shelf (OTS) components, whether proprietary or open-source, are similar. But in the latter case, availability of the source code should allow the integrator greater latitude to mitigate and control the risks. The risks include:

- An increasing gap between the frozen system-specific version and the new versions of the component.
- The disappearance of the support company.
- Technical risks due the component's failures.

There are also risks associated with the terms of the license. Here, open source licenses have some specificities that must be understood, such as the contamination effect of the GPL license.

From a technical viewpoint, the main challenge is to produce a dependability case that is accepted by the Certification Authority. For COTS components, the case has to be prepared with the support of the supplier, and still necessitates a strong involvement of the integrator. For OSS components, additional scenarios become possible: a consortium of integrators may share part of the effort required by certification, as soon as they have a common interest into a given open source product.

3. THE CERTIFICATION CHALLENGE

The *RIS* Working Group examined the various certification standards that were relevant to the application domains of its members: avionics systems (DO-178 B [3], ARP 4754 [4]), railway systems (CENELEC 50128 [5]), space systems (ECSS-Q-40A [6]), nuclear systems (IEC 60880 [7]), as well as a generic standard (IEC 61508 [8]). Whatever the standard, the associated requirements and recommendations depend on the criticality level of the software component: the higher the level, the more demanding the standard. The classification into levels, determined from the impact a failure may have on the system, was found quite homogeneous (see the correspondence we established in Table 1).

Table 1. Software Criticality Levels

	Railway systems	Avionics systems	Space systems	Nuclear systems
No impact	SIL 0	E	/	/
Impact on the system	SIL 1-2	C-D	critical	B-C
Loss of human lives	SIL 3-4	A-B	catastrophic	A

Our analysis is that the use of OSS is not realistic at the highest levels (e.g. SIL 3-4 for railway systems) – unless the software component was purposely developed to meet the certification requirements, and turns out to be distributed under an open source license for some strategic reasons. Since the requirements are very stringent, it is not possible to fulfill them *a posteriori*. Intermediate levels (e.g., SIL 1-2) are quite conceivable, but the integrator will have to spend some effort to build appropriate documentation, and perform additional validation and design rework activities. Some standards only define the objectives to be reached (e.g., DO-178 B) while others provide recommendations on the methods to be used (e.g., CENELEC 50128). Our analysis is that whatever the application domain, the same methods can be used to fulfill comparable objectives. This leaves open the possibility, for consortium of users, to share part of the required effort. Obviously, for the lowest levels (e.g., SIL 0), the use of OSS components should not be a problem (at least from a certification viewpoint).

As mentioned in the ARP 4754 document, the criticality level can be reduced if appropriate architectural features are used. As an example, triple redundancy may be used to implement a level A avionics component based on level C components (note, however, that the dissimilarity and independence of the three components must be established with an A assurance level). In our opinion, the ability to build critical systems from less critical components, through architectural solutions, is the key to allow the introduction of OSS. Once again, it should be possible to identify generic (not domain-specific) solutions for hosting OSS. Two of them, namely system partitioning and component wrapping, are briefly discussed in the next section.

4. HOSTING ARCHITECTURES

The hosting architecture should address different problems:

- The system has to be protected from the OSS failures.

- The OSS functionalities may be too abundant (compared to the needs of the critical system), or they may necessitate some adaptations.
- The architecture should be able to cope with the evolution of components (long term maintenance).

In order to prevent error propagation from unreliable components to critical ones, a classical solution is partitioning. The system is partitioned into subsystems such as the failure of any subsystem is confined into this subsystem. The subsystems have the criticality of their most critical component. *Physical* partitioning corresponds to a strict segregation of subsystems, while *logical* partitioning enable software of different criticalities to coexist on the same execution platform. Logical partitioning involves both spatial (e.g., via memory protection mechanisms) and temporal (e.g., via scheduling policies, watchdogs) isolation. Such techniques, widely used in critical systems, are relevant from the perspective of hosting OSS, as well as COTS, components.

Another protection technique is wrapping. A wrapper encapsulates a software component, enabling to filter and control invocations of the component's services, and to incorporate error detection and recovery mechanisms. Hence, wrapping is appropriate to adapt the OSS interface to the system's needs (e.g., by restricting the set of used functionalities), to limit the impact of component evolution on the architecture (only the wrapping layer has to be reworked when the component is changed), and to add protection mechanisms. Examples of fault tolerance wrappers for real-time executive supports can be found in [9, 10]. Once again, we believe that part of the effort to develop such wrappers could be shared by consortium of users, because there are common needs whatever the application domain. Wrapping can be applied to both OSS and proprietary software components, but the achievable degree of protection is strongly dependent on the access to the source code: sophisticated error detection and recovery mechanisms require observability and controllability of the internal state of the target component.

5. VALIDATION OF OSS

One manifesto of the open-source movement [2] expresses the following idea: "Given enough eyeballs, all bugs are shallow." According to the author, given the large number of users "eager" to contribute, every bug should be quickly located and fixed.

Not surprisingly, this view has generated much controversy (see e.g. [11, 12]) and there are strong arguments showing that the claim is over-optimistic. Note that, in practice, we observe that many successful OSS are developed and maintained following a more centralized approach, with most of the validation effort relying on an organized board of experts. Anyway, from the perspective of certification, the existence of a large number of "eyeballs" is not sufficient for justifying confidence on the OSS. Hence, the integrator will have to look for more convincing evidence, and to supplement the case by additional validation effort.

Whatever the certification standard, testing plays an import role in producing evidence.

Conformance testing aims at verifying that the OSS conforms to its specification. The test documentation must ensure traceability between functional requirements and test cases. Unfortunately, the test suites provided in open-source distributions are often impossible to exploit, because they have been determined in an *ad hoc* manner, without any concern for traceability analysis. Worse, there is sometimes nothing such as a software requirements document. For OSS products distributed by support companies, it may be the case that testing has been designed more rigorously, based on an elicitation of requirements. But the test suites and associated documentation are generally not included in the distribution, because they are part of the strategic know-how of the company. Fortunately, the problem can be mitigated for OSS products implementing interface standards. As soon as the interface specification is publicly available, consortium of users may share the effort to produce conformance tests that can be exploited for certification purposes. A good example is the Open Group Consortium[3], from which POSIX conformance test suites can be obtained.

Besides conformance testing, we believe that *robustness testing* is an important issue from a dependability viewpoint. Robustness testing checks the OSS behavior in the presence of faults or stressing operational conditions. It may serve several purposes:

- comparing the robustness of candidate products. Given a family of similar products, robustness testing results can contribute to the decision of which one to select for integration in the system.
- characterizing the failure modes of a selected component. The test results may then support subsequent design decisions, like the design of wrappers supplying protection mechanisms.
- Assessing the effectiveness of implemented wrappers (in that case, the tested artifact is the wrapped OSS).

Some results can already be found for a number of executive supports, COTS or OSS: microkernels [13], operating systems [14], midlleware [15].

[3] http://www.opengroup.org

Incidentally, they show that open-source executives are not less robust than proprietary ones.

Depending on the target criticality level, more formal verification techniques should also be considered.

Automated *static analysis* allows properties of the source code to be proven. Examples of properties include compliance with coding standards, or the absence of errors like buffer overflows, out-of-bounds arrays access or race conditions for concurrent tasks. Real-time properties can also be addressed. As an example, in [16], static analysis is used to determine the worst case execution times for an open-source real-time kernel.

Model-checking involves checking that a model, specified under the form of a state automaton, satisfies a certain property (usually specified as a temporal logic formula). Typical use of model-checking is for the verification of protocols. Ideally, model-checking should be performed at the specification level, before the protocol is implemented. However, it has also proven useful to verify existing protocols *a posteriori* [17, 18]. In this case, access to the source code is necessary to build a proper abstraction (i.e., the model fulfills the property only if the original source code also fulfills it).

All these techniques may be used to produce common certification material for an existing OSS.

6. CONCLUSION AND RECOMMENDATIONS

The conclusion of the Group is that OSS products are a strong opportunity for critical systems integrators. Their use in operational systems is quite conceivable, with appropriate architectural solutions to lower the criticality level, and actions to reach the certification standard for that level.

It was clear from the beginning that the introduction of OSS in critical system would require a pro-active approach. The open-source movement has emerged with no particular concern for critical systems, and it is up to us to invent the means to take advantage of this movement. In particular, making OSS products compatible with a certification process cannot be achieved for free. Also, it was felt important by the Group to issue recommendations not only on how to *use* OSS, but also how to *contribute* OSS. If OSS is a strategic concern, then critical system actors should consider entering the "virtuous circle" so as to support the movement. Ideally, measures to promote OSS in critical systems would include:

- Intiating an evaluation center for OSS.

  The center would launch evaluation campaigns for some OSS of interest and make the results publicly available. The center would be a means, for critical system players, to share information on relevant products such as executive supports or protocols. It would also enable OSS developers to receive feedback on their product.

- Initiating a common case for certification.

  The view expressed in this paper is that part of the material to be produced can be exploited whatever the application domain, as soon as the standards impose similar requirements for the OSS. It would be necessary to initiate a project to demonstrate this idea, with partners from different application fields, both system suppliers and assessors. The project would focus on one OSS of interest, a target criticality level (say, the intermediate levels in Table 1), and would investigate the feasibility of satisfying the certification requirements by means of a common set of methods.

- Demonstrating architectural principles to host OSS

  Hosting architectures will be based on redundancy, partitioning and wrapping. However, these architectural principles are too general and cover a wide spectrum of solutions: there is a need for more precise recommendations. A small subset of solutions should be investigated, prototyped and validated on a common platform. A candidate platform is the Integrated Modular Avionics (IMA), which is characterized by an open architecture using standardized interfaces.

  A contribution to the community would then be the availability of open-source wrappers, implementing protection mechanisms for OSS components.

- Promoting open-source development environments

  In this paper, we have focused on OSS used as components of critical systems. But OSS can also penetrate the development environments used to produce critical software.

  OSS development toolsets would present many advantage, including independence on monopolistic support, easier integration of tools through non-proprietary interfaces, and ability to benefit from technological advances from the academic world. We recommend that projects be launched to investigate viable alternatives to the proprietary development environments currently in use.

These recommendations would require a strong involvement of the critical system industry, as well as political and financial support from public organizations. However, we believe the effort is worth while.

ACKNOWLEDGEMENTS

This paper reports on the results of a collaborative work performed in the framework of the *RIS* network. We wish to thank all our colleagues who contributed to the Working Group on "OSS and Dependability": Béatrice Bérard (LSV), Philippe Coupoux (Technicatome), Yseult Garnier (SNCF), Serge Goiffon (Airbus), Georges Mariano (INRETS), Vincent Nicomette (LAAS-CNRS), Luc Planche (Astrium), Isabelle Puaut (IRISA), and Jean-Michel Tanneau (Thales). We are also grateful to the *RIS* Advisory Board, and particularly its coordinator Jean Arlat, for their constant support and constructive comments throughout the life of the Working Group.

REFERENCES

[1] B. Bérard, P. Coupoux, Y. Crouzet, P. David, Y. Garnier, S. Goiffon, G. Mariano, V. Nicomette, L. Planche, I. Puaut, J-M. Tanneau, and H. Waeselynck, *Logiciel libre et sûreté de fonctionnement – cas des systèmes critiques*, P. David and H. Waeselynck (Eds), Hermes Science, ISBN 2-7462-0727-3, 2003.

[2] E.S. Raymond, "The Cathedral and the Bazaar", *First Monday*, vol. 3, no. 3, March 1998. http://www.firstmonday.dk/issues/issue3_3/raymond/index.html

[3] RTCA / DO178B, "Software Considerations in Airborne Systems and Equipment Certification", 1992.

[4] SAE – ARP 4754, "Certification Considerations for Highly-Integrated or Complex Aircraft Systems", 1995.

[5] CENELEC EN 50128, "Railway applications — Communication, Signalling and Processing Systems — Software for Railway Control and Protection Systems", 2001.

[6] ECSS-Q-40A, "Space Product Assurance – Safety", 2002.

[7] IEC 60880, "Software for Computers in the Safety Systems of Nuclear power stations", 1986.

[8] IEC 61508-3, "Functional Safety of Electrical/Electronic/Programmable Electronic Safety-Related Systems. Part 3: Software requirements", 1998.

[9] E. Anceaume, G. Cabillic, P. Chevochot, I. Puaut, "A flexible run-time support for distributed dependable hard real-time applications", *Proc. of the 2nd IEEE International Symposium on Object-Oriented Real-Time Distributed Computing (ISORC'99)*, pp. 310-319, St Malo, France, May 1999.

[10] M. Rodriguez-Moreno, J-C. Fabre, J. Arlat, "Wrapping Real-Time Systems from Temporal Logic Specifications", *Proc. 4th European Dependable Computing Conference (EDCC-4)*, A. Bondavalli and P. Thévenod-Fosse (Eds), Springer Verlag, LNCS no. 2485, pp. 253-270, 2002.

[11] N. Bezroukov, "A Second look at the Cathedral and the Bazaar", *First Monday*, vol. 14, no. 12, December 1999. http://www.firstmonday.dk/issues/issue4_12/bezroukov/index.html

[12] J. Viega, "the Myth of Open Source Security", *Earthweb.com*, may 2000. http://www.developer.com/open/article.php/626641

[13] J. Arlat, J-C. Fabre, M. Rodriguez, F. Salles, "Dependability of COTS Microkernel-Based Systems", *IEEE Trans. on Computers*, vol 51, no. 2, pp.138-163, February 2002.

[14] P. Koopman, J. DeVale, "Comparing the Robustness of POSIX Operating Systems", *Proc. 29th Int. Symp. On Fault-Tolerant Computing (FTCS-29)*, Madison, WI, IEEE CS Press, pp. 30-37, 1999.

[15] E. Marsden, J-C. Fabre, "Failure Mode Analysis of CORBA Service Implementations", *Proc. IFIP/ACM Int. Conf. on Distributed Systems Platforms (Middleware'2001)*, Heidelberg, Germany, 2001.

[16] A. Colin, I. Puaut, "Worst-Case Execution Time Analysis of the RTEMS Real-Time Operating Systems", *Proc. 13th Euromicro Conf. on Real-Time Systems*, Delft, NL, pp. 191-198, June 2001.

[17] K. Havelund, A. Skou, K.G. Larsen, K. Lund, "Formal Modeling and Analysis of an Audio/Video Protocol: An Industrial Case Study Using UPPAAL", *Proc. 18th IEEE Real-time Systems Symposium (RTSS'97)*, San Francisco, CA, pp. 2-13, December 1997.

[18] B. Bérard, L. Fribourg, "Automated Verification of a Parametric Real-time Program: the ABR Conformance Protocol", *Proc. 11th Int. Conf. Computer-Aided Verification (CAV'99)*, Springer Verlag, LNCS no. 1633, pp. 96-107, 1999.

TRUSTING STRANGERS

Open Source Software and Security

Carl E. Landwehr
Institute for Systems Research, University of Maryland, College Park, MD, USA

Abstract: The issues of trusting software, certifying security, and the relative merits of open and closed source software as a basis for critical systems are discussed. It is concluded (i) that neither approach in itself can assure the absence of security flaws or sabotage, (ii) that better methods are needed for assuring the properties of products without respect to the people or process used to create them, and (iii) that system architects should exploit what they know they don't know, as well as what they do know, in composing system architectures.

Key words: security, trust, certification, open source, closed source

1. SOFTWARE AND TRUST

We trust many artifacts that we do not personally investigate or even understand. Most of us probably understand how a rowboat or a bicycle works, and we can usually see all of its functioning parts. But using a car, an airplane, or almost any modern appliance involves relying on technology that we don't examine directly and which in many cases we understand only at some surface level. Few of us understand the detailed calculations and inspections that underlie the safety of public buildings in which we enjoy concerts and films or the microwave ovens in which we may cook dinner. We in fact rely on the anonymous strangers who design, build, deliver, and in some cases maintain that artifact, as well as the processes that are in place in our society to reward or punish them.

Software is an unusual sort of artifact in that it has little physical substance, yet it can convey information, possibly sensitive information, and it can control physical devices. It has a significant cost of design and implementation, yet very low cost of replication. Very minor changes in its physical realization can cause major changes in system behavior. Though a great deal of money is spent on it, it is rarely sold. Usually it is licensed, customarily under terms that relieve the producer from nearly all responsibility for its correct functioning.

2. CERTIFYING SECURITY

There are many perspectives for contrasting open and closed source software: purchase price, maintenance cost, reliability, performance, safety, interoperability, and so on. The focus here is from the security perspective, from which we consider the response of software to potential acts of malice.

Safety critical systems for public use frequently depend on certification of process combined with some degree of inspection and testing. These processes, particularly when combined with both the threat of legal liability for the consequences of accidents attributed to poorly engineered products, and the possibility of customers avoiding products and companies whose products have proven unsafe, seem to work reasonably well. There are not regular reports of airplanes falling from the sky or trains colliding because of faulty software. Continued vigilance in these domains is of course required.

Unfortunately, these processes do not seem to be operating so well with regard to security. The possibility of malicious use, or the malicious insertion of subtle flaws that might later be maliciously exploited is not in general contemplated by the certification processes applied in safety.

There are, of course, regular and increasing reports of security failures in systems throughout the world. The increasingly common malicious acts of creating and distributing worms and viruses primarily exploit accidentally introduced flaws in widely distributed software. Economic incentives (e.g. for platforms from which to send spam or mount distributed denial of service attacks) motivate the covert installation of malicious, remotely controllable software on vulnerable platforms.

There are also mechanisms for certifying the security properties of software. The primary mechanism at present is the provided by the "Common Criteria" scheme, which provides a somewhat complex means to specify the security properties and assurance level required of some particular component and to evaluate whether those properties are present in some particular target of evaluation.

There are two significant problems with this scheme: one is that at the levels of assurance most commonly sought, the source code of the system is never even looked at by the certifiers; their tasks are primarily to assure that the system's specifications are properly in order (and often these are created strictly for the certification process), to perform some level of testing of security functions, and to see that mechanisms are in place to assure that the software delivered is the same as what was evaluated. Yet the kinds of software flaws most commonly exploited by today's attacks are not likely to be discovered without access to the source code. Second, this scheme remains component-oriented, while security remains a system property. This is not to say that the scheme is without merit, but it is very definitely limited in what it can achieve, and its cost-effectiveness has never been assessed.

But in a world where the headlines are being made by suicide bombers, nations continue to engage in well-funded intelligence gathering activities, and daily electronic transfers of funds in the US Fedwire system alone average more than $1 trillion, simple software flaws are not the only concern in assessing software security. Software that may wind up in critical systems may be the target of specific attacks. Indeed, a recent book asserts that the U.S. made sabotaged pipeline control software available for the Soviet Union to obtain more than twenty years ago, and this software in the end triggered a major pipeline fire in Siberia. While I have no direct knowledge of the truth or falsity of this report, it is difficult to deny that that famous fire might have been triggered in this way. An expert might well be able to hide such software sabotage so that it is not even visible in the source code, using methods like those documented in Ken Thompson's famous Turing lecture. Software can be highly inscrutable even if the source code is available; the effects of asynchronous operations and feature interactions are notoriously difficult to understand.

3. OPEN VS. CLOSED

Do these considerations weigh on one side of the balance or the other for open source software?

Open source software has the advantage that any interested party can apply arbitrary tools to investigate it, to rebuild it, and to modify it to suit specific needs. It may be compiled by different compilers and linked by different linkers and the results compared. It can be examined by an arbitrary third party in as much detail as the sponsor can afford. But liability is unlikely to be present as a potent force in this case, since the user takes on the responsibility of composing, and potentially changing, the software. Control over the input to the source code may be uncertain, since it may have contributions from around the globe. And the fact that the proverbial "thousand eyes" could examine it does not mean they will, or that all of those eyes will be friendly -- they may be looking for holes, or places to insert subtle back doors. There is ample evidence that flaws can persist unseen in source-available software for decades. People may donate effort to creating open source software, but the evidence to date is that, except in a few notable cases (e.g., OpenBSD), they won't donate very much effort to providing competent security review of it.

Closed source software has the benefit of the producer's economic interest in the product. This interest should not be underestimated; it is (or can be) a powerful force for assuring product quality in a competitive marketplace. It can drive strong measures for control of software development, for testing of software prior to release, for configuration control of the released product and for prompt repair of defects. It is the value of the product in the marketplace, and hence its value as a corporate asset, that can justify this investment. Regardless of one's view of the result, it is certainly significant that after years of shrugging off security concerns as irrelevant to the market, since January 2002 Microsoft has apparently invested heavily in improving its programming practices from the standpoint of security and in changing the tradeoffs it makes in determining what features to enable by default. Nevertheless, even lacking the source code, hackers continue to find and exploit security flaws in Microsoft and other closed source software products. Further, commercial software development is increasingly a global enterprise, even if it is conducted within one corporation.

4. CONCLUSIONS

I propose three general conclusions from these observations:

1. Caveat emptor. Neither the open source model nor the closed source model has done a very good job of producing "bullet-proof" software except when someone has been willing to make a significant investment for that purpose. Exposing the source code does nothing per se to improve its security properties. Neither does hiding it.
2. Seek product and architectural assurance rather than process assurance. As software, closed or open source, is developed by groups of people in many diverse locations around the world, it will become increasingly difficult to have confidence that a particular critical system is secure because its software was produced by people you trust or by people using a process you trust. Rather, we need stronger methods for examining the actual code run on critical systems to assure that it has the intended properties, and where we can't gain that assurance, we need architectural methods to limit the damage it can cause.
3. Exploit what you know, and what you know you don't know, about the software in your system. If you are using open source software, take advantage of the opportunity to review it, consider whether you should reconfigure it or rebuild it. If you are dealing with a vendor of closed

source software, investigate the development processes used, consider the possible motivations of the developer, take account of any independent evaluations of the software, or the lack thereof. Use this information to develop a system architecture that manages the risks you know about.

ACKNOWLEDGMENT

Thanks to my Maryland colleague Michael Hicks for helpful comments on a draft of this note.

AN INTERDISCIPLINARY PERSPECTIVE OF DEPENDABILITY IN OPEN SOURCE SOFTWARE

Cristina Gacek
School of Computing Science, University of Newcastle upon Tyne, Newcastle upon Tyne, UK, NE1 7RU

Abstract: Open Source Software (OSS) development needs to be considered during software development as to whether to develop an OSS packages, and/or whether to develop with OSS. In this paper we briefly summarize the various characteristics that can be used to describe an OSS project and then explore the possible relationships between OSS products/projects and dependability.

Key words: open source software; dependability, project's characteristics; interdisciplinary.

1. INTRODUCTION

In the last 6 years, there has been a considerable amount of interest and discussions surrounding Open Source Software (OSS) development as a viable option to be considered during software development. The focus is two-fold. On one hand there is developing OSS packages, and on the other there is developing with OSS. When embarking on a new software development task, or continuing the development of an existing software package, individuals and corporations have to make an explicit decision on whether to make this software open source or not. On the other hand, existing OSS, similarly to Commercial off the Shelf (COTS) packages, can be considered to be used within various projects as a stand-alone package, as a reusable component, or as a platform. Unlike COTS, OSS can also be used as a starting point for changes and evolution.

Considerations of developing OSS or with OSS have not been limited to systems without very stringent dependability requirements, making it imperative to evaluate the links between OSS and dependability. This has triggered discussions with respect to using OSS in the context of high dependability requirements, as well as evaluating whether there are lessons to be learnt from OSS development that can help improve dependability in software development at large.

1.1 Context

The observations and insights discussed here are a result of work in the DIRC (Interdisciplinary Research Collaboration in Dependability) project (UK EPSRC Grant GR/N13999) and further research in the topic, including several students' dissertations at the University of Newcastle upon Tyne.

A range of OSS projects were studied taking into account considerations from Computing Science, Social Sciences, Psychology, Economics, and Law. The number of projects investigated was just below 100, varying from very large and well known ones to fairly small and new ones.

Within DIRC, OSS was investigated by a multidisciplinary team to establish whether this was a silver bullet that could significantly improve dependability. It quickly became clear that the term Open Source was used differently by various people: some focused on the licensing model, many meant only that the source code was visible, far fewer identified the motivation and redundancy (of reviewing) aspects which looked as though they could actually change what was developed (DIRC 2004). Upon further investigation, it also became clear that the way in which various projects implement the "open source model" varies greatly. Most of these findings are discussed in section 2.

Later studies in OSS provided greater insight into various characteristics of OSS projects and how these are interrelated (see section 3).

2. WHAT IS OSS?

Open Source is not a precise term. Some characteristics are common to all OSS projects, but there are much more of these that vary considerably from project to project. Some of these characteristics do exist in traditional (closed source) projects too, although they are likely to be more visible in OSS projects. Previous work has looked into these in more depth (Gacek and Arief, 2004).

The main commonalities among OSS projects are:

- adherence to the Open Source Definition (OSD, 2004);

- and the fact that developers are always users.

  The main variable characteristics are:

- project starting points;
- motivation;
- community:
  - balance of centralization and decentralization,
  - how their meritocratic culture gets implemented,
  - and whether the contributors are co-located or geographically distributed, and if so to what degree;
- software development support
  - modularity of the code,
  - visibility of the software architecture,
  - documentation and testing,
  - process of accepting submissions:
    - choice of work area
    - decision making process
    - submission information dissemination process,
  - and tool and operational support;
- licensing;
- and size of community and code base involved.

As highlighted above, OSS projects' characteristics can vary greatly, but that is true of all software projects. Hence, this taxonomy of characteristics can be equally applied to OSS and traditional software development projects, as depicted in table 1, adapted from Gacek and Arief (2004).

A key conclusion from the findings above is that it would not be meaningful for example to compare OSS development with traditional (closed source) software development. Any further studies and conclusions have to be based on more specific terms. The projects under study must always be further qualified by a description of their relevant details.

3. OSS AND DEPENDABILITY CONSIDERATIONS

When discussing OSS products and dependability, there are two facets to be considered. OSS products might need to be evaluated for use in a high dependability context. Additionally, OSS products provide a fertile ground for investigating how various project characteristics can impact dependability. Both of these aspects are discussed below.

Table 1. Software Projects' Characteristics (adapted from Gacek and Arief (2004))

Characteristic	**Open Source**		**Traditional**	
	Common	**Variable**	**Common**	**Variable**
Adherence to the OSD	✔		N/A	N/A
Developers are users	✔			✔
Starting points		✔		✔
Motivation		✔	✔	
Community				
Balance of centralization and decentralization		✔		✔
Meritocratic culture		✔		✔
Geographical distribution		✔		✔
Software development support				
Modularity		✔		✔
Visibility of software architecture		✔		✔
Documentation and testing		✔		✔
Accepting submissions				
Choice of work area		✔		✔
Decision making process		✔		✔
Submission information dissemination process		✔	N/A	N/A
Tool and operational support		✔		✔
Licensing		✔		✔
Size		✔		✔

3.1 Evaluating the dependability of OSS products

The term OSS usually tends to be associated with a few notorious products, such as Apache and Linux, which are far from being the average OSS product. Just like with traditional software, no assumptions can be made about the dependability of an OSS package without further knowledge about the product itself, and the process and methods used while deriving it.[1]

Typical stereotypes about OSS products/projects that relate to dependability are:

1. OSS products contain fewer faults because they have been reviewed by many people.
2. OSS products are more secure because they have been reviewed by many people.
3. OSS products have little to no design documentation available.
4. Having little design documentation available does not impact an OSS project as negatively as it would a traditional one. The reason being that

[1] We have run studies to look into OSS versus traditional software by OSS fans and by OSS sceptics. All of which reached this same conclusion.

OSS developers contribute towards development for their joy and pleasure, and consequently are less likely to leave the project than an employee to change jobs.

5. OSS products are developed by hackers in their free time, who only submit code for consideration once a high standard of quality has been achieved.

An assumption about OSS projects behind both items 1 and 2 above is that their code is extensively reviewed. The reality is that the vast majority of OSS projects consist of a single developer (as can be seen by visiting the very popular hosting sites SourceForge (2004) and Freshmeat (2004)), thus this assumption is invalid.

Item 3 above is an over generalization. It is true that most OSS products have very little documentation available, but there are successful OSS projects that have even created a sub-project dedicated to documentation. It is noteworthy that it is more common to find user and installation manuals than design documentation.

Stereotypes 4 and 5 above rely on the assumption that OSS contributors work for their pleasure in their free time. This assumption is fairly outdated. Many large corporations have employees contributing towards OSS products as part of their paid job. An immediate consequence is that these contributors are as likely to leave the OSS project as any employee in a traditional environment (making item 4 invalid). Another consequence is that these individuals are under higher pressure to deliver the product sooner and might be unable to strive for excellence (as is the assumption behind item 5).

Consequently, evaluating the dependability of an OSS product needs to be done on a case by case basis. Just like with traditional software, even different versions and releases of the same product must be considered individually.

An interesting related issue is that of who would be responsible for pursuing certification of OSS. The best model for this is yet to be identified, yet the same way that companies have been contributing towards the development of OSS products for their advantage; they could also work towards providing needed certification. How to provide the right incentives such that this certification gives companies the proper motivation is still an open question.

3.2 Deriving dependability insights from OSS products

Studies of individual OSS products can be used to derive insights into dependability in general. These are easier to conduct than studies of traditional (closed source) software projects. Much of the information related to OSS projects is available electronically to the public, although at times requiring a considerable amount of time and effort to locate. Sources include the projects' web sites with descriptions of the projects, various versions of the software, and logs of various mailing lists documenting public email exchanges. It should also be noted that in most cases, the key players within OSS projects are quite receptive to queries by students and researchers and very willing to help.

Recent work with students at the University of Newcastle upon Tyne has started looking for correlations among some OSS projects' characteristics. To date, one strong correlation has been found to hold. It shows that the quality of the documentation available and the readability of the source code are directly related. Other possible correlations are being pursued.

Beneficial findings from studies in OSS projects can be validated in other settings. Depending on the character of those findings, plans can also be drawn towards replicating positive results within a traditional development environment.

4. CONCLUSIONS

An analysis of different modes of working among OSS projects makes it clear that there are many technical, psychological and sociological facets involved and furthermore that most of these could also be deployed in traditional software development projects.

A key conclusion from the findings discussed in this paper is that it is not meaningful to bundle all OSS projects and products together. For example, comparing OSS development with traditional (closed source) software development yields no significant result. Studies, discussions, and conclusions have to be based on more specific terms than just open source or traditional software development. These must always be further qualified by a description of the relevant details being considered.

Evaluating the dependability of an OSS product needs to be done on a case by case basis. No generalization can be made. Still OSS projects provide a good ground for investigating what different (combinations of) characteristics of software development models yield more dependable results. Findings from such investigations can then be implemented in other OSS and/or in traditional software development projects.

REFERENCES

DIRC, 2004, Interdisciplinary Research Collaboration in Dependability (last accessed 13 May 2004); http://www.dirc.org.uk/index.php.

freshmeat, 2004, freshmeat.net: Welcome to freshmeat.net (last accessed 13 May 2004); http://freshmeat.net.

Gacek, C., and Arief, B., 2004, The many meanings of open source, IEEE Software. 21(1): 34-40.

OSD, 2004, OSI's Open Source Definition (last accessed 10 April 2004); http://www.opensource.org/docs/definition.html.

SourceForge, 2004, SourceForge.net: Welcome (last accessed 13 May 2004); http://sourceforge.net.

IS ACADEMIC OPEN SOURCE SOFTWARE DEPENDABLE?

Shigeru Chiba
Tokyo Institute of Technology, W8-50, Ohkayama 2-12-1, Meguro-ku, Tokyo 152-8552, Japan
chiba@acm.org

Abstract I have been developing several open source products as part of my academic research projects and a few of them has obtained a large number of users. In this paper, I present my experience of such open source software, OpenC++ and Javassist, and mention my thought about whether or not academic open source software can be dependable.

Keywords: Java; C++; Open Source Software.

1. My experience of OpenC++

OpenC++ [3, 1] is an extensible C++ compiler based on computational reflection [10]. This software has two versions: version 1 and version 2, which are quite different software products although they share the same name.

OpenC++ version 1 [3] released in around 1993 can be regarded as a language providing a mechanism called runtime metaobjects. The runtime metaobjects are objects that can intercept method calls and field accesses to other objects. This ability is useful for implementing a number of language extensions such as dependability, distribution, and persistence. OpenC++ was one of the first languages that provided runtime metaobjects with semi-production quality and have been widely used as a research platform for implementing various language extensions by using metaobjects [6, 11].

Fabre et all [6] used OpenC++ version 1 for implementing automatic object replication, which significantly improves dependability of software against host failure. Their idea was that metaobjects intercept all method calls to mission-critical objects and send copies of the method calls to corresponding backup objects running on different hosts. If that mission-critical objects become down, the backup objects are substituted for the original objects. Because of OpenC++, this replication mechanism could be easily implemented and thus the developers of that mechanism could focus their concerns on higher-level issues such as replication policies and execution performance.

OpenC++ version 2 [1] was released in 1996. It is a toolkit of source-to-source translator in C++ although the programming interface was constructed with the concept of metaobjects. From the academic viewpoint, OpenC++ version 2 was a system using a technique called compile-time reflection, which dramatically reduces runtime penalties due to metaobjects, compared to others in particular OpenC++ version 1.

OpenC++ version 2 has been widely used. Since 2000, more than 6,000 copies of this software have been downloaded by both academia and industry. For example, Fabre's group again used OpenC++ version 2 and developed a checkpointing system for improving dependability [7].

Although OpenC++ was an academic product, its quality was acceptable enough to build real applications. However, maintaining OpenC++ to be compatible to the latest specifications of the C++ language needed tremendous efforts. In particular, supporting C++ templates was a hard task and thus OpenC++ has not fully supported C++ templates yet; OpenC++ can process a program using templates but metaobjects cannot intercept template classes. The limitation of development resources is a major problem of academic open source software.

OpenC++ version 2 is now on http://opencxx.sourceforge.net and it is maintained by a group of volunteers since 2003. This is mainly because it has been getting difficult more and more for me to have time to maintain OpenC++ these years. Since the goal of academic software development is to prove that some idea is realistic and right, maintaining software after the research project finished is usually difficult.

2. My experience of Javassist

Javassist [2, 5] is a bytecode engineering toolkit for Java. The development of this software started in 1998 as a research project of reflective computing in Java and this software was first released in 1999. We are currently using this software as a research platform of aspect-oriented programming systems [9, 4, 8].

A unique feature of Javassist is that it allows the developers to manipulate a class definition (i.e. a class file) at the bytecode level without detailed knowledge of the specifications of Java bytecode. They need only the knowledge of the Java language. Javassist provides source-level abstraction, through which the developers can manipulate bytecode. Javassist automatically translates class-file manipulation described at source-level vocabulary into the equivalent manipulation at bytecode level.

A typical application of Javassist is to implement a component providing a non-functional concern such as persistence and synchronization. Using such a component is troublesome since developers must carefully insert a number of method calls in the client components so that the client components can appropriately call methods in that component. Javassist can be used for automatically inserting such method calls. This automation can avoid wrongly inserting method calls and thus decreasing stability and dependability of the software.

Since 2000, more than 6,800 copies of Javassist has been downloaded. Recently, Javassist recorded more than 500 downloads per month in the fourth quarter in 2003. The development of Javassist since 2003 is being hosted under the umbrella of JBoss.org, which is an open source project developing the JBoss J2EE server and several complement products. JBoss is a commercial-quality open source software and it has the third biggest share in the J2EE server market. Since JBoss internally includes Javassist and it has more than 7,000 downloads per month, the number of the Javassist users is huge if such indirect users are included.

The relatively larger user base of Javassist than OpenC++ worked well for improving the quality of the software. In general, a larger user base can find a larger number of bugs so that it can improve the stability of the software. A few people among the Javassist users have contributed source code to Javassist for extending the functionality.

3. Academic open source

An academic project is a good framework for developing innovative software. It is usually easy to release the resulting products to the public as open source software. Releasing open source software is rather motivated in an academic project since the goal of academic project is often to propose a new idea and convince people that the idea is right and useful. Open source software is a great promotion tool for showing the idea to people.

On the other hand, an academic project is not a good framework for maintaining open source software and improving the quality of that software. Developing a commercial-quality software is not a goal of most academic projects. If a primary developer of the software is a student or a post-doctoral researcher, she would leave the project in a few years. Moreover, the lifetime of the project itself is usually less than five years. Thus, keeping the developers in the team and continuing maintenance is not easy.

Some might think open source software could be maintained by volunteers. In fact, OpenC++ is currently maintained by a group of volunteers. However, volunteer-based maintenance is not sufficient to catch up the rapid evolution of the specifications of the C++ language, for example. The resources of the volunteer group is limited for maintenance. This is not surprising. While developing new software is exciting and it can attract talented developers, maintaining existing software is usually boring and hence developers do not want to spend a large amount of their time.

I have an interesting experience. The OpenC++ mailing list sometime receives a message from people who are new to the project. They take a very quick look at the source code of the software and usually say that the style of the source code is very old-fashioned (they do not know that the source code was written more than eight years ago!) and hence the source code must be completely rewritten. Otherwise, they say that the software should be redesigned by using today's XML technology or something similar. However, if we say "OK, your suggestion is right. Can you kindly do that work and check new source code in the CVS?", then they say "Ah.. I don't have time to write code for your project (since I am a very important guy and hence busy). The only contribution I can do now is to give my (variable) consultation to the project." In most cases, this is their last message post to the mailing list.

To make academic open source software dependable, we need another kind of framework for the maintenance phase. An academic project can be a cradle of open source software but it cannot take care of the software after it grows up. Professional open source proposed by Marc Fleury of JBoss Inc. can be such a follow-up framework. In his framework, developers are paid by a company that is selling technical supports of their open source software. Thus they must spend 50% of their work time for maintenance and technical supports of the software. However, they can use another 50% for extending the software or developing a new version of the software. In other words, 50% for money and 50% for fun.

There are high-quality academic open source software. However, keeping that quality after the initial development is difficult. Since keeping the quality is mandatory to use open source software as part of highly dependable software, we need a framework, such as professional open source, for motivating developers to maintain the software.

Today, some industrial people regard open source software just as inexpensive software. However, the cost of using open source software would go up if the software can be used as a dependable component. Dependability is expensive. The users must pay directly or indirectly developers of the software so that the developers can be motivated for the maintenance.

References

[1] Chiba, S., "A Metaobject Protocol for C++," in *Proc. of ACM Conf. on Object-Oriented Programming Systems, Languages, and Applications*, SIGPLAN Notices vol. 30, no. 10, pp. 285–299, ACM, 1995.

[2] Chiba, S., "Load-time structural reflection in Java," in *ECOOP 2000*, LNCS 1850, pp. 313–336, Springer-Verlag, 2000.

[3] Chiba, S. and T. Masuda, "Designing an Extensible Distributed Language with a Meta-Level Architecture," in *Proc. of the 7th European Conference on Object-Oriented Programming*, LNCS 707, pp. 482–501, Springer-Verlag, 1993.

[4] Chiba, S. and K. Nakagawa, "Josh: An Open AspectJ-like Language," in *Int'l Conf. on Aspect Oriented Software Development (AOSD'04)*, pp. 102–111, 2004.

[5] Chiba, S. and M. Nishizawa, "An Easy-to-Use Toolkit for Efficient Java Bytecode Translators," in *Proc. of Generative Programming and Component Engineering (GPCE '03)*, LNCS 2830, pp. 364–376, Springer-Verlag, 2003.

[6] Fabre, J., V. Nicomette, T. Perennou, R. J. Stroud, and Z. Wu, "Implementing Fault Tolerant Applications using Reflective Object-Oriented Programming," in *Proc. of the 25th IEEE Symp. on Fault-Tolerant Computing Systems*, pp. 489–498, 1995.

[7] Killijian, M. O., J. C. Ruiz-Garcia, and J. C. Fabre, "Portable Serialization of CORBA Objects: A Reflective Approach," in *Proc. of ACM Conf. on Object-Oriented Programming Systems, Languages, and Applications*, ACM SIGPLAN Notices vol. 37, no. 11, pp. 68–82, 2002.

[8] Nishizawa, M., S. Chiba, and M. Tatsubori, "Remote Pointcut – A language construct for distributed AOP," in *Int'l Conf. on Aspect Oriented Software Development (AOSD'04)*, pp. 7–15, 2004.

[9] Sato, Y., S. Chiba, and M. Tatsubori, "A Selective, Just-In-Time Aspect Weaver," in *Proc. of Generative Programming and Component Engineering (GPCE '03)*, LNCS 2830, pp. 189–208, Springer-Verlag, 2003.

[10] Smith, B. C., "Reflection and Semantics in Lisp," in *Proc. of ACM Symp. on Principles of Programming Languages*, pp. 23–35, 1984.

[11] Stroud, R. J. and Z. Wu, "Using Metaobject Protocols to Implement Atomic Data Types," in *Proc. of the 9th European Conference on Object-Oriented Programming*, LNCS 952, pp. 168–189, Springer-Verlag, 1995.

OPEN SOURCE IN DEPENDABLE SYSTEMS: CURRENT AND FUTURE BUSINESS MODELS

Cyrille Comar and Franco Gasperoni
AdaCore/ACT Europe
8 rue de Milan, 75009 Paris, France
comar@act-europe.com
gasperoni@act-europe.com

Abstract This article begins by describing the legal foundations of business models in the software industry. It then introduces the Free Software (FS) and Open Source Software (OSS) movements, and surveys various business models found in the FS/OSS based on them. A special emphasis is placed on the applicability of these business models to industries that produce dependable systems. This article concludes by exploring a FS/OSS co-op model that could enable the development of software components for dependable systems.

Keywords: Business Model, Free Software, Open Source Software, Co-op, Safety-Critical Software, Integrated Modular Avionics.

1. Introduction

This section provides the legal background to understand business models commonly adopted in the computer software industry. It then explains the Free and Open Source Software movements and how they relate to dependable systems.

Legal Background

Copyright is the exclusive legal right to copy, distribute, modify, display, perform, rent or more generally exploit a work by its copyright holder. Copyright applies to software works. In the context of software, both source code and binaries are protected by copyright. Loading a copy of the software onto a computer is considered copying. Only the copyright holder of a software program is allowed to copy, modify, make derivative works, and distribute the software. Anybody else needs permission from the copyright holder. In the software industry this permission is called a software license.

Nothing requires the copyright holder of a software work to give a license, or to give the same license to all possible users. Copyright holders can, at their discretion, charge a fee in exchange for a copy of the software work and its attached license. In this case what the recipient is buying is not the software per se but a copy of it. Virtually all software products are sold this way.

The software license specifies the conditions under which the recipient can (and more often, cannot) copy, distribute or modify the copy of the software received.

Free Software and Open Source Software

The *Free Software* (FS) movement created by Richard Stallman in the early 80's aims to "preserve, protect and promote the freedom to use, study, copy, modify, and redistribute computer software, and to defend the rights of FS users" [1]. To protect the freedoms of FS, Richard Stallman created the GPL (General Public License) [2].

In this respect, FS is no different from proprietary software sold by companies like Microsoft. A FS program comes with a license (the GPL), just as does software from "closed-source" software vendors. The big difference between the GPL and closed-source software licenses is that the GPL is written to favor the users of FS, while the license of closed-source software vendors is written to allow as little as necessary, and to favor the closed-source software vendor. Specifically, the GPL allows:

- Copying with no restrictions of any kind;

Furthermore in the case of redistribution the GPL requires:

- Redistribution of original software with sources;
- Redistribution of derived works with full sources.

Note that the term "free" in Free Software is intended to connote "freedom" but is often misinterpreted as "no cost". As a result the term *Open Source Software* (OSS) was coined to address this problem. Given the rapid gain in popularity of the FS/OSS movement, unscrupulous software vendors have claimed their programs to be "Open Source" by simply adjoining the sources along with their binaries - while imposing draconian restrictions on what could be done with those sources. Such actions repudiate the notion of freedom that founded the FS/OSS movement.

To counter such abuse, the Open Source Initiative (OSI) was created to unambiguously define the term "Open Source Software" [3]. This non-profit corporation defines "OSS", and lists a number of approved OSS licenses that match the definition. There are many approved OSS licenses. In addition to the GPL, examples include: the BSD License, the MIT License, the Apache Software License, the Mozilla Public License. There are over 50 approved OSS licenses enumerated on the OSI site [4].

FS/OSS and Dependable Systems

FS/OSS projects have blossomed due to the synergy created by openly sharing software and ideas. The FSF/UNESCO Free Software directory contains over 3,000 packages from visible projects such as GCC (the GNU Compiler Collection) to Gnome (the GNU desktop [5]). The SourceForge site alone hosts over 80,000 projects accessed by nearly 850,000 registered users [12].

As opposed to most existing FS/OSS, the software in a dependable system cannot be reduced only to a set of sources with build scripts and instructions. Evidence of dependability also resides in the availability of other artifacts, such as requirement documents, system models, design specs, proofs of correctness, test suites, verification and validation processes. In the most critical safety and/or security contexts, these kinds of evidence are formalised as certification materials to be provided according to the requirements of a recognized, often international, standard. The creation and evolution of the software component in a dependable system must be part of an auditable and repeatable process with stringent quality requirements.

These aspects of system development are not the primary concern of FS/OSS projects. This does not mean that FS/OSS programs are not dependable. It does mean that a record of quality assurance measures used to achieve dependability in a FS/OSS application is often not readily available. The focus of a FS/OSS project is typically to offer a useful, reliable software program to a given community.

Given that FS/OSS projects have shown that they can produce high-quality, widely available software programs for the benefit of all, it is natural to wonder how people building dependable systems can leverage, or even contribute, to the FS/OSS movement. In [6] the authors analyze this question in the area of safety-critical systems. The question they ask is: "What would be the benefit of using FS/OSS in safety-critical systems, and under what conditions can FS/OSS be used"?

In the remainder of this article we look at business models that have sprung up in the context of FS/OSS and analyze their relevance to the production of dependable software. We conclude by elaborating one of them and examining how it might be adapted to the benefit of the dependable software industry.

2. Business Models and the Computer Industry

The business models underlying most of the traditional computer industry rest, at least initially, on the notion of supplier scarcity. Put simply, there are three basic types of scarcities: product, expertise, and infrastructure.

An example of software product scarcity is the MS Windows operating system: you can purchase MS Windows only from Microsoft. An example of hardware product scarcity is the Pentium-compatible microprocessor: you can purchase Pentium chips from Intel, the originator of the Pentium design, or AMD. An example of expertise scarcity is the expertise required to manage a large IT (Information Technology) project: you can purchase this expertise from companies such as IBM Global Services, EDS, Cap Gemini, and a few others. An example of scarcity of infrastructure is the infrastructure developed by Dell in the PC industry. The PC industry has become a commodity industry, i.e. an industry with an abundance of suppliers. Thanks to its infrastructure, Dell has evolved from a garage-like operation to the PC industry leader.

In closed-software products, initial scarcities can be made into long-lasting ones thanks to the creation of technical entry barriers that give rise to monopolies or oligopolies. This phenomenon is well described in [7].

3. Business Models of FS/OSS

In contrast to traditional scarcity-based models as described in the previous section, the FS/OSS movement has created economies of abundance leading to a "community/network effect". In the "network effect", a community of software developers is created. This community, and the mind-share that is associated with it, is leveraged to sell products, expertise, infrastructure, advertising space, or some mixture of these.

The purpose of this section is to explore some business models involving FS/OSS. It will also examine how the three previously mentioned kinds of scarcities (product, expertise, infrastructure), along with the "network effect", are used to generate revenue. The list given here is by no means exhaustive.

Pure FS/OSS Product

As for any software product, there is no restriction on the price that can be charged for software licensed under a FS/OSS license. In this model the FS/OSS vendor limits itself to selling a standalone, self-contained set of FS/OSS programs with perhaps some minimal installation help.

Recipients of FS/OSS can buy one copy of the software and install/run it on as many machines as they like. This means that the conventional sell-per-unit business model does not work very well for FS/OSS since FS/OSS licenses favor an economy of software abundance. Furthermore, recipients of FS/OSS programs have themselves the freedom to redistribute copies of the software product and to charge for it. This limits the amount that the initial vendor can charge to pretty much commodity prices, unless the FS/OSS product is both one-of-a-kind and sold in low volume to address specialized business needs.

Thus, this business model leverages solely on scarcity of infrastructure (assembling of proper FS/OSS packages and redistribution). Most commercial GNU/Linux distributions until recently were based on this pure FS/OSS product commodity price model. Because the infrastructure required for this kind of operation is easily available, this type of business model has been abandoned by a number of GNU/Linux distributors.

For developers of dependable systems, this business model is not particularly attractive or relevant. Development of dependable software is an expertise-intensive task usually employing sophisticated technology. As such, buying a CD-ROM at commodity prices with little or no associated service is not particularly interesting for two reasons. Either the FS/OSS product is a sophisticated toolset (in which case it is critical that high-quality service accompany the product, regardless of its FS/OSS status), or it is a component, such as a library or operating system to be embedded in the final dependable system (in which case getting a CD containing sources is nice, but not nearly enough to meet the customer's need for evidence).

Dual License Product

In this model, the FS/OSS work is distributed at no cost under the terms of the GPL, as well being sold under a different license to customers who do not want to be bound by the terms of the GPL. This model is available only to the copyright holders of the software, and leverages product scarcity. It is viable only when the software being sold is included, in whole or in part, in another application that is in turn sold by a customer under terms different from the GPL. If a customer were to include in his own work FS licensed under the GPL, then his application would be considered a derivative work of the FS, thereby forbidding redistribution unless the whole application were licensed under the GPL.

MySQL, a database, and Cygwin, a UNIX-like environment for Windows, are licensed this way. This is an interesting illustration of the fact that the copyright holder can distribute the same version of a software work with different licensing conditions.

With respect to dependable systems, this business model rests on vendor lock-in. It has the advantage, relative to the completely proprietary model, of offering the sources of the product at no extra cost. It may also leverage a larger community of users and perhaps additional expertise independent of the vendor. Apart from these, it offers no significant advantage over a proprietary software model. Its appropriateness to industries developing dependable software depends more on the relevance of the product and associated services than on any enhancement of value due to the business model.

The Proprietary FS/OSS Product

This business model is an oxymoron, or we could call it the have-your-cake-and-eat-it-too business model. In this model the software vendor assembles a set of FS/OSS and proprietary applications, and markets the bundle on the basis of perceived synergy among them. The vendor uses the conventional charge-per-unit model where the unit price can be higher because of the scarcity created by the proprietary components in the bundle. Some GNU/Linux distributors have adopted, often temporarily, this business model.

This model is so anchored in the conceptual milieu of proprietary software business that it offers no advantage to the customer over the conventional closed-software model.

FS/OSS Leveraged Hardware

With the advent of 64-bit chips such as the Itanium from Intel [8] a number of hardware vendors have announced 64-bit workstations running (sometimes customized versions of) Linux. An interesting example is the SGI Altix platform [9]. In this business model hardware vendors leverage the Linux "network effect" to offer high-performance servers at premium prices.

Bundling a FS/OSS operating system (OS) and related software components, along with services covering the complete platform, is an interesting offer to developers of dependable software: the entire system on which their application rests becomes open for inspection. The QA and other documents typically needed when developing dependable software are not available, but for certain types of dependable systems having access to the OS source code allows a dependable system vendor to create an in-house team to qualify and tailor the OS according to the dependable system requirements. The additional support provided by the hardware vendor for the platform (and typically bundled into its premium pricing) is a differentiating factor for customers developing dependable systems, compared to commodity hardware with little or no vendor support.

Infrastructure Provider

Companies such as VA Software [10] with its OSDN (Open Source Development Network, Inc.) [11] leverage scarcity of infrastructure to provide an OSS development website, SourceForge [12] with a large repository of FS/OSS projects for whom the basic service is free of charge, while advanced services come at a fee. OSDN delivers more than 222 million page views and reaches 12 million unique visitors per month. On the strength of this network effect, some of its revenue is indirect from web advertising. Other online revenue comes from per-user annual subscriptions that give access to advanced services on the SourceForge.net web site, such as advanced search capabilities, priority technical support, project monitoring, etc. The annual cost per user is low (less that USD 50 in 2004).

VA Software also sells SourceForge Enterprise Edition [13] to manage and execute offshore and distributed team development. The SourceForge application itself does not appear to be FS/OSS. VA Software leverages the free service it provides to the FS/OSS communities to sell and promote its SourceForge product.

This business model is interesting for developers of dependable system that have a large and possibly distributed development teams. Leveraging the experience with collaborative development in the FS/OSS community and using the same infrastructure that was created to support it can be an attractive solution.

Pure Service

In this model a service company builds expertise around a number of FS/OSS works and helps its clients with installation, support, use, maintenance, upgrades and adjustments or customizations that may be needed. This business model is based on a relative abundance of software, but scarcity of expertise, to market service. An example is Alcove, a European company providing professional FS/OSS services [14]. Another interesting example in this domain is what IBM is doing with Linux with over 2,000 Linux-skilled IBM Global Services professionals [15, 16].

Offering service, and in this case expertise, is certainly interesting in the context of dependable systems development, if the consultants being engaged are experts and contributors to the FS/OSS being used in the construction of the dependable system. The difference between this business model and that of "regular" service companies is that in the FS/OSS case consultants can inspect and contribute to the development of the FS/OSS product. As such they are in a position to provide a deep level of know-how to the client developing a dependable system.

Leveraged Service

A leveraged service is an expertise-based service that facilitates the effective application of a FS/OSS product to specific business needs. This product/service combination is typically sold as a yearly subscription comprising the FS/OSS toolset with upgrades, high-quality toolset support and online consulting from toolset specialists. GNAT Pro, the FS development environment for the Ada programming language used in mission- and safety-critical systems is an example [17].

We use the GNAT Pro offering to illustrate the value proposition of this model. GNAT Pro customers receive a high-quality FS product accompanied by service directly from Ada experts and the GNAT Pro developers. The GNAT Pro experts serve as partners to the customer's development team. They work closely with the customer team to help them make optimal use of GNAT Pro and to assist them with all aspects of their Ada software development. As part of that dialogue the GNAT Pro engineers regularly address issues such as code optimization, programming language semantics, multi-language systems, and code organization. In addition to the benefits stemming from a high-quality product, this level of service leads to higher productivity and reduced risk in projects using GNAT Pro.

This business model leverages the subtle combination of two scarcities: scarcity of the FS/OSS expertise and scarcity of the FS/OSS quality assurance (QA) infrastructure. In the case of GNAT Pro, the GNAT Pro development team has built a sophisticated QA infrastructure comprising over 30,000 real-life test cases (a total of over 6 million lines of Ada source code) and automated capabilities for execution and evaluation of the tests, supporting nightly integration, regression testing and analysis on multiple platforms.

This business model works for FS/OSS used in fairly to highly technical software projects requiring sophisticated tools, libraries, and other software components, along with a high degree of expertise, and of confidence in the reliablility of the products. The software deployed in a dependable system is often of this sort. As a result, this business model is well-suited for industries producing highly-dependable software. What's more, this business model is in the interest of the companies ultimately responsible for the software used in dependable systems because it aligns their interests with those of their tool vendors. A company developing software for a dependable system is interested in receiving a high-quality product with high quality service in order to develop its dependable application. The only way a FS/OSS company can secure recurring revenue with this business model is by ensuring that the customer renews his subscription. This will happen only if the customer is happy with the technology and the service he receives: unlike for closed-software, the FS/OSS product alone provides no vendor lock-in.

OSS Co-Ops

The Eclipse Foundation [18] and the Apache Software Foundation [19] have an interesting and unconventional business model.

Eclipse is an open, extensible IDE (integrated development environment) built on a mechanism for developing, integrating, and running modules called plug-ins. Put it another way, Eclipse is a platform providing a common IDE infrastructure for tool providers to plug-in their tools.

The Apache Software Foundation provides support for the Apache community of open-source software projects such as the Apache HTTP server.

Both the Eclipse Foundation and the Apache Software Foundation are non-profit organizations. They are characterized by a collaborative, consensus-based organization and development process. They form a tightly-coupled community of developers and users governed by an open and pragmatic software license. We call these types of organizations OSS cooperatives or OSS co-ops.

A general-purpose co-op is an association formed and operated for the benefit of those using it. Its business purpose lies more in cost reduction than in revenue generation. The roots of the co-op concept lie in the work of Peter Kropotkin in 1902 [21]. In his book Kropotkin describes how in Siberia animals, instead of competing for resources, have to work together to stay alive. Throughout his book, Kropotkin stresses that cooperation is the main factor in evolution, rather than the competing forces posited by Darwin and his adherents.

It is precisely this drive for cooperation to solve a mutual problem, too hard or too costly to solve alone, that is the business case for OSS co-ops. The idea of industrial cooperation is not new. The Eurofighter consortium [22] is a good example of cooperative effort across aerospace companies and nations. What is novel, and what the FS/OSS movement has shown, is that this idea can be applied to the development of software.

In the next section we look into how this concept of OSS co-ops can be put to work in the development of software for dependable systems.

4. OSS Co-Ops and Dependable Systems

In this section we explore, through an example, how the OSS co-op business model could lead to a new model for the development of software components in dependable systems.

Example: Integrated Modular Avionics

Our example is set in the avionics industry - an industry where dependable software is crucial. Until recently, the avionics industry has relied on federated architectures where separate avionics subsystems (computers) each perform a dedicated function. With the constant increase in aircraft functionalities, computational requirements, and corresponding embedded software, the life-cycle cost of this federation of individual systems has led aerospace companies and program offices to seek alternative approaches. The main solution is a move towards generic computing platforms that can run multiple applications concurrently, possibly at different levels of safety criticality. This approach, known as Integrated Modular Avionics (IMA), results in a reduced number of subsystems (computers) and reduced weight [23, 24]. One of the outcomes is the need for an operating system to support the IMA software architecture.

When an aeronautics company FlightEX wants to supply IMA-compatible avionics software, for instance a flight management system (FMS), they need to re-engineer their current FMS software to execute under an IMA-compatible operating system (OS). The re-engineering effort of their FMS is within the core competence of FlightEX since the FMS represents an important part of its avionics software know-how. On the other hand, creating and maintaining an IMA-compatible OS layer is not part of the usual activities of FlightEX. Since this is a requirement for new avionics programs, it must be done. To solve this dilemma FlightEX has adopted the following strategies:

- Follow the conventional "do-it-yourself" approach. Use internal resources to design, develop, provide certification evidence, and maintain the IMA-compatible OS.

- Purchase a commercial off-the-shelf (COTS) OS and adapt it to be IMA-compatible along with providing all the certification artifacts necessary for its deployment in avionics applications.

- Team up with commercial off-the-shelf (COTS) OS vendors to provide avionics guidance and funding for the development of IMA-compatible OSes.

Example Continued: What to Do for the OS?

Faced with the absence of IMA-compatible OSes it is tempting for FlightEX to develop its own OS, or internally adapt an existing one. On the positive side, the OS specifications can be customized to match the exact needs of FlightEX. Furthermore, the first steps for the development of such an OS are based on the company's detailed avionics know-how. On the negative side, internal resources are diverted from the core avionics focus of FlightEX, in addition to the necessity for long-term maintenance of the home-grown OS and the related expertise. Further, the adapted FMS, which is one of the company's core products, runs the risk of being less flexible to deploy in other IMA architecture implemented over a different OS choice.

Faced with this unpleasant situation a number of avionics companies have transferred the commercial rights of the IMA-compatible OS to a commercial vendor. The idea being that the vendor can sell the IMA-compatible OS to other avionics companies and, with the resulting revenue, ensure long-term maintenance and evolution of the OS. This approach is based on the insight that the IMA-compatible OS alone will not be the key differentiating factor when competing for avionics projects.

Following a proprietary COTS-only approach has its own risks. In fact, a commercial offering can live for as long as it is profitable. This is an issue when the required expertise and related investments are high and the customers few. This, along with the viability of the COTS supplier, is a risk factor when software choices must stand for decade-long projects. In addition, there are potential geo-political concerns: European avionics companies may need to avoid COTS OSes restricted by US export regulations and vice-versa. See [6] for a complete discussion of the risks related to the use of COTS in avionics software.

5. Conclusion: Towards an OSS Co-Op

In addition to the home-grown or the COTS approaches described above, a cooperative approach may provide an interesting middle ground. Instead of going alone, or relying on a third party, aeronautics companies and others sharing similar OS needs, can cooperate towards a common OS. The objective would be to ensure long-term availability to all co-op members of the OS along with a reduction in their overall costs of deployment.

The OSS co-ops such as Apache and Eclipse offer an interesting model for sharing the development and maintenance effort as well as the ownership of the software. They also provide interesting ideas on how to manage software independence from any particular member of the co-op. In the case of the avionics industry, the co-op model needs to be enhanced to take into account the specificities of safety-critical software (creating and sharing certification material, putting in place a strict QA infrastructure for software evolution, etc.)

- Sharing the source code is insufficient. Other things need to be shared and jointly owned, in particular certification materials.

- A strict QA infrastructure needs to be put in place as part of the evolution process.

As in the Apache and Eclipse cases, an independent organization made of its co-op members can play the leading role in hosting and maintaining the overall infrastructure, as well as guaranteeing the quality and independence of the certification material that is shared by co-op members. The software would be available as OSS and made available publicly, to spread its use and allow third part vendors to adapt their toolset easily. To encourage others to become members of the co-op, certification artifacts along with support and expertise as detailed in the "leveraged service" business model would be provided to members of the co-op for their projects.

This software co-op business model leverages the economics of sharing which has made the success of the FS/OSS movement. A COTS OS vendor may even get it started by pitching its own OS, in order to gain a decisive competitive advantage over its competitors. A fantasy?

References

[1] http://www.fsf.org/

[2] http://www.gnu.org/copyleft/gpl.html

[3] http://www.opensource.org/

[4] http://www.opensource.org/licenses/

[5] http://www.gnu.org/

[6] Logiciel libre et sûreté de fonctionnement, by Philippe David and Hélène Waeselynck Editors, 2003, Lavoisier. In French.

[7] The Gorilla Game, by Geoffrey A. Moore, Paul J. Johnson, and Tom Kippola, 1998, Harper Business Publisher.

[8] http://www.intel.com/products/server/processors/server/itanium2/

[9] http://www.sgi.com/servers/altix/

[10] http://www.vasoftware.com/

[11] http://www.osdn.com/

[12] http://sourceforge.net/

[13] http://www.vasoftware.com/products/index.php

[14] http://www.alcove.com/

[15] http://www.ibm.com/linux/

[16] http://www-5.ibm.com/services/be/pdf/linux_services_opportunity.pdf

[17] http://www.gnat.info/

[18] http://www.eclipse.org/

[19] http://www.apache.org/

[20] http://www.eclipse.org/

[21] Mutual Aid: A Factor of Evolution, by Peter Kropotkin, 1902. Available from Porter Sargent Publisher (December 1976). Also at http://socserv.socsci.mcmaster.ca/ econ/ugcm/3ll3/kropotkin/mutaid.txt

[22] http://www.eurofighter.com/

[23] DO-255: Requirements Specification for Avionics Computer Resource, RTCA, 2000. Available at http://www.rtca.org/onlinecart/product.cfm?id=193.

[24] ARINC 653-1: Avionics Application Software Standard Interface, ARINC, 2003. Available at https://www.arinc.com/cf/store/catalog_detail.cfm?item_id=495.

AN OPEN-SOURCE VHDL IP LIBRARY WITH PLUG&PLAY CONFIGURATION

Jiri Gaisler
Gaisler Research, Första Långgatan 19, 413 27 Göteborg, Sweden

Abstract: An open-source IP library based on the AMBA-2.0 AHB/APB bus is presented. The library adds "plug&play" capability to the AMBA bus, while maintaining compatibility with existing AMBA cores. The library is both vendor and technology independent, and has support for several commercial tool-chains.

Key words: IP cores; VHDL; system on chip; SOC; plug&play; SPARC; AMBA; PCI

1. INTRODUCTION

To shorten the development time of complex system-on-chip (SOC) devices, IP-core based design methodology is increasingly being used. However, integrating third-party cores from different suppliers can require significant adaptation and harmonization of both functional and logistical (tool-oriented) interfaces. Procurement and licensing conditions, NDA agreements, and royalty issues must also be resolved, and can be equally challenging.

One approach to solve these problems has been through the development of open-source IP cores, such as the LEON SPARC processor [1] (ESA & Gaisler Research) or the many cores developed by OpenCores.org [2]. While these open-source developments are interesting and promising on their own rights, they do not solve the combined functional and logistical problems with third-party IP reuse as described above. The procurement and licensing issues are simplified, but several technical issues persist. The LEON processor consists of a set of IP cores with harmonized interfaces and simulation/synthesis scripts, but the model implements only one major function (processor). The OpenCores group provide many different cores, but neither the functional nor logistical interfaces are well harmonized.

The development of the GRLIB open-source IP library is a new attempt to address the reuse problems. The library consists of configurable IP cores with common interfaces and package structure. This paper will describe the rational and some implementation details of this new library.

2. GRLIB CONCEPTS

2.1 Overview

The GRLIB IP Library intends to enhance the development of SOC devices by providing reusable IP cores with common functional and logistical interfaces. Common functional interfaces means that the cores implement the same on-chip bus interfaces, and use the same configuration and technology mapping methods. Common logistical interfaces means that the IP cores are coherently packaged in a common distribution, and use the same scripting method for compilation and synthesis.

A key aspect has been to insure vendor independence at both core and tool level. The library is designed to be easily portable to different CAD tools and target technologies. It does also not depend on a vendor specific inter-face or technology which needs to be licensed or procured. The library is also designed to allow contributions or extensions from other parties. Each contributor is assigned a unique vendor name and ID, and can add cores to a well defined and separated part of the library.

The overall concept of GRLIB is thus to provide a standardized and vendor-independent infrastructure to deliver reusable IP cores. The sections below will outline how the various parts of this infrastructure has been implemented.

2.2 Library organization

GRLIB is organized around VHDL libraries, where each IP vendor is assigned a unique library name. Using separate libraries avoids name clashes between IP cores and hides unnecessary implementation details from the end user. A library typically contains a number of packages, declaring the exported IP cores and their interface types. All vendor-specific files such as simulation and synthesis scripts are contained in a vendor-specific area, and automatically merged into a combined script by a global makefile. Adding and removing of libraries and packages can thus be made without modifying any global files. This also insures that modification of one vendor's library cannot will not affect other vendors.

The initial release of GRLIB can generate scripts for the Modelsim simulator, and the Synopsys, Synplify and Xilinx XST synthesis tools. Support for other CAD tools can easily be added.

2.3 On-chip bus

The GRLIB is designed to be "bus-centric", i.e. it is assumed that most of the IP cores will be connected through an on-chip bus. The AMBA-2.0 [3] AHB/APB bus has been defined as the common on-chip bus, due to its market dominance (ARM processors) and because it is well documented and can be used for free without license restrictions.

GRLIB uses VHDL record types to group related bus signals. Each AMBA unit only uses two record signals to connect to the bus, one record with all inputs and one record with all outputs. The AMBA bus is multiplexed (Figure 1), and each AMBA unit drives a separate record signal to the arbiter, which selects the active unit to drive the shared bus.

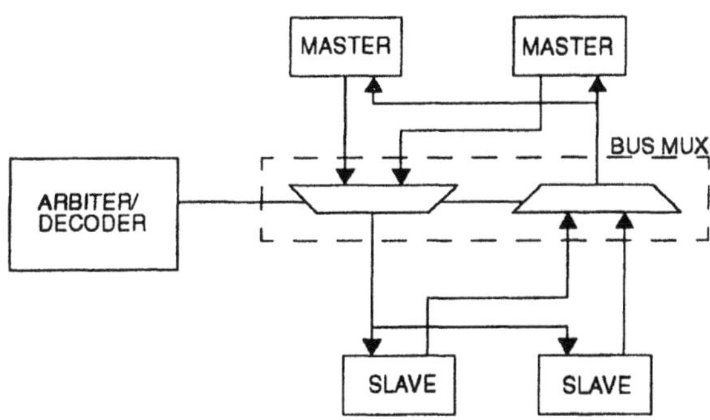

Figure 1. AMBA AHB Bus Multiplexers

2.4 Distributed address decoding

Adding an IP core to the AHB bus is however not as straight-forward as just connecting the bus signals. The address decoding of AHB is centralized, and a shared address decoder and bus multiplexer must be modified each time a core is added or removed. To avoid dependencies on a global resource, and allow SOC design to be as simple as putting together LEGO bricks (!), distributed address decoding has been added to the GRLIB cores and AMBA AHB/APB controllers.

In a standard AMBA system, a fixed address decoder generates a chip select for each AMBA slave. In the GRLIB AMBA system, each instantiated core is assigned an address space through VHDL generics, and this information is routed to the address decoder together with the other bus signals in the output record. The address decoder does not have a fixed chip select generator, but automatically builds the chip select logic from the information received from the slaves. In this manner, the chip select generator always corresponds to the current configuration! Since the address space information is passed through VHDL generics, they will be constant and allow an efficient synthesis of the chip select logic. Using generics also allows an IP core to be instantiated several times with different parameters.

The example below shows two instantiation of the same UART device:

```
uart1 : apbuart -- UART 1
generic map (apbndx => 1, apbaddr => 16#200#, irq => 3)
port map (rstn, clkm, apbi, apbo(1), uartin1, uartout1);

uart2 : apbuart -- UART 2
generic map (apbndx => 2, apbaddr => 16#300#, irq => 4)
port map (rstn, clkm, apbi, apbo(2), uartin2, uartout2);
```

2.5 Interrupt steering

A problem with AMBA and most other on-chip buses is that interrupt steering is not defined in the bus specification, and must be solved in a system-dependent ad-hoc manner. GRLIB therefore provides a unified interrupt handling scheme by adding 32 interrupt signals to the output record of the AMBA modules. Similar to the address space definition, a VHDL generic is used to select which interrupt the unit should drive. The remaining interrupt signals are simply driven with zero. The arbiter ORs the 32-bit interrupt vector from each unit together into a combined 32-bit vector, and sends it out on the input records. The AMBA unit that implements an interrupt controller can then monitor the combined interrupt vector and generate the appropriate processor interrupt. In this way, interrupts can be generated regardless of which processor or interrupt controller is being used in the system, and does not need to be explicitly routed to a global resource. The scheme also allows that interrupts are shared by several cores and resolved by software.

2.6 Plug&Play capability

A broad interpretation of the term "plug&play" is the capability to detect the system hardware configuration through software. Such capability makes it possible to use software application or operating systems which automatically configure themselves to match the underlying hardware. This greatly simplifies the development of software applications, since they do not need to be customized for each particular hardware configuration.

The information which is needed for plug&play capability includes the type of cores that are attached to the local bus, how they are configured, which address range they are mapped to, and which interrupt they drive. In the well-know PCI [4] bus, this information is stored in the "configuration space" and accessed through special configuration read/write cycles.

In order to bring "plug&play" capability to AMBA, functionality to access the configuration parameters is needed. This functionality must be provided without modification to the basic bus protocol, or compatibility with the large infrastructure of AMBA compliant third-party IP cores would be lost. This rules out the addition of new bus cycle types, such as the configuration read/write cycles on PCI.

In GRLIB, the address mapping configuration is sent from all cores to the AMBA address decoder, where it is used for chip select generation. By providing the remaining plug&play information (core type and interrupt steering) in the same way, the address decoder contains the full system configuration. The decoder is designed to automatically concatenate the configuration information from all AHB devices are into a small configuration prom, by default placed at the top of the address space. Any AHB master can then read the system configuration using standard read cycles, and a plug&play operating system can be supported.

To provide the plug&play information from the AHB units in a harmonized way, a configuration record for AMBA AHB devices has been defined (Figure 2). The configuration record consists of 8 32-bit words, where four contains configuration words defining the core type and interrupt routing, and four contain so called "bus address registers" (BAR), defining the memory mapping.

The configuration word for each device includes a vendor ID, device ID, version number, and interrupt routing information. The BARs contain the start address for a segment allocated to the device, a mask defining the size of the segment, and information whether the segment is cacheable or prefetchable. The configuration record can contain up to four BARs and the core can thus be mapped on up to four distinct memory segments.

By identifying the cores through a vendor and device ID, a mapping between the VHDL library assignment and vendor ID can be established. Each vendor receives a unique vendor ID, and can add cores and device IDs without conflicts with other vendors.

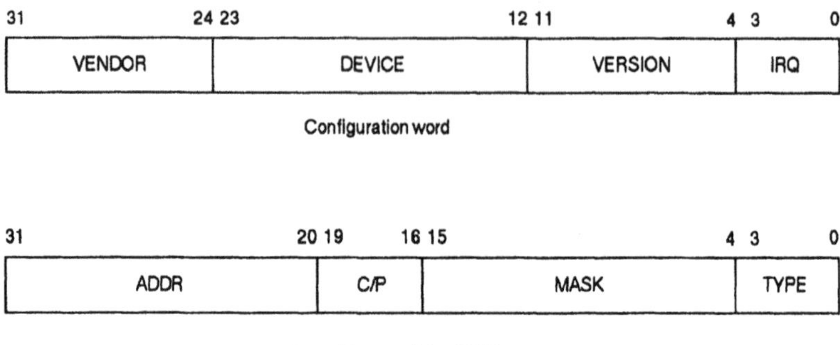

Figure 2. AMBA AHB configuration record

2.7 Portability

Mapping IP cores to the desired target technology is normally handled by the synthesis tool, but does not work for technology specific mega cells such as embedded memories, hard multipliers or pads. GRLIB is intended to be technology independent, and therefore provides "portability" API for these type of blocks. The API is implemented as a component with a VHDL generic to select the target technology. In the architecture of the component, VHDL generate statement are used instantiate the corresponding macro cell from the selected technology library. For RAM cells, generics are also used to specify the address and data width, and the number of ports. Below is an example of a pad and a single-port ram with technology selection.

```
entity outpad is
  generic (tech, level, slew, voltage, strength : integer := 0);
  port (pad : out std_ulogic; i : in std_ulogic);
end;

entity syncram is
  generic (tech : integer := 0; abits, dbits : integer := 8 );
  port (
    clk      : in std_ulogic;
    address  : in std_logic_vector((abits -1) downto 0);
    datain   : in std_logic_vector((dbits -1) downto 0);
    dataout  : out std_logic_vector((dbits -1) downto 0);
    enable   : in std_ulogic;
    write    : in std_ulogic);
end;
```

The portability API includes components such as single-port ram, two-port-ram, dual-port ram, single-port rom, clock generators and pads.

2.8 Availability

A working beta version of GRLIB has been available since early 2004. The library includes cores for AMBA AHB/APB control, the LEON3 SPARC processor, 32-bit PC133 SDRAM controller, 32-bit PCI bridge with DMA, 10/100 Mbit ethernet MAC, 8/16/32-bit prom and sram controller, generic UART, modular timer unit, interrupt controller, and a 32-bit GPIO port. Memory and pad generators are available for Virage, Xilinx, UMC, Atmel, and Actel.

The first public version will be made available during Q2 2004, and released under GNU GPL.

3. CONCLUSIONS

GRLIB has been developed to simplify both the development and reuse of open-source IP cores. By specifying common functional interfaces, new cores can easily be added and immediately reused. The logistical interface support several commonly used CAD tools, and can easily be extended. The distributed address decoding allows to design an modify complex SOC designs without having to modify any global controller or decoder. To enhance portability, an API to map technology-specific macro cells has been defined. To simplify software development and debugging, a plug&play capability has been added. By organizing GRLIB according to vendors, modification or addition of IP cores can be done without side-effects. By providing the library freely under the GNU GPL license, immediate access is provided to both academia and commercial companies.

REFERENCES

[1] LEON2 home page, http://www.gaisler.com/leon.html
[2] Opencores home page, http://www.opencores.org
[3] AMBA Specification 2.0, ARM Ltd, May 13, 1999, http://www.arm.com
[4] PCI Local Bus Specification, Revision 2.1, June 1, 1995, PCISIG

LINUX: A MULTI-PURPOSE EXECUTIVE SUPPORT FOR CIVIL AVIONICS APPLICATIONS?

Serge Goiffon and Pierre Gaufillet
AIRBUS France - Avionics and Simulation Products, 316 route de Bayonne, 31060 Toulouse Cedex 03, France

Abstract: Software plays an important role in modern aircraft. Criteria like portability, reusability, cost savings, maintainability, lead suppliers of equipment and functions to adopt standards. Integrated Modular Avionics is the new paradigm for the avionics world. The ARINC 653 standard has been chosen as the application programming interface, despite the predominant position of POSIX standard in other industries. Nevertheless, both standards have different but complementary approaches, and a multi-purpose adaptable open source software like Linux could be a good candidate to host avionics applications.

Key words: Linux, POSIX, ARINC 653, Open Source, avionics application, DO-178B

1. NEW TRENDS IN CIVIL AVIONICS

The amount of embedded software in modern aircraft has continuously increased over the past 30 years. Today, the complexity of avionics functions has reached a point where a classical "make all from scratch" development strategy is superseded. Future aircraft will continue to embed more and more software. Embedded avionics equipment will tend to become more and more a generic platform whose goal will be to provide allocation and control of computing resources needed by avionics functions : CPU, memory and input/outputs. This new trend is known as Integrated Modular Avionics.

In this challenging industrial context, PDS[1], like operating systems, are a key factor to reduce the time to market of avionics applications: introducing an hardware abstraction layer solves the problem of hardware component obsolescence, and adopting industrial standards, like POSIX[2], or avionics standards, like ARINC 653[3], ensures durability and portability of applications.

Nevertheless, this new trend leads to an increase in the certification cost that is not always compatible with the use of a PDS. This is so because the product does not necessarily fulfill the quality development process required by DO-178B[4], and the equipment supplier may not accept the extra cost to achieve conformance. The quasi monopolistic position of the PDS supplier may further compound the problem.

In this context, the Linux open source model can provide an alternative solution: low cost access to technology, freedom to modify the source code to adapt it to avionics constraints. But it also raises new questions that need to be addressed: ability to comply with avionics hardware components and embedded constraints, and availability of certification material.

2. POSIX VS. ARINC 653

The ARINC 653 standard has been chosen as the avionics application programming interface for future aircraft, despite the predominant position of the widely used POSIX standard in other industries. ARINC 653 first issue was published in 1997. One year before, POSIX standard real-time extensions were approved as an international standard, ISO/IEC 9945-1:1996 (including1003.1b, 1003.1c) and in 1998 the first real-time profile standard, IEEE Std 1003.13-1998 was published, enabling POSIX to address embedded real-time applications and smaller footprint devices.

POSIX and ARINC 653 not only offer different programming interfaces, but also carry different design concepts listed in Table 1.

[1] Previously Developed Software

[2] POSIX stands for Portable Operation System Interface

[3] ARINC 653 is document describing the avionics application software standard interface

[4] DO-178B is a RTCA document "Software Considerations in Airborne Systems and Equipment Certification". It provides guidance on designing, specifying, developing, testing, and deploying software in safety-critical avionics systems.

Table 1. Comparing POSIX and ARINC 653

POSIX	ARINC 653
Event driven execution model	Cyclic based execution model
Multi-processing, multi-threading execution model	Same as POSIX but terminology used is partition for process, and process for threads
Priority preemptive scheduling for processes and threads	Within partition time slice : priority preemptive scheduling of A653 processes with deadline management
No temporal partitioning	Temporal partitioning : fixed allocation of time slices to partitions in a repetitive time frame pattern
I/O interrupt driven	I/O polling and I/O partitioning
Memory segregation	Same as POSIX but terminology is spatial partitioning
Socket	Sampling and queuing ports on I/O
Inter Process Communication	Sampling and queuing ports on RAM
Mutex and condition variables	Buffer, blackboard, semaphore, event
Timers	No timers like POSIX but API service to wait for timeout
Signal management	Health monitoring

In ARINC 653, partitioning is a key concept allowing to host multi-criticality level applications[5] and ensures that whatever the behavior of a partition, it shall not perturb, either directly nor indirectly, the execution of other partitions. This fault isolation mechanism is the basis to build an incremental certification demonstration.

The choice of ARINC 653 has consequences on the development process of applications. Like all newly adopted standards, it lacks tools and interoperability features with existing development platforms (mostly based on UNIX/POSIX). On the contrary, Linux and its conformance to industrial standards, has allowed to built over years, a collection of tools (the GNU development toolset is a revealing example) to ensure interoperability and allow native development models.

3. EMBEDDING LINUX IN AVIONICS EQUIPMENT

Linux has shown over the past 8 years, the ability to adapt to a wide range of architectures, from multi-processor mainframes to embedded platforms, allowing interoperability of applications with the rest of the world. Linux is supported by a large community of developers, testers, and

[5] An application is made of one or more partitions, executed on the same or different modules.

its success and durability also relies on the adoption of standards. In addition to supporting many hardware platforms, the new 2.6 kernel release offers soft real-time characteristics with good performances.

Recently, the Avionics and Simulation Department of Airbus, has investigated, for a research project, the possibility of switching from a POSIX real-time COTS operating system embedded on a real equipment (with soft real-time constraints), to a standard Linux kernel. The main objectives to achieve were:

- to acquire a good knowledge of kernel internal mechanisms, so as to be able to port it to specific embedded equipments, and adapt/develop drivers for specific avionics I/O devices,
- to limit the effort of porting existing applications to the new platform,
- to draw up an inventory of available documentation from the point of view of the certification process.

The porting of Linux has followed the six main steps described below:

1. adapt low level hardware services to specific hardware components: boot sequence (no BIOS), interrupt controller, real-time clock management, RS232 serial link (for console debugging).
2. downsize the kernel footprint in order to make it compatible with the limited hardware resources of the avionics equipment.
3. build a kernel image (with ram disk and console output capabilities) including minimal root file system with the busybox[6] tool. Such a configuration provides a standalone machine with limited functionality.
4. include Ethernet driver and TCP/IP stack so that embedded equipment can be seen as a diskless computer. Such a configuration provides distant file system mounting capability, and allow debugging with gdb, automated test suites launching, etc ...
5. adapt/migrate existing hardware specific drivers from the previous COTS operating system to Linux (avionics buses, wired input/outputs, FLASH, EEPROM). This step is achieved by looking for mechanisms in Linux kernel that are similar to the ones used in the COTS kernel (synchronization of tasks, communication between tasks, timeouts management). During this step, a simple FLASH file system was implemented to suppress cache disk latency and allow direct execution of application code from FLASH.

[6] BusyBox provides a fairly complete UNIX command environment for any small or embedded system. It was first released by LINEO team, but is today maintained by Erik Andersen (www.busybox.net)

6. migrate existing applications. This simply led us to recompile and build applications with GNU tools in the new Linux environment. The code had to be reworked for parts that were not compliant to POSIX API.

The results of this study showed no technical obstacle, or incompatibility with avionics hardware, which would prevent the embedding of the Linux kernel. However, it has been noticed that major subsystems like Memory Manager, Virtual File System, Network, and Inter-Process Communication, turn out to be unnecessarily complex compared to the needs in critical embedded systems. The main problem we identified remains a significant work of reverse-engineering in order to produce the certification material required by DO-178B (coding standards, design documents, traceability, code coverage, ...).

4. FUTURE WORK

Today, Linux offers much more than what embedded avionics applications would need. The kernel uses complex algorithms and dynamic resource allocation mechanisms to optimize system resource usage, whereas critical embedded systems need simple, deterministic behavior. It may require a significant effort to gain a fine understanding of the kernel design, possibly rework part of it, and produce a dependability case that is accepted by the Certification authority.

Future work could then focus on kernel design, reverse-engineering and validation activities (see [1] for a more complete analysis of the use of open source software in critical embedded systems):

- introduce temporal partitioning mechanisms and implement A653 API services.
- include static pre-allocated system resources in the kernel. Resources are set up once at system initialization time and remain valid until module reset.
- increase system modularity by allowing the use of simpler or dedicated software components (memory management, scheduling, file system).
- keep the kernel as close as possible to the Linux current development tree (no forking): only introduce changes that gain acceptance from the Linux community,
- use/develop tools to reverse-engineer the code and build missing certification material (software design, dynamic behavior of system, analysis of partitioning mechanisms, ...).

- apply validation methods like model checking or formal proof of properties on safety related parts.
- characterize the system robustness or fail-silent behavior with fault injection techniques.

REFERENCES

[1] B. Bérard, P. Coupoux, Y. Crouzet, P. David, Y. Garnier, S. Goiffon, G. Mariano, V. Nicomette, L. Planche, I. Puaut, J-M. Tanneau, and H. Waeselynck, *Logiciel libre et sûreté de fonctionnement – cas des systèmes critiques*, P. David and H. Waeselynck (Eds), Hermes Science, ISBN 2-7462-0727-3, 2003 (in French).

A JOURNEY TOWARDS AN OSS-AWARE ORGANIZATION

Jean-Michel Tanneau
Thales Research & Technology, Domaine de Corbeville - 91404 Orsay - France

1. INTRODUCTION

For integrator of software intensive systems, open source software (OSS[1]) comes with two kind of opportunities: those which address its operational level, through the use of OSS components within systems, and those which may influence, or be part of, its R&D strategy, through appropriation and application of the "value creation" mechanisms, fundamentals of OSS.

In other words these two families of opportunities come to light respectively by considering: OSS as a product (technical object), and OSS as an open organizational system, with its objective, its structures (mostly informal), its techniques & processes, and most importantly, its socio-cultural sub-system (e.g. value system, motivations, group dynamics).

Nota: the scope of this paper is restricted to the first family of opportunities, i.e. those related to the use of OSS in systems. In short, the second family aims at: a) increasing the productivity and enhancing the quality by applying OSS specifics (such as development process, re-use, sharing, synergy, personal involvement on a voluntary basis, meritocraty) to internal developments, b) strengthening the durability of R&D investments related to core business, and c) allowing a sharing and co-operation on

[1] By open source software, we mean software which license complies with the Open Source Definition as managed and promoted by the Open Source Initiative (http://opensource.org)

generic and non-core business technologies (which stands for succeeding in freeing previously internally developed technology and making it evolve in the open source world).

2. USE OF OSS

OSS is also a COTS (with C:= Component) ...

In the business of the systems integrator, the entry of OSS in the landscape is more an evolution of the current situation, characterized by COTS[2] Based Systems, than a revolution as it had been when COTS were introduced. To assess OSS related opportunities, we propose to conduct a competitive analysis, OSS Vs COTS, through criteria that have motivated the use of the latter.

If the generalized use of COTS mainly responds to a cost reduction requirement (under the pressure of customers[3]), the integrator has additional demands. It expects COTS:

- To fulfil technical requirements related to target systems[4], and to provide the best possible capability in terms of feature, effectiveness and quality.
- To come with a support that must be reactive and of high quality.
- To be available at the *right* time and stay available and supported for a *long enough* period of time in order to defer obsolescence issues (to minimize the technology refresh phases[5]).
- To be the least possible intrusive as regards to the system architecture.

... with new opportunities...

By comparing OSS and COTS at coarse grain, and from the perspective of systems integrator, OSS ranks higher according to:

- ***Cost***: besides the no license nor royalty fee, it has to be noticed that the cost of some execution environments[6] may significantly decrease (e.g.

[2] By COTS, we mean "proprietary" Commercial Off The Shelf.
[3] In the US defense market, the secretary of Defense W. Perry mandated the use of COTS in 1994.
[4] Which is not so obvious as it could appear.
[5] Such expectation is commonly met in organizations having to manage long term maintenance, as in the Defense and Aerospace domain, where systems are commonly kept in operational condition for a 20 years period (or even more).
[6] Defined as the computer, the networking, the operating system, and possibly middle-ware.

from a proprietary Unix workstation to a x86/Linux[7]); the same with transfer cost[8] and cost related to get support (see below).

- ***Support***: in addition to knowledge bases that live on the Web, the free and direct access to developers, generally provides very efficient support in terms of quality and reactivity. In other respects, the free and open access to the technology allows support and engineering companies to gain deep knowledge on it, and to do business with it. This leads to the creation of a local professional support market ruled by an expertise based competition (opening the market).

- ***Adaptability and Testability***: the possibility to tune the OSS component (e.g. to enhance it with specific feature) permits to meet closely the system's requirements. In addition, access to the source code enables fine testing (unit testing, coverage testing) where with COTS only black box testing is possible (besides relying on editor's information and claims).

- ***Interoperability and standards***: most of the OSS components implement standards or are based upon them. Compared to a closed-proprietary technology, the main benefits are: an easier and cleaner integration of components, more stability in time, a decrease of the transfer cost (for technology refresh phases). Moreover, as far as distributed environments engineering and more generally Component Based Software Engineering (CBSE) is concerned, the definition and description of the component and its interfaces and services is straightforward and trustable with OSS, making it a first-class candidate for integration in Component and/or Service Based Architecture.

But the main differentiating factor between both types of components, and maybe the greatest opportunity related to OSS, is:

- ***Independence towards COTS & editors***

The introduction of a COTS in a system leads to a dependency link which induces the integrator to a loss of control on the system and its life cycle.

On the system: as a black box the content and behavior of the COTS is uncertain, the system relies on it and the integrator has to deal with this

[7] The Moore's law outcome applied to these x86 architectures and the fact that they are commonly used by the OSS community, have both contributed to make it possible.

[8] Defined as the cost to remove and replace the component.

situation without any hold on the COTS editor. In other respects, COTS evolution is generally "(mass-)market" driven which may change its features and take it away of our requirements.

On the system's life cycle management: the removal of the COTS from the editor's catalogue imposes its replacement (even if technically such a replacement is not justified); the system's life cycle is constrained with the COTS roadmap and is subjected to its veracity. Therefore, to gain confidence, before selecting a component, the integrator wishes to get information about its editor; such information encompasses the financial situation of the editor, its market positioning and sharing, its global strategy, its commercial strategy, and the roadmaps of products under consideration on which integrator may ask editor to commit itself through agreement. Experience learnt us to be suspicious about the information released by editors, sometimes because it is in their own interest to disinform, but most often because they are subject to the law of a continuously and suddenly restructuring market (concentration and emergence of monopolistic positions). More than the uncertainty related to editors' information, it is the future of these editors which is uncertain (except for the two or three major ones). Such uncertainties on COTS and editors are major risk items for the system integrator.

If this dependency between system and COTS lifecycles is manageable with one COTS, what about a system including about ten or so ones, each of them evolving at its own speed and technically depending on others ?

In the context of OSS, the dependency is significantly different as far as component's durability & availability is concerned, as well as its evolution and its related information.

The availability of an OSS, in a given release, is guaranteed; there is no provisioning issue as what has been released under an OSS license will stay usable as OSS for ever (component can not vanished). As a result, the integrator and/or the client is in a position to better control the system's lifecycle, in particular its technology refresh plan which thus can be "technology gap clearing" oriented, rather than being subject to editors diktats.

As there is no or few economic pressure on the components' maintainers, they thus favor technology, innovation, adherence to standard, and interoperability criteria to drive the evolution of their software; that is what integrator is generally expecting.

As for COTS, different information related to OSS under consideration is needed to gain confidence before selecting one. Maintainers use strategy of transparency, which is a key success factor in the OSS ecosystem;

furthermore information is checkable (through many sources: forum, development trees...).

- ***Deployment***

The recent work in Component Based Software Engineering (CBSE) addresses either COTS and OSS, but

... and new risks

Although OSS as an external component meets the same needs than COTS and comes with additional opportunities (that turn to address the main drawbacks of COTS), it also comes with additional risks.

Licenses and Intellectual Property Rights (IPR)

Each OSS comes with its license, either written by the software's author or chosen from the set of available OSS licenses, which specifies the rights of users but also their obligations, especially in case of redistribution (which is the situation of an integrator). Where some licenses authorize the use of OSS software within a proprietary product (e.g. Apache Software License, BSD like licenses), others, often quoted "viral licenses", state that "works based on" the component they cover, must be released and distributed under the terms of the same licenses; the figurehead of such kind of license is the GNU General Public License (GPL). The issue for the integrator using a component covered by such a license in a system is to know whether or not this latter (or part of it) falls under the term "work based on", defined as "derivative work" in the GNU GPL; in other words, the point is to know whether or not IPR are affected. It is tricky to give a straightforward answer to this question as the definition of "derivative work" in the American IP code[9] is fuzzy enough (and not dedicated to software) to allow controversy between lawyers. Furthermore and besides the "viral licenses" issue, some OSS licenses are incompatible between them, making it impossible for the covered software to co-exist into a larger system.

From the above discussion, it is obvious that the system integrator using OSS has to address very carefully the legal issues. In the system design phase, the component selection process will have to arbitrate between candidates, taking in account potential conflicts that could be raised through OSS license: incompatibility between OSS, conflict with internal IPR policy, conflict with IPR terms of the contract covering the system under consideration (e.g. in case of IPR transfer from integrator to client). Moreover such a legal analysis, in addition to be carried out for all candidate

[9] See Copyright Act, at 17 U.S.C. §101

components in a generic way, has to refine in the context of targeted software architecture to take care of the "derivative work" concern.

To control legal risk related to use of OSS, the organization can set up internal policy or directive to ensure that legal analysis has been conducted; but "law", if necessary isn't sufficient if not known by stakeholders (even layers and legal experts), therefore, to become normal practice, communication and awareness campaigns should not be underestimated.

Warranty & Liability

OSS is delivered without any warranty (provided "AS IS") and authors liability is often restricted to the minimum. Users of the software shall take over the entire responsibility; where the user is an integrator he shall be liable for the customer. Compared to COTS, where warranty is minimum and editor's liability is often limited to the license fee, the additional risk of using OSS is minimal.

Diffuse and unequal (in terms of global quality) supply

When selecting a component to be part of a system, it enters in this system life cycle (system development and integration, deployment and maintenance phases) through plans which are established according to information available at that time (e.g. its roadmap). Therefore such a selection is a critical decision which can have serious consequences if the choice appears to be a wrong choice (i.e. a component which wouldn't behave as expected and planed, or which would suddenly vanish); hence, accurate information is needed and that's the role of the evaluation process.

This process applies per products segment[10] and aims at: a) providing the picture of the supply (for each component under evaluation, get the current situation and the mid-term[11] forecast with a given level of confidence, from the technical and business points of view) and b) constructing a vision of trends (technology, supply and demand). This work is done by a group of experts, in the covered technology as well as in application domains targeted, with the support of a purchaser-negotiator to deal with COTS/editors and an expert knowledgeable about OSS world. According to the evolution of the segment, more precisely the evolution of one of its decisive variables (technology, supply), such a process has to be re-run periodically.

[10] A products segment groups together all candidates round a given technology or service (e.g. RDBMS, GUI toolkits, J2EE Application Servers).

[11] Horizon: 2 – 3 years.

In a products segment, one may find tens of possible OSS candidates, at different stages of maturity (takeoff, maturity, decline), at different levels of quality (in implementation, architectural design, documentation), with different attractiveness for developers (one to tens) and for users (individuals, academics, large organizations).

If effectiveness and technical feature of OSS are assessed in the same way as COTS (definition of criteria[12] and their weighting[13], then rating[14]), the novelty is the ability to assess its quality (quality of the implementation) through dedicated workbench encompassing: unit testing, coverage testing, compliance to coding rules, design audit (compliance to software engineering best practices, e.g. dependencies, cycles); this opportunity not only allows to assess the component's reliability but its easiness to be integrated and replaced (intrusiveness assessment) in a larger architecture and its ability to evolve (based on its architectural reflections).

The technical side is one facet of the selection decision making, others being support and durability (the ability to last and to evolve). To this aim an OSS dedicated evaluation (sub-)process has to be set up to investigate the project through its organization (key success factors), its reactivity, the related support supply (community based and professional).

From such evaluation process, a list of recommended OSS components is drawn up that will serve as a reference for system architects in their components selection decision making process; all of the information collected during the evaluation is gathered in a knowledge base, accessible to all of the stakeholders (developers, integrators, testers, architects), which will become richer from uses of the components in different systems.

Continuous evolution (compared to stability)

OSS is continuously evolving to integrate both bugs fixes and new features. According to its stage (in the life cycle) and maintainer's policy, the frequency of releases varies from one per day/week for projects in the taking-off phase to one per 6 months for mature projects. Where such effervescence is good for reliability and enhancement of the software, it is considered as an issue compared to the stability needed in system development; trade-off should be reached between both.

This "continuous evolution" feature also requires the integrator to set up a strong version and configuration management policy to manage

[12] Criteria covers the technology features and the adherence to standards (if any concerned) of the segment under investigation.

[13] Weights mirror relative importance of features, from a general point of view (technology) and/or a particular one (targeted application domain).

[14] Rates are collective decisions backed by study of documentation, individuals experience, mock-up.

components embedded in the systems (i.e. in addition to home-made source, all of the OSS core source code and subsequent patches, either released by the OSS project and home-made ones, that have been applied to get the actually used component).

According to the size of the organization, a single point of procurement can be defined to be in charge of: getting the original releases of selected components (integrity concern) with subsequent patches, getting on touch with projects evolutions, testing and assessing added-value of new releases, preparing customized packaged version (taking account of target HW and SW contexts, delivering internally to the organization the validated versions and possibly providing additional internal support services.

3. CONCLUSION

In this paper we do not intend to promote the idea of COTS replacement by OSS, we do consider OSS as a new source of provisioning and are convinced that both of them may and should co-exist in a larger system; the decision to choose between an OSS and a COTS component should be pragmatic, taking in account the technical features and the industrial concerns (e.g. cost, support, long-term maintenance).

OSS is a disruptive item in the "traditional" way a system integrator works, its introduction should be grasped as organizational changes that affect some of the organization's sub-systems. There is no "one best way" to know what need to be changed and how, in Thales we have chosen to follow a diagnostic approach to answer both questions (the second one not being addressed in this paper).

For the "what", we followed a competitive analysis of the two solutions, COTS and OSS. We first addressed the opportunities then the risks related to the use of OSS; to minimize and to control each of the latter, and therefore to be in a position to benefit safely from OSS, we have pointed out changes: a legal analysis process (OSS license analysis and global legal analysis at system level), a dedicated OSS evaluation process (taking care of the project organization and its stakeholders in addition to the product), a reinforcement of configuration management policy, and a single point of procurement. Such changes address different organization's sub-systems: the "techniques" one, to create and adapt process & policy at production and management/support level, the "culture" one, to change preconceived idea, and to a less extend the "structure" sub-system (to emphasize role of informal structures and networking as change agents).

How to implement such changes is contingent to the organization, taking account of its business, its strength/weakness and its core competencies (learning and adaptability capacity). But as a change management process, great care has to be taken in communicating and training about the changes, in "crystallizing" them through policies and behavior, in getting and keeping the continuous commitment of top level management (sponsor), and keeping available and motivated a dedicated network of individuals to champion and support all the process.

Topic 13

Interdependencies of Critical Infrastructures

Organiser:

Rune Gustavsson
Blekinge Institute of Technology, BTH, Sweden
Rune.Gustavsson@bth.se

Our society depends increasingly on reliable and sustainable infrastructure. Due to globalisation and deregulations those infrastructures are becoming more and more interdependent and intervened. A good example of this interdependency is the emerging embedding of ICT (Information and Communication Infrastructures) into power nets.

Existing power nets have proved to be unexpectedly vulnerable as we have recently witnessed by large and costly power blackouts in Europe and the US. Vulnerabilities of Internet are also a well known costly and alarming fact of, e.g., e-business. As a matter of fact, we also know that power blackouts also cause break-downs of information networks. We also have indications that malicious Internet code (virus or Trojans) might have caused, or contributed to, power blackouts.

The following papers were selected for presentation; however, final papers were not available at press time:

Power networks as a critical infrastructure
Nouredine Hadjsaid

Distribution generation as a stabilization factor of power grids
Christophe Andrieu

The role of supporting information infrastructures of a virtual utility
Rune Gustavsson

Challenges of future virtual power grids
Nouredine Hadjsaid

Topic 14

Social Robots: Challenges for Machine Intelligence

Organisers:

G. Giralt
LAAS/CNRS, France
giralt@laas.fr

R. Chatila
LAAS/CNRS, France
chatila@laas.fr

Front-line current developments in Robotics concern a vast spectrum of domains where close human-robot interaction plays a paramount role. These domains encompass Service (public-oriented, tour guide,...), Assistive (medical care, elderly care-taking, physically impaired,...) and Personal Robots (household, companions, entertainment,...).

Usually referred as Human Friendly Robotics and Human Centered Robotics, all those application cases emphasize the crucial aspect, well captured by Social Robots, of Human-Robot interaction issues where humans are most often non-expert users and by-standers. The very nature of this interaction brings to the forefront machine-intelligence central research issues of advanced Cognitive Robotics with key themes blending a large range of topics from embodiment and appearance to open-ended learning and decisional autonomy.

Overviews and focused presentations will address in particular the European IST FET project COGNIRON.

SOCIAL ROBOTS: CHALLENGES FOR MACHINE INTELLIGENCE

Domain outline, main trends and issues

Raja Chatila, Georges Giralt
LAAS-CNRS, Toulouse, France

Front-line current developments in Robotics concern a vast spectrum of domains where close human-robot interaction plays a paramount role. These domains encompass Service (public-oriented, tour guide,...), Assistive (medical care, elderly care-taking, physically impaired,...) and Personal Robots (household, companions, entertainment,...).

Usually referred as Human Friendly Robotics and Human Centered Robotics, all those application cases emphasize the crucial aspect, well captured by Social Robots, of Human-Robot interaction issues where humans are most often non-expert users and by-standers. The very nature of this interaction brings to the forefront machine-intelligence central research issues of advanced Cognitive Robotics with key themes blending a large range of topics from embodiment and appearance to open-ended learning and decisional autonomy.

Hence, we have to confront a most highly challenging research framework encompassing a large set of technical themes in the demanding human-centered application perspective:

- i) Multimodal communication: bi-lateral, appearance, context, behavior,...
- ii) Perception: active, semantics, gestures, person identification,...
- iii) Robot Motion: proximity with humans, cooperative tasks,...
- iv) Learning: open-ended modalities, skill acquisition, understanding the universe of action, user tuning,...

v) Autonomous decision: intentionality, planning, task reasoning, cooperative activities,...
vi) Dependability: safety, reliability, communication and operating robustness,...

The nine papers presented address these key themes bringing in results and on-going developments with a particular mention to Japan's two large-scale programs on Humanoïd Robots and the European IST FET project COGNIRON.

The organization in three sessions, *Overview and Challenges, Human Robot Interaction, and Learning and Cognition*, aims to provide room for in depth thematic discussion with a concluding final panel stressing critical issues related to human-robot interaction and robot dependability, with machines endowed with salient features in the areas of decisional autonomy and open-ended learning.

DEVELOPMENT OF HUMANOIDS AND NEW BUSINESS STRUCTURE

Hirochika Inoue
Digital Human Research Center, AIST, Japan

This talk introduces some of the recent research and development of humanoid, and discusses the problems, approaches and applications for the next generation humanoid.

First, the humanoid research efforts at the University of Tokyo group, which the author has long been committed, are introduced. It includes various small robots created by the remote-brained approach, full-size humanoids designed as integrated intelligent systems, and a humanoid with a flexible spine structure. Second, the results of a Japanese national project for humanoid robotics will be shown. This five-year project, referred to as the HRP project, was carried out as the platform-based studies for humanoid and human friendly robotic applications. We have succeeded in building a new humanoid platform to serve as technical infrastructure for R&D. The project has also challenged to realize five application scenarios, such as humanoids performing plant inspection routines, humanoid service workers in hospital environments, humanoid drivers that can operate ordinary construction machinery, cooperative tasks with human workers in outdoor environments, and controlling a home-sitting humanoid operated remotely using a PDA.

The new hardware platform HRP-2 and the software platform OpenHRP provide a common research tool not only for fundamental scientific studies but also for practical application studies. The humanoid platform changes a starting point of our humanoid R&D, enables new approaches, opens new possibilities of humanoid related business, and contributes to develop the human-robot symbiotic society.

Technical problems to be solved, approaches for further developments, sorts of applications, business models, and a roadmap, towards the next generation, will be discussed. And the structure of future robot business will be figured out.

TOWARDS ROBOT COMPANIONS

Raja Chatila
LAAS-CNRS, 7 av du Colonel Roche, 31077 TOULOUSE Cedex 4, France

We address the challenges of developing a new generation of robots that would be acting along with humans in their daily life and sharing their space.

In order to interact efficiently with humans in changing situations and to be able to accomplish various tasks, such robots should exhibit cognitive capacities for environment understanding, situation awareness and assessment, learning, and decision-making.

The talk will discuss the concepts and approaches for achieving these capacities. The robot being initially endowed with an elementary set of sensor data processings and motor actuation, it builds sensory-motor representations by associating perceptions with actions. This process is based on distributed multiscale representations that are incrementally built through a reinforcement learning mechanism. Situations, defined as associations of spatial layouts and temporal sequences are learned in the same manner. The robot behavior is driven by the need to increase a value function.

ROLES OF ROBOTS IN HUMAN SOCIETY: CHALLENGES AND CASE STUDIES

Kerstin Dautenhahn
Adaptive Systems Research Group
Univerisity of Hertfordshire, Department of Computer Science, UK

My talk will discuss different possible roles of robots in human societies, focussing on studies that we carried out in the Aurora project (http://www.aurora-project.com/). Challenges identified, and lessons learnt from studying interactions between robots and children with autism will be presented in the broader context of service robotics, with a particular focus on "a robot in my house" scenario which is central to the Cogniron project.

HUMAN-LIKE MOTION FROM PHYSIOLOGICALLY-BASED POTENTIAL FIELD

O. Khatib, J. Warren, V. De Sapio, L. Sentis
Artificial Intelligence Laboratory, Department of Computer Science, Stanford University, USA

The challenge of synthesizing motion behaviors is a long-standing problem in robotics. With the recent advent of complex humanoid systems, this challenge grows ever demanding. Due to their anthropomorphic design, humanoids should move in a human-like manner to facilitate movement within man-made environments and to accommodate interaction with their biological counterparts. Common control strategies for emulating human motion involve generating joint space trajectories or learning specific motions, but these approaches require off-line computations and do not generalize well to related tasks. There is a pressing need for a framework where natural motion is generated in real-time for a large range of tasks.

From observations of human motion, it is apparent that people perform many different behaviors while executing a task. These secondary criteria are the essence of natural human motion, affecting not whether but how the task is achieved. With this as motivation, we have developed a prioritized multiple task control framework that in real-time dynamically decouples each task. Equipped with this control framework, we propose a general methodology to discover the innate subtasks of human motion. These behaviors are initially identified by hypothesis or direct observation. By designing targeted motion capture experiments that excite these behaviors, we then confirm or refute their presence and ascertain their importance relative to other tasks.

We will illustrate this methodology by examining the muscular effort required to perform positioning tasks. In general terms, it is evident that humans avoid overexertion in commonplace motions. However, this concept is not easily quantified, nor is its relative importance to other behaviors clear. By utilizing biomechanical models for neuromuscular dynamics and control, we demonstrate that humans seek to minimize the muscular effort (normalized by torque capacity) needed to compensate for gravity while performing positioning tasks. While there are additional behaviors that characterize human motion, we believe that effort minimization is particularly significant. To this end, we conducted preliminary experiments to investigate the manner in which humans address muscular effort while performing tasks. In these experiments, we observe a strong trend that the gravity torques are balanced over the various joints in a manner that is correlated to the available torque capacity at each joint.

Based on these observations, and past use of muscle-level weighted norm criteria in the biomechanics community, we conjecture that postural motion involves the minimization of a muscle effort potential. Our results suggest a robust relationship between human motion and task level minimization of this muscle effort potential. By using this potential to define the posture field, we can utilize the posture space to minimize effort in real-time while performing any primary task. Moreover, the flexibility of our control framework will easily incorporate other behaviors upon identification. By establishing this basis, we expect to capture the characteristics that drive most of natural human motion.

A DIALOG BASED INTERACTIVE ROBOT

Gerhard Sagerer
Universitaet Bielefeld, Technische Fakultaet, Angewandte Informatik, Germany

Recently the research in robotics has started to focus on the development of service robots that serve people in natural office or home environments, e.g., robots for household work, as tour guide or for elderly care. Such a robot has to exhibit cognitive capabilities such as to understand human activities and to behave socially. Two of the key issues in realizing these ambitious goals are recognition of user attention and multi-modal dialog management. In the following we are going to take a closer look at these two points with the implementation of the home-tour scenario as example.

The central idea of a home-tour scenario is that the user buys a service robot, unpacks it at home and familiarizes it with this environment by showing it different rooms and objects. This can be considered as a basic scenario in the application of a service robot.

To start the interaction the robot has to first detect the user who intends to interact with it and keep contact with him/her. Questions that need to be answered here include how to find human figures against the background, how to distinguish robot's communication partner from other persons present and how to keep contact with the communication partner during the interaction.

For our mobile robot BIRON (Bielefeld Robot Companion), we developed a multi-modal framework for detection and observation of humans based on multi-modal anchoring which allows simultaneous tracking of multiple persons. It efficiently integrates data collected by different types of sensors: 1) A laser range finder detects humans' legs and provides data about the location of the person (distance and direction to the robot). 2) A pan-tilt camera is used to recognize human faces and torsos. The height and the location of the person can be estimated with this information. 3) Stereo microphones locate sound sources. BIRON can robustly detect persons in its vicinity by incorporating information from depth, visual and auditory cues this way.

If the user is standing in front of BIRON, speaking and looking at it, BIRON will presume that the current user intends to communicate with it and starts to focus on him/her. Once the interaction has started, the robot's focus remains on this person even if he/she is not speaking. BIRON signals its attention to its communication partner by turning its camera or/and itself to the person. The first user studies show that most users take this behavior as very human-like.

Apart from an attention mechanism a natural communication also requires to take as many communicational cues into account as possible. Generally, human beings tend to point to objects that they are verbally referencing. Especially in the home-tour scenario both gesture and speech can be involved, e.g. when the user shows the robot, say, his/her TV set. In order to understand utterances, which require association of the physical object with its name spoken by the user, the robot has to be able to combine information acquired from both modalities. On the side of the system output, the robot also needs to present the result of its processing in a multi-modal fashion. For example, if the robot has detected more than one object in the direction when dereferencing a user's gesture a clear object-name association becomes difficult. In this case we are planning to integrate a feature that allows the robot to ask clarifying questions and to point to the ambiguously detected objects.

Thus, in the future design of our multi-modal interaction scheme we will not only incorporate multi-modal cues in the process of understanding but also in the active process of producing feedback. We expect that this strategy will enable a more flexible dialog which is currently one of the key issues in dialog system design and has direct impact on social abilities of service robots.

TRACKING HUMANS

Ben Kröse, Taylan Cemgil, Wojciech Zajdel, Zoran Zivkovic
Informatics Institute, University of Amsterdam, Netherlands

In a human-inhabited environment it is essential that a robot which interacts with humans is able to keep track of them when they move around in the environment. This is not an easy job. Multiple people may be in the robot's vicinity, sometimes a person leaves the vicinity of the robot and re-enters some time later. Two issues are essential in tracking: localization and identification. Multi-modal cues (audio, visual, maybe radar) may be used for the task. In this paper we restrict ourselves to visual cues and present our work to track people with a vision system.

The first step in the tracking process is the detection of a human in its field of view. Current research assumes either a static camera, so that everything which moves is categorized as human, or assumes models which make it possible to detect humans with a moving camera. Our approach assumes a static camera for the detection, and uses a background modeling technique. After candidates have been detected, they are tracked with a color-histogram-based object tracking algorithm. A new robust algorithm will be presented that presents a natural extension of the well known 'mean-shift' procedure. The new algorithm simultaneously estimates the position of the local mode and the covariance matrix that describes the approximate shape of the local mode. Local features, such as color histograms or spatial features are used for identification.

A second problem occurs if a person disappears and reappears in a camera image. The robot has to answer the question: "is this the person which I saw before or a new person?". To answer this question is not easy, especially if the (light) conditions vary among different observation locations, or if the time between observations is very long (weeks..). The color histograms or spatial features used for identification within an image might not be valid anymore. Cognitive reasoning techniques are needed which take into account the context, such as position of the robot, or time between observations. We present a probabilistic framework to deal with this reasoning problem. We show that novel techniques in the field of dynamic Bayesian networks can be used to do fast and reliable tracking in these situations.

LEARNING AND COOPERATIVE MULTIMODAL HUMANOID ROBOTS

Ruediger Dillmann
IRF, Karlsruhe University, Haid-und-Neu-Str. 7, Karlsruhe, Germany

In this talk a brief overview on the German Collaborative Research Center on Humanoid Robots is given. The research topics focused by the collaborative research center are multimodal man machine interaction, learning of motion, skills and tasks, man-robot cooperation, perception and action and mechatronics and controls for a human like torus consisting of 2 redundant arms, 2 dexterous 5-finger hands, a head with eyes and ears, a neck and a spine.

Over a period of 10 years it is envisaged to elaborate and establish basic methodologies and technology for humanoid robots to act and cooperate close with humans in a dayly living environment. An integrated perspective towards continuous humanoid interaction gaining multimodality adaptivity, redundancy and flexibility is proposed.

Programming, cooperation and interaction with a humanoid robot is assumed to be multimodal which means to let the user program the robot simply by speech, gesture or demonstrating a task. The robot observes, interprets and then tries to imitate and to learn the performed user action.

On the basis of a redundant humanoid 2 arms type, a robot system equipped with an active stereo head and a microphone array observation of the demonstrated task is realised as a first prototype using an active vision system. Grasping of objects is detected with the help of data gloves and active vision. The system interprets and stores the observed actions, segments them into meaningful sequences in a given context. Due to sensor errors and the complexity of the intended interaction, the system generates queries concerning intention, manipulation and objects. Motion catch techniques in combination with learning capabilities are combined towards imitation learning and active observational learning strategies.

The project will be outlined and actual research work and results will be discussed.

FROM GEOMETRIC TO COGNITIVE MAPS - A KEY ELEMENT FOR PERSONAL ROBOTS

Roland Siegwart, Shrihari Vasudevan, Adriana Tapus
Autonomous Systems Lab, Swiss Federal Institute of Technology Lausanne (EPFL) CH-1015 Lausanne, Switzerland

Environment representation and situation awareness are key issue for personal and service robotics. Recent research in mobile robotics mainly concentrated on environment representations for efficient and robust navigation (e.g. Simultaneous Localization and Mapping). However, personal robots need competences that go beyond navigation and thus environment representations that include relationships and semantics of objects. Only this will enable personal robots to reason about the environment and develop cognitive competencies.
Many methods have been proposed to represent an environment in the framework of autonomous navigation, from precise geometric maps based on raw data or lines up to purely topological maps using symbolic descriptions. Each of these methods is optimal concerning some characteristics but can be very disappointing with respect to other requirements. However, none of them is able to cope with the large variety of environments that humans encounter in their daily live.

Most current approaches make a trade-off between precision and global distinctiveness. Precision and distinctiveness have a strong link with the level of abstraction of the features used for navigation (fig.1). Raw data represent the lowest level in the hierarchy of abstraction. Localization and mapping with raw data can result in high precision, but the required data volume scales very badly with the size of the environment, the distinctiveness of the individual data points is very low and semantic information cannot be integrated. An example of such an approach is Markov localization [Fox98, Thrun01]. The second level of abstraction

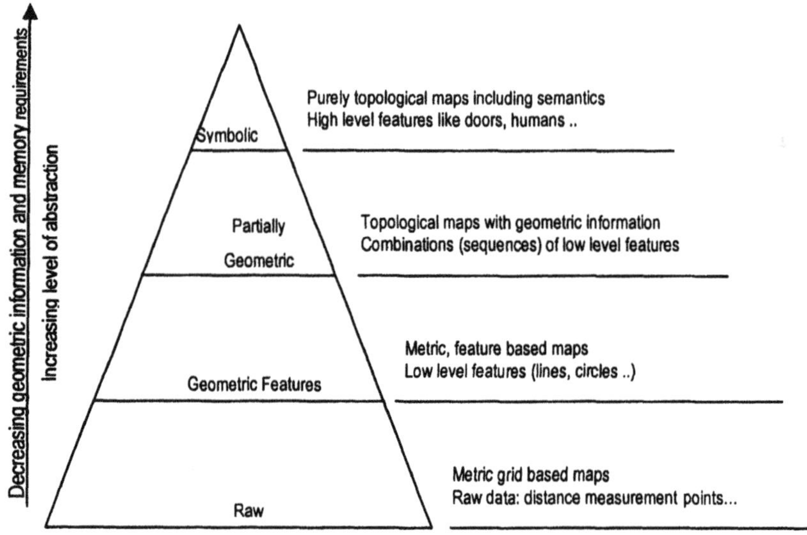

Figure 1: *This figure depicts the hierarchy of abstraction levels towards cognitive maps. More we go up in the hierarchy, more we reduce the geometric information and we increase the distinctiveness and semantics information. For localization and mapping, geometric precision and distinctiveness is of importance, whereas for the development of cognitive competencies, semantics and relations between objects come forward.*

corresponds to geometric features (lines, edges). The stochastic map technique to SLAM [Leonard92, Castellanos99, Dissanayake01] and the multi-hypothesis localization [Arras03] are typical examples belonging to this level. These approaches still feature high precision with reduced memory requirements, but have shortcomings concerning global distinctiveness and unmodeled events and are still purely geometrical. Partially geometric features correspond to the third level of the hierarchy. Representations using partially geometric features are for examples fingerprints (a sequence of low level features) described in [Lamon01, Lamon03], but also more bio-inspired approaches [Arleo00, Berthoz97, Hafner00] using neural networks, e.g. the work by Hafner [Hafner00] uses a neural network to create a topological map of the environment based on images of an omni-directional camera. On the highest abstraction level the environment is represented by a symbolic description. This can be very compact and distinctive, but reliable tools for extraction of high level features and appropriate concepts for probabilistic high-level knowledge representations are still under development.

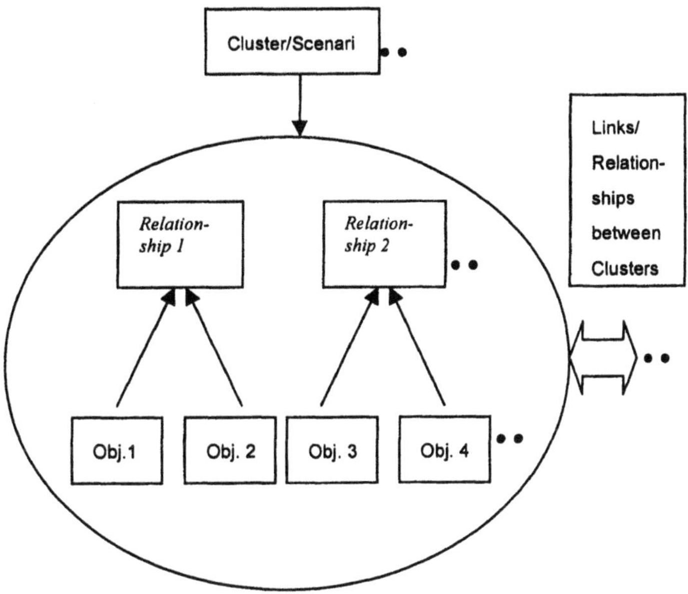

***Figure 2**: Cognitive Map: Relationship between objects – from relationships to scenarios*

The aim of the present work is to suggest and discuss a multilevel representation approach for robust and compact environment representation with the goal of establishing cognitive maps for future service and personal robots. This is realized by integrating different level of abstraction and representations in a common framework for navigation and interaction. For example, to get from the airport to a given room in a hotel, maps of the city streets and of the hotel are necessary, but also knowledge about transportation systems and much more. Clearly, this task requires different representations and levels of abstraction for planning and decision-making. A crucial point is then the linkage between the different levels of abstraction so that the representation remains coherent over time. In the multi-level representation we propose, the mobile robot uses the most suitable level of abstraction, depending on the task it has to accomplish and the certainty about its pose. Moreover, depending on the actual situation, it has to be able to switch from one level to another (see figure 1).

In this paper we will discuss the possibility to integrate most recent results in mobile robot navigation in a multi-level hierarchical representation and we will present our first attempts towards multi-resolution, multi-representation maps. The presentation starts with a general description of the proposed framework. We will then discuss typical sensors used in mobile robotics and their impact to the environment representation. Firstly our approach combining low-level features for local metric and fingerprints for global topological localization and mapping will be presented and highlighted with experimental results. Secondly our concepts towards cognitive representation are presented. The cognitive maps or mental maps – term introduced for the first time in [Tolman48] – permit an encoding of the spatial relations between relevant locations or objects within the environment. More details with regards to the cognitive maps can be found in [O'Keefe78]. The cognitive maps can be viewed as topological representations (see figure 2). The main idea is to combine objects and their relationships in a probabilistic object-graph model in order to enable planning and reasoning on an abstract level. Preliminary simulation results will outline this approach, its potential and related challenges.

REFERENCES

[Agrawal94] Rakesh Agrawal and H.V. Jagadish, *"Algorithms for searching massive graphs,"* IEEE Transactions on Knowledge and Data Engineering, VOL 6, No 2, April 1994.

[Arleo00] Arleo A. and Gerstner W. (2000), "Spatial Cognition and Neuro-Mimetic Navigation: a model of Hippocampal Place Cell Activity", Biological Cybernetics, 83, 287-299

[Arras03] K.O.Arras, Castellanos, J.A., Schilt, M. and Siegwart, R., *"Feature-based multi-hypothesis localization and tracking using geometric constraints,"* Robotics and Autonomous Systems, 1056 (2003) 1-13, 2003

[Berthoz97] Berthoz A. (1997), *"Le sens du mouvement"*, Editions Odile Jacob, Paris, 1997

[Castellanos99] Castellanos J.A., Tardos J.D., *"Mobile Robot Localization and Map Building: A Multisensor Fusion Approach,"* Kluwer, 1999.

[Chaib-Draa98] Chaib-Draa, B. and Desharnais, J. *"A Relational Model of Cognitive Maps"*, International Journal of Human-Computer Studies, 49, 181-200, 1998

[Charniak91] Eugene Charniak, *"Bayesian Networks without Tears,"* AI Magazine – AAAI 1991

[Cohn02] Anthony Cohn, Aphrodite Galata, David Hogg, Derek Magee, Bernd Neumann, *"Conceptual framework and knowledge representation tools for temporal and spatial context,"* Technical Report, CSL IST – 2000 – 29375, 2002.

[Crowley89] J. Crowley, *"World modeling and position estimation for a mobile robot using ultrasonic ranging,"* Proc. of IEEE Int. Conf. on Robotics and Automation, pp. 674--680, Scottsdale, AZ, May 14-19, 1989.

[Dissanayake01] Dissanayake, Newman, Clark, Durrant-Whyte and Csorba, *"A Solution to the Simultaneous Localization and Map Building (SLAM) problem"*, IEEE Trans. On Robotics and Automation, Vol 17, No.3, June 2001

[Finn01] Finn V Jensen, *"Bayesian Networks and Decision Graphs"*, Springer Verlag, 2001

[Fox98] Fox, D., *"Markov Localization: A Probabilistic Framework for Mobile Robot Localization and Navigation,"* Ph.D. Thesis, Institute of Computer Science III. Bonn, Germany, University of Bonn, 1998

[Guo02] H. Guo and William H. Hsu. *"A Survey of Algorithms for Real-Time Bayesian Network Inference,"* AAAI/KDD/UAI-2002 Joint Workshop on Real-Time Decision Support and Diagnosis Systems. Edmonton, 29 July 2002

[Hafner00] Hafner V.V., *"Learning Places in Newly Explored Environments,"* in Meyer, Berthoz, Floreano, Roitblat and Wilson (Eds.), SAB2000 Proceedings Supplement Book, Publication of the International Society for Adaptive Behavior, Honolulu, 2000

[Lamon01] Lamon, P., I. Nourbakhsh, et al., *"Deriving and Matching Image Fingerprint Sequences for Mobile Robot Localization,"* Proc. of the IEEE International Conference on Robotics and Automation (ICRA), Seoul, Korea, 2001

[Lamon03] Lamon, P., Tapus A., et al., *"Environmental Modeling with Fingerprint Sequences for Topological Global Localization"*, Proceedings of the International Conference on Intelligent Robot and Systems (IROS03) Las Vegas, USA, 2003.

[Leonard92] J.J. Leonard, H.F. Durrant-Whyte, *"Directed Sonar Sensing for Mobile Robot Navigation,"* Kluwer Academic Publishers, Dordrecht, 1992.

[Martinelli03a] Martinelli A and Siegwart R., *"Estimating the Odometry Error of a Mobile Robot during Navigation,"* accepted at the European Conference on Mobile Robots (ECMR 2003), Warsaw, Poland, September 4-6, 2003

[Martinelli03b] Martinelli A, Tomatis N. et al, *"Simultaneous Localization and Odometry Calibration"*, Proceedings of the International Conference on Intelligent Robot and Systems (IROS03) Las Vegas, USA, 2003.

[Martinelli03c] Martinelli A and Siegwart R., *"Convergence of a Relative Map Filter for SLAM"*, submitted at the ISRR03, Siena, Italy.

[O'Keefe78] O'Keefe, J. and Nadel, L. (1978). *"The Hippocampus as a Cognitive Map"*, Clarendon Press:Oxford.

[Pearl86] Judea Pearl, Fusion, *"Propagation and structuring in belief networks,"* Artificial Intelligence, Vol 29, Issue 3 (September 1986), pages 241 – 288

[Thrun01] S. Thrun, D. Fox, W. Burgard, and F. Dellaert, *"Robust Monte Carlo Localization for Mobile Robots,"* In Artificial Intelligence (AI), 2001.

[Tolman48] Tolman, E. C. (1948), *"Cognitive maps in rats and men"*, Psychological Review, 55:189-208.

[Tomatis02] Tomatis N., Nourbakhsh I. and Siegwart R., *"Hybrid Simultaneous Localization and Map Building: Closing the Loop with Multi-Hypotheses Tracking."* In Proceedings of the IEEE International Conference on Robotics and Automation, Washington DC, USA, May 11 - 15.

CENTIBOTS: VERY LARGE SCALE DISTRIBUTED ROBOTIC TEAMS

[1] Kurt Konolige, Charlie Ortiz, Regis Vincent, Benoit Morisset, Andrew Agno, Michael Eriksen
[2] Dieter Fox, Benson Limketkai, Jonathan Ko, Benjamin Stewart, Dirk Schulz
[1]SRI International, USA; [2]University of Washington, USA

We describe the development of Centibots, a framework for very large teams of robots that are able to perceive, explore, plan and collaborate in unknown environments.

Centibots teams currently consist of approximately 100 robots, which can be deployed in unexplored areas and which can efficiently distribute tasks among themselves; the system also makes use of a mixed initiative mode of interaction in which a user can easily influence missions as necessary.

In contrast to simulation-based systems which abstract away aspects of the environment for the purposes of exploring component technologies, the Centibots design reflects an integrated end-to-end system.

GPSR Compliance
The European Union's (EU) General Product Safety Regulation (GPSR) is a set of rules that requires consumer products to be safe and our obligations to ensure this.

If you have any concerns about our products, you can contact us on

ProductSafety@springernature.com

In case Publisher is established outside the EU, the EU authorized representative is:

Springer Nature Customer Service Center GmbH
Europaplatz 3
69115 Heidelberg, Germany

www.ingramcontent.com/pod-product-compliance
Ingram Content Group UK Ltd.
Pitfield, Milton Keynes, MK11 3LW, UK
UKHW022316190726
13856UKWH00001B/36

* 9 7 8 1 4 7 5 7 8 8 9 3 8 *